The Carbon Emission Liability Mechanism

Baoming Yang

The Carbon Emission Liability Mechanism

A New Solution for Global Carbon Neutrality

中国经济出版社
CHINA ECONOMIC PUBLISHING HOUSE

Springer

Baoming Yang
Tongji University
Shanghai, China

Translated by
Quanju Qiu
Shandong University of Science
and Technology
Qingdao, China

ISBN 978-981-96-3611-2 ISBN 978-981-96-3612-9 (eBook)
https://doi.org/10.1007/978-981-96-3612-9

Jointly published with China Economic Publishing House
The print edition is not for sale in China (Mainland). Customers from China (Mainland) please order the print book from: China Economic Publishing House.

This work was supported by China Economic Publishing House.

Translation from the Chinese Simplified language edition: "新公共物品原理与全球碳中和解决方案" by Baoming Yang, © China Economic Publishing House 2023. Published by China Economic Publishing House. All Rights Reserved.

This Springer imprint is published by the registered company Springer Nature Singapore Pte Ltd.
The registered company address is: 152 Beach Road, #21-01/04 Gateway East, Singapore 189721, Singapore

Dedicated for those fighting against global climate change

Preface

"We're on the highway to climate hell with our foot still on the accelerator." António Guterres, the UN Secretary-General, voiced his concerns in his opening speech at the COP 27 conference.

As the world's largest and most influential climate conference, Conference of the Parties (COP) held its 27th session officially in Sharm El-Sheikh, Egypt on November 6, 2022, with more than 35,000 participants across the globe, including government representatives, observers and civil societies as well as more than 70 national leaders, and generated massive amount of carbon dioxide.

Since 2022, tens of millions of people across the globe have suffered the effects of climate extremes: devastating floods in Pakistan have killed at least 1,700 people and displaced 8 million; scorching summer heatwaves in many parts of Europe have resulted in over 10,000 fatalities; and withering droughts in East Africa have threatened food security for 37 million people. The wake-up call of the climate crisis is sounding closer and closer.

"Humanity has a choice: cooperate or perish." Guterres said, "It is either a Climate Solidarity Pact -or a Collective Suicide Pact.".

COP 27 ultimately concluded with a two-day extension after many rounds of intensive negotiations, and an agreement called the *Sharm el-Sheikh Implementation Plan (SIP)* was unveiled at the closing ceremony. One of the significant achievements was that the long-pending "Loss and Damage" funding had been established, but the sources of the funding have yet to be negotiated, rendering it an unimplemented agreement in intent.

How will the global climate change be tackled? Where does the international community's path to global carbon neutrality lead to? Humankind, still a tiny sampan adrift in the vast ocean, finds itself in a predicament, with multiple captains vigorously negotiating for control.

On September 22, 2020, Chinese President Xi Jinping solemnly announced at the 75th Session of United Nations General Assembly that China would be committed to hit peak emissions by 2030 and carbon neutrality by 2060, marking a pivotal step forward in the Nationally Determined Contributions (NDCs) of major global economies to carbon emission reduction, and one of the key milestones in the global fight against climate change.

China's "3060" dual carbon targets has officially commenced, with the year 2021 marking the inaugural year for striving for carbon neutrality in China. For the next four decades, "dual carbon" will serve as the pivotal theme underlying the economic life of every organization, enterprise and household within Chinese society.

As the global climate crisis intensifies, carbon emissions have emerged as the most central topic in the international community. Consequently, international cooperation and international negotiations revolving around carbon emissions have persisted for nearly three decades. However, in the climate landscape where developed countries dominate the rules of the game on carbon emissions, the disparities between developing countries, represented by China, and developed countries in Europe and the United States, have not diminished despite their shared interests, therefore, the progress toward carbon neutrality within the international community remains sluggish, and the time for achieving the optimal global climate goals is getting less and less. How can the international community not only achieve the global climate goals, but also transform carbon emissions into a win-win scenario that takes into account the interests of developing countries and all stakeholders? This requires profound wisdom and groundbreaking advancements in the climate change economics and global solutions to carbon neutrality.

In a report released in March 2021, the International Renewable Energy Agency (IRENA) pointed out that by 2050, global investment in renewable energy would be expected to surge by 30%, amounting to $131 trillion. Given China's current share of approximately one-third of global carbon emissions and the current exchange rate, the investment in renewable energy within China alone would require a total of 283 trillion yuan. According to China International Capital Corporation (CICC), China's total green investment by 2060 is estimated to reach 139 trillion yuan. This volume of investment exceeds the historical scale of investment in any sector in China, highlighting the immense challenges not only China but also governments worldwide face. It is evident that relying solely on traditional sources of finance and adopting a passive stance will render the achievement of global climate goals elusive. Therefore, the international community must reach a consensus in the understanding of the nature of climate change and devise a sound top-level design to find a more efficient and equitable pathway towards carbon neutrality.

The establishment of a more effective carbon emission management system and the utilization of more effective policy instruments to promote decarbonation in China continue to be a pivotal concern, influencing its development over the next four decades. So it is with the international community, which also faces an urgent need to address this issue promptly. At present, the international community relies on two major policy instruments, carbon emission allowances and carbon taxes, to facilitate carbon emission reduction and achieve carbon neutrality. However, both theoretical and practical analyses have revealed significant limitations exist in these two instruments: they are not only inefficient, complex to design, but also lack fairness and involve high operational and regulatory costs in spite of incomplete coverage, difficulties in establishing standards and in assessing actual impacts. Consequently, it is challenging to achieve international coordination and consensus. Worse still, the economic burden of decarbonation over the past decade has been excessively high, which is unbearable for the international community. Therefore, there is an urgent need to explore a fairer, more scientific and efficient third pathway forward.

Climate change confronts the governments with a daunting task: not only must they design a comprehensive decarbonation system, but they also face significant operational challenges in executing the current decarbonation efforts. Carbon emission accounting, for instance, necessitates substantial government investment and rigorous checks, yet data issues persist. Despite over two decades of persistent efforts, carbon regulation remains confined to a limited number of industries, such as coal-fired power industry, which falls far short of what is required for achieving carbon neutrality. Consequently, the international community urgently needs to accelerate its steps in response to climate change.

This book innovatively introduces a groundbreaking Carbon Emission Liability Mechanism (CELM), establishing a novel carbon emission liability (CEL) framework. It explores a third way towards global carbon neutrality by conducting a comprehensive analysis of global climate change from a multidisciplinary perspective, covering law, sociology, economics, digitization, and science and technology. The CELM-based "1+1" Global Carbon Neutrality Solution involves the establishment of two systems: Global Decarbonation System and Global Green Energy Supply System. The two systems are supported by four self-operating sub-systems: Carbon Ticket Management System (CTMS) for carbon footprint management, Negative Carbon Trading Market (NCTM) for carbon offset and financial support, Global Energy Internet (GEI) for delivering global green energy, and International Electricity Trading Market (IETM) for global energy trading. By operating the two systems and four sub-systems globally, we try to realize the following goals:

1. To establish a novel legal theory for global carbon neutrality, along with the fundamental principles to address the urgent challenges posed by climate change. We try to establish a new type of fairer, more efficient and rational underlying logic for climate change economics and jurisprudence, and to provide theoretical support for the establishment of a new international order of global carbon neutrality that can achieve the temperature limit targets set by the Intergovernmental Panel on Climate Change (IPCC).
2. To establish a real-time, accurate and robust system for social carbon footprint data. The carbon footprint data across the entire society will be recorded in real time, ensuring their accuracy and completeness, so as to provide crucial data and arithmetic support for the accurate calculation of carbon emissions of individual commodity and organization, for the assessment of carbon emissions of various construction plans, and for the formulation of effective carbon policy instruments by the governments.
3. To establish a NCTM that promotes bidirectional incentives (negative incentives for carbon emissions and positive incentives for low-carbon practices and carbon removals). By harnessing the market mechanism, the incentives can be interconnected, leading to accelerated decarbonation in both directions.

4. To establish a "1+1" Global Green Energy Supply System, that is, "Global Energy Internet + International Electricity Trading Market". This system aims to address the challenges of randomness, volatility and consumption difficulties associated with zero-carbon green energy. By accelerating the substitution of fossil fuels, we seek to establish a more stable and sustainable power supply system globally, significantly enhancing the availability of electricity and energy in underdeveloped regions. Our efforts align with the decarbonation system, ultimately propelling us towards global carbon neutrality.
5. To significantly reduce the administrative burden and complexities associated with dual carbon targets for national governments. By establishing a self-operating and self-driven national-level management system for carbon emissions and carbon neutrality, we seek to address the challenges and minimize the costs involved in monitoring, reporting and verification (MRV). This will not only expedite the participation of the entire society in actions for decarbonation, but also accelerate the pace of decarbonation in China and globally.
6. To assist the international community to limit global average temperature increase to 1.5 °C set by IPCC ahead of schedule. The CELM will contribute significantly to the IPCC's goal of achieving global net-zero CO_2 emissions by 2050 and ensure that the total amount of new global carbon emissions will be within the designated control target, thereby safeguarding the Earth's warming within the critical 1.5 °C limit and preserving our planet's safety.
7. To transform the huge input and costs associated with global carbon neutrality into positive outcomes. In the current context of stagnant globalization, the international community is facing a huge challenge in restarting economic growth after the pandemic. The path towards global carbon neutrality outlined by the CELM offers a way forward for the international community, enabling process towards global carbon neutrality without incurring a heavy financial burden. The comprehensive green transformation can not only bolster the current economy but also address the challenges posed by generational accounting.
8. To resolve conflicting carbon tariffs in the international trade. The CTMS, built upon the CELM, can provide reliable carbon footprints. Furthermore, the pricing mechanism for "International Negative CO_2", coordinated multilaterally, can resolve numerous disputes over carbon leakage in international trades and reduce the number of conflicts arising from mechanisms like the EU's Carbon Border Adjustment Mechanism (CBAM).
9. To generate a substantial new revenue stream for governments. Shortage of funds often poses a challenge for governments to promote carbon neutrality. However, under the CELM, the governments, as the initial issuers of carbon sales, can obtain large revenues through the negative carbon market, which can be utilized to support the green transition and optimize social distribution. If China were to establish itself as the world's largest negative carbon trading and output market, it would stand to gain immense revenues and settlement incomes from the trading market. This would enable the Chinese government to allocate a larger proportion of these revenues towards bolstering support for technologies, projects and enterprises associated with carbon reduction.

10. To assist China in fulfilling its climate ambitions and emerging as a pivotal leader in addressing global climate challenges. For nearly three decades, China has borne significant international scrutiny to reduce carbon emissions. With its green energy capacity and the advantages of the Ultra-High Voltage transmission grid (the Energy Internet), successful implementation of the CELM could enable China to fulfill even more ambitious climate goals and establish it as a forefront nation in tackling global climate change, thereby making more significant contributions in areas such as carbon neutrality policy-making, carbon pricing, and carbon finance.

Furthermore, the principles underpinning the CELM can be elevated to form a novel theory for public goods. This theory would offer a robust theoretical foundation and a solution framework for a multitude of complex issues involving public goods with spatial and temporal externalities. Additionally, it can be further developed and applied to address the challenges posed by larger-scale and more intricate public goods within the international community, thereby serving as a significant benefit to humanity.

Acknowledgements After graduation, I joined the Shanghai Construction Group, where I engaged in project management within the engineering sector. This period coincided with the rapid expansion of China's infrastructure construction since the early 1990s, revealing both the developmental challenges and inefficiencies within the industry. A study by a prominent domestic real estate firm indicated that during the peak of China's construction boom, "an alarming proportion (70%) of world's illegally and legally felled wood went to China, with 70% of that destined for construction sites", used for formwork, support, and decorative materials. Due to the extensive management practices at that time, a significant portion of the wood was wasted. The construction industry in China was at its peak, and every 1% reduction in wood waste across the nation's construction sites could translate into a 0.5% decrease in global deforestation. Witnessing this state of affairs instilled in me a profound sense of responsibility and a clear mission: to leverage advanced management concepts and technologies to transform the operational landscape of the construction sector in China, to enhance the quality of management and reduce resource waste. In 1999, driven by this vision, I established Lubansoft, initiating a journey dedicated to the exploration and promotion of digitalization in both engineering and urban planning sectors. Initially, we channeled all available resources into the research and development of Building Information Modeling (BIM) technology. Over the ensuing two decades, our commitment has remained steadfast, aiming to enhance the fine and intensive management practices within China's construction sector, to achieve intelligent and sustainable development in the sector, and foster harmony between industry and nature. Though the development and promotion of BIM digital technology over the past two decades have been challenging, I have given it my all and never let up in my efforts.

I pursued my master's degree in Engineering at Tongji University and later obtained my doctoral degree in Technical Economics, with a focus on industrial institutional economics. The research conducted for my doctoral thesis, along with my long-term observations and reflections on institutional economics, coupled with over two decades of entrepreneurial experience in the digital technology sector, has endowed me with valuable insights. Firstly, it has become evident that industrial institutional economics holds immense potential. Many of the challenges faced in the development of China's industries, including aviation, industrial software, chips, and artificial intelligence, stem from issues in top-level design of industrial strategies and policies. These shortcomings lead to a lack of systematic support, an unsupportive environment, and insufficient conditions for industrial growth. Secondly, one of the primary reasons for the systemic issues within these industries is the influence of cognitive capacities of academic circles and policymakers. A lack of fundamental understanding of the principles of industrial development (First Principles) means that the correct foundational theories are neither identified nor established, leading to misguided top-level designs that impede the healthy development of the industry.

The ongoing struggle against climate change exemplifies these institutional challenges. Due to fundamental theoretical deficiencies and a failure to build effectively upon the work of predecessors, despite over three decades of concerted global efforts by countless researchers, managers, and policymakers, significant progress has remained elusive, exacting a heavy toll. This has severely constrained economic growth and made it difficult to achieve the temperature control goals set by the international community.

Due to the collaboration with Green Construction Center of Tongji University, I have gained a deep understanding of the international community's efforts to respond to climate change. On one hand, I was concerned about the increasingly severe climate issues; on the other hand, I firmly believed that there will be significant breakthroughs in the research of climate change economics and institutional economics. The path to global carbon neutrality should not be so arduous, and progress should not be so slow. This conviction has sparked a strong interest in me, leading me to organize a team and invest resources. I eventually stepped away from the company entirely and redirected my personal funds into what was arguably the most challenging project in human history: combating climate change.

Fortunately, our team has quickly yielded promising results, and we were pleasantly surprised by some significant breakthroughs in both theory and methodology. After all, this is a direction that countless experts and policymakers from a multiple of disciplines in the internation community have been striving to address for over three decades. Through exchanges and discussions with numerous professionals, I have become increasingly convinced that our research holds substantial value in addressing climate issues.

Throughout the progression of our research, we have received assistance and support from many quarters. Without their support, the advancement and the numerous findings presented in this book would not have been possible. I would like to express my sincere gratitude to them.

First and foremost, I thank God for his selection and guidance. As someone outside the immediate circle of experts, I never anticipated having the opportunity to contribute in such a significant field and to make a difference in addressing one of the greatest challenges facing humanity. Our team has made rapid progress, achieved major breakthroughs and generated numerous important research findings in less than two years, which would be unimaginable without divine inspiration and guidance.

Among all individuals, the first person I would like to express my gratitude is my wife, Lu Lianhua. When I conceived the plan to study climate issues and carbon-neutral solutions, she immediately understood the gravity of the current climate situation and the essence of my ideas, offering her unwavering support. During the time when the pandemic was prevalent, both my company and family life were facing numerous challenges, but her backing allowed me to step back from business operations, set up a team, and invest considerable resources into researching the most pressing challenge in the world: climate change. Without her full support and encouragement, I would not have had the perseverance and courage to pursue a cause without caring rewards and success for such a long time. Beyond her moral support, Lu Lianhua has provided substantial administrative support for the project, as well as participating in multiple rounds of proofreading, contributing significantly to the enhancement of the quality of this book.

My supervisor, Professor Huang Yuxiang (former Dean of the School of Economics and Management at Tongji University), is an important participant in the project, and I find it difficult to express my gratitude adequately. Professor Huang supports me not because I was his student, but due to his deep expertise in public economics, which makes him acutely aware of the innovation, rationality, and feasibility of theories and methods such as the transfer of carbon emission liability. Therefore, he has offered me boundless encouragement. Since the inception of the project, Professor Huang has selflessly provided the project team with relevant theoretical knowledge in economics and public finance, helping us save a considerable amount of time in understanding various aspects of China's public economic policies. He serves as an important academic advisor to our research, providing academic standards, identifying issues, and offering suggestions on each new argument we propose. Despite his advanced age of 83, he has meticulously revised many drafts of our research reports, word by word, and has engaged in deliberate deliberation and serious discussion of every minor professional issue with us. Despite physical hardships, family matters, and numerous difficulties, Professor Huang has earnestly striven to assist us. His rigorous academic spirit, affirmation, and full support for our research work have been a tremendous source of motivation and strength for the entire project team and me. To this day, he continues to interact with the project team to discuss the entirety of our research topic.

Professor Feng Shenhong, Deputy Secretary of the Party Committee of Tongji University has provided us with significant support in Tongji University.

Throughout the process, the research team has worked collaboratively, pooling everyone's wisdom. Professor Shi Qian, Secretary of the Party Committee of the School of Economics and Management at Tongji University, along with Professor Han Chuanfeng, Director of the Think Tank for Sustainable Development and New Urbanization at Tongji University, as well as Professor Liu Xinghua, have provided supervision, academic governance, and assistance in popularizing the research findings. Particularly, Professor Han Chuanfeng has made substantial contributions to the platform construction, the organization of academic demonstrations, and the provision of research resources during the course of the project.

My colleague, He Lingtong, has taken on a multitude of work and undertaken an enormous workload. She has overcome numerous challenges to successfully complete relevant tasks. These tasks included theoretical system improvement, data analysis, material sorting and editing, and coordination. Additionally, He Lingtong has been responsible for the overall project management for the publication of this book, executing the responsibilities with high efficiency and quality. Mr. Xu Peizheng, a researcher in our team, has demonstrated great enthusiasm and effort in the research, particularly in areas such as the Global Energy Interconnection and power market reforms. Mr. Xu Peizheng has also contributed significantly to data collection and provided essential support for various thematic research components of the entire project.

Moreover, I would like to extend my gratitude to Mr. Liu Xinyi, President of the Shanghai International Group and former President of the Shanghai Pudong Development Bank. Throughout the entire research process, Mr. Liu Xinyi has provided the project team with substantial professional guidance, suggestions, encouragement, and support. He has facilitated our communication with numerous relevant government departments and assisted in connecting us with many experts who offered valuable feedback on our research reports, dedicating a significant amount of his time to these efforts. Additionally, Mr. Liu Xinyi has imparted invaluable advice on how to effectively exchange academic ideas with government departments and how to present policy recommendations, which has been extremely beneficial to me. These contributions have played a crucial role in the realization and application of our academic concepts and research findings.

I would also like to thank Ms. Yang Yanqing, Director of the Planning and Development Department at the Shanghai Artificial Intelligence Laboratory and former Director of Yicai Research Institute. Professor Yang Yanqing has offered many academic suggestions on the research of our project and facilitated numerous opportunities for presenting our research findings within the academic community.

Furthermore, I am grateful to Professor Xiao Jianzhuang, Vice President of Guangxi University and former Director of the Green Construction Research Center at Tongji University, for his contributions to this project. Our collaborative research on the calculation of carbon emissions in the engineering sector has driven our team to dive into this project. Professor Xiao has dedicated significant efforts to promoting and applying the research findings of this project.

Professor Zhu Dajian of Tongji University is a renowned expert in the field of climate issues and public policy in China. He has provided enthusiastic guidance to our research, offering numerous academic suggestions and consistently encouraging and supporting the innovative ideas and critical thinking of new scholars.

My youngest son, Yang Zetian, is a senior in high school and has begun studying economics. Influenced by the adults around him, he has developed an interest in climate issues and carbon neutrality, alongside a strong awareness of the importance of a low-carbon lifestyle. In 2022, ten government departments and commissions in Shanghai jointly organized the inaugural Youth Dual Carbon Proposal Competition. Encouraged by parents, Yang Zetian and three of his classmates formed a research group to participate in the competition with the theme "Establishing a Household Carbon Account Mechanism and Mobilizing Public Participation in Carbon Reduction", winning an award. Their social research findings and proposed mechanisms represent significant innovations compared to the current carbon inclusion framework. This book draws upon the results of their social research projects, underscoring the importance of fostering green environmental values and lifestyles among young people.

I would also like to extend my thanks to Yu Hui, who has dedicated a considerable amount of time to proofread this book, thereby contributing to its textual quality.

I would like to thank Dr. Jiao Yi for his meticulous review of this book and for providing many insightful suggestions.

Finally, we would like to thank Mr. Mao Zengyu, the President of Economic Press China, for his support for this book. We also thank editors Ms. Jiang Li, Ms. Jiang Jing, and Ms. Liu Shihuo, who was responsible for the output of the versions in foreign languages, for their assistance and support during the editing and publishing process.

The editorial team proofread every word, making significant efforts to present the most accurate and comprehensive content to our readers.

There are countless individuals who have provided us with support and assistance in our work, and it would be impossible to list them all. Here, I would like to extend my sincere thanks to each and every one of them.

Competing Interests The author has no competing interests to declare that are relevant to the content of this manuscript.

Research Team

Led by Dr. Yang Baoming, this project boasts a team of esteemed researchers, including He Lingtong, Han Chuanfeng, Huang Yuxiang, Shi Qian, Liu Xinghua and Xu Peizheng.

As the project's lead, Dr. Yang Baoming is responsible for the core theoretical research and final outcomes, guiding the overall compilation of the book.

Ms. He Lingtong coordinates the editorial work of the book, contributing to the writing of Chaps. 1, 3, parts of Chaps. 5 and 6, oversees the verification of all references as well as the production of data charts and tables, and participates in the overall proofreading.

Mr. Xu Peizheng, primarily focusing on research related to the power market reform within this project, contributes to the writing of parts of Chap. 10 and the appendices, while also assisting in the proofreading of the entire book.

Prof. Huang Yuxiang serves for the project as the senior consultant in economics, responsible for reviewing the outcomes of the project in line with professional theories. He provides suggestions for improvement and optimization, and actively participates in the discussion on crucial issues, ideas and theories.

Professors Han Chuanfeng, Shi Qian and Liu Xinghua actively engage in numerous seminars throughout the duration of this project, offering invaluable guidance and numerous suggestions and insights. Their contributions significantly enhance the research outcomes and the overall quality of the book.

July 2023

Contents

Chapter 1
Goals, Progress, Issues and Challenges of Global Carbon Neutrality

Climate change has emerged as one of the major challenges affecting global development in the twenty-first century. It exerts unprecedented impacts globally, including frequent climate disasters, altered weather patterns leading to food production crises, and rising sea levels, creating catastrophic risks that are affecting countries across the globe without discrimination. Governments and social organizations are increasingly aware of the urgency to take decisive actions to address this dire situation.

Since 1992, when the United Nations Framework Convention on Climate Change (UNFCCC) was signed by over 150 countries and the European Economic Community, the pursuit of global carbon neutrality has been ongoing for nearly three decades. Nearly 100 economies worldwide have proposed carbon neutrality targets of varying degrees. However, due to the disparities in development stages, perceptions and institutional frameworks among these economies, the intensity and effectiveness of their carbon neutrality efforts vary significantly. Notably, the tendency to politicize the climate change has slowed down the process towards global carbon neutrality. As the gravity and urgency of climate change intensify, it is crucial to recognize that we share one Earth and inhabit a common world. Therefore, we are expected to embrace the vision of building a community with a shared future for mankind, to be united to tackle the pressing issue of climate change, and to actively engage in self-help efforts.

1.1 Goals of Global Carbon Neutrality

The UN Climate Change Conference and the UN Intergovernmental Panel on Climate Change (IPCC) stand as the most influential international organizations addressing climate-related issues.

The UN Climate Change Conference, commonly known as the Conference of Parties to the UNFCCC, or COP for short, is the world's largest and most important

B. Yang, *The Carbon Emission Liability Mechanism*,
https://doi.org/10.1007/978-981-96-3612-9_1

annual climate-related conference. The COP is held under the leadership of the UNFCCC and aims to bring together countries that are parties to the UNFCCC every year to discuss strategies for jointly addressing climate change. Notably at the COP 21 held in Paris on December 12, 2015, 195 countries adopted *The Paris Agreement*, which outlined a unified global action to address climate change after 2020. Article 2 of *The Paris Agreement* explicitly committed to "holding the increase in global average temperature to well below 2 °C above pre-industrial levels and pursuing efforts to limit the temperature increase to 1.5 °C above pre-industrial levels, recognizing that this would significantly reduce the risks and impacts of climate change". Furthermore, Article 4.1 of *The Paris Agreement* stated that "in order to achieve the long-term temperature goal set out in Article 2 … to achieve a balance between anthropogenic emissions by sources and removals by sinks of greenhouse gases in the second half of this century, on the basis of equity".

The UN Intergovernmental Panel on Climate Change (IPCC) was jointly established in 1988 by the World Meteorological Organization (WMO) and the United Nations Environment Programme (UNEP) to provide political leaders with periodic scientific assessments concerning climate change, its implications and risks, as well as to put forward adaptation and mitigation strategies.

In October 2018, the IPCC released a report titled *Special Report: Global Warming of 1.5 °C*, focusing on the impacts of global warming of 1.5 °C above pre-industrial levels. The report stated that limiting global average temperature increase to 1.5 °C by the end of the twenty-first century would require rapid, far-reaching and unprecedented transitions in all aspects of society. The report found that limiting global warming to 1.5 °C rather than 2 °C clearly benefits humans and natural ecosystems, significantly reducing the risks of long-term or irreversible climate change. According to the report, the global response to warming of 1.5 °C comprises "rapid and far-reaching" transitions in land and ecosystem, energy, urban and infrastructure, and industrial system. By 2030, global net anthropogenic CO_2 emissions must decline by about 45% from 2010 levels, ultimately reaching net zero emissions by the year 2050. This implies the necessity of removing CO_2 from the atmosphere to offset residual emissions. At the same time, the IPCC has also emphasized the unprecedented challenges posed by keeping warming within 1.5 °C. A temperature control target of within 1.5 °C, and net-zero emissions by 2050, constitute the global goal for carbon neutrality (Fig. 1.1).

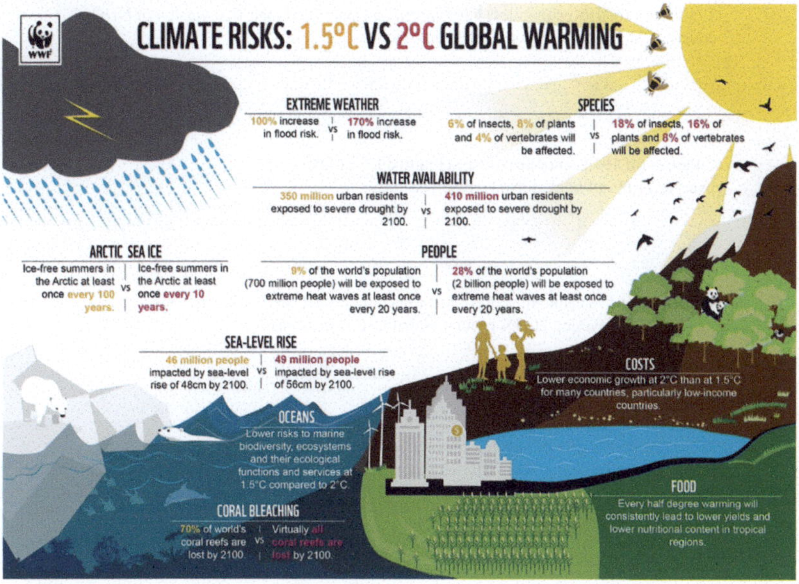

Fig. 1.1 Climate risks: 1.5 °C vs. 2.0 °C global warming (*Source* IPCC)

1.2 Progress Towards Global Carbon Neutrality

1.2.1 Carbon Reduction Commitments of Parties to The Paris Agreement

The Paris Agreement, ratified in 2015, set forth the ambitious goal of achieving carbon neutrality, but progress towards this goal has been slower than anticipated. As of May 31, 2023, according to Climate Watch, 195 Parties (comprising 194 countries and the EU) out of a total of 198 economies (the EU is treated as a single economy) have signed *The Paris Agreement* and submitted their initial Nationally Determined Contributions (NDCs), covering 94.3% of total global greenhouse gas (GHG) emissions. Furthermore, all Parties are obliged to submit Long-Term Low Greenhouse Gas Emission Development Strategies (LT-LGEDS), of which 62 Parties have submitted LT-LGEDS, covering 71.6% of total global GHG emissions. Additionally, 109 Parties have explicitly mentioned their intention to reduce the total GHG emissions up to 2030, accounting for 80.5% of the total global GHG emissions. In accordance with the terms of the Agreement, Parties are required to update or submit their NDCs every 5 years, and currently 176 Parties have updated or submitted the second version of NDCs, covering 80.5% of the total global GHG emissions (see Fig. 1.2). According to the *Emissions Gap Report 2022* released by UNEP in October 2022, only a few countries, such as Australia, Brazil, Indonesia, and Republic of Korea, have updated

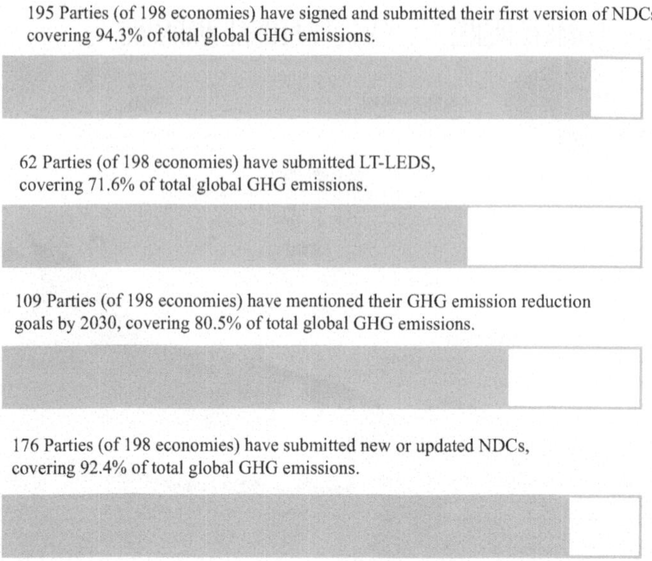

Fig. 1.2 Implementation of *The Paris Agreement* (*Source* Climate Watch)

their NDCs after the COP 26 conference held in October 2021, and submissions account for 0.5 $GtCO_2e$ of the total.

In addition, Climate Watch has been diligently monitoring commitments of countries around the world to carbon neutrality target. As of May 31, 2023, a total of 91 economies (representing 95 countries) have announced zero-carbon targets, covering 78.9% of global GHG emissions. Of these, 21 economies have enshrined their net-zero targets into law, covering 15.5% of global GHG emissions; 49 economies have outlined zero-carbon targets in their national policies, covering 57.5% of global GHG emissions; and 19 economies have launched explicit zero-carbon initiatives, covering 4.4% of global GHG emissions. Unfortunately, 106 economies remain without zero-carbon plans, covering 22.7% of global GHG emissions, mainly located in Africa, Central Asia and certain Latin American countries (see Fig. 1.3).

Of the 91 economies that have announced zero carbon targets, the vast majority (60 economies) have set their targets in 2050, consistent with that stipulated in *The Paris Agreement*, covering 30% of global GHG emissions; and 9 economies have announced a zero-carbon target before 2050, covering 1.8% of global GHG emissions; and 15 economies have set their targets beyond 2050, covering 1.8% of global GHG emissions (see Fig. 1.4). Economies with zero carbon emission announcement by and before 2050, as targeted in *The Paris Agreement*, account for only one-third of global GHG emissions.

It has been eight years after the signing of *The Paris Agreement*, but compliance remains challenging. At present, while each country has made an announcement to achieve net zero carbon emissions, the actual implementation hinges on the effectiveness of the mechanism design and the enforcement capabilities of individual nations.

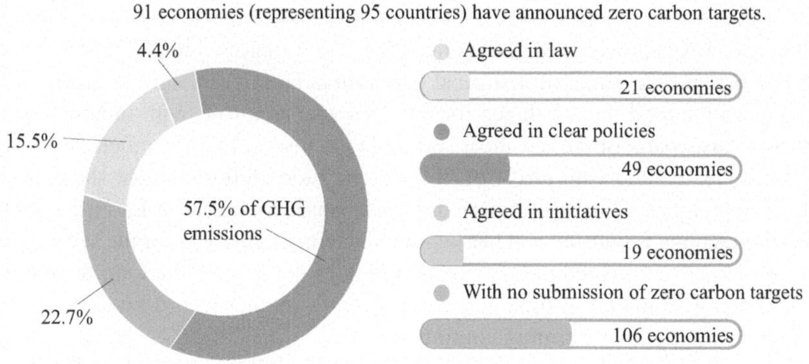

Fig. 1.3 Zero carbon announcement

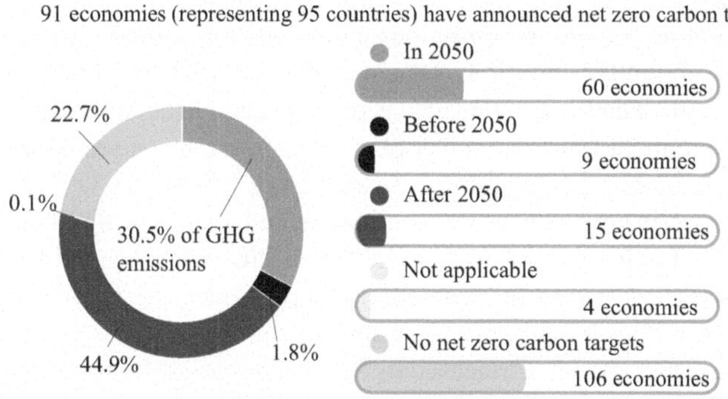

Fig. 1.4 Year of net zero carbon emissions

Assessing the compliance status of *The Paris Agreement* reveals that there is significant pressure to attain net zero carbon emissions by 2050, indicating a substantial gap towards achieving global carbon neutrality.

1.2.2 Global Climate Change and Carbon Emissions

In April 2023, the World Meteorological Organization (WMO) released the report titled *State of the Global Climate 2022*. The report indicates that the eight years 2015 to 2022 are likely to be the eight warmest years on record due to increased concentrations and accumulated heat of GHGs. In 2022, extreme heatwaves, droughts and devastating floods have already affected millions of people and caused billions of dollars in damages. The signals and impacts of climate change are becoming increasingly evident. Sea level continued to rise in 2022, reaching a new record high. Since January 2020, global mean sea level has risen by nearly 10 mm, approximately

10% of the overall rise in sea level since satellite measurements began in 1993. In the European Alps, records of glacier mass loss were shattered in 2022. Mass losses were far beyond the range of historical variability. The Greenland Ice Sheet ended with a negative total mass balance for the 26th year in a row, with intense surface melt over large parts of the ice sheet and large ice losses. In September, heavy rain (not snow) associated with post-tropical cyclone Fiona fell on the ice sheet, also a first for September. This would mark the third consecutive year of La Niña. Such a triple-dip La Niña is unusual and has kept global temperature low for the second year in a row. However, this temporary fluctuation does not reverse the long-term trend, and it is merely a matter of time before we witness another record-breaking hottest year. Obviously, global warming continues.

On March 7, 2023, the International Energy Agency (IEA) released its *CO_2 Emissions in 2022* report. The report showed that global energy-related CO_2 emissions grew by 0.9% or 321 Mt in 2022, reaching a new high of over 36.8 Gt (see Fig. 1.5). CO_2 growth in 2022 was well below global GDP growth of 3.2%, reverting to a decade-long trend of decoupling emissions and economic growth that was broken by 2021's sharp rebound in emissions. Despite the global rise in carbon emissions in 2022 due to extreme weather events such as droughts and heat waves, as well as an unusually large number of nuclear power plant shutdowns, increased deployment of clean energy technologies helped prevent an additional 550 Mt in CO_2 emissions. In 2022, global growth in emissions was lower than feared, thanks to significant growth in clean energy technologies such as renewables, electric vehicles, and heat pumps. Without this increased growth in clean energy deployment, the annual increase in energy-related emissions would have been almost triple.

On March 20, 2023, the IPCC released its Sixth Assessment Report titled *Climate Change 2023: Synthesis Report*. The report revealed that over the past century, the combustion of fossil fuels, along with unequal and unsustainable energy and land use, has led to a steady rise in global temperatures, currently standing at 1.1 °C above pre-industrial levels. Consequently, this has resulted in more frequent and intense extreme weather events, posing increasing risks to natural ecosystems and human populations across all regions of the globe. As warming increases, food and water security become increasingly critical, particularly when coinciding with other

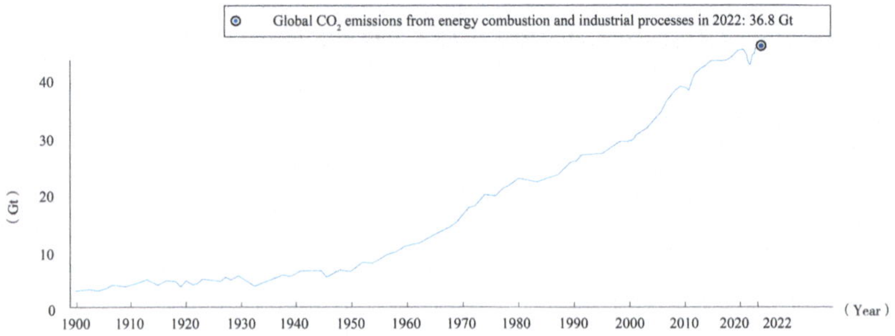

Fig. 1.5 Global CO_2 emissions and their annual change, 1900–2022 (*Source* IEA)

adverse events such as pandemics or regional conflicts. The challenges of achieving global carbon neutrality have become even more acute as GHG emissions continue to rise. The current pace and scale of efforts, along with existing plans, are insufficient to address the challenges posed by climate change. In the face of the growing climate challenges, the report states that all sectors will need to make full, rapid and sustained reductions in GHG emissions this decade if global temperature increase is to be kept to within 1.5 °C of pre-industrial levels, and urgent actions are required to halve emissions by 2030. Ultimately, the IPCC proposed the concept of "climate resilient development", which necessitates the integration of climate change adaptation measures with efforts to reduce GHG emissions.

In recent years, despite the energy crisis triggered by extreme weather events, the Russian-Ukrainian conflict, and the pandemic, the intensity of global carbon emissions has declined. Nonetheless, global carbon emissions continue to reach record highs every year, far beyond the goals of "achieving net zero and limiting global average temperature increase to 1.5 °C by 2050".

1.2.3 Current State of Global Carbon Pricing Mechanism

To cope with the ever-increasing GHG emissions, countries are exploring the feasibility of restricting carbon emissions and guiding the whole society towards carbon reduction by means of a pricing mechanism: carbon pricing. Establishing a sound, reasonable, affordable and coordinated carbon pricing mechanism has emerged as a crucial aspect of the global response to climate change.

Carbon pricing is a mechanism by charging emitters for each ton of CO_2 equivalent released, mainly including: Carbon Tax, Emission Trading System (ETS), Carbon Crediting Mechanism, Internal Carbon Price and so on.

In May 2023, the World Bank released a report titled *State and Trends of Carbon Pricing 2023*". The World Bank has been tracking the carbon market for around two decades, and the annual report of *State and Trends of Carbon Pricing* is now in its tenth year. When the first report was published a decade ago, only 7% of global emissions were covered by either a carbon tax or an ETS. In 2023, as highlighted in the 2023 report, almost a quarter of global GHG emissions (23%) are now covered, but in recent year, the growth has not exceeded 1%. As of April 2023, there have been 73 carbon pricing mechanisms (carbon taxes and ETSs only) in operation globally, and the introduction of carbon pricing instruments remains an ongoing effort in various countries and regions across the globe, albeit with sluggish progress.

The countries that have introduced carbon taxes or ETSs are mainly high-income countries located in Europe and North America, and their carbon prices are higher than those of low-income countries. The vast majority of high-income countries have carbon prices above USD 50/ton and largely exceed USD 15/ton, while low- and middle-income countries have carbon prices largely below USD 10/ton. Nonetheless, there is still a large gap compared to the price of carbon that would support a global carbon neutrality goal. The High-Level Commission on Carbon Prices concluded in

2017 that carbon prices needed to be at the level of USD 40/metric tons of carbon dioxide (tCO_2) to USD 80/tCO_2 in 2020 and reach USD 50/tCO_2 to 100/tCO_2 by 2030 to be on track to keep temperatures below 2 °C—the upper end of the limit agreed upon in *The Paris Agreement*. Adjusting for inflation allows a more direct comparison with current carbon prices—prices would need to reach USD 61 to USD 122 by 2030, which is higher than the current carbon prices in the vast majority of regions (see Fig. 1.6).

Carbon pricing mechanism has become a pivotal instrument in achieving climate goals. Despite the fact that Finland imposed the world's first carbon tax in 1990, over three decades ago, there remains a significant gap, far beyond the goals stipulated in *The Paris Agreement* and temperature targets set by the IPCC in terms of the number of countries involved, the amount of GHG emissions, and the level of carbon pricing implemented.

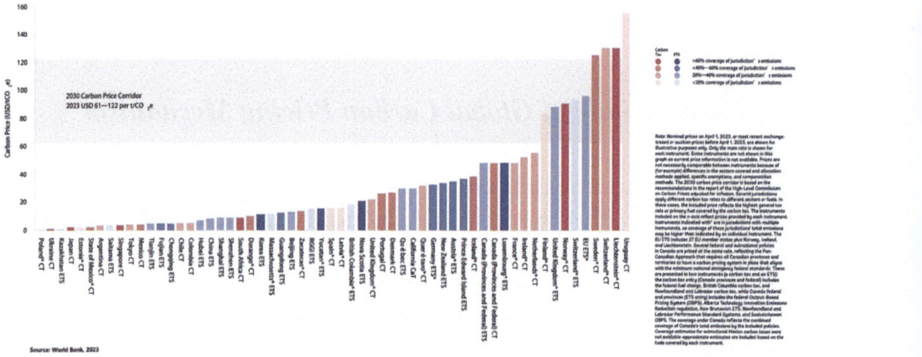

Fig. 1.6 Prices and coverage across ETSs and carbon taxes (*Source* World Bank. *Note* Nominal prices on April 1, 2023, or most recent exchange-traded or auction prices before April 1, 2023, are shown for illustrative purposes only. Only the main rate is shown for each instrument. Some instruments are not shown in this graph as current price information is not available. Prices are not necessarily comparable between instruments because of (for example) differences in the sectors covered and allocation methods applied, specific exemptions, and compensation methods. The 2030 carbon price corridor is based on the recommendations in the report of the High-Level Commission on Carbon Prices adjusted for inflation. Several jurisdictions apply different carbon tax rates to different sectors or fuels. In these cases, the included price reflects the highest general tax rate or primary fuel covered by the carbon tax. The instruments included on the x-axis reflect prices provided by each instrument. Instruments indicated with* are in jurisdictions with multiple instruments, so coverage of those jurisdictions' total emissions may be higher than indicated by an individual instrument)

1.3 Issues and Challenges Facing Global Carbon Neutrality

Climate change has garnered widespread consensus at the global level, leading governments to engage in the pursuit of global carbon neutrality through various measures such as signing agreements, committing to carbon neutrality, and adopting relevant carbon pricing instruments, etc. However, the progress made so far remains insufficient when compared to the remaining time available to mankind and the immense time cost already incurred. Humanity still faces enormous challenges in achieving global carbon neutrality.

1.3.1 Increased Frequency and Severity of Global Climate Disasters

Global warming is an indisputable reality, and the extreme weather events it triggers are breaking records. *The Global Climate Status Report (2022)* released by the China Meteorological Administration (CMA) showed that the year 2022 witnessed a significant increase in the number of global meteorological disasters, primarily characterized by high temperatures and severe droughts during the summer of the northern hemisphere as well as widespread torrential rainfall and flooding across various regions. Europe, China, the United States, Japan, Pakistan and India suffered record-high temperatures and unprecedented heatwaves. Specifically, droughts ravaged the United Kingdom, France, Romania and China while Pakistan, Brazil, eastern Australia, India, Bangladesh and Republic of Korea were hit by devastating floods caused by intense rainfall. Extreme events, such as high temperatures, droughts and floods, have profoundly disrupted the daily life of every human being on Earth, while causing tens of billions of dollars in damages and further contributing to the energy crisis and global carbon emissions. This is the Earth's warning to mankind, which awakens public awareness of the climate crisis and the looming climate tipping points, and further sounds the alarm that time is running out for mankind.

1.3.2 1.5 °C Temperature Control Window May Be Closing

On October 27, 2022, the United Nations Environment Programme (UNEP), together with the Copenhagen Climate Centre and other institutions, released the Emissions Gap Report 2022 titled *The Closing Window: Climate Crisis Calls for Rapid Transformation of Societies* (see Fig. 1.7). The report found that the international community stands still far from the Paris target, with no credible pathway to achieve the 1.5 °C goal. Despite the decision by all countries at COP 26 in 2021 to strengthen NDCs, the NDCs submitted in 2021 reduce projected global greenhouse gas (GHG) emissions by only 0.5 gigatons of CO_2 equivalent ($GtCO_2e$), less than 1% of the

Fig. 1.7 Cover of emissions gap report 2022

projected global emissions in 2030. "This report tells us in cold scientific terms what nature has been telling us, all year, through deadly floods, storms, and raging fires: we have to stop filling our atmosphere with greenhouse gases, and stop doing it fast," said Inge Anderson, Executive Director of UNEP. "We had our chance to make incremental changes, but that time is over. Only a root-and-branch transformation of our economies and societies can save us from accelerating climate disaster."

In March 2023, the IPCC released its Sixth Assessment Report titled *Climate Change 2023: Synthesis Report*. According to the report, global GHG emissions in 2030 associated with the implementation of NDCs announced prior to October, 2021 would make it likely that warming will exceed 1.5 °C during the twenty-first century and would make it harder to limit warming below 2 °C. There are still gaps between the projected carbon emissions resulting from implemented policies and those outlined from NDCs, and financial flows fall far short of what is needed to achieve climate goals across all sectors and regions. Among the scenarios and model pathways evaluated, the best estimate indicates a global warming of 1.5 °C between 2021 and 2040. Notably, the Copenhagen Climate Center, in particular, projects a global warming of 1.5 °C by August 2034 based on its calculations.

1.3.3 Contradiction Between the Long-Term Goal of Carbon Neutrality and the Short-Term Goal of National Development

GHGs are the largest public goods, and carbon neutrality is a global medium- and long-term goal. However, governments across the globe are confronted with diverse development issues: economy, employment, energy security and so on. Especially in the midst of global downward economic landscape interwoven with global stagflation and recession, the pursuit of carbon neutrality often finds itself relegated to the backburner. Tim Gould, Chief Energy Economist at the International Energy Agency, has expressed concern that "following *The Paris Agreement*, investment in the energy transition is increasing in developed countries and China, while spending in other developing countries and emerging markets remains still stuck at the 2015 level, and that to jointly address energy and climate issues, it will be impossible if emerging developing economies could not catch up with."

Certainly, the window for global temperature control targets is being closing at an accelerating rate due to the "procrastination" of governments, and the long-term goal of carbon neutrality is becoming increasingly urgent.

1.3.4 Politicization of Carbon Neutrality and Increasing Complexity in Climate Negotiations

Energy use is the primary source of carbon emissions and is closely tied to human's economic development and living standards. Carbon emissions are essentially related to development. A period of rapid industrial development will witness a huge increase in carbon emissions. Therefore, carbon neutrality, once proposed, has become an important tool in the global political game. As a global public good, meaningful carbon emission reduction requires the concerted efforts of all countries in the world. However, liability sharing and fundraising have become the focus of the political game. As national interests continue to diverge, the landscape of international climate negotiations has become increasingly complex and intricate, from the relatively straightforward division between developed and developing countries in the early stage to a highly complex negotiating pattern today, with the coexistence of North–South camps and various blocs established on the basis of diverse interests. As a result, the outcomes achieved in the international climate negotiations over the past three decades have been negligible compared to the time and efforts invested.

1.3.5 Sluggish Development in Basic Theories of Climate Change Economics

Economic Growth and Climate: The Carbon Dioxide Problem, published by William D. Nordhaus in 1977, marked a pivotal moment in integrating climate issues into economic analysis, laying the foundation of climate change economics as a distinctive branch within the broader discipline. In 1992, Nordhaus put forward the Dynamic Integrated Model of Climate and the Economy (DICE), which was used to estimate the optimal path of capital accumulation and reduction of GHG emissions. In 1996, Nordhaus, in cooperation with Yang Zili, developed the Regional Integrated Model of Climate and the Economy (RICE), which allowed different countries to evaluate climate-change policies, taking into account their own economic trade-offs and self-interests. On October 8, 2018, the Royal Swedish Academy of Sciences awarded William Nordhaus the Nobel Prize in Economics for his contribution to the integration of climate change into long-run macroeconomic analysis.

Apart from Nordhaus, there are not many economists engaged in the field of climate change economics. Yet no insightful economic theories that provide more theoretical support for policy design are proposed.

1.3.6 Carbon Neutral Policy Instruments Still in Exploration

Currently, the countries in the world are exploring diverse combinations of policy instruments to promote the process of carbon neutrality, mainly including carbon pricing instruments such as carbon taxes, carbon emission rights, internal carbon price, carbon subsidies, and some non-pricing instruments. However, several questions remain unanswered: Which policy instrument is most efficient and cost-effective? Which combination of policy instruments yields the best results? Is there an optimal combination of policy instruments among countries? Given that the application of carbon policy instruments in various countries is still in its infancy, and several constraints exist, including limited application timeframes and scopes, as well as disparities in institutional frameworks, development levels, and cultural perspectives across nations, the assessment of the effectiveness of carbon neutral policy instruments has not yet been able to provide a satisfactory answer.

1.4 The Decisive Factor in Global Carbon Neutrality: The Realization of China's Dual Carbon Targets

In 2005, China surpassed the United States to become the world's largest carbon emitter; in 2013, China's per capita carbon emissions surpassed those of the European Union; and in 2021, China's per capita carbon emissions exceeded those of developed countries. Despite a declining trend in carbon intensity, China's emissions still significantly outweigh those of major economies in the world. The total amount and the intensity of carbon emissions make China a key factor in the process of global carbon neutrality.

China's commitment to climate action is unequivocal. It ratified the United Nations Framework Convention on Climate Change (UNFCCC) by the National People's Congress (NPC) on November 7, 1992, and joined the international collaboration on global carbon neutrality, actively fulfilling its liability to reduce carbon emissions. In 2020, China announced its ambitious "3060" dual carbon targets, aiming to achieve carbon peaking by 2030 and carbon neutrality by 2060. Since the introduction of the targets, China has made a sound, orderly and solid commitment to the goal of carbon peaking and carbon neutrality, set up a dual carbon "leader group", and basically established the "1+N" policy system for carbon peaking and carbon neutrality. The carbon market has operated in an orderly manner, and the green and low-carbon transformation of energy resources has continued to be promoted, which has sent positive signals to the international community and strengthened the international community's confidence in the prospects for global climate governance. China is expected to become a decisive force in global carbon neutrality.

1.4.1 Current Status of Carbon Emissions in China

According to *CO_2 Emissions in 2022*, a report released by the IEA, in 2022, global energy-related CO_2 emissions reached a new high of 36.8 Gt, while energy-related emissions in China decreased 23 Mt to around 12.1 Gt (see Fig. 1.8), accounting for about one-third of the total global carbon emissions. According to IEA's *Global Energy Review: CO_2 Emissions in 2021*, on a per capita basis, CO_2 emissions were an average of 8.4 tons in China in 2021, exceeding the average in advanced economies and far exceeding that in other emerging market and developing economies (see Fig. 1.9). Since the twenty-first century, China's carbon emission intensity has continued to decline, and by 2021, the carbon emission intensity of GDP declined in China, falling to 0.45 tons of CO_2 per USD 1000 of GDP, but it is still the country with the highest carbon emission intensity among the major economies in the world (see Fig. 1.10).

1.4.2 Progress in China's Dual Carbon Policy

In 1992, China became one of the first parties to sign the United Nations Framework Convention on Climate Change (UNFCCC). After that, China has not only established a national coordinating body dedicated to addressing climate change, but also implemented a series of policies and measures in response to climate change aligned with its national sustainable development. These efforts have significantly

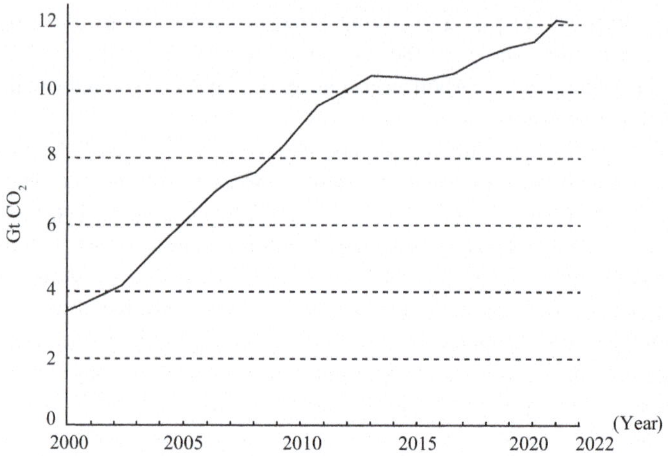

Fig. 1.8 CO_2 emissions in China, 2020–2022 (*Source* IEA)

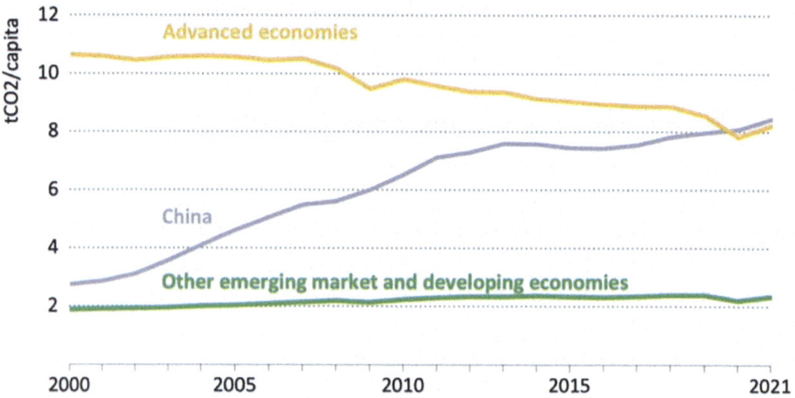

Fig. 1.9 CO_2 emissions per capita by region, 2000–2021 (*Source* IEA)

contributed to mitigating and adapting to climate change. Regarding the issue of climate change, China adheres to the principles of "common but differentiated responsibilities, equity, and respective capabilities", and resolutely defends the rights of the vast number of developing countries, including itself. In 2002, the Chinese Government ratified *The Kyoto Protocol*, and in 2007, it formulated *China's National Program for Responding to Climate Change*, which outlined the specific objectives, fundamental principles, key areas and measures to tackle climate change by 2010, and requested that the energy consumption per unit of GDP in 2010 be reduced by 20% compared to the 2005 level. Additionally, in 2007, fourteen national organs, including the Ministry of Science and Technology (MOST), the National Development and Reform Commission (NDRC), jointly formulated and released the *China's*

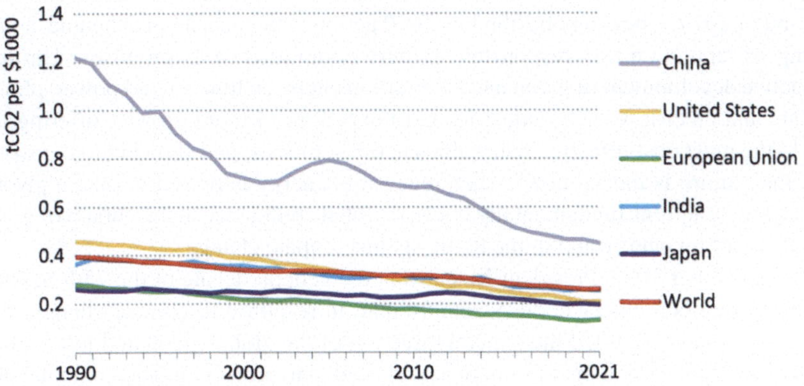

Fig. 1.10 CO_2 emission intensity of GDP, 1990–2021 (*Source* IEA)

Special Action on Science and Technology for Coping with Climate Change, which outlined the objectives, key tasks and safeguards for the advancement of science and technology, as well as the enhancement of independent innovation capabilities in the field of climate change adaptation by 2020. This marked the first comprehensive policy document addressing climate change in China, and also represented the first national program on climate change in developing countries.

In November 2013, China unveiled the *National Climate Change Adaptation Strategy*, the first strategic plan dedicated to adaptation to climate change, which systematically organized the systems and policies for addressing climate change. In June 2015, China submitted a document entitled *Enhanced Actions to Climate Change—China's Intended Nationally Determined Contributions* to the Secretariat of the UNFCCC, which defined the ambitious goals by 2030: to achieve the peaking of carbon dioxide emissions around 2030 and making best efforts to peak early; to lower carbon dioxide emissions per unit of GDP by 60% to 65% from the 2005 level; to increase the share of non-fossil fuels in primary energy consumption to around 20%; and to increase the forest stock volume by around 4.5 billion cubic meters on the 2005 level. Additionally, China remains committed to taking proactive measures to adapt to climate change, and elevating its capacities in risk resistance, prediction and early warning, disaster prevention and mitigation. As the world's largest developing country, China's diligent efforts to achieve the goals of the Convention have been recognized by the international community. In fact, according to reports from 18 NGOs, including the World Wide Fund for Nature (WWF), China has already surpassed its "fair share" in its climate change action targets.

With China's vigorous efforts, countries around the world reached *The Paris Agreement* in 2015, a milestone in the fight against climate change. China advocated for the greatest interests of developing countries in terms of nationally determined contributions, financing, technical support and transparency, etc. In 2016, China took the lead to sign *The Paris Agreement* and actively promoted its implementation. By the end of 2019, China had fulfilled its 2020 action targets ahead of schedule, solidifying its reputation as a responsible country committed to its promises. Through the active development of green and low-carbon energy, China's wind power, photovoltaic and electric vehicle industries have experienced rapid growth, offering the world the most cost-effective renewable energy solutions, and showing to the world that the "future is indeed now" when renewable energy is poised to play a pivotal role. China's actions fundamentally boosted global confidence in the pursuit of green and low-carbon energy and in the battle against climate change.

In September 2020, President Xi stated at the general debate of the 75th Session of the United Nations General Assembly that, in response to climate change, *The Paris Agreement* signified the general direction of the global green and low-carbon transition, representing the minimum action needed to protect our shared homeland, the Earth, and that all countries must take decisive steps forward. At the same time, China announced its intention to scale up its Intended Nationally Determined Contributions (INDCs) by adopting more vigorous policies and measures and aim to have CO_2 emissions peak before 2030 and achieve carbon neutrality before 2060. China's solemn commitment had aroused great responses around the globe, and received a wide range of positive feedbacks from the international community. On a number of major international occasions since then, President Xi Jinping had repeatedly reiterated China's dual carbon targets and emphasized resolute implementation. In particular, at the Climate Ambition Summit held in December 2020, President Xi further announced that by 2030, China aimed to lower carbon dioxide emissions per unit of GDP by 65% from the 2005 level, to increase the share of non-fossil fuels in primary energy consumption to around 25%, to increase the forest stock volume by around 6 billion cubic meters on the 2005 level, and to make the total installed capacity of wind and solar power reach more than 1.2 billion kilowatts. President Xi also emphasized that China, a country always committed to its promises, would take the new development concept as its guide, promote a comprehensive green transformation of economic and social development in the context of high-quality development, and implement the above goals in a practical manner so as to make greater contributions to the global response to climate change.

In June 2022, China released the *National Climate Change Adaptation Strategy 2035*, which put forward the guiding principles, core objectives and fundamental approaches for adapting to climate change in the new era. The document divided its focus into two dimensions: natural ecosystems and economic and social systems, based on the varying degrees of exposure and vulnerability to the adverse impacts and risks of climate change across various fields and regions. The document pinpointed crucial areas including water resources, terrestrial ecosystems, oceans and coastal zones, agriculture and food security, health and public health, infrastructure and major projects, urban habitat, and sensitive secondary and tertiary industries. Additionally, the document underscored the necessity of establishing a multi-level regional pattern which adapted to climate change, integrating climate adaptation with territorial spatial planning. It proposed climate adaptation actions tailored to eight regions and key strategic regions such as Beijing-Tianjin-Hebei, the Yangtze River Economic Belt, the Guangdong-Hong Kong-Macao Greater Bay Area, the Yangtze River Delta and the Yellow River Basin. These efforts had provided vital guidance and a solid foundation for China to adapt to climate change.

By the end of 2022, a comprehensive "1+N" policy system has been established through a series of documents, featuring clear objectives, a rational division of labor, robust measures, and seamless integration. This system strives to attain carbon peaking and neutrality, fostering a favorable collaboration model among all stakeholders and consistently driving progress towards achieving the dual carbon targets.

The "1" in the system refers to the *Working Guidance*: In October 2021, the *Working Guidance for Carbon Dioxide Peaking and Carbon Neutrality in Full and Faithful Implementation of the New Development Philosophy* and the *Action Plan for Carbon Dioxide Peaking Before 2030* were released successively, which provided a top-level blueprint for achieving the dual carbon targets, and played a pivotal role in the "1+N" policy system, a prominent development that would set directions and provide political guidance for China's efforts to decarbonize. These two documents clearly outlined the timetable, roadmap and construction plan for carbon peaking and carbon neutrality.

The "N" in the system refers to the action plans and measures: The working guidance on the dual carbon targets released by the State Council clearly outlined the path to carbon reduction, safeguard measures as well as additional support measures. Since then, targeted action plans and measures have been developed for key sectors and key industries. The key sectors covered energy structure, industrial transition, urban and rural construction, transportation, agriculture and rural areas while key industries included coal, oil and gas, iron and steel, non-ferrous metals, petrochemicals, chemicals, and building materials. Additionally, a series of supplementary plans and measures have been subsequently formulated in science and technology, financing, statistics and accounting, and talent cultivation. Furthermore, individual action plans for carbon peaking have been tailored for each of 31 provinces, autonomous regions and municipalities.

1.4.3 Achievements in China's Carbon Neutrality Process

1. China's carbon emission intensity continues to decline

According to the report released by the IEA, since the twenty-first century, China's carbon emission intensity has been on a consistent decline, and by 2021, the carbon emission intensity of GDP declined in China, falling to 0.45 tons of CO_2 per USD 1000 of GDP, but it remains the highest among the major economies in the world (see Fig. 1.10). Based on the research and calculation by CICC, China's carbon intensity in 2020 declined by 48.4% compared with the 2005 level, leading to a accumulated reduction in CO_2 emissions of about 5.8 Gt. Furthermore, energy consumption intensity decreased by 28.7% from 2011 to 2020. *China Ecological Environment Status Communique 2021* released by the Ministry of Ecology and Environment indicated that the preliminary calculation of CO_2 emissions per 10,000 yuan of GDP in China reduced by 3.8% compared with the 2020 level. Moreover, according to the *Statistical Bulletin of the People's Republic of China on National Economic and Social Development in 2022*, CO_2 emissions per 10,000 yuan of GDP (calculated at prices in 2020) decreased by 0.8% compared with the 2021 level.

China's energy structure is heavily reliant on coal-fired power, coupled with a vast network of industrial infrastructure that operates below international efficiency standards. As a leading manufacturing country, China holds a pivotal role in the global supply chain, producing a significant share of manufactured goods. China has spent substantial efforts and paid high prices in reducing carbon emissions.

2. Eco-environmental construction and carbon removal capacity enhancement

(a) Over four decades, China has contributed a quarter of the world's new greening land

China adheres to the concept of building a shared community of life between human beings and nature, and has taken practical measures to protect forests and land use, and achieved remarkable results. In March, 2023, the Office of the National Greening Commission released the *Communiqué on China's Land Greening in 2022* (hereinafter referred to as the *Communiqué*), which showed that in 2022, China made significant strides in environmental restoration, having successfully afforested 3.83 million hectares, planted grass to enhance the conditions of 3.214 million hectares of land, and implemented sand prevention, control, and rock desertification management over an area spanning 1.8473 million hectares. According to the *Communiqué*, in 2022, China comprehensively promoted the systematic management of mountains, water, forests, fields, lakes, grasses and sands, and carry out large-scale actions to green the national territory, with obvious results. Throughout the year, a total of 262 various types of activities were organized under the "Internet + Compulsory Tree Planting for All" program. Currently, China boasts 231 million hectares of forests, achieving a forest coverage rate reaching 24.02%, and its vast grasslands span 265 million hectares, with a comprehensive grassland vegetation coverage rate of 50.32%.

(b) China has reduced air pollution nearly as much in seven years as the US did in three decades

On June 14, 2022, Bloomberg published a report titled *China's Clean Air Campaign Is Bringing Down Global Pollution*, in which it said "China has reduced air pollution nearly as much in seven years as the US did in three decades". Citing data from the Energy Policy Institute at the University of Chicago, Bloomberg indicated that in eight years, from 2013 to 2020, the number of harmful particulates in the air in China fell by 40%, which was quite a feat, almost as much as what the U.S. did in three decades after enacting the *Clean Air Act*, a 44% drop in pollution levels. The international community is increasingly acknowledging China's noteworthy achievements in combating climate change and reducing air pollution.

3. Rapid increase in the share of green energy and the fast development of green energy technologies

(a) Rapid increase in the share of green energy

China's low-carbon energy transition is gaining momentum, as the production of clean energy continues to accelerate, and the share of non-fossil energy consumption steadily rises. In 2022, China's newly installed capacity of wind and photovoltaic power hit 125 million kilowatts, while the annual installed capacity of renewable energy reached 152 million kilowatts, accounting for 76.2% of the country's newly installed capacity. This significant milestone marked the emergence of green energy as the primary source of China's new power generation. By the end of 2022, the installed capacity of renewable energy had surged 1.213 billion kilowatts, accounting for 47.3% of the total installed capacity of power generation, an increase of 2.5 percentage points compared with the 2021 level. For years, China has led the world in terms of installed scale for wind power, photovoltaic power, hydropower and biomass power generation. Furthermore, 77 nuclear power units had been in operation or under construction, with a combined installed capacity of 83.35 million kilowatts, ranking second globally. In 2022, renewable energy sources contributed 2.7 trillion kilowatt-hours (kWh), accounting for 31.6% of the total electricity consumption of the whole society, an increase of 1.7 percentage points compared with that of 2021. Therefore, renewable energy sources play an increasingly critical role in ensuring energy supply. Notably, China's renewable energy power generation capacity in 2022 was equivalent to reducing domestic CO_2 emissions by about 2.26 Gt.

(b) World leader in green energy technologies

China's renewable energy technologies continue to maintain a global leading position. The global center for new energy industry has further shifted towards China, where key components produced by China, such as photovoltaic modules, wind turbines, gearboxes, account for about 70% of the global market share. Remarkably, in 2022, the exports of wind power and photovoltaic products assisted in reducing CO_2 emissions in other countries by approximately 573 Mt.

China's photovoltaic industry boasts the most complete industrial supply chain and robust industrial support in the world. Its upstream and downstream components form a synergistic linkage, ensuring obvious advantages in both production capacity and output volume, which lays a solid foundation for exports. At the same time, China's photovoltaic industry remains at the forefront of technological innovation, establishing global technological leadership and paving the way to seize opportunities in the international market. In addition, digital technology and intelligent technology have accelerated the digital transformation and upgrading of manufacturing industry, and significantly improved production efficiency. In 2022, PV module exports reached 154.8 GW, representing a 74% increase compared with that in 2021. The export value totaled USD 42.375 billion, a year-on-year growth of 65.45%, which made an important contribution to the global response to climate change, and provided support for the realization of affordable Internet access with PV in over 20 countries.

China's wind power industry has fostered a comprehensive international business chain, covering technology research, development, construction, equipment supply, testing and certification, ancillary services and other aspects that have now matured significantly. According to the statistics released by the Chinese Wind Energy Association of China Renewable Energy Society, in 2022, China's newly installed (shipment) capacity of wind turbine exports reached 2.29 million kilowatts, with a cumulative (shipment) capacity of exports of 11.93 million kilowatts. These exports have successfully gained a foothold in 49 countries across 5 continents.

According to the *Energy Technology Perspectives 2023* released by the IEA, the report listed statistics of manufacturing capacities of mature renewable energy technologies as of 2021, including offshore wind energy, onshore wind energy, solar energy, electric vehicles and other aspects of the industry chain. Notably, China's manufacturing capacity accounted for more than 50% in the global share. Among them, manufacturing capacity for offshore wind energy components accounted for 70% in the global market, with specifically 53% for towers, 73% for nacelles and 84% for blades; manufacturing capacity for onshore wind energy components accounted for 59% in the global market, with specifically 55% for towers, 62% for nacelles and 61% for blades; manufacturing capacity for solar PV components accounted for 85% in the global market, with specifically 96% for wafers, 85% for batteries, and 75% for modules; manufacturing capacity for electric cars and battery components accounted for 71% in the global market, with specifically 68% for cathode, 86% for anode, 75% for batteries and 54% for electric cars; manufacturing capacity for fuel cell heavy-duty trucks components accounted for 47% in the global market, with specifically 45% for fuel cell trucks and 48% for fuel cell systems; manufacturing capacity for heat pumps accounted for 39% in the global market; and manufacturing capacity for electrolysers accounted for 41% in the global market (see Fig. 1.11).

4. UHV grid technology and the world's energy Internet

As of late 2020, China had "14 UHV alternating current (UHVAC) lines and 16 UHV direct current (UHVDC) lines" in operation, and was constructing "2 UHVAC lines and 3 UHVDC lines", totaling 35 UHV projects with a total length of 48,000 km. The transmission capacity across the provinces and regions had reached 140 million kilowatts (kW), with a cumulative power transmission capacity of over 2.5 trillion kilowatt-hours (kWh). Notably, China had constructed a 1150 kV overhead line spanning from Zhundong, Xinjiang to Wannan, Anhui Province, with a transmission distance of 3300 km. This line stands as a world leader in terms of the highest voltage level, the largest transmission capacity, the farthest transmission distance and the most advanced technology level.

By May 2022, the world's first ±800 kV UHVDC demonstration project, the Yunnan-Guangdong UHVDC project, had cumulatively transmitted clean hydropower from Yunnan to Guangdong, the load center of the Pearl River Delta (PRD), exceeding 300 billion kWh, equivalent to saving 86.4 million tons of standard coal, or reducing CO_2 emissions by 0.23 Gt, SO_2 emissions by 1.66 Mt, nitrogen

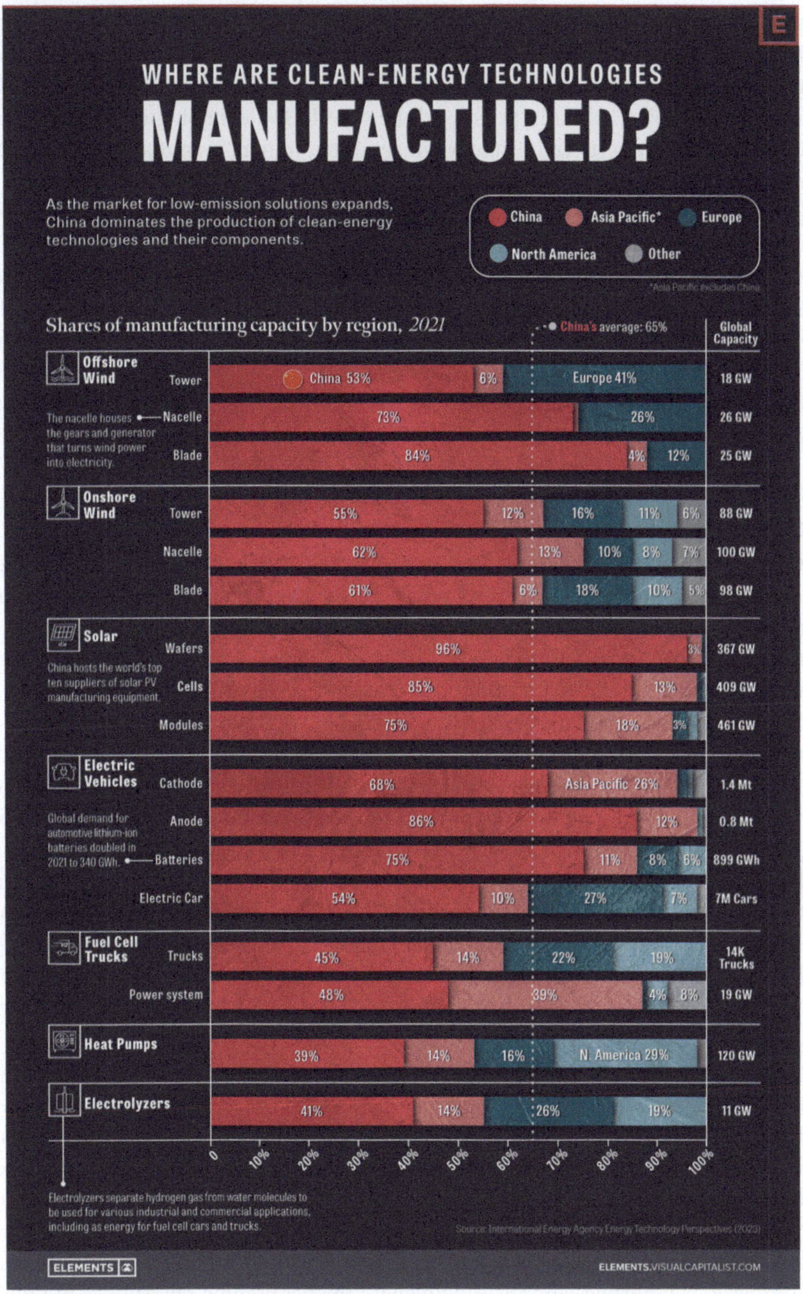

Fig. 1.11 China's global share of clean energy technology capacity in 2021 (*Source* Drawn based on the report by the IEA)

oxide emissions by 0.830 Mt and dust emissions by 43.2 Mt. This significant achievement optimizes the resources allocation between the east and west, realizes their complementary benefits and significantly contributes to China's dual carbon targets.

At present, China has fully possessed the core UHV technologies with independent intellectual property rights and a full set of equipment manufacturing capacity, thus seizing the strategic, technological, equipment and standard high grounds in UHV. State Grid has mobilized dozens of scientific research institutions, universities, over 200 equipment manufacturing enterprises, and over 500 construction units, totaling hundreds of thousands of talents, to collaborate in the R&D and construction of UHV projects. These efforts have led to the breakthroughs in 310 key technologies, and the spearheading of the development of 75 international and 788 national standards. China's undisputed leadership in UHV technology will play a crucial role in the forthcoming energy interconnection revolution and the global pursuit of carbon neutrality.

5. Carbon market and green finance development

China has been striving to explore the pivotal role of carbon market mechanisms in national decarbonation, and has been conducting pilot projects for eight years in eight provinces across the country. On July 16, 2021, the national carbon emission trading market officially opened. The first compliance cycle included 2162 key emission units in the power generation industry, covering about 4.5 Gt of CO_2 emissions, making it the largest carbon market in the world. Transaction data showed that in 2022, the national carbon market saw a total traded volume of 50.8895 Mt of carbon emission allowances, amounting to a total turnover of 2.814 billion yuan. Of this, the annual listed agreement transaction volume reached 6.219 Mt, with an annual turnover of 358 million yuan. The highest transaction price stood at 61.60 yuan per ton while the lowest 50.54 yuan per ton. And the closing price on the final trading day of the year was 55.00 yuan per ton, representing a 1.44% increase compared with that on the final trading day of the previous year. The annual bulk agreement transaction volume totaled 44.6705 Mt, with an annual turnover of 2.456 billion yuan.

By the conclusion of 2022, the cumulative turnover of carbon emission allowances in the national carbon market amounted to 230 Mt, and the cumulative turnover amounted to 10.475 billion yuan. Notably, on December 22, 2022, the cumulative turnover in the national carbon market exceeded the significant milestone of 10 billion yuan (Fig. 1.12).

In 2022, the trading activities in the national carbon trading market predominantly took place at the beginning and the end of the year. Specifically, the transaction volume in January–February and November–December comprised 19% and 66% respectively of the overall annual trade volume.

Overall, the basic framework for the national carbon trading market has been preliminarily established, and its effectiveness in encouraging enterprises to reduce GHG emissions and accelerate green and low-carbon transition has emerged gradually.

In terms of the construction of carbon trading market, as the carbon pricing mechanism matures through further enhancements to the carbon market, the behavioral

National Transaction of Carbon Emission Trading

July 16 -Dec. 31, 2021

Transaction Data in National Carbon Trading Market

Type of transaction	Highest price (yuan/ton)	Lowest price (yuan/ton)	Closing price (yuan/ton)			Volume (tons)	Turnover (yuan)	Means of transaction
			December 31, 2021	December 30, 2022	Price limit			
CEA	62.29	38.50	51.23	54.22	5.84%	30,774,596	1,451,471,161.73	Listing agreement
						148,014,754	6.209,758,861.26	Bulk agreement
						178,789,350	7.661,230,022.99	Subtotal
Total as of December 31, 2021						30.774,596	1,451,471,161.73	Listing agreement
						148,014,754	6.209758,861.26	Bulk agreement
						178,789,350	7,661,230,022.99	Total

National Transaction of Carbon Emission Trading

January 4 -Dec. 30, 2022

Transaction Data in National Carbon Trading Market

Type of transaction	Highest price (yuan/ton)	Lowest price (yuan/ton)	Closing price (yuan/ton)			Volume (tons)	Turnover (yuan)	Means of transaction
			December 31, 2021	December 30, 2022	Price limit			
CEA	51.50	50.54	54.22	55.00	1.44%	6,218,972	357,855,798.67	Listing agreement
						44,670,521	2,456,148,895.61	Bulk agreement
						50,889,493	2,814,004,694.28	Subtotal
Total as of December 30, 2022						36,993,568	1,809,326,960.40	Listing agreement
						192,685,275	8,665,907,756.87	Bulk agreement
						229,678,843	10,475,234,717.27	Total

Fig. 1.12 Transaction data in National Carbon Market in 2021 and 2022 (*Source* Shanghai Environment and Energy Exchange)

patterns of each market participant will be affected. This, in turn, will reshape the enterprises' profit outlook and help them embrace low-carbon technology into the cornerstone of their competitive edge.

6. International recognition

As the world's largest carbon emitter, China faces immense pressure from the international community. However, its proactive response to climate change has also garnered widespread praise from the international community. In particular, after General Secretary Xi Jinping formally proposed the "3060" dual carbon targets at the General Debate of the 75th Session of the UN General Assembly, a number of international experts, including Jeffrey Sachs, an American renowned economists, Tim Adams, former Under Secretary of U. S. Department of the Treasury, Lord Adair Turner, former Chair of the Financial Services Authority of the United Kingdom, and Edmond Alphandry, former Finance Minister of France, have all lauded China's significant commitment to carbon neutrality. This shows that China is at the forefront of global efforts to combat climate change, exhibiting a responsible and encouraging attitude that is highly gratifying.

On February 21, 2023, Nobel Sustainability Trust, based in Stockholm, Sweden, announced that Mr. Xie Zhenhua, China's Special Envoy for Climate Change, had been awarded the "Special Prize for the year 2022" for his exceptional contributions to global cooperation and climate change. Mr. Xie, on behalf of China, has attended world climate change conferences and exhibited outstanding leadership in coordinating the positions of all parties and fostering consensus and cooperation. In his statement, Mr. Xie emphasized that this was not just a personal honor, but also served as a recognition of China's contribution to climate change mitigation and sustainable development.

1.4.4 Challenges to China's Dual Carbon Targets

China has made great achievements in combating climate change and reducing carbon emissions over the past two decades. However, as the world's largest carbon emitter, accounting for about one-third of the global total carbon emissions, it is still facing huge domestic and international challenges.

1. Difficulty in obtaining carbon footprint data of all materials, products and services in the whole society

Within the vast landscape of society, billions of materials, products, and services exist, each with its unique carbon footprint data. The diversity of commodities and the intricate industrial chain render the collection and disclosure of carbon footprint data a costly and arduous task.

Furthermore, carbon footprint data are inherently dynamic. Even for the same product, carbon emissions can vary significantly between enterprises. Additionally, within a single enterprise, data fluctuations occur due to advancements in production technology and processes. Therefore, it is challenging to accurately capture the recent average societal carbon emission level. Additionally, the sheer volume of data involved presents a significant systematic challenge for data collection efforts.

The absence of accurate values of carbon emission factors for a wide range of materials, products and services, coupled with the lack of dynamic data of each organization's carbon footprints, poses the following challenges:

(a) It hampers the accurate assessment of carbon emissions associated with project plans, engineering design proposals, and technical plans.
(b) It complicates the development of effective top-level and sector-specific policy instruments.
(c) It impedes the selection and investment of projects since green finance fails to play a better role.
(d) It makes it difficult to allocate carbon emission liability and distribute carbon reduction tasks effectively.

2. Difficulties in the selection and implementation of policy instruments

The government aims to accelerate corporate emission reduction through the implementation of carbon taxes and carbon emission allowances. However, due to a lack of comprehensive and accurate carbon footprint data, it is challenging to determine which approach, carbon taxes or carbon markets, is more effective. As a result, the progress in implementation has been slow.

(a) Setting carbon pricing (carbon tax rates and carbon price for emission rights) poses a formidable challenge for the government, as it grapples with the complexities of determining fair pricing across a wide range of products and industries.
(b) Designing the allocation method for carbon emission allowances is a complex endeavor, as it necessitates a delicate balancing interests among multiple parties, making it a challenging task.
(c) The management of operational processes presents significant difficulties. Preventing carbon data falsification is a major challenge, and the associated costs of monitoring, reporting, and verification (MRV) are substantial. Additionally, ensuring fairness and integrity throughout the control process is a complex task, fraught with inherent challenges related to governance and anti-corruption measures.

3. How to establish a carbon market that is aligned with carbon neutrality objectives, and how to upgrade the top-level design

The current role played by the carbon market remains relatively limited despite the official launch of the trading pilot program in Beijing on March 28, 2012, over a decade ago, and the subsequent establishment of eight provincial trading pilots across the country. By the end of 2022, the cumulative transaction turnover had reached only 16.146 billion yuan. Even after the establishment of the national carbon trading market in July 2021, the trading scale remained relatively small, with a cumulative transaction turnover of 10.475 billion yuan by the end of 2022. This indicates that the current domestic carbon market plays a minor role within the broader carbon neutrality framework. Due to the lack of effective guidance of academic theories, China has been emulating carbon market schemes from Western countries. The top-level design of the carbon market lacks a clear direction towards the ultimate goal of carbon neutrality. It focuses primarily on the allocation of carbon emission allowances, making it difficult to scale up and play a crucial role in carbon emission reduction. It also struggles to address the conflicting interests between the government and the corporations, as well as between different regions and provinces, thereby hindering the achievement of market unity.

4. How to attract more green finance investments

To achieving the ambitious "3060" dual carbon targets, China requires an investment of approximately 200 trillion yuan. Where will the funds come from? Relying solely on fiscal investment for such a massive amount is not realistic. It is crucial to find alternative funding sources that avoid imposing a significant burden on the macro economy and to create effective incentives for green investors. This necessitates a series of groundbreaking designs, including the utilization of carbon-related big data and comprehensive innovation in the top-level design of the carbon market.

5. How to promote carbon reduction across society in a faster, more cost-effective and efficient manner

To achieve the "3060" dual carbon targets, China must mobilize the entire society to participate in carbon reduction efforts, including every social organization and all consumers that contribute to carbon emissions. Currently, efforts have primarily focused on a limited number of carbon-intensive sectors such as coal-fired power companies, with limited effectiveness. The current situation is that the front end enterprises bear the burden of carbon reduction costs, while the back end of the industry chain and consumers remains largely indifferent to carbon reduction. In addition, the scope for carbon reduction in the front end enterprises has already been limited, as their production and carbon emissions are largely determined by the entire industry chain.

Every organization, company, and individual that consumes energy or utilizes materials and services from suppliers with carbon emissions should be considered a carbon emitter, thereby assuming the liability for carbon reduction and contributing to emissions mitigation. The primary driver of carbon emissions is not investment and production but rather consumption. Therefore, the liability for carbon reduction falls upon every organization, every company, and every individual. Carbon reduction management should swiftly expand its scope to encompass every organization, every company, and all consumers within the society.

To achieve the dual carbon targets, it is imperative to accelerate the establishment of a comprehensive carbon reduction system across the society. However, the current carbon reduction system, primarily focusing on the coal-fired power industry, confronts numerous challenges, chief among them being the scarcity of theoretical and conceptual guidance.

6. Climate issues may become a variable that influences China's international relations.

Based on the outcome of the United Nations Climate Change Conference COP27, which concluded on November 20, 2022, it is apparent that climate issues have progressively emerged as a major topic in international relations, leading to unfavorable implications for China.

7. How can China report its annual progress towards carbon peaking and carbon neutrality to the world?

China has surpassed the United States to become the world's largest CO_2 emitter, making it a significant focus of global climate concerns. The international community will closely monitor China's progress towards carbon peaking and carbon neutrality, expecting annual reports that are accurate, comprehensive, credible, and persuasive in terms of data and outcomes. This underscores the urgent need for China to establish a robust and compelling data system that showcases substantial achievements and compelling evidence.

8. Addressing carbon border adjustment and developing a low-carbon economy

The European Union's Carbon Border Adjustment Mechanism (CBAM) has been launched and is scheduled to commence trial operation in 2023. It is crucial for us to have well-defined strategies and plans in place. Presently, apart from advocating for our interests and collaborating with developing countries, we lack a comprehensive and systematic set of measures to effectively address this situation, which may potentially create more barriers for our export trade.

International carbon border adjustments impose clear requirements on the quality of our low-carbon economy. To remain the competitiveness of Chinese exports, it is imperative that they are not only cost-effective and of high quality, but also are low-carbon or even zero-carbon products. Furthermore, it is essential to provide credible, authoritative and compelling carbon footprint data.

As a major manufacturing nation, the international carbon border adjustment mechanism presents both opportunities and challenges for China. However, given the current absence of an effective carbon reduction system within our country, the predominant impact tends to be more negative. Nonetheless, with the exercise of sufficient wisdom and foresight, we have the potential to shift its impact from a passive to an active stance.

Firstly, China is also a massive market for imported products and resources, with a significant volume of fossil fuel imports. The impact of carbon tariffs can be largely offset by this factor.

Secondly, once China establishes a robust carbon reduction management system, it can enhance its international influence on climate issues. If we successfully develop a comprehensive carbon footprint big data system and establish a sound carbon market framework, under a consumer liability mechanism, it is the consuming countries that should bear the primary economic liability for carbon reduction.

Thirdly, it can facilitate the promotion of high-quality economic development domestically. Carbon border adjustments ultimately assess the economic quality, restraining products with high carbon emissions while paving the way for the rise of low-carbon economies. To improve its economic quality, China must leverage this driving force and the evolving international trade regulations, transforming from a passive stance to an active one.

9. How to respond to the competition in the industry chains of international green energy and carbon neutrality technologies

As the world embarks on the journey towards carbon neutrality, the market for green energy technologies and carbon neutrality-related technologies is poised to create a vast industrial chain, emerging as a pivotal sector in the global new economy. China has already established a significant advantage in areas such as photovoltaics, wind energy, and ultra-high voltage transmission. It is crucial for China to expedite global market expansion, enhance its market share, and elevate its position in the international green energy industry. Securing a leading edge in technologies like carbon capture, utilization, and storage (CCUS) is of paramount importance for China's journey towards carbon neutrality.

10. How to effectively transition the energy mix and increase the share of renewable energy sources

To achieve the dual carbon targets, China is crucially expected to reduce the share of fossil fuels and significantly increase the share of renewable energy sources.

Currently, fossil fuels account for approximately 85% of China's energy mix, but by 2060, non-fossil energy sources are expected to comprise 80% of the entire energy consumption system in China.

The challenge lies in the recent extensive investments in coal-fired power, making it difficult to phase out. The establishment of infrastructure for renewable energy, such as transmission grids and energy storage facilities, will take time. Therefore, it is necessary to quickly raise funds and accelerate the substitution of renewable energy sources.

The recent Russia-Ukraine conflict has underscored the significance of energy security for nations across the globe. China, heavily reliant on imported fossil fuels, has a significant import dependency of around 70% for crude oil and approximately 50% for natural gas. While China possesses relatively abundant coal resources, the issue of resource scarcity remains prominent. Given the critical nature of resources security, China must accelerate the development of renewable energy sources.

In the current international landscape and amidst the challenges posed by climate issues, striking a balance between traditional energy investments and expediting the energy transition process is not only beneficial for accelerating carbon neutrality but also significantly enhances energy strategic security. Renewable energy, as a local resource, should also be considered when contemplating energy strategic security. A substantial portion of renewable energy in the future will be distributed and installed in a decentralized manner. Traditional energy facilities, such as coal-fired power plants, are vulnerable to pinpoint attacks, while the transportation security of fossil fuels is also relatively low. In contrast, distributed renewable energy sources exhibit greater resilience and flexibility.

Chapter 2
Philosophical, Sociological and Legal Discussions on Global Climate Change

Human first paid direct attention to climate change in the 1970s. In 1979, the World Meteorological Organization (WMO) convened the first World Climate Conference and endorsed plans to establish a World Climate Programme (WCP), through reasonable means of climate resources, to foresee and prevent potential changes in climate and to protect climate environment and resources. In 1988, the Intergovernmental Panel on Climate Change (IPCC) was established with the joint efforts of the United Nations Environment Programme (UNEP) and the WMO. It is an institution focusing on scientific consultation about international negotiations and regulations over climate change. At the same time, the negotiations for the United Nations Framework Convention on Climate Change (UNFCCC), under the promotion of the IPPC, were initiated in 1990. And UNFCCC was finalized and opened for signature in 1992 and officially entered into force in 1994.

The UNFCCC pointed out that every country should contribute to mitigating climate change, albeit with responsibilities allocated under the principle of "common but differentiated responsibilities", wherein developed countries should take the lead in adopting measures. Since then, the Conference of the Parties (COP) has been held annually, commencing in Berlin, Germany, in 1995. Then, at the third Conference in 1997, *The Kyoto Protocol* was adopted. These two documents (*The UNFCCC* and *The Kyoto Protocol*) have laid the legal foundation for global cooperation in combating climate change.

Given the inherent complexity of global climate change, in the absence of a profound understanding of its essence and a definitive optimal solution, countries tend to focus primarily on the immediate costs involved. An awkward reality is that some vested interest groups, especially developed countries within the OECD, prioritize their own interests as their starting point. Consequently, the lingering North–South division between them and developing countries, represented by China and members of the G77, has not been significantly bridged yet, and over the past three decades, there has been little tangible progress made in international negotiations and cooperation efforts.

B. Yang, *The Carbon Emission Liability Mechanism*,
https://doi.org/10.1007/978-981-96-3612-9_2

In recent years, with constant breakthroughs in the new energy technologies, the international community has increasingly focused on environmental improvement. Most countries, such as China, America, European countries, Japan and India, have developed their own timetables for Nationally Determined Contributions (NDCs) to carbon peaking and carbon neutrality. Despite persisting conflicts among vested interest groups, the global antagonism surrounding climate change has been greatly eased. Moreover, given that the international community could find optimal strategies for decarbonation mechanisms and international collaboration, it will be greatly promising for humanity to solve climate problems. Before that, it is imperative to conduct in-depth discussions on climate change from philosophical, sociological and legal perspectives to identify the greatest common denominator among nations and establish critical consensus. Only by these efforts can we establish the most effective global collaboration mechanism and accelerate carbon neutrality.

2.1 Climate and Environment: Human Challenges and the Tragedy of the Commons

There is an increasing consensus among humanity that, without concerted efforts to address climate and environmental issues, the Earth may become inhospitable to human life within a few generations. Frequent climate disasters, the rising sea level, health problems caused by air pollution and constant viral outbreaks send us a signal that we should take immediate actions right now. Today, the mainstream international community is devoting itself to environmental improvement by the approaches of reducing carbon and pollutant emissions while other pioneers are exploring alternative approaches, for instance, Elon Musk, an American entrepreneur who is committed to colonizing Mars in search of a new habitat for humanity.

According to the *Climate Change 2023* released by the IPCC in 2023, to limit the global warming to 1.5 °C above pre-industrial levels, the whole world is estimated to emit 500 Gt of CO_2 from the start of 2020. Giving the annual carbon emissions of 36 Gt worldwide in recent years, the global emission budget will be exhausted in about 12 years, specifically by 2034. Therefore, to limit the global warming to 1.5 °C, all nations are expected to make concerted, rapid, and sustained efforts to reduce GHG emissions within this decade. At the same time, if humanity aims to halve GHG emissions by 2030, emissions should be reduced from now.

So, who should be granted this limited space for development? The atmosphere, as a global public resource, inevitably turns into the "tragedy of the commons" due to its shared nature where individuals strive to occupy more while others are left with less. And the approach to securing a larger share heavily depends on the international landscape. The current approach involves regulations accompanied by negotiations, yet redemption and even wars are also viable alternatives as well. Because of the balance of power among major countries with nuclear weapons, world wars will not break out temporarily. However, intensifying regional conflicts are inevitable.

It is reasonable for humanity to harbor pessimism. Whether considering the inherent greed of human nature or the logical deduction of the "tragedy of the commons", climate disasters caused by global warming seem almost inevitable. The increasingly frequent extreme weather events send us a warning that climate disasters are already knocking on our windows, threatening to burst into our homes at any moment.

Since 1992, when representatives from 154 countries signed the UNFCCC at the United Nations Headquarter and initiated official international cooperation, global negotiations on climate change have been conducted for over three decades. But we have yet to witness significant essential progress, and the promised $100 billion fund from developed countries for decarbonation in developing countries remains largely unfulfilled. The adoption of an aspirational "loss and damage" fund resolution at COP 27 represents a significant milestone, marking for the first time funding for climate-induced loss and damage has been officially incorporated in the agenda of the COP meetings. It advocates various existing sources, including financial institutions, to provide funding to developing countries, particularly those vulnerable to climate change, in order to compensate for the "loss and damage" caused by climate disasters. However, this resolution fails to include specific operational details such as the amount of funding, mechanisms to ensure its availability, and a timeline for the implementation. All of the above gaps shed light on the extreme challenges faced by the global community in addressing climate change.

The key indicator of climate change is CO_2, and the debate regarding whether the global warming is caused by CO_2 has persisted for over three decades. In fact, the greatest achievement of this ongoing debate has been the general increase in public awareness of environmental protection, instead of fostering international collaboration to tackle climate problems or reduce carbon emissions. Climate impacts may seem remote to the average public, but air quality and smog are daily concerns that cause greater anxiety. Coupled with economic development, addressing environmental problems and improving quality of life have become urgent priorities for governments and the public worldwide. And the public eagerly awaits more actions from their governments. Climate and environmental problems are closely related to humanity. Combustion of fossil fuels not only emits CO_2, but also releases lots of pollutants, severely impacting the people's lives. Therefore, both governments and the public are eager to improve the situation.

After three decades, the necessary awareness and material basis for improving global climate have been established. Coupled with breakthroughs in clean energy and global energy interconnection, humanity has the potential to set aside differences and conflicts and jointly explore solutions to addressing global climate change.

Time is indeed effective in resolving certain problems. Over the years of debate, the emergence of revolutionary technologies, changes in perception and the emergence of new challenges have altered the original landscape. However, as time passes, the pressure on governments is mounting as the window of opportunity for addressing climate problems is narrowing.

2.2 Starting Point of Consensus on Climate Change: Building a Community with a Shared Future for Mankind

Why hasn't controversy reached a consensus in the past three decades? The international community's solution to global climate problems, predominantly driven by developed countries, has persisted in treating countries unequally in terms of carbon emission rights, disregarding the rights of all nations to develop collectively. These conflicts of interests and positions are evident, pervasive, enduring, and challenging to resolve.

Fortunately, thanks to technological breakthroughs and humanity's increasing demand for better social and environmental quality, this problem has been mitigated. Humans are now poised to find better solutions to address this problem before fundamental conflicts arise.

Building a community with a shared future for mankind is reflected in the fact that mankind not only lives on the same Earth, but also is in the same boat. To address global climate change, developed countries are also expected to recognize the rights of developing countries to pursue development.

The vision of a community with a shared future for mankind proposed by the Chinese Government is not only aligned with historical trends but also strikes a chord with developing countries. If the Chinese Government succeeds in finding an innovative approach to achieve carbon peaking and neutrality ahead of schedule in the context of both development and decarbonation, it will greatly enhance China's international status.

2.3 Carbon Emission Rights and Human Rights

The three decades of disputes over climate change has demonstrated that carbon emission rights are closely related to human rights and the right to development of a country. In addressing climate change, the most crucial is how to fairly share the liability for carbon emissions and allocate carbon emission rights. However, any slight deviation from the current path can lead us into a dead end with no solution in sight.

In scenarios where the cost of clean energy is much higher than that of fossil fuels or the supply of clean energy is insufficient, carbon emission rights are intricately related to regional development. Among the several proposals put forward at the Copenhagen Climate Conference in December 2009, the IPCC's proposal was considered as the most equitable. However, the allocated per capita carbon emissions for developed countries were still four times higher than those for developing countries. It is noteworthy that in the past century, the per capita carbon emissions in developed countries were 7.5 times higher than those in developing countries. The allocation lacked any legal basis or humanitarian sentiment displayed by affluent and influential countries in this context and was bound to be rejected by developing countries at large.

In 2006, Albert Gore, then Vice President of the United States, launched his documentary film *An Inconvenient Truth*, in which he played a key role both behind the scenes and on screen. Accompanied by a book of the same title, the release stirred significant resonance across Western countries. The film primarily addressed the impact of industrialization on global climate change and human survival, earning the Best Documentary Feature Award at the 79th Academy Awards. Accordingly, Gore was awarded the Nobel Peace Prize in 2007 for his contributions to the environmental advocacy. As the Nobel Committee remarked, "Al Gore has for a long time been one of the world's leading environmentalist politicians. He is probably the single individual who has done most to create greater worldwide understanding of the measures that need to be adopted."

Ironically, Gore's household produced a significant carbon footprint. According to a report from the Tennessee Center for Policy Research in the United States, Gore's mansion in Tennessee consumed a total of 190,000 kWh in less than a year, spanning from February 3, 2006, to January 5, 2007. While the average annual electricity consumption for households in this area was only 15,600 kWh, and the average household in America consumed 10,700 kWh per year. Gore devoured more than ten times the national average, guzzling more electricity in one month than an average local family used in an entire year.

There were several heated swimming pools in Gore's mansion, requiring continuous electricity consumption for water heating to maintain optimal swimming temperatures at all times. The electricity consumed solely for pool heating in a single year was sufficient for other American households for six years. Alarmingly, in 2017, according to data collected by the Tennessee Center for Policy Research in the United States, the Gore household's electricity consumption not only failed to decrease but actually increased, soaring to twenty-one times the national average.

How different countries and ethnicities are perceived regarding carbon emission rights is a crucial issue in the field of human rights. In the realm of human rights concerning carbon emissions, developed nations must shift their perspectives. Instead of exploiting the interests of developing countries through the allocation of carbon emission rights and the implementation of carbon border adjustment mechanism, developed countries should embrace market-based methods to purchase carbon credits and pay greater costs to obtain higher levels of carbon emissions.

China, as a current major emitter, bears a significant responsibility. To change this situation, China must not only vigorously defend its legitimate interests in the international climate arena but also take proactive actions. Only by doing so can China gradually secure the initiatives and not lag behind in the global efforts towards combating climate change.

2.4 Who Should Bear the Liability for Carbon Reduction: Producers or Consumers?

Climate change has been studied by both academia and governments for over three decades. Yet, the allocation of carbon reduction liability among nations remains unclear, along with the allocation of liability among organizations (carbon emission rights), between producers and consumers, and between the wealthy and the impoverished. These crucial matters have yet to be convincingly addressed with sound theory and logic.

Incredibly, whether the liability falls on producers or consumers has not been seriously discussed in the international climate negotiations over the past three decades. Instead, the focus has predominantly been on the mechanism of producers bearing the liability, with many regarding it as unquestionable. However, research conducted in this book reveals that this mindset is a pivotal reason why global carbon neutrality efforts have stagnated. Now is the time for a reevaluation and redefinition! Otherwise, the prevailing notion of producers bearing the liability will continue to impede global carbon neutrality efforts.

2.4.1 Carbon Emission Liability in the International Trade

Based on calculations, China emerged as a net exporter of carbon emissions in the international trade. In 2018, China's exports embodied 1.53 Gt of CO_2 emissions, while imports embodied 542 Mt of CO_2 emissions. The net export of CO_2 emissions in foreign trade accounted for approximately 10.5% of the country's total emissions. Among these, exports to the European Union embodied 270 Mt of CO_2 emissions, accounting for 17.6%, while exports to the United States embodied 286 Mt of CO_2 emissions, accounting for 18.7%. In contrast, imports from the European Union and the United States embodied 31 Mt and 44 Mt of CO_2 emissions, respectively, thus confirming China's status as a net exporter of CO_2 emissions.

China primarily imports high-tech products and services such as software and chips, while exporting mainly low to medium-end industrial products like clothing apparel and machinery. As a manufacturing powerhouse, China's net export of carbon emissions is substantial. Who should bear the liability for the carbon emissions generated by the international trade, the importing country or the exporting country? Is the assertion reasonable that "whoever emits bears the liability" (producer liability) advocated by Europe and the United States?

If academia and policymakers fail to devise a scientific theory and a series of policy instruments that are both fair and efficient, it will be a lengthy process to reduce carbon emissions relying solely on individual self-awareness. Therefore, academia and policymakers have the responsibility to research and develop rational liability mechanisms from top to bottom. This requires multidisciplinary research spanning humanities, law, and economics to identify the most reasonable and beneficial international liability mechanisms for addressing the issue.

2.4.2 The Rationality of Consumers Bearing the Liability

From an economic perspective, the mechanisms of both producers bearing the liability (producer liability) and consumers bearing the liability (consumer liability) theoretically yield similar outcomes for an efficient market. Ultimately, the cost of carbon emissions will be transferred to the end consumers, becoming part of the total product cost. However, in the case of carbon emissions, both energy and electricity supply markets and international trade are non-efficient markets. From an efficiency standpoint, the mechanism of consumer liability is more conducive to the design and implementation of emission reduction systems and is easier to clarify liability relationships when designing policy instruments and governance schemes. Economics can prove that the mechanism of consumer liability enjoys higher governance efficiency and fairness under current international trade and market conditions in various countries. Consumers are the ultimate end of product production and distribution, while the production process and chain can be lengthy. It is easier to identify consumers, who bear the liability, and subsequently design related mechanism.

From a humanistic and moral perspective, it is rational for consumers to bear the liability. Both producers and intermediate service providers generate carbon emissions, but all to satisfy consumers' demands. Conversely, when consumers do not need specific products and services, the associated carbon emissions in the production process will not occur logically. When society has the ability to internalize external social costs into product costs through calculation, the mechanism of consumer liability becomes natural. Consumers bear all costs of general products, including the costs of materials, processing, transportation, and services. Of course, regarding carbon emissions, we don't mean that producers do not need to bear the liability, but rather consumers' right to know the truth and the right to choose drive producers to bear the liability naturally through market mechanism. Producers with carbon emission intensity exceeding industry averages will be at a competitive disadvantage in terms of cost and brand reputation. Under the mechanism where consumers bear the main liability, producers' liability remains clear and significant. High-carbon emitters may even be directly eliminated.

From a legal perspective, the mechanism of both producer liability and consumer liability are rational from the standpoint of fairness. But consumers should bear the main liability for cost burden, as this is the inherent logic of the market. Considering fairness, consumers generally bear the average level of industrial emissions, whereas producers with excessive emissions will bear the consequences accordingly.

2.5 Balancing Interests of Nations and Regions: The Impossible Triangle of Climate Governance

A major trilemma in global climate governance, dubbed the "impossible triangle" by some scholars, revolves around the tension among globalized governance, governance efficiency and equity, and national sovereignty. The negotiations at various global climate conferences revolve around seeking a balance within this impossible triangle. *The Paris Agreement* marks a pivotal transition from a top-down, mandatory emission allocation system to a bottom-up, voluntary emission reduction commitment system, signifying a challenging evolution involving the balance of fairness, efficiency, and national interests. The top-down governance model, with its enforcement capabilities, may guarantee governance efficiency to some extent. However, the bottom-up approach, though respecting the will and development needs of each country, may compromise the interests and fairness of all countries due to the temporal and spatial externalities of climate issues, potentially sacrificing efficiency. To truly address global climate change, the international community must work on three dimensions.

1. Cruciality of global coordination: Given historical factors and varying stages of national development, it is imperative to establish a framework which adheres to the principle of "common but differentiated responsibilities" among countries and regions. However, there are significant challenges in quantifying the emissions and implementing this framework. Some countries emit less while others emit more, so it becomes difficult to achieve the goals. Therefore, global coordination includes not only the coordination in the allocation of emissions, but also the coordination in technology, talent, project development, carbon markets, and financing among countries, forming a comprehensive global framework that ensures optimal efficiency.

   The global carbon reduction efforts over the past three decades have shown that a sole focus on the allocation of liability and emission rights leads to ineffective solutions. Therefore, the international community should focus on more consensus points conducive to global carbon neutrality, such as exploring more efficient carbon reduction mechanisms, technological cooperation, building a global energy Internet, and constructing international carbon markets, which would make it easier for governments to pursue their goals.
2. High efficiency on the basis of relative fairness: Addressing global climate change necessitates both comprehensive and timely actions. High governance efficiency must be achieved to meet the ambitious targets proposed by the IPCC. Efficiency mechanisms demand rigorous constraints and enhanced coordination, requiring all parties to bear liability and make contributions. Negotiating among 200 countries worldwide is a daunting task, so finding the greatest common denominator for the international community should be based on fundamental principles. To foster consensus, this greatest common denominator should not include the allocation of carbon emission rights. Theoretically, efficient paths exist, but the

challenge lies in identifying several fundamental principles that all nations are willing to acknowledge and uphold.

3. National commitments and actions: Climate change involves not only the quantity of carbon emissions but also issues of industrial collaboration, financial investment, economic growth, and welfare rights. All actions must align with the will of individual countries. The United Nations does not yet have the capacity to enforce the law, and coordinating actions involves intricate interest balances and operational details, making it extremely challenging.

This also indicates that national sovereignty plays a crucial role in the climate governance landscape, and the political nature of climate change profoundly shapes the international climate governance system and governance efficiency. In times of brute force, such issues may escalate to war for resolution. In the present era, however, resolving this issue requires finding the greatest common denominator for the international community while also finding more common interests. If countries can directly reap current macro-positive benefits from carbon reduction, it will be easier to solve the issue.

Unfortunately, over the past three decades, the international community has failed to innovate and advance beyond the fundamental theories, and top-level designs concerning carbon emissions, a public good, have remained confined to the notion that carbon reduction will incur significant immediate costs, with intangible future benefits. This has led climate negotiations in the international community being used as tools for power struggles, which is the greatest tragedy of the international community in the past three decades. Little do people realize that if the international community were to transcend previous thoughts and focus on common interests and innovation, momentous changes could be achieved.

Developing countries believe that developed countries, theoretically, acknowledge their moral responsibility for climate change and the obligation to assist developing countries, but there is a significant gap between their tangible actions and stated promises. They are neither willing to introduce substantial reforms to the international mechanisms nor to take more active domestic measures. Developed countries, on the other hand, argue that developing countries should not be exempted from mandatory obligations to reduce emissions. There is still a significant gap in the understanding of the nature of the issue between the two sides, as developed countries view climate change as a technical issue, whereas developing countries believe that global warming is a consequence of excessive consumption by developed countries. Carbon emission rights are essentially a matter of redistributing interests within the international community, which is equivalent to the right to development.

As time progresses and technological breakthroughs are made, shared interests will eventually prevail. A well-designed decarbonation system can foster an all-win scenario for all parties involved. With improving conditions, it is crucial for developed countries to change their mindset, embrace the vision of building a community with a shared future for mankind, and adopt a more equitable approach to achieving the goals.

2.6 God's Perspective: Solution to Global Climate Change

Assuming God wanted to give humanity another chance and create a Noah's Ark, how might God design a solution to climate change? How might God arrange the process towards global carbon neutrality?

Firstly, God will set a goal. The decarbonation process would be structured around the warming control targets proposed by the IPCC. In the divine blueprint for humanity, there is a high likelihood that the following fundamental principles would be established:

1. Humanity is a community with a shared future, where each country and social group of people are equal. The survival of each group is intertwined with that of all others, and no country or ethnic group can exist independently. No nation or group should prioritize its own interests at the expense of those of others, otherwise it will lead to consequences detrimental to all. All humans are born equal, which is not only reflected in the political, democratic, and electoral aspects that governments have traditionally emphasized, but also extends to carbon emission rights, a pivotal aspect of equal right.
2. Both producers and consumers share the liability. Producers are obliged to control carbon pollution, while consumers are accountable for the social costs associated with carbon emissions. For consumers, liability follow the benefits. Therefore, producers and consumers share a common liability for carbon emission reduction.
3. Consumers have the freedom to choose. The flow of air is free on earth, and the right and liability related to carbon emissions should also be transparent and able to flow freely. In other words, consumers should have the right to know and to choose, which means they should have access to transparent information regarding the carbon emissions of products. One of the important tasks of the government is to ensure that the carbon footprints of all products in society are made clear and accessible to consumers.
4. The environmental-friendly production organizations survive. To meet climate targets, production needs to be optimized. Earth's resources, including atmospheric resources, are extremely limited. Through a low-cost market mechanism, it is essential to reward high-quality and low-carbon production capacity while eliminating inferior and high-carbon capacity.
5. It is essential to provide adequate incentives to all actions and organizations that enhance carbon removals capacity. This is to encourage more organizations and individuals to participate in actions that enhance carbon removals capacity and contribute to solving climate issues. Therefore, it is crucial for the government to design adequate incentive mechanisms.
6. It is necessary to minimize the impact on current economic development. In addressing climate change, we must confront these challenges head-on, without avoiding realistic challenges. By focusing on tangible, immediate practical benefits, we can successfully rally the entire nation's efforts to reduce carbon emissions.

7. Rich countries and wealthy individuals should assume greater liability. Rich countries must be liable for their historical emissions, while wealthy individuals, who tend to consume more, must take on more liability. Rich countries and wealthy individuals should provide financial assistance to less-developed regions, aiding in poverty alleviation and green transformation.

In designing this framework, God undoubtedly considers the overall situation, equality of human rights and the pursuit of common development.

2.7 China's Liability in Addressing Global Climate Change

In 2020, President Xi Jinping solemnly announced China's "3060" dual carbon targets at the United Nations General Assembly, demonstrating China's climate ambition and the liability of a major power. As the liability for addressing global climate change has aligned with China's aspiration for high-quality development, the Chinese Government can advance with giant strides confidently.

Based on its current technological and industrial strengths in green transformation, China can confidently assume a leading role in tackling global climate change.

Firstly, China's vision of building a community with a shared future for mankind serves as a fundamental prerequisite for addressing global climate change. With a high-level perspective and a commitment to overall interests, China's philosophy demonstrates the responsible demeanor of a major power. This vision is poised to garner support from an increasing number of countries and actively guide the comprehensive resolution of climate change.

Secondly, China has emerged as a global leader in clean energy technological capabilities and production scales. The technological capabilities, industrial chain completeness, production scale, and market share of China's photovoltaic and wind energy industries are all at the absolute forefront of the world. China's green energy industrial capabilities will facilitate a faster transition to renewable energy and China may even become a decisive force in global transition to green energy.

Thirdly, China's pioneering energy Internet, based on ultra-high-voltage transmission technology, has steadily become mature and operational. The concept of global energy Internet represents a remarkable innovation and potentially one of the most significant inventions after the information Internet. Imagine the possibility of desert-spanning photovoltaic power plants, which can supply uninterrupted energy to three regions (each covering 8 time zones)[1] each day. This vision outlines an extraordinary technological blueprint.

Fourthly, China has the capability to propose the most equitable and efficient solutions to global carbon neutrality, such as the CELM theory and Global Carbon Neutrality Solution proposed in this book, which will steer us forward towards addressing climate change. The CELM theory and its solution can not only propel the

[1] There are 24 time zones in the world, which can be divided into 3 regions, each covering 8 time zones—a note by the translator.

realization of China's "3060" dual carbon targets, but also establish an international carbon market with significant influence on global carbon neutrality goals. At the same time, it provides the most efficient operating system for the early achievement of global carbon neutrality, which helps realize the temperature control targets set by the IPCC, and provide significant funding for the process of global carbon neutrality, thus making crucial contributions to the holistic resolution of global climate challenges. It is also the best practice of China's vision of building a community with a shared future for mankind.

Given the current conditions, China possesses sufficient soft and hard power to actively pursue, engage, and invest in global climate change. By enhancing its participation in the formulation of regulations, China can achieve significant outcomes and play a decisive role in promoting its economic development and elevating its international status.

2.8 Major Variables in Current Climate Change

As we ushered in 2022, climate issues have surged to the forefront of global discourse, exacerbated by the resurgence of the COVID-19 pandemic and the prolonged Russia-Ukraine conflict. With the European Union imposing economic sanctions on Russia, coal-fired power plants in the Europe were restarted, resulting in a sharp decline in the carbon price within the EU. It suggested that the international community was more concerned with economic recovery, seemingly relegating climate change to the backburner.

However, the truth should be the contrary.

Firstly, the global climate disasters in 2022 should serve as a wake-up call for humanity. In May 2022, extreme heatwaves swept through northern India, with temperatures soaring to a record-breaking 49.2 °C in certain regions of Delhi. The average maximum temperature in May surpassed the highest recorded temperature in India over the past 122 years.

According to Roxy Mathew Koll, a Climate Scientist at the Indian Institute of Tropical Meteorology, while atmospheric factors do contribute to heatwaves, global warming is the underlying driver that intensifies extreme weather in India. An analysis conducted by the World Weather Attribution (WWA) organization, reported by the Associated Press, reveals that heatwaves that affect vast geographical areas for extended durations are extremely rare, and the heatwave event in Delhi can be considered a once-in-a-century occurrence. However, due to escalating global warming caused by climate change, the likelihood of such heatwaves has increased by 30 times.

Arpita Mondal, a Climate Scientist at the Indian Institute of Technology says that according to her research, if global warming is 2 °C above pre-industrial levels, heatwaves similar to the current one could potentially occur at most once every five years. Mondal said, "This is what's happening now, but it's a sign of future climate change."

And the results of another study suggest that the figures above may still be conservative. An analysis published by the Meteorological Office in the United Kingdom says that climate change has made heatwaves 100 times more likely, and that these "scorching climatic phenomena" could occur as frequently as every three years.

Despite the threat of COVID-19 pandemic and wars, climate change has never receded and remains the greatest and most enduring threat to humanity, posing costly challenges both in the present and in the future. Undoubtedly, climate change remains a pressing issue that demands the urgent and concerted actions of all mankind. While COVID-19 pandemic and wars are transient, climate change will continue to accumulate and become worse as CO_2 concentrations in the atmosphere continue to increase. It is superficial and short-sighted to disregard the urgency of addressing climate change.

Secondly, the Russia-Ukraine conflict has shown us that the key to strategic energy security lies in phasing out fossil fuels. One of the key points of the Russia-Ukraine conflict is its impact on the global energy landscape. Russia's resilience in a protracted war is attributed to its robust energy and agriculture resources. Had the EU managed to replace a significant portion of fossil fuels with clean energy in the previous decade, resulting in a significantly lower dependence on fossil energy, it would have likely adopted a more proactive stance in the Russia-Ukraine conflict.

The urgency of transitioning away from fossil fuels has become even more evident with the energy crises that have occurred in many parts of the world in recent years. This sentiment is widely echoed by many leading experts, including Nicholas Stern, a renowned British authority on climate change economics. Therefore, the assumption that the recent surge in coal-fired power use in EU countries signifies an abandonment or delay of carbon neutrality targets is a complete misunderstanding. In fact, the temporary increase in coal-fired power use is precisely a response to the short-term energy crisis, which, instead, emphasizes the dire need to accelerate the transition from fossil fuels. This is also the paramount lesson that China should learn from the Russia-Ukraine conflict: to accelerate the substitution of fossil energy and drastically reduce its overall usage.

Carbon neutrality involves the substitution of fossil fuels with renewable energy alternatives. The transition not only ensures domestic supply, but also closely aligns with the enhancement of China's energy security. Currently, China imports 70% of its oil and 50% of its natural gas, while its coal reserves are projected to last for a limited number of years based on China's current consumption rates. Strategic energy security is the sword of Damocles for China, making the prompt replacement of fossil fuels a crucial priority in its national policies. Leveraging solar energy in deserts, wind energy offshore, and achieving complete substitution of fossil fuels through global energy Internet across time zones represents the long-term solution.

Third, the greatest opportunity to restart the economy after the pandemic lies in the energy transition and the development of a low-carbon economy. The three-year span has profoundly reshaped societal perspectives, significantly altering social consumption concepts. The public is now more conservative, with lower income expectations and diminished consumption desires. Against this backdrop, the transition towards a green economy emerges as the most effective and impactful economic driver to restart the economy.

Fourthly, the energy revolution towards clean and renewable energy must continue unabated. The demand for high-quality human development remains eternal. In particular, China's current development has reached a stage where both the economy and the people prioritize quality. Fossil fuels, while being a significant contributor to climate change, also play a crucial role in reducing environmental pollution and improving environmental quality. Currently, fossil fuels are not merely energy products, they are also highly valuable and extensively used raw materials for chemical products, therefore, burning them as energy sources is a great loss of human production resources. It is thus in the best interest of human society to maximize the utilization of fossil fuels, more or even completely, as raw materials for chemical products.

At the same time, energy revolution brings new and strategic opportunities for industrial upgrading, economic transformation and the development of new industries. We should never miss such a national strategic opportunity.

Fifthly, it is the need for China to cooperate and develop with the West. If China excels in achieving carbon neutrality and gains recognition and support from numerous developing countries, Europe and the United States will inevitably seek cooperation with China. After all, China accounts for 1/3 of global carbon emissions and is a decisive factor in the global climate.

After years of dedicated efforts, China now possesses the strength and resilience to play its role effectively. It is advisable for China to utilize carbon emission reduction to transform its economy and emerge as a climate leader. With a changing perception and a firm grasp of opportunities, China is well positioned to reshape the landscape. What China requires now is a top-level Chinese solution that is both fairer and more efficient in addressing global carbon neutrality.

From this, we can conclude that China's pursuit of carbon neutrality is not only a liability borne by a major country in responding proactively to global climate change, but also a choice based on a series of considerations, including energy security strategy, high-quality economic transformation, seizing the forefront of new energy industry, sustainable development, and accelerated ecological and environmental protection, etc. Therefore, it is a chance to seize a leading position in the new wave of economic transformation, thereby advancing China's further development.

2.9 Cherish the Achievements, Clarify Human Goals and Accelerate Actions

As green energy technology advances as well as information and digital technologies proliferate, the international community stands poised to address the global climate crisis through a shared commitment to the common good. Developed countries should not harbor selfishness, while developing countries should be proactive to accelerate the upgrading of energy technology and fossil fuel substitution. Under the coordination of the United Nations, the international community should harness the collective wisdom of all mankind, transcend the past limitations and embrace their respective liability. Only by this way, can the international community be fully capable of realizing the goals set by the IPCC ahead of schedule, ensuring a brighter future for all mankind.

Chapter 3
Current Development and Practice: The Economics of Climate Change

Global warming is universally perceived as a survival challenge. With governments worldwide successively declaring the advent of "climate emergency", urgent and robust climate policies are needed to respond to this challenge. Regardless of misleading remarks on climate change and its future implications from some agencies, there remains a consensus among humanity to actively tackle this challenge. While climate change is indeed real, anthropogenic, and will exert significantly adverse effects, it is imperative to acknowledge that climate policies can have profound effects on macroeconomic stability and social welfare, with both potential benefits and drawbacks. Therefore, it is crucial to weigh the impacts of both to devise policies that maximize welfare benefits.

After over three decades of negotiations, the constraints of global climate issues have become evident and widely agreed upon. The conclusion reached by the IPCC is broadly acknowledged worldwide, that is, to limit global average temperature increase to 1.5 °C in the twenty-first century and achieve net-zero emissions by 2050. Therefore, the economic studies on climate change strive to identify the optimal pathway within these constraints.

However, the reality is that the pathway and implementation plan for global decarbonization remain unclear because, despite three decades of negotiations, the focus remains primarily on carbon taxes and emission rights, failing to come to the point. Additionally, the sluggish progress in global decarbonation indicates that these plans are insufficiently effective to achieve the optimal target of limiting global average temperature increase to 1.5 °C, proposed by the IPCC.

B. Yang, *The Carbon Emission Liability Mechanism*,
https://doi.org/10.1007/978-981-96-3612-9_3

3.1 Definition of Climate Change from the Perspective of Economics

The temporal and spatial externalities of carbon emission refer to the fact that current carbon emissions can have lasting effects on human survival, spanning decades (temporal) while emissions in one region, such as Antarctica, can affect the melting of Arctic ice and the survival of polar bears (spatial). This stands in stark contrast to other forms of pollution, which tend to be merely localized. The emissions of a single ton of CO_2 in any part of the world have an equal global impact, affecting all countries and populations. Meanwhile, the consequences of carbon emissions are delayed, with current emissions still affecting the climate decades or even hundreds of years later, placing a burden on future generations in the form of climate shocks. Notably, a significant portion of the carbon in the atmosphere today originates from the emissions produced in the industrialized countries of Europe and the United States over a century ago. The externalities of carbon emissions make it perhaps the most intricate "tragedy of the commons" dilemma in economics. Accurately calculating the costs of temporal and spatial effects poses numerous technical challenges. Furthermore, the externalities of carbon emissions also underscore the fact that humanity is a community with a shared future, a great vision championed by China, which also emphasizes the necessity of a globally unified carbon market. Therefore, the transfer of liability and the handling of carbon emissions resulting from the international trade are inevitable.

Distinct from those of typical public goods, the externalities of carbon emissions exhibit characteristics of large-scale and super-systemic impacts, indicating that carbon emissions, through production chain and global trade, mutually and circularly affect all organizations and individuals. An organization's carbon emissions are not autonomous, but triggered by downstream demands. Upstream carbon-emitting products become integral component of downstream products, leading to the question: how should liability be allocated between upstream and downstream entities? This fact indicates that the carbon market confined to a single industry is almost ineffective, rendering the conventional liability mechanism of "whoever produces is liable; whoever emits is liable" questionable in addressing carbon emissions.

Nicholas Stern, former Chief Economist for the World Bank and a renowned scholar in the economics of climate change, published a 700-page report titled *The Economics of Climate Change: The Stern Review* (hereinafter referred to as *The Stern Review* for short) for the British Government in October 2006 (see Fig. 3.1). *The Stern Review* pointed out that climate change is the largest and most widespread market failure in history, posing exceptional challenges to economics.

The negative (temporal and spatial) externalities of carbon emissions make the private sectors particularly less motivated to participate in the fight against climate change, which also render the adjustment mechanisms in the free market comparatively ineffective. Therefore, the design of an efficient policy instrument to mitigate their negative externalities is the key to solving climate change. In contrast to the negative externalities of carbon emissions, technological advances in green energy sector

Fig. 3.1 The cover of *The Economics of Climate Change: The Stern Review*

and carbon capture, utilization, and storage (CCUS) capabilities exhibit significant positive externalities in tackling climate change, necessitating urgent implementation of incentivizing policies to encourage investors to invest more in carbon reduction technologies. Overall, governments need to devise a systematic policy instrument to mitigate the negative externalities of carbon emissions while enhancing the positive externalities of carbon reduction technologies.

Another intricate challenge for policymakers is that climate change, brought about by carbon emissions, involves a large number of players at many levels. The main players in the game include international interest groups, countries, governance sectors, economic sectors, enterprises, individual consumers and so on, accordingly affecting all countries, industries, businesses and the entire global population of 7 billion. Therefore, it is not easy to find an equilibrium solution that can balance the interests of the players at multiple levels and can span a long duration. Accordingly, the quest for the most effective and equitable public policy stands as the biggest challenge for economic academics. Moreover, the large-scale complexity of carbon emissions is not only reflected in this, but also in the fact that the impacts of climate catastrophe are global, and the impacts on economic life are enduring and intricate.

Currently, economic theorists propose three primary approaches to solving problems like the "tragedy of the commons":

The first is to privatize property rights. Over the past three decades, one of the primary solutions to global climate change, spearheaded by the IPCC and dominated by the West, has centered on the allocation of carbon emission rights. However, in practice, a pie of 500 Gt of carbon emissions to be divided among nearly 200 countries is a highly complex task, and efforts in this direction are doomed to fail.

Three decades of large-scale, unsuccessful negotiations on climate change have demonstrated the limitations of this approach.

The second is to realize public management through legal rule-making by a coalition of conventions. This approach requires an overarching regulatory authority, and in fact the IPCC has done a great deal of work, but unfortunately, owing to its inability to find a fair, effective, and feasible solution, it has failed to secure its position as an international body with legal enforcement authority. The annual UN Climate Conference, attended by approximately 40,000 participants, has also failed to formulate a unified and enforceable legal framework for decarbonation as well as an operational system that can be implemented practically. Ironically, the UN Climate Conference has become one of the weakest and most carbon-intensive climate actions, and arguably one of the least effective human efforts to address climate change.

The most promising approach is the third one, which allows communities and groups to self-organize, self-govern, and to devise a system for allocating public resources through collective bargaining. The significant contribution of the UN Climate Conference lies in the unanimous recognition of the global climate risks faced by humankind, igniting a universal desire to solve these issues and assume related liability. An increasing number of major emitters have pledged to reduce emissions, even aiming for carbon neutrality. These are the fruits of self-organization and self-governance. If the pledges for emission reduction committed by these leading emitters can be fully achieved, there is considerable hope for achieving carbon neutrality globally.

As mentioned in Sect. 1.2.1, as of May 31, 2023, 195 Parties (194 countries plus the EU) have submitted their initial Nationally Determined Contributions (NDCs). Carbon reduction pledges already cover 94.3% of global GHG emissions, making a remarkable milestone in the international community's efforts to address climate change over the past decade.

Since climate change is a global problem, a "commons" challenge that transcends national boundaries, it is challenging to balance the interstate interests, as evidenced by three decades of global climate negotiations. However, pollution problem, contrary to carbon emissions, tend to be more localized and domestic, even sometimes confined to a single village. Paradoxically, this localized nature provides a significant impetus to address the climate problem. In history, development before governance is a common path to industrialization in various countries, with limited impacts and generally confined within national borders. Consequently, there are fewer obstacles in terms of self-will, self-organization and self-management at this level.

This is also a pivotal factor in China's shift of attitudes, from moderate to determined, towards carbon emissions. The predominant societal contradiction in China has evolved, now centered on the gap between the people's escalating aspirations for a better quality of life and the unbalanced, inadequate development, where the significance of environmental quality is steadily gaining prominence. A few years back, the smog that blanketed major cities was so severe that even financial abundance could not fully compensate for the lack of happiness. As people's economic standing improves, they become increasingly motivated to environmental self-governance, ultimately leading to a significant reduction in carbon emissions. This pattern of evolving practices and strategies for decarbonation is evident not only in China but also in developed nations.

Currently, many large carbon emitters have announced their timelines for achieving carbon neutrality, largely driven by the desire to foster high-quality development and enhance their citizens' happiness index. In this way, carbon emission reduction has become a conscious behavior, which significantly contributes to the solution of global climate change. What this tells us is that finding a carbon–neutral solution that benefits both the country and its people is pivotal in addressing global climate change.

Once the intricate challenge of resource allocation among nations is resolved, addressing issues within a country becomes more manageable, as there is a governing authority, namely the national government, overseeing the rulemaking process.

3.2 Fundamental Theories of the Economics of Climate Change

For a considerable duration, governments and economic academia have primarily relied on the Pigouvian Tax principle and the Coase Theorem as the fundamental economic theories for addressing the externalities of public goods. The Pigouvian Tax principle maintains that the government internalizes the costs of externalities into private costs through taxation, or that the costs of production should include the part that causes damage to society, so as to achieve the optimal allocation of social resources. On the other hand, the Coase Theorem focuses on the determination of property rights for public goods and ensures the optimal allocation of resources through efficient transactions in the market.

These two theories have served as the basis for the design of climate policy instruments for over three decades.

3.2.1 The Pigouvian Tax Principle

The Pigouvian Tax was first proposed in 1928 by Arthur Pigou, the eminent British welfare economist (1877–1959). According to his view, the reason for the failure of allocation of resources is due to the inconsistency between private costs and social costs of the economic parties, so that private optimization leads to social non-optimization. According to Pigou, the key to maximizing efficiency lies in that private costs should equal social costs. The optimal allocation of resources cannot be achieved by whoever takes advantage, whether private costs or social costs. When social costs are lower than private costs, i.e., social benefits disproportionately than private sectors, it is also undesirable. The Pigouvian Tax addresses this imbalance by levying a tax on polluters, tailored to the extent of harm caused by their pollution. This tax serves to bridge the gap between private costs incurred by polluters and the corresponding social costs, thus equating the two. The Pigouvian Tax exerts a corrective effect on external diseconomies by correcting the external costs of production and consumption by means of taxation, so that the costs of the product provided by the enterprises are equal to their social costs.

The Pigouvian Tax operates as a specific tax. The amount of the tax is equal to the difference between the marginal social cost and the marginal private cost, i.e.

$$\begin{aligned}\text{Marginal Social Cost} = & \text{ Marginal Private Cost} \\ & + \text{ Social Loss (External Cost)}\end{aligned}$$

Theoretically, a Pigouvian tax has the potential to facilitate an efficient allocation of resources and achieve a Pareto optimality in pollution.

However, determining who bears the burden of this tax, producers or consumers, poses a technical challenge. Ultimately, the dynamics in the market dictate that both producers and consumers will shoulder the tax burden. This manifests in producers' reduced profits and consumers' diminished consumer surplus. The distribution of this tax burden between producers and consumers hinges on the elasticity of demand and supply, with the less elastic party incurring a higher proportion.

Due to the low elasticity of demand in the energy market, consumers primarily shoulder the tax burden. Consequently, it does not significantly matter whether the carbon tax is imposed at the production or consumption stage. Ultimately, it can be inferred that the carbon tax, essentially the cost of carbon emissions, falls upon the consumers.

In an ideally uniform market, the distinction between producer and consumer liability for a carbon tax is negligible, yet the ultimate burden ultimately lies on the consumers. However, in practice, because of the need to address cross-border trade relations and non-market-based pricing mechanisms, such as electricity tariffs, the adoption of consumer liability is of a great advantage, and even a necessity. Because failure to levy the tax on consumers disrupts market signals, leading to confusion and preventing the internalization of external costs. And to deal with the externalities of public goods like environmental pollution and carbon emissions, it is essential to incorporate social costs into their internal costs.

Regarding carbon emissions, developed countries in the West tend to emphasize producer liability, while a large number of research reports released by the IPCC also propose solutions based on producer liability. Meanwhile, scholars from developing countries still have yet to conduct sufficient research on the differences between producer and consumer liability.

3.2.2 The Coase Theorem

The Coase Theorem, developed by Ronald Coase, a winner of the 1991 Nobel Prize in Economics regarding property rights, holds that, to address the externalities of public goods, provided that property rights of such externalities are explicitly defined, stakeholders could engage in transactions guided by the principles of a free market. Crucially, if transaction costs are zero, the market will naturally achieve an optimal allocation of resources. The Coase Theorem further points out that, in the above situation, no matter how property rights are initially distributed, market transactions will invariably lead to optimized resource allocation.

Coase strongly advocates against excessive government involvement in addressing the problems brought out by public goods. Instead, he envisions that under the condition of well-defined property rights, the problems could be efficiently tackled through market transactions, negating the need for government intervention through taxation to mitigate externalities. Consequently, Coase vehemently opposes the implementation of the Pigouvian Tax as a solution to externalities, arguing that it represents excessive government meddling and lacks practical feasibility. He further criticizes the Pigouvian Tax as being theoretical and divorced from real-world scenarios, labeling it as "blackboard economics". Coase believes that the Pigouvian Tax places immense demands on government capacity and integrity, but in reality, it is challenging to operate and attain optimal resource allocation.

The Coase Theorem provides a framework for addressing externalities through a market-driven mechanism, such as trading of pollution rights. One key advantage it offers over the Pigouvian Tax is its reduced reliance on government information and competency, thereby minimizing the risk of market distortion. Notably, external costs often involve complexities beyond that one party harms the other. Penalizing and prohibiting the behaviors of one party may also unreasonably harm that party itself, and taxing one party alone is not necessarily a good solution.

However, the market-driven Coase Theorem also faces significant limitations, especially for a large-scale and complex system such as climate change, and it is challenging for the government to design an effective and practical program based on the Coase Theorem. First of all, the application of the Coase Theorem requires clear definition of property rights, while it is extremely difficult to reasonably allocate carbon emission rights across countries, regions and enterprises. Over three decades of international negotiations on climate have shown that this is an impossible solution, not to mention that there also exist problems such as difficulty in measuring or monitoring, etc.; and secondly, when transaction costs are excessively high, for example, due to insufficient regulations or costly monitoring and implementation, market transactions become unfeasible. Finally, while theoretically the Coase Theorem suggests that when the transaction cost is zero, no matter how the initial property rights are allocated, the optimal allocation of social resources can be achieved; but the equitable allocation of carbon emission rights, which represent the fundamental right to development, remains a pressing concern. This is also an important reason why there has been no progress in the agreement on global carbon emissions so far.

Upon observing the current practices in the carbon market across diverse nations, it becomes evident that the granting of carbon emission rights varies significantly from country to country and even within regions. Some nations offer emission rights freely, while others auction them. Moreover, in the temporal dimension, the concept of carbon emission rights, even within the same country or region, can vary drastically across different time periods. Consequently, establishing a standardized object of transaction and an efficient trading market for carbon emission rights within a country, poses significant challenges, let alone globally.

The key relates to our comprehension of the Coase Theorem. The essence of the Coase Theorem lies in providing conceptual framework, rather than prescriptive methodologies. In his article "The Problem of Social Cost", Coase repeatedly emphasizes that tailored solutions to particular issues hinge on thorough on-site investigations, and it is impossible to use a simple model on the blackboard to solve all the real social problems. The ideas inherent in the Coase Theorem are everlasting and remain the most valuable source of ideas in solving modern environmental challenges, such as climate change. However, implementing effective strategies demands that governments creatively adapt Coase's principles to fit the unique characteristics of climate change.

In particular, while Coase's original cases focus on relatively simple public goods, the contemporary challenges of climate change present a significantly more intricate scenario, encompassing temporal and spatial externalities, vast scales, and immense complexity. Coase's brilliance lies in his foresight that each problem of social public goods requires a tailored analysis, devoid of rigid, one-size-fits-all solutions. However, subsequent generations have fallen short in this regard, adhering to rigid approaches, which has led to a frustrating situation where, despite the immense investments and research, significant progress in climate change economics remains elusive.

3.2.3 William Nordhaus' Solution to Climate Change

William Nordhaus, an American scholar who won the 2018 Nobel Prize in Economics for his contributions to the economics of climate change, has been one of the most influential economists in this field in recent decades. He argues strongly for a shift away from emission permits to a taxation on carbon emissions. Nordhaus is a Sterling Professor of Economics at Yale University, where he rose to fame by co-authoring *Economics* with Paul Samuelson. His research interests span a wide range of topics within resource and environmental economics, including energy economics, environmental economics, and the economics of climate change.

In the mid-1990s, Nordhaus introduced the Integrated Assessment Model (IAM), a global quantitative model which describes the interaction between economic dynamics and climate change. Over a span of more than 15 years, he integrated diverse disciplines, such as energy, environment, resources, climate, meteorology, and economics, into the explanatory framework of economics, resulting in a Dynamic Integrated model of Climate and the Economy (DICE Model). The model attempts to analyze the circular flow in which the economic system generates CO_2, the emitted CO_2 triggers changes in the ecosystem, and the changes subsequently affect the economic system. Given its vast scope, intricate design and complexity, accurately gauging the model's applicability remains a challenge.

At that time, the impact of human economic activities on the atmosphere and organisms had begun to emerge. In 1977, Nordhaus published an article titled "Economic Growth and Climate: The Carbon Dioxide Problem", which highlighted the imminent problem posed by the impact of human economic activities on the global climate, urging recognition of its gravity. Despite its brevity, the article covered a range of issues related to the characteristics of CO_2, international cooperation in emission reduction, policy instruments, uncertainty, etc. Many of the concerns expressed in the article have gradually materialized in reality over the past three decades, including the challenges in international cooperation and the inherent uncertainty in analytical studies.

The diligent and sustained efforts contribute to Nordhaus being awarded the Nobel Prize in 2018, solidifying his enduring influence. Currently, the mainstream tool for studying climate change, the Integrated Assessment Models (IAM) for Climate Change, remains firmly rooted in the framework of the DICE model and is widely used to simulate the intertwined evolution of the economy and the climate, as well as to assess the economic implications of relevant climate policies, such as the imposition of carbon taxes.

Nordhaus' contribution lies in his formulation of the methodology to address climate change, while there are no groundbreaking achievements in the ideas on the economics of climate change. Although his ideas on the economics of climate change may not have achieved groundbreaking status, the theoretical model has nonetheless made everyone feel that humanity is one step closer to achieving the goal of a sustainable global economy. The Royal Swedish Academy of Sciences said in a statement: "William D. Nordhaus and Paul M. Romer have designed methods for addressing some of our time's most basic and pressing questions about how we create long-term sustained and sustainable economic growth."

Nordhaus is also clearly correct in arguing that humanity should respond with progressive policies when faced with the effects of climate change. Calculations show that the impacts of a higher carbon price on macroeconomy should not be underestimated, especially when the policy instrument employed is simple and compulsory. This stance sharply contrasts with the radical conclusions advocated by Professor Stern at the London School of Economics in the United Kingdom. Nordhaus' core idea, which has been adopted by the U.S. government, serves as the theoretical cornerstone for the various policies implemented by various U.S. administrations to deal with climate change, exerting a far-reaching influence on the global response to climate change.

The calculations of the three U.S. administrations on carbon pricing have been heavily influenced by his findings. Paradoxically, the calculations of the three administrations are widely different and none of them have been implemented. This indicates that while Nordhaus' methodology holds academic merit, it still encounters significant obstacles in translating its theory into practical policy outcomes.

Nordhaus gives two reasons for the uncertainty about the economic effects of climate change:

On the one hand, policy measures aimed at reducing GHG emissions have to work through the economic system; on the other hand, climate change can also have an impact on the production processes and final outputs of the economic system, such as droughts leading to food shortage.

In fact, it took Nordhaus and his team about 15 years to make this assertion. As economists, they needed to understand the intricacies of ecosystems and to make judgments about what to trade off and put into the model.

The subsequent development of DICE model brought the analysis closer to reality. The model divides the world into 10 distinct regions, with large carbon emitters like the US and China represented as independent regions, while other regions contain multiple countries. They make choices under their respective conditions, responding to three scenarios: no cooperation, limited cooperation, and full cooperation.

This is the key why the Nordhaus team goes towards a wrong direction. It is inherently radical to try to build a computable mathematical model incorporating economic, environmental and climate systems. Even if such a model could theoretically function, it would be exceedingly difficult to generate results that are both realistic and applicable. Although the modeling incorporates numerous systems and factors, it still fails to account for a significant portion of the complexities involved. Given Nordhaus' relatively moderate stance on decarbonation, it's inevitable that climate activists have identified numerous flaws in his arguments. He vigorously criticized Stern, a leading proponent of radical carbon reduction measures, highlighting numerous unreasonable assumptions in Stern's approach. However, Nordhaus' own modeling methodology, with perceived irrationalities in his trade-offs and assumptions, has also been easily scrutinized and criticized.

Despite his Nobel Prize, Nordhaus' ideas have faced continuous challenges in recent years. In fact, the practicality and real-world applicability of his research remain questionable.

The core idea, governing Nordhaus' solution to climate change, is rooted in the Pigouvian Tax, which attempts to solve the social external costs of carbon emissions through taxation. However, this economic thinking lacks significant innovation and breakthrough. Nordhaus' most noteworthy contribution lies in the establishment of an algorithmic model that explores the interaction between climate change and macroeconomics, trying to quantify and calculate the control of all climate-related issues. However, he places undue optimism in the mathematical model established. In the context of current realities, its practical value appears limited and its applied results are not particularly commendable. Over the past decade, Nordhaus' research on the economics of climate change has primarily focused on analyzing the impact of hypothetical policies on economic and social scenarios, rather than designing actual solutions. Consequently, deriving the most efficient solutions directly from his work is not feasible. Carbon taxation, as a strategy for reducing emissions, possesses numerous inherent limitations and challenges. Unfortunately, Nordhaus did not devote adequate attention or research to these issues. These limitations significantly constrain the applicability of carbon tax programs, while carbon emission trading schemes have gained prevalence in the international community.

3.2.4 The Stern Report

Nicholas Stern, former President of the Royal Economic Society and former Chief Economist of the World Bank, released the influential and momentous *The Stern Report* on climate change in 2006, which analyzed the financial, social and environmental impacts of climate change. *The Stern Report* has made an important contribution to assessing the impacts of climate change and enriching the economics of climate change, with far-reaching implications for global climate governance. *The Stern Report* has earned Stern a reputation as "the founding father of global policies on climate change". Notably, Stern has been focusing on China in his long-term research, and he believes that China has played a pivotal role in promoting the global agenda on sustainable development as well as combating climate change.

The Stern Report assesses the economics of moving to a low-carbon global economy, focusing on the medium to long-term perspectives, and drawing implications for the timescales for action, and the choice of policies and institutions. It also evaluates the potential of different approaches for adaptation to changes in the climate and specific lessons for the UK, in the context of its existing climate change goals.

The conclusions of *The Stern Report* are summarized as follows: (1) Climate change could have very serious impacts on growth and development. (2) There is still time to avoid the worst impacts of climate change, if we take strong action now. (3) The costs of stabilizing the climate are significant but manageable; delay would be dangerous and much more costly. (4) Action on climate change is required across all countries, and it need not cap the aspirations for growth of rich or poor countries. (5) A range of options exists to cut emissions; strong, deliberate policy action is required to motivate their take-up and (6) Climate change demands an international response, based on a shared understanding of long-term goals and agreement on frameworks for action.

Stern states clearly, "The investment that takes place in the next 10–20 years will have a profound effect on the climate in the second half of this century and in the next. Our actions now and over the coming decades could create risks of major disruption to economic and social activity, on a scale similar to those associated with the great wars and the economic depression of the first half of the 20th century." Stern's policy recommendations are radical, calling for early and strong actions and investment across all countries, with profound macroeconomic implications looming large in the near future.

The Stern Report has exerted great influence and gained the recognition from a considerable number of governments, prestigious organizations and scholars alike. However, it has also drawn scrutiny from some scholars, particularly William Nordhaus, a Yale University professor, who challenged its scientific rigor and validity. Nordhaus argued that a conventional economic analysis of climate change suggests a "gradual" approach to emission reduction, starting with modest cuts and scaling up as economic and technological advancements occur. He criticized *The Stern Report* for exaggerating risks and adopting an overly extreme discount rate, leading to parameters that diverge significantly from reality. According to Richard Tol, an economist at Princeton University in the United States, Stern chose the most pessimistic findings when assessing the impacts of global climate change on water supply, agriculture, health, and insurance. In addition, the protective role played by structures such as breakwaters is ignored when assessing the impacts of rising sea level. "This is a good report, but it contains too many assumptions." Partha Sarathi Dasgupta, a leading economist, further commented on *The Stern Report*, "Stern's conclusion that immediate and drastic emission reductions are needed to combat climate change is not a scientific fact, and the model is parameterized with a very low discount rate of 0.1%, which means that the current generation will have to save 97.5% of its income for future generations, which is simply absurd." He therefore criticized the study more of a political report than an academic one.

Undoubtedly, putting aside the debate over the scientific validity of quantitative economic analysis in *The Stern Report*, the threat of climate change has been recognized as one of the most serious challenges facing the world. *The Stern Report* has played a key role in shaping this global consensus, and its influence has broadened with the intensity of the discussions it has sparked. In April 2008, the research team led by Stern released another report titled *Key Elements of a Global Deal on Climate Change*. Serving as a complement to *The Stern Report*, this report reiterated the urgency for immediate global action, highlighting that any delays in the present would impose immeasurably high costs on governance in the future. It further suggested that global policymaking on climate change should satisfy three basic principles: effectiveness, efficiency and equity.

In 2009, Stern published an article on the World Bank's official website entitled "Low-carbon growth: the only sustainable way to overcome world poverty". He argued that the three great challenges of the twenty-first century were the battle against poverty, the management of climate change and the fight against the economic downturn. He contended that the transition to low-carbon development could bring new jobs and economic growth in the present, while enhanced energy efficiency could contribute to income augmentation. Further, low-carbon technologies could offer promising avenues for growth and employment, potentially enabling even the poorest countries to leapfrog right over traditional energy consumption patterns, thereby saving the costs associated with establishing extensive power grids. Smarter grids not only improve energy efficiency but also facilitate the use of new technologies while minimizing power transmission costs. Additionally, new energy sources might empower some impoverished yet resource-rich countries to gain a comparative advantage in low-carbon development.

On October 26, 2021, in a lecture to mark the 15th anniversary of the publication of the landmark report *The Stern Report*, Stern, who co-chaired the Global Commission on the Economy and Climate, told the media, "The drive for net zero emissions, over the next two or three decades, will result in the biggest and most fundamental transformation in the global economy that has ever occurred during peacetime."

3.2.5 Review of Basic Theories on the Economics of Climate Change

The authoritative academic theories on public goods introduced in the preceding paragraphs provide an important foundation for current and future theoretical research on the economics of climate change, and these theories are indispensable for government and future generations to solve the climate issue. However, despite their significance, these theories have not yet to come up with feasible and practical solutions to the challenges posed by climate change, which encompasses temporal and spatial externalities as well as large-scale and super-systemic impacts. Therefore, it is imperative that we build upon the work of our predecessors and strive for significant innovations and breakthroughs in order to confront the real challenges posed by global climate change.

Pigou and Coase did not have the opportunity to analyze and study topics such as climate change at that time, and hence, were unable to offer ready solutions for government consideration. Research conducted by Nordhaus and Stern, in fact, is an extension and development of Pigouvian Tax theory, but lacks major breakthroughs in the fundamental theory. Their focus primarily revolves around the establishment and calculation of macroeconomic models, emphasizing the measurement of long-term social costs and the determination of the reasonable value of current carbon price through the application of discount rate. First of all, such research holds immense value, assisting governments and the academia in establishing a quantitative cognition of the intricate relationship between the cost of emission reduction and macroeconomy. Unfortunately, a significant discrepancy exists between their research findings, leaving the academia and the governments perplexed. Nordhaus and other researchers, with the aid of the models, have arrived at roughly similar conclusions, indicating a favorable approach for carbon tax pricing: if a macro-level carbon tax is employed to reflect a nation's commitment to decarbonation, the price should gradually increase from its current level, to the mid-teen dollar, and to approximately USD 100 per ton by 2100. Nevertheless, these models fail to provide the governments with a definitive roadmap for implementing an effective tax pricing and achieving the desired reduction target. Meanwhile, the Stern proposal appears too radical, and its projected macroeconomic costs are even prohibitively high at the moment for the governments to adopt.

Therefore, the most authoritative economists on climate change have failed to come up with effective and implementable solutions to global carbon neutrality. Despite compelling or alarming data presented, the fact is that, to date, they have not been adopted in any policy instrument by governments. This is primarily because foundational concepts and meticulously crafted economic models, relative to a complex public goods issue such as climate change, are inadequate to assist in creating carbon reduction strategies, let alone directly devise viable solutions.

A major challenge for the Pigouvian Tax is its inability to standardize pricing globally, as there exists no authoritative algorithm or conclusive pricing framework. Currently, the guiding principle for decarbonation revolves around "costs to the previous generation, benefits to the future ones (away from damages)", which makes the discount rate an insurmountable problem for the Pigouvian Tax on climate change. Due to the temporal and spatial nature of the externalities, in discounting social costs in the distant future, different discount rates can yield significantly disparate outcomes, even tens of times, in carbon pricing. The lack of consensus on the discount rate stemming from these externalities undermines the practicality of the Pigouvian Tax's principles in decarbonation. Furthermore, achieving consensus on the calculations of long-term social costs is unlikely due to the fact that it is based on too many assumptions. The implementation of a carbon tax program demands extensive governmental capacity and international collaboration, yet the three-decade history of the Climate Conference suggests that governments may not always be as effective as hoped.

In the context of carbon emissions, Coase's theory also encounters unsolvable problems. The allocation of carbon emission rights poses a significant challenge, and the sheer number of stakeholders and the complexity of the macro-level impacts make it impossible to find a good formula for defining property rights, and the probability of successful negotiations is close to zero, as evidenced by the history of the United Nations Climate Change Conference over the past three decades. Despite the establishment of 35 carbon markets globally since the opening of the European Union's carbon trading market in 2005, the operation of the markets has not achieved significant success, playing a relatively limited role in reducing carbon emissions.

The method and theory employed by Nordhaus and Stern exhibit significant similarities. Stern favors a radical approach, displaying a strong tendency towards the calculations of forward social costs and the application of a specific discount rate, yet his current macro-impact analysis falls short. In this regard, Nordhaus adopts a more pragmatic stance and advocates for a gradual approach. The divergence between the two scholars also lies in in their tactics, as reflected in the scale of their respective proposals. Both, however, have failed to offer the international community a viable, comprehensive solution towards global carbon neutrality.

3.3 Crucial Challenges for the Economics of Climate Change

To provide an economically efficient solution to carbon emissions, the typical "tragedy of the commons" issue, several relationships need to be clarified:

First, it is imperative to clarify property rights. The right to emit is an embodiment of property rights. Clarifying the ownership of these rights can significantly alleviate the problem, and efforts towards this end are already underway by the IPCC as well as European and American nations. However, the challenge lies in how to allocate the privilege to emit the next 500 Gt of carbon into our planet's atmosphere, which is the globally interconnected public asset. What theoretical framework should guide this allocation? Apart from the coercion of warfare, there is no consensus on this matter. Conversely, the ownership of "negative carbon/negative CO_2" assets, such as forest carbon removals or those created by CCUS facilities, is inherently unambiguous, preventing any disputes over their ownership. The choice of which property rights to prioritize in addressing climate change will ultimately dictate the success or failure of the program to reduce carbon emissions.

Secondly, it is essential to clarify the liability for the externalities resulting from carbon emissions. The question arises: who should shoulder the burden of these social costs, the consumers or the producers? The IPCC, along with European countries and America, has consistently advocated for producer liability. This approach is reflected in the way the West approaches both the allocation of carbon emission rights and the imposition of carbon tariffs.

In a unified free market, it can be deduced that the effects of the two liability mechanisms, producer liability and consumer liability, are in fact unified, and the ultimate outcome is a shared liability that adjusts the interests of both parties, therefore, the difference between the two mechanisms is not significant. Whether it is a carbon tax program or an emission right program, under an efficient market, the producer liability mechanism will also transfer the liability to consumers. However, the allocation of emission rights among countries, regions and enterprises in a planned economy will lead to the confusion of market signals, the failure of market mechanism, and the undermining of consumers' right to know and right to choose. Simultaneously, tariff barriers in the international trade hinder the efficiency of the international trade market, preventing effective transmission of price signals.

It is noteworthy to highlight that in the international trade, especially on climate (carbon emissions) change, the two distinct liability mechanisms exhibit significantly varied effects. Specifically, under the frameworks of allocating emission rights and imposing carbon tariffs, along with the producer liability system, the integrity of liability, rights and benefits associated with product production and consumption is divided, leading to potential manipulation and exploitation of benefits.

When considering carbon emissions, the delicate balance between government intervention and market forces is paramount, and much debate surrounds the interplay and jurisdictional scopes of these two entities. Both entities must be leveraged to their fullest potential, yet a misallocation of responsibility can lead to inefficiencies. Their interplay in allocating carbon emission rights is prominently infective, as shown in the underdeveloped state of the carbon market and the reluctance to rigorously implement a carbon tax, highlighting the need for a more balanced and strategic approach.

Thirdly, it is necessary to design an efficient pricing mechanism to calculate the external costs. Once clarifying the mechanism of liability, how to price the external costs of carbon emissions becomes a pivotal task. Our aim is not only to effectively promote decarbonation, but also to ensure that the impacts on the macro-economy and consumer acceptance remain within the affordable range.

In countries that have adopted the carbon pricing mechanism, the governments typically resort to a carbon tax, or a trading system for carbon emission rights, or a combination of both. However, these approaches encounter significant challenges. Currently, 40 countries and regions have implemented carbon tax programs, which while having some effect, are not fundamental solutions. China, for instance, has yet to activate a carbon tax. Although the government has attempted to analyze the quantitative relationship among carbon tax pricing, decarbonation, and macroeconomy using computational models, the actual interplay among these factors remains unclear. Technological conditions, energy patterns, and macro-impact mechanisms have been changing considerably, and it is difficult for the algorithmic model to keep pace. The carbon tax pricing program faces more problems and will be analyzed in more details later. The trading system for carbon emission rights aims to control carbon emissions and price carbon emission trading. Nearly two decades of practice in the trading market for carbon emission rights has proved that, due to the high uncertainty in the allocation of carbon emission rights and the limited coverage of the industries, the carbon emission right program fails to accurately reflect the cost of carbon emissions, and is insufficient to promote efficient emission reduction. Additionally, the program places significant demands on government capacity and incurs substantial regulatory costs.

Fourthly, information on carbon emissions from markets and products (carbon footprints) should be real-time, accurate and complete. Achieving this will facilitate the development of relatively fair and efficient policies and institutional designs. One of the reasons why various stakeholders negotiate and it is difficult to improve the effectiveness of carbon reduction is that the information on carbon footprints is not real-time, accurate and complete enough, i.e. information asymmetry. Given that society has embraced the era of big data and intelligent cloud computing, this issue holds a digital and informative solution. Significant time was lost until the introduction of the CELM theory in this book.

Fifthly, the relationship between government intervention and market mechanism should be coordinated. In order to realize net-zero global carbon emissions (carbon neutrality), both the role of the government and the role of the market should be brought into full play, with a greater emphasis on the market's function. The government's role and value primarily lie in establishing an effective system and utilizing market incentives to motivate more participants to collaborate for the goal of emission reduction. The government's role should not be centered on allocating carbon emission rights or designing carbon pricing mechanisms. Given the government's limited capacity and resources, and it is not enough to rely solely on its administrative power to distribute reduction tasks. In particular, prolonged and extensive administrative intervention on market players has obvious negative impacts on the macroeconomic system, and abruptly shutting down power supplies directly disrupts production. Instead, our objective should be to maximize social welfare. Manufacturers with carbon emissions per unit of output below the industry average should face no restrictions, while those exceeding the average should face stringent controls or even the revocation of their operating licenses. Only through a market-based mechanism can we achieve the survival of the fittest and ensure that efficient producers replace inefficient ones in terms of energy consumption and carbon emissions.

Sixthly, the power of every individual in the society must be harnessed to its fullest. The right to emit carbon is the basic right of every individual, and so is the liability to reduce carbon emissions. Realizing global carbon neutrality requires not only the efforts of the government and energy companies, but also the participation of everyone in the society. Obviously, global carbon reduction is related to every member of the society. When consumers adopt a thrifty lifestyle and avoid excessive and high-carbon packaging, they significantly reduce wasteful production activities, thereby cutting down significant carbon emissions. Similarly, if each enterprise in the industrial chain can produce the same output with less energy and resource consumption, and if every link in the chain contributes to carbon reduction, the overall potential of society becomes immense.

It is important to use mathematical models to calculate the impact of carbon pricing on the macroeconomy, but they alone cannot furnish the government with a direct and feasible top-level system for decarbonation. Therefore, carbon pricing represents a secondary concern, not the most pressing matter. Instead, the design of a comprehensive top-level system holds greater significance.

Our approach to carbon neutrality must incorporate the perspectives from sociology, jurisprudence, and economics, that is, from a broader perspective and with a deeper sense of humanity. Crafting a solution that is fair, efficient, and feasible is indeed a challenge, but it is not an impossibility. We must break free from the academic constraints of climate change economics over the past three decades and surmount our own thinking limitations.

3.4 Research Status and Achievements of the Economics of Climate Change

Over the past three decades, the economics of climate change has been the hottest and most carbon-intensive field of research in academic history, with an extensive array of papers and reports published worldwide. Governments, academic and research organizations have invested huge resources in research, but strangely enough, the results have been very disappointing. The annual United Nations Climate Conference amounts to a mere war of words, lacking convincing insights and viable solutions.

Notably, the research conducted by economists and institutes contributes significantly to carbon emissions, yet fails to help the United Nations or governments solve many practical problems. This phenomenon is profoundly regrettable, not just due to the substantial financial investment and direct carbon emissions, but primarily because it impedes progress in tackling global climate change.

Currently, the research efforts of climate change economists across various countries primarily revolve around the following aspects.

3.4.1 *Integrated Research of Economic Model and Climate Science Model*

Climate change continues unabated and the costs of governance continue to rise, leading to a concentrated public dialogue on these costs. However, the cost of climate disruption is merely one facet, as climate policies themselves incur substantial costs that increase with each enhanced commitment and target. The core challenge, from a welfare and cost–benefit analysis perspective, lies in identifying the optimal point where the combined costs of climate change and its policies are minimized.

Developing sound and rational climate policies requires economic models that accurately capture the dynamics of climate change. Over the past two decades, a group of economists, spearheaded by William Nordhaus who won Nobel Prize, have undertaken extensive research, trying to integrate economic models with climate science models. This integrated modelling enables a precise measurement of the interplay between climate change and macroeconomy under different pathways of emission reduction and different combinations of policy strategies. Numerous studies have emerged in this area, with several notable climate-economy models, especially the influential DICE model by William Nordhaus.

3.4.1.1 Choice of Warming Target: How Many Degrees

The Stern Report, the leading report on the economics of climate change, came to the sensationalized conclusion that climate change could cost as much as 20% of per capita consumption now and in the future, a conclusion that William Nordhaus pointed out was highly misleading as it exaggerated the risks posed by global warming.

Despite its controversy, *The Stern Report* offers a systematic solution to global climate change, including increased taxation in the environmental field. Furthermore, it highlights the urgency of investing 1% of global GDP annually in combating climate change to mitigate its potentially devastating impacts.

The question of how much and how quickly governments should respond to climate change remains unsolved. *The Stern Report* provides much of the basic information, but fails to answer the question well. In an interview with the *Neue*

Zürcher Zeitung in January 2020, William Nordhaus asserted that achieving the goal of "limiting global average temperature increase to 2 °C above pre-industrial levels" was impossible, and he noted that he was not alone in this prediction, with half of the simulations showing the same conclusion. He also stated that the "2 °C target" had been set without considering the costs involved.

The IPCC strongly urges countries worldwide to choose the option of limiting global average temperature increase by the "1.5 °C target", warning if we fail, the number of people suffering severe disasters will rise by hundreds of millions. William Nordhaus, on the other hand, has argued that the macroeconomic and social welfare costs of achieving the "2 °C target" are prohibitively high. Of course there are many more controversial options for controlling temperature rise, many of which have been quantitatively analyzed with vast data, computational theories, and analytical results, yet none has provided a convincing solution. Currently, several large countries are setting their own carbon–neutral yearly targets, which, if achieved, are expected to help realize the "2 °C goal" proposed by the IPCC.

3.4.1.2 Calculation of Carbon Price (Social Cost of Carbon)

The calculation of carbon price (social cost of carbon) serves as a key indicator in addressing carbon emissions, and substantial efforts and resources have been invested in its calculation, yet the outcomes vary significantly. The cost of a single ton of CO_2 ranges from a few dollars to hundreds, spanning a gap of several dozen-fold, which sparks considerable debate. Obviously, it is difficult to reach a unanimous consensus on the long-term social cost attributed to carbon emissions. Therefore, it is necessary for the present emission organizations to assume liability for future costs. Notably, the selection of a different discount rate could result in a drastic deviation from the current carbon price, rendering such calculations nearly futile.

3.4.1.3 Practical Significance of Economy-Climate Modeling

Nordhaus' goals are highly idealized and of infinite value if they can be effectively achieved. But the theoretical framework is intricate, whereas the real-world context is stark. There remains a significant gap to bridge before economic modeling can advance to the practical level of accurately capturing the complexities of climate change.

There are two significant limitations that hinder research efforts in this area. Firstly, climate science models and climate economic models are inherently encumbered with an extensive array of assumptions and conditional parameters. Despite the quest of governments and humanity to achieve quantitative analysis of such intricate systems, there remains a substantial gap in determining whether these models can accurately and quantitatively mirror reality. Many minor factors are neglected, and the questions arise: What are the weights of the neglected factors, and could they potentially trigger a butterfly effect? Can the interaction mechanism of various subsystems be accurately restored and modeled? We need enough time to verify and answer these questions. Secondly, there are many parameters in the algorithmic model whose values are often highly subjective, in particular, the discount rate in economic models, where aggressive or moderate choices often lead to a significant variance of over 10 times in the calculation results. This variance significantly distances the results from reaching consensus and gaining acceptance among policymakers.

Since the emergence of climate change, human's response to it has been increasingly diverse. The research significance of climate economic modeling has begun to diminish when emission reduction targets become clearer. The selection of warming targets and the calculation of carbon price (social cost of carbon) are no longer as pivotal as theoretical economists once believed, and the calculation based on the long-term social cost has become less significant. To calculate economic costs resulting from breakthroughs in green energy and carbon reduction technologies, as well as actual warming, is beyond the expertise of economists, and it is even difficult for interdisciplinary teams of professionals to yield convincing results. Accordingly, the goal of the calculation has shifted from pricing carbon in the present based on long-term social cost to maximizing the input–output efficiency of achieving carbon neutrality by the mid-twenty-first century. That is to say, the more pressing issue at hand is to identify the most cost-effective policy pathways in alignment with their committed targets. These two calculation goals are profoundly different, and the latter is the real challenge that climate change economics should prioritize.

3.4.2 Price Coordination Mechanism: Carbon Taxes and Carbon Cost Measurement

Carbon taxes are one of the two most highly regarded policy instruments, and William Nordhaus was one of the most vocal proponents.

The Finnish carbon tax program, initially implemented in 1990, spans over three decades. Although carbon taxes have significantly contributed to the reduction of carbon emissions, their effectiveness and value have been somewhat limited. Two primary approaches for carbon taxes exist. The first one directly levies taxes on carbon emissions or on carbon content, providing a direct reflection of the emissions generated. However, this approach demands sophisticated measurement technologies, resulting in higher implementation costs. Consequently, it has been adopted by only a few countries, such as Poland and the Czech Republic. The second levies taxes according to the total amount of fuel consumption or its carbon content, which is simpler and has been widely adopted by most countries, such as Finland, Denmark, the United Kingdom, Japan, etc. Nevertheless, this approach is not conducive to incentivizing enterprises to adopt advanced technologies to reduce carbon emissions.

Carbon tax is grounded in the principle of Pigouvian Tax, which aims to achieve the optimal allocation of resources through the internalization of social cost. However, accurately measuring social cost in this context can be challenging and misleading for policymakers. Given the vast complexity of externalities of carbon emissions, which span temporal and spatial dimensions, estimating the social cost of such large-scale public goods decades later remains a formidable task. The resulting calculations are often questionable in their applicability, rendering the input–output ratio highly uneconomical.

There is a significant amount of domestic and international research into carbon pricing mechanisms based on carbon taxes, and numerous papers have been published in this field. These studies primarily fall into two categories: the first examines the appropriate level of carbon tax from the perspective of social cost, while the second analyzes the macroeconomic implications of various carbon tax levels. However, in practice, neither of these has yielded a dynamically feasible carbon tax program that can be readily implemented by governments.

3.4.2.1 Estimating the Social Cost of Carbon (SCC) in the United States

To determine the carbon tax standard (carbon price), it is imperative to estimate the forward SCC. Carbon price, as the American economist William Nordhaus explains, is the discounted value of the SCC in each respective period. President Joe Biden announced, at the start of his administration, that he would begin measuring the SCC. In fact, this is not the first time that the United States has measured the SCC. All three recent American presidents, Obama, Trump, Biden, have done so, which shows the importance of carbon cost measurement. However, their starting points for this measurement differ. Obama and Biden aim to promote the implementation of carbon taxes, while for Trump, it is to withdraw from the global climate agreement. This exemplifies how the same policy instrument can be utilized by politicians for varying purposes and in diverse manners.

The Obama administration conducted a carbon cost measurement in 2010, and the results at that time were converted to about USD 26 per ton in 2020. Following an updated calculation in 2016, this figure rose to USD 42 per ton. Conversely, upon taking office in 2017, Trump recalculated the cost of carbon, yielding a significantly lower figure of USD 7 per ton, primarily focusing on the domestic costs within the United States. Subsequently, the Biden administration resumed the estimates initiated by the Obama administration, setting the carbon cost at USD 51 per ton. Facing these adjustments under the Biden administration, Trump is once again attempting to utilize legal avenues to halt Biden's carbon pricing program.

Professor Huang Yuxiang at Tongji University analyzed the behavior of the three successive U.S. administrations and concluded that the U.S. aims to utilize carbon taxes to reduce emissions. The Republican Party advocates a minimal or even no tax, while the Democratic Party advocates a high tax rate. Notably, the cost of carbon per ton has fluctuated extensively, from USD 42 to USD 7, and now stands at USD 51. What accounts for such a significant disparity? The method used in the U.S. should be the conventional Cost Benefit Analysis (CBA), which monetizes the social cost incurred by carbon emissions and then discounts them with the social discount rate to form carbon price. This price then serves as a basis for decision-making by calculating, balancing the benefits of carbon reduction policies against the associated costs. It is natural because the neoclassical economics predominates in the U.S, and they view carbon emissions as merely an external effect of market resource allocation, requiring monetary quantification to restore market equilibrium. While CBA as an analytical framework is generally undisputed, its application as a sophisticated tool for decision-making, particularly in the context of public goods like carbon emissions, can be extremely biased or even erroneous, since carbon emissions affect global economic and social development. First of all, it is difficult to choose a consistent methodology in the monetization of social cost, and the choice of social discount rate is even more divergent. For instance, the Obama administration chose a discount rate of 3%, while Trump may advocate 6%, which would have a significant impact on the present value of carbon. It must be noted that the present value of a dollar after 50 years later, discounted at 3%, is $ 0.23, while the present value, if discounted at 6%, is only $0.06. The discount rate for long-term benefits reflects intergenerational equity, often a subject of value judgments rather than empirical agreement. These calculations are arranged on the basis of obtaining future benefits from present inputs, which would be redundant if a carbon reduction mechanism could obtain sufficient present benefits.

Estimates of the price of carbon also vary widely in academic circles. Nicholas Stern, the British economist who is recognized as the father of climate change economics, estimated the carbon price to be 266 USD per ton, while Nordhaus arrived at a much lower price of 37 USD per ton, employing a higher discount rate. This notable divergence in neo-classical economic thinking begs the question: how can the CBA methodology be harnessed to further delve into this research?

Bill Gates, the founder of Microsoft, recognized the inefficiency of the existing approach and spearheaded the proposal of the "Green Premium" concept to replace carbon pricing methods based on social cost. The idea is to set a net-zero carbon emission target, and then calculate the financial implications of immediate governmental action versus inaction. The objective is to choose the measures associated with the minimal "premium". This is actually the Cost Effectiveness Analysis (CEA) under the CBA framework. The average cost of carbon, as estimated by the CICC Global Institute based on the green premium, stands at approximately 377 yuan per ton (equivalent to USD 58 per ton).

The actions taken by the three U.S. administrations show that, in terms of the design of government policy instruments, for public goods such as carbon emissions, the cost of carbon is very important to carbon pricing and forms a fundamental cornerstone in the entire design of carbon–neutral policy instrument.

In this book, it is argued that carbon tax is a pivotal policy instrument for internalizing the externalities of public goods, particularly carbon emissions. Indeed, it is already being applied in some European countries and brings success to some degree. However, this traditional approach, at least, is not the most efficient, especially in allocating transnational producer and consumer liability. Therefore, it should not be deemed as the ultimate or the sole policy instrument for governments to achieve carbon neutrality. Carbon emissions are special international public goods, and it is unrealistic to expect that 200 countries around the world will agree on a single value for the cost of carbon, given the different calculations made by the three U.S. administrations. Moreover, the estimation of the cost often originates not from the market mechanism, but from academic circle. Many parameters, such as the discount rate, forward loss value, estimation duration, etc., are subjective judgment, without absolute correctness. Historically, power and war have been the means to address similar issues, but in today's multipolar world, consensus-building is increasingly challenging. In addition, the logic for determining the carbon price (carbon tax) based solely on the cost of carbon is not clearly related to the government's goal of achieving carbon neutrality, but only establishes the basis for collecting the tax, which is worth considering.

In summary, the issue of carbon cost, like the allocation of carbon emissions across countries, has been debated for three decades, yet a convincing theoretical basis or definitive calculation remains elusive. Therefore, carbon pricing, like the allocation of carbon emissions, must be inherently flawed, and it is time for a change in thinking.

3.4.2.2 Coordination of Carbon Taxes with Economic Development and Decarbonation

The calculation of carbon cost extends beyond mere the calculation of forward cost. The imposition of a carbon tax will inevitably trigger a certain degree of inflation across the macroeconomic landscape, a concern that the governments take seriously in assessing the economy's resilience. Given the rigidity of carbon pricing which is based on carbon taxes, carbon emitters have to pay the corresponding forward social cost, often resulting in high carbon pricing. Moreover, in the current economic climate, it is challenging for governments to adopt this approach.

The academic community has conducted extensive research on the macroeconomic, industrial, and consumer impacts of carbon taxes, leveraging their proficiency in extrapolating vast data results through elaborate mathematical models. Over the years, this research has been remarkably prolific. However, the findings suggest that the overall macroeconomic implications of a carbon tax are significant, leading to a subdued response from governments regarding carbon tax initiatives. Given the current global economic downturn and the challenges in reviving economies, countries are understandably reluctant to add further strain.

Merely calculating the cost of carbon is insufficient; we must also consider the intricate relationship between carbon pricing and emission reduction. Climate science has established clear limits on total emissions and a timeline for achieving net-zero emissions. Carbon taxation, as a policy instrument, must align with this emission reduction process, or it will be costly and ineffective. Carbon taxation faces significant challenges in this regard. As a tax policy, it requires stability, however, the difficulty in synchronizing carbon pricing with the emission reduction process as well as the complexity of coordinating policy mechanisms between the two are key reasons why governments exercise caution in employing carbon taxation as a policy instrument.

3.4.2.3 Real Constraints on Global Economic Development Imposed by the Current Global Climate Change

Up to now, the development of carbon tax instruments has faced a dramatic change in the conditions of the climate problem. The real constraints on economic development imposed by the global climate problem, have undergone a significant shift. The core constraints are the stringent limits on total carbon emissions and the timeframes outlined by the IPCC: a mere 500 Gt of emissions remaining after 2020, with the goal of achieving net-zero emissions by 2050. The core constraint is no longer the forward social cost of carbon emissions, which is inaccurate and no longer meaningful. Instead, we are expecting a system that offers flexibility, allowing for the adjustment of a few, or even a single variable, and enables us not only to achieve the two goals proposed by the IPCC, but also to be both macroeconomically friendly and equitable.

This book aims to navigate this intricate dilemma and overcome the challenges that lie ahead.

3.4.2.4 Consumer Liability: Acquiring Fundamental Data Is Not a Problem

One of the significant technical factors, alongside political considerations, that prompts the international community, including China, to emphasize producer liability is the challenge of acquiring fundamental data on the carbon footprints of products and organizations. In the absence of readily accessible information regarding the carbon content of final products, consumer liability becomes impractical to implement. Consequently, carbon taxes or carbon emission rights tend to be implemented primarily in upstream energy companies, where such measures are more feasible.

However, in the era of big data and digital intelligence, the technical problems can be readily addressed through a cross-disciplinary, top-level integration mindset.

If accurate data on carbon footprints can be obtained, data on the carbon content of commodities and the emission intensity of enterprises can be accessed efficiently at anytime and anywhere, and the consumer liability mechanism can be activated. Consumers and manufacturers with higher emission intensity than the average can take the liability first, and administrative measures can even be taken to design the relevant indicators to ensure their role in carbon reduction.

With the support of information digital technology, the allocation of international and domestic carbon liability, grounded in a consumer liability mechanism, can be effectively resolved.

3.4.2.5 Problems and Limitations of Carbon Tax Policy Instrument

Carbon tax, a policy instrument rooted in national sovereignty, holds the potential to significantly reduce emissions, both from an economic viewpoint and in line with the practice of international carbon tax.

Despite its recognition by the esteemed climate economist Nordhaus, the carbon tax policy instrument faces notable limitations and challenges, evident in the following aspects:

1. Pricing is challenging. The pricing of a carbon tax originates from the forward social cost of carbon, which inherently relies on numerous assumptions that are often subject to disagreement. Furthermore, the intricate interplay of climate impacts on the economy and society necessitates a considerable number of assumptions and oversights. Decades of research into discounting have revealed that even minor variations in the choice of discount rate can lead to starkly different final outcomes, thereby significantly diminishing the practical applicability of carbon tax pricing theories. Moreover, the determination of carbon price is intricately intertwined with both the forward social cost of carbon emissions and the current fluctuations in the costs of carbon mitigation technologies as well as the cost competitiveness of green energy technologies. This intricate interplay renders it impossible to rely solely on the traditional social cost principle (the Pigouvian Tax) for a solution. Carbon pricing also necessitates dynamic adaptation to macroeconomic effects and the emission reduction process, rendering its implementation challenging even with the combined efforts of economists' calculation abilities and the legislation of carbon tax.
2. The transmission mechanism of carbon price remains suboptimal. Electricity, a pivotal basic industry integral to national economy and people's livelihoods, serves as a fundamental resource for both daily living and production. To ensure a secure, stable, and adequate supply of electricity, numerous countries, including China, have imposed stringent price controls. In China, electricity price is not fully market-oriented, relying primarily on planned pricing. Consequently, when a carbon tax is imposed at the upstream stage of the industrial chain, specifically the production link, the market mechanism is obstructed, failing to effectively communicate signals to the downstream market. This lack of consumer perception undermines the market's role in efficient resource allocation, resulting in a non-efficient market state. Under such conditions, upstream production costs rise significantly, often to an unsustainable level, heavily impacting economic growth. Meanwhile, downstream consumers remain unaware and unable to adjust their consumption structure, patterns, or culture accordingly. Without successful consumer participation in emission reduction efforts, the overall efficiency of these efforts is diminished. Furthermore, the international trade, also characterized as a non-efficient market, experiences a similar "obstruction" in the value of the carbon tax due to tariff barriers.

3. The correlation between the pricing of carbon tax and the overall amount of emission reduction remains ambiguous. While economic and mathematical models can quantify this correlation, it is commonly acknowledged that establishing a direct correlation between the two is challenging. Within a short timeframe, it is difficult to ascertain the precise impact of carbon taxes on emission reduction, and their effectiveness in controlling carbon neutral process is not as apparent or satisfactory. Furthermore, when the government observes that emission reduction rates are either too rapid or too sluggish and seeks to dynamically adjust the carbon price to align with these changes, the process becomes complicated because carbon tax, as a policy instrument, requires legislative procedures for modification.
4. A carbon tax, inherently a policy concerning national sovereign, faces significant challenges in achieving international synergy due to the complexity of legislative mechanisms and processes across nations. The need for global climate governance to foster collective efforts is paramount, yet the coordination cost among countries for such a policy is prohibitively high. Consequently, it becomes arduous to formulate a unified international strategy to mitigate carbon emissions. Furthermore, the promotion of an international carbon border adjustment mechanism, akin to CBAM, would clash with the WTO policy framework, thus potentially igniting disputes among nations and making it difficult or costly to coordinate globally.
5. The utilization of carbon tax funds remains ambiguous. Once the revenue generated from the carbon tax is integrated into the financial system, standardizing and controlling its allocation becomes challenging, often resulting in disputes regarding the allocation rights across various sectors. Notably, during the current financial strains experienced by countries, the risk of misappropriation significantly increases, hindering efforts towards emission reduction. Ideally, the public anticipates that carbon taxes would be invested in carbon reduction initiatives, innovative incentives, and subsidies to foster the development of related technologies.
6. Balancing regional interests can pose significant challenges, particularly when it involves navigating the complexities of compensating energy-producing provinces for the additional costs imposed on their enterprises by carbon taxes, while also determining how to fairly allocate the liability among regions that consume energy.
7. Formulating carbon tax policies for industries is a complex task. The diverse characteristics of each sector, its varying reduction effects and its impact on the cost structure of each industry necessitate careful consideration of whether to adopt a uniform or differentiated carbon tax approach. A uniform approach may not be feasible, while a differentiated approach faces greater challenges and costs. Additionally, imposing a higher tax could have devastating effects on some industries and macroeconomic operations, while a too-low tax may have minimal impact on emission reduction.
8. Legislative challenges and rigid policy adjustments pose obstacles to the pursuit of carbon neutrality. Given the dynamic nature of this ambitious goal, ongoing

observation is essential, particularly regarding its macroeconomic implications, which demand prompt and flexible adjustments. However, the adjustment of a carbon tax policy faces intricate legislative hurdles, lengthy procedural cycles, and huge costs. This results in practical difficulties when it comes to dynamically adjusting the carbon tax rate, revealing a lack of flexibility within this policy instrument.

9. Calculating the impact of carbon taxation on GDP growth proves challenging, hampered by the complexity of various variables and the rapid evolution of technological factors that are challenging to fully incorporate into the analysis. Existing mathematical models, even those developed by renowned domestic and foreign research teams, have exhibited considerable inaccuracies in assessing the economic repercussions of carbon taxes, thereby limiting the reliability of their predictions. To effectively regulate the process of carbon neutrality, the government must rely on a policy instrument that offers greater control, flexibility for dynamic adjustments, and the ability to readily quantify its impacts on economic growth.
10. Carbon taxation fails to consider the interests and incentives of carbon removal organizations. Carbon taxes primarily target carbon emitters, imposing social external cost on them and serving primarily as a one-way punitive measure for carbon reduction. However, to expedite the carbon neutrality process, this unidirectional incentive is insufficient. Climate change involves both carbon emissions and carbon removals, yet the tax policy instrument lacks the capacity to establish a benefit mechanism or incentive system for carbon removal organizations. Carbon removals, a sector deserving robust development, is crucial in achieving carbon neutrality. Hence, even with the implementation of a carbon tax, the carbon market cannot be discarded. Comparatively, the carbon market offers a more straightforward design for a bidirectional incentive system that encompasses both reward and punishment.

In summary, based on theoretical and empirical perspectives presented in this book, it is argued that a carbon tax may not be the optimal instrument. At present, China has yet to activate this instrument, and it is suggested that its application in China will not be considered subsequently.

3.4.3 Quantitative Emission Reduction Mechanism 1: Allocation Approaches for Carbon Emission Allowances

To solve the public goods problem grounded in the Coase Theorem, a pivotal step is to establish clear property rights. In the context of climate change, this primarily concerns the allocation of carbon emission rights. Numerous scholars in the field of climate change economics have conducted extensive research and proposed various methodologies. Among these, the most extensively studied approaches are outlined below.

1. Historical intensity-based approach. Based on the historical production data and emissions of an enterprise, the emissions per unit of product are calculated and used as a benchmark for yearly reduction.

Advantages: This approach allows for emission adjustments in line with changes in product output, incentivizing enterprises to conserve energy and reduce emissions through the gradual lowering of emission standards.

Disadvantages: The approach can lead to what is known as "whipping the fas cow," where enterprises may be unfairly penalized due to changes in market conditions and product inconsistencies. Additionally, it can result in government intervention extending into the most micro-level aspects of the economy.

2. Baseline approach. With reference to the overall emission data of the industry, this approach involves setting a standard for emission intensity within an industry. Allowances are then issued based on this standard. The average emission level of the industry in each year is measured annually to ensure fairness.

Advantages: Allocation of allowances is adjusted with changes in product output, thereby encouraging technological advancement and eliminating outdated practices.

Disadvantages: However, it may not be suitable for industries with significant differences in production processes. Additionally, determining the industry average can be technically challenging and involve a considerable workload.

3. Historical emission-based approach. Allowances are issued directly on the basis of historical emissions. This approach is particularly applicable in industries where horizontal comparisons are challenging or not feasible.

Advantage: It is simple and feasible.

Disadvantages: There is a limitation in the ability to assess historical emissions, and it is difficult to determine the annual reduction.

4. Auction-based approach. Carbon emission allowances are acquired through market-driven means, and the government receives revenue from the auctioning process.

Advantages: By employing an auction-based system, policymakers can minimize the chances of introducing distortions in the market. Since the auctioning process is straightforward, convenient, and highly effective, it ensures that allowances are sold to the highest bidder. The auction system not only provides the government with a novel source of public revenue, but also offers flexibility in compensating consumers or communities for any adverse impacts. Additionally, it rewards those who take proactive measures to reduce their emissions.

Disadvantages: The auction system has limited effectiveness in preventing carbon leakage and does not adequately compensate for losses incurred due to stranded assets.

The current dilemma confronting research on quantitative mechanisms stems primarily from the highly problematic nature of its underlying preconditions. The allowance system, inherently an administrative framework with a strong planned economy backbone, encounters numerous intractable technical challenges. Moreover, its complexity, inefficiency, and lack of fairness render large-scale implementation challenging. As a result, it is feasible only in a select few large power plants, not across all societal organizations, due to the enormity of the project. This significantly undermines the effectiveness of the decarbonation system, limiting the government's ability to target a broad range of industries and enterprises.

The Coase Theorem aims to harness market mechanisms to address issues concerning public goods, with minimal government intervention. However, the allowance method, a widely adopted policy instrument by the international community, inherently involves significant and intricate government involvement. This high demand on government capabilities and resources stands in stark contrast to the original intent of the Coase Theorem. Consequently, subsequent trading arrangements fail to capture the advantages of the Coase Theorem in mitigating carbon emissions, which is obviously against Coase's original vision.

Therefore, we must seek a new direction, one that fosters larger-scale and more efficient emission reductions. And we are compelled to explore novel policy instruments with innovative thinking.

3.4.4 Quantitative Emission Reduction Mechanism 2: Carbon Emission Trading Market and Carbon Market

Climate change economists firmly maintain that the carbon market is a pivotal market element in addressing the climate crisis, rivaling only the carbon tax. Though the market mechanism for carbon emission rights emerged later, it has significantly outpaced the carbon tax in terms of development. In China, the carbon emission trading market has undergone several years of local pilot projects and culminated in the launch of a national carbon market, whereas the carbon tax remains unimplemented to this day.

Through the allocation of carbon emission rights and the regulation of the market, the government endeavors to minimize the overall societal cost of emission reduction and achieve the most efficient allocation of market resources. The carbon trading market, which is based on carbon emission rights, has garnered significant scholarly attention in the field of climate change economics. While we maintain a strong optimism regarding the potential of the carbon market, the current reality falls short of our expectations.

The carbon market based on carbon emission rights has been operational for more than two decades, yet its global progress has been sluggish, yielding unsatisfactory results. The current global carbon market primarily revolves around trading carbon emission rights, encompassing a portion of certified emission reduction (CERs) products. In terms of operational efficacy, it is evident that the carbon market based on emission rights alone is insufficient to shoulder the liability of achieving global carbon neutrality.

China's carbon market has yet to transcend the confines of international practice, trailing behind the European carbon market in terms of progress. Starting in 2013, seven provinces and cities in China launched pilot carbon markets, and by July 16, 2022, the national carbon market was officially launched. By the end of 2022, a total of 230 Mt of emission allowances had been traded in the national carbon market, amounting to a cumulative turnover of 10.475 billion yuan. However, the current carbon market mechanism is plagued with significant inherent issues, rendering it incapable of supporting the investment demand of nearly 200 trillion yuan and the realization of the "3060" dual carbon targets. Precisely due to the underwhelming performance of the carbon market, society has become increasingly skeptical about the significance and role of leveraging the carbon pricing mechanism to facilitate the attainment of decarbonation targets and even carbon neutrality in various countries.

The adoption of carbon market is theoretically grounded in the Coase Theorem, which posits that upon clarifying property rights for public goods, the optimal allocation of resources is entrusted to market mechanisms. Government entities have a keen interest in the allocation of such property rights. However, over two decades of international operations have revealed that the Coase Theorem has often been superficially misinterpreted, leading to widespread incorrect applications.

The current international and Chinese carbon markets primarily operate on the basis of carbon emission rights. China's national unified carbon trading market is explicitly designated as a market for trading these rights. However, the inability of governments, both internationally and in China, to devise an optimal top-level system stems from a misguided understanding of the theoretical and fundamental premises underlying the carbon market. The excessive focus on determining and allocating carbon emission rights has led to numerous shortcomings in the trading market for carbon emission rights. The allocation methodology is heavily influenced by planned economy principles, lacking a scientific allocation scheme. Additionally, high operational and verification costs, coupled with susceptibility to corruption, have contributed to low operational efficiency and non-significant emission reduction effects. In fact, Coase himself was deeply concerned about excessive government involvement in addressing the externalities of public goods and had significant doubts about the government's ability and positive impact in policy implementation. Regrettably, the current state of the international carbon market for emission rights suggests that economists and policymakers are utilizing the Coase Theorem in a manner that Coase himself would have strongly opposed. While this may appear ironic, it is indeed a widespread reality.

Due to the substandard outcomes of the previous carbon market trial, China holds the perspective that achieving carbon peaking and neutrality necessitates multifaceted support. To this end, the central government has categorized these supports into seven key domains and numerous subcategories, thereby establishing a "1+N" policy framework. The carbon market, as a minor component within this comprehensive support system, serves primarily as a supplementary measure. For it to truly exert its intended impact, the carbon market, as well as carbon allowances, must be integrated with overall emission control, which has yet to occur. Consequently, in the journey towards carbon peaking and neutrality, both domestically and globally, the carbon market can only play a supplementary, rather than a foundational or leading, role.

China's market mechanism is not particularly well developed. In such an economy where the market-driven system is not fully matured, it is very difficult to achieve emission reduction through the carbon market. Although enhancing the carbon market could be a potential option, it is unrealistic to expect significant outcomes from it. While many experts consider the carbon market a crucial tool in attaining China's dual carbon targets, in reality, it only plays a supplementary and regulatory role. Furthermore, it is not realistic to determine the carbon price through carbon market trading. In a market economy, market players tend to accept prices, rather than determining them, as prices are a reflection of the balance between supply and demand; when supply tightens, prices rise, and when supply loosens, prices fall.

The carbon market operates similarly, being predominantly government-led. When the allocation of allowances by the government is tighter, prices tend to rise; conversely, a looser allocation results in lower prices. All transactions within this market involve accepting prices, not discovering them. Attempting to determine the price through transactions alone is impractical. Organizing production based on prices discovered through such transactions would inevitably lead to distortions in resource allocation.

The emergence of ordinary commodity markets typically stems from market forces, devoid of government coercion, thereby leading to lower transaction costs compared to administrative pricing. Conversely, the trading of emission rights in the carbon market relies heavily on the intervention of government coercive measures, such as administrative oversight. This results in significantly higher transaction costs in carbon market pricing compared to those associated with carbon taxes.

The above perspectives aptly capture the contemporary pulse of the carbon market. While these observations may appear reasonable for a trading market, which has failed due to excessive intervention of the planned economy, they are obviously too biased for the role that the trading market itself can play. This specific market differs from others, as markets with distinct top-level designs yield diverse outcomes. It is shortsighted to underestimate the role of the market mechanism due to the shortcomings in the current carbon market. Just as we cannot undermine the decisive role of the stock exchange market on scientific and technological innovation, a carbon market with a sound design can yield similar results. For the carbon market to effectively contribute to emission reduction and technological advancement, it is crucial to perceive the essence of the matter, abide by its principles, and discover the right pathway. The research in this book has revealed that there exist serious problems with the theoretical basis of the current carbon market, which has led to major flaws in the current top-level design across various countries. By identifying these critical problems and making necessary improvements, we can truly unleash the pivotal potential of the carbon market.

3.4.4.1 Failure of the Coase Theorem

The design idea of the carbon market for carbon emission rights originates from Coase's theory of public goods, widely recognized in academia as the Coase Theorem. The Coase Theorem states that the externalities associated with social public goods can be solved through the clear definition of property rights and the efficient functioning of markets. However, when applied to the pressing issue of climate change, empirical evidence proves the failure of the Coase Theorem.

There are two primary reasons.

On one hand, the extent to which property rights can be defined poses a challenge. Coase, utilizing a simplified model of public goods, demonstrated that when property rights are unequivocally defined, an efficient market with minimal transaction costs can facilitate optimal allocation of social resources through transactions. He further argued that regardless of the initial allocation of property rights, efficient market transactions can still achieve this optimal allocation. While this suggests that the initial allocation may not be paramount, in the context of carbon emissions, it holds immense significance. Given that carbon emission rights are perceived as the right to development, their allocation becomes a pivotal concern for all stakeholders, often representing the most formidable hurdle to overcome.

The negotiations spanning the past three decades highlight a critical shortcoming: the lack of definitive clarity in the allocation of emission rights, both internationally among nations and domestically within regions and enterprises. This obscurity derives from the inherent complexities of climate change, both temporally and spatially, rendering a precise definition of property rights elusive. This deviation from clarity is a stark contrast to the idealized modeling of property rights outlined in the Coase Theorem. Ideally, under the Coase Theorem, the total carbon emissions (500 Gt), as established by the IPCC, would be precisely apportioned to individual countries, which would be measurable and regulated if each country strictly adheres to the rules. However, over three decades of global endeavors have demonstrated that such a precise allocation remains an unattainable ideal.

It is also evident that, even within a country's borders, the allocation of carbon emission rights does not meet the standards set by the Coase Theorem. The annual allocation of emission rights to industrial organizations, a common practice in all countries, fails to align with genuine property rights, regardless of the methodology employed. What is often perceived as property rights is, in reality, a rationing authority granted to enterprises by the government, a power derived from planning rather than grounded in objective reality. This significant deviation is a far cry from the definition of property rights outlined in the ideal model of the Coase Theorem.

On the other hand, the carbon market based on carbon emission rights has proven to be insufficiently effective.

Let's illustrate this through a simplified model grounded in the Coase Theorem. Imagine there are industrial enterprises located upstream of a river, engaging in production and emissions. Meanwhile, a fishing company auctions for the fishing rights and emission rights pertaining to this river. For the Coase Theorem to be operational, the coordination of the transaction between these upstream enterprises and the fishing company must be successful. Provided property rights are explicitly defined, the market has the innate ability to self-regulate prices, with transaction costs approximating zero. This scenario aptly demonstrates the validity of the Coase Theorem, indicating that the market can operate efficiently when property rights are straightforward and unambiguous.

The global climate problem is so far removed from the idealized model of the Coase Theorem since its property rights cannot be clearly defined. The severely substandard object of transaction and the vast number of counterparties involved result in exceedingly high transaction costs within the trading market, thereby impeding the development of an efficient market. Consequently, there is little prospect of directly applying the principles of the Coase Theorem to address the pressing climate issue.

However, we cannot ignore, let alone deny, the value and importance of Coase's ideas on property rights. The Coase Theorem remains one of the most important fundamental theories for us to solve the climate problem, but it requires significant innovations in the context as complex and intricate as climate change.

3.4.4.2 Non-market Factors in the Carbon Market

The current allocation mechanism of carbon emission rights across various countries is essentially a governmental mandate, a typical model in planned economy, rather than a standard market-oriented property right. This approach is severely inefficient and unfair, a fact that has been thoroughly evidenced by the practices in various nations, including China. Notably, in 2021, many cities in China encountered a restriction of electricity consumption, which not only hampered production but also severely disrupted the smooth functioning of the macro-economy, serving as a direct reflection of the policy's consequences.

The consequences brought out by restricting electricity consumption in China in 2021 illustrate that breaking down emission reductions through administrative measures pays heavy prices. Administrative measures, such as unregulated restrictions on the electricity consumption across virtually all enterprises, or the allocation of energy use rights solely based on tax payments, are ineffective in achieving efficient resource allocation. For some enterprises, the costs of electricity restrictions are immense. For example, a globally renowned cell phone manufacturer is highly dependent on a specific component in its entire industrial chain, and a mere one-minute power outage in the production of that component requires two to three days of re-commissioning. As a result, in some places last year, the power supply was restricted twice a week, resulting in its production being possible only on one day a week. However, for enterprises with insufficient orders, even three or four days of weekly production is sufficient.

The government should leverage the price mechanism to guide emission reduction entities with low cost to assume the primary liability for emission reduction, thus minimizing the overall cost of achieving this goal. This market-driven approach is undoubtedly a more rational solution.

From an economic perspective, an efficient policy instrument for decarbonation should primarily establish a rational liability mechanism that clarifies social costs and effectively internalizes external costs into product costs. This approach ensures the establishment of a robust reduction mechanism. However, the current mechanism for carbon emission rights lacks such functionality.

The mechanism for emission rights confronts significant challenges in balancing international interests. The protracted international dispute over carbon emission rights, spanning three decades, underscores its flawed direction. It was only after *The Paris Agreement* introduced a bottom-up framework for nationally determined contributions to emission reduction that tensions in the international community began to ease. Internal allocation of carbon emission rights within a country is inherently flawed, and it is disheartening to see stakeholders still fighting over securing greater carbon emissions. Numerous teams have invested substantial resources in exploring various allowance allocation methods, but many of these are largely ineffective and, ironically, emit a considerable amount of carbon. Therefore, the mechanisms relying on carbon emission rights are inefficient and hardly equitable, necessitating a complete overhaul of the current approach.

The IPCC proposed a program at the Copenhagen Climate Change Conference that considers the interests of developing countries. However, under this program, the per capita carbon emission stock of developed countries stands at 7.5 times that of China, and their future carbon emission allowances remain 3.5 times higher, reflecting a considerable disparity and unfairness.

The international community must adopt a more scientific and market-driven approach to tackle the challenge of decarbonation. The policy instruments implemented by governments should be comprehensively refined to ensure fairness and efficiency across countries, regions, organizations, and individuals.

3.4.4.3 Problems and Limitations of the Carbon Market Based on Carbon Emission Rights

1. Carbon emission rights allocated through free allowances are non-standard commodities, posing significant challenges in their marketization.

Currently, the system operates by distributing a substantial number of allowances freely or by auctioning a minor portion. Unused allowances are then sold in the carbon market. However, these free allowances essentially constitute a form of non-marketable entitlement, a product of planning economy, making their marketization a daunting task. If they are to be traded, the pricing mechanism is uncertain, hindering the growth of the carbon market. Moreover, it is difficult to unify and standardize the carbon emission rights issued by different national and regional governments. Even within the same country, allowances issued in different years vary significantly in connotations and substance, rendering them unsuitable for asset management and operation.

2. Detecting carbon price signals remains a challenging task.

The current allowance-based system for carbon emission rights in various countries obscures numerous market and cost signals, thereby rendering carbon pricing non-market-driven. Consequently, the current carbon price is scarcely aligned with the social value of carbon reduction or the actual cost of carbon removals, impeding its potential as a pivotal tool in achieving carbon neutrality.

On May 18, 2023, the carbon price in China's carbon market stood at 56 yuan per ton, and the volume traded in China's carbon market comprised about 2% of its total carbon emissions. Is the price of carbon in China at that point really 56 yuan/ton? If we compare the total amount of carbon emissions in China to the total amount traded for the whole year, the price of carbon in China is less than 1 yuan/ton.

Carbon market in China suffers from excessive decentralization, having one market in each province, which artificially compounds the trading. The lack of standardization is profound, leading to inflated market transaction costs and significantly diminishing the market's effectiveness. Recognizing this, in April 2022, the Chinese Government advocated for the establishment of a national unified carbon market, alongside with a comprehensive regulatory framework. This initiative aims to facilitate the seamless circulation of factors, including a standardized carbon trading platform.

3. It is difficult to internationalize the trading of carbon emission rights.

Due to the fact that carbon emission rights are authorized and strictly regulated by governments within a country or a region, their inherent value lacks standardization, making it challenging for them to become a viable international trading commodity. Consequently, the establishment of an international carbon market faces significant difficulties. As Hainan International Carbon Market embarked on its construction in March 2022, the primary question arose: What is the object of transaction? Given the limited scale of domestic transactions over the years, how can this market be promoted to an international level? This is the initial concern that requires consideration.

4. It is difficult to contribute to the development of green finance and to give full play to the key role of finance in the green transition.

Green finance can guide the flow of capital to low-carbon green, resource-saving technological and ecological industries. The development of green finance requires good investment products and input–output expectations.

Despite its seven or eight years of piloting, China's domestic carbon market has struggled to foster the development of a green financial market due to issues with its mechanism, limited scale, and underlying transactional products. As a result, social investors, financial institutions, and individual investors have yet to enter the market. It is evident that the development of green finance requires robust products and suitable transactional objects, which carbon emission rights currently fail to adequately fulfill.

5. The carbon market is ineffective in providing meaningful incentives for the growth of the carbon removal industry.

In fact, it significantly hinders the development of carbon removal organizations. The fundamental nature of carbon emission rights and carbon removals is vastly different; one is a government-allocated allowance, while the other actively removes carbon from the atmosphere. This stark contrast in nature makes it challenging for the carbon market, if it focuses primarily on emission rights, to foster the advancement of the carbon removal industry, which is precisely the sector the government aims to cultivate.

As stipulated in the regulations, CCERs utilized for quota settlement and offsetting must simultaneously satisfy two prerequisites: first, the offsetting ratio must not exceed 5% of the settled emission allowances; second, they must not originate from emission reduction projects that are already subject to national allowance management.

Regrettably, the national carbon market established in 2021 has been explicitly defined as a "trading market for carbon emission rights", necessitating the government's urgent need to redesign the carbon market from the top as soon as possible.

3.4.5 Carbon Border Adjustment Mechanism

The proposal of carbon border adjustment mechanism is deeply rooted in a complex historical context. For over three decades, the European Union, as a primary advocate in addressing climate change, has been critiquing developing nations, particularly China, for their rapid increase in carbon emissions and perceived inadequacy in implementing effective policies to reduce them. The EU's intention has been to utilize carbon-related mechanisms as a lever to potentially constrain the economic growth of these developing countries.

Due to the transboundary nature of climate change, effective governance necessitates global collaboration, yet the prevalence of "free-riding" among smaller and economically disadvantaged nations is noteworthy. Developed nations, striving to lower emissions to enhance air quality and climate resilience, have encountered this phenomenon and it becomes a pressing challenge that scholars and policymakers alike are keen to address. To mitigate carbon leakage, Europe's Carbon Border Adjustment Mechanism (CBAM) has successfully completed all legislative steps and is now in the process of implementation.

Currently, the international carbon market predominantly revolves around carbon emission rights, with significant disparities in carbon pricing stemming from the diverse policy strengths across various nations. For instance, in 2023, China's domestic comprehensive carbon trading price hovered around 56 yuan per ton, whereas the carbon price in the EU typically exceeded 60 Euros per ton, and in some cases, even surpassed 100 Euros per ton (see Fig. 1.6). This discrepancy in carbon pricing could be further exacerbated by the inconsistency in the allocation of free allowances. Due to this vast price gap, Western countries have highlighted the issue of "carbon leakage", referring to the economic unfairness that arises when carbon prices drive the capital and enterprises in developed nations to countries with lower carbon prices, thereby adversely affecting the economic interests of capital-exporting nations. Against this backdrop, the European Union has advocated the establishment of an international CBAM as a potential solution.

To mitigate climate change, the EU took significant strides in 2020 by adopting *The European Green Deal* on January 15th. This landmark agreement set ambitious goals, including a reduction in GHG emissions by 50% to 55% by 2030, compared to the 1990 level, and the attainment of carbon neutrality by 2050. In July 2021, the EU Council introduced the Carbon Border Adjustment Mechanism (CBAM), a proposal for a carbon tariff, aimed at implementing these climate targets. On March 15th, 2022, during a meeting of Economic and Financial Affairs Council (ECOFIN), Finance Ministers of the 27 Member States approved a proposal for an EU carbon tariff, advocated by the French Council Presidency. French President Emmanuel Macron announced the news on his personal social media account. Shortly after, on April 25th, 2023, the EU Council voted to adopt the CBAM, which officially came into force on May 17th, 2023.

The initial sectors to be encompassed by this mechanism are steel, cement, aluminum, fertilizers, electricity, and hydrogen. The focus is primarily on direct emissions stemming from the production process as well as indirect emissions (resulting from the utilization of purchased electricity, steam, heat, or cold in the manufacturing process), particularly in the cement, electricity, and fertilizer industries. Additionally, a limited number of downstream products are also included. Importers of these goods are required to compensate for the carbon price difference between the producing country and the EU's emission trading system.

While the EU maintains that the CBAM aims to safeguard EU industries from the threat of carbon leakage, thereby enhancing the competitiveness of domestic companies under the EU carbon tax, the reality is that imports from countries with higher carbon emissions are subject to taxation. This approach is likely to have a more significant impact on countries like China, which have traditionally been major exporters of such goods to the EU. Deloitte's analysis reveals that Russia tops the list, while China closely follows, in terms of trade volume impacted by the carbon tariff. Specifically, China's affected trade volume is akin to approximately 2% of the EU's exports in 2019, a value of roughly €6.5 billion.

Similar to CBAM, William Nordhaus, the 2018 Nobel Prize winner in Economics, proposed the idea of a "Climate Club". This club is structured around two fundamental rules: a coordinated agreement for emission reduction among participating countries, and corresponding penalties for countries that do not fulfill their obligations. The core provision of the agreement is the pricing mechanism, specifically, the establishment of an internationally agreed-upon target price for carbon emissions. The simplest and most effective measure to penalize non-participating countries is to impose tariffs on products imported from non-participating countries. The ultimate goal of employing a uniform carbon tariff as a punitive mechanism within the Climate

Club is to promote proactive action by countries to reduce carbon emissions. The EU-CBAM is already on its way, and the G7 Climate Club has entered a substantive phase. In December 2022, the G7 released the Climate Club's Objectives and Terms of Reference, planning to set up a Climate Alliance centered on an "International Target Carbon Price" and to impose a uniform carbon tariff on imports from non-participating countries. Once the EU-CBAM and G7 Climate Club are implemented, Chinese exporters of key commodities such as steel and aluminum will see a significant 30% increase in costs and a drastic drop in competitiveness, prompting the Chinese Government to formulate an urgent response.

Currently, the implementation of CBAM-like programs faces several pivotal challenges. Firstly, it is intricate to establish a globally standardized target price for carbon emissions, along with determining the criteria and modalities for implementing a uniform carbon tariff. This endeavor encompasses numerous complexities, including the historical context of countries and regions, the responsibilities of both developing and developed nations, and the disparities in national carbon pricing policies. Secondly, the question of who will administer the funds and their intended usage remains controversial. Thirdly, there are considerable technical hurdles in validating carbon footprint data. Lastly, it is challenging to harmonize the conflict of rules with the WTO agreement, and it needs to further justify the legitimacy of carbon tariff barriers.

Moreover, carbon tariffs also involve the historical context of carbon emissions in both developed and developing countries, as well as the allocation of liability between producers or consumers. Carbon emission right extends beyond the realm of economics, intersecting with sociology and jurisprudence.

While carbon tariffs, if enforced, are undoubtedly conducive to reducing carbon emissions, the impediments to their implementation require further attention and resolution to ensure their effectiveness. Unilateral mechanisms, such as the G7 Climate Club and CBAM, lacking sufficient international coordination, are likely to encounter opposition from numerous countries, thus intensifying existing tensions. Carbon tariffs in the aviation sector, which were the EU's initial attempt to introduce such a measure, encountered significant resistance from countries like the United States, Russia, China, and India, ultimately making their implementation challenging.

3.4.6 Regional Liability and Economic Impacts of Emission Reduction

The liability mechanism for decarbonation has a significant impact on the regional interests among inter-provincial areas within a country, which has prompted extensive research from scholars. Currently, the prevalent analytical method centers on producer liability, facilitating the quantitative assessment of numerous inter-regional impacts. However, securing a universally acceptable solution remains challenging.

This challenge stems from the problematic assumptions underlying the producer liability perspective, which often hinder the attainment of sound analytical outcomes.

The investment in green transition and the input in emission reduction in energy resource regions and carbon removal provinces pose a significant challenge, representing a crucial theoretical breakthrough that needs to be addressed.

The resource endowment varies across regions, resulting in diverse original divisions of labor. For some regions, energy is their primary industry, while others primarily utilize energy. The substantial cost of decarbonation begs the question of who will bear the burden. In an effectively functioning market, the joint liability of energy-producing provinces and consumer provinces would mitigate the issue, yet price signaling in the current market is inefficient, and the conflicts of interest among provinces and regions are more apparent.

It is clear that a consumer liability mechanism would offer significant advantages and be more practical in terms of macroeconomic stability, fairness, and decarbonation.

3.4.7 Subsidy Policy for Neutral Technology Industries

Within the comprehensive industrial system for carbon neutral technologies, numerous technological domains necessitate significant technological advancements and risk-bearing investments. To foster these advancements, the government must offer robust incentives across diverse fields, encompassing green energy technology, energy storage solutions, smart grid infrastructure, CCUS technology, and carbon management information systems.

Carbon reduction technologies, owing to their beneficial externalities, deserve robust incentives, a necessity that cannot be overstated.

The question lies in how to ensure these incentives are maximized in their effectiveness. Further, how can government financial resources and carbon neutral funds be optimally allocated to yield the best possible inputs and outputs? Both academic and policy design studies are crucial in addressing these challenges. Furthermore, the specifics of implementation hold paramount importance. The Chinese Government, renowned for its ability to centralize efforts and achieve significant outcomes, has long relied on financial subsidies as a powerful tool. However, in its subsidy programs for photovoltaic, wind power, and new energy vehicles, challenges have arisen. Issues such as subsidy misappropriation and fraud have become increasingly prevalent, garnering widespread criticism from society. A notable example is the special investigation conducted by four ministries, including the Ministry of Finance, which uncovered subsidy fraud amounting to 9270.7 million yuan among 93 major enterprises specializing in new energy vehicles.

Should a product utilizing advanced technology be subsidized? If so, what is the most effective means of subsidy? Should it be a direct, production-based subsidy, preferential tax incentives, or financial policy support? Alternatively, are there other programs that could be utilized? It's crucial to note that the efficiency of incentives and administrative costs vary significantly across different policy tools. Could the amount of policy subsidies exceed the cost of production for a given product? Additionally, how can we mitigate fraudulent subsidy claims and ensure that subsidies are not allocated to non-existent products or those that fail to reach consumers? The design of the subsidy amount, process, policy, and implementation system plays a pivotal role. Therefore, it's imperative to have a clear understanding of the principles before designing any subsidy program. Otherwise, the policymakers may inadvertently design a policy program that compromises its efficiency and management, ultimately leading to issues in both policy effectiveness and management.

The scarcity of research projects and rigorous academic discussions in this area leaves many questions unanswered, particularly regarding the issues surrounding financial subsidies. Given the vast sums involved, the prevalence of cheating and corruption in subsidy programs has been a concern that demands our utmost attention. It is imperative for academics to delve deeper into this topic, engaging in rigorous research, argumentation, and debate.

One noteworthy example is Shanghai's incentive program offering free license plates for new energy vehicles. This program effectively subsidizes consumers directly, allowing them to avoid the significant cost of auctions for new vehicle license plate in Shanghai, which often exceeds 100,000 yuan. Additionally, it saves consumers the immense time and effort required to successfully acquire a license plate through auction.

However, the role of certain existing subsidy policies on industrial technological progress can be potentially negative. If the primary motivation for an incentive policy revolves around subsidies, it can create a situation where, under a quantitative subsidy mechanism, the less an enterprise invests in R&D, the lower the product quality and cost, potentially leading to maximized profits. This adverse incentive scenario must be rigorously avoided in both policy design and implementation. The government should persist in offering policy incentives for advanced technologies and products that exhibit positive externalities. Therefore, there is room for further refinement in the specific incentive measures and methodologies. The key lies in whether policy subsidies can effectively internalize product costs and foster a tighter integration between products, consumers, and markets.

What incentives are appropriate for each of the important technology industries that are conducive to carbon neutrality? Research in this area is also critical, as governments need theoretical support and data analysis to guide policy design. This represents a significant contribution and value of academia. However, it is unfortunate that academia has conducted limited research on these aspects.

Empirical evidence suggests that, regardless of other industries' practices or the efficacy of subsidy policies in the new energy sector, subsidy policies are often inefficient and face numerous challenges, including issues related to government integrity. Generally, governments should minimize reliance on direct subsidy policies and instead focus on effectively internalizing the costs of negative externalities. By doing so under market mechanism, technological advantages with positive externalities can be reflected in market competition, ultimately leading to optimal outcomes.

3.4.8 Summary

The intricate economics of climate change pose significant research challenges, resulting in a lack of substantial impact from current research efforts, whether it be carbon taxes or carbon markets. The international community has even questioned the practical relevance of climate change economists' work, dubbing it as "spherical chickens in a vacuum" after exhaustive theoretical analyses. Moreover, the complexity of climate issues has tested neoclassical economic research, with the idealized and simplified theoretical models struggling to accommodate the multi-faceted nature of the climate problem. However, we cannot overlook the invaluable role that economic ideas and theories play in addressing the problems concerning public goods. Instead, we must stand higher and see further on the shoulders of our predecessors. By adding bricks and mortar to the well-laid foundation of previous work, we can make our own contribution. Therefore, economists should not despair in the face of climate change, as there is still much potential for progress.

3.5 Carbon Taxes: International Practices

A carbon tax is an environmental tax levied on carbon-based fuels (such as coal, gasoline, and diesel) and collected from fossil fuel producers or consumers, or directly on CO_2 or other GHG emissions. This tax serves as a pivotal policy instrument in reducing carbon emissions, and numerous economists advocate for it as the most effective means to mitigate carbon emissions.

3.5.1 Development of International Carbon Taxes

The concept and practice of carbon tax first emerged in Europe, significantly advancing environmental tax reforms across the continent. Leveraging this momentum, European nations embarked on reforms centered around "carbon tax and energy tax". Finland pioneered carbon tax in 1990, while other Nordic countries like Norway, Sweden, and Denmark implemented it in the 1990s. Subsequently, Switzerland and other European nations followed suit. In recent years, carbon tax has gained traction in Asia and Africa as well. South Africa became the first African nation to introduce a carbon tax, while the Singaporean Government announced plans to levy one in 2019, marking the inception of carbon tax in Asia. Currently, Singapore's carbon tax covers industries that contribute up to 80% of the country's local GHG emissions.

According to the World Bank, as of April 2023, a total of 40 countries/regions around the world have implemented carbon taxes, covering 5.5% of global GHG emissions. In 2022, countries where carbon taxes are implemented collected about

\$29 billion in carbon tax revenues, accounting for 31% of global carbon pricing benefits, a slight increase from the 2021 level of \$28 billion.

3.5.1.1 Tax Rates

Carbon tax rates e xhibit significant disparities among nations, ranging from USD 0.08/tCO_2e in Poland to USD 155.86/tCO_2e in Uruguay. Uruguay started to collect a carbon tax in January 2022, but its carbon tax rate is extremely high, with USD 137.29/tCO_2e and USD 155.86/tCO_2e in 2022 and 2023 respectively. The overall carbon tax rate is low, with carbon tax rates in nearly half of the countries lower than USD 25/tCO_2e, and, except for Uruguay, only the developed countries in Northern Europe have a carbon tax rate exceeding USD 50/tCO_2e. In Asia, Japan and Singapore are the only countries with established carbon tax systems, and their tax rates remain at a comparatively low level.

Certain countries have implemented varying tax rates for distinct taxable entities. For instance, Iceland and Denmark impose lower taxes on F-gases compared to general fossil fuels, whereas Finland and Luxembourg levy higher taxes on transportation fuels and diesel than on other fossil fuels.

At the initial stage of the implementation of a carbon tax, countries usually set a lower level of tax rate to minimize the adverse impact on the competitiveness of their products, and then gradually increase the tax rate in multiple phases to ensure the effectiveness of emission reduction. For example, Japan raised its carbon tax rate in three phases over three and a half years to avoid a sharp increase in its tax burden.

3.5.1.2 Taxation Basis

There are primarily two models for determining the taxation basis of a carbon tax. The first model directly taxes carbon emissions or carbon content, which effectively reflects the emissions of the primary emitter. However, this approach imposes higher demands on measurement technology and incurs greater implementation costs, making it currently adopted only by a select few countries like Poland and the Czech Republic. Alternatively, the second model taxes based on the total fuel consumption or its carbon content, which is simpler and thus adopted by most countries, including Finland, Denmark, the United Kingdom, and Japan. Nevertheless, this model may not adequately incentivize enterprises to adopt advanced technologies for decarbonation.

3.5.1.3 Tax Collection Process

At present, three primary models govern the implementation of carbon taxes during the tax collection process. Firstly, there is the production-based taxation model, which targets solely the production of fossil fuels. Countries such as Iceland, Japan, and certain Canadian provinces adhere to this approach. Secondly, there is the consumption-based taxation model, which taxes only the consumption of fossil fuels. Poland and the United Kingdom, for instance, employ this method. Lastly, there is the dual taxation model, which levies taxes on both the production and consumption of fossil fuels simultaneously. The Netherlands exemplifies this approach, imposing taxes on producers, importers, distributors, and consumers of fossil fuels. The production-based tax is advantageous in terms of administration and minimizing social resistance, yet it faces challenges in effectively transmitting price signals to consumers, thereby limiting the regulatory impact of the carbon tax. Conversely, the consumption-based tax aligns with principles of tax fairness and is instrumental in raising awareness among enterprises and consumers regarding energy conservation and emission reduction. However, it encounters difficulties due to the widespread dispersion of taxpayers, posing challenges for control. Currently, the majority of countries opt for levying carbon taxes at the production stage.

3.5.1.4 Tax Benefits

The imposition of a carbon tax, levied on fuel consumption (carbon content) or carbon emissions from the production process, can potentially lead to double taxation when coupled with other taxes, and double control when integrated with carbon trading programs. Furthermore, owing to the varying regulation degrees of environmental policies across nations, a carbon tax may undermine the international competitiveness of energy-intensive enterprises and export-oriented industries. To safeguard the global competitiveness of domestic industries, virtually every country has implemented Specialized Tax Measures for Industry, entailing varying degrees of subsidies and incentives. For instance, European countries offer carbon tax exemptions to enterprises participating in the EU carbon trading market. Canadian provinces grant partial exemptions to energy-intensive industries, such as aviation and transportation. Danish enterprises enjoy differential tax concessions based on their net CO_2 tax burden (inclusive of rebates) relative to sales, while enterprises enrolled in the Voluntary Emission Reduction Agreement (VERA) are eligible for tax reductions and exemptions. In the Netherlands, social, educational, and non-profit organizations can receive tax rebates up to 50% of their tax payable. In Sweden, some energy-intensive enterprises are entitled to tax reductions and exemptions, and as the tax rate increases over time, the percentage of such reductions and exemptions also increases, effectively counterbalancing the rising tax burden on enterprises.

3.5.1.5 Revenue Use

Global revenues from carbon taxes were estimated at $29 billion in 2022, and have remained low for the previous two years. In order to maintain carbon tax revenue neutral, a number of countries have incorporated these revenues into their general budgets and subsequently implemented tax rebates to the general population. Finland, for example, offers rebates to energy-intensive industries; while Denmark uses part of the revenue from carbon tax to subsidize residential usage of natural gas and electricity, and part of it is used to provide rebates for enterprises paying VAT or subsidize their energy-saving investments. The United Kingdom rebates taxes through three avenues: reducing the national insurance premiums paid by enterprises for their employees, increasing the subsidies for investment in energy-saving and environmental protection technologies, and setting up a carbon fund. However, investigation shows that the effectiveness of these tax rebate is not ideal. A survey conducted by U.S. journalists among citizens in Canada and Switzerland, both countries that have implemented nearly revenue-neutral carbon pricing, revealed that in Canada, some provincial residents receive a one-time carbon rebate as part of their annual tax payments, while Swiss residents perceive the rebate as a discount on their health insurance premiums.

3.5.1.6 Carbon Tax Effectiveness

A carbon tax, while ensuring emissions are lower than in a no-tax scenario, faces significant uncertainty in achieving absolute reduction in carbon emissions. This is evidenced by Haites' empirical analysis of emission reduction in Nordic countries such as Sweden and Norway from 1981 to 2007, which revealed that the carbon tax reduced emissions by 2.8% to 4.9% compared to the no-tax baseline. However, the absolute amount of carbon emissions in Finland, Denmark, Sweden, and Norway did not show a substantial decline after the implementation of the carbon tax, or the decline was significantly smaller than after joining the carbon market. In 2012, Australia introduced a carbon tax, but in 2014, the Senate of the Australian Federal Parliament voted 39–32 to repeal the tax, effectively scrapping the legislation that had been in effect since 2012. Australian Prime Minister Tony Abbott argued that the carbon tax imposed a significant cost of AU$9 billion annually on businesses, yet had minimal impact on reducing CO_2 emissions. He further contended that repealing the tax would lower market costs for businesses, enhancing their competitiveness.

3.5.2 *Progress of Carbon Tax in China*

As far back as 2002, the National Bureau of Statistics of China (NBS) and Statistics Norway conducted a joint project to assess the impact of a carbon tax on China's economy and GHG emissions. This project developed a computable general equilibrium (CNAGE) model for China, which provided a quantitative analysis of the impact of a carbon tax on China's economy and GHG emissions. The study reveals while a carbon tax would significantly reduce CO_2 emissions, it would also adversely impact China's economic conditions, particularly in the short term, with substantial costs.

However, in the long run, the negative impacts of such a tax are expected to gradually diminish. For a developing nation like China, the economic cost of introducing a carbon tax to mitigate GHG emissions is indeed substantial.

In July 2008, the Energy Foundation initiated a project titled "Research on China's Carbon Tax", while the Institute of Fiscal Science under the Ministry of Finance established a research team to delve deeply into the topic. This team conducted extensive research on carbon tax, exploring its feasibility and implementation strategies from theoretical, policy, and technological perspectives. Their findings were published in a series of papers.

In May 2010, leading experts from the National Development and Reform Commission (NDRC) disclosed in an industry conference that the NDRC and the Ministry of Finance (MOF) had jointly crafted a special report titled "Design of China's Carbon Tax Framework", which outlined the proposed framework for China's carbon tax system, including its functional positioning and related taxes, the roadmap for implementation, as well as the proposals for supporting measures. The report concluded that the optimal time for introducing a carbon tax in China would be around 2012, with an initial focus on taxing enterprises rather than individuals. The expert group emphasized that, as CO_2 emissions serve as the basis for tax calculation, a quantitative approach and a fixed tax rate are deemed appropriate. Furthermore, the carbon tax revenue should be channeled towards subsidizing energy-efficient and environmentally sustainable industries and enterprises. Regarding tax rates, the report proposed two options: either a "10 yuan/ton in 2012, increasing to 40 yuan/ton by 2020" or a "20 yuan/ton in 2012, rising to 50 yuan/ton in 2020, and 100 yuan/ton by 2030". These proposals, once publicized, sparked widespread societal interest and discussion.

During the two sessions[1] held in 2008, 2009, and 2010, there were proposals advocating for the introduction of a carbon tax.

In 2013, following the directive of the CPC Central Committee and the State Council, the Ministry of Finance, the State Taxation Administration, and the Ministry of Environmental Protection collaborated to formulate the *Environmental Protection Tax Law of the People's Republic of China (Draft for Review)* through thorough investigation and research. This new tax system, which superseded the existing sewage charges, pioneered the integration of a CO_2 emission tax, commonly known as the "carbon tax", for the first time.

This measure has sparked intense societal responses. The opposition to implementing the carbon tax is primarily led by a group of economists who rely on traditional economic frameworks for their calculations. Their analysis suggests that introducing a carbon tax would inescapably harm the interests of ordinary citizens to a significant extent. These economists fear that traditional energy enterprises might shift the burden of the carbon tax onto the general public, especially affecting the overall welfare of low-income groups and leading to a decline in their standard of living.

---

[1] Two sessions refer to National People's Congress (NPC) and Chinese People's Political Consultative Conference (CPPCC)—a note by the translator.

Based on a number of indicators, including China's level of economic development and tax burden, a Shanghai-based research group came to an important finding that the imposition of a carbon tax would inevitably trigger a decline of social welfare, which fell by about 2% in urban areas and by about 1.7% in rural areas.

Eventually, the former Legislative Affairs Office of the State Council, after repeated consultations with industry experts and the general public, finalized the *Environmental Protection Tax Law of the People's Republic of China (Draft)*, excluding the CO_2 emission tax. In the explanation of the draft, it is stated that "the levy of environmental protection tax on CO_2, which is controversial among various stakeholders, will be temporarily excluded from the scope of taxation". Wang Fengchun, Deputy Director of the Bill Office of the NPC Environment and Resources Committee, explained in an interview that "China is currently prioritizing the establishment of a national carbon trading market. Including the carbon tax in the environmental protection tax law would create a degree of functional overlap, which is the primary reason for its exclusion from the draft for public consultation". On January 1, 2018, the *Environmental Protection Tax Law of the People's Republic of China* officially came into effect, without incorporating a carbon tax.

While the Ministry of Finance diligently delved into the carbon tax framework, China launched a pilot trading program for carbon emissions in seven provinces (cities), including Beijing, Tianjin, Shanghai, Chongqing, Hubei, Guangdong and Shenzhen in 2011, thus kicking off a long journey of exploration. Ultimately, the carbon market "won" in China.

In January 2023, Taiwan enacted the *Climate Change Response Act*, intending to introduce a carbon tax on major emitters and a CBAM-style carbon tariff on imported goods with a significant carbon footprint. However, the precise modalities for implementing these two carbon taxes have yet to be finalized.

3.6 Carbon Market: International Practices

At present, from the perspective of global carbon market practices, carbon market refers to the Emission Trade System (ETS). The ETS, also known as carbon market, is an effective policy to encourage the reduction of GHG emissions. Carbon emission right refers to the right to use the atmosphere or atmospheric capacity, i.e. the right to emit GHGs such as CO_2 into the atmosphere.

3.6.1 Development Status of Global Carbon Market

Carbon market refers to the market in which carbon emission rights are traded as the object of assets, and the establishment of the ETSs directly influences whether the carbon market can effectively reflect the value of carbon emission rights. Furthermore, it significantly impacts the effectiveness of achieving ultimate reduction targets.

In 2005, the European Union officially adopted the "cap-and-trade" model, resulting in the establishment of the first regional emissions trading system: EU ETS, which authorized countries to use Certified Emission Reduction (CER) credits. Since then, other regional ETSs have gradually emerged.

In March 2023, the International Carbon Action Partnership (ICAP) released *Emissions Trading Worldwide: 2023 ICAP Status Report.* The report shows that by January 2023, the number of ETSs in operation has more than doubled, growing from 13 to the current 28, and so too did the share of global emissions covered by an ETS, which jumped from 8 to 17%, following the increase from below 4 gigatons in 2014 to the current 9 gigatons. An additional 20 ETSs are under development or consideration, particularly in Latin America and Asia.

Over the past two decades since the inception of carbon markets, while the establishment of ETSs in various countries has been gradual (see Fig. 3.2), revenues generated from carbon trading have witnessed remarkable growth. This growth is attributed to the consistent rise in allowance prices, the introduction of auctioning mechanisms, the increasing share of allowances auctioned, and the continuous expansion of the carbon market. Consequently, in 2022, revenues from global carbon market hit a record high of $63 billion. Since 2008, the global ETSs have raised over $224 billion in funding, with over half of that amount generated in 2021 and 2022 alone. Notably, the EU carbon market, the world's largest carbon trading system in terms of volume and turnover, leads globally in carbon allowance revenues, accounting for nearly 65% of the global total (see Fig. 3.3).

Despite the global energy crisis in 2022, sparked by the Russia-Ukraine conflict, leading to a surge in energy prices and exacerbating inflationary pressures, the global ETSs remained largely resilient to broader economic shocks, maintaining similar allowance prices at the end of 2022 compared to the 2021 level.

In the medium and long term, it is expected that the global carbon market will show a steady improvement in breadth and depth, as well as in the development of international cooperation. Primarily, the construction and planning of carbon markets at national and regional levels will be steadily advanced, resulting in a wider geographical influence and expansion of scope. Furthermore, individual carbon markets are expected to continuously optimize their mechanisms, as exemplified by the growing number of industries incorporated, comprehensive coverage of GHG, a phased reduction in the allocation of free allowances, and a timely increase in the proportion of auctions.

Furthermore, ETSs are generating record level of revenues that can be used to both deliver further GHG reductions and to alleviate the burden on low-income communities and households, either directly via rebates or indirectly, such as funding energy efficiency improvements in state housing.

Almost two decades have elapsed since the inception of the first carbon trading market in 2005. Despite the consistent increase in the number of carbon trading

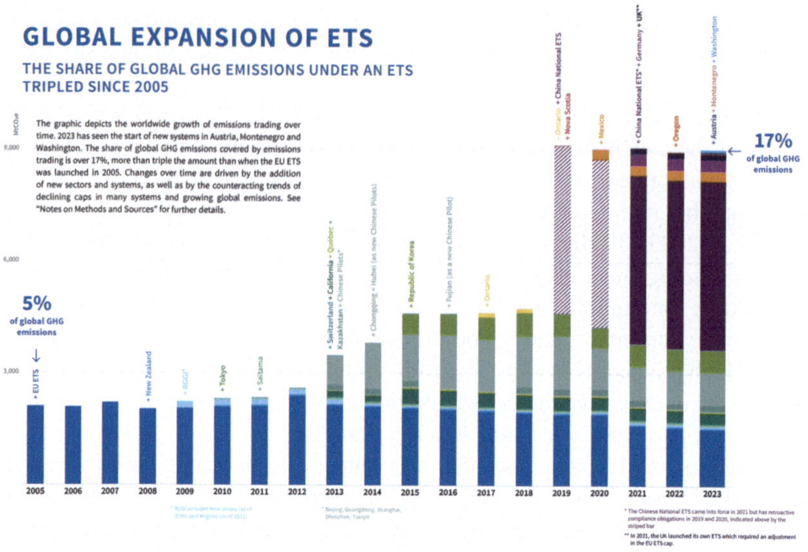

Fig. 3.2 Global expansion of ETSs (*Source* ICAP)

Fig. 3.3 Development of allowance prices in global primary ETSs (*Source* ICAP)

markets, the emissions they cover, and the value of transactions, these figures remain relatively modest in absolute terms.

This book takes the EU ETS as an example to introduce the intricacies of its operation mechanism.

3.6.1.1 Aggregate Control and Allocation Mechanism

EU ETS was officially established on January 1, 2005 in accordance with *Directive 2003/87 EU*. Its primary objectives are to internalize environmental costs, transform the environment into a production factor for paid utilization driven by market forces, and through the establishment of the European Allowance (EUA) trading

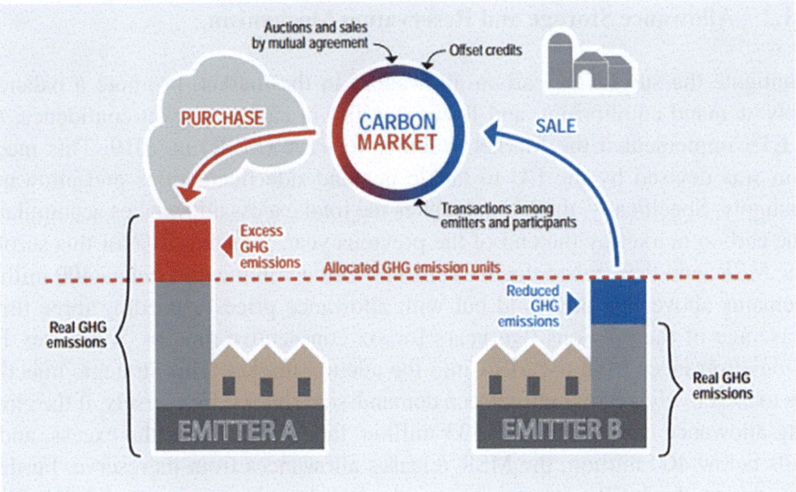

Fig. 3.4 Cap and trade diagram

market, efficiently allocate environmental resources. Additionally, it aims to promote the development of energy-saving and emission reduction technologies, ultimately minimizing operational costs for enterprises while safeguarding the climate and environment.

The EU ETS stands as the world's pioneering and largest multinational emissions trading system, representing the most developed carbon market globally. It encompasses all EU member states, along with Iceland, Liechtenstein, and Norway, involving approximately 10,000 companies across the power, manufacturing, and aviation sectors. Notably, it covers roughly 40% of the EU's total GHG emissions.

The EU ETS utilizes a "cap-and-trade" approach (as depicted in Fig. 3.4), offering an effective financial incentive for companies to minimize their carbon emissions.

Cap: The European Union sets an aggregate emission target, imposes a cap on the aggregate emissions of enterprises included on the limit list, and progressively reduces this cap year by year. Especially in the third phase, a Linear Reduction Factor (LRF) is introduced to ensure a steady annual decline in total carbon emissions.

Allowance: Enterprises on the list are granted carbon emission allowances, either free of charge based on specific criteria or through auctions. Initially, most allowances were awarded without cost, but the proportion allocated for free has been steadily decreasing, prompting the adoption of a compensatory auction system. The methodology for free allocation has also shifted from a historical emission basis to a more baseline-oriented approach.

Trade: Carbon market participants who exceed their allocated emissions must purchase EUAs from those who have generated fewer emissions. Conversely, companies that emit below their allowances have the opportunity to profit by selling their EUAs in the carbon market.

3.6.1.2 Allowance Storage and Reservation Mechanism

To mitigate the surplus of carbon allowances in the market, promote a balanced supply–demand equilibrium, and foster stability in carbon market confidence, the EU ETS implemented the Market Stability Reserve (MSR) in 2019. This mechanism was devised by the EU to tackle demand-side fluctuations and allowance oversupply. Specifically, the EU calculates the total excess allowances accumulated in the carbon market by the end of the previous year, transfers 24% of this surplus to the MSR, and then, when the market's allowance volume dips below 400 million or remains above that threshold but with allowance prices exceeding three times the average of the previous two years for six consecutive months, it releases 100 million allowances from the MSR into the auction market. This strategic injection aims to effectively address unforeseen demand-side shocks. Conversely, if the circulating allowance count surpasses 833 million, the MSR absorbs the excess, and if it falls below 400 million, the MSR releases allowances from its reserve. Furthermore, during the MSR's inception year, the EU directly incorporated 900 million allowances, originally intended for auction in 2019–2020 but not sold in 2014–2016, into the MSR. This integration mitigated the imbalance between carbon allowance supply and demand resulting from sluggish demand and an influx of international carbon credits in the aftermath of the 2008 financial crisis.

3.6.1.3 Measurement, Reporting and Verification (MRV) System

This system is an important source to obtain allowance data in the EU ETS, underpinning and sustaining the overall effective functioning of the EU ETS. It adheres to fundamental principles that include:

Integrity: The cornerstone of EU ETS measurement lies in the integrity of emission sources and source streams. Each operator is required to submit a comprehensive, site-specific measuring methodology within their measurement plan.

Consistency and Comparability: The measurement plan functions as a dynamic document, requiring regular updates as measurement methods evolve. Arbitrary alterations to the measurement methods are prohibited to maintain consistency over time.

Transparency: Data collection, compilation, and calculation must adhere to stringent transparency standards. This means that all data and the methods used to obtain and utilize them must be documented transparently, with all relevant information securely stored and retained so as to be fully accessible to authorized third parties.

Accuracy: Operators must prioritize the accuracy of the data, striving for the highest level of accuracy. The measurement processes should be technically feasible and cost-effective, avoiding unnecessary expenditures.

Methodological Integrity: Operators are required to utilize the methodologies outlined in their approved measurement plan to accurately determine emissions in their annual emissions report. This ensures the integrity of the reported data. The annual emissions report must then undergo verification by an independent, accredited verification body to further safeguard its authenticity.

3.6.1.4 Strict Compliance and Penalty Mechanism

The EU requires member states to conduct an annual assessment of the compliance status of enterprises within the EU ETS. The regulation stipulates that compliant enterprises must submit, within a designated timeframe each year, a report verified by a third-party detailing their emissions as well as the equivalent total amount of emission allowances in the previous year. Failure to do so will result in being deemed non-compliant and subject to penalties imposed by the respective governments. These penalties primarily consist of:

1. Financial penalties, a fine of 100 euros per ton of excess emissions.
2. Public disclosure of the defaulting enterprise's name.
3. A requirement of the defaulting enterprise to make up for the excess emission allowances of the current year in the subsequent year. That is to say, after the defaulting enterprise pays the fine, any remaining excess carbon allowances that cannot be offset will remain and accumulate, without exception, until the following year. Furthermore, these enterprises will be required to pay 1.08 times the amount of allowances equivalent to the excess emissions.
4. Continuous improvement: Operators must establish robust monitoring procedures. Where feasible, e.g. to a higher level, the operators must submit regular reports on their potential for improvement. In addition, the operators are expected to respond to the recommendations of the verifier.

3.6.1.5 Carbon Financial Mechanism

The EU ETS boasts robust financial characteristics, operating as an integrated market that simultaneously launches futures and spot transactions since its inception. Pursuant to the EU's *Markets in Financial Instruments Directive II*, carbon emission rights are classified as financial instruments, necessitating the reporting of daily and weekly conditions for both emission rights and their derivatives. Primarily, EU carbon allowance futures are traded on the Intercontinental Exchange (ICE), and by the end of the second phase of the EU ETS, carbon futures constitute a substantial share, nearing 90%, of the total allowance trading volume. Numerous financial institutions actively participate in the EU ETS, assuming the role of counterparties to regulated entities, thereby playing a pivotal role in ensuring the smooth functioning of the market.

3.6.1.6 Step-by-Step Implementation Mechanism

To ensure its sound development, the EU ETS has undergone four distinct phases of development (see Table 3.1 and Fig. 3.5), during which the market system has been continuously optimized and enhanced.

In its initial phase (2005–2007), the EU ETS covered only CO_2 emissions from power generators and energy-intensive industries. Almost all allowances were given to businesses for free and the penalty for non-compliance was €40 per ton. It is noteworthy that the total emission limit of 2096 $MtCO_2e$ in this phase was set on the basis of estimates. As a result, the total amount of allowances issued exceeded that of the actual emissions and, with supply significantly exceeding demand, in 2007 the price of allowances fell to zero.

The second phase (2008–2012) coincided with the first commitment period of *The Kyoto Protocol*, and saw a slight decrease in the EU ETS emission limit to 2049 $MtCO_2e$. The proportion of free allocation fell slightly to around 90%. The aviation sector was brought into the EU ETS. However, the 2008 economic crisis led to emissions reductions that were greater than expected. This led to a large surplus of allowances and credits, which weighed heavily on the carbon price throughout phase 2.

The third phase (2013–2020) witnessed major adjustments to the EU ETS, with the introduction of a single EU-wide cap on emissions in place of the previous system of national caps. More sectors and greenhouse gases were included: petrochemicals, ammonia, ferrous and non-ferrous metals, gypsum and aluminum production. Auctioning, up to 57%, was taken as the default method for allocating allowances (instead of free allocation). In addition, a Linear Reduction Factor (LRF) was introduced, and emission allowances have been declining at a rate of 1.74% year-on-year (see Fig. 3.6).

Phase 4 (2021–2030) aims to fulfil the ambitious goal of cutting GHG emissions by 55% relative to the 1990 level by 2030 proposed by the European Green Deal. To this end, the EU ETS has undergone significant adjustments, with the emission limit tightened to 1,572 MtCO2e, and the LRF revised upwards from 1.74% to 2.2%, ensuring an annual reduction of 43 Mt in carbon allowances. Concurrently, the MSR mechanism has also been further strengthened, doubling of the intake for the MSR (the ratio of allowances included in the MSR to the total allowances in circulation) from 12 to 24% until 2023. Starting in 2023, allowances held in the MSR were limited, and excess volumes became invalid. Moreover, the EU Parliament is contemplating further measures: potentially adjusting the LRF to 4.2% in 2024, instantly slashing allowances by 1.19 million tons, and intake of the MSR maintained at 24% until 2030, all aimed at accelerating the achievement of emission reduction targets. Carbon allowance prices have surged rapidly in Phase 4 in response to the imminent reality and expectation of intensified efforts to reduce emissions. While the price trend in the second half of 2021 largely reflected the impact of gas supply shortages in Europe, the underlying drivers were the intensified emissions reductions, the decreased emission allowances, and the ensuing tightening of market expectations, all contributing to an upward trajectory in carbon prices.

Table 3.1 Four phases of the EU ETS

	Goal of the phase	Greenhouse gases	Geographic scope	Sectors	Cap	Allowance management	Market regulation
Phase 1 (2005–2007)	Piloting the system, establishing the infrastructure and carbon market	CO_2	EU27	Power plants over 20 MW, oil refining, steel, cement, glass, lime, brick making, pottery making, paper making	2058 Mt of CO_2	95% of allowances for free	Joint Implement (JI), clean development mechanism (CDM)
Phase 2 (2008–2012)	−8% emissions reduction relative to 1990 levels	CO_2	EU27 Norway Iceland Lichtenstein	Same as Phase 1 plus Aviation in EEA	1859 Mt of CO_2	90% of allowances for free	Limiting JI, CDM project quality; Limiting offset quantity
Phase 3 (2013–2020)	−21% emissions reduction relative to 2005 levels	CO_2, N_2O, PFC	EU27 Norway Iceland Lichtenstein	Plus aluminum, petrochemical, ammonia, nitric acid, oxalic acid, glyoxylic acid production, carbon capture, management and transportation, CO_2 underground storage	2084 Mt of CO_2 in 2013, with a linear annual reduction of 1.74%	For power plants, 100% of allowances by auctioning; For manufacturing sector, 80% of allowances for free, with an annual reduction to 30% in 2020	Further limiting JI, CDM project quality; Establishing MSR
Phase 4 (2021–2030)	−43% emissions reduction relative to 2005 levels	CO_2, N_2O, PFC	EU27 Norway Iceland Lichtenstein	Same as Phase 3	Linear annual reduction of allowance decrease of 2.2%	For power plants, 100% of allowances by auctioning; 43% of total allowances for free, with an annual reduction to 0 in 2026	No offset

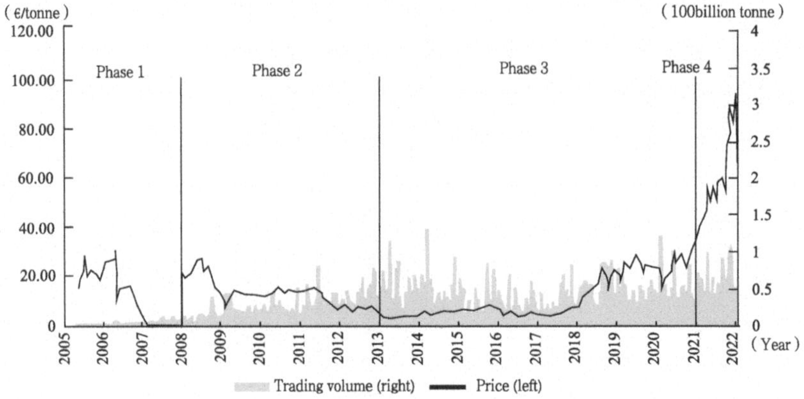

Fig. 3.5 Futures trading price and volume in the EU ETS (*Source* CICC Research Institute)

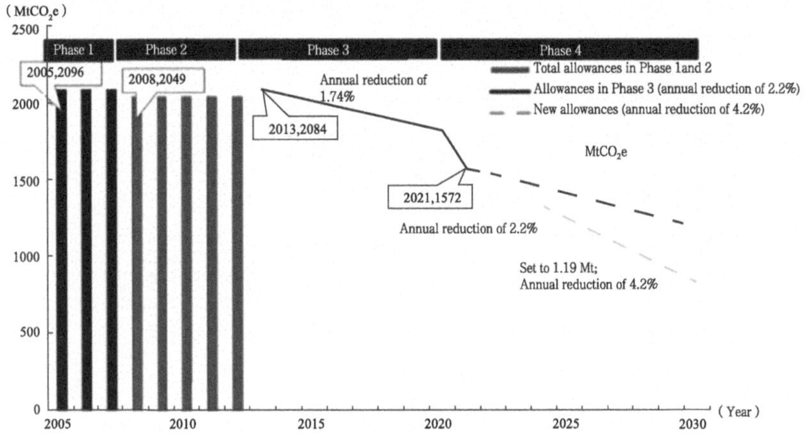

Fig. 3.6 Emission allowances and reduction pathway in each phase (*Source* CICC Research Institute)

The ETS fundamentally caps the total carbon emissions, thereby instilling a discernible downward path for emissions. However, this certainty in emissions reduction comes at the expense of uncertainty in carbon pricing.

3.6.2 China's Carbon Market Practice: High Enthusiasm, Harsh Reality

China's domestic carbon market has been operating on a trial basis in decentralized markets at the provincial level, on a very small scale since the launch of regional pilot program in 2011. Since then, China has conducted trading pilots in eight provinces and municipalities, including Beijing, Shanghai, Guangdong, Shenzhen, Hubei, Chongqing, Tianjin, and Fujian, covering sectors such as electricity generation, iron and steel manufacturing, chemicals, and metal smelting. As of December 31, 2022, these eight pilot markets have completed a cumulative total of 448.57 million tons of allowances traded online, and reached a trading volume of about 12.212 billion yuan. Detailed transaction data for each regional carbon market is presented in Table 3.2.

On July 16, 2021, Shanghai witnessed the historic establishment of the national carbon market, and the first transaction on emission rights was successfully concluded. In the subsequent year, 2022, the national carbon market recorded a total volume of Chinese Emission Allowances (CEA) amounting to 5,088.95 tons, accompanied by a total turnover reaching 2.814 billion yuan. By the end of 2022, the cumulative volume of allowances in the national carbon market reached 230 million tons, with the cumulative turnover surpassing 10.475 billion yuan. Despite China's position as the world's largest carbon emitter, the turnover and volume in its national market reveals a disproportionately small impact. It is widely recognized that the current carbon market is too small in scale, limited in coverage, and inadequate in total volume control. Consequently, it exerts minimal pressure on enterprises to reduce their emissions and contributes marginally to the overarching goal of achieving carbon neutrality.

Furthermore, the current carbon pricing system falls short of serving as an authentic signal. Out of China's total carbon emissions of approximately 12 billion tons, the trading volume barely scratches the surface, not exceeding 1 billion tons. Alarmingly, the overwhelming majority of carbon allowances are allocated free of charge, leaving only a fraction—a mere few hundred million tons—subject to trading. This glaring disparity utterly fails to mirror the genuine price signal that the carbon market ought to embody, deviating significantly from the social cost of carbon emissions. The carbon price fluctuates dramatically with the number of free allowances

Table 3.2 Transaction data for each regional carbon market (as of December 31, 2022)

Pilot markets	Date of opening	Total volume (ten thousand ton)	Total turnover (100 million yuan)
Beijing	2013.11.28	1817.02	12.28
Tianjin	2013.12.26	2411.68	5.97
Shanghai	2013.11.26	1944.83	6.38
Shenzhen	2013.6.18	5545.11	14.22
Guangdong	2013.12.19	21,414.05	56.39
Hubei	2014.4.2	8543.66	21.35
Chongqing	2014.6.19	1056.72	0.99
Fujian	2016.12.22	2124.01	4.54

allocated: scarcity drives prices up, whereas abundance pushes them down. Consequently, this pricing mechanism, which corresponds to a mere fraction of the total emissions, lacks the robustness of a genuine market system and is unlikely to effectively incentivize widespread emission reductions across society. Moreover, its implications for the macroeconomy have been substantial, underscoring the urgency for a more comprehensive and effective carbon pricing strategy.

The empirical evidence is already clear that the current carbon market for carbon emission rights needs fundamental change.

The sluggish progress observed in this carbon market stems primarily from its traps within the Western experiences, coupled with a dearth of advanced economic theories grounded in climate change to steer its development. The advent of the CELM theory presents a pivotal opportunity to alter this landscape. It offers a chance for China to establish an international carbon market that could potentially lead the world.

Events Review: Various regions in China are competing to build carbon markets

1. Guangzhou has significantly escalated its endeavors towards establishing a robust carbon futures market. On September 14, 2021, Guangdong released the *Guangdong Action Plan for Deepening the Reform of Market-based Allocation of Capital Elements*, a blueprint outlining the strategic direction to foster the development of the Guangdong-Hong Kong-Macao Greater Bay Area's emission trading market, leveraging the existing Guangdong carbon emissions trading framework. The plan also advocates for enhancing Hong Kong and Macao investors' participation in Guangdong carbon market and instituting a framework for transboundary carbon emissions trading. This transboundary trading platform paves the way for qualified international investors to engage in emission rights trading within Mainland China, utilizing either foreign exchange or Renminbi (RMB).

   Furthermore, on November 5, 2021, a collaborative effort by four key departments, including the Ministry of Industry and Information Technology, issued the *Guiding Opinions of Four Departments on Strengthening Industry Integration and Cooperation to Promote Green Development of Industry.* This document underscores the support for the Guangzhou Futures Exchange to build a carbon futures market under the guidance of the China Securities Regulatory Commission (CSRC). It encourages the active and steady progression of the research and development pertaining to carbon emission futures, and advocates for the standardization of carbon financial services.
2. Hainan has launched its construction of an international carbon trading center. On April 14, 2018, a pivotal milestone was reached with the issuance of the *Guiding Opinions of the CPC Central Committee and State Council on Supporting Hainan to Comprehensively Deepen Reform and Opening Up*, which expressly advocated for the legal establishment of an international trading hub in Hainan, encompassing a broad spectrum, including energy, shipping, commodities, property rights, equity, and notably, carbon emission rights. This groundbreaking initiative marked the first official proposal to foster an international carbon trading

center in Hainan. Consequently, the construction of such a market has been strategically positioned on the agenda.

In July 2019, Hainan convened a meeting on the establishment of an international trading market for carbon emission rights, emphasizing the market's adherence to the central government's vision of positioning Hainan as an "internationalized" hub for carbon emissions trading. This meeting also underscored the exploration of avenues to attract foreign investors.

On February 7, 2022, with the consent of the Hainan Provincial Government, the Financial Bureau of Hainan Province issued the *Approval on the Establishment of Hainan International Carbon Emission Trading Center Limited*, greenlighting the initiation of preparatory work for its establishment. This pioneering venture is poised to be registered in Sanya.

3. On July 16, 2021, the national trading market for carbon emission rights started online trading. The power generation industry became the first industry to be included in the national carbon market, with more than 2000 key emission units included. Promptly at 9:30 a.m., the carbon emission trading system of the Shanghai Environment and Energy Exchange (SEEE) showed that the opening price of carbon trading was 48 yuan per ton. Moments later, the first transaction was successfully concluded at 52.78 yuan per ton, totaling 160,000 tons in volume and generating a turnover of 7.9 million yuan. By the conclusion of 2022, the cumulative volume of carbon emission allowances in the national carbon market reached 230 million tons, and the cumulative turnover amounted to 10.475 billion yuan. Remarkably, on December 22, 2022, the cumulative turnover exceeded the monumental threshold of10 billion yuan.

3.6.3 Main Problems and Urgency of Change in the Current Carbon Market: A Case from China

At present, China's domestic carbon market is dominated by trading of carbon emission rights, most of which are free allowances, which are not yet capable of achieving dual carbon targets. The government grants free allowances to carbon emitting enterprises, which can be sold if they can't use them up, and enterprises with insufficient allowances need to purchase them to maintain and increase their production. The allowance-based approach to carbon emission rights, a form of planned economy, exhibits considerable diversity across nations, with China primarily administering its system through provinces and cities. This has led to policy inconsistencies, regional imbalances, and difficulties in achieving a sound and equitable system.

The current carbon emission trading system serves as a market-driven policy instrument aimed at mitigating carbon emissions. Its primary objective is to ensure the efficient allocation of carbon emission allowances, thereby controlling the overall carbon footprint and minimizing societal costs associated with emission reduction efforts. However, the argument that carbon emissions trading system is market-driven is not accurate. Instead, it represents a hybrid approach, blending elements of market economy within a predominantly planned framework, which inherently harbors significant internal challenges. The determination and allocation of total emission allowances follow a planned approach, while the exchange of surplus or deficient emission rights among organizations exhibits a partial market character. This dual nature gives the system an unconventional flavor. Nevertheless, the efficacy of carbon emissions trading hinges critically on the design intricacies of national carbon market mechanisms. Factors such as the total emission allowances, the way of allocating the initial emission allowances, as well as the coverage of the industries included have an important impact on trading price, market scale, and ultimately, the costs and outcomes of emission reduction efforts.

In Sect. 3.4.5, we have thoroughly surveyed the current research landscape and developmental trends of the international carbon market. Building upon this foundation, we now delve deeper into several pivotal issues that warrant further exploration.

3.6.3.1 Influence of Total Amount of Allowances

The total amount of carbon emission allowances refers to the quantity available for trading within the carbon market. An increase in this value signifies a more lenient cap imposed by the market, resulting in a lower carbon price, reduced mitigation costs, but a weaker impact on emissions reduction. Conversely, a decrease in the value indicates a stricter cap, leading to higher carbon prices, greater mitigation costs, and a stronger emission reduction effect. However, this straightforward logic fails to hold true in numerous scenarios due to the profound influence the current mechanism exerts on the macroeconomy, coupled with the absence of a robust scientific algorithmic foundation for determining the total emission allowances. Climate economists have invested significantly in developing algorithmic models, aiming to integrate macroeconomic factors, climate physics, and carbon price impacts into a single, precise framework. Despite these efforts, these models often fall short of providing decisive support to policymakers due to myriads of assumptions surrounding macroeconomic, climatic, and technological mitigation impacts, as well as the inability to include numerous influential factors.

Therefore, establishing a direct correlation between the total amount of allowances and the carbon neutrality process poses a significant challenge.

3.6.3.2 Influence of Allowance Allocation Approaches

There are three primary approaches for allocating initial carbon emission allowances: the "grandfather" approach, which involves free allocation based on historical emissions; the "benchmarking" approach, where allowances are granted freely according to emission intensity benchmarks and the compensation auction approach.

The Regional Greenhouse Gas Initiative (RGGI) of the United States has been using auctions as the main means for allocating allowances, and the EU ETS has been adopting paid allocation through auctions since its third phase, a practice that promotes fairness. Prior to this, from 2009 to 2013, the EU ETS granted allowances freely, a practice that often lacked robust price signals, contributing to an overabundance of free allowances. This, in turn, triggered a steep decline in carbon prices and hindered market vitality. A comparable scenario has emerged in China's carbon market over the past few years.

The current object of trading in the carbon market revolves around "carbon emission rights", with their allocation posing a significant challenge, one that may not yield a universally perfect solution. The Coase Theorem underscores that within a market mechanism where transaction costs exist, the initial allocation of property rights is directly related to the trading efficiency of the final market. Consequently, the rational allocation of emission allowances forms the cornerstone for the effective operation of the entire carbon market.

However, a pivotal issue arises from the inherent disparity of government power, as national and regional governments vary significantly from one another. This disparity complicates the harmonization of carbon emission rights within and across countries, leading to high operational complexity and hindering the formation of a globally unified market. The inability to achieve domestic unity renders carbon emission rights unsuitable as a commodity for market trading, further impeding their potential to drive meaningful carbon reduction efforts. Given these challenges, it is foreseeable that the development of the carbon market based solely on carbon emission rights has likely completed its intended mission, necessitating the exploration of alternative approaches to advance the cause of carbon reduction.

3.6.3.3 Influence of the Coverage of Allowances

Research shows that the nature and role of the trading market for carbon emissions are also quite relevant to its coverage of industries. Currently, both domestic and international carbon markets are constrained in their ability to cover a wide range of industries, with the domestic market facing particular challenges. Specifically, due to limitations in acquiring accurate carbon data, the domestic market is restricted to covering solely the coal-fired power sector, a situation that poses significant problems. Both theoretical arguments and practical observations suggest that the positive impact of the trading market remains modest, while its negative consequences may outweigh the benefits.

The influence of carbon emissions trading, when confined to a single or a select few industries, on the overall efficiency of resource allocation within society is notably constrained or may even exhibit negative effects. A tangible example illustrating this phenomenon is the case of China's carbon emissions trading market.

China's trading market is currently confined to the coal-fired power industry, a total of more than 2,000 enterprises. As a result of carbon emission controls, coal-fired power enterprises are facing an escalation in the cost per kWh of electricity generated, leading to heightened losses. The burden of these carbon-related costs fails to be effectively passed down through market mechanisms, thereby dampening the incentive for these enterprises to generate power. Consequently, numerous regions in the country have resorted to pulling the plug to limit the use of electricity, which profoundly restricts the development of macroeconomy.

This case shows that the carbon emission trading restricted solely to coal-fired power enterprises is a costly resource allocation mechanism. Its optimality hinges on the ability of the carbon market to facilitate resource allocation across the entire society, enabling the organizational unit with the lowest marginal cost of carbon reduction to shoulder the burden of emissions. However, the current carbon emission market operates in a manner that reduces carbon emissions at the societal node with the highest marginal cost, yielding an outcome completely opposed to the government's aspirations.

3.6.3.4 Problems with the Current Carbon Market for Emission Rights

In Sect. 3.4.4, an in-depth analysis of the academic problems pertaining to the carbon emission rights has been conducted. Upon integrating the insights gained from this section with those presented in Sect. 3.4.4, it becomes evident that China's carbon market for emission rights continues to confront a myriad of challenges and issues.

1. The determination and allocation of allowances entail substantial policy-related expenses, impeding the pace of advancement in both the expanse and intensity of decarbonation due to the substantial capacity and investment prerequisites demanded of governments.
2. Marked by substantial MRV costs, the process is further hindered by inadequate data accuracy, steep regulatory expenses associated with MRV, and recurrent instances of data manipulation. The absence of an effective self-monitoring mechanism akin to that employed for Value-Added Tax (VAT) exacerbates the issue.
3. The control and trading system encompasses a notably limited number of enterprises, resulting in a sluggish pace of carbon reduction. Firms within regulated sectors face minimal scope for emission cuts, whereas an overwhelming majority of societal organizations, exceeding 99%, remain oblivious to the urgency of carbon reduction efforts.
4. The scope of industries and enterprises subject to control remains inadequately narrow, hindering the optimization of resource allocation. Should the carbon market remain exclusive to a select few industries and merely thousands of enterprises, the macroeconomic cost of carbon reduction would be disproportionately high, while the benefits derived from optimized resource distribution would be significantly limited.
5. The level of marketization within the regulatory policy framework is insufficient, and the effect of good money driving out bad money is not obvious. Consequently, carbon emission allowances risk stifling the growth of high-quality enterprises, and it remains uncertain whether any allocation method will be favorable to high-quality production capacity.

6. The absence of a sizable carbon finance market poses a significant challenge. Amidst a pressing global shortfall of funds for the transition to a green economy, the international community eagerly anticipates the carbon finance market to serve as a pillar of support. However, the current market's daily trading volume, which hovers around a mere few thousand dollars, falls far short of the scale required to effectively address this crucial task.
7. The lack of a comprehensive system encompassing both positive and negative incentives for decarbonation and sequestration undermines efforts to curb emissions. The carbon pricing mechanism, anchored in carbon emission rights, suffers from ambiguity, with unclear directions for price fluctuations and a persistent low carbon price level. This has resulted in inadequate motivations for carbon reduction and innovation initiatives. While the government endeavors to adjust prices through complementary measures, achieving scientific and reasonable pricing remains a formidable challenge. A carbon trading market centered on "negative carbon" targets holds significant promise in mitigating these issues, as it directly targets carbon neutrality.
8. The equity of inter-provincial allowances remains unresolved. The current allowance-based carbon market risks exacerbating spatial disparities in emissions, known as the inter-provincial carbon equity problem. Notably, under the producer liability mechanism, these disparities are more pronounced than those under the consumer liability approach. Variations in economic development, industrial and energy structures across provinces, coupled with the national carbon market's impact on inter-provincial mobility of factors like capital and labor, lead to significant differences in allowance trading volumes, trading positions (sellers or buyers), and economic consequences among provinces. This phenomenon, known as the inter-provincial allocation effect, underscores the complexity of achieving equity.

Beyond the aforementioned challenges, China's carbon market for emission rights confronts numerous other issues, many of which have persisted for an extended period, suggesting the need for a fundamental transformation.

The concepts of "carbon emission rights" and "carbon neutral liability" (negative carbon, carbon sequestration, and carbon capture) are two distinct concepts. The current carbon market operates as a trading platform for carbon emission rights, not for carbon neutral liability (negative carbon), thereby failing to directly align with the ultimate goal of carbon neutrality. Therefore, there is an urgent need to change the top-level design of the carbon market, transitioning from a system centered on trading emission rights to one that focuses on trading carbon neutral liability, specifically targeting "negative carbon" achievements.

This transformation will have profound implications on the global march towards carbon neutrality. Adhering to the "3060" dual carbon target, the balance between carbon emissions and sequestration must be fully reciprocal, from start to finish. Consequently, the trading target of the carbon market, grounded in the pursuit of carbon neutrality, ought to center on the "negative carbon" products.

Currently, the carbon emissions trading system serves as an initial policy instrument. Aligned with the aspiration of achieving carbon neutrality, it is imperative for every enterprise to embrace the accountability of maintaining carbon balance. This necessitates a gradual shift from the notion of "carbon emission rights" towards the liability of fostering "carbon neutrality". In instances where enterprises possess "carbon emission liability stock (CEL stock)", they ought to purchase "negative carbon" as a means to neutralize and offset, thereby fostering a comprehensive, global closed-loop system.

In the future, the carbon exchange should be a trading place for negative carbon transactions, where enterprises that generate carbon emissions trade with those that mitigate and reduce carbon, with the focus shifting from carbon emission rights to negative carbon products. Enterprises with carbon emission liability (CEL) purchase "negative carbon" credits within the exchange, while enterprises with reduced CEL will offer them for sale, ensuring a balanced market where supply and demand converge at equilibrium.

In conclusion, to overcome existing constraints and foster innovation, embracing a negative carbon market grounded in the CELM theory presents a promising solution to the aforementioned challenges.

3.7 The Road to Carbon Neutrality: Carbon Taxes or Carbon Market

To foster decarbonation, there's a universal agreement on the necessity to internalize the external costs associated with carbon emissions. However, the approach to tackle this issue remains a matter of contention. Among the prevalent international carbon policy instruments, carbon taxes and carbon markets stand out. The question lingers: which is superior, or should they be combined? This debate has persisted for over three decades. Advocates within the monetary sector favor carbon taxes as they expand the tax base and augment revenue streams. Conversely, those in the financial sector prefer the carbon market because it creates a huge green financial carbon market, a new area where financial markets can make a big difference. The Chinese Government embarked on piloting a carbon market in 2011, yet refrained from implementing a carbon tax instrument, primarily due to concerns over its potential impact on the macroeconomy, which might have been overly exaggerated.

Irrespective of the policy instrument selected, the meticulous design of the specific policy program holds immense sway over its eventual outcome. Illustratively, the decision pertaining to the carbon tax rate—whether to incrementally intensify it prior to easing or vice versa, and its application on the production or consumption end—is fraught with nuance and can elicit vastly disparate effects. The existing carbon market, rooted in carbon emission allowances, remains significantly constrained in scope.

The carbon market does not exclusively encompass the present framework centered on carbon emission rights; rather, it can be tailored to encompass diverse trading subjects beyond these allowances. Furthermore, the allocation of carbon emission rights within the current carbon market framework poses intricate questions: What is the distribution mechanism? How abundant are the free allowances? Are they dispensed to the production or consumption sectors? These aspects are all delicately nuanced.

Thus, the selection of a policy instrument by a nation's government is intricately intertwined not only with its macroeconomic implications but also significantly influenced by the interplay and outcomes of academic debates.

Carbon tax operates as a price coordination mechanism, where the government sets the price of carbon, whereas the market determines the amount of emission reduction. Conversely, the carbon market functions as a quantitative mechanism, where the government prescribes the emission reduction targets, and the market subsequently determines the carbon price. The specific policy design underpinning these two mechanisms profoundly influences their respective impacts on the carbon neutrality journey and economic growth, yielding distinctively different outcomes.

Zhang Xiliang, head of the Technical Expert Group on the Overall Design of China's Carbon Emission Trading System and director of the Institute of Energy, Environment and Economics at Tsinghua University, advocates that the carbon market aligns more seamlessly with market-oriented principles. He argues that the uncertainty surrounding carbon taxes primarily stems from the unpredictability of emission reduction volumes, whereas the carbon market's uncertainty revolves around price fluctuations. When evaluating from the vantage point of comprehensive carbon emission management, Zhang contends that the carbon trading market emerges as a more reliable instrument.

Nobel laureate William Nordhaus, through comparative analysis, argues that a price coordination mechanism for a carbon tax would be more effective than the mechanism for quantifying carbon emission rights in *The Kyoto Protocol*. First, a price coordination mechanism allows for easier and more flexible integration of the economic costs and benefits associated with emission reduction, whereas the methodology in *The Kyoto Protocol* lacks a clear correlation to the ultimate environmental or economic goals. Second, carbon taxes are more effective in the face of large uncertainties, as their benefits manifest in a relatively linear fashion compared to the costs incurred. Moreover, quantitative controls, as employed under the emissions target approach, tend to induce high volatility in carbon market prices. In contrast, a carbon tax not only has a higher potential to generate revenue but also mitigates distortions caused by existing tax systems. Lastly, by refraining from fostering rent-seeking behaviors through artificially induced scarcity, a carbon tax minimizes the risks of corruption and financial fraud.

The intricate mechanisms of price coordination (carbon taxes) and quantitative regulation (carbon emission rights), which are currently in practice, have undergone meticulous scrutiny in Sects. 3.4, 3.5, and 3.6 of this book. Both systems, however, manifest significant drawbacks and encounter insurmountable challenges when confronted with the multifaceted nature of decarbonation. Despite any attempts at refinement, they fall short of comprehensively addressing the pressing climate crisis we confront. Indeed, the prevailing carbon tax program and carbon market initiatives across various nations, whether focusing on the pricing strategy of carbon taxes or regulating emissions volumes, confront a common obstacle: the government's inability to exert full control over these mechanisms. This limitation stems from the inherent complexity of managing decarbonation efforts. When one crucial aspect remains unmanageable, the overall effectiveness of these measures becomes predictably constrained.

Nordhaus' analysis of the carbon tax policy instrument primarily centers around international harmonization, overlooking the myriad challenges confronted by carbon pricing mechanism at both the international and domestic levels. Within individual countries and regions, the design of policy instrument, particularly the prevalent carbon tax strategies, faces significant hurdles. Moreover, the complexities at the international level are exacerbated, as demonstrated by the challenging journey of global tariff harmonization over the past three decades. Similarly, the progress of carbon market based on carbon emission rights has been very unsatisfactory, and the professionals do not recognize that the current carbon market plays a key role in the overall carbon neutrality process.

As a result, the current policy instruments, whether the quantitative control mechanism or the price coordination mechanism, exhibit substantial limitations. It is imperative that we should seek a more effective third alternative, transcending the confines of existing ideologies. This necessitates embracing more robust technological advancements, fostering groundbreaking innovations within the program framework, and devising strategies to bypass prevailing challenges. Our aim should be to create a system that is more powerful than the traditional mechanisms of carbon taxes and carbon markets. Additionally, this program must embody simplicity in execution, fairness, and efficiency, while ensuring the feasibility of international coordination.

I am convinced that the path we embark upon holds immense promise.

3.8 True Propositions of Global Climate Change

In essence, due to the complexity and specificity of global climate change, it is very challenging to unify the diverse viewpoints and perspectives of governments, professional bodies, and experts across various disciplines. Achieving consensus on pertinent issues and viable solutions is hindered by disparate stances and outlooks, leading to a situation where the goal is overshadowed by disputes over localized interests. Regrettably, few individuals strive to address the root causes, with many remaining entrenched in debates. As UN Secretary General Guterres remarked at the opening of COP27, "We are on a highway to climate hell with our foot still on the accelerator". This is a true reflection of the evolution of global climate change over the past three decades, particularly the outcomes of annual climate conferences.

After three decades of extensive human research on climate, it is imperative that we converge on the pivotal issues at hand. Through the lens of economic analysis of climate change and with a profound understanding of our shared human destiny, it is high time to crystallize the essence of the climate challenge and strive for a comprehensive consensus among all stakeholders.

In this book, it is proposed that the real economic proposition of the current global climate change is to seek for a fair and efficient pathway for decarbonation, given the explicit target of mitigating carbon emissions set forth by the IPCC: to cap total global carbon emissions to 500 Gt after 2020 and achieve net-zero emissions by 2050. With the collective commitment of nations to these dual-carbon objectives, it advocates for a holistic yet localized approach to investing in carbon reduction measures, with the aim of minimizing the overall cost of this endeavor.

Such a proposition for the economics of climate change would help us to get out of the research dilemma and focus on solving the real problems, achieving more consensus and realizing the goals to which the big governments have committed themselves. With the right proposition, the academic search for solutions and solutions will be relatively easy.

With this proposition in mind, let us look back at the applicability of these mainstream policy instruments. The first approach, rooted in the principle of Pigouvian Tax, employs a carbon tax. For a considerable period, the international community has emphasized its significance in addressing externalities by internalizing social costs into the pricing of goods. However, it is evident that the method of calculating the carbon price (carbon tax) through forward social costs is no longer applicable. This is primarily due to the subjective nature of selecting a social discount rate, leading to a huge difference in the results. Moreover, the calculation of forward costs is not very relevant to the goal of carbon neutrality. Hence, a transition is imperative, from a carbon pricing framework based on forward social costs to one centered on carbon reduction or neutrality targets. The second approach is based on the Coase Theorem, which tackles externalities by establishing carbon emission rights. Nevertheless, effectively allocating national sovereign carbon emission rights, implementing carbon tariffs, and mitigating their macroeconomic impacts pose significant challenges, thereby hindering optimal efficiency.

In addressing the pressing global climate issue, policy instruments heavily enmeshed in national sovereignty face significant constraints, including the carbon tax tool, rooted in price regulation, and the carbon market for carbon emission rights, grounded in quantity regulation. The crux of the matter lies in the necessity to transcend the intractable trilemma of "global collaboration, equity and efficiency, and national sovereignty". To navigate this complex landscape, we must relinquish reliance on policy instruments heavily weighted with national sovereignty connotations, such as carbon taxes and emission allowances. Instead, the optimal global carbon–neutral pathway can escape this impossible triangle.

So far, the international community has been dissatisfied with the economic framework addressing climate change. Both practical outcomes and theoretical research have met with skepticism, as economists are often perceived as overly idealistic and theoretical in their approach, failing to adequately grapple with the intricacies of the climate crisis. Are climate change economists doing a "nursery test" by placing great emphasis on carbon pricing? The theory is correct, but it does not work. What's more, the costs of the policy far outweigh the benefits.

3.9 The Third Pathway: Global Carbon Neutrality Solution from a Consumer Liability Perspective

In order to solve the true proposition of the climate problem, this book proposes to adopt a more market-driven policy instrument, that is, the third pathway for the global climate challenge: to establish a mechanism that empowers consumers to take liability. It uses digital and informational technologies to establish a complete carbon footprint big data, and establish a negative carbon trading market which supports social organizations to offset carbon emissions. Furthermore, it proposes to integrate pricing mechanisms and progressively internalizing the social costs of carbon emissions, thereby incentivizing green technological innovations and ultimately driving society towards global carbon neutrality. This represents the cornerstone of the mechanism outlined within this book.

Only with a more market-driven consumer liability mechanism, coupled with a negative carbon market system, bolstered by the transformative prowess of information technology and big data capabilities, as well as unparalleled clarity regarding global carbon footprints, can we coordinate international reduction efforts. The question of imposing carbon tariffs on international trade necessitates a negotiation process centered on establishing phased-in international negative carbon pricing, which, given the genuine commitment of relevant stakeholders to addressing the climate crisis, is destined for successful solution. The liability mechanism outlined in this book endeavors to streamline the complexity of the global climate challenge, identifying the broadest common ground, thereby facilitating efficient resolution of the intricacies surrounding international trade, domestic carbon reduction efforts, and the delicate balance of interests and responsibilities. Furthermore, it adeptly addresses the daunting challenge posed by the seemingly impossible triangle of climate action.

Under the third pathway, numerous intractable issues confronted by previous policy instruments can undergo significant improvement, if not outright resolution, both at the international and domestic levels.

1. The moral high ground. Large producers are subjected to carbon taxes and moral condemnation for their pollution practices, yet this approach fails to yield a viable solution to the pressing issue. The prevailing international discourse surrounding carbon emissions has proven ineffective in uniting key players like Europe, the United States, and China under a cohesive carbon reduction program.

   Regarding the externalities of carbon emissions, a fundamental question arises: Should the liability lie with producers, whose emissions ultimately impact consumer welfare, or with consumers, whose demand fuels production and subsequent emissions? Moral judgments, though seemingly straightforward, have historically been one-sided, prompting reflection on why this is the case. The substantial resources and time invested by the international community in establishing producer liability mechanisms finally made everyone realize the necessity to reassess this issue.

Consumer liability mechanism enhances the rationality of the overall accountability system by acknowledging that consumers, who ultimately contribute to carbon emissions through their consumption choices, should bear a share of the cost to offset these emissions. Both consumers and producers ought to be subjected to moral scrutiny.

2. Market failure I: carbon tariffs. Western developed countries, as tax collectors, do not have a clear explanation of the mechanisms of liability for carbon emissions, including power, pricing, ownership rights and usage patterns. This ambiguity constitutes an unjustifiable trade barrier and a violation of WTO regulations. When taxed parties, primarily developing countries, lack a clear comprehension of this liability mechanism, they are left uncertain on how to navigate the situation, inadvertently positioning themselves as the subject of criticism.
3. Market failure II: planned economy in energy market. In many countries, notably China, the energy market operates under a stringent planning regime, characterized by predetermined oil prices and standardized electricity prices. This structured approach poses significant challenges in effectively conveying price signals from upstream policy instruments, ultimately contributing to policy inefficiencies and failures. Historical endeavors to mitigate carbon emissions through policy instruments have often grappled with this entrenched issue. Instead, the consumer liability mechanism will arrange the liability sharing and emission reduction effect better through the market forces.
4. Government failure I: the allocation of carbon allowances. This is basically an unsolvable problem. The reality is that all social organizations are emitters, and with such a complex web of stakeholders, it is really difficult for the government to solve emission reduction through the allocation of carbon emission rights, which fails to achieve the optimal allocation of resources. Moreover, the government's capacity is inherently constrained, and the associated workload costs can be prohibitively high for society to bear. Furthermore, concerns over government integrity and transparency in the allocation process persist, exacerbating the challenges. Therefore, it is necessary to establish an effective market to realize the Pareto optimality in social resource allocation.
5. Government failure II: the measurement of the impact on macroeconomy. The inadequacies in liability mechanisms and the malfunctioning of price transmission systems pose significant threats to the validity of macro-market equilibrium calculations. These shortcomings render many calculations redundant, as they overlook crucial factors such as interest rate fluctuations, rapid technological advancements, and policy interventions. More critically, market failures in price signaling lead to inaccurate calculations, further complicating the picture. The

biggest problem faced by the government at present is that it is unable to understand the mechanism of the impact of decarbonation on the macro economy, and it is worried that the impact will be too great.

6. Social mobilization for carbon reduction. The current reliance on policy instruments such as carbon taxes and carbon markets based on emission rights has inherent limitations. These mechanisms primarily impact a limited scope of enterprises and organizations, falling short of the comprehensive engagement required to achieve the ambitious climate goals that necessitate the participation of all sectors of society, from individuals to corporations. Governments must recognize this shortcoming and seek innovative strategies that can effectively mobilize the entire societal fabric towards carbon reduction.

If the Government can only incentivize the 2000–3000 major carbon emitters, but cannot mobilize all organizations and members of society to participate in carbon reduction, the impact of decarbonation will be too small. An efficient and inclusive mechanism must be devised to fully mobilize the community to participate in carbon reduction, and publicity alone is far from enough.

Moreover, it impacts the speed of carbon reduction. Without the full mobilization of society, the current carbon market remains constrained in its ability to generate funds, leaving developing nations burdened with carbon tariffs imposed by developed countries. Furthermore, the scarcity of funds hinders the creation of effective incentives for carbon reduction technologies, further stalling progress. To overcome these obstacles and accelerate the pace of carbon reduction, we must seek innovative solutions beyond the traditional frameworks of carbon taxes and emission rights-based market.

Chinese scholars in climate change economics ought to prioritize top-level ideological research, engaging more thoroughly with domestic and international theories within the lens of consumer liability. This book reveals that, when societal carbon footprint data is exhaustive and its value and potential are fully harnessed, an exceptionally effective policy instrument emerges, even amidst local market inefficiencies and national sovereignty-related policy hurdles. This instrument, essentially, revolves around "a mechanism whereby consumers shoulder the costs of carbon emissions, while the backend of the industrial chain takes accountability for the overall carbon footprint generated at the frontend." This innovative framework holds the key to addressing numerous challenges in the ongoing pursuit of carbon neutrality and accelerating the global transition towards this goal.

By leveraging the synergies between government intervention and market forces, the external social costs associated with global public goods can be seamlessly internalized into product pricing, fostering their circulation on a global scale and thereby resolving numerous issues along the way.

In the past, achieving global collaboration in climate governance has proven elusive, hindering the progression of carbon neutralization efforts across nations. This predicament resembles the tale of the emperor's new clothes, where no one dares to challenge the status quo due to the divergent interests of countries on the international stage. Countries have tended to approach climate change economics from their individual vantage points, with climate experts in developing nations often struggling to uncover the root causes of global climate issues, pinpoint their most pressing aspects, or get the global maximum common denominator. The political rivalries among nations have inadvertently spilled over into the realm of climate actions. However, with China having made significant strides in various key areas of the green energy transition, it now finds itself in a more influential position. If Chinese academics can assume a leadership role in advancing top-level theoretical frameworks, it stands to reason that China's solutions to climate challenges will be even more effective and impactful.

Under the premise of consumer liability, the liability system can be logically and comprehensively justified. The relationship between liability and rights, spanning international, regional, industrial chain, as well as carbon emission and absorption domains, becomes increasingly objective, facilitating the establishment of a market-driven processing mechanism. This robust theoretical foundation paves the way for the design of an integrated management system for decarbonation, ready for swift progression into practical implementation.

It is worth emphasizing that within the mechanism of final consumers paying the bill, in a relatively efficient market, the equitable distribution of liability across society remains unaffected. This approach fosters reasonable accountability among societal members, without imposing undue burden on consumers, thereby aligning with the principles of the Coase Theorem.

In an efficient market, producers assuming liability and consumers assuming liability yield similar outcomes, as costs are distributed between them, with the less elastic party—typically the consumer—bearing a greater share. Despite variations in the implementation of tax systems across nations, be it charged at the upstream end (production), at the downstream end (consumption), or segmented taxation, the overall outcomes remain largely consistent. In China, VAT is administered in a segmented manner, whereas in countries like the United States and Japan, taxation primarily targets consumers, bypassing producers.

The notion that consumers assume the total cost of a product's production processes poses no logical problems. In fact, a consumer liability mechanism offers a superior approach to addressing cross-border liability sharing (such as carbon tariffs), regional liability arrangements, and market failure in the upstream electricity market. Furthermore, it alleviates the complexities and expenses associated with government operations, presenting a more effective resolution to intricate relationships and challenges.

Chapter 4
The Origin of Global Climate Change

A comprehensive overview of global climate change, coupled with an assessment of previous generations' endeavors in the economics of climate change, will enable us to more accurately delineate humanity's most paramount challenge and establish a robust foundation to explore theories and devise solutions.

To genuinely tackle the global climate crisis, we must adopt the first principles thinking in our quest for solutions. That is, the prerequisite for finding the most equitable and efficient solution to global climate change is to first define the fundamental postulates and axioms underpinning it. Only by courageously confronting the essence of climate change, both the academia and the international community can achieve groundbreaking innovations through interdisciplinary collaboration, integrated research, and logical deduction, thereby substantially elevating the academic standards of climate economics. Such advancements will ensure that the formulation of policy instruments rests on a firm theoretical basis. Regrettably, over the past three decades of climate research within the international arena, there has been a notable scarcity of studies that deeply delve into the underlying logic of global climate change and analyze the essence of the problem at hand, let alone derive actionable solutions.

The academic journey of climate change over the past three decades has been fraught with setbacks, similar to a tragic narrative. For an extended period, national interest groups have instrumentalized the climate issue, interpreting it from disparate angles to steer humanity's course, rather than genuinely striving for solutions. Concurrently, a myriad of organizations and individuals within the climate research sphere have capitalized on academic, official, and market opportunities in the climate arena, prioritizing the creation of academic, political, commercial, and financial demands and supplies that are detrimental to addressing the climate challenge. These endeavors and resource inputs have failed to meaningfully mitigate climate change; instead, they have inadvertently contributed to heightened carbon emissions. The fear of disruptive innovations and the reluctance to relinquish established territories have hindered further progress. Therefore, the evolution of the climate issue shows

B. Yang, *The Carbon Emission Liability Mechanism*,
https://doi.org/10.1007/978-981-96-3612-9_4

not only the socio-economic tragedy of the commons, but also the profound human tragedy.

The window to take urgent climate action is closing rapidly, and it is time to get to the root of the problem and accelerate the search for an innovative pathway that genuinely tackles the root cause.

4.1 Two Postulates of Global Climate Change

To address the pressing global climate issue and attain the internationally aspired target of limiting global average temperature increase to 1.5 °C, as stipulated in the reports by the IPCC and the consensus forged at successive United Nations Climate Conferences, it is plausible to deduce that the international community has implicitly embraced two postulates regarding climate change, i.e., in order to solve the climate problem, the international community must attain these two goals. Hence, the attainment of these dual goals stands as a prerequisite for addressing the climate challenge.

Postulate 1 The total net increase in global carbon emissions from 2020 onwards is constrained to 500 Gt

The total net increase in global atmospheric carbon cannot exceed a certain amount.

The IPCC reports state that to limit global warming to 1.5 °C or less, the world can only afford a total net increase in emissions of mere 500 Gt of CO_2, measured from the beginning of 2020. However, currently, the global annual emissions hover around 36 Gt. If this rate persists, humanity risks depleting its entire allowable carbon budget within the next twelve years.

The net increase in carbon emissions is related to total carbon emissions as well as carbon absorption (CCUS-like and forestry carbon removals).

$$\begin{aligned}&\text{Net increase in carbon emissions}\\&\quad = \text{total carbon emissions} - \text{carbon absorption}\end{aligned}$$

Therefore, the governments must work on two aspects to realize the ambitious carbon control goal: firstly, to minimize carbon emissions and design a two-way incentive mechanism to accelerate the decarbonation process; secondly, to foster the expansion of carbon removals and incentivize the development of technologies and industries associated with carbon removals. As low-cost carbon capture technologies make breakthroughs and the high utilization value of CO_2 continues to evolve, the prospects for carbon removals industries look promising. This development has the potential to significantly alleviate the pressure on governments to curb emissions.

Postulate 2 It is expected to realize global net-zero emissions by 2050

After the total concentration of CO_2 in the atmosphere approaches a critical threshold, it becomes imperative for the world to attain net-zero or even negative carbon emissions by a specified deadline, and the IPCC has set the ambitious target of 2050 as the pivotal year for the international community to achieve global net-zero emissions.

This milestone's establishment rests upon a robust foundation of extensive research and analysis, fostering a consensus among nations worldwide.

Under the leadership of the United Nations, the international community has relentlessly pursued the attainment of these two goals. The annual United Nations Climate Change Conference, the flagship event galvanizing worldwide efforts to combat climate change, marked its 27th iteration by the conclusion of 2022 (COP 27). At each conference, approximately 40,000 national delegates and technical experts from nearly 200 nations worldwide engage in exhaustive deliberations and reach compromises on the allocation of liabilities and operational frameworks for achieving these goals. While notable agreements have emerged from these gatherings, a significant disparity persists between these accomplishments and the full realization of the two goals.

China's "3060" dual carbon targets stand as a vital component in the pursuit of global carbon neutrality. However, its path to achieving this ambitious target remains under active exploration, and the current mechanism is so inefficient and has such a disproportionate impact on the macroeconomy that we cannot yet be optimistic about achieving China's dual carbon targets and the global climate goals.

4.2 Seven Axioms of Global Climate Change

This book presents seven basic ideas on which the international community should reach consensus in order to solve the global climate problem. These seven ideas are self-evident and can be called "axioms". This is the starting point for solving the global climate problem and the basis for achieving global carbon neutrality. From a rational and scientific point of view, the international community should face no difficulty in reaching a consensus on these seven points. However, the reality is that despite their clarity, the past three decades have witnessed a persistent divide among nations, stemming from diverse interests and stances. Meanwhile, the history of the fight against carbon emissions over the past three decades shows that we still need to make continuous efforts to push the international community to reach a consensus on these seven pivotal axioms, otherwise it will significantly hinder humanity's capacity to meaningfully address the global climate issue.

Axiom 1 Mankind is a community with a shared future

Human beings live on the same planet, and combating climate change is a common challenge facing mankind. No one can survive the climate crisis alone, nor is it ethical to abandon anyone in this endeavor. Therefore, it is a prevailing trend to be united to tackle climate change, as the following consequences of this global issue transcend borders and affect us all alike.

1. If the Earth is no longer fit for human existence, the impact on human beings will be indistinguishable;
2. A fluctuation of one ton of CO_2, whether emitted or absorbed, in any corner of the world, contributes equally to altering the Earth's climate system.;
3. Every country, every organization, and every individual need to work together to address the world's pressing climate challenges.

Axiom 2 Everyone on Earth has equal rights to carbon emissions

Every country and every race have the same right to development. There should be no unfair rules that some individuals or groups are allowed to emit more while others are only allowed to emit less. When considering both historical cumulative emissions and current per capita emissions, it becomes evident that the impoverished in less developed nations emit significantly less than the rich in wealthier countries. In the prevailing international landscape, these unfair rules face significant challenges in achieving a consensus, making it even more difficult to propose and implement effective solutions to address the pressing issue.

Therefore, it is imperative to recognize that while the rich may have the capacity to emit more, they must also bear a heavier financial burden commensurate with their responsibility for environmental impacts.

Axiom 3 Consumers take liability

Consumers are primarily liable for carbon emissions generated from the production of goods and services, i.e. they bear the financial burden (cost) for the resulting carbon absorption. Production, not an end in itself, is inherently driven by consumer demand. Any costs, associated with material sourcing, energy consumption, manufacturing, transportation, and service delivery incurred during production, are integrated into product costs, which are subsequently passed on to consumers. Furthermore, the costs of mitigating environmental pollution, including air carbon pollution and carbon sequestration, will also be borne by consumers.

The fact that consumers are primarily liable does not exclude producer liability. Consumers' purchasing decisions can indeed influence producer behaviors, fostering a competitive environment where only the most sustainable and responsible producers thrive. Consequently, carbon emissions generated during the initial stages of the industrial chain will ultimately be addressed by those at the backend. By emphasizing consumer liability, we do not aim to absolve producers of their duties but rather leverage market mechanisms to distribute carbon emission liability across the entire industrial chain in a more equitable and efficient manner. After all, the more scientific and rational allocation of liability will ultimately strengthen society's overall capacity to address these challenges.

Axiom 4 Developed countries and rich individuals should bear greater liability

According to the statistics from the Global Carbon Project, the historical carbon emissions of G7 nations, up until 2020, account for 44% of the world's total carbon emissions. Furthermore, Chancel's research reveals that the world's richest, accounting for 1% of the population, produce 23% of the global carbon emissions from 1990–2019. Notably, in 2019, the richest, accounting for 1% of the world's population, emitted 101 tons of carbon per capita, 144 times more than those of the lowest income earners, accounting for 20% of the world's population.

Rich countries hold a disproportionately large share of total historical carbon emissions, and given their substantial annual per capita emissions, they ought to shoulder a significantly greater burden in the pursuit of carbon reduction.

Meanwhile, financing the green transition poses a major challenge, necessitating substantial investments to advance the global carbon neutrality agenda. Consequently, the rich in rich countries should invest a higher proportion of their income towards carbon reduction efforts compared to the poor.

Moreover, addressing the global climate crisis, safeguarding planetary security, and fostering a superior living environment for humanity stands to bring more substantial marginal benefits to rich nations and individuals alike.

In 1992, representatives of 154 countries signed the *United Nations Framework Convention on Climate Change* at United Nations Headquarters. The Convention stipulates that all countries should work together to combat climate change, but with "common but differentiated responsibilities". Specifically, developed nations are called upon to lead the way and assume greater responsibility.

Axiom 5 Consumers have the right to know and the right to choose

Consumers have the right to know the carbon emissions of products and the right to choose low-carbon products. It is evident that these rights hold immense potential in driving societal-level carbon reductions. In fact, mandatory carbon labeling systems in certain countries have demonstrated remarkable effectiveness in this regard.

However, these two rights are rendered worthless if consumers lack the means to access carbon emission information. A major hindrance to the establishment of a robust carbon responsibility mechanism lies precisely here, as a comprehensive and efficient carbon footprint tracking system remains elusive. If technological advancements could ensure seamless access to carbon footprint data across all products, empowering consumers with the knowledge they need, the mechanism would work effectively. Armed with the right to know and choose, consumers could, in turn, invert the carbon liability along the industrial chain, thereby addressing many of the prevailing challenges and fostering a more sustainable future.

Axiom 6 "Real Negative CO_2" is a global standard commodity that can be traded freely around the world

One ton of “Real Negative CO_2” signifies the removal of an equivalent amount of CO_2 from the Earth’s atmosphere, achieved either naturally through forests, wetland carbon sinks, etc., or technologically via CCUS technology.

The removal of a single ton of CO_2, regardless of its origin, contributes equally to mitigating the global climate impact. Consequently, “Real Negative CO_2” emerges as the cornerstone asset underpinning carbon reduction mechanism, evolving into a viable and resilient carbon asset. Organizations striving for carbon neutrality can purchase internationally certified “Real Negative CO_2” from diverse sources worldwide to offset their carbon footprint.

It is critical to find the underlying elements that drive both positive and negative incentives for decarbonation, which is the key to an efficient carbon reduction mechanism. Currently, CCERs and carbon emission rights are unable to support the global pursuit of carbon neutrality.

Axiom 7 Market forces should be fully leveraged

Precisely due to the vast scale and intricate nature of carbon emission reduction, which is a public good inherently characterized by temporal and spatial dimensions, the increased involvement of governments often complicates the search for the greatest common denominator, hindering the achievement of global synergy. Conversely, with minimal government intervention and a streamlined mechanism, we can more effectively pursue the greatest common denominator among the international community. In such a scenario, it becomes evident that market forces will assume a paramount role, guiding and facilitating carbon reduction efforts.

Accordingly, the government should devise a fair and efficient policy framework that fully harnesses market forces to achieve carbon neutrality. The current arrangement of carbon emission rights across nations and the allocation of such rights to domestic enterprises face challenges in standardization and market integration. Furthermore, carbon taxation, as a sovereign policy, encounters difficulties in unifying standards and integrating into global markets. To overcome these obstacles, we must explore more efficient market mechanism and optimal strategies that foster seamless synergy among global market mechanism, international multilateral policies, and governmental interventions.

The Two Postulates and Seven Axioms of global climate change (carbon neutrality) are the cornerstones that underpin the global carbon market and the Carbon Emissions Liability Mechanism (CELM) proposed in this book, serving as the basis for the derivation and design of our proposed solution system aimed at achieving global carbon neutrality.

Chapter 5
New Carbon Emission Liability Mechanism

Drawing upon the two Postulates and seven Axioms of global climate change outlined in Chap. 4, this book embraces global carbon neutrality as its paramount goal, with the vision of Building a Community with a Shared Future for Mankind. It endeavors to deduce and identify the most effective pathway towards this goal, amidst the prevailing international consensus, and subsequently introduces an innovative Carbon Emission Liability Mechanism (CELM). The CELM, rooted in a global perspective, establishes two fundamental assumptions and three basic principles, thereby paving the way for the establishment of a novel global carbon neutrality system and fostering a fresh international order centered on carbon emission reduction.

5.1 Two Assumptions

Assumption 1 Governments of all countries are obligated to achieve the carbon neutrality targets they have pledged to the international community

According to the IPCC report, there is a total global budget of 500 Gt of carbon emissions after 2020, and we must control the total amount of carbon emissions in order to limit global average temperature increase to the crucial 1.5 °C safety threshold.

As of May 31, 2023, data from Climate Watch reveal that 195 economies worldwide have signed the Paris Agreement and submitted their initial Nationally Determined Contributions (NDCs), covering 94.3% of global GHG emissions.

The UNFCCC report highlights a concerning reality: even if all countries fully fulfill their NDCs, the aim of holding the increase in the global average temperature

B. Yang, *The Carbon Emission Liability Mechanism*,
https://doi.org/10.1007/978-981-96-3612-9_5

to well below 2 °C above pre-industrial levels, and even more so, to 1.5 °C as unanimously agreed upon in the Paris Agreement, remains elusive. Conversely, the report projects that the current process towards global carbon neutrality could lead to a global average temperature increase of 2.4 to 2.6 °C by 2100. Furthermore, the UNFCCC estimates that developing nations will necessitate a cumulative investment ranging from US 5.8 trillion to US 5.9 trillion by 2030 to achieve the current NDCs targets.

According to the above reports, it will be a formidable challenge to achieve the ideal neutrality target. Nevertheless, it is reassuring to note that governments are committed to their NDCs and are earnest in honoring their pledges. The impediments posed by inadequate funding and technological limitations can potentially be addressed through the collaborative efforts of the international community.

China has committed to the "3060" dual carbon targets, aiming for net-zero carbon emissions by 2060. Given the current progress, this target presents a formidable challenge. Since China is the world's largest carbon emitter and the second-largest economy, its success in achieving carbon neutrality is decisive for the realization of the global target. The journey ahead is undoubtedly long and winding, yet the Chinese government is resolute in its commitment, recognizing that failure to do so could diminish China's international standing. To meet this ambitious goal, every organization and individual within Chinese society must embrace their liability, not just in mitigating emissions but striving towards carbon neutrality.

In fact, China possesses robust technical and industrial foundations that are well-suited for achieving this goal. Presently, the greatest hurdle lies in identifying the most efficacious route to carbon neutrality, i.e., a top-level design for decarbonation that is both fair and efficient, so that carbon neutrality can be achieved as early as possible without compromising economic growth. This is the challenge that this book endeavors to provide solutions.

Assumption 2 Governments of all countries are dedicated to establishing a fair and efficient decarbonation policy system

Over the span of three decades, the history of the climate issue underscores a distressing reality within the international arena: the climate discourse has been plagued by an imbalance, skewed more towards vested interests than shared liability, and fraught with conflicting positions rather than mutually beneficial cooperation. Within individual nations, the distribution of benefits among various interest groups in the emissions reduction endeavor surpasses the urgency of advancing the overall goals, while the pursuit of commercial gains often eclipses the imperative to tackle underlying problems. In the face of the life and death of human destiny, the elusive attainment of solidarity stands as a challenge, which is really a sorrowful tragedy for our humans.

To genuinely tackle the pressing global climate challenge, the international community necessitates a collective of global organizations that are sincerely motivated by a sense of equity to shoulder the liability for the well-being of all inhabitants on this planet. It is yet uncertain whether China's vision of "building a community with a shared future for mankind" will emerge as a pioneering force in leading the world towards carbon neutrality. Conversely, if the European Union's CBAM strays from the path of international trade cooperation and the multilateral framework designed for global carbon neutrality, it is doomed to foster an environment of increased confrontation and strategic maneuvering within the international community.

The realization of a country's NDCs goals requires a governing group that is liable for the international community and loyal to the country and willing to be impartial in the face of huge distribution of benefits. This group must enact legislation fairly, and possess the capability to harness the most advanced governance concepts and adopt the most progressive policy alternatives. Yet this poses a formidable challenge for every nation, as both economic and academic interests can often hinder the pursuit of carbon neutrality, necessitating the vigilant attention of all societal sectors. The fluctuating positions and carbon pricing strategies of successive U.S. administrations, each influenced by the sway of interest groups, serve as a testament to this complex interplay of factors.

An effective carbon reduction policy requires some entities to bear the financial burden, some entities to collect data on production and carbon emissions from each organization, so as to ensure the equitable distribution of liability among social organizations and households. All of these initiatives require robust legal backing and a delicate balancing of interests among various stakeholders, posing a formidable test for every government.

Under the leadership of the United Nations and with the influence of the international community, it is assumed that governments will rise to these challenges, reach compromises, and create international synergies based on equitable principles within the international community.

During the United Nations General Assembly in September 2020, the Chinese government pledged a resolute commitment to the ambitious "3060" dual carbon targets, and we hold steadfast faith in its timely, if not accelerated, attainment. The Chinese government boasts a formidable advantage in decision-making efficiency, coupled with a vast reservoir of experience in centralizing efforts, ensuring that the journey towards carbon neutrality will be no exception to this proven track record.

5.2 Three Basic Principles

Based on the conclusions in Chaps. 3 and 4, the book proposes three basic principles that underpin the new CELM, aimed at charting the optimal course towards global carbon neutrality. These principles are rooted in a profound knowledge of the nature of climate change, the axioms and the assumptions for the success of achieving global carbon neutrality.

Principle 1 Consumers bear the economic burden of carbon emissions, and the back-end of the industrial chain takes liability for the total amount of carbon emissions of the front-end

The establishment of this principle serves as the cornerstone for constructing an efficient decarbonation system for the whole society.

Who should be liable for carbon emissions and pay the bills economically is the primary issue in the design of decarbonation mechanism, which will determine the efficiency and value of emission-cutting mechanism.

After clarifying the main body liable for carbon emissions and the principle of liability allocation, it will become much easier to design the subsequent solution.

The production of a product passes through many links in the industrial chain, involving the cooperation of several, or even dozens or hundreds of enterprises, before it finally reaches the hands of consumers. Theoretically, the carbon emissions of each product can be calculated precisely, but its production process may involve up to thousands of participants, rendering the definition of carbon emission liability, which affects all stakeholders, a pivotal challenge in emission reduction system.

Should it be whoever emits is liable for carbon emissions (producer liability) or whoever consumes pays (consumer liability)? Should the downstream of the industrial chain be liable for the emissions generated by their upstream partners?

What comes to mind most readily is whoever emits is liable, and the current carbon reduction mechanism is indeed based on this principle, but its outcomes have been underwhelming. In an ideal, efficient market, such a program is feasible. But the problem is that the global production and trade ecosystem is not an efficient market. There are major tariff barriers in international trade, and the domestic market is not a unified market, besides, government intervention, through planning and control, heavily influences the industrial chain. Consequently, the mechanism of producer liability grapple with market failure.

This book contends that the market principle of assigning liability to those who benefit or consume represents a more efficient approach, poised to play a pivotal role within the carbon reduction framework. Ultimately, the concept of consumer liability enjoys the strongest legal and economic backing, and when complemented by an effective solution to capturing carbon footprint data, it emerges as the most efficient mechanism for tackling the overall issue.

It is paramount that producers are held accountable, but grounded in the fundamental principle where consumers bear primary liability, with back-end producers effectively serving as consumers to the front-end ones. Any organization in the industrial chain whose carbon emission intensity exceeds the average level of society will be directly liable. As long as we can establish a set of effective system to acquire carbon footprint data, it is easy to realize effective control and efficient carbon reduction, and ensure equitable distribution of liability across society.

Under the principle of consumer liability, consumers have the right to know and the right to choose (Axiom 5 of Chap. 4). The ability to know inherently compels consumers to consider two pivotal aspects: the cost implications and the moral obligation towards environmental protection. Consequently, they are inclined to select products that align with their personal interests while also benefiting the community, thereby establishing an orderly system of liability that extends from the back end of the industrial chain to the front end.

Upon the establishment of a robust consumer liability mechanism, the decarbonation liability system can be meticulously reconstructed, ultimately yielding a self-driven and self-regulating carbon reduction framework. By harnessing an efficient system to allocate and transfer liability, clarity, fairness, and rationality in accountability can be attained within the whole society, fostering both system-driven and voluntary initiatives towards carbon reduction.

Under the consumer liability mechanism, a carbon fee is incorporated into the pricing of goods.

i.e.:

$$\begin{aligned}\text{final selling price of goods} &= \text{product price} + \text{tax} \\ &+ \text{carbon fee (the amount of carbon liability in the product} \\ &\times \text{bon price)}\end{aligned}$$

Terminal retailers will be liable for collecting the carbon fee from consumers, and will also be liable for the final CEL carbon ticket offsetting, thus closing the loop of carbon liability in the whole industrial chain. In the future, a carbon fee will be included to the receipts, clearly indicating both carbon footprint in the product and the corresponding fee to be collected. Additionally, a growing number of countries will adopt regulations on carbon labeling, mandating that each commodity package display its embodied carbon, safeguarding consumers' right to know and right to choose.

Principle 2 Organizations whose carbon intensity exceeds the average level of industry should be immediately liable, that is, all organizations should balance the input and output of carbon tickets, and be liable for offsetting any CEL stock

The production and sales process within each organization is, through the purchase of diverse production materials, equipment and services from upstream providers as well as the employment of labor forces, to complete the production of a product, and to sell the product subsequently. Integral to these activities is the inevitable process of carbon emissions. Upstream suppliers provide it with production materials, equipment or services, all of which consume energy and generate carbon emissions in the process of their production, transportation and service delivery. Therefore, the CELM theory holds that when an organization purchases production materials, equipment and services from upstream suppliers, it is not merely purchasing the resources themselves but also inheriting the embedded costs and carbon emission liability associated with these resources. Similarly, upon selling the product, it transfers a portion of this carbon liability along with the product. This constitutes a comprehensive societal carbon footprint journey, wherein carbon footprint data permeates every stage of production and trade. If we have a robust, universally accessible system that records carbon footprint data, we could figure out the carbon liability of each final product, as well as decompose the carbon liability among individual organizations.

To streamline the tracking and allocation of emission liability among all organizations and consumers in the whole society, according to the CELM theory, a certificate to document the amount of carbon emission liability associated with each product and service is developed, known as "carbon emission liability (CEL) ticket", or simply "carbon ticket" or "red ticket". This certificate meticulously records the amount of CEL (carbon footprints) for each market transaction. Concurrently, a national management system for carbon ticket data is designed to record the carbon ticket data from each transaction, creating a complete carbon footprint big data of the whole society.

The "carbon ticket" contains the names and codes of both transaction parities, the product's name and code, trading volume, CEL amount per unit, and the total CEL amount. It is similar to the VAT invoice issued by national tax authorities in China, but it is a separate note that only records and confirms the amount of CEL associated with a transaction. Notably, this ticket does not record the total amount of carbon emission charges, but rather concentrates exclusively on the amount of carbon liability within the product.

The carbon ticket issued by the supplier is called an output ticket, whereas the carbon ticket received by the purchaser is called an input ticket, both sharing an identical format. For an organization, the output ticket issued by a supplier functions as an input ticket for a purchaser. Over a given period, the organization accumulates numerous input tickets, collectively representing its total CEL-Input, and issues a corresponding number of output tickets, forming its total CEL-Output. The amount of CEL of any organization is determined by calculating both its CEL-Input and CEL-Output. Naturally, due to the dynamics of upstream and downstream transaction negotiations, the total values of these inputs and outputs will not be exactly equal, resulting in a difference. This difference serves as an indicator of the extent to which an organization is liable for the cost associated with its carbon emissions.

The national CEL Carbon Ticket Management System (CTMS) records the transfer of CEL, or carbon footprint, among all parties involved in each transaction in the whole society. Through legislative measures, the government will mandate that all transactions involving the transfer of carbon tickets must be registered within the national unified CTMS. Consequently, each organization's production and business activities generate comprehensive CEL-Input and CEL-Output data, ensuring a comprehensive and accurate record of their carbon footprint.

The country will enact legislation to define a clear equation:

Carbon emissions for which the organization is liable = Total amount of CEL received from upstream (CEL-Input) − Total amount of CEL transferred downstream (CEL-Output) A negative value represents the "negative carbon" asset of the organization, which is viewed as a positive asset. The organization can sell its "negative carbon" asset in the trading market, thereby gaining economic benefits. This serves as a positive incentive from the government, encouraging the production of low-carbon products.

Conversely, a positive value indicates the amount of CEL of the organization, which is considered as a negative asset or liability. In such cases, the organization must assume the liability for achieving carbon balance and purchase "negative carbon" from the trading market to neutralize and offset its emissions.

Principle 2, based on Principle 1 (consumers take the primary liability for carbon emissions), clarifies the amount of carbon emission liability and the mechanism to assume liability across each node of the entire industrial chain. It also ensures the implementation of Principle 1. Producers within the industry chain should strive to reduce their carbon emission intensity (carbon emissions per unit of output). When this intensity falls below the industrial average, producers are exempt from bearing the additional cost associated with carbon liability. Furthermore, if their emissions are markedly lower than the industrial average, they can sell negative carbon and get double rewards from the market: cash reward and an increased brand premium, reflecting their commitment to social liability.

Generally, the carbon emission intensity among producers of the same type of product in each industry will be normally distributed, with an identifiable industry-wide average (or median) emission intensity. Producers whose carbon emission intensity exceeds the average will issue carbon output tickets to their downstream customers, and the amount of CEL accepted by these downstream customers will generally not exceed the industrial average, unless the producers reduce their original price, thereby maintaining the overall price competitiveness. Therefore, as long as an effective carbon pricing mechanism is established, the carbon emissions associated with a product can be effectively monetized and effectively integrated into the total cost of the product, thereby internalizing the carbon emission costs.

For downstream customers, the total price they pay for a product comprises the original product price plus a carbon fee.

For producers, the total cost of the product encompasses the original product cost plus a carbon fee. By striving to refine their production technology in order to mitigate carbon emissions, producers reap two significant benefits: firstly, a reduction in the cost associated with carbon emissions, and secondly, an enhancement of their brand value through demonstrating social liability.

Such a mechanism would enable all organizations (enterprises) to strive to reduce carbon emissions, mitigate the total cost increase caused by carbon fees, and enhance their price competitiveness. This, in turn, fosters a dynamic within the industry chain where each organization exerts pressure on its upstream organizations (supply side) to cut emissions, in response to the pressure exerted by downstream organizations (demand side). This concerted effort shapes a virtuous cycle for carbon emission reduction which is interconnected and mutually restrained across the entire industry chain, ultimately completing a closed loop driven towards emission reduction within the entire industrial chain.

What is a carbon neutral organization? It is one that achieves a delicate balance between CEL-Input and CEL-Output. This initial step involves ensuring that the emission intensity remains at or below the industrial average, promptly addressing any imbalances that arise. The subsequent step entails transitioning to a state of non-emission, self-neutralization, and offering "zero-carbon" products and services to society. The carbon ticket system serves as a straightforward management tool, empowering relevant government departments, organizations, and individuals alike to quantify their carbon footprints. This system ensures that the carbon footprint record within the entire society is transparent, precise, real-time, and comprehensive, thereby quantifying the carbon emission liability of each organization and individual. With this clarity, the carbon reduction targets for all parties become unmistakably clear.

The operation of CTMS system will greatly promote the carbon reduction efforts of the whole society, while minimizing the cost of national investment. Notably, it will significantly alleviate the challenge of ensuring integrity in the management of carbon emissions across the entire society.

This principle effectively internalizes the external costs of carbon emissions into product pricing, thereby fostering a competitive landscape where energy-efficient and low-carbon economic entities thrive, adhering to the principle of "survival of the fittest". In this environment, organizations with inferior technology, high energy consumption, and significant carbon emissions incur steeper carbon costs. Meanwhile, the quantification of the carbon footprint across all products establishes a benchmark for evaluating corporate social liability and business ethics, creating both economic and ethical pressure for companies to strive for carbon neutrality. Consequently, enterprises are compelled to speed up their carbon reduction efforts, ultimately accelerating the pace of societal decarbonization.

Our research reveals that the methodology employed by the CELM addresses the intricate challenge of calculating carbon emissions across diverse industries. At present, the calculation of carbon emissions needs to design a set of very complex algorithms and indicators, which needs to be completed by numerous professional consulting institutions, resulting in a time-consuming and energy-consuming endeavor that may not always guarantee scientific rigor and precision. However, with the introduction of CELM approach, we envision a future where financial professionals or cashiers will be empowered to autonomously calculate CEL within their organizations, that is, the addition and subtraction of CEL-Input and CEL-Output, which is very easy and convenient.

Principle 3 The carbon trading market facilitates the engagement of organizations in "negative carbon" transactions, enabling them to offset their CEL. The pricing of this "negative carbon" is dynamically set by the market mechanism

Organizations which exceed the industrial average carbon emission intensity, need to periodically (on a quarterly basis) purchase negative carbon from the carbon market to offset their CEL, therefore, the carbon trading market plays an important role in the overall social decarbonation system. The CTMS aims to provide carbon footprint data and determine the amount of CEL for which an organization should be held accountable. At its core, the carbon trading market serves a dual purpose: to provide the organizations with the source (i.e., negative carbon) to offset their CEL and the cost to bear the liability (i.e., carbon pricing). Carbon trading market is the most important carrier of carbon pricing. In this way, the core of carbon reduction system for the whole society revolves around a complementary 1 + 1 framework: "CEL Carbon Ticket Management System + Negative Carbon Trading Market", both rooted in the principles of CELM. Notably, the core object of trading within the CELM-based NCTM is exclusively on "negative carbon", distinguishing it from traditional carbon emission allowances (CEA) in ETS or voluntary certified emission reduction products like CCERs.

It is appropriate for all organizations to engage in offsetting settlements on a quarterly basis, taking into account both the workload and convenience of managing carbon assets for enterprises and the transactional settlement cycle within the industrial chain.

It is very reasonable to determine the carbon emission price through the carbon trading market. This approach not only facilitates the effective mitigation of carbon emissions but also incentivizes investments in carbon removal activities, such as forestry initiatives, as well as the research, development, and deployment of carbon capture, utilization, and storage (CCUS) technologies.

The prevailing carbon trading market, which revolves around the trading of carbon emission allowance, should shifted to the trading of "negative carbon" as soon as possible. This shift would seamlessly bridge the gap between the bilateral carbon emissions (carbon source) and carbon removal markets (see Fig. 5.1).

The trading of "negative carbon" products in carbon market offers several advantages as following:

1. Standardization. Standard products facilitate the establishment of both unified domestic and international market. Furthermore, they pave the way for the development of a certification system recognized by the international community, ensuring seamless adoption and dissemination of standards across the global community. The standardization of carbon products is a decisive factor in establishing a robust international carbon market.
2 Timeliness. Price tends to be timely and dynamic. And the costs of negative carbon (carbon neutrality) are dynamic, quickly responsive to market supply and demand, leading to an efficient price discovery mechanism.
3. Fairness. The market-driven approach outperforms the administrative mechanism. Carbon taxes and ETS often give rise to technical complexities, unintended

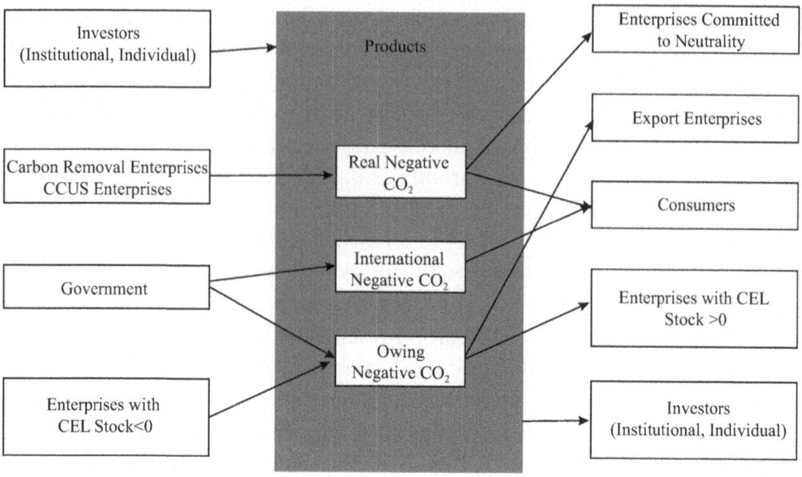

Fig. 5.1 Negative Carbon Trading Market (NCTM) based on the CELM

inequities and corruption problems. Furthermore, their implementation imposes demanding requirement on government capacity and resource investment.

4. Accurate price signals. The trading market for carbon emission allowances in China, which has been in trial operation for seven or eight years, recorded an average carbon price of 56 yuan/ton in 2022. This price disparity, approximately tenfold lower than that of the EU, stems from the non-market-oriented nature of carbon emission rights. The amount of free allowances issued significantly influences the carbon price, rendering it an imperfect reflection of the true cost per ton of carbon emissions. In contrast, the trading price within a negative carbon market directly reflects the actual cost per ton of carbon emissions, providing a stable and unambiguous price signal.
5. Low pricing cost. The cost of the government to devise and administer carbon taxes and carbon allowances is substantial, with collection cost and MRV cost adding to the burden. Furthermore, the market fails to effectively convey price signals, hindering its efficiency. In light of the macroeconomic landscape and the ongoing emission reduction progress, the government adopts an approach similar to monetary interest rate pricing, which, within the framework of a negative carbon market model, minimizes regulatory complexities and associated costs.
6. Strong incentive effect on decarbonation and related technology development. The negative carbon trading market directly connects "carbon emissions" and "carbon removals", facilitating both positive and negative reinforcements. The marketplace ensures real-time and precise reflection of costs and benefits associated with carbon reduction, providing corporate decision-makers with unambiguous economic leverage and quantifiable incentive structures. Notably, the funds contributed by end-consumers for their carbon emissions are directly channeled through the trading market to carbon removal enterprises and enterprises

with lower carbon emission intensity compared to industrial average, thereby minimizing the inefficiencies and complexities of capital management.

In order to establish a carbon reduction liability system within society, the carbon pricing mechanism derived from negative carbon trading presents compelling advantages over traditional carbon taxes or market-based pricing. Chapter 8 provides an exhaustive top-level design blueprint for the CELM-based NCTM.

5.3 Determination of Carbon Emission Liability Under the CELM Framework and Its Comparison with Current Schemes

5.3.1 Carbon Emission Accounting Mechanism of Current Schemes

Carbon emission accounting standard constitutes a pivotal element within the global emission reduction ecosystem. It serves as the cornerstone for implementing carbon taxes and facilitating transactions within ETS. At various hierarchical levels, the primary objects of carbon emission accounting encompass countries/regions, provinces and cities, industrial parks, enterprises, individual projects, and even products. Notably, the methodologies and standards employed in the accounting process vary across different nations and regions.

5.3.1.1 International Carbon Emission Accounting Standards

Currently, relevant carbon emission accounting standards issued by authoritative international organizations cover a broad spectrum, including countries, enterprises (organizations), products and services, as well as individuals (see Table 5.1).

The *IPCC Guidelines for National Greenhouse Gas Inventories*, published by the IPCC, are universally acknowledged and extensively employed guidelines for national GHG emission inventories to date, including six primary categories of GHG, mainly CO_2. The current applicable versions are the *2006 IPCC Guidelines for National Greenhouse Gas Inventories* (hereinafter referred to as *The IPCC Guidelines*), published in 2006, and the *2019 Refinement to the 2006 IPCC Guidelines for National Greenhouse Gas Inventories,* published in 2019. The emission factor method provided in *The IPCC Guidelines* is the most prevalent approach for GHG emissions, which combines information on the extent to which a human activity takes place (called activity data, or AD) with coefficients which quantify the emissions or removals per unit activity (known as emission factors, or EF). The basic equation is therefore:

Table 5.1 International carbon emission accounting standards and norms

Accounting levels	Name of standards and norms	Time	Application scope	By	Methods
End consumption carbon emissions	IPCC Guidelines for National Greenhouse Gas Inventories	2006 and 2019	Countries	IPCC	Emission factors
	ISO 14064	2006	Enterprises and projects	ISO	Monitoring and auditing of existing terminal emission sources for enterprises or projects
	GHG Protocol	2004	Enterprises and projects	WRI/ WBCSD	
Full life cycle carbon emissions	PAS 2050	2008	Projects	BSI	Establishing databases and models to account for carbon emissions throughout the life cycle of products/services
	ISO 14040/14044	2006	Projects	ISO	
	Product and Supply Chain GHG Protocol		Projects	WRI/ WBCSD	
	ISO 14067	2013	Projects	ISO	

GHG emissions (kg of GHG) = activity data (TJ) × emission factor (kg of GHG/TJ), where activity data indicate the extent of energy consumption caused by human activities, while the emission factor is the amount of GHGs emitted per unit of heat generated.

To calculate CO_2 emissions in the process of energy consumption, the above equation can be further elaborated as follows:

$$\begin{aligned}
&CO_2 \text{ emissions (kg of } CO_2) \\
&\quad = \text{activity data (TJ)} \times \text{emission factor (kg of } CO_2/\text{TJ)} \\
&\quad = \text{fuel consumption (kg)} \times \text{lower calorific value (TJ/kg)} \\
&\qquad \times \text{potential emission factor (kg carbon/TJ)} \\
&\qquad \times \text{carbon oxidation factor} \times 44/12
\end{aligned}$$

Among them, fuel consumption refers to the physical energy consumption, with solid and liquid energy typically measured by mass unit, whereas gaseous energy is measured by volume unit. Lower calorific value refers to the heat released by the sample per unit mass, under constant volume conditions, in excess oxygen until the combustion products are composed of oxygen, nitrogen, CO_2, sulfur dioxide, gaseous water and solid ash. The potential emission factor is carbon content per unit calorific value. The carbon oxidation factor measures the percentage of carbon that is actually oxidized to CO_2 when combustion occurs. 44/12 is the conversion coefficient of carbon (with atomic weight 12) to CO_2 (with molecular weight 44).

Emission factors are also known as carbon emission factors. When selecting these factors for various fuel types, it is advisable to consider the recommendations outlined in the IPCC Guidelines, which are called default values.

In March 2006, the International Organization for Standardization (ISO) introduced the ISO 14064, a series of standards which provide a complementary set of frameworks to quantify, monitor, report and verify GHG emissions. This standardized approach to calculating and verifying emission data ensures consistency, transparency and credibility in the quantification, monitoring, reporting, validation and verification processes of GHG emissions at the organization and project levels. By adhering to these standards, governments and enterprises can effectively measure and control their GHG emissions.

The GHG Protocol, also known as the "Greenhouse Gas Accounting System", is an authoritative and influential GHG emission accounting program developed by the World Resource Institute (WRI) and the World Business Council for Sustainable Development (WBCSD). Over a decade-long partnership, these two organizations have convened over 170 multinational stakeholders from diverse sectors, including business, politics, and environmental groups from across the globe. This collaborative effort has culminated in the creation of such program.

The GHG Protocol is mainly composed of four distinct but interrelated standards, transcending a solitary accounting framework. It constitutes a series of standards, guidelines and calculation tools tailored for enterprises, organizations and projects, enabling them to quantify and report GHG emissions. These standards, guidelines and calculation tools are independent and mutually complementary, forming the cornerstone for accounting and reporting GHG emissions by enterprises, organizations and projects to help foster the global transition towards a low-carbon economy. This series can provide standardized methods to account GHG emissions for enterprises or emission reduction projects, thus further reducing accounting costs. Additionally, it equips enterprises and organizations with the foundational data and accounting methodologies necessary to engage in both voluntary and mandatory carbon reduction endeavors.

The most important standards in the system are the following three standards: *GHG Protocol Corporate Accounting and Reporting Standard* (2011), or *Corporate Standard* for short, *Product Standard* (2011) used to understand the full life cycle emissions of a product, as well as *Corporate Value Chain (Scope 3) Standard* (2011).

To help delineate direct and indirect emission sources, improve transparency, and provide utility for different types of organizations and different types of climate policies and business goals, three "scopes" (scope 1, scope 2, and scope 3) are defined for GHG accounting and reporting purposes in *Corporate Standard.*

Scope 1: Direct GHG emissions

Direct GHG emissions occur from sources that are owned or controlled by the company, for example, emissions from combustion in owned or controlled boilers, furnaces, vehicles, etc.; emissions from chemical production in owned or controlled process equipment.

Scope 2: Electricity indirect GHG emissions

Scope 2 accounts for GHG emissions from the consumption of purchased secondary energy (including electricity, steam, heating and cooling). Purchased electricity is the common form for ordinary enterprises, which is defined as electricity that is purchased or otherwise brought into the organizational boundary of the company. Scope 2 emissions physically occur at the facility where electricity is generated.

Scope 3: Other indirect GHG emissions

Scope 3 emissions are a consequence of the activities of the company, but occur from sources not owned or controlled by the company. Some examples of scope 3 activities are production of purchased upstream materials, commuting of staff.

To put it simply, Scope 1 covers the direct emissions produced by the enterprises during their own production and operation. Scope 2 includes the emissions generated by the energy purchased by the enterprises, mainly the department which purchase electricity. Scope 3 includes all emissions produced by enterprises, excluding those falling under Scope 1 and Scope 2.

5.3.1.2 China's Carbon Emission Accounting Standards

To enhance the GHG accounting system, the National Development and Reform Commission has devised a comprehensive, three-tiered approach for the nation, local governments, and enterprises, emphasizing direct reporting of GHG emission data by pivotal enterprises. By formulating tailored guidelines for accounting and reporting emissions of key industries, the Commission has laid a cornerstone for advancing carbon emissions trading, establishing robust corporate GHG reporting systems, and refining the overall GHG statistical accounting framework.

In 2010, the National Development and Reform Commission organized relevant departments and research institutes to compile the *Guidelines for the Compilation of Provincial Greenhouse Gas Emission Inventories (Trial)* based on the IPCC Guidelines, which has been widely used in the calculation of provincial and local GHG inventories, providing technical support for local GHG mitigation plans and peak pathway design.

In 2013, the National Development and Reform Commission issued the first batch of guidelines for accounting and reporting GHG emissions in 10 industries, marking the commencement of a trial phase. Subsequently, in the latter part of 2014 and the middle of 2015, the Commission extended this initiative by releasing the second batch of guidelines for accounting and reporting GHG emissions specifically designed for enterprises in four additional industries, followed by the third batch encompassing ten more industries.

The first batch of guidelines in 2013 include:

1. *Guidelines for Accounting and Reporting GHG Emissions of Chinese Power Generation Enterprises (Trial)*
2. *Guidelines for Accounting and Reporting GHG Emissions of Chinese Power Grid Enterprises (Trial)*

3. *Guidelines for Accounting and Reporting GHG Emissions of Chinese Steel Enterprises (Trial)*
4. *Guidelines for Accounting and Reporting GHG Emissions of Chinese Chemical Enterprises (Trial)*
5. *Guidelines for Accounting and Reporting GHG Emissions of Chinese Electrolytic Aluminum Enterprises (Trial)*
6. *Guidelines for Accounting and Reporting GHG Emissions of Chinese Magnesium Smelting Enterprises (Trial)*
7. *Guidelines for Accounting and Reporting GHG Emissions of Chinese Flat Glass Enterprises (Trial)*
8. *Guidelines for Accounting and Reporting GHG Emissions of Chinese Cement Enterprises (Trial)*
9. *Guidelines for Accounting and Reporting GHG Emissions of Chinese Ceramic Enterprises (Trial)*
10. *Guidelines for Accounting and Reporting GHG Emissions of Chinese Civil Aviation Enterprises (Trial)*

The second batch of guidelines in 2014 include:

1. *Guidelines for Accounting and Reporting GHG Emissions of Chinese Oil and Gas Enterprises (Trial)*
2. *Guidelines for Accounting and Reporting GHG Emissions of Chinese Petrochemical Enterprises (Trial)*
3. *Guidelines for Accounting and Reporting GHG Emissions of Chinese Independent Coking Enterprises (Trial)*
4. *Guidelines for Accounting and Reporting GHG Emissions of Chinese Coal Enterprises (Trial)*

The third batch of guidelines in 2015 include:

1. *Guidelines for Accounting and Reporting GHG Emissions of Paper and Paper Product Manufacturers (Trial)*
2. *Guidelines for Accounting and Reporting GHG Emissions of Other Non-Ferrous Metal Smelting and Rolling Processing Enterprises (Trial)*
3. *Guidelines for Accounting and Reporting GHG Emissions of Electronic Equipment Manufacturing Enterprises (Trial)*
4. *Guidelines for Accounting and Reporting GHG Emissions of Machinery and Equipment Manufacturing Enterprises (Trial)*
5. *Guidelines for Accounting and Reporting GHG Emissions of Mining Enterprises (Trial)*
6. *Guidelines for Accounting and Reporting GHG Emissions of Food, Tobacco and Alcohol, Beverage and Refined Tea Enterprises (Trial)*
7. *Guidelines for Accounting and Reporting GHG Emissions of Public Building Operating Units (Enterprises) (Trial)*
8. *Guidelines for Accounting and Reporting GHG Emissions of Land Transport Enterprises (Trial)*

9. *Guidelines for Accounting and Reporting GHG Emissions of Fluorine Chemical Enterprises (Trial)*
10. *Guidelines for Accounting and Reporting GHG Emissions of Enterprises in Other Sectors (Trial)*

In addition, since 2013, the National Development and Reform Commission has released 12 batches of 200 voluntary GHG emission methodologies, which form the cornerstone of China's Certified Carbon Reduction (CCER) accounting system and predominantly align with the methodology under the Clean Development Mechanism (CDM). Nevertheless, the prevailing approach falls short of catering to the evolving demands of industries and enterprises. Consequently, the Ministry of Ecology and Environment, in collaboration with local associations and societies, continues to solicit methodologies from across the society.

It is evident that the operational and maintenance expenses associated with these accounting methodologies across numerous industries are substantial, posing challenges for maintaining scientific rigor and relevance to technological advancements and management requirements.

5.3.1.3 Current Challenges in Carbon Emission Accounting

1. The accounting standards are not clear.

The accounting of the actual carbon emissions necessitates comprehensive information spanning the full life cycle, encompassing raw materials, manufacturing processes, and electricity usage. However, the intricacies of these processes vary vastly across industries, resulting in distinct carbon emission profiles. Steel production, for instance, encompasses six to seven intricate stages, necessitating precise calculations of emissions in each stage. Similarly, the production of a single product in the chemical industry might involve entirely different raw materials and processes, leading to differing emission levels. In the cement industry, the daily monitoring of magnesium oxide and calcium oxide content in clinker adds another layer of complexity, not only requiring sophisticated measurement techniques but also generating vast amounts of data. While China has introduced GHG accounting methodologies for numerous industries, these efforts fall short of comprehensively covering all sectors and keeping pace with rapid technological advancements. In short, the accounting standards in industries are not clear, which poses challenges for carbon emission accounting.

2. Carbon emission factors are seriously deficient.

In the existing system of carbon accounting standards, there are two carbon accounting methods: accounting-based and measurement-based respectively, which can be concisely categorized into three main types: emission factor method, mass balance method and actual measurement method. Among these, the emission factor method stands out as the most universally applicable and prevalent approach. Nevertheless, the current scenario in China reveals a critical shortage of domestic carbon emission factors, characterized by scattered management and sluggish updates. Both internationally and domestically, the existing carbon emission management framework fails to establish a comprehensive, accurate, and real-time dynamic database of carbon emission factors.

Taking the construction industry as an example, a significant milestone was achieved on September 8, 2021, when the Ministry of Housing and Urban–Rural Development promulgated the national standard titled *General Code for Energy Efficiency and Renewable Energy Application in Buildings* (hereinafter referred to as the *Code*). This landmark regulation, which came into effect on April 1, 2022, has for the first time mandated the inclusion of carbon emission accounting in the design documentation of buildings. Since then, each construction project is expected to calculate carbon emissions across three stages: material production and transportation, construction and demolition, as well as operation. However, a formidable challenge lies ahead: the construction engineering industry faces a glaring deficiency in the database of carbon emission factors for its myriad materials and equipment, with information and data being woefully incomplete. At present, various industries have published data on carbon emission factors, but for the engineering industry, the comprehensiveness, real-time updates and accuracy of the data are far from enough.

3. Accounting capacity is insufficient.

The prevailing accounting standards are marked by insufficient clarity, compounded by a dire shortage of a comprehensive emission factor database. Additionally, there exists a substantial disparity in emission calculation methodologies, while the industry is gravely understaffed with qualified carbon accounting professionals and inspectors.

Pursuant to the current regulations, enterprises are mandated to independently calculate and submit their carbon emission reports, which are then subjected to verification by government-appointed agencies. Nonetheless, the vast majority of enterprises lack the necessary accounting expertise to fulfill this obligation independently, resorting instead to engaging third-party institutions. This reliance on external entities, while feasible, imposes a substantial financial burden on enterprises and the society at large, rendering the cost of carbon accounting unsustainable.

4. The cost of carbon accounting is unbearable to the whole society.

At present, the annual trading volume of China's carbon emission market is merely 4 billion to 5 billion yuan. With the inclusion of other industries to compliance carbon market, experts estimate that 200,000 professionals dedicated to carbon accounting will be needed, which is unimaginable. This immense demand translates into an annual labor cost of approximately 40 billion yuan, vastly outstripping the market's current value of roughly 10 billion yuan, posing an unsustainable economic burden on society.

5. It is difficult to supervise data verification.

The carbon market for emission allowances is built on the basis of carbon emission data, and the authenticity of data is the stable and solid foundation upon which this market system is constructed. Precision in carbon accounting, though important, often proves elusive due to its inherent complexities. Normative documents, such as verification guidelines, are deeply intertwined with the unique production characteristics of various industries and enterprises, exhibiting a high degree of specialization and considerable inter-industry disparities. Consequently, managers within environmental departments at the grassroots level grapple with the challenge of swiftly and comprehensively grasping inspection points within a limited timeframe, posing a significant hurdle to the effective oversight of emission data. Furthermore, the inability to continuously monitor carbon content data, coupled with extended data intervals, perpetuates challenges in process supervision. Moreover, it is impossible for verification agencies and authorities to monitor at any time. Additionally, the current framework, wherein carbon emission rights mean the cost of emissions, inadvertently fosters incentives for data fabrication among enterprises, thereby exacerbating the difficulties in supervising data integrity.

5.3.2 Comparison of the Determination of Carbon Emission Liability Under the Current Scheme and the CELM Framework

Currently, the international community grapples with a pivotal challenge in carbon emission reduction management: the absence of a comprehensive, accurate, and dynamic database for full-product emission factors. Emission organizations encounter substantial costs in conducting carbon data inventories, coupled with issues of poor data quality and a struggle to eradicate fraud, hindering the acquisition of reliable emission data and impeding the expansion of decarbonation management. Moreover, the difficulties associated with securing carbon emission data, its suboptimal quality, and prolonged verification processes significantly contribute to the sluggish pace of integrating other high-emission industries into the national carbon market.

Carbon emission accounting is the basis to implement carbon taxes and carbon emission trading. Under the current emission management framework, it is necessary to accurately verify and scientifically calculate the actual life-cycle carbon footprint of an organization and a product, thereby clarifying its liability for carbon emissions undertaken by the organization. The accounting work corresponding to the current carbon accounting strategy and methodology poses significant obstacle and bottlenecks. Notably, the thermal power generation sector has already encountered numerous challenges in acquiring carbon emission data. As we endeavor to extend carbon emission management to more industries, such as steel, cement, and aluminum, we will face formidable difficulties in terms of accounting workload, costs, and data supervision, making these endeavors seem almost insurmountable.

The purpose of carbon accounting is to allocate clear liability for carbon emissions to individual organizations and products. However, to achieve this clarity, we have other option, instead of carbon accounting, such as through market trading mechanism, to produce a more reasonable and accurate verification of carbon emission liability for the whole society. This represents a pivotal insight offered by this book. While the international community is actively pursuing two primary paths for carbon reduction—carbon taxes and carbon emission trading market, both require precise calculation for each organization and product, a task that is challenging and hindered by the aforementioned difficulties.

Under the CELM framework, a novel, scientifically sound, rational, and efficient mechanism for verifying carbon emission liability can be constructed, grounded firmly in market dynamics. Essentially, the CELM framework embodies an aggregate control approach, wherein the internal liability framework within the economic system arises organically through the workings of the market mechanism.

Without taking into account import and export trade, the verification of CO_2 emissions/carbon sources at a national level can be directly grounded in the current national GHG accounting system, and the total amount is exactly the same.

Once carbon sources are integrated into the economic production system, transactions among various organizations not only spur the circulation of logistics, capital, and taxation but also introduce the transfer of carbon emission liability, facilitated by carbon tickets within the CTMS. To meet consumer demands, each entity within the industry chain offers low-carbon products and services, engaging in emissions reduction competitions with peers by adopting footprint management strategies and selecting suppliers who provide low-carbon raw materials.

The specific allocation of carbon emission liability for each economic activity (transaction) is determined through negotiation among the parties involved, bypassing the need for complex calculations or government intervention. Instead, the market mechanism proves to be the most efficient in self-regulating the distribution of carbon liability. The ultimate determination of an organization's carbon emission liability lies in the subtraction between the total CEL input tickets and total CEL output tickets, a straightforward calculation that can be effortlessly managed, tracked, and analyzed utilizing an intelligent digital system.

The innovative CELM framework abandons the scientific accounting mechanism for actual carbon emissions, and avoids the challenges of intricate data acquisition for carbon inventories and verification at the individual organization level. Once the total amount of carbon sources is clarified and integrated into the economic system, it becomes more reasonable and efficient to harness the market mechanism to allocate carbon emission liability. This approach fosters digital and intelligent management facilitated by information systems (see Table 5.2).

Table 5.2 Comparison of the determination of carbon emission liability between the current scheme and the CELM framework

Items	Current scheme	The CELM framework
Determination of carbon emission liability	Based on carbon emission data measured by scientific approach	Based on market mechanism
Total amount of CO_2 emissions at the national level	Measured by source data	Calculated by carbon source data, with the total amount consistent with the current scheme
Acquisition of CO_2 emissions data at the organization level	Mainly referencing the GHG accounting methods promulgated by the IPCC, the National Development and Reform Commission has introduced GHG accounting methods for 24 industries, fostering scientific calculation and precise measurement practices	Upon the integration of total carbon source data into the economic system, market-based liability is allocated to all societal organizations through transactions within the industrial chain, enabling the precise determination of each organization's share of liability
Data value of CO_2 emission liability at the organization level	With the exception of carbon sink organizations, CO_2 emissions are generally positive for organizations	The carbon emission liability is the subtraction between the input and the output of carbon tickets, which can be either positive or negative
Advantages of carbon emission data acquisition	Despite the existence of rigorous methodologies, there is a notable absence of purely scientific practical applications, leading to high operational costs that often exceed societal capabilities. Consequently, these methodologies fail to offer any tangible advantage	The allocation of liability through market transactions is rational, cost-effective, and highly operable, with minimal carbon accounting and regulatory expenses, virtually approaching zero. This approach presents a significant advantage overcurrent approach
Difficulty in acquiring carbon emission data	The cost associated with conducting carbon inventories is exceedingly high, and the current methodologies and expertise are insufficient to support the comprehensive acquisition of carbon emission data across society and the entire industry	All transaction data is recorded in a digital carbon management system
	The lack of accessibility to carbon emissions data for all organizations poses a challenge, as the aggregated data from individual organizations often does not align with the national emission data, leading to inconsistencies in the overall picture	There are barely no difficulties encountered. The cumulative carbon liability data from all organizations seamlessly aligns with the national emission data, ensuring there are neither overlaps nor carbon leakage

Chapter 6
National Decarbonation System Based on the CELM and Its Implementation Plan

At present, the global decarbonation system is inefficient, hindering the swift progress towards carbon neutrality. Beyond the scarcity of robust foundational theories in climate change economics, two pivotal issues persist at the solutional level: First, the absence of an efficient, autonomous and self-driven big data system for the whole society's carbon footprints, coupled with the opacity of carbon neutrality information in the whole society, creates obstacles for policymakers in crafting effective strategies and for consumers in making informed choices. Secondly, the dearth of potent positive and negative incentives for both "carbon emissions" and "carbon removals" undermines progress. The current emission trading market primarily revolves around the distribution of emission allowances, while the CCER system, being a relative reduction mechanism, fails to accurately target actual emissions and sequestration, thereby limiting its effectiveness. Consequently, it is undeniable that the existing international carbon reduction system has been operating inefficiently for over two decades, with minimal tangible outcomes.

Based on the new CELM, the book introduces a "1+1" Decarbonation System encompassing "Carbon Ticket Management System + Negative Carbon Trading Market" (see Fig. 6.1), which is easier to implement and can foster collaborative carbon reduction efforts across society.

The national Carbon Ticket Management System (CTMS) based on the CELM can obtain real-time, quantitative, accurate and exhaustive big data on social carbon footprints at minimal cost, significantly bolstering the efficiency of decarbonation management across the whole society. Three decades of inefficient decarbonation endeavors have underscored the urgent need for a comprehensive, efficient carbon footprint data system, grounded in robust mechanisms and methodologies. Such a system must harness data and technology to establish clear data definitions and liability. Given the current advancements in information and digital technologies, and building upon China's successful "Golden Tax Project" experience in value-added tax, this feat is entirely achievable. Crucially, it necessitates daring to transcend the

B. Yang, *The Carbon Emission Liability Mechanism*,
https://doi.org/10.1007/978-981-96-3612-9_6

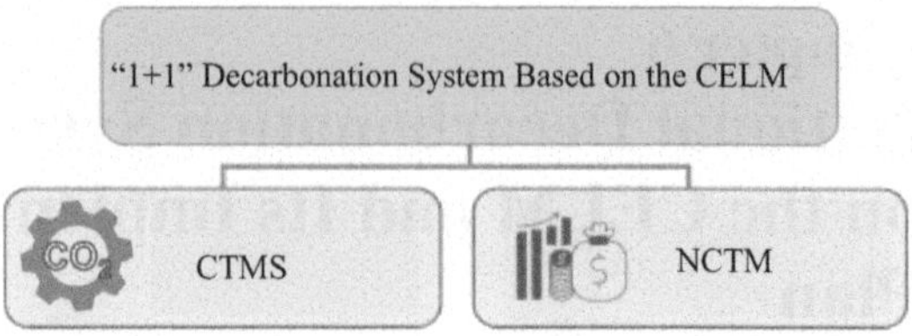

Fig. 6.1 "1+1" Decarbonation system based on the CELM

ideological constraints of the past three decades and embracing the courage and ingenuity required for innovation.

We introduce a Negative Carbon Trading Market (NCTM) based on the CELM, and create a bidirectional incentive framework encompassing both "carbon emissions" and "carbon removals" dynamics. This innovative approach fosters a genuinely efficacious carbon pricing system, surpassing the limitations of existing market for carbon emission rights. It transcends the inefficiencies inherent in government-centric allocation of carbon allowances, whereby departments at various levels manage the total societal carbon footprints. Instead, it harnesses the potency of data analytics, systemic strength, and market forces, empowering society to achieve efficient carbon reduction.

This chapter will focus on the "1+1" Decarbonation System based on the CELM and its implementation plan.

6.1 "1+1" Decarbonation System Based on the CELM

The CELM-based "1+1" Decarbonation System is composed of two interconnected sub-systems: the national "Carbon Ticket Management System (CMTS)" and the national unified "Negative Carbon Trading Market (NCTM)". These two subsystems collaborate seamlessly to constitute a comprehensive national framework for mitigating carbon emissions.

The most important function of the national CTMS lies in its comprehensive recording of societal carbon footprint data, which help clarify the share of CEL for each product, and confirm the CEL of each organization. This system ensures no carbon leakage occurs. Once the quantity of carbon sources is registered into the system, the subsequent transfer process ensures that each organization's liability is clearly defined and accounted for.

The pivotal role of the national unified NCTM is to offer a compensatory product, namely negative carbon, which enables organizations to offset their accumulated CEL. While generating revenue through carbon fees, the government fosters an efficient trading platform where low-carbon emitting entities and carbon removal organizations can monetize their efforts, thereby contributing to the closure of the entire societal loop for carbon reduction.

6.1.1 National Gold Carbon Project: The CTMS

The national CTMS is similar to the value-added tax invoice system (Golden Tax Project) in its approach, overseeing the carbon footprint data of social organizations, extending even to individual households. This system ensures that every transaction undertaken by an organization undergoes rigorous scrutiny, with every input and output of CEL tickets being meticulously recorded and tracked through its circulation records.

We can call this data system "Gold Carbon Project" or "Gold Carbon System".

The organization utilizes the input and output of CEL tickets, similar to the input and output of taxes in corporate value-added tax system. In fact, the design of the CTMS draws inspiration from the value-added tax system, and under the national government's tight grip on the sources, the intricate transactional layers across the entire industrial chain remain impervious to tax evasion. Likewise, with robust national management at the sources, there is no need to worry about carbon ledger leakage (domestic carbon leakage). Therefore, the liability will fall on specific organizations within the industrial chain. The amount of CEL recorded on the input/output CEL tickets is mutually agreed upon through negotiation between transaction parties, yielding carbon footprint data that is unparalleled in accuracy, fairness, and reasonability. This precision stems from the authenticity of the data provided by the upstream and downstream entities within the entire industrial chain, which are interlocked and objective, rendering fabrication impossible. Furthermore, the aggregate CEL remains constant under systemic control, eliminating errors. While CEL can be transferred in the market, their total volume remains unchanged, underscoring the system's high degree of accuracy and reliability.

The national CTMS oversees each organization's carbon ledger. It is imperative that the data within this system be seamlessly integrated with the tax system, facilitating data sharing and enabling rigorous verification of every transaction's carbon footprint. However, amidst the current trend, numerous entrepreneurial and research teams are engaging in overly complex endeavors by exploring blockchain technology for carbon footprint tracking, overlooking the core essence of effective carbon data management.

6.1.2 Carbon Stock Offsetting: The National Unified NCTM

Government departments and carbon removal organizations (including forestry departments, CCUS organizations, etc.) contribute to societal sustainability by offering negative carbon products through the NCTM. These products serve as a counterbalance to the carbon footprints of organizations, effectively reducing their carbon stock. The free-market bidding mechanism governs the acquisition of these negative carbon products, fostering an efficient bilateral market where "carbon emission" and "carbon removals" seamlessly interface, constituting a robust two-sided marketplace for carbon neutrality. In this ecosystem, carbon removal organizations garner direct revenue from the negative carbon market, while carbon-emitting entities directly pay for their emissions.

The NCTM distinguishes itself sharply from the prevailing international market for carbon emission rights, both in essence and in its functions. While the latter revolves around allocating and trading emission rights, thereby establishing a monetary value for the right to emit, the former focuses on the exchange of negative carbon products, thereby assigning a tangible cost to carbon emissions. Furthermore, the latter aims to facilitate the transfer of carbon emission rights, whereas the former strives to attain carbon neutrality.

The carbon pricing in the NCTM dynamically determines the societal cost of each ton of CO_2 emitted, leveraging market forces to objectively mirror the current emission expenses. This pricing is not a discounted estimation of future societal burdens but rather a carbon cost price that harmoniously integrates the targets of carbon neutrality with economic growth. This is completely different from the nature of carbon price in China's trading market for emission rights, where most of the allowances are allocated for free, and only a very low proportion of carbon emission rights need to be obtained through trading. Consequently, the actual average societal emission cost needs to be calculated separately, which is far lower than the actual trading price of about 55 yuan/ton in the current national carbon market. Therefore, carbon price signals are very unclear and inaccurate.

Under the CELM, in principle, there are no restrictions placed on any organization's carbon emissions. Provided they are willing to purchase negative carbon products to offset their CEL, the normal economic operations remain unhampered by administrative interventions. This approach fosters greater autonomy among social organizations in their business planning endeavors.

6.2 Implementation and Operation Plan of CELM-Based Decarbonation System

To guarantee the equitable, efficient, and cost-effective functioning of the national "1+1" Decarbonation System, it is imperative to devise a comprehensive set of implementation plans that showcase the vitality and innovativeness of the system. Currently, the international arena is inundated with diverse decarbonation mechanisms and methodologies, leading to substantial sunk costs and the emergence of numerous vested interest groups. Navigating through this complex landscape to effect meaningful change poses significant challenges.

CELM-based Decarbonation System is a theory rooted in the fundamental nature of global climate change, with the ambition to formulate an efficient implementation plan for achieving carbon reduction objectives.

6.2.1 Formulate a CEL System by National Legislation

National legislation has paved the way for a robust framework by enacting a series of laws and regulations, including the *National Carbon Emission Reduction Management System*, the *Carbon Ticket Management Law*, and the *Operation Management Measures for the Negative Carbon Trading Market*. These legislative measures aim to establish a comprehensive CEL system that encompasses all sectors of society, clearly defining the roles and liability of social organizations within the carbon ticket system. Furthermore, they outline the fundamental principles governing the system's operation and address various legal considerations. The main purpose of the legislation is to establish the following core principles:

1. End consumers bear the cost of carbon emissions, and the back end of the industrial chain is liable for the total carbon emissions of the front end.

   This principle, the basis for the design of decarbonation system, clarifies the CEL across the whole society, marking a transition from a producer-centric to a consumer-centric approach.
2. Organizations exceeding the industrial average in carbon intensity are obligated to promptly assume their CEL. To maintain equilibrium, these entities must balance their input and output of CEL tickets, and those with accumulated carbon emissions must actively neutralize their footprints and purchase negative carbon products from the carbon market, thereby contributing to the overall decarbonization effort.

   It is crucial to establish a regular settlement mechanism, for instance, on a quarterly basis, for every carbon-emitting organization. If an organization is able to successfully transfer all of its CEL-Input to downstream entities, it achieves carbon neutrality and avoids incurring additional emission costs. Conversely, when the difference between the input and output of CEL tickets is positive, indicating a surplus of CEL, the organization must purchase negative carbon products from the carbon market to offset its CEL and fulfill its liability. If this difference is negative, signifying that the organization's carbon emission intensity falls below the industrial average, it possesses a surplus of negative carbon, which can be directly sold in the carbon market, thereby rewarding its low-carbon initiatives with incentive income.
3. The carbon emission flow data of all transactions are recorded in the CTMS.

   The big data of carbon footprints in all transactions is recorded in the CTMS, providing a robust foundation for the effective implementation of the government's policies and the seamless operation of the societal-wide carbon emission reduction system.

6.2.2 Establish a CTMS Platform Covering All Sectors of Society to Achieve Full Management of Carbon Footprint Data

The state shall develop and establish a nationwide CTMS, similar to the VAT invoice system (Golden Tax Project), which shall oversee the carbon footprint data of entire social organizations, extending even to individual households. This system necessitates that every organization meticulously documents the input and output of carbon tickets in every transaction.

The government assigns each organization a unique CEL account, and it is suggested to directly adopt the prevailing organizational credit code, promoted by the government, as its carbon account code. This approach facilitates seamless integration with other pivotal social management systems.

Via the implementation of the "Golden Carbon Project" or "Golden Carbon System", the government attains dynamic, precise, and comprehensive big data pertaining to national carbon emissions. This enables the creation of a premium national database for carbon emission factors, which subsequently underpins various decarbonation management endeavors through the utilization of this robust big data system.

From an operational competency and rationality standpoint, the fiscal and tax systems should be entrusted with the responsibility of overseeing the carbon ticket management system. Firstly, the finance department should administer the revenues generated from carbon fees. Second, the carbon ticket system and the VAT system share more applications for integration, data sharing and verification. Given that the VAT system is already well-established, complete with robust organizational and talent frameworks, its operational efficiency is unparalleled, ensuring seamless integration and optimized performance.

Government departments release "Owing Negative CO_2" products proportional to the number of carbon sources into the negative carbon trading market, where these products can be acquired by carbon-emitting organizations to offset and settle their carbon stock, thereby generating revenues for the governments through negative carbon sales. The revenues from selling negative carbon products are integrated into the fiscal system, which adopt a two-track system for revenue and expenditure and ensure comprehensive utilization. Therefore, it is advisable to be integrated into the fiscal and tax system.

6.2.3 Verification and Input of Carbon Source Data

Under the CTMS, the government departments merely need to verify the carbon emissions per unit of production and supervise the total emissions of carbon-emitting organizations, effectively regulating the total carbon footprints of the society. Given the limited variety of carbon sources and the relatively stable carbon content per unit of production, the primary contributors—coal, oil, and gas companies—render the task of quantifying carbon sources straightforward and cost-effective for the government.

Chapter 7 will discuss in details the management plan for carbon-emitting organizations and their data.

After the carbon emissions per unit of production and the total number of carbon sources are verified, the related government department issues a carbon output ticket to the emitting organization in the CTMS, simultaneously logging the data into the system.

One of the key strengths of the CTMS lies in its ability to streamline regulatory expenses once carbon source data is registered into the system. Adhering to the principles of free market trading, the system will reasonably allocate the total amount of CEL across the economic landscape. The total carbon emission data of the entire system is always constant, eliminating errors, carbon leakage and double counting, ensuring self-correcting accuracy. This approach mitigates the most vexing issues of data verification and excessive costs that plague current decarbonation system designs.

6.2.4 Self-Operation of the CTMS

The circulation of the input and output of CEL tickets meticulously documents all trading activities across the entire social spectrum. When engaging in the exchange of products and services, both parties proactively manage carbon tickets, thereby integrally weaving them into the fabric of trading contracts. This seamless circulation process is devoid of governmental intervention, ensuring that no matter how the carbon emissions circulate, there are always organizations in the industrial chain to take liability, alleviating concerns of carbon leakage for the government. Theoretically, it is not difficult to prove that if the government maintains a firm grip on the carbon sources, and free trading, through the market mechanism, is conducted within the intermediate link of the industrial chain, the carbon footprint data obtained by the transaction negotiation is the most feasible. For regulatory bodies, the current task of verifying carbon emissions across various organizations is cumbersome, a factor that has limited the decade-long carbon market pilot primarily to a select few coal-fired power companies.

It is evident that the CTMS exhibits remarkable efficiency and autonomy, resulting in minimal operational, supervisory, and MRV costs incurred by government departments. In contrast, the allowance-based trading market is burdened with significantly higher MRV expenses, since it stems from fundamentally different operational logics and thus yields vastly divergent levels of operational complexity and effectiveness.

6.2.5 Establish a National Unified NCTM Based on the CELM

Social organizations consistently engage in quarterly settlements through the carbon ticket system, necessitating the establishment of a national negative carbon trading market to facilitate the supply of offsetting products: "negative carbon". Organizations with a positive value in their emission stock purchase "negative carbon" products from this market to offset their CEL, thereby fulfilling their obligations towards carbon neutrality. Conversely, organizations with a negative value in their emission stock can profitably sell "negative carbon" products in the market. The government only issues carbon output tickets, instead of carbon input tickets, and is the largest "negative carbon" supplier in the carbon market, generating substantial revenue for the state. Furthermore, carbon removal sectors, including forestry organizations and Carbon Capture, Utilization, and Storage (CCUS) entities, can monetize their efforts by selling "negative carbon" products in the carbon market, generating investment income.

Therefore, it is necessary to establish a negative carbon trading market based on the CELM, enabling social organizations to purchase "negative carbon" products to balance their carbon accounts, and offset their accumulated CEL. The negative carbon trading market under the CELM is very different from the current market that primarily revolves around carbon emission rights. The main product traded within this market is "negative carbon", a concept elaborated upon in Chap. 8.

Prior to the carbon market's accessibility to institutional and individual investors, the total quantity of "negative carbon" products introduced by the government into the market is determined as follows:

$$\begin{aligned} &\text{Total amount of Owing Negative } CO_2 \\ &= \text{total carbon sources} - \text{total carbon removals} \end{aligned}$$

The government will prioritize the allocation of "negative carbon" from carbon removal organizations to be used to offset carbon stock.

Once the carbon market is accessible to both institutional and individual investors, the government can introduce "negative carbon" products tailored to the evolving demands for carbon asset investment. Furthermore, the government can control and regulate the carbon price in response to economic growth, carbon asset investment demands and carbon neutrality process. In this CELM-driven carbon market, the role and position of the government is similar to the relationship between the government and the RMB, which can influence the macroeconomy through the currency interest rate.

The "1+1" society-wide carbon management system based on the CELM will serve as the cornerstone for effective emission reduction across all sectors of society.

The government should establish a national unified negative carbon trading market through legislation, thereby terminating the fragmented operations of various pilot markets and the CCER market, so as to prevent resource dispersion and chaos of emission reduction systems.

The government should enact legislation outlining the principles for top-level design as well as core operational and management regulations for the negative carbon trading market, thereby solidifying its legal standing. This market should be accessible to all market players, including carbon asset operators, and should facilitate the free trading, leading to the emergence of an authentic carbon pricing mechanism. As the principal driver of carbon neutrality, the national government assumes the role of a "owing negative carbon" contributor within the carbon market. Meanwhile, as the issuer of carbon output tickets, it also represents the negative carbon input corresponding to various carbon sources, thereby exerting significant influence over carbon pricing dynamics within the market.

6.2.6 Each Organization Settles Its CEL on a Quarterly Basis

Each social organization regularly calculates and settles its CEL through the carbon ticket management system and the negative carbon trading market. Organizations with a positive value are obliged to purchase "negative carbon" products from the carbon market as a means of offsetting and assuming their CEL. Conversely, those with a negative value have the opportunity to sell "negative carbon" products, thereby reaping low-carbon incentives and benefits. This approach mirrors the fundamental principles of the value-added tax's routine final settlement, albeit with a crucial distinction: VAT is typically deducted but not refunded, except some products, such as exports and software products, which allow for refunds as stipulated by special industry policies.

Quarterly settlement is more appropriate, and it is not necessary to settle like the VAT on a monthly basis, since there is a time cycle for the operation of product sales, contract settlement, and the intricate management of carbon ticket inputs and outputs. Besides, the convenience of organizing the settlement process, alongside social operating costs, should be considered.

For the organizations with negative values, the government departments should exercise supervision to avoid counterfeiting and arbitrage, which, while generally not as prevalent, is still a concern but far more manageable than during the initial phase of the VAT system. Since the carbon emission cost is factored into the overall transaction price, individual organization' incentive to falsify information is diminished, albeit arbitrage with downstream entities remains possible. Nonetheless, the comprehensive data in the carbon ticket system enables the development of a robust audit and verification subsystem. By cross-checking data with the VAT system, this subsystem possesses formidable verification capabilities, adept at detecting and alerting against arbitrage practices.

For organizations that have carbon stock yet failing to fulfill their obligations to timely settle, the government can devise penalty measures to underscore the gravity of adhering to prompt settlement regulations. For instance, upon repeated delays in meeting payment deadlines, penalty interest will accrue, calculated based on the offset amount. Upon exceeding a predetermined threshold of delays, collaborative efforts with the business administration departments will escalate sanctions, culminating in the revocation of the organization's business license if necessary.

6.2.7 *The End-Sales Organization Collects Carbon Fees When the Products Are Sold*

After the completion of all links of product manufacturing, the product is subsequently distributed to the end-sales organization via the circulation chain, ultimately reaching consumers. At this time, the carbon ticket associated with the product can no longer continue to flow, as the end-sales organization sells the product to consumers while simultaneously imposing the carbon fee onto them. The methodology for determining the carbon fee levied by retail organizations on consumers is outlined below:

$$\begin{aligned}\text{Final selling price} &= \text{product price} + \text{tax} + \text{carbon fee}\\ &= \text{product price} + \text{tax} + \text{the amount of CEL in product}\\ &\quad\times \text{carbon price}\end{aligned}$$

In the future, retail organizations will incorporate an item of a carbon fee into the purchase invoices provided to consumers, which will disclose the amount of CEL of the product and the total carbon fee. Consumers are fully informed and empowered to make conscious choices, and their choices will be an important driving force for emission reduction. A growing number of countries have begun to establish management system to label carbon content in the commodities, mandating the labelling of a product's carbon content on its packaging and specifications, subject to government supervision and verification.

Organizations offer products and services to end consumers, and consumers pay carbon fees directly for the CEL associated with goods and services. That is to say, organizations that sell products and services charge carbon fees to end consumers. Furthermore, these organizations utilize the funds collected from carbon fees to procure "negative carbon" products through the carbon market, effectively offsetting their carbon emissions, and make regular quarterly settlement in the carbon ticket management system.

When retail organizations collect carbon fees from consumers, some rules and regulations are expected to be formulated to govern their practices and prevent bidding up price. For example, they should adhere to the fundamental principles of transparency in carbon liability and unification in charging standards.

To prevent retail merchants from engaging in unfair pricing practices, mitigate disputes, and maintain order within the consumer landscape, organizations collecting carbon fees during product sales must adhere strictly to the regulations and guidelines established by the state. Specifically, the unit price of carbon fees levied on consumers by sales organizations ought to be legally mandated. This price can be benchmarked against the average closing price of the national carbon market from the preceding month. Moreover, the government should announce the carbon price standard for commodity carbon fees in each month, serving as the sole prevailing national price.

The government can draw valuable insights from the successful implementation of specific practices related to collecting carbon fees for end-consumption, notably exemplified by Shanghai's methodology for collecting sewage treatment fees for public utilities (see Sect. 6.7 for details).

6.2.8 Accounting of the Carbon Account in the Organization

The circulation of CEL tickets in the market can be analogized to the exchange of goods and services, albeit representing a unique class of "negative commodities" intended for offsetting and transferring environmental costs shared among societal entities. Within the accounting framework, the inclusion of the "carbon ticket" as an accounting subject, with a physical unit of kilograms and a value unit denoted in yuan (negative), signifies the embedding of these costs. This approach incentivizes organizations to minimize their costs by actively reducing or neutralizing carbon emissions.

The carbon ticket management system is seamlessly integrated with the VAT system, streamlining accounting data processing for organizations and facilitating verification efforts by government regulatory bodies.

The organizational carbon account, including all social units that engage in inputs and outputs (enterprises, institutions, farmers and households), should cover all organizational cells of the whole society. Decarbonation is a social imperative, and only when every organization and every individual are mobilized and truly bear the CEL, can we achieve optimal efficiency in reducing carbon emissions across society.

6.3 Establish Household CEL Carbon Accounts and Promote Carbon Reduction for All

In the process of carbon neutrality in the whole society, it is far from enough to rely on social organizations and governments to assume liability. Merely innovating governmental mechanisms and fostering continual technological advancements in production sectors, while crucial, falls short of fully addressing the challenge. It is equally imperative to strengthen the CEL at the consumption side and to instigate the reform of consumption pattern. At the heart of this endeavor lies the pivotal role of encouraging residential decarbonation. In response, Chinese provinces and municipalities have embarked on an active campaign, leveraging the carbon-inclusive mechanism and investing significant resources into its development and promotion. However, despite these efforts, the overall outcome remains unsatisfactory. This elicits a question: What constitutes the genuine key to engaging households nationwide in decarbonation efforts?

6.3.1 The Need to Promote National Carbon Reduction

Household carbon emissions are important sources of social carbon footprints. According to the *Report on Tackling Climate Change (2020): Promoting New Climate Momentum*, GHG (particularly CO_2) emissions stemming from household consumption in China account for 52% of China's total GHG emissions, surpassing even industrial emissions. As the living standards of Chinese households continue to improve, this figure will continue to rise, and carbon emissions from newly purchased consumer goods are one of the main sources of household carbon emissions. Given the substantial role that households play in the national carbon landscape, achieving carbon neutrality necessitates the engagement and participation of every household across society.

Household carbon emissions stem from residents' daily consumption habits, including both direct carbon emissions and indirect carbon emissions. On a daily basis, direct carbon emissions arise from the purchase and consumption of energy carriers like coal, oil, natural gas, and electricity, as well as personal transportation, to fulfill necessities such as hot water, lighting, electrical appliances, and automobile fuel. Conversely, indirect carbon emissions are associated with non-energy goods and services, encompassing essentials like food, clothing, housing, leisure and entertainment activities, transportation, and communication.

Households at different levels of consumption not only differ greatly in the total amount of carbon emissions, but also in the composition of carbon emissions.

Dario Kenner, the author of *Carbon Inequality: The Role of the Richest in Climate Change*, coined the term "Polluter Elite" to refer to the wealthiest segments of society that indulge in substantial consumption of fossil fuels or adopt lifestyles characterized by high carbon footprints, thereby exerting a disproportionately large influence on the climate. Despite their relatively small numbers, the environmental impact of these "polluter elites" is profound.

In May 2022, the National Academies of Sciences of the G7 states issued *Decarbonization: The Case for Urgent International Action*, noting that the G7 accounts for nearly half of cumulative global carbon emissions and currently accounts for about 25% of global CO_2 emissions. According to a study by French economist Lucas Chancel, the share of carbon emissions contributed by the richest 1% of the world grew from 13.7% in 1990 to 16.9% in 2019, 5.4 percentage points higher than that of the poorest 50% of the global population. In 2019, the richest 1% of the world emitted 101 tons of carbon per capita, 72 times more than the lower 50% of the lower-middle income group (see Fig. 6.2). In 2019, China's per capita carbon emissions stood at 8.0 tons, of which the per capita carbon emissions of the top 10% of the high-income group were 38.0 tons, 13.6 times that of the lower 50% of the lower-middle group (see Fig. 6.3).

Chancel has estimated that "An 11-min flight emits no fewer than 75 tonnes of carbon per passenger once indirect emissions are taken into account (and more likely, in the 250–1000 tonnes range). At the other end of the distribution, about one billion individuals emit less than one tonne per person per year. Over their lifetime, this group of one billion individuals does not emit more than 75 tonnes of carbon per person."

The "polluter elites", whose lifestyle inherently entails substantial carbon emissions through extravagances such as multiple mansions, luxury automobiles, yachts, private jets, and frequent travel, monopolize a significant portion of the world's resources. Consequently, the attainment of carbon neutrality for humanity as a whole necessitates a collective shift or at least advocacy for alterations in their high-carbon consumption patterns and lifestyles.

At the consumer end, the IPCC report underscores the potential for a 40–70% reduction in GHG emissions by 2050, contingent upon the implementation of right policies, infrastructure, and technologies aimed at transforming individual lifestyles and behaviors.

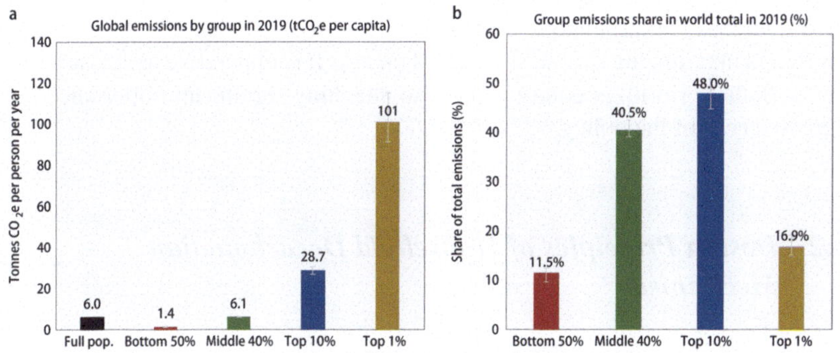

c

Global emissions inequality in 2019: summary table

	Number of individuals (million)	Average (tonnes CO_2 per capita)	Threshold (tonnes CO_2 per capita)	Share (% total)
Full population	7,710	6	<0.1	100%
Bottom 50%	3,855	1.4	<0.1	11.5%
incl. bottom 20%	1,542	0.7	<0.1	2.3%
incl. next 30%	2,315	1.8	1.1	9.2%
Middle 40%	3,084	6	2.8	40.5%
Top 10%	771	29	13	48%
incl. top 1%	77.1	101	47	16.9%
incl. top 0.1%	7.71	425	125	7.1%
incl. top 0.01%	0.771	2,332	566	3.9%

Source: Lucas Chancel. Global carbon inequality over 1990-2019.

Fig. 6.2 Global distribution and percentage of per capita carbon emissions by income group

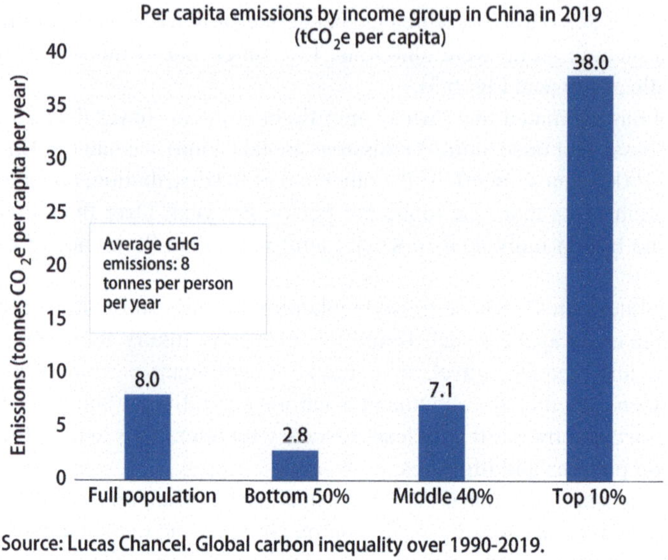

Fig. 6.3 Distribution of carbon emissions by income group in China in 2019

The household decarbonation mechanism must strike a balance between ensuring fairness and maximizing overall societal efficiency. It is imperative to devise a robust framework that prioritizes equity while also attaching significant importance to the progressiveness of the policy.

6.3.2 Design Principles of Household Decarbonation Mechanism

The design of household decarbonation mechanism must adhere to the following principles.

1. High efficiency in emission reduction and system implementation.

The household decarbonation mechanism has a pervasive impact on every household. The effectiveness of this mechanism necessitates a comprehensive consideration of several pivotal aspects:

First, the mechanism must ensure a high level of efficiency in decarbonation. This necessitates harnessing market mechanisms and leveraging digital capabilities to heighten societal awareness regarding carbon emissions and significantly influence the dynamics of household expenditure costs. A prevalent observation from nation-wide resident surveys reveals that while individuals express considerable concern about climate issues, they often fail to adjust their lifestyles and consumption patterns, mistakenly believing they have already contributed sufficiently and that the CEL does not solely rest on their shoulders. The underlying cause of this disconnect lies in the absence of a system that quantifies individual and household CEL, coupled with an efficient market-driven mechanism to enforce the liability with appropriate rigor.

Secondly, the household decarbonation mechanism involves substantial implementation costs, yet it must achieve a correspondingly high level of efficiency. As this mechanism touches upon every household in society, it is imperative that its operation and implementation not only align with their interests but also minimize the inconvenience and workload imposed upon residents. Otherwise, it risks encountering difficulties in gaining widespread public support.

2. Fairness and progressivity.

The social cost of carbon emissions is substantial, and the equitable allocation of this liability is of paramount importance. The quality of the system design significantly impacts both the positive and negative aspects of its societal benefits. It must embody fairness, ensuring that it does not exacerbate the stress of low-income households but rather contributes to their well-being. Conversely, the cost imposed on wealthier individuals should be relatively higher, reflecting the progressive nature of the policy. To achieve this, implementing a progressive system of per capita carbon emissions, similar to the tiered structure of individual income tax rates, is imperative.

3. It is conducive to achieving common prosperity and building a better society.

The prevailing concept of common prosperity could easily be misinterpreted as a mere redistribution of existing wealth, a mindset that is perilous and prone to fostering anxiety among the affluent and entrepreneurs regarding their property security—a detriment to stable economic growth. Instead, during the societal transition towards a green economy, the strategic adjustment of incremental asset distribution mechanisms and the refinement of liability allocation systems offer a promising blueprint for guiding diverse societal strata towards a mutually beneficial path to "a better society". The pursuit of carbon neutrality objectives pervades every facet of our economy and way of life. When crafted properly, the decarbonation mechanism can evolve into a potent policy instrument, significantly contributing to building a better society. Recognizing the substantial fiscal implications of carbon fees across society, governments have a unique opportunity to harness this revenue stream for income redistribution and enhancing social equity, a worthy endeavor deserving of their utmost attention.

6.3.3 Current Carbon Inclusion Schemes, Progress and Limitations

In China's current decarbonation system, the carbon inclusion mechanism assumes a pivotal role in fostering a shift towards eco-friendly consumption patterns and culture among consumers, garnering significant attention from local governments. This mechanism strives to motivate individuals and micro, small, and medium-sized enterprises (MSMEs) to embrace low-carbon practices, champion green consumption, and foster the adoption of a green and low-carbon lifestyle. Consequently, it propels enterprises towards low-carbon transformation and upgrading, ultimately enhancing the overall level of low-carbon development across society.

6.3.3.1 The Concept of Carbon Inclusion

The fundamental principle of carbon inclusion is to use mobile Internet, big data, blockchain and other cutting-edge digital technologies to quantify, record and verify diverse eco-friendly and low-carbon behaviors undertaken by the public, communities, micro, MSMEs, covering their actions across clothing, food, housing, consumption, travel, etc., according to carbon inclusion standards or methodologies. Subsequently, these efforts translate into individual emission reduction achievements, which are recorded in a carbon ledger. By leveraging emission reduction trading, policy incentives, and market motivations, a virtuous cycle of green living feedback is established, rewarding emission-reducing behaviors. The carbon inclusion mechanism strives to ignite and sustain public enthusiasm for actively engaging in carbon neutrality initiatives, making tangible the contributions of every group and individual towards achieving the dual carbon goals. This approach embodies the essence of ecological civilization and the concept of national action.

6.3.3.2 Progress of Carbon Inclusion Mechanism

At the national level, *China's Policies and Actions for Addressing Climate Change (2022)* and *Progress on the Implementation of China's Nationally Determined Contributions (2022)* both propose to explore an innovative mechanism of voluntary emission reduction, that is, carbon inclusion, to encourage the whole society to participate in decarbonation.

At present, China's carbon inclusion mechanism can be divided into two types: government-led and enterprise-led. The former is primarily propelled by local governments, whereas the latter is mainly initiated and established by financial institutions and e-commerce platforms. Despite minor variations, the operational modes of these various carbon inclusion mechanisms largely converge, with a strong reliance on the carbon inclusion platform as their cornerstone. Through data integration with public institutions or e-commerce platforms, the emission reduction of public low-carbon behaviors under low-carbon scenarios is calculated according to the corresponding methodology. Subsequently, based on predetermined rules, corresponding carbon credits are awarded. These credits empower the public to exchange commercial concessions and access public services within the carbon inclusion platforms. Furthermore, they can be utilized for carbon offsetting, or even traded in the carbon trading market to offset the carbon emissions of the enterprises with higher emissions.

Wuhan is the pioneering city in China to explore the carbon inclusion mechanism. In 2013, Wuhan unveiled the *Wuhan Low-carbon Pilot Implementation Plan*, which laid the foundation for the subsequent introduction of the innovative "carbon points system" in 2014, aiming to use the "carbon currency exchange mechanism" to guide the residents to live a low-carbon life and promote low-carbon consumption. This is one of the earliest urban carbon inclusion projects in China, providing valuable, hands-on experience for the development of carbon inclusion mechanism. Subsequently, an array of provinces and cities, including Guangdong, Hebei, Shaanxi, Tianjin, Zhejiang, Jiangsu, Jiangxi, and Shandong, have embarked on their own pilot projects.

Guangdong Province is the first to integrate carbon inclusion mechanism with carbon market trading. In April 2017, the Development and Reform Commission of Guangdong Province enacted the *Interim Measures for the Administration of Certificated Emission Reduction Under the Carbon Inclusion Project*. It pointed out that certified voluntary emission reductions, generated by low-carbon activities such as reducing GHG emissions and increasing GHG removals, which are voluntarily implemented by enterprises or individuals within the pilot regions of the carbon inclusion projects in Guangdong Province, are allowed to access the carbon trading market.

In December 2022, eight departments, including the Shanghai Municipal Bureau of Ecology and Environment, jointly issued the *Work Plan for the Construction of Carbon Inclusion System in Shanghai*, and clearly proposed to "formulate offset rules to guide the integration of carbon inclusion efforts into Shanghai's carbon emission trading market via an offset mechanism, and to support and encourage the enterprises to purchase carbon inclusion emission reductions and settle their carbon emissions through the offset mechanism". In May 2023, the *Allocation Plan of Shanghai 2022 Carbon Emission Allowances,* issued by the Shanghai Municipal Bureau of Ecology and Environment, clearly stated that Shanghai carbon emission reductions (SHCER) have been included within the scope of offsetting.

The carbon inclusion mechanism fosters the public's enthusiasm for embracing green and low-carbon lifestyles, thereby catalyzing widespread citizen engagement in carbon emission reduction efforts. It further propels citizens' transition from mere awareness of low-carbon practices to actual low-carbon behaviors, with each individual's participation in emission reduction contributing significantly towards the achievement of the dual carbon targets.

6.3.3.3 Problems and Limitations of Carbon Inclusion Mechanism

Regardless of the specific type of carbon inclusion mechanism employed, they essentially focus on individual consumption and establish personal carbon accounts, therefore, there inherently exist certain limitations.

1. Individual consumption not only revolves around personal consumption, but also reflects the division of labor in household. Family is the cell of society, and family roles reflect different division of labor, shaping the unique pattern of consumption. In different family structure, the consumption of different role is different. For example, the household's water, electricity and fuel bills are paid by the same person, either the wife or the husband. Besides, the wife usually pays the bills for groceries, whereas the husband usually pays the bill for electronics purchases. Consequently, while individual carbon footprint data might appear modest, the cumulative emissions of a household can be substantial, rendering individual incentives insufficient. Energy consumption, a pivotal contributor to household carbon emissions, is predominantly a family-based phenomenon, intricately tied to family size and family structure. As such, personal carbon accounts fall short in comprehensively capturing and analyzing these family-level dynamics.
2. The current approach to carbon inclusion for emission reduction lacks scientific rigor, incurs substantial implementation costs, and exhibits limited sustainability. The mechanism outlines specific low-carbon consumption scenarios and green behaviors, and formulates accounting methods for related low-carbon behaviors, which are linked to the credits of green low-carbon behaviors under the carbon inclusion mechanism. Typically, the accounting of low-carbon behaviors is usually to establish a baseline consumption scenario to get the baseline carbon emissions, subsequently calculating the emissions associated with green, low-carbon alternatives to derive a relative reduction. This reduction is a relative concept. However, both theoretical analysis and historical practice show that the relative emission reduction mechanism tends to be unsuccessful, because of its lack of scientific rationality and high costs associated with its implementation.

   Given the diverse range of factors influencing individuals' consumption habits, including family environment, family structure, regional customs, and living habits, it becomes challenging to establish universally applicable standard baseline behaviors. Consequently, the scientific rationality of carbon emission reduction for green low-carbon behaviors is problematic, and it is not suitable to be included in the carbon market for trading.

   What's more, keeping track of a person's carbon consumption is challenging, costly and not sustainable.
3. The current carbon inclusion mechanism inadequately captures the comprehensive picture of an individual's total carbon emissions. By solely focusing on identifying and rewarding low-carbon behaviors within specific consumption scenarios, it overlooks a vast array of consumption activities that contribute to an

individual's overall carbon footprints. As a result, the system fails to provide a full and accurate reflection of individual carbon consumption. For example, the rich may engage in a wider variety of consumption scenarios, and thus accumulate more decarbonation data, whereas those who genuinely lead low-carbon lifestyles, often practicing frugality and minimizing consumption, may have fewer opportunities to earn points due to their limited consumption scenarios. Consequently, the personal carbon account data generated by this system do not give a true picture of individual carbon emissions.

6.3.4 Application Basis of Household CEL Carbon Account

The book argues that adopting the household CEL carbon account mechanism, as opposed to the individual carbon account, is a more fitting approach to reducing overall societal carbon emissions. The research underscores that China's household CEL carbon account framework possesses a solid foundation for implementation.

In 2022, ten government commissions in Shanghai, including Shanghai Municipal Education Commission and Shanghai Municipal Development and Reform Commission, collaboratively launched the "2022 Shanghai Youth Dual Carbon Proposal Competition", and a team of four from the First Affiliated Middle School to Tongji University set up a dual carbon research group, with the theme of "Establishing a Household CEL Carbon Account Mechanism and Mobilizing Public Participation in Carbon Reduction". They conducted a social survey and gave relevant proposals and suggestions. The research group conducted a social survey utilizing the SoJump App,[1] posing 22 questions and collecting 648 valid responses. The analysis of the questionnaires revealed several key insights: 93.06% of the respondents acknowledged that addressing climate change is a shared liability and everyone should play a role. Notably, 83.33% expressed willingness to compromise on their quality of life to reduce carbon emissions, with over half indicating a readiness for proper adjustments. 80% were unaware that their consumption habits significantly contributed to high carbon emissions. Furthermore, 62.04% of participants expressed their willingness to pay additional carbon fees as a means of reducing emissions. Lastly, 52.47% advocated for designing a household carbon reduction mechanism based on per capita emissions (Fig. 6.4).

6.3.5 Design and Implementation of Household CEL Carbon Account Mechanism

The fundamental purpose of the carbon inclusion mechanism is to integrate individuals and households into the carbon reduction framework. Currently, China lacks a

[1] SoJump (also known as wenjuanxing) is a Chinese company that provides online, self-designed questionnaire and related services since 2005. It is widely popular in China—a note by the translator.

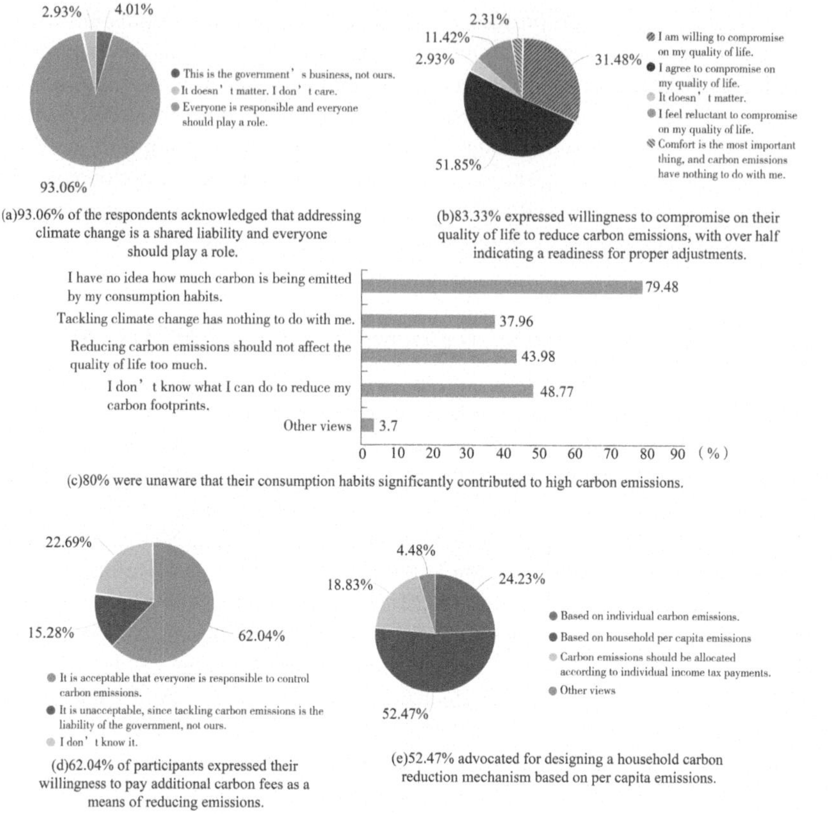

Fig. 6.4 Research conclusions

unified national system for carbon inclusion, prompting various regions and entities, notably local governments, Internet platforms, and banks, to embark on their own initiatives by establishing carbon accounts. However, these existing carbon accounts primarily focus on individuals rather than households, with inconsistencies in statistical principles, standards, and behavioral data that fail to align with the household consumption patterns. Consequently, they inadequately motivate the public to reduce emissions and tap into the potential of consumption-driven change. Family serves as the fundamental unit of society and the cornerstone of daily life, what's more, individual consumption habits and preferences diverge significantly. Since much of our consumption occurs within the family context, encompassing consumption of household energy, food, daily necessities, and transportation tools, a shift towards household-based carbon accounts becomes paramount. Such an approach fosters a stronger sense of universality and shared liability, with household CEL carbon accounts offering more statistically significant records, statistics, and analysis. The design of a household CEL carbon account, therefore, not only resonates with practicality but also holds immense practical value.

1. To establish carbon accounts on a household basis for end consumers.

In the CTMS, a carbon account is established for every household where household consumption data is collected, including the direct energy consumption data of the household and the indirect carbon emission data stemming from the personal consumption activities of its members.

2. To connect account data and consumption data.

By connecting the household registration management system and population data from the Bureau of Public Security, the CTMS can directly generate a household CEL carbon account and automatically place family members into a unified carbon account.

Indirect carbon emissions can be automatically counted in the household CEL account, covering a variety of energy consumption, such as water, electricity, coal, etc., therefore, the household carbon emission data can be automatically calculated.

Direct carbon emissions can be connected with the online payment data of family members, and any consumption can automatically retrieve the associated carbon emission data of the product or service, which is integrated into the household CEL carbon account.

3. Statistics and analysis of household CEL carbon account.

Household CEL carbon account records and calculates household carbon consumption behaviors and decarbonation efforts, offering a visual representation of carbon consumption data that facilitates comprehensive statistics, analysis, and traceability. This allows family members to access and review their household's carbon footprints at any time, fostering a heightened awareness among the public regarding carbon reduction. Understanding the sources of carbon emissions becomes more intuitive, empowering families to adopt a low-carbon lifestyle.

4. To encourage households to become carbon removal units.

Households play a dual role in the carbon cycle, serving as both significant emitters and potential carbon removal units. In rural areas, numerous families engage in the management of land, trees, orchards, ponds, and other natural resources that possess substantial carbon removal potential. With the establishment of a national carbon removal certification system, the carbon removal capabilities of these household-managed resources undergo rigorous verification. Once verified, these carbon removal units can be leveraged as valuable assets, enabling households to participate in negative carbon trading market and generate income from their environmental contributions.

5. Progressive management of carbon price per capita household to achieve annual settlement and secondary distribution.

Analogous to the annual settlement of individual income tax, the household CEL carbon account will undertake the settlement at the end of each year. Adhering to the principle of equity, the government establishes a unified national benchmark for per capita carbon emissions and devises a regulatory framework featuring a progressive carbon pricing system, possibly modeled after a two-tiered structure. Taking the national per capita emission level of 8.0 tons of CO_2 in 2019 as the baseline, the household CEL carbon account automatically tallies annual household emissions to derive per capita carbon emissions of the household. Households exceeding the 8.0-ton threshold will be subject to tiered pricing. Specifically, emissions exceeding the set standard but falling within the first tier will incur an additional carbon fee, calculated at the first tier's rate, which is low and keeps the financial burden on households manageable. Should emissions surpass the first tier's limit, the excess will be charged at the second tier's price, which is a multiple of the first tier's rate. This framework can be extended to encompass third or more tiers, with each subsequent tier imposing an exponentially higher carbon price, further incentivizing households to reduce their carbon footprints. That is, under the CELM, the rich individuals can consume more and generate more carbon emissions, but they must bear the corresponding liability in a progressive manner. If the annual household emissions per capita is below 8.0 tons, the government grants a subsidy, ensuring that low—and middle-income households not only escape additional carbon fees, but can receive additional subsidies for their low-carbon lifestyle. These subsidies come from the progressive payments made by the wealthy for emissions exceeding their allotted threshold. According to Chancel's data (see Fig. 6.3), if per capita carbon emissions remain unchanged, merely 10% of high-income groups would have to pay excess carbon fees, while 90% would have access to subsidies to cover the additional carbon cost of household consumption under the consumer mechanism.

In addition, more incentive mechanisms can be designed based on per capita household carbon emissions, such as offering rewards to zero-carbon families and green families, or giving play to the role of carbon neutral model families. Such initiatives will further propel the adoption of low-carbon consumption patterns and lifestyles nationwide.

6.3.6 Advantages of the Household CEL Carbon Account Mechanism

The household CEL carbon account mechanism has great advantages compared with the current carbon inclusion mechanism.

1. Being sounder and more rational.

The household CEL carbon account mechanism aligns more closely with the realities of household carbon emissions. To account for, analyze, and supervise carbon emission behaviors and data on a household basis accurately reflects the fact that various daily consumption activities are centered around families. This approach enhances operability, feasibility, and provides more meaningful statistical analysis.

2. Generating strong national decarbonation effect.

The main body of decarbonation efforts will be extended to the families and family members, fostering widespread participation in practical decarbonization initiatives. This approach aims to cultivate carbon-reducing behaviors and habits among all individuals, thereby accelerating the overall pace of carbon emission reduction.

3. Incentivizing manufacturers to produce eco-friendly products through consumer choice.

When consumer choice matters, a culture of low-carbon consumption emerges, which, through the price mechanism, incentivizes manufacturers across the industrial chain to produce eco-friendly products. This market-driven approach operates autonomously, resulting in a more efficient and sustainable outcome.

4. Gaining benefits and producing positive feedback.

By subsidizing households that reduce their carbon emissions, we can align low-carbon practices with economic incentives and societal values. This creates a virtuous cycle that encourages more families and individuals to join the ranks of low-carbon advocates, thereby expanding the army of eco-conscious actors.

5. Forming a low-carbon and energy-saving consumption culture.

By analyzing household CEL carbon accounts, we could understand the sources of carbon emissions, and guide the cultivation of a low-carbon and energy-efficient consumption culture.

6. Being highly efficient and of low implementation cost.

Leveraging the government's CTMS system, the household CEL carbon account mechanism can seamlessly integrate with relevant government platforms and major banking payment systems. This facilitates automated data collection, processing, cost calculations, and annual settlements, making the process highly convenient and accessible, thereby readily garnering the support of all residents.

7. Playing an important role in implementing common prosperity and building a better society.

Poor households tend to consume less, resulting in lower per capita carbon emissions, whereas rich households consume more, inherently leading to higher per capita carbon emissions. The cost of these emissions should be equitably distributed across society. By implementing a system based on per capita carbon emissions, rich families and those with significant carbon footprints can be obliged to shoulder a greater liability for mitigating their environmental impact.

8. Providing reference for national low-carbon policies.

Household CEL carbon account data serves as a valuable resource for analyzing consumption patterns, identifying trends in consumption development, and exploring the underlying factors influencing these structures. This information provides crucial support for the formulation of effective low-carbon policies in China.

To sum up, the international community should vigorously promote the household CEL carbon account mechanism based on the CELM. Such an endeavor can effectively address the inefficiencies and financial burdens associated with current carbon inclusion mechanisms.

6.4 Treatment Plan for the Input and Output of Carbon Source Organizations

The primary types of carbon source organizations are comprised of fossil energy enterprises, involving coal, oil, natural gas and other energy resources that are under state ownership. And the largest exporter of carbon sources in the economic sense is the national government. Domestic energy production enterprises and those engaged in energy importation can be classified as carbon source organizations for management.

Carbon source organizations contribute to social carbon footprints in two distinct aspects: firstly, through the carbon emissions generated by their own production and operational process; secondly, by virtue of the carbon content inherent in the production and subsequent sale of their energy products.

The CEL in the energy products, as shown in the CEL input tickets of the carbon source organizations, is obtained by multiplying the total amount of resources and the unit carbon emissions and the state serves as the exporter. Since the energy resources are owned by the state, this conforms to the actual situation.

As the preeminent exporter of carbon sources, the state possesses significant CEL output tickets but no corresponding input ticket, thereby enabling the input of vast amount of negative carbon into the trading market. This results in a huge carbon–neutral revenue right (similar to the right to collect taxes). The CEL mechanism can function as a huge revenue stream for the country (similar to the carbon tax source), and it is completely determined by market transactions, ensuring fairness and high operational efficiency. This revenue can be invested in multiple avenues, including green energy projects, carbon reduction projects, subsidies and carbon funds that facilitates "negative carbon" operations within carbon trading market, functioning as a purchaser of "negative carbon" which is similar to projects such as forest management and carbon sequestration, thereby supporting these endeavors. Section 13.5 of this book will delve into the proposed allocation of government carbon fee revenues, emphasizing the need for legislative oversight in managing this revenue fund, including dedicated earmarking for specific purposes.

The meticulous management of carbon source organizations by the government is paramount, necessitating a holistic approach that invigorates large enterprises while relaxing control over small ones. It is imperative to progressively broaden the scope of regulations, enhancing the precision with which carbon sources are managed.

This should entail the comprehensive and gradual integration of not only coal mines, oil fields, and natural gas enterprises but also a diverse array of carbon-emitting organizations like fertilizer plants, cement factories, livestock farms, and enterprises utilizing materials for fuel production (including charcoal makers). By doing so, we can ascertain the specific carbon emissions per unit of each fuel, tightly control the emission sources, and minimize carbon leakage.

Compared with the current MRV, CELM-based management and data processing poses significantly fewer challenges in terms of enterprise number and data accounting. This method boasts not only simplicity but also reduced verification complexity and heightened accuracy, making it a more viable and efficient approach.

6.5 Data Processing for Carbon Emissions in Imports and Exports as Well as Carbon Tariff Under the CELM

Carbon reduction management system in a responsible country should include the management of carbon emissions associated with both imports and exports. Currently, the functioning of decarbonation systems across countries remains independent, posing significant challenges in achieving synchronization, plagued by a dearth of unified standards. Up to now, it is still impossible to connect and share carbon footprint data worldwide. Therefore, it is necessary to devise tailored decarbonation management programs for imports and exports.

Amidst the intensifying global push towards carbon neutrality, CBAM has finally taken effect in the European Union after years of protracted debate and negotiation. Navigating the carbon disputes that arise in international trade poses a formidable challenge to the continued globalization and sustainable development of international trade. The prevailing CBAM-like frameworks have encountered significant resistance, with even the United States voicing strong opposition. Consequently, theories and schemes rooted in the concept of CELM present the most promising avenue for addressing the pressing issue of carbon tariffs in international trade.

The impact of carbon emissions transcends national borders, necessitating international and global cooperation in carbon reduction efforts. The advent of CTMS that operate on an international scale and facilitate cross-border collaboration holds immense promise. Under this mechanism, those nations or entities that demonstrate lower costs in carbon reduction and carbon sequestration will assume greater liability in carbon mitigation tasks, consequently earning greater negative carbon income. Such an incentive mechanism fosters a healthy international competition in carbon reduction and carbon absorption technologies, thereby accelerating technological advancements and propelling the pace of global carbon reduction.

6.5.1 Carbon Data Processing for Imports

After the CTMS is fully launched, the processing of carbon data pertaining to imported commodities will be processed in different stages and with tailored schemes.

In scenarios where countries are not integrated with the data system for product carbon footprints, the carbon emission content of imports is generally determined using the standardized data from domestic database for carbon emission factors. Subsequently, the government department, with the support of the CTMS, issues a CEL output ticket to the importing organization. For the country concerned, these importing organizations are classified as carbon source organizations, and the carbon content of imported goods contribute to the country's overall data of carbon sources.

Another possible scenario arises when foreign exporters can provide authoritative and accurate data on the carbon content of their products, or when a mutual recognition agreement on the carbon content of commodities exists between the two countries. In such cases, the national unified procedures for verifying the carbon content of imported goods, or the mutual recognition agreement, would be adhered to.

There is another scenario where a standardized system for carbon footprints has been integrated between countries. If the management system for carbon footprints is unified with that of the exporting country, resulting in a systematic opening-up, mutual recognition, and data sharing, then the commodity carbon footprint data from the exporting country can be seamlessly integrated into the CTMS of the importing country.

6.5.2 Carbon Data Processing for Exports

If China's exporting enterprises fail to continuously transfer CEL tickets to the importing country, they are regarded as end-sales organizations and obliged to complete the offset and settlement of CEL domestically. This is not only a necessity to shoulder international liability for climate change but also a pivotal step towards enhancing China's high-quality development standards.

Chinese goods exported to the EU should be offset and settled in China according to the carbon price standard stipulated by the EU. The enterprises must pay carbon fees in China and deliver relatively "zero carbon goods" to the EU, which will be a very important principle for the management of carbon emissions of Chinese commodity exports. In the event that carbon fees are not settled domestically, according to the CBAM principle, the enterprises need to pay carbon tariffs to EU countries, resulting in the loss of national carbon fee revenue. Consequently, all future exports to countries that impose carbon tariffs will be governed by this framework.

6.5.3 Coping with the CBAM

With the globalization of the "1+1" framework of "carbon ticket management system + negative carbon trading market", rooted in the CELM, it effectively addresses the challenge of carbon tariffs in the international trade. By harmonizing data standards and unifying carbon pricing between trading partners, the issue of carbon tariffs vanishes. Conversely, when one party, akin to the current EU's CBAM, pioneers the move, it introduces numerous complexities, including the intricate procedures for levying, allocating, and utilizing carbon tariffs in international trade, which are elaborated upon in pertinent sections of Chap. 10. Should China spearhead the advancement of an international negative carbon trading market, it would indeed confront similar challenges upon importing goods. However, the pivotal advantage lies in the fact that the carbon emission fee is settled within China's jurisdiction, thereby granting China the initiative. Presently, China finds itself in a passive position within the EU's CBAM framework, having to advocate for the discussion of CBAM tariff barriers under the WTO framework.

Countries worldwide should promptly establish a standardized international "1+1" system rooted in the CELM, which, can effectively address challenges concerning carbon tariffs akin to the EU's CBAM. By solely negotiating the phased pricing structure of "international negative carbon" and mutually abiding by these agreements, nations can significantly diminish the complexity of negotiations and facilitate a smoother consensus-building process.

6.5.4 Carbon Tariffs for China's Imports

If China accelerates the construction and development of a negative carbon trading market based on the CELM, and systematically incorporates the cost of carbon emissions (carbon price) into all domestic products, two primary scenarios emerge in managing imported products.

In the first scenario, imported products have already paid carbon fees through either a carbon tax or offsetting within a negative carbon trading market in the exporting country, for example, in the EU where the carbon price exceeds that in China. Their products can directly enter the Chinese market. Provided they provide credible carbon footprints and evidence for carbon fee payment, they are eligible for exemption from carbon tariffs.

In the second scenario, imported products are not subject to carbon pricing mechanisms, such as a carbon tax or a negative carbon trading market, in their exporting countries, or the carbon price is notably lower than that of China. In this case, once China establishes a robust carbon market, it may consider imposing carbon tariffs on these imported products. However, China should clarify that the revenue generated from these tariffs will be invested in green energy and carbon reduction initiatives within the exporting countries. This approach ensures mutual benefits, as the reinvestment of revenues from carbon tariffs fosters eco-friendly growth in the exporting nations. The advantages for China, arising from this strategy, are twofold:

Firstly, the investment country, China, will be in charge of the entire investment, financing and construction process. This includes the design, execution of the general contract, and the provision of essential equipment, all originating from China.

Secondly, this approach aims to bolster the competitiveness of Chinese products globally. As China's carbon market matures rapidly and carbon prices escalate, there is a risk of carbon leakage within China, potentially undermining the competitiveness of Chinese enterprises' offerings in both domestic and international markets, accordingly, this approach helps prevent carbon leakage in China. This issue, similar to EU's carbon tariffs, needs to be considered in advance.

6.6 Trial Operation and Implementation of the CELM

Generally speaking, the CELM is a national decarbonation system, and the government needs to coordinate the operation of the national "carbon ticket management system" and the "negative carbon trading market", thereby ensuring the full functionality of the CELM and fostering a tangible reduction in emissions.

However, a notable gap persists between theory and practice. Individuals frequently harbor doubts regarding the transition to new systems, which often commences with modest pilot projects before gradually expanding their scope of implementation. For instance, a localized pilot is undertaken to validate the system's theoretical foundations and software reliability. However, given that CELM theory is inherently driven across the entire supply chain, such localized pilots can inadvertently lead to incomplete data issues. In China, numerous provincial and municipal carbon markets have been undergoing pilot testing for over a decade, yet they have struggled to yield satisfactory results. The lackluster performance has hindered the effective realization of emission reduction goals, thereby casting doubt on the overall progress of the decarbonation system. The fluid nature of CO_2, the expansive scope of the supply chain, and the shortcomings encountered in the primary carbon market pilots collectively suggest that a localized approach may not be suitable for an effective carbon reduction system, including the carbon market itself.

The current pilot project on carbon market has encountered two pivotal challenges that have hindered its success. Firstly, there exist profound problems within the top-level design, rendering any pilot project, regardless of its scale, inherently unlikely to achieve success. Secondly, the limited scope of these pilot projects has led to a multitude of problems that are difficult to generalize and apply to the broader, larger system. Consequently, this narrow focus often fosters cognitive biases and misconceptions.

Consequently, the development and operation of the CELM ought to be entrusted to the department specifically mandated by the central government. A more effective approach would be to commence nationwide operations concurrently. During the initial trial phase, it is advisable to set the carbon price at zero, focusing initially on the circulation of carbon tickets. This strategy ensures minimal exposure to potential risks and resistance that may arise from larger-scale pilot endeavors.

6.6.1 Trial Operation of the CELM

There are two possible pilot schemes for the CELM.

6.6.1.1 Scheme I: Trial Operation in the Electric Power Industry Chain

Following the implementation of the "1+1" framework by the government, the government issues CEL output tickets to coal enterprises according to their carbon source data. Specifically, whenever a coal enterprise supplies coal to an electric power company, it must accompany the delivery with a CEL ticket, which is then passed on to the power grid company upon the subsequent supply of electricity. Conversely, renewable energy sources like photovoltaic and wind power, upon delivery to the grid company, are exempt from or carry minimal CEL tickets. When the power grid company distributes electricity to electricity retailers, it issues a CEL ticket to these entities. Subsequently, when selling electricity to end-users, the retailers levy a carbon fee that is commensurate with the overall carbon content. Notably, during the pilot phase, this carbon fee is being trialed at a significantly reduced rate to facilitate a smooth transition.

In this way, the CEL tickets circulate within the entire power system, allowing for continuous evaluation during the trial operation stage. This iterative process enables the timely identification of problems and their subsequent improvement, thereby enhancing the overall effectiveness and achieving desirable outcomes.

Within this scheme, the trial operation of the negative carbon trading market can draw upon valuable experiences from the established market for carbon emission rights, such as the design of trading rules and the development of trading systems. Given the standardization of negative carbon products, the negative carbon trading market under the CELM bypasses the need for pilot projects in provinces, allowing the direct establishment of a unified national carbon market.

6.6.1.2 Scheme II: Nationwide Trial Operation at Zero Carbon Price

In the trial operation stage, the carbon price can be initially set at zero, solely retaining the flow of pure carbon tickets. This approach significantly minimizes the operational risk associated with the CELM. With the carbon price set at zero, it eliminates the formation of price signals that might otherwise disrupt the transactional links of the industrial chain and the broader macroeconomy, allowing solely for the circulation of carbon footprints within the system. Despite the absence of monetary transactions, the operation of pure data facilitates the visibility of carbon footprints for various industries and enterprises, alongside industry-specific and enterprise-level carbon emission-related indicators. The transparency and digitization of these carbon emission data play a pivotal role in fostering more effective carbon reduction efforts. Consequently, the operation of the CELM can be considered risk-free. In contrast to the current trading market for carbon emission rights, which primarily encompasses the power industry and has encountered numerous challenges, resulting in significant macroeconomic impacts and prompting several regions to limit their electricity supply, the CELM offers a more comprehensive and stable solution.

Based on the above analysis, China can embark on a nationwide trial operation of the CELM with manageable risks and a swifter manifestation of its full potential. During the initial phase of this national trial, the system will solely focus on the flow of carbon input and output tickets, with the carbon price set at zero yuan. This approach allows for the accumulation of valuable experience and data throughout the trial operation period. Should the process remain free of major issues, a thorough evaluation can pave the way for the prompt implementation of a comprehensive "1+1" system.

6.6.1.3 Feasibility of Trial in a Single City and a Single Industry

The "1+1" Decarbonation System based on the CELM, when applied solely within a single city or industry for trial operations, is unlikely to yield significant results. This is due to the fundamental nature of the CELM, which is designed as a comprehensive carbon reduction framework encompassing all organizations and goods across society. As no industry operates in isolation, it inherently interacts with other industries and regions through transactions. Consequently, limiting the system's scope to a single region or industry omits crucial data from these interconnected processes. While carbon emission data within the targeted industry and region can indeed be accurately gathered, it becomes challenging to procure comprehensive data on products and services sourced from other provinces and cities. The incompleteness and potential inaccuracies of such data significantly increase the processing workload, compromising data accuracy and ultimately diminishing the overall operational effectiveness of the CELM. Hence, it is not feasible to employ the CELM as a pilot program confined to a solitary industry or region.

6.6.1.4 Initial Strategy and Plan of CELM Operation

Theoretically, the operation of the CELM exerts minimal direct influence on the broader macroeconomic system. This is attributed to the system's design, which evenly distributes carbon emission costs across the entire economy. Consequently, the impact on individual organizations remains negligible, resulting in a similarly muted overall macroeconomic effect. On the contrary, the CELM can be harnessed to enhance macroeconomic operations and elevate economic quality.

In practical operation, given the inherent uncertainty of the impact on the economy during the initial operational phase, it is advisable to initiate the price of negative carbon at a low level or even at zero. Following a period of trial operation, this price can be gradually increased to reflect the actual cost of achieving carbon neutrality. This process of carbon price increase necessitates a protracted timeline, taking into account factors such as domestic macroeconomic resilience, international product competitiveness, and the progression towards achieving dual carbon targets. To ensure a smooth and stable transition, a dedicated committee of experts and a research and design department should be established to oversee the regulation of carbon prices, thereby mitigating the risk of systemic shocks.

6.6.2 Controlling Illegal Profits Made by Falsely Issuing Carbon Tickets

The CTMS possesses a robust capability for early detection of abnormal situations, with its data being intricately interlinked through various layers. Nevertheless, it cannot entirely eradicate the potential for arbitrage perpetrated by illegitimate entities. In this regard, the VAT system offers valuable experience, as it has successfully mitigated the prevalence of illegal VAT activities over time. By leveraging a combination of "system + technology", the VAT system has effectively curbed fraudulent VAT arbitrage. Similarly, the operation of CTMS can benefit from this approach. On one hand, legislation is essential to impose a degree of oversight on the fraudulent issuance of carbon tickets and to raise the legal consequences for such violations. On the other hand, harnessing technological solutions to address the issue and minimize manual supervision, such as integrating with the VAT system for data verification, can be highly effective in preventing arbitrage of false carbon tickets.

6.6.3 Integration with the VAT System

The value-added tax system in China is arguably one of the most formidable tax systems in the world. By integrating the data of the carbon ticket system with the VAT system, we can enable cross-verification of carbon ticket data, thereby facilitating the development of an efficient and streamlined audit and verification system. To optimize the implementation efficiency of this system, it is advisable that the operation of the CELM be entrusted to the financial system. Meanwhile, the Ministry of Ecology and Environment should spearhead the design and formulation of management regulations, while the financial department oversees the execution of the carbon ticket system.

6.7 Case Study: Collection of Sewage Treatment Fees in Shanghai and Its Significance to the Collection of Carbon Fees

6.7.1 History of the Collection of Sewage Treatment Fees in Shanghai

In 1976, Shanghai Municipal Drainage Management Office was established as an independent institution responsible for sewage collection, transportation and treatment, as well as the operation and management of flood prevention and drainage in the central city.

Since the reform and opening up in 1978, in order to speed up the construction of infrastructure and the management of water environment, and safeguard urban flood prevention security, the management system and operational mechanism of the drainage industry in Shanghai have been constantly adjusted and optimized.

On November 4, 1986, the Shanghai Municipal Government passed the *Interim Measures for the Collection of Fees for Urban Drainage Facilities in Shanghai*, and the drainage fee was levied at 0.12 yuan /m^3. It marked a pivotal shift from exclusive government funding for drainage management expenses towards a more equitable sharing model involving the state, collectives, and individuals.

In 1987, Shanghai started the construction of the first phase of the combined sewage treatment project, with a total investment of 1.6 billion yuan, augmented by a significant loan of 160 million US dollars from the World Bank. As a condition attached to this financial support loan, the World Bank proposed that a dedicated drainage enterprise, rather than a traditional public institution, should oversee the operational management of the sewage system upon completion. Furthermore, it advocated for the establishment of a drainage charge system.

In December 1995, Shanghai Municipal Drainage Co., Ltd. was established, and Shanghai drainage charges underwent a transition from traditional institutional charges to operational charges.

On December 7, 1995, the Shanghai Municipal People's Government promulgated the *Measures for the Administration of the Collection of Drainage Facilities Fees in Shanghai*, explicitly stating that the Shanghai Municipal Engineering Administration Bureau is the administrative department responsible for the collection of drainage fees, and the Shanghai Municipal Drainage Co., Ltd. is responsible for the collection and management of drainage fees.

In December 1996, the *Regulations of Drainage Management in Shanghai* was enacted to re-establish the Shanghai Municipal Drainage Management Office, which clarified the separation of supervision and management subjects. Subsequently, in 2004, the Shanghai Municipal Bureau of Water Resources transferred the administrative responsibilities pertaining to drainage enterprises to the Urban Investment Corporation, successfully achieving the separation of drainage management and operational functions.

In 2016, the *Implementation Measures for the Collection and Use of Sewage Treatment Fees in Shanghai* was issued, marking a pivotal shift in the nature of sewage treatment fees, which were transformed into administrative charges.

Sewage treatment fees constitute a vital source of non-tax revenue for the government, with the Shanghai Municipal Bureau of Water Resources entrusting water supply companies to collect these fees from all users across Shanghai. The entirety of these collected fees is then remitted to the government, where they are incorporated into its fund budget management framework for dedicated purposes.

The charge consists of two components: water supply fees and sewage treatment fees, which are calculated as follows:

$$\text{Water supply fee} = \text{water consumption}\left(\text{m}^3\right) \times \text{unit price}\left(2.25\ \text{yuan/m}^3\right);$$

$$\text{Sewage treatment fee} = \text{water consumption}\left(\text{m}^3\right) \times 0.9 \times \text{unit price}\left(2.0\ \text{yuan/m}^3\right).$$

Among them, 0.9 is the internationally accepted displacement coefficient, indicating that the sewage volume generated corresponds to approximately 90% of the water supplied. The total charge is the sum of the two components (Fig. 6.5).

Meter reading	Last meter reading	684	This meter reading	713	Water consumption
	Meter state	Normal			29
Water supply fee	Annual cumulative water consumption(m^3)	Current water consumption (m^3)	Unit price (yuan/m^3)		Amount (yuan)
	In 2023, the accumulated water volume for your household has reached 29 m^3, while there is 191 m^3 available remaining for the first-tier usage.	First-tier 29			65. 25
sewage treatment fee	Water consumption (m^3)	Unit price (yuan/m^3)	Calculation method		Amount (yuan)
	29				52. 20
Previous balance (yuan)		0. 04	Current amount (yuan)		117. 45
Carry-over of small amount		0. 09	Amount payable (yuan)		¥117. 40
Note:	Our company has received the water fee of 101.3 yuan paid by your account in February 2023, thank you!				
Note:	2023 settlement period: March 2023 to February 2024				

Fig. 6.5 Water bill for residents of Shanghai, China (selected)

6.7.2 Administrative Procedures for Price Adjustment of Drainage/Sewage Treatment Fees

Due to rising prices, improved treatment standards and increased investment, the unit cost of sewage treatment has undergone numerous adjustments throughout the years.

Pursuant to the *Measures for the Administration of the Collection and Use of Sewage Treatment Fees* jointly promulgated by the Ministry of Finance, the National Development and Reform Commission and the Ministry of Housing and Urban–Rural Development, the standards for collecting sewage treatment fees shall be formulated in accordance with the principle of ensuring the smooth operation of sewage treatment facilities, covering the expenses of sludge treatment and disposal, and allowing for reasonable profits. Additionally, the opinions of local departments in charge of pricing, finance and drainage at and above the county level shall be incorporated. Before implementation, these standards must be submitted to the respective level of people's government for approval. Furthermore, urban drainage authorities are mandated to transparently disclose the rationale, entities subject to collection, standards, procedures, legal obligations, and other pertinent details surrounding the collection of sewage treatment fees.

In Shanghai, residential sewage treatment fees are included in the *Shanghai Pricing Hearing Catalogue*, mandating that the pricing and adjustment of sewage treatment fees must undergo the rigorous pricing hearing process. This process involves conducting hearings and engaging in various forms of consultation to solicit opinions and suggestions from all stakeholders. Only upon obtaining the approval of the municipal government, following these comprehensive hearings, can the collection standards for sewage treatment fees be adjusted. The collection of such fees in Shanghai is thus governed by a transparent and inclusive framework.

6.7.3 The Collection of Sewage Treatment Fees in Shanghai

From March 1, 2016, the sewage treatment fees paid by units and individuals within the service scope of Shanghai sewage treatment facilities have been collected by public water supply enterprises, acting as agents designated by the Shanghai Municipal Bureau of Water Resources. The entirety of these fees is subsequently remitted to the municipal treasury, where they are allocated as special funds. The Shanghai Municipal Bureau of Water Resources ensures transparency by annually disclosing the revenue and expenditure pertaining to municipal sewage treatment fees. In 2021, the city successfully collected 2.673 billion yuan in sewage treatment fees and disbursed 4.08 billion yuan towards sewage treatment service expenses.

The expenditure incurred for sewage treatment significantly surpasses the income generated, necessitating price adjustments in subsequent years. These adjustments aim to facilitate the construction of sewage treatment projects and water environment treatment efforts, while also addressing the funding shortfall for the construction, operation, and maintenance of sewage treatment facilities.

6.7.4 Reference for Carbon Fee Collection at the Consumer End

The historical experience and practice of collecting sewage treatment fees (drainage fees) in Shanghai serve as a valuable benchmark for the government in devising consumer-end collection methodologies and mechanisms. Its comprehensive collection framework, robust administrative management system, and transparent pricing procedures at the terminal can offer insightful guidance.

Given the substantially larger scope of carbon emission charges, which encompass various commodities and consumption activities, the government must build upon the existing framework of public service expenses while striving for innovation. In crafting the fee system, the government should prioritize enhancing efficiency, minimizing administrative overheads, and mitigating potential resistance from the public.

Carbon fees should be collected by each point-of-sale organization, with minor adjustment to existing sales receipts by listing a separate item: carbon fee, which offers two key advantages: firstly, consumers perceive it as an individual cost rather than a product price increase, fostering a sense of shared liability for carbon reduction. Secondly, it significantly enhances public awareness of decarbonation by visibly showcasing the emissions and associated fees for every purchase, thereby motivating individuals to adopt eco-friendly practices. Moreover, this approach addresses the prevailing issue of excessive packaging in high-end goods, where the carbon footprints and cost of packaging often outweigh the product itself. Once carbon emission cost, as a separate item, is included in the total product cost, market forces and heightened consumer consciousness will naturally drive a reduction in wasteful packaging, leading to a more sustainable consumption pattern.

Currently, online payment has been widely popularized. By integrating consumers' personal electronic payment accounts with their respective household CEL carbon accounts, the data of household CEL carbon accounts will become increasingly complete and accurate. This integration serves as a solid cornerstone for implementing a tiered charging policy tailored to individual households, using both the household unit and per capita carbon emissions as the benchmarks. As a result, the carbon fee policy will evolve into a more refined and effective framework.

Currently, China's electricity prices encompass various non-tax revenues approved by the State Council, which are integrated into the cost of electricity. These include funds allocated to support reservoir immigration (for large and medium-sized projects), renewable energy initiatives, and rural electrification loans, among others. Notably, the Three Gorges Water Conservancy Project adds an additional 1.5 fen per kWh in Shanghai. Consequently, the sales price of electricity comprises a multi-faceted formula that incorporates the on-grid electricity price, transmission and distribution fees, transmission and distribution losses, as well as government-mandated funds. Specifically, the sales price is formulated as: sales price = on-grid electricity price + transmission and distribution fees + transmission and distribution losses + government funds + additional charges. At present, government funds are included in the price, with no separate item listed, resulting in a lack of transparency and a strong call for social reform. Drawing parallels from the longstanding tradition of separately billing sewage treatment fees alongside water bills, we contend that integrating carbon emission fees as a distinct item within the electricity price would not only enhance clarity but also garner widespread acceptance from consumers.

Chapter 7
Carbon Ticket Management System (CTMS)

Carbon Ticket Management System (CTMS) is one of the two core systems within the CELM-based "1+1" Decarbonation System, functioning as a comprehensive big data platform that meticulously tracks and manages the carbon footprints of every commodity across society. It clarifies the CEL of all organizations and individuals in the whole society, thereby furnishing crucial data pillars that underpin the decarbonation system in the whole society. Research shows that the global climate challenge has proven intractable over the past three decades, primarily due to the enigmatic nature of carbon footprint data. Solving the challenge in this complex, information-scarce black box scenario has been akin to a blind man attempting to comprehend the grandeur of an elephant. The introduction of CTMS, rooted in the CELM, unleashes immense potential by illuminating these previously obscured facets.

The cornerstone tasks pertaining to CTMS operation encompass the management of carbon sources and their organizations as well as carbon removals (carbon sinks) and their organizations, along with the system's overarching design and operational framework. These vital aspects will be the focal points of our subsequent discussions in this chapter.

7.1 Carbon Source Organizations and Carbon Source Management

Based on the CELM theory, effective governance of carbon source organizations and their data by the government paves the way for seamless integration into the CTMS. Once the precise carbon liability metrics are inputted into the system, the subsequent management of societal carbon emissions becomes self-sustaining, facilitated by market-driven transactions. The CTMS excels in capturing the comprehensive, end-to-end carbon footprints of every product in real-time, ensuring data accuracy and completeness. With a robust foundation of reliable carbon source data, the

B. Yang, *The Carbon Emission Liability Mechanism*,
https://doi.org/10.1007/978-981-96-3612-9_7

CTMS enhances the efficiency and effectiveness of carbon reduction management, significantly streamlining the current carbon management landscape and realizing substantial savings in societal costs associated with carbon data management.

Hence, the management of carbon source organizations and carbon sources is paramount. The establishment of a fair and efficient management system for both carbon source organizations and carbon sources forms the cornerstone for ensuring the accuracy of CTMS system data.

7.1.1 Types of Carbon Source Organizations

There are many types of carbon source organizations. Given the diverse nature of carbon source organizations, a strategic approach to their management is crucial. This can be achieved through a phased implementation, initially focusing on larger entities and gradually extending to smaller ones. By incrementally expanding the scope of control, a more comprehensive and inclusive management system can be realized, ensuring a more holistic and effective oversight.

7.1.1.1 Major Types of Carbon Source Organizations

1. Energy resource organizations

Coal, oil, natural gas and other energy production enterprises, along with charcoal and other fuel production enterprises, are carbon source enterprises. The government must implement a unified management framework for these enterprises nationwide, measuring and making their production output and carbon content per unit of production available for public. Energy import enterprises are also included. Considering China's substantial imports of coal, oil, and natural gas, these import enterprises, initially acting as both traders and carbon source organizations, should be granted carbon output tickets. In a scenario where an internationally recognized CTMS data standard emerges, facilitating seamless data exchange and sharing among nations, the process would be further streamlined, allowing for direct utilization of CEL figures from the CTMS system in the exporting countries. Nevertheless, ongoing spot checks and rigorous verification of carbon data remain vital, which will become an important task implemented by the customs in the future.

Fossil energy supply enterprises are the most important type of carbon source organizations. According to the *Global Carbon Budget 2022*, released by the by the Global Carbon Project international science team, "total global CO_2 emissions of 40.6 Gt are projected for 2022", while 90% from fossil carbon, therefore, the management of carbon source data from such organizations represents the foundational tier of carbon data governance across society.

2. Intermediate emission organizations

The fertilizer industry, despite not being categorized as an energy sector, necessitates inclusion in carbon management efforts since their products produce chemical reactions in farmland to produce CO_2 during use. The innovation and use of agricultural fertilizers have revolutionized crop productivity and the quality of agricultural products. However, their process of production and use is accompanied by substantial GHG emissions, primarily consisting of CO_2, ammonia, and nitrogen oxides. Notably, CO_2 emissions surpass 70% of the total emissions generated during the production of fertilizers.

The country will establish a standardized framework for assessing carbon emissions per unit product across various fertilizer products throughout their production and utilization cycle and publicly disclose a unified standard value. Furthermore, comprehensive statistics on the aggregate carbon footprints will be compiled, factoring in both production capacity and carbon emissions per unit product, and these data will be integrated into the CTMS.

The cement industry stands as one of the most significant contributors to carbon emissions from intermediate production processes. Notably, in 2020, China's cement sector emitted approximately 1.466 Gt of carbon, constituting a substantial 14.3% of China's total carbon emissions. This placed it second only to the steel industry, which accounted for roughly 15% of national carbon emissions, highlighting the cement industry's pivotal role in carbon reduction efforts and emphasizing its status as a key sector for mitigation strategies.

The carbon emissions generated in the production process of the cement industry stem primarily from two primary sources. Firstly, an overwhelming 80% to 85% of cement raw materials comprise limestone. The decomposition of carbonate in the raw materials in the kiln results in the release of CO_2, accounting for a significant 55% to 70% of the total carbon emissions throughout the entire production cycle. Secondly, the combustion process necessitates the consumption of vast amounts of fuel. It is estimated that the production of one ton of cement and one ton of cement clinker currently emits approximately 617 kg and 866 kg of CO_2, respectively. Additionally, substantial amounts of secondary energy are also consumed during the grinding of raw clinker.

The carbon source data of intermediate emission organizations constitutes a crucial component of their overall carbon emissions. The government departments should oversee this data, issue CEL output tickets, and integrate them into the CTMS. It should be noted that the carbon content of external materials, such as purchased energy materials and electricity, is indicated by the CEL input tickets which show the amount of CEL undertaken by the upstream entities, and is freely traded and transferred within the CELM, alleviating the need for specific government intervention in their management.

3. Animal husbandry organizations

According to the statistics from the Food and Agriculture Organization of the United Nations (FAO), the livestock sector contributes significantly to global emissions, accounting for 9% of total CO_2 emissions and an 18% of GHG emissions, thereby positioning it as a pivotal carbon-emitting industry. The primary sources of carbon emissions within the animal husbandry industry stem from direct processes, including vast quantities of manure and urine generated from livestock breeding, CO_2 exhaled by livestock and poultry during respiration, intestinal gas emissions, as well as emissions originating from various wastes and pollutants that accumulate during the livestock and poultry breeding processes.

The state ought to establish carbon emission standards tailored specifically for individual pigs, cows, sheep, and other livestock and poultry species. These standards can serve as a benchmark for pig farms, sheep farms, dairy cattle farms, and so forth, enabling each facility to determine the carbon emissions per animal. Consequently, the aggregate carbon footprints of a farm can be easily calculated by multiplying the number of livestock by their respective carbon emission standards.

4. General import enterprises

Imported products inherently carry a carbon content and need to be acknowledged as a contributor to carbon emissions. The government faces two distinct approaches in addressing this issue, as outlined in Sect. 6.5. If the CEL recognized by China is settled in the exporting country, the Chinese Government will refrain from levying additional charges on the importer. Conversely, if this is not the case, the pertinent administrative authorities in China will issue CEL output tickets to import enterprises.

Import enterprises should provide credible evidence of the carbon content associated with their imported goods. In situations where a definitive carbon content cannot be ascertained, the products will be subject to the standard carbon content value prescribed by the Chinese Government.

5. Waste departments

The waste sector mainly engages in solid waste landfill treatment, biological treatment, incineration and open combustion, wastewater treatment, etc. According to the *Third National Communication on Climate Change of the People's Republic of China*, carbon emissions generated from waste treatment activities in 2010 amounted to 800 tons, accounting for 0.09% of the total CO_2 emissions for that year.

6. Other organizations

Forests, although often perceived as carbon removals, can also contribute to carbon emissions, particularly in instances of forest fires. These emissions are ideally suited for deduction within carbon removal management frameworks.

As carbon management practices continue to evolve and become more sophisticated, governments have the opportunity to progressively expand and deepen the scope of their interventions in order to achieve substantial carbon reductions.

7.1.1.2 Are Fossil-Fuel Plants Carbon Sources?

Under the prevailing approach to carbon emission control, fossil-fuel power plants often take center stage. However, the CELM theory presents a starkly contrasting view. Under the CELM, fossil-fuel plants are not classified as carbon sources. They are responsible for energy conversion, converting fossil energy (primary energy) into electric energy (secondary energy), thereby occupying an intermediary position in the energy chain. Consequently, they are not deemed the primary source of carbon emissions. However, coal-fired power plants are indeed large carbon emitters and are still important targets for carbon reduction efforts, but with different perspectives. The utilization of energy and the application of carbon absorption technology have become the key factors.

In terms of carbon reduction for enterprises such as fossil-fuel plants, the CELM introduces a dual-way incentive mechanism in the market, addressing the following two aspects:

- Firstly, it incentivizes the enhancement of energy efficiency and the reduction of carbon intensity in electricity generation. By improving energy efficiency, enterprises can lower their overall production costs, resulting in reduced output to the grid company and higher profit margins per unit of production. This, in turn, fosters price and brand competitiveness (greener enterprises), ultimately enhancing the competitiveness of their products in the market.
- Secondly, carbon removals produced by the application of carbon absorption technology should be certified as "Real Negative CO_2". Under the CELM, the power plant already assumes their normal liability for decarbonation, and the employment of additional carbon-absorbing devices should be rewarded separately. The quantity of negative carbon assets approved by a carbon removal certification entity can be used to offset CEL within the corporate carbon account or traded for profit in the carbon market.

7.1.1.3 Efficiency of Carbon Source Data Management of the CTMS

The MRV cost under the current management mechanism for carbon emission rights is huge and prone to problems.

In contrast, under the CELM, there are fewer carbon source organizations, thereby drastically decreasing the administrative burden and complexity faced by the government. This streamlined approach facilitates more precise and effortless access to carbon source data for the authorities. One key advantage of the CELM over the CTMS lies in its integration with the carbon footprint big data system. By ensuring robust carbon source management and accurate data input, the CELM enables the swift, comprehensive, and precise collection of societal carbon footprint data, achieving remarkable efficiency.

7.1.2 Verification of Carbon Source Amount of the Organizations

The verification of the total amount of carbon sources in the carbon source organization constitutes the cornerstone for establishing the carbon footprint data of the whole society. The methodology used by the government to calculate and issue carbon output allowances to these organizations is rooted in the formula:

$$\begin{aligned}\text{Amount of carbon source} &= \text{output of carbon source products}\\ &\quad \times \text{ carbon content per unit carbon source product}\end{aligned}$$

The output of carbon source products is facilitated by the VAT system, which streamlines the verification process. This approach ensures greater accuracy by cross-referencing enterprise-reported figures, thereby minimizing audit efforts and enhancing overall efficiency.

The determination and verification of carbon content per unit carbon source product are likewise fairly straightforward, primarily relying on chemical formulas that yield relatively consistent values. These values can be rigorously tested and validated by government-accredited testing institutes, ensuring their authenticity. In managing test reports, stringent measures must be in place, as evidenced by several fraud cases reported in China in 2021. While containing such incidents may not pose immense challenges, the system necessitates gradual reinforcement and refinement to plug any potential loopholes and safeguard integrity.

On April 8, 2022, the National Dual Carbon Leading Group held an online meeting to crack down on carbon emission data fabrication, reported issues related to carbon market data fabrication and urged to crack down on carbon emission data fabrication and promote the healthy and orderly development of the carbon market.

The meeting pointed out that achieving carbon peak and neutrality is a major strategic decision made by the Central Committee of the Party with President Xi at the core after careful consideration. The carbon market stands as a vital market-driven mechanism pivotal to advancing dual carbon initiatives, wherein carbon emission data forms the cornerstone of trading activities, and data quality serves as the lifeblood of this market. The discovery of data fabrication by certain intermediary service agencies has gravely undermined market fairness, disrupted orderly market functioning, eroded market confidence, and significantly threatened the healthy development of the carbon market. This, in turn, has severely impeded the systematic promotion of dual-carbon endeavors, with repercussions that are exceedingly detrimental and necessitate stringent measures for eradication.

The meeting stressed that all relevant departments across regions should attach great importance to the problem of data fabrication. By adhering to a problem-centric approach and maintaining a "zero tolerance" stance, stringent measures must be taken to rigorously investigate and handle fraud cases, thereby creating a formidable deterrent and resolutely preventing the recurrence of data fabrication. Strengthening inspection and oversight is imperative to effectively rectify identified issues, thoroughly investigate the liability of concerned units and individuals, and encourage mutual learning through self-assessment and corrective actions. Additionally, conducting timely special inspections with a "look-back" perspective is necessary. Leveraging the implementation of rectification efforts as a catalyst, a robust problem-detection mechanism should be established, enhancing routine supervision, tightening accountability, solidifying liability across all stakeholders, and ultimately fostering the healthy, stable, and long-term development of China's carbon market.

Leveraging CTMS-based carbon data management significantly reinforces the benefits of a "system + technology" framework, enabling substantial mitigation of issues and substantial reductions in management costs.

7.1.3 Certified Reduction of the Amount of Carbon Sources

Certain enterprises, notably coal-fired power plants, employ cutting-edge technologies to diminish carbon emissions per unit of carbon source. Without considering the carbon absorption device, their emissions are notably below industry standards, indicating a lower carbon intensity per unit of carbon source compared to the initial authorized carbon content for energy resource organizations. This means that the carbon input of upstream energy resource enterprises is larger than the actual carbon emissions per unit of carbon source of enterprises. To address this, the government should introduce a certification process for verification and reduction, so as to encourage the transformation towards carbon reduction technologies within the industrial chain and the adoption of new energy utilization technologies.

Moreover, the verification of certified reductions necessitates the establishment of a set of strict procedures and systems.

The verification of certified reduction should establish a set of strict procedures and systems.

7.1.4 Management Strategy: Focus on Large Emitters and Relax Control Over Small Ones, and Gradually Deepen and Expand

Under the CELM, as long as the carbon source data in the CTMS is accurate and complete, the carbon reduction system of the whole society can automatically operate and be very effective. Therefore, the management of carbon source organizations and their associated data management holds paramount importance.

The carbon source organizations should be comprehensively managed, given their diverse categories. In executing this management, a phased approach is advisable, prioritizing larger organizations while giving freedom to the smaller ones. By gradually expanding the scope of control, a more comprehensive management of carbon source organizations can be achieved, steadily approaching the goal of capturing 100% of total carbon source data. It's important to recognize that this overall management is a gradual process, requiring patience and strategic planning. Specifically, focusing on managing the major fossil energy carbon sources, namely coal, oil, and natural gas, can effectively control an estimated 90% of total carbon emissions. This approach stands in contrast to the current emphasis on coal-fired power industry alone, demonstrating that the CELM-based decarbonation program can prioritize larger organizations while giving freedom to the smaller ones in the real sense.

Management schemes tailored for different types of carbon source organizations and their corresponding data vary greatly. On the basis of the foundational knowledge gained from managing fossil energy carbon sources, gradually establishing and improving the management system of various carbon sources will not be too challenging in terms of technical difficulty and execution difficulty.

When establishing various carbon source management systems, it is imperative to ensure that there is no overlap or omission of items. This meticulous approach is crucial for achieving a system that is both scientifically sound and practically efficient, guaranteeing accurate data and seamless implementation.

7.1.5 Design and Capability Improvement of the Supervisory System

With the increase of carbon price, the carbon cost associated with the carbon liability will be integrated into product pricing, fostering significant stakeholder interests. In the past two years, China has witnessed a surge in carbon emission data fabrication cases, with reputable consulting firms involved, significantly hindering the progress towards the nation's dual carbon goals. Consequently, enhancing the regulatory framework is paramount in addressing this issue.

Firstly, optimizing verification procedures and systems is crucial. The verification framework must be continuously adapted to evolving circumstances and challenges, undergoing gradual refinement and enhancement to ensure its effectiveness.

Secondly, strengthening management and evaluation of certification entities is imperative. More rigorous regulations should be implemented for managing these units, particularly for third-party institutions found guilty of fabrication. Penalties should be escalated, ranging from fines to disqualification and potentially even criminal prosecution, thereby raising the cost of violations.

Thirdly, harnessing the vast data of the CTMS is vital, ensuring openness, transparency, and enhanced public scrutiny. The CTMS encapsulates the carbon footprint data of entire societal organizations, and the carbon emission factor database it generates should be accessible to the public, bolstering data transparency and fostering stronger public oversight. Additionally, the system should be augmented with advanced data analytics and early warning capabilities to further refine its functionality.

7.2 Carbon Removal Organizations and Carbon Removal Management

Carbon neutrality does not mean zero carbon emissions; instead, it refers to achieving net-zero emissions. There are emissions, but there is also absorption that offset those emissions, resulting in net-zero emissions. Consequently, the role of carbon removal organizations (enterprises), or carbon sink organizations (enterprises), is vital. The application of Carbon Capture, Utilization, and Storage (CCUS) technology will be essential in the future progress towards achieving carbon neutrality.

China must promptly incentivize the carbon removal organizations to contribute to carbon reduction efforts through the carbon market, encouraging the research and development as well as application of carbon reduction technologies. At the same time, it is necessary to strengthen the management of carbon removal organizations and the certified carbon removals. The implementation of Chinese Certified Carbon Sink (CCCS) system should be prioritized on the agenda as soon as possible.

7.2.1 Types of Carbon Removal Organizations

A diverse array of carbon removal organizations exists, and below, we present an introductory overview and analysis of their primary types.

1. Forestry organizations

Both newly established forests and existing forests should be included in carbon removal organizations for certification. Certified "Real Negative CO_2" amounts can be traded in the carbon market, enabling forest managers to directly receive financial benefits.

Forest managers need to invest substantial resources and costs into the maintenance, upkeep, fire prevention, and anti-poaching efforts of existing forests. To ensure better protection of existing forests and validate their substantial carbon absorption value, a stronger incentive mechanism must be established. Recognizing the carbon removal capacity of existing forests and gaining immediate returns for their conservation efforts are crucial for their protection and for ensuring they continue to play a significant role in carbon absorption.

At the same time, confirming the carbon removal asset value of existing forests is beneficial for addressing inter-regional transfer payment issues and serves as a necessary policy measure for achieving nationwide carbon neutrality. In regions abundant in forest resources, provincial and municipal governments are actively organizing their own certification and trading. There should be prompt coordination at the national level. Instead of decentralized development by various regions, efforts should be focused on accelerating the creation of a unified national carbon market with standardized criteria, enhancing the liquidity and value realization of carbon removal assets in a larger and cohesive market.

The carbon fixation capacity of existing forests is generally not certified. Instead, the certification focuses on the annual increase in carbon fixation.

Forests not only play a crucial role in carbon fixation but also contribute significantly to preventing soil erosion, improving the environment, and protecting ecosystems. The government should establish immediate incentive mechanisms to actively encourage afforestation.

If a forest with certified carbon-removal capacity is subsequently cut down, exploited, or damaged by natural disasters such as wildfires after a certain period, the amount of carbon it fixes will be released back into the atmosphere. Therefore, it is essential to have objective and accurate continuous certification and management in place. This also presents management challenges, such as the risk of the organization managing a forest going bankrupt, ceasing operations, or being acquired, which can create uncertainties in its ongoing management. Therefore, from the perspective of effectiveness, it is preferable for the certification of forest carbon removals to be managed by government authorities. The current carbon fixation capacity should be granted based on the assessment of the total carbon removals in the region's forest. Thus, if the forest area in a region decreases during the year, the certification authority should grant carbon emission amount rather than carbon removal amount. This approach provides both positive and negative incentives for local governments to protect forests and enhance carbon fixation.

Local authorities should allocate the annual carbon removal amount to local carbon removal organizations, implementing rewards and penalties, so as to ensure dynamic and effective local management.

The certification mechanism for forest carbon removals should be coordinated at the national level, with unified standards that achieve international recognition to ensure long-term sustainable development value. Currently, provinces and cities are developing carbon removal methodologies, but significant challenges remain regarding their scientific validity, consistency, and efficiency.

2. CCUS organizations

Enterprises utilizing technological equipment for carbon capture and absorption are key carbon removal organizations to be developed in the future. Currently, the cost of using such absorption equipment remains relatively high, approaching one thousand yuan per ton. In the future, producing "Real Negative CO_2" will become a major industry. The international community needs to invest significant research and development resources in CCUS to enhance technology, scale up operations, and significantly reduce the cost of carbon absorption.

The global community is tasked not merely with attaining carbon neutrality but also with eliminating the staggering 1.74 trillion tons of carbon emissions that have accumulated in our atmosphere since the industrial revolution, adhering strictly to the dictates of climate governance. By further exploring the added value of CO_2 as a production resource, the carbon capture industry stands poised to unlock immense potential for future expansion and development.

China must develop CCUS as a strategic future industry, rapidly achieving global leadership in technology and production scale. A large-scale CCUS industry can not only help China accelerate its progress toward carbon neutrality but also enable the sale of "Real Negative CO_2" in the global carbon market, bringing a multitude of benefits.

Firstly, it will help China establish an international carbon market. In the future, who will lead in addressing global climate change—China, the U.S., or Europe? Who will create the most influential international carbon market? Having a substantial supply of "Real Negative CO_2" available for sale and trade is one of the keys to the prosperity and development of the global carbon market. If China achieves a high production of "Real Negative CO_2", establishing an influential carbon market will naturally follow. In March 2022, Hainan embarked on the construction of an international carbon market, a move fueled by the undeniable importance of CCUS-derived "Real Negative CO_2" products. It is challenging to innovate significantly in the trading of carbon emissions rights, and the carbon market for emission rights is doomed to gradually decline in significance.

Secondly, it will propel the growth of international carbon finance, as global investments in climate change mitigation are anticipated to surpass an astounding USD 200 trillion over the next four decades. This presents a formidable opportunity for China to establish itself as the preeminent international carbon market, enhancing its influence in the realm of carbon finance. By developing a broader array of carbon financial derivatives, China can secure a larger market share and assume a leadership position, further solidifying its role in global climate action.

Thirdly, it will increase China's foreign exchange earnings. By selling "Real Negative CO_2" in the global carbon market, China can generate substantial foreign exchange earnings.

In the context of carbon neutrality, the overall price of CCUS represents the cost of carbon emissions. Reducing the cost of CCUS is crucial in the carbon neutrality process. Experts have analyzed the substantial potential for cost reduction in CCUS, identifying three key aspects for addressing this challenge: firstly, by relentlessly fostering technological innovation and upgrading existing technologies; secondly, by augmenting production scales to harness economies of scale; and thirdly, by continually advancing CO_2 utilization technologies, thereby enhancing the application value of CO_2 as a vital production resource.

3. Wetlands, marine mangroves, and other biomass operational organizations that function in carbon absorption

Organizations with carbon absorption capabilities and contributions should be included in management and certified for their "Real Negative CO_2" quantities, allowing them to receive incentives. This approach is highly beneficial for the overall goal of carbon neutrality.

The certification process for these types of carbon removals confronts challenges similar to those encountered with forest carbon removals, pertaining to sustainable and effective management.

7.2.2 Certification of Carbon Removal Capacity for Carbon Removal Organizations

To achieve global carbon neutrality, it is crucial to vigorously develop the carbon removal industry, therefore, it is important for the products of carbon removal enterprises, "Real Negative CO_2", to be comprehensively, accurately, and promptly certified.

The standard unit for "Real Negative CO_2" is the removal of 1 ton of CO_2 from the atmosphere, denoted as: -1 tCO2e. This definition is clear and precise, with 1 ton of CO_2 serving as the standard product and quality, therefore, "Real Negative CO_2" is a standardized product.

The core of carbon removal management lies in the certification of "Real Negative CO_2" output. Once the amount of "Real Negative CO_2" is verified by an authoritative certification body, a certification document, also known as a "green ticket", should be issued to the owner of the "Real Negative CO_2" assets, which corresponds to the "red ticket" indicating CEL. The "green ticket" and "red ticket" have a compensatory relationship, meaning they can offset each other.

The certification of "Real Negative CO_2" should encompass all existing assets. Assets capable of producing "Real Negative CO_2" should be treated uniformly. Comprehensive coverage should be provided to carbon removal enterprises to broaden the scope of incentives.

The certification of carbon removal of existing carbon removal assets should be based on the following principles:

- Principle of Additionality: This principle requires that carbon removal resources, such as forest resources, need to involve annual management and maintenance investments. Some natural resources, such as oceans and the Loess Plateau, should not be certified for a specific organization if they do not require additional management and maintenance investments, even if their carbon fixation impact is significant. The carbon removal benefits from this portion belong to the national government and are not traded in the carbon market, so as to avoid issues related to property rights and certification, and mitigate market challenges, aligning with the principle that those who invest should be the ones who benefit.
- Principle of Incrementality: Previously generated carbon removal resources are not certified. Instead, only the new increase in the amount of carbon removals each year is certified. For instance, the existing carbon fixation number of mature forests is generally not certified. Instead, only the annual increase in carbon fixation is certified. This approach is necessary to maintain consistency in carbon management systems and advance the marketization of negative carbon.

With current technological methods, the carbon removal certification system based on the CELM is simpler and easier compared to the CCER system. It presents lower certification difficulty and offers higher levels of objectivity and standardization. The CELM focuses on absolute emission reductions, while CCER deals with relative emission reductions. The nature of the two systems differs significantly, although there are some areas of overlap. Certification under the CELM is notably simplified to a considerable extent, resulting in much higher objectivity and accuracy.

Once the basic information of forestry projects is certified, annual certification can be conducted using advanced technologies such as satellite imagery and drone-based photogrammetry, ensuring objective and accurate assessments. It is important to note that while forest area can increase, it may also decrease due to various factors. For a given area, the contribution to carbon reduction is determined by the net increase in carbon removal. This involves complex data processing and requires the establishment of a fair and efficient certification system.

For facility-based CCUS projects, technologies like the Internet of Things (IoT) can accurately monitor equipment performance, ensuring objective and precise data. The certification of carbon removal amount for these projects also requires a robust system to prevent data manipulation and fabrication, supporting the sustainable development of the industry.

The establishment, certification, and process supervision of carbon removal projects must be systematized to ensure high efficiency, low costs, and minimal issues. Therefore, it is essential to develop a scientifically rigorous carbon removal certification system.

7.2.3 Establishment of Chinese Certification System

The goal of China's certification system should be clear: it should aim for international recognition, advance towards the establishment of a significant international carbon market, and enhance China's role in global climate governance. This effort is not only for advancing the domestic carbon neutrality process and carbon market.

Strict penalties should be in place for data falsifiers, as such incidents have already occurred. To improve and strengthen the certification system, it is necessary to clarify the liability of the parties involved, consulting firms and certification bodies. A system for cross-validation should be established to reduce loopholes in the entire system, enhancing fairness while also improving efficiency. China has accumulated considerable methodological experience in CCER and has established a solid foundation. The CTMS based on the CELM inherently possesses advantages in data capability. However, to develop an internationally advanced certification system based on the CELM theory, greater efforts are still needed.

For China's carbon removal certification to gain international recognition, it is essential for China to establish an internationally accepted "Real Negative CO_2" certification system at an early stage. This endeavor involves actively promoting the development of international carbon removal certification system, coupled with the relentless enhancement of certification standards. Furthermore, China must strive to assist the international community in constructing authoritative national "Real Negative CO_2" certification systems. It also includes cultivating a number of internationally recognized certification consulting agencies, training skilled professionals to ensure high credibility. By securing a prominent position in this field, China will lay a solid foundation for the establishment of an international carbon market.

The registration system for carbon removal certification is crucial. After the amount of carbon removals (Real Negative CO_2) certified through a specific process, the carbon removal data must be recorded in the registration system. This system integrates with the carbon ticket management system and the negative carbon trading system, supporting a closed-loop operation for the entire carbon reduction framework.

The registration system for carbon removal certification is a national carbon asset management system coordinated by the government. It is designed to support the registration of newly created carbon removal assets, facilitate the trading and transfer of these assets within the carbon market, and handle data processing for CEL accounting, offsetting and settlement in the carbon ticket management system. This system could be developed and managed by the Ministry of Ecology and Environment, which oversees current carbon emissions. Furthermore, the system data needs to be integrated with international carbon market data and carbon management systems.

7.2.4 Promoting the Development of Carbon Removal Certification System Internationally

Based on its domestic successes, China should actively advance the internationalization of its carbon removal certification system. The goal of China's negative carbon trading market should be targeted at the international market, and the certification of the core trading asset, "Real Negative CO_2", must meet international standards. Whether it's forest carbon removals or CCUS technologies, China has the opportunity to become the largest global player in these industries, therefore, forging ahead into international markets is essential.

Moreover, it is essential to advance the establishment of a unified international system for "Real Negative CO_2" certification. The certification of "Real Negative CO_2" output quantities needs to be recognized by the international community. "Real Negative CO_2" refers to the removal of 1 ton of CO_2 from the air and could become an internationally accepted standard product.

The domestic negative carbon certification system should aim to achieve three goals:

- Firstly, products certified as "Real Negative CO_2" domestically should gain international recognition. This is a core foundation for building the international carbon market and an essential element for China to address international carbon tariffs (similar to CBAM).

- Secondly, Chinese certified carbon removal system should be able to be exported internationally to serve more cooperating countries. In particular, it could complement the "Belt and Road" initiative, not only exporting services but also enhancing its influence in global climate governance.
- Thirdly, it equips China with the capability to play a pivotal role in formulating regulations pertaining to international climate governance. Throughout the past three decades, China's presence in global climate dialogues, particularly in academic and standard-setting forums, has been relatively modest, yielding limited influence. Consequently, it is imperative that efforts be intensified to effect a transformation in this regard.

Therefore, it is essential for the relevant Chinese government departments to take the lead, coordinate academic expertise in the field of climate change, and accelerate the shift of focus and resources from the CCER domain to the development of an international standard certification system.

7.2.5 CCER Should Not Be Restarted: Discussion on the Certified Emission Reduction Mechanism

With the domestic carbon market in China being sluggish, Chinese Certified Emission Reduction (CCER) has emerged as one of the most prominent segments in the dual carbon market, serving as an alternative trading asset beyond carbon emission allowances. After the National Development and Reform Commission suspended CCER registration in 2017, there has been strong demand to restart CCER market trading domestically. This would allow many low-carbon project owners to benefit, and provide business opportunities for professionals in the dual carbon industry. In the past three years, tens of thousands of carbon consulting firms have viewed CCER certification and trading as the biggest market opportunity. Will their aspirations be fulfilled?

CCER is the Chinese version of carbon credits. Research findings indicate that, given the overall direction of transformations in the future carbon market, CCER should not be restarted due to its lack of objective standards, compromised sustainability, high technical and execution costs, incompatibility with international standards, and misalignment with development trends of carbon market. Moreover, its cost-effectiveness is low, giving rise to numerous challenges and issues.

7.2.5.1 Development History and Current Status of CCER

According to the *Measures for the Administration of Carbon Emissions Trading (Trial)* (*Order No. 19 of the Ministry of Ecology and Environment*), CCER refers to the quantified and certified GHG emission reductions from projects within China, such as renewable energy, forestry carbon removals, and methane utilization, which are registered in the national trading system for voluntary GHG emission reductions.

Based on the global impact of GHGs, the varying reduction potential and costs across different countries, and the differing economic costs of global cooperation and emission reductions, *The Kyoto Protocol* introduced three flexible mechanisms for GHG reduction: the Clean Development Mechanism (CDM), Joint Implementation (JI), and Emissions Trading (ET). Among these, JI and ET are mechanisms for cooperation between developed countries, while CDM facilitates cooperation between developed and developing countries.

As to Clean Development Mechanism (CDM), developed countries engage in project-level cooperation with developing countries by providing funding and technology, in exchange for certified emission reduction (CER), which are used by developed countries to fulfill their reduction commitments under *The Kyoto Protocol*.

According to the statistics from World Bank, from 2002 to the end of 2020, there were over 18,000 registered carbon credit projects globally, covering approximately 4.3 Gt of CO_2. About half of these projects were issued under the CDM, with the other half coming from various other international standard systems.

China's CCER trading began in 2012 when the National Development and Reform Commission issued the *Interim Measures for the Administration of Voluntary Greenhouse Gas Emission Reduction Trading* (referred to as *The Interim Measures*) and the *Guidelines for the Validation and Certification of Voluntary Greenhouse Gas Emission Reduction Projects*. These documents established the workflow for voluntary emission reduction projects, initiating the issuance of CCER in China. In 2015, the national information platform for voluntary emission reduction trading was officially launched, marking the formal start of CCER trading.

China's CCER is primarily based on CDM projects. The first CDM project in China was the Huitengxile Wind Farm in Inner Mongolia, which was registered in June 2005. Since the registration of the regional energy center project by Beijing Shangzhuang Gas-fired Cogeneration Company in June 2017, no new CDM projects have been registered in China. During the rapid development phase of CCER, favorable prices stimulated a boom in CDM project trading. Over 12 years, a total of 1478 Chinese projects were issued, generating a cumulative 900 million tons of carbon assets, with a trading volume amounting to several billion dollars.

After a brief period of prosperity, the CCER program suddenly came to a halt in 2017.

On March 17, 2017, the National Development and Reform Commission (NDRC) issued an official announcement, *Temporary Halt on Accepting Applications for the Recordation of Greenhouse Gas Voluntary Emission Reduction Trading Methodologies, Projects, Emission Reductions, Verification and Certification Bodies, and Trading Institutions*, highlighting that "during the implementation of the *Interim Measures*, there have been issues such as low trading volumes of GHG voluntary emission reductions and some projects failing to meet standard requirements." Nonetheless, CCER projects that had been successfully recorded were still permitted to engage in transactions.

Concurrently, the NDRC announced its intention to revise certain clauses within the existing *Interim Measures for the Administration of Voluntary Greenhouse Gas Emission Reduction Trading* to address these concerns.

Analysts have pointed out that during the implementation of the *Interim Measures*, there were issues such as low trading volumes of GHG voluntary emission reduction and the non-standardization of certain projects. First, there is an imbalance between supply and demand for existing CCER projects, where the demand from local carbon markets and corporate voluntary emission reduction efforts has been insufficient to absorb the emission reductions from registered CCER projects. Second, concerns have been raised over the quality of data from some individual projects.

Since the *Interim Measures* were initiated for revision in 2017, CCER has been on hold for nearly six years. Although the processes for recordation and issuance have been suspended, the market trading of certified emission reductions that are already in circulation has continued.

The proactive control exerted by the authorities over the development of CCER suggests that significant issues have been detected. As we consider the possibility of restarting CCER verification and trading, the question arises: have these issues been sufficiently addressed?

7.2.5.2 CCER Operational Mechanism and Challenges

The inception of the CCER was historically inevitable, serving a pivotal role in the early stages of international decarbonation efforts. However, as the low-carbon technology industry develops and the carbon reduction system evolves, there is a critical need for a substantial upgrade to the incentive system for certified emission reductions. Industry experts and managers must acknowledge that incremental tweaks to the existing framework will not suffice to sustain its vitality or support its continued growth.

1. The CCER verification mechanism is a product in history

At present, the management of CCER in China adheres to the regulations in *The Interim Measures* released in 2012. These measures stipulate that CCER should be grounded in specific projects and must demonstrate authenticity, measurability, and "additionality."

Internationally, the concept of "additionality" is defined that the emission reductions achieved by CCER projects are additional, compared to the "baseline." This implies that without the support of external CCER initiatives, the project and its reductions would encounter obstacles related to financial performance metrics, funding channels, technical risks, market adoption, and resource availability, making it nearly impossible for the project to succeed on its own merits. Furthermore, according to *The Interim Measures*, the "baseline" and "additionality" of CCER projects should be established and substantiated using methodologies that have been officially recorded by the national authorities. These methodologies are guidelines, endorsed by the National Development and Reform Commission, used to determine project baselines, argue for additionality, calculate emission reductions, and devise monitoring plans. The determination of "baseline" and "additionality" relies on an intricate knowledge base and verification process, leading to considerable complexity and high costs associated with the verification of CCER projects.

The process of establishing "additionality" for CCER projects across various methodologies generally involves four key dimensions (steps): the certification of pioneering projects, barrier analysis, investment analysis, and analysis of widespread adoption. Through a series of evidence submission, investigation, and argumentation, the government must separately confirm and assess the "baseline" of the proposed project, identifying any commercialization hurdles, assessing whether investment returns fall short of established benchmarks, and evaluating the potential for commercial viability. As a rule, the additionality argumentation of CCER projects requires that the power generation sector's benchmark rate of return should not exceed 8%, yet most wind and photovoltaic projects boast an internal rate of return (IRR) that is higher than 8%. Projects with an IRR below this threshold have typically received forms of subsidies or achieved state-fixed price, indicating that they do not confront inherent commercialization barriers (as their rates of return are market-accepted), thus deviating from the original purpose of CCER and lacking in additionality.

In the case of wind and photovoltaic sectors, which were once the backbone of CCER, technological advancements and a substantial scaling up of industry have led to a significant reduction in the cost of unit production. These sectors now even rival traditional coal-fired power in terms of price competitiveness, rendering the CCER mechanism largely obsolete. Additionally, within the CCER system, emission reductions from sources such as forests, wetlands, and coastal mangroves are purely carbon removals and are well-suited for integration into the China Certified Carbon Sink (CCCS) system.

2. The offset mechanism of CCER and carbon emissions

Currently, the CCER offset mechanisms in various regional pilot markets across the country are operating independently, with each locality having its own policies regarding requirements for offsetting allowances, type restrictions, time period limitations, and proportion limits. The offset ratio ranges from 2 to 10%. It is anticipated that the national trading market for carbon emission rights will eventually introduce the CCER system as an offset mechanism, though the timing of this restart and the specific policies for offsetting allowances, type restrictions, time period limitations, and proportion limits remain uncertain.

According to the current regulations set by the authorities, upon the restart of CCER, enterprises will be able to offset up to 5% of their own emissions by purchasing the corresponding certificates. This regulation imposes significant limitations on the development of CCER, implying that the market demand for CCER is greatly reduced, leading to a situation where it becomes a less attractive option. The management and maintenance of the vast certification system formed by hundreds of methodologies are an unbearable burden for sustaining the existing certification system.

3. Challenges with the CCER mechanism

Firstly, the standards for baseline determination, additionality, and emission reduction accounting suffer from poor objectivity, complexity, and low operational feasibility, which impedes the establishment of international norms. Consequently, the mechanism operates with low efficiency and a poor return on investment.

The certification of additionality in CCER is particularly complex and lacks standardization, making it difficult to gain international recognition. Determining the baseline for emission reductions is also a complicated technical process with nebulous standards. Many solutions and standards developed and recognized by experts may quickly become outdated due to rapid changes in industry, technology, and macro-policy. These challenges contribute to the complexity and impracticality of the CCER system.

From the perspective of operational difficulty and efficiency, the limited market vitality and challenges in internationalization of CCER diminish its potential for growth and promotional value. Similar to carbon emission rights, the difficulty in standardization leads to the intractable issue of inter-country recognition. If applied only within a single country, the input–output ratio is unreasonable.

The entire CCER system requires extensive support from methodologies, with high costs for verification processes and regulatory oversight. Coupled with the 5% limitation of the offset mechanism, the development of CCER is severely restricted, making the investment unviable under any circumstances. We should not continue to focus on CCER and should explore more innovations for addressing climate change.

Currently, there are over 200 methodologies for voluntary emission reduction registered in China, with numerous methodologies within the same field but a lack of unified, authoritative methodologies for similar source projects. For example, there are nine local standards for forestry projects (including those under application).

Such a complex system cannot be scaled up and is unlikely to gain international recognition, preventing the formation of an international market.

Secondly, the CCER incentive targets relative emission reductions, not absolute carbon absorption. Many projects do not actually absorb carbon from the atmosphere and are no longer the focus of carbon reduction incentives in the current stage. The development of CCER was initially motivated by the need to incentivize and subsidize early green and low-carbon projects, addressing the issue of insufficient returns on these projects. While it had significant value in the early stages of international carbon reduction efforts, its practical significance is now much reduced. With the cost of per kilowatt-hour generated from solar and wind power now below that of coal-fired power, the value of CCER has significantly diminished. Carbon reduction incentive policies must now directly target carbon absorption, focusing on actions and technologies that genuinely remove carbon from the atmosphere.

Thirdly, CCER has a significant overlap and conflict with other emission reduction tools and mechanisms. Currently, the ambiguous rules for policy coordination between the carbon trading system and the market transactions for green electricity, as well as the mechanisms for purchasing green power certificates, allow companies to develop renewable energy projects like wind and photovoltaic power to potentially reap dual benefits from CCER trading and green electricity transactions for the same project. The task of streamlining and resolving conflicts among green power, green certificates, carbon allowances, CCER, and energy using rights to optimize their combined impact on energy savings and carbon reduction has emerged as a critical challenge for current management.

Restarting CCER would bring additional complexity to the government's agenda. The current direction of carbon reduction efforts should not involve adding more policy instruments but rather streamlining, simplifying, and unifying the existing ones.

Fourthly, as decarbonation mechanisms evolve and the internalization of carbon costs becomes more established, it is imperative to reevaluate and streamline phase-specific incentive programs to maintain competition fairness and to conserve public finances. As the application and expansion of carbon taxes and trading mechanism for carbon emission rights, particularly with the operation of the "1+1" system based on the CELM, the social cost of carbon emissions will gradually be reflected in the actual cost of all goods, effectively internalizing the external cost of carbon emissions. As this internalization advances, it is crucial to ensure that low-carbon projects do not receive preferential treatment over others, as this could disrupt market pricing and fairness. Low-carbon projects and products already have the potential to gain a competitive edge through reduced overall costs and can further benefit from enhanced brand value and consumer preference through transparent carbon labeling and cost disclosures. Moving forward, the value of CCER-related projects should be embedded within the total cost of goods. The economic justification for CCER subsidies is tenuous, and the overlapping and cumulative effects of multiple policies lead to ambiguous mechanisms and diminished returns on investment. If additional incentives are needed, they should be provided through fiscal measures, such as tax reductions or low-interest financing, rather than allowing certified emissions reductions to generate profits in the carbon market.

7.2.5.3 Differences Between CCER and CCCS

The distinction between CCER and CCCS (Chinese Certified Carbon Sink) lies in the fact that "negative carbon" products adhere to a global standard. Removing one ton of CO_2 from the atmosphere anywhere in the world holds the same significance and value globally. A carbon market based on "negative carbon" indicators is more likely to form a unified global market, which is conducive to accelerating the overall progress of global decarbonation.

Currently, the market confuses CCCS with CCER, which is increasingly unsuitable for the needs of the carbon neutrality process. It is high time to differentiate between the two concepts. In fact, they are entirely different in nature. The production of "negative carbon" by "carbon removal" enterprises is pivotal to achieving carbon neutrality. Therefore, the "carbon removal" industry, which produces "negative carbon," is becoming increasingly important, and CCER should quickly step aside from the historical stage.

Carbon removal refers to the process, activities, and mechanisms by which carbon dioxide (CO_2) is removed from the atmosphere. This is primarily achieved through the absorption and storage of CO_2 by forests, wetlands, oceans, soils, and increasingly through CCUS technologies. Research indicates that China's carbon removal capacity is on the rise. According to studies conducted by the Chinese Academy of Sciences on carbon budget projects, China's current terrestrial carbon storage is equivalent to 36.3 Gt of CO_2, with an annual carbon fixation rate ranging from 1 to 4 Gt of CO_2, accounting for 10% to 40% of anthropogenic carbon emissions. This contribution is significant and should not be overlooked. It is estimated that forests will reach their peak carbon fixation capacity by 2060, after which the fixation rate will decline. This underscores the critical role that ecosystem, such as forestry, plays in the vision of carbon neutrality, and carbon removal projects are poised to assist China in achieving its carbon neutrality objectives.

Analyzing from the dimension of physical properties, carbon removal refers to the removal of CO_2 from the atmosphere, while CCER refers to the reduction of CO_2 emissions relative to a baseline. Carbon removal represents negative carbon emissions, directly offsetting positive carbon emissions and is directly aligned with carbon neutrality. CCER's carbon emission reduction is a relative reduction, which differs significantly from the removal of CO_2 from the atmosphere in terms of physical meaning. While from the perspective of trading target in the carbon market, carbon removals (negative carbon) have objective standards, suitable for trading. The relative carbon emission reduction of CCER is a non-objective standard that requires a complex set of methodologies and a significant investment of human and material resources for measurement and verification. The concept and standards of negative carbon can be globally unified, ensuring that market pricing reflects the global interest. Therefore, "negative carbon" has the potential to become the dominant product in future carbon markets. It is imperative that we focus our efforts and resources on building a robust negative carbon certification system, which represents the correct path forward.

The "Real Negative CO_2" certification system, compared to CCER, has the following characteristics:

1. Unlike CCER, which certifies emission reductions, the "Real Negative CO_2" system verifies genuine carbon sequestration. It exclusively certifies projects and quantities that directly remove carbon from the atmosphere.
2. There is no requirement for additionality in the "Real Negative CO_2" system. Any carbon removal project that requires investment, ongoing cost maintenance, and development is considered an effective negative carbon industry and is eligible for incentives.
3. The "Real Negative CO_2" system focuses solely on certifying incremental carbon removal, excluding the certification of existing carbon stocks. For carbon removal entites like forests and mangroves, it certifies only the annual incremental carbon removal. In contrast to the current CCER system, the "Real Negative CO_2" system is much simpler and more valuable. It does not need to account for intangible concepts like investment baselines and additionality, and the standards remain stable over time.

4. The more negative carbon products, the better, without being constrained by offset ratios. All "Real Negative CO_2" can be traded in the carbon market for sale. Any entity that emits carbon can purchase negative carbon to offset 100% of their emissions.

7.2.5.4 CCER Transformation: From CCER to CCCS

Ignoring the relative carbon emission reductions within CCER, it is imperative to strengthen the certification system for "negative carbon" and "carbon removal" within CCER.

Currently, there is a collective understanding across society for carbon reduction. As numerous emission reduction technologies emerge, each enterprise has the opportunity to innovate in carbon reduction through technological and management advancements. However, these emission reduction technologies depend on national certification for incentivization, which would lead to a significant social cost and is no longer a realistic approach. Moreover, carbon reduction has evolved into a social liability rather than a direct reward mechanism. An ideal and sustainable subsidy policy for new technologies should be transparent, with minimal operational difficulty, and designed to eliminate the potential for "fake subsidy" loopholes. As the mechanism for internalizing the societal cost of carbon emissions matures, these challenges will be resolved effectively, and there is no reason to maintain the inefficient and potentially chaotic CCER-like mechanisms.

The international decarbonation systems in the future will center on two key aspects: first, to refine the internalization of carbon emission costs to ensure the system is more objective, equitable, efficient, and low-cost, thereby guiding the development of a low-carbon economy and expediting decarbonation; second, to incentivize carbon absorption directly, with a clear emphasis on absolute carbon absorption rather than relative carbon reduction. These two mechanisms work in tandem to accelerate the global carbon neutrality process. They do not overlap or conflict and consider the positive and negative incentives of all relevant parties, making them both efficient and fair.

Undoubtedly, we should intensify our efforts to foster a certified carbon removal system that is directly aligned with carbon neutrality and can be executed with high efficiency. The certification system of CCER should be discontinued, and resources and efforts should be redirected towards strengthening the construction of the "Real Negative CO_2" certification system. The restart and continued operation of the CCER mechanism would introduce confusion into the carbon emission reduction system of the entire society, leading to increasing overlap, conflicts, and irrationalities.

Certainly, within CCER-related projects, those that can produce "Real Negative CO_2" should be integrated into the new certified carbon removal system for certification, allowing relevant organizations to directly engage in the negative carbon market for profit.

7.2.5.5 CCER Trading Market Should Not Be Restarted

Based on the comprehensive analysis, CCER is not suitable as a trading asset in capital markets due to its inherent characteristics, making it difficult to align with the mainstream carbon markets internationally. Consequently, it is not advisable for government departments to continue investing resources in the construction of other fragmented carbon markets or specialized CCER trading platforms, as this could easily lead to another unsuccessful endeavor.

CCER trading market fragmentizes the market landscape and disperses resources. In the short term, the size of the Chinese carbon market is not substantial. The current annual trading volume of the trading market for carbon emission rights stands at mere tens of billions of yuan. However, according to the negative carbon market scheme based on the CELM theory, the trading volume could soar to one to five trillion yuan, and potentially expand to ten to twenty trillion yuan if it successfully evolves into an international platform. The current size of the Chinese carbon market is significantly smaller than the stock market, and further segmenting it into numerous smaller entities would be detrimental. The overall value of the carbon market would suffer greatly.

Currently, the construction of China's carbon market is in urgent need of consolidating the various provincial markets into a single, unified national carbon market with a focus on negative carbon. This approach should be directed towards the goal of an international carbon market, rather than establishing a new CCER trading market or other fragmented markets. The current practice, which lacks confidence in the top-level design theory, has led to significant costs through repeated attempts and experiments. With the introduction of the CELM and its solution, there is no longer any need to revive CCER.

CCER trading market disrupts market mechanism efficiency in resource allocation. The primary purpose of the carbon trading market is not speculative capital manipulation but rather efficient market resource allocation, which is essential for enhancing macroeconomic and social welfare. The objective of government-led carbon market construction is to reduce the overall social cost of carbon reduction. Market fragmentation would severely undermine the core principle of carbon market construction, with carbon emission trading between coal-fired power companies having minimal value in terms of resource allocation efficiency. The government aims to integrate all organizations and individuals that emit or absorb carbon within society, facilitating effective resource allocation. Only by directly connecting the "carbon emissions" and "carbon removals" in the entire society can resource allocation efficiency be maximized.

A standalone CCER trading market cannot achieve significant scale. The inherent limitations of CCER, which result in a 5% cap on the proportion of carbon allowances it can offset, preclude the possibility of its market size growing substantially. Currently, the annual trading volume of the national trading market for carbon emission rights is only in the tens of billions, which means the CCER market will never exceed 5 billion yuan in size, rendering it largely insignificant. The government should focus on identifying better carbon asset targets: those that are simple, standardized, and have a large scale without limitations. The ideal asset in this context is "negative carbon."

As a relative reduction in emissions, CCER is unlikely to establish international standards, thereby posing a barrier to its internationalization. Its development potential is limited, and the return on investment is disproportionate. Ultimately, carbon neutrality aims for international coordination, and mechanisms that cannot establish international standards will not be effective on a global scale.

The proliferation of methodologies, numbering in the hundreds, presents significant challenges in management and operation, with issues of integrity and rent-seeking proving difficult to resolve. Since CCER represents relative emission reductions, different industries and sectors require the development of distinct methods for verification, certification, and calculation, leading to excessive management costs and an array of operational issues. The proposal to train 200,000 CCER auditors and promote a thriving training industry is fundamentally flawed in logic. Given the annual volume of only tens of billion yuan in the carbon market, under the 5% offset mechanism, the CCER market is only several hundred million yuan. However, the annual labor cost for 200,000 auditors would be approximately 40 billion yuan, an absurdly inflated figure. This is a delusional market that is far removed from reality. The carbon neutrality industry is meant to address the climate crisis, which poses a threat to human survival, not to create artificial commercial markets.

7.2.5.6 Outlook for CCER Policy Trends

CCER was initiated in response to the international community's need to launch a large number of carbon emission reduction projects. Now it has declined due to its limitations and an increasing number of issues. But its phase-specific historical mission has been completed. With the improvement of the international decarbonation system, especially the emergence of the new theoretical system for addressing climate change, the CELM theory and the global carbon neutrality scheme, the CCER has fulfilled its historical mission and there is no need to restart it.

Many original CCER projects are low-carbon products that are extremely beneficial for decarbonation across society. The positive externalities of these products are highly deserving of incentives. As the internalization of the societal cost of carbon emissions becomes more sophisticated, the market competitiveness and development capabilities of low-carbon products will increasingly rely on their own market competitiveness for better development, rather than relying on mechanisms like CCER, which currently necessitates enormous social costs to subsidize.

The focus of international decarbonation and carbon neutrality efforts should be to establish and improve the internalization of the societal cost of carbon emissions across society, placing various technology industries under a relatively fair mechanism for selection. This approach will minimize the impact on the macroeconomy and maximize the increase in social welfare.

In summary, the CCER market should not be restarted. China should allocate more resources to the construction of certified carbon removal system to achieve better development and prospects.

At present, if the positive externalities of CCER low-carbon projects still necessitate supplementary incentive mechanisms, it would be more suitable to employ fiscal and financial policy instruments for this purpose. These instruments are straightforward to implement and have lower execution difficulties and costs. For instance:

1. Introducing tax incentives, which could encompass both value-added tax (VAT) and income tax. These incentives are based on the project's output and do not require complex certification processes, leading to more favorable administrative costs and efficiency.
2. Providing low-interest financing. This can be achieved through policy-oriented low-interest financing offered by green finance funds, supporting project development.
3. Implementing other high-efficiency supplementary mechanisms. For example, in Shanghai, electric vehicles are exempt from the hefty 100,000 yuan registration fee, which represents a substantial subsidy policy that directly benefits end users and has been highly effective.

These policies are tailored to specific projects and can even provide direct subsidies to end users, offering high efficiency and reducing issues such as fraud and rent-seeking. They have low administrative costs and also have a more positive impact on the industry. The emergence of fraud and rent-seeking issues in China's new energy market is largely due to unreasonable institutional arrangements.

7.3 Design of Carbon Ticket Management System

To expedite global carbon reduction efforts, streamline the precise formulation and implementation of policies, and provide robust data support for carbon emission reduction management across various industries, it is crucial for government agencies to swiftly acquire comprehensive big data on the carbon footprint of society. Consequently, there is an urgent need to expedite the construction and operationalization of a Carbon Ticket Management System (CTMS) based on the CELM.

The essential aspects of the architecture and functional design for a CTMS system platform that encompasses the entire society are as follows.

7.3.1 National CTMS

The Carbon Ticket Management System (CTMS) is a centralized digital big data platform for carbon footprint data and decarbonation management across all organizations, materials, products, and services within the country. It is managed by the central government policy departments and operates with regional government subsystems. The CTMS plays a critical role in national decarbonation management.

All carbon emissions data related to the transactions of goods and services within society are recorded and processed within this system. Once operational, the CTMS can aggregate carbon footprint data for every organization, every material, product, and service. It can also analyze and compile carbon emission data at various levels of granularity throughout the production process of the supply chain.

Each organization is assigned a CEL carbon account, serving as the unique ID for national carbon data management. It is recommended to reference the unified social credit code for this purpose, and a comprehensive carbon ledger should be established for each organization based on the carbon account.

The CTMS system shares similarities with the national tax system, both using input and output data to determine an organization's CEL. The CTMS can also be referred to as the "Golden Carbon System" or the "Golden Carbon Project." It is anticipated that the construction of the Golden Carbon Project will fundamentally alter the progress of China's "3060" dual carbon targets.

7.3.2 Carbon Tickets and Their Management

7.3.2.1 Definition of Carbon Tickets

Carbon tickets, or CEL carbon tickets, serve as documentary evidence, detailing the transfer of CEL within the lifecycle of a product or service transaction, as agreed upon by the transacting parties. These tickets are the bearers of comprehensive social carbon footprint data, and they are meticulously maintained within the national Carbon Ticket Management System (CTMS).

CEL Output ticket: When a supplier delivers goods or services, they not only provide a Value-Added Tax (VAT) invoice to the purchaser for payment but also issue a carbon ticket. This carbon ticket meticulously records the quantity of CEL transfer within the product or service, and it is registered as an output ticket in the supplier's carbon account. This action signifies that the supplier has shifted the liability for offsetting carbon emissions associated with the product or service to the purchaser.

CEL input ticket: Alongside the VAT invoice received as payment evidence from the supplier, the purchaser also receives a carbon ticket. This carbon ticket is then recorded as an input ticket in the purchaser's carbon account. This act signifies that the purchaser has taken on the liability for offsetting the carbon emissions corresponding to the product or service.

For an organization, the carbon tickets issued by its upstream suppliers are considered as input tickets, while the carbon tickets it issues to its customers or users are treated as output tickets.

Except for the output tickets issued by the government to carbon source organizations, in any transaction stage, the issuance of output tickets or input tickets is determined in accordance with the principle of market equality, through negotiation and agreement between the trading parties. This is not determined by the algorithms of a specific methodology or by simple front-end aggregation and statistics, but is entirely based on the principle of free trade. As long as the downstream purchasing parties accept them, an organization can issue more output tickets than its input tickets, which typically indicates that the organization's product has a lower carbon intensity than the industry average. Conversely, an organization may issue fewer output tickets than its input tickets, which typically suggests that its product has a higher carbon intensity than the industrial average.

The amount of carbon emissions for which an organization should be liable is the total of its input tickets minus the total of its output tickets. This is settled on a quarterly basis to ensure that the organization's carbon liability balance is zero. If the result is negative, it can be considered "negative carbon" and sold in the carbon market to generate revenue. If the result is positive, the organization must purchase "negative carbon" from the market to offset it. Therefore, from the perspective of an organization's liability for carbon emissions offsetting, it is in its interest to receive fewer input carbon tickets and issue more output carbon tickets.

7.3.2.2 Carbon Ticket Content and Format

The content and format of carbon tickets are standardized by the national management authorities. All operations and management related to carbon tickets are conducted within the Carbon Ticket Management System (CTMS), which exclusively utilizes electronic tickets, eliminating the need for any paper-based documentation.

The detailed information recorded on a CEL ticket includes: ticket serial number, seller details, buyer details, product code, name, specification, quantity, CEL per unit, CEL, and issuance information such as checker and operator (Fig. 7.1).

The seller issues the ticket in the CTMS, and the purchaser confirms the receipt of the ticket in the CTMS.

7.3.2.3 Carbon Ticket Issuance Rules

The issuance and circulation of carbon tickets must ensure the real-time, accurate, and complete management of social carbon footprint data, preventing unscrupulous organizations from profiting from loopholes. Government authorities will formulate

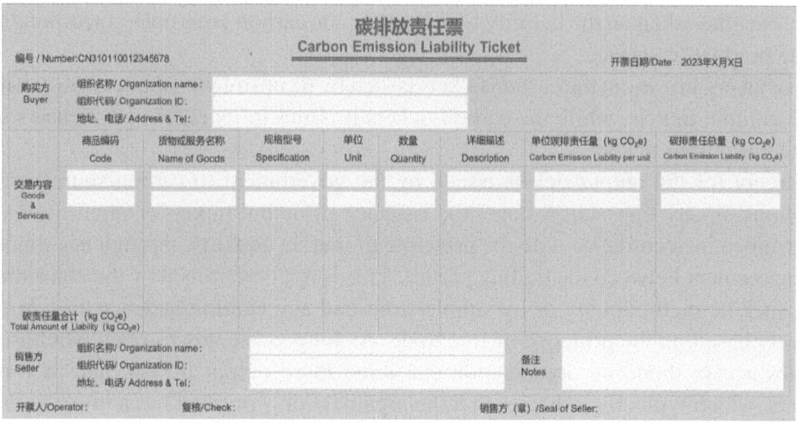
碳排放责任票
Carbon Emission Liability Ticket

编号 / Number:CN310110012345678

开票日期/Date: 2023年X月X日

购买方 Buyer
组织名称/ Organization name:
组织代码/ Organization ID:
地址、电话/ Address & Tel:

交易内容 Goods & Services	商品编码 Code	货物或服务名称 Name of Goods	规格型号 Specification	单位 Unit	数量 Quantity	详细描述 Description	单位碳排责任量 (kg CO_2e) Carbon Emission Liability per unit	碳排责任总量 (kg CO_2e) Carbon Emission Liability (kg CO_2e)

碳责任量合计 (kg CO_2e) Total Amount of Liability (kg CO_2e)

销售方 Seller
组织名称/ Organization name:
组织代码/ Organization ID:
地址、电话/ Address & Tel:

备注 Notes

开票人/Operator: 复核/Check: 销售方（章）/Seal of Seller:

Fig. 7.1 Carbon ticket sample

specific regulations and policies to ensure the legitimacy and smooth functioning of the carbon ticket system. The following rules should be clearly defined.

1. The issuance and circulation of carbon tickets should be based on real transactions

Carbon tickets follow the transaction process, not the physical goods. Both physical goods and services carry carbon emission liability. Carbon tickets are related to standard tax invoices but are not the same and must be issued independently. In addition, carbon tickets must specify the carbon emissions generated by a particular product or service transaction and provide the quantity of the product or service. The quantity should be determined by the transaction contract and should correspond to the carbon emission liability associated with the carbon ticket.

Carbon tickets are not allowed to be issued falsely or in a circular manner for the purpose of speculation. False issuance of carbon tickets for speculative purposes will be treated as a serious illegal act, akin to falsely issuing VAT invoices. Government management departments and judicial authorities will jointly formulate relevant legal systems.

2. Guarantee of correspondence and accuracy

A transaction contract may be split into multiple parts according to the delivery schedule, but the product quantity and CEL on each carbon ticket should match. The aim is to create accurate carbon footprint data and carbon emission factors that can be used by the entire society, providing data support for comprehensive carbon emission management.

3. Complete and accurate content information

All entries on carbon tickets must be complete and accurate. The CTMS employs an intelligent review system to verify the reasonableness of submitted carbon tickets and provides feedback to the users. In case of errors, a certain fine can be imposed to enhance the quality of carbon ticket operations and reduce data discrepancies.

4. Validity principle

The carbon ticket becomes effective when the seller issues it to the purchaser, who then confirms it. This carbon ticket is then recorded in the organization's carbon account for settlement and inclusion in the carbon ticket database.

Once the carbon ticket system is operational, it is inevitable that many issues will arise. Through practical application, the rules for operating the carbon ticket system can be continuously improved.

7.3.2.4 Processing Examples of Input and Output of Carbon Tickets

Example 1 Processing of input and output of carbon tickets for a construction company's contract project

The Project Department B of Construction Group A has undertaken the construction contract for the SH Center project from the Urban Investment Company of City SH. The contract covers a construction area of 500,000 square meters and a contract value of 10 billion yuan, with a contract carbon ticket volume of 1 million tons, meaning the contracting party accepts carbon input tickets worthy of 1 million tons.

After five years of construction, the project is completed and delivered.

During the five-year construction period, Construction Group A received a total of 20,000 carbon tickets from various material, equipment suppliers, and subcontractors, totaling 900,000 tons of carbon. Specifically, in the first year, they received 100,000 tons, in the second year, 150,000 tons, in the third year, 150,000 tons, in the fourth year, 200,000 tons, and in the fifth year, 300,000 tons.

Construction Group A has been engaging in periodic process settlement and final project settlement with the Urban Investment Company of City SH throughout the construction process. How does the Project Department B of Construction Group A handle the input carbon tickets for the SH Center project?

Within the CELM, the carbon ticket circulation volume between trading parties is determined through negotiation and can also be explicitly outlined in the contract. For this project, the SH Urban Investment Company will delineate the CEL as a distinct bidding item in the tender documents. There are two distinct bidding approaches: (1) Fixed CEL: The tender documents will define a fixed threshold for the project's allowable carbon emissions, and all bidders will propose their bids based on this predetermined value. Under this situation, the client will select the winning bidder based on the lowest construction and installation cost. (2) Open competition: The tender documents will permit a competitive bidding process for the carbon emission quantity. The winning bid will be selected based on the lowest total construction and installation cost combined with the lowest carbon fee. The amount of carbon emissions is then established in the contract based on the bidding outcome, and the client will only accept carbon input tickets that are in line with the stipulations in the contract. The contract will also delineate the conditions and principles governing the issuance of the contractor's carbon output tickets during the project's progress. These provisions will form indispensable contract clauses within the broader context of societal decarbonation, and the clauses related to carbon ticket handling will become a pivotal component of the contractual agreement.

Under the CELM, the general contractor also adopts a similar approach when selecting suppliers. In addition to meeting the technical specifications of the products and services as required by the tender, the general contractor selects suppliers based on the lowest total carbon fee and product price.

Given that the project duration is 5 years, process settlement is necessary. To comply with government requirements for all organizations to settle their carbon accounts on a quarterly basis to minimize financial tie-up in carbon fees, the Project Department B of Construction Group A, with the assistance of the group's finance department, will sort out and analyze the carbon input tickets received each quarter. According to the project schedule and the carbon ticket handling clauses in the contract, they will aim to issue carbon output tickets as early and as frequently as possible. If the carbon output tickets issued during each stage exceeding the input tickets, this results in a "negative carbon" on the carbon tickets, indicating a business surplus, with positive net cash flow. The finance department will categorize this surplus as the income earned by the project department. If the carbon output tickets issued are less than the input tickets, the project department will accumulate carbon emissions, indicating a business loss, with negative cash flow. The finance department will categorize this carbon fee loss as a loss induced by the project department.

The project department of the contracting party (the Urban Investment Company of City SH) will control the acceptance of carbon input tickets according to the progress of the project and the terms of the contract.

Throughout the various stages of the carbon ticket circulation between the parties, each carbon output ticket issued by the contracting party (Construction Group A) will specify the project name, the total amount of carbon tickets, and the construction area corresponding to the carbon amount (not the total contract construction area). After the final settlement of the project, the total CEL from all the carbon tickets will sum up to the contractually agreed total, which in this case is 1 million tons. Therefore, Construction Group A will issue carbon output tickets totaling 1 million tons. The total construction area from all the carbon tickets will add up to the total contract construction area of 1 million square meters. It is particularly important to note that in the CELM-based CTMS, the product delivered by the construction contractor is the construction project, and the unit of delivery is the construction area. Therefore, the construction company issues carbon output tickets with the product unit being the construction area.

The cumulative carbon input tickets received by Project Department B from its suppliers and subcontractors amounts to an impressive 900,000 tons, culminating in a remarkable achievement of 100,000 tons of "negative carbon". This exceptional outcome underscores the project company's adeptness in meticulously managing carbon emissions during the procurement of materials and equipment, as well as in the selection of subcontractors, surpassing the contractual benchmarks. As a result, the realized 100,000 tons of carbon negative can be capitalized upon by being traded in the carbon market, thereby increasing the profit. Given the prevailing carbon price in China's vibrant carbon markets, which stands at approximately 60 yuan per ton, it can provide a potential revenue boost of 6 million yuan to Project Department B. To streamline and optimize these financial transactions, the finance department of Construction Engineering Group A oversees the centralized disposal across all projects within the group's unified CEL carbon account. This centralized approach ensures that the market value equivalent to 6 million yuan, derived from the carbon negative achievement, is duly allocated to Project Department B's overall profit, while maintaining the ownership of the 100,000 tons of carbon negative assets within the company's portfolio. The entire process is meticulously conducted by the company's finance department.

Example 2 Processing of input and output of carbon tickets for research projects conducted by university research teams

A dedicated research team led by professors and Ph.D. candidates from TJ University embarked on an ambitious research endeavor for the SH Municipal Government, titled "Fostering Carbon Neutrality in the Yangtze River Delta Region". This project, valued at 1 million yuan, concluded successfully after a yearlong journey. Throughout the execution of the project, the research team managed its financial resources, allocating funds to various vital expenditures. These expenditures included 100,000 yuan for transportation, 50,000 yuan for printing materials, 30,000 yuan for office electricity, 50,000 yuan for replacing five malfunctioning computers, 50,000 yuan for organizing meetings, and 30,000 yuan for expert consultations. Concurrently, the project has acquired a total of 200 input tickets from upstream suppliers, representing 100 tons of carbon emissions. How should the research team and the university manage the input of carbon tickets?

Two distinct scenarios emerge.

Scenario 1: If the tender document from the SH Municipal Government stipulated that the project fee encompassed carbon costs and the purchaser (SH) declined to accept carbon tickets, the research team must neutralize the necessary carbon in their project. Specifically, they should procure 100 tons of negative carbon from the carbon market, valued at 6000 yuan (calculated at 60 yuan per ton), to offset their emissions. To facilitate this process, the university's finance department can deduct the 6000 yuan from their allocated funds and manage the acquisition and settlement of the carbon offsets, ensuring compliance and efficiency.

Scenario 2: If the project fee excludes carbon fees and the tender document explicitly allows for the transfer of input tickets of 100 tons to the SH Municipal Government, the research team should issue the corresponding output tickets alongside a VAT invoice to the government.

In the scenario where the research team receives an excess of carbon tickets of 20 tons beyond the stipulated amount (totaling 120 tons), they should assume liability for the additional emissions. To offset this imbalance, they must purchase 20 tons of negative carbon from the carbon market, costing 1200 yuan. The university's finance department would deduct this amount from the team's funds and administer the settlement of the additional carbon offset.

If upstream suppliers furnish input tickets of 80 tons during the project, and the team subsequently issues output carbon tickets of 100 tons to the government, it effectively generates a 20-ton carbon negative surplus. As recognition for this achievement, the university rewards the team with an additional 1200 yuan, and the university is responsible for managing the entire process, encompassing carbon offsetting, sales of the carbon negative surplus, and investment and management of carbon assets.

Summarizing the two cases, it is essential to emphasize that the amount of CEL carbon tickets in the industrial chain is definite through negotiations, forming a component of future contractual and commercial terms. They are not derived from formulaic calculations or exhaustive equipment-based monitoring. And only such a system can appeal to all members of the society, incorporating them into the carbon reduction system and driving carbon reduction efforts throughout.

7.3.3 *Main Functions of the CTMS*

7.3.3.1 For Social Organizations (Enterprises)

1. Recording transaction data flow of input tickets in the CEL carbon account

The CTMS seamlessly receives and reviews input tickets issued from upstream suppliers. Upon satisfactory review, the system promptly confirms and acknowledges these tickets, and then the system generates and issues output tickets to downstream customers.

Besides summarizing and analyzing the input and output of carbon tickets, it can also provide real-time access to carbon stock data.

2. Outputting carbon footprint data for their diverse product portfolio

The CTMS meticulously allocates carbon liability metrics to each product within the organization's extensive portfolio, ensuring a precise alignment with the total amount of CEL.

Recognizing the complexity of product range in a business organization, which may span thousands of unique items and may utilize diverse energy sources, the system expertly facilitates the intricate matching, corresponding, and decomposition of these multifaceted elements.

Moreover, the CTMS boasts advanced multidimensional statistical analysis capabilities. It offers flexible statistical analysis based on diverse criteria, including varying time periods, specific materials used, individual products, and distinct service categories.

3. Facilitating efficient quarterly settlement and liquidation of carbon stocks

The CTMS streamlines the quarterly settlement and liquidation of carbon stocks for organizations. For organizations holding carbon stocks, the system enables them to procure negative carbon from the negative carbon trading market. Subsequently, the

CTMS expertly performs hedging and write-offs (carbon offsets) between existing carbon stocks and the acquired negative carbon products, effortlessly updating the organization's carbon stock inventory and negative carbon data.

For those carbon accounts that generate a surplus of negative carbon, where carbon output exceeds input, the CTMS facilitates the sale of these excess negative carbon products on the carbon market.

4. Facilitating negative carbon trading directly via CTMS

The CTMS serves as a direct channel to the carbon market trading system, seamlessly bridging the data gap between the two systems. When an organization finds itself with either a surplus or deficit in carbon stocks, the system promptly facilitates connections to the carbon market. For organizations with positive carbon stocks, the CTMS enables the purchase of negative carbon products to facilitate settlement. Conversely, for those with excess negative carbon products, the system streamlines the sale process, offering a potent incentive for organizations committed to low-carbon practices.

5. Establishing a comprehensive social carbon emission factor database through statistical analysis of the social benchmark for carbon emissions of various materials and products

The CTMS empowers users to query the prevailing social benchmark for carbon emissions associated with diverse products. These benchmarks, commonly known as carbon emission factors, are invaluable tools for assessing carbon emissions of project proposals and engineering design schemes.

6. Management of carbon removals

Enterprises investing in carbon removal projects can leverage the CTMS to manage their endeavors with precision. Upon successful verification by government-approved certifying authorities, these enterprises obtain certificates representing the amount of negative carbon products granted by the government. These negative carbon products can then be utilized to offset the organization's carbon emissions.

The CTMS further enhances this process by integrating with the National CEL Carbon Asset Registration System, facilitating carbon asset registration and write-offs.

7. Management of carbon assets

Organizations can proactively manage their carbon assets by strategically purchasing or selling them on the carbon market. They can also capitalize on price fluctuations and forecasts to invest in future carbon products and others. Through carbon asset management, organizations can not only minimize carbon emission costs but also engage in profitable investment arbitrage. The carbon finance market, coveted by nations worldwide for expansion, faces challenges due to limitations in current tools and top-level designs. Nevertheless, the CELM-based NCTM emerges as a capable contender, poised to overcome these hurdles.

The CTMS also plays a pivotal role by providing organizations with access to comprehensive price curves and insightful trend analysis results.

8. Functioning as a carbon management command center

The CTMS can aggregate and visually present the most crucial data that organizational leaders prioritize, and then transform these complex data into intuitive graphical representations, facilitating decision-making and directing carbon management for organizational leaders.

7.3.3.2 For Households

1. Integrating with population databases to establish household CEL carbon accounts

The CTMS integrates with population databases, fostering the creation of individualized household CEL carbon accounts. This integration consolidates the carbon footprint of each family member into a unified account. This not only lays the groundwork for family-level carbon emission management but also equips governments with a robust, systematic tool to effectively implement consumer-centric carbon reduction policies.

2. Monitoring total carbon emissions, carbon removals, and carbon stocks in household accounts

The CTMS enables monitoring aggregated carbon emission data of a family, including total carbon emissions, total carbon removals, and carbon stocks. It can analyze carbon emissions across various categories such as food, transportation, clothing, etc., and present them in visual charts, thus creating easy comprehension of carbon data for a family.

3. Controlling household carbon removals

In rural areas, a large number of farmers contract forests and therefore generate carbon removals, which can become an important source of income for families in the future. Therefore, it's imperative to manage family carbon removal data. Certified by government-approved verification agencies and received negative carbon certificates issued by the government, these carbon removals transform into family assets that can be sold for monetary value at opportune times.

4. Carbon asset investment: Purchasing and selling "negative carbon" and aspiring for zero-carbon families

Families dedicated to the pursuit of zero-carbon living, embodying their commitment to carbon neutrality, can harness the power of the CTMS to acquire negative carbon from the carbon market. By doing so, they effectively offset their household carbon emissions, transforming into exemplary families achieving carbon neutrality (zero-carbon families) and actively contributing to societal sustainability efforts.

Additionally, families can engage in carbon asset investment through the CTMS, and purchase and sell at the right time to earn margins, which can become a significant option for families to hedge against currency inflation.

7.3.3.3 For Government Departments in Charge of Carbon Management

1. Facilitating transparent access to transaction records of input and output of carbon tickets

Leveraging the CTMS, governmental carbon management departments can efficiently conduct comprehensive summaries and sophisticated statistical analyses on transactions associated with individual carbon accounts, empowering them with real-time insights into carbon stocks as well.

Furthermore, the CTMS' robust backward tracing functionality enables a holistic view of the carbon footprint of any organization or product, spanning the entire lifecycle.

2. Conducting basic data input and meta-analysis of carbon sources

Governmental carbon management departments issue output tickets to various carbon source enterprises.

Multi-level authorization should be considered for basic data input of carbon sources, aligning with the administration system. Verification and confirmation of data input can be conducted by governmental management departments at various levels, with large-scale state-owned enterprises collaborating with central authorities and local energy companies collaborating with local governments.

The CTMS also supports advanced meta-analysis for basic data of carbon sources, enabling powerful aggregations and insights across multiple dimensions, such as time, regions, energy types, and industries.

3. Reviewing and analyzing carbon account settlement and payment

The CTMS possesses the capability to review and conduct statistical analyses of monthly (or quarterly) settlement and payment transactions across all organizations.

4. Multifaceted statistical analysis of carbon emissions

The system facilitates comprehensive statistical analyses tailored to diverse dimensions, encompassing time periods, organizations, materials, products, and service categories.

Additionally, it incorporates a robust sorting function, enabling the categorization of industries based on crucial indicators like total carbon emissions, carbon emission intensity per ten thousand yuan of output value, and emission intensity per unit of production (e.g., tons in steel and cement sectors, gross floor area in construction), thereby providing support for policy design.

5. Data application

The CTMS can accurately and completely output carbon footprint data of various materials and products, providing accurate basic data for carbon emission management across the society and the development of green finance.

6. Conducting statistical analysis of the social benchmark values of carbon emissions for all products, and establishing carbon emission factor database for various industries

The system pioneers the development of a dynamic and precise factor database for societal carbon emission management, addressing a pivotal challenge in contemporary practices. Instead of solely relying on societal forces, the establishment of this factor database must be with the help of digitization and informatization, and the CTMS can accomplish this milestone.

7. Implementing intelligent verification of carbon tickets

The system can implement basic intelligent verification and analysis for each carbon ticket and provide feedback to issuing organizations, enhancing ticket quality and preventing risks.

8. Providing analysis and early warning against abnormal situations and anti-carbon ticket fraud

Where there is interest, there are challenges. Therefore, the CTMS can draw on the experience of the VAT system, which has long been addressing fraud, to swiftly develop its own response capabilities as best as it can.

For instance, the system can track and trace the carbon footprint of every organization and product, spanning the entire production lifecycle.

As a fully digital system in all respects from inception, the CTMS faces significantly reduced supervision challenges compared to paper-intensive systems like VAT, boasting inherent strength in monitoring and fabrication prevention and thus relatively less regulatory pressure.

9. Empowering government with AI-driven decision support

Leveraging the big data on societal carbon footprints, the system constructs sophisticated models to delve into historical patterns, anticipate carbon reduction trajectories, and offer policymakers invaluable insights into carbon mitigation strategies and their macroeconomic implications. Notably, it presents reliable intelligent forecasts for future carbon pricing frameworks.

10. Navigating carbon tariffs

The CTMS ensures export enterprises have access to precise and verifiable carbon footprint data for their products. With the cooperation with national carbon markets, this capability preempts domestic carbon emission costs, safeguarding against unnecessary carbon tariffs imposed by foreign nations. As the EU's CBAM comes into force, posing a challenge to China's international trade, the "1+1" framework emerges as the optimal countermeasure. Consequently, the CTMS must promptly develop dedicated functionalities and applications to effectively manage carbon tariffs.

11. The CTMS: A governmental hub for carbon management

The CTMS should establish a governmental hub for carbon management to provide at-a-glance and dynamic views of key indicators, with timely alerts for abnormalities.

These key indicators include total carbon emissions, total carbon removals, settlement and payment, industry-specific conditions, dynamic conditions like critical consumer-side data, and trend charts for major indicators.

12. Achieving fully electronic (paperless) operation

The CTMS distinguishes itself by operating with a significantly reduced carbon footprint compared to the VAT system, achieving complete electronization right from inception. By eliminating the reliance on paper documents, it fosters a low-carbon carbon ticket management system. In contrast, the VAT system, burdened by the excessive use of paper invoices and consequently high carbon emissions, is still in the midst of transitioning towards paperlessness. The CTMS, however, bypasses this interim phase, embracing full paperlessness, electronization, and digitization immediately.

7.3.4 Essential Capabilities of the CTMS

1. Unparalleled data capacity

To record the exhaustive carbon footprint data of society, a mammoth volume of information must be efficiently managed, necessitating a colossal data capacity. To fulfill this requirement, the implementation of a robust, multi-tiered storage architecture, integrating high-performance databases, data lakes, and data warehouses, is paramount.

2. Ensuring data security and confidentiality

As the CTMS accumulates a substantial volume of data over time, its significance escalates, becoming a cornerstone for China's carbon neutrality efforts and economic advancement. Recognizing the paramount importance of these data, which encompasses national economic security and vital interests, safeguarding its confidentiality and security assumes utmost priority.

The security measures for big data systems, including disaster preparedness, cyber-attack prevention, and data leakage safeguards, must attain the pinnacle of information system security protection standards. Furthermore, it is imperative to establish multiple offsite data centers for disaster recovery.

A comprehensive data security protection framework must be devised, accompanied by stringent regulations governing data utilization and secondary development, thereby fostering a robust legal landscape that safeguards data security.

3. Efficient data processing and swift response

Given the immense societal demand for data querying and statistical analysis, the CTMS must possess exceptional processing capabilities and great computing power.

4. Early warnings against abnormal situations

The CTMS can promptly alert and autonomously address abnormal situations, such as irregularities in carbon footprint records and query anomalies, efficiently identify suspicious carbon accounts and tickets as well. A dedicated professional team, coupled with a continually updated knowledge base of anomaly judgment rules, further strengthens the system's intelligent analysis capabilities.

5. Robust capabilities for secondary development, interfacing with external systems, and compatible with other systems.

The CTMS ought to offer robust API (Application Programming Interface) and SDK (Software Development Kit), alongside other secondary development toolkits, to the public domain, empowering seamless integration into diverse digital management systems. Therefore, the system must carry rigorous permission control and data desensitization capabilities.

The system's direct integration capabilities extend to, but are not confined to, critical national systems such as the National CEL Carbon Asset Registration System, National Carbon Market Trading System, National Institution Code System, National Population Management Data System, National VAT System, National Macroeconomic Analysis System, and Banking Payment System.

6. Empowering data mining and AI-driven analysis

The carbon footprint big database holds a giant amount of data with immense value, transcending mere carbon emission management. It also holds profound potential for application in diverse domains, including national economic management, industry regulation, and corporate governance, catering to the needs of governments, industry authorities, and enterprises alike.

To harness this potential, the database must boast optimized table structures and view designs. Furthermore, it should enable the efficient generation of knowledge graphs and support the integration of advanced AI algorithms, like integrable large-scale models, aimed at unleashing the full potential of data mining and automating application.

7.3.5 Seamless Integration with Carbon Exchange Platforms for Account Settlement

The direct and seamless integration of the CTMS with carbon exchange platforms is paramount. During each settlement cycle, organizations are mandated to undertake carbon account settlement, where those in possession of carbon tickets must procure negative carbon products from the market for carbon offsets, while those with negative carbon stocks capitalize on them by selling them for profit. Consequently, establishing a frictionless link between the CTMS and the carbon market is imperative, facilitating regular settlement processes for societal organizations.

The CTMS also enables the management of carbon assets for social organizations. Based on its carbon emission needs and carbon asset investment, an organization can purchase or sell carbon assets, negative carbon, in advance. Hence, it's crucial to easily access the carbon exchange from the CTMS to trade negative carbon products and manage carbon assets efficiently.

7.3.6 Integration with Taxation Systems

The integration of the CTMS with the Golden Tax System is a necessity. These two sets of data, when combined, can provide vital insights for government's macro-management, serving as a crucial tool for decision-making.

Given the financial significance of carbon tickets, the CTMS must incorporate robust mechanisms to combat fraud and arbitrage. By interfacing with taxation systems, the system enhances data verification and analysis across the supply chain.

Special emphasis must be placed on the integration of the CTMS with the Golden Tax System, particularly in aligning organization codes, material codes, and ticket numbers, which requires meticulous design to ensure data interoperability and exchange efficiency. Relatively, the CTMS has higher management requirement compared to the Golden Tax System.

7.3.7 Developing an Intelligent Coding System Tailored to CTMS Requirements for Materials, Products, and Service

To streamline the analysis of carbon footprints across the entire spectrum of materials, products, and services within the society and accurately assess industry-wide benchmarks for specific categories, a unified and intelligent coding system spanning all materials, products, and services is essential. This system should facilitate big data processing, enabling the higher-dimension and finer-granularity exploitation and utilization of the big data.

The coding system's core requirements encompass:

1. Recording and analyzing carbon footprint data for an organization (enterprise).
2. Granular product-level carbon footprint analysis.
3. Allowing statistical analysis of the normative social carbon emission values for product groups, and the establishment of a factor database of social dynamic carbon emissions.

The GS1 standard currently dominates the market with its widespread adoption as an international benchmark. Due to the current VAT system's less stringent coding requirements, it has not adopted the GS1 standard. Whether the CTMS should adopt the GS1 standard or other coding standards remains to be studied, issues need to be considered include:

First, whether the GS1 fully meets the CTMS's needs for data processing and analysis.

Second, whether the GS1 fully aligns with the need for digital transformation of the society at large. In the future, with so many digital systems in China, unifying the encoding of master data is extremely urgent.

7.3.8 *Anti-fraud Capabilities of the CTMS*

The CTMS, based on the CELM, inherently presents a lower risk landscape for fraud compared to traditional VAT systems, yet it necessitates unwavering vigilance. Carbon tickets, seemingly merely manifest the embodied CEL in commodities but ultimately impose carbon emission costs on products. Therefore, they, akin to the VAT, can be considered as equity certificates. Given the evolving carbon emission management system, governments have already addressed several instances of carbon data fraud.

The input and output of carbon tickets of social organizations are both managed within the national CTMS, making it relatively easy to ensure data authenticity. By linking with the VAT system, the CTMS anti-fraud capabilities are further strengthened, but inevitably encountering fraud.

7.3.8.1 Potential Fraud Scenarios

One concerning strategy employed by fraudulent enterprises involves establishing downstream enterprises to whom they transfer substantial carbon tickets, falsely portraying negative carbon emissions that are then monetized. These downstream enterprises may be legitimate enterprises with genuine transaction histories or shell companies solely created for arbitrage purposes. Additionally, a layered scheme of fraud may emerge, where downstream enterprises issue fictitious carbon tickets to their own downstream partners, creating a complex web of arbitrage and circulation. In such scenarios, enterprises at the end of this chain, burdened with carbon stocks, are unlikely to fulfill their settlement and payment, while those at the forefront profiting from the arbitrage.

7.3.8.2 Analysis of Illegal Arbitrage

While legitimate enterprises with operational realities would typically refrain from participating in carbon arbitrage schemes due to the increase in product costs, those on the brink of bankruptcy or closure may view such maneuvers as a desperate attempt to generate profit. Consequently, premeditated, multi-layered arbitrage scams emerge as a more probable threat.

Analysis and recognition of the intelligent anti-fraud system empowered by the CTMS: Introducing an intelligent anti-fraud system module in the initial phase of the CTMS, harnessing global big data analytics, can significantly enhance the system's ability to detect such schemes.

1. The system conducts rationality analysis on enterprises with negative carbon emissions, scrutinizing their carbon emissions per unit output or yield against industry peers. Any notable deviations, indicating potential anomalies, trigger further inquiry into the underlying reasons, such as the adoption of advanced carbon reduction technologies or green energy usage. By combining systematic data analysis with field inspections, the system ensures precise identification of irregularities. Additionally, historical data analysis flags unusual changes, facilitating problem detection through both data analytics and on-site verification.
2. The system delves into the intricate layers of the transaction chain, conducting multi-faceted data analysis until carbon neutrality is achieved. Such arbitrage scams inherently involve upstream enterprises arbitraging while downstream ones evading liability. If the CTMS tracks large carbon stocks in downstream enterprises accompanied by irregular settlements, these indicators serve as red flags, prompting immediate anti-fraud investigations into upstream enterprises with reported negative carbon emissions. In this manner, the CTMS demonstrates robust analytical prowess and early warning capabilities, making fraudulent arbitrage endeavors exceedingly challenging to execute.
3. The CTMS meticulously scrutinizes stark disparities between carbon emission input and output. Both disproportionately high and low ratios can serve as signs of potential abnormality, necessitating extended data analysis to mitigate associated risks.

In conclusion, armed with its comprehensive data of carbon footprints across the transaction chain, the CTMS boasts formidable problem detection and prevention capabilities, effectively limiting overall risks of fraud and arbitrage. It can regularly screen enterprises that either report unusually large carbon stocks or maintain significant carbon stocks without corresponding settlements, serving as a potent tool in curbing fraudulent arbitrage practices across the board.

In conclusion, both international and domestic carbon markets have witnessed numerous cases of carbon emission data falsification and fraud, necessitating heightened vigilance.

7.3.9 Making Data Interfaces Available to Organizations Across the Society

The CTMS possesses a vast and detailed big data repository of socio-economic activities, providing detailed carbon footprint data and powerful analytical tools for organizations and individuals across the society. It offers two sets of data: carbon footprint and the social cost of carbon. To support and mobilize all members joint efforts in contributing to carbon peaking and carbon neutrality, the system should provide scalable API data interfaces and SDK development toolkits to external information systems.

Furthermore, the data generated by the CTMS will become a significant data asset for macroeconomics, which could be developed to create numerous data products and powerful new productivity tools, playing a crucial role in macroeconomic development and regulation.

Of course, careful planning and design are necessary when facing different entities and applications, what data should be provided, as well as how data desensitization should be handled.

Chapter 8
Negative Carbon Trading Market (NCTM)

Eight provinces and municipalities in China have progressively ventured into carbon markets as pilot projects, yet their progress remained modest over the past decade. The scene shifted dramatically following the announcement of China's ambitious "3060" dual carbon targets (achieving carbon peaking by 2030 and carbon neutrality by 2060), reigniting a surge of interest and renewed efforts towards establishing carbon markets nationwide. However, hindered by the nascent state of theories guiding their construction, the development of these markets has yet to yield substantial breakthroughs.

The NCTM (Negative Carbon Trading Market) scheme based on the CELM, coupled with the Carbon Ticket Management System (CTMS), the most significant policy instruments for carbon reduction, will assist us in successfully building China's carbon markets and becoming a driving force in the pursuit of domestic and global carbon neutrality.

8.1 Top-Level Design for the National Negative Carbon Trading Market

The NCTM based on the CELM, distinct from conventional carbon trading markets that primarily focus on CEL, introduces a novel paradigm in terms of transaction objects, trading mechanisms, and market functionalities. Given the lack of a well-established theoretical system or practical experience worldwide, the significance of a meticulously crafted top-level design for fully leveraging the critical role of the NCTM cannot be overstated (Fig. 8.1).

B. Yang, *The Carbon Emission Liability Mechanism*,
https://doi.org/10.1007/978-981-96-3612-9_8

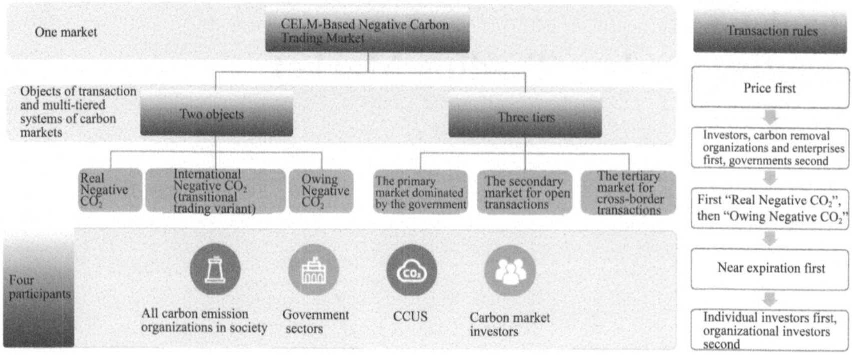

Fig. 8.1 Top-level design of the CELM-based negative carbon trading market

8.1.1 Building a Unified National Carbon Market (One Market)

Extensive research and practical applications have conclusively shown that reforming China's carbon trading market necessitates the establishment of a nationwide, unified carbon market grounded in the CELM theory, with "negative carbon" as its core transaction object. Only such an approach can address the current state of fragmentation and limited scale that characterizes the market for CEL. The global carbon reduction landscape demands a more comprehensive alignment with the diverse aspirations of achieving carbon neutrality worldwide, and a unified, large-scale carbon market offers a platform for optimal resource allocation.

The transaction object of "negative carbon" is inherently geared towards the ultimate objective of carbon neutrality, providing a gradual yet steadfast path towards this goal. In contrast, carbon emission rights, as government-mandated instruments designed to manage total emissions at specific junctures, serve different purposes and thus yield different outcomes. In 2015, the COP 21 and the CMP 11, which were held in Paris, established a mechanism of common but differentiated responsibilities, with major countries committing to Nationally Determined Contributions (NDCs) for carbon reduction. From then, the selection and design of policy instruments against carbon emissions should shift comprehensively towards carbon neutrality, simplifying many challenges at the same time.

8.1.1.1 Nationwide Unified Carbon Market

Negative carbon, defined as the removal of one ton of CO_2 from the atmosphere, represents a standardized process that carries equal significance for global carbon neutrality, regardless of its geographical location. This standardization paves the way for the establishment of unified national and global carbon markets.

If China emerges as a pioneer in fostering a "negative carbon" market, it will undoubtedly secure the initiative in the international carbon market landscape. The establishment of a unified carbon market is crucial, which will even be of greater strategic significance for China if the country gains dominance in the globally unified carbon market.

Having conducted a decade-long series of local pilot projects centered on carbon emission rights, China's nationwide carbon market embarked on its inaugural journey in July 2021. In stark contrast, the NCTM, grounded in the CELM, can be implemented nationwide from its inception, circumventing the need for the pilot projects across provinces and cities. Moreover, this direct approach mitigates risks inherent in the market's nascent stages, with aspirations firmly set on forging an internationally unified carbon market directly.

Leveraging the synergy between the NCTM and the CTMS, the former, during its initial phase, can facilitate risk-mitigated endeavors such as a modest carbon pricing scheme or even offering carbon allowances free of charge for trial operations, thus minimizing potential macroeconomic disruptions. The adoption of regional pilot models within the CELM-based carbon trading market is ill-suited due to the likelihood that issues encountered may not adequately reflect national-scale challenges, thereby necessitating the avoidance of such potentially misleading approaches.

Upon establishing a nationwide carbon market grounded in the CELM, the process of phasing out smaller, fragmented, and comparatively less influential provincial and municipal carbon markets centered on carbon emission rights can be expedited. This pivotal move will empower China to ascend to the pinnacle of the globally unified carbon market, bringing into full play the advantages in its vast carbon market and substantial carbon-negative production capabilities, as well as strengths in renewable energy sector and the China Energy Internet, built upon Ultra-High Voltage (UHV) technology. This comprehensive strategy will position China as a global leader in the realm of international negative carbon trading.

8.1.1.2 Vision, Mission, and Goal of the CELM-Based Carbon Market

For an endeavor to better fulfill its vitality and value, it must possess great cause genes. China's CELM-based carbon market is no exception, adhering steadfastly to the principles of fairness and efficiency while striving to support the construction of a community with a shared future for all mankind. It embarks on this journey with a visionary outlook, embracing a broad and long-term perspective with ambitious vision, mission and goal.

Vision: To attain global carbon neutrality, rendering our planet a more beautiful and habitable home for humanity.

Mission: To elevate China's carbon market to one of the most crucial parts in the global carbon neutrality.

Goal: To achieve global carbon neutrality five years ahead of schedule, by 2045.

Values: Upholding fairness, efficiency and positivity, and fostering global collaboration towards a brighter future.

The CELM-driven decarbonation system will profoundly reshape the global landscape of climate issues, ushering in a new era where China, once being accused in the realm of global climate governance, now stands poised to lead the charge towards achieving global carbon neutrality and contribute significantly to building a community with a shared future for mankind.

8.1.2 Transaction Objects of Carbon Market (Two Objects)

At the crux of the CELM-based carbon market lies the cornerstone concept of "negative carbon", which includes two pivotal trading objects. These objects, in their evolution, can be further divided into three distinct categories in phases.

1. Real Negative CO_2 (Trading Code: RN.CO_2)

Real Negative CO_2 (or real negative carbon) represents the equivalent of CO_2 removed from the atmosphere by carbon removal (or carbon absorption) organizations with real costs associated with carbon absorption. These organizations encompass governments and enterprises managing forests, professional CCUS (Carbon Capture, Utilization, and Storage) enterprises equipped with advanced carbon absorption facilities, as well as a diverse array of other organizations and individuals possessing carbon absorption capabilities. The quantity of "Real Negative CO_2" must be meticulously verified by internationally recognized certification bodies and registered within the national-level carbon asset management system, ensuring its status as a globally standardized commodity with universally consistent significance and value standards for advancing global carbon neutrality, transcending geographical boundaries.

In the initial phase, the primary demand for "Real Negative CO_2" emanates from advanced enterprises, particularly those with stringent moral and ethical commitments to environmental preservation, such as renowned IT giants (Alibaba, Tencent, Huawei, among others), software enterprises, and pivotal central state-owned corporations. These enterprises, inherently low-carbon in nature with minimal carbon emissions, especially in terms of carbon emission intensity, are poised to surpass their corporate carbon neutrality ahead of schedule. They are also motivated to purchase the "Real Negative CO_2" at relatively high prices in the carbon market to offset their CEL and thus achieve corporate carbon neutrality. Therefore, they take the lead in assuming their social liability for carbon neutrality, and often earn favorable ESG (Environmental, Social, and Governance) ratings from the international community.

The trading price of "Real Negative CO_2" within the carbon market is dynamically determined through market-based transactions, taking into account the actual costs incurred, as well as supply and demand volumes of both sides. As the number of carbon removal organizations proliferate and the cost associated with the CCUS technologies decreases, the price of "Real Negative CO_2" is anticipated to undergo a swift and pronounced decline.

Prior to the price of "Owing Negative CO_2" fully aligning with the actual costs of carbon absorption, there arises a distinct demand for "Real Negative CO_2" from export-oriented enterprises, seeking to circumvent border measures imposed by Europe and the United States, as exemplified by the EU's CBAM (Carbon Border Adjustment Mechanism). By purchasing "Real Negative CO_2", Chinese exports achieve carbon neutrality and thus transform into zero-carbon products, thereby evading potential carbon tariffs levied by importing nations under any pretext. However, given the elevated price of "Real Negative CO_2" during its initial stages, the International Negative Carbon, a virtual negative carbon solution, can serve as a viable transitional option through strategic trading negotiations.

Carbon removal organizations leverage the revenue generated from the sale of "Real Negative CO_2" to sustain their operations and generate organizational profits. This, in turn, fuels continuous production and technological advancements, ultimately leading to increased output and a consistent reduction in costs.

In scenarios of supply–demand imbalances, particularly acute shortages of "Real Negative CO_2" within the carbon market, governments can intervene by selling virtual "Real Negative CO_2" futures to stabilize the market. Crucially, these futures must be promptly produced and ready for offsetting, so as to uphold international credibility.

The purchases of "Real Negative CO_2" by export enterprises to achieve carbon neutrality in their products will undoubtedly lead to a notable surge in their actual costs. Nevertheless, three strategic approaches can effectively alleviate this burden: Firstly, embracing innovative technologies and refined management practices to expedite carbon reduction efforts and alleviate carbon emissions. Secondly, incorporating carbon fees into product prices and thereby charging from foreign import enterprises, which subsequently pass them on to downstream consumers, manifesting the "consume liability" principle. Lastly, governmental intervention through targeted tax adjustments, akin to previous export tax rebates which reduce VAT and income taxes on profits, can reduce export costs and bolster the competitiveness of domestic products' prices.

The significance of "Real Negative CO_2" products cannot be overstated, as they serve as the cornerstone for advancing the international carbon market. China's endeavor to establish an international carbon market regards "Real Negative CO_2" as its transaction object. Enabling foreign carbon emitters to procure these products from China's market merits the acknowledgment of local authorities, as it represents the tangible removal of one ton of CO_2 from the atmosphere. After the establishment of the CELM-based NCTM, China should promptly establish dedicated teams to publicize the CELM concept and China's NCTM blueprint, aiming for widespread international recognition, potentially even from the United Nations, thereby fostering the development of a globally preeminent international carbon market within its borders.

Because of the initial premium associated with "Real Negative CO_2", it is plausible that a transitional trading alternative, "International Negative CO_2" (Trading Code: $IN.CO_2$), may emerge, which means periodic carbon prices recognized in international trade. The EU's CBAM is setting the price of carbon during the transition phase.

Notably, the price of "International Negative CO_2" lies below the actual price of "Real Negative CO_2" but exceeds that of the "Owing Negative CO_2" mentioned below, facilitating periodic mutual recognition in international trade. Products meeting this threshold are eligible for exemption from carbon tariffs, therefore, exporters are exempted from tariffs by acquiring "International Negative CO_2" for carbon offsetting. As the greatest manufacturer and a significant exporter, China's carbon market must brace itself for the imminent tide of carbon tariffs.

Chinese export enterprises confront two pivotal challenges in navigating the EU's CBAM:

- Firstly, they must ascertain the CBAM's carbon price standard and proactively engage in domestic carbon offsetting, adhering to the CBAM-approved carbon price that safeguards against carbon tariff imposition.
- Presently, the EU's CBAM operates unilaterally, with self-made carbon pricing for imports dictated by the price in the European carbon markets, hovering between 80 and 100 Euros per ton, a substantial figure. Export products with competitive carbon emission intensities may evade tariff losses, yet those lacking such advantage will encounter significant competitiveness erosion. Ideally, a reasonable international carbon trading price should emerge from a multilateral framework, where periodic carbon prices are collaboratively determined and upheld to.
- Secondly, accurately quantifying a product's carbon emissions is crucial. The CTMS offers authentic, reliable, and verifiable data on products' carbon footprints, addressing the dual challenges posed by carbon tariffs in trade with Europe and the United States.

2. Owing Negative CO_2 (Trading Code: ON.CO_2)

"Owing Negative CO_2" refers to the "negative carbon" that is directly imported into the carbon market by the government, which does not actually remove CO_2 out of the atmosphere, but is available to social organizations to offset their carbon emissions. The government departments are the first issuers of carbon output tickets, with a large amount of carbon output tickets to sell, but no input tickets, thus the government has a lot of "negative carbon" to sell in the carbon market. The revenue generated from the sale of "negative carbon" by government departments is injected into the "National Carbon Neutral Fund", which is used for appropriate inputs to promote the national carbon neutrality process. Therefore, as the overall authority responsible for carbon neutrality, government departments are entitled to receive this revenue. The CELM-based carbon market has created a good model for the collection of the national carbon fees, which, being reasonable and efficient, opens up a huge financial source for the government departments and provides strong investment backing for the green economic transition.

The annual amount of "Owing Negative CO_2" that the government inputs into the carbon market is equivalent to the total amount of CEL that the entire macro-economy needs to offset, which is roughly equal to the total amount of carbon sources minus the total amount of "Real Negative CO_2" that is exported by the carbon removal organizations. The carbon pricing of "Owing Negative CO_2" in the first phase of the CELM is equivalent to an oligopolistic market pricing mechanism. Fortunately, this oligopoly is the national government. The government will comprehensively set the price according to the macroeconomic performance and carbon neutrality process, starting from the principle of maximizing social welfare, which is very beneficial to both the government and the whole society.

When a large amount of funds invested in carbon assets enters the carbon market, the government can increase the input of "Owing Negative CO_2" to obtain more funds for carbon reduction. However, the government needs to manage the funds properly and subsequently handle the repurchase.

The price of "Owing Negative CO_2" will be much lower than that of "Real Negative CO_2" in the initial stage, and even zero pricing can be used during the trial period. Gradually it converges to the price of "Real Negative CO_2" year by year. The function of "Owing Negative CO_2" is to facilitate the government to gradually incorporate the cost of carbon emissions into the economic system: firstly, it allocates the CEL to the overall economy and the whole society, ultimately to the consumers. Secondly, it obtains funds for carbon reduction, which can be invested in carbon reduction projects and technological innovation and upgrading. However, considering the affordability of the real economy and avoiding inflation, a long-term process is needed to gradually increase the carbon price. All enterprises with a CEL stock will have to purchase "Real Negative CO_2" or "Owing Negative CO_2" from the carbon market to balance their carbon input and output and bear the liability for emission reduction.

The "Real Negative CO_2" in China's carbon market is an internationally traded carbon asset product, while the "Owing Negative CO_2" serves as a policy instrument for domestic carbon control and reduction. As the cost of CCUS decreases and the requirements for carbon control and reduction increase, the price of "Owing Negative CO_2" will gradually rise and finally become consistent with the price of "Real Negative CO_2". At this point, all transaction objects in the carbon market will become "Real Negative CO_2", and "Owing Negative CO_2" will have completed its historical mission, exiting the stage of carbon neutrality, which signifies that we will have achieved carbon neutrality for the whole society. Therefore, until the price of "Owing Negative CO_2" aligns with the prevailing market price of CCUS, which is the price of "Real Negative CO_2", it serves as a tradable product for domestic carbon-emitting organizations to fulfill their carbon reduction obligations, therefore, it is only suitable for transactions among domestic carbon emitters. The revenue from "Owing Negative CO_2" belongs to the national government and is used for investments related to carbon reduction, as detailed in Sect. 13.5.

The core transaction objects of the NCTM under the CELM consist of two products, and with variations, there will be three products in the longer term. In a prosperous international carbon market, financial derivatives will also gradually increase.

8.1.3 Multi-tier Carbon Market (Three Tiers)

The government, as the largest exporter of carbon emissions, inputs "Owing Negative CO_2" into the carbon market, while the carbon removal organizations input "Real Negative CO_2" into the carbon market, forming the primary market. The secondary market involves all carbon market participants conducting transactions within the domestic carbon market. The tertiary market involves transactions among international carbon market participants. China's carbon market is expected to be the earliest to form a fully equipped carbon market with three tiers based on the CELM, which is crucial for China to establish a global carbon market financial center.

The primary market in the first stage is mainly an oligopolistic market dominated by the government. This is related to China's state-owned system for energy resources, which may be different in other countries. As the maintainer of atmospheric public goods, the government can solve the problem of carbon source output through legislation. The government inputs "Owing Negative CO_2" into the carbon market, while carbon removal organizations input "Real Negative CO_2" into the carbon market, forming the primary market.

The amount of "Owing Negative CO_2" input by the government into the carbon market = the total carbon sources − the total amount of "Real Negative CO_2".

In the first stage, the amount of "Real Negative CO_2" is limited, requiring the government to provide sufficient amount of "Owing Negative CO_2".

Because the government is the maintainer of atmospheric public goods and the primary issuer of carbon tickets, it holds a natural monopoly position in the CELM-based carbon market. The government can regulate the carbon market in a relatively orderly and precise manner, and the government's pricing power will be strong, providing the market with clear expectations.

When the production of "Real Negative CO_2" exceeds the amount of "Owing Negative CO_2", the carbon market will transition towards a fully market-oriented form.

The secondary market is a trading market that includes all relevant parties involved in the carbon market. Participants in the secondary market freely match and trade, making it an open and free trading market. The secondary market should embrace social investment institutions and individual investors as early as possibly, which will activate the market, enhance fundraising capabilities for carbon reduction projects, and expand the scale and influence of green finance in the financial market.

Through proactive government regulation, the secondary market can avoid significant fluctuations in carbon prices. In the CELM-based NCTM, the government can fully and effectively control market prices. If the secondary market develops well, carbon assets can become an important asset for investment institutions and households, serving as a hedge against currency inflation for investors and even potentially replacing real estate, the so-called financial reservoir, to some extent.

The tertiary market is the international carbon market. The carbon market is expected to become the financial market with the most potential and international financial influence after the oil market. The international carbon market has great potential for development, and China should strive to make progress. To take the lead in establishing an international carbon financial market, China enjoys many favorable conditions: the largest carbon emission scale; the leading production scale and strength in the renewable energy industry chain, such as photovoltaic sector; the greatest potential for renewable energy production; and advanced technology in the Energy Internet (especially ultra-high voltage technology).

Due to inconsistent standards and difficulties in quantifying value, the internationalization of carbon markets based on carbon emission rights is currently challenging to achieve. Although the Certified Emission Reduction (CER) products from Clean Development Mechanism (CDM) projects can be traded internationally, there are more problems and countries have imposed significant restrictions, making it difficult for them to develop. The fundamental reason is that the standard line for emission reductions and the recognition of additionality are considered artificial, making it hard to reach a consensus and achieve a unified market. The transaction object of "Real Negative CO_2" in the CELM-based carbon market is not plagued by similar issues and is an excellent transaction object for the international carbon market.

Subsequently, capital derivatives can be added to the secondary and tertiary markets, including the introduction of carbon futures products to provide additional tools for capital risk management. This will enhance market vitality and capital volume, strengthening support for the real economy.

8.1.4 Market Participants (Four Types)

The CELM-based NCTM exhibits a high level of inclusivity towards participating entities. Its objective is to allow more entities to participate while maintaining the stability of the carbon market, thereby fostering a market atmosphere where the whole society is involved in carbon reduction. This approach aims to pool more resources into the cause of green economic transformation. There are four main types of market participants as follows.

1. Government departments. The government is the primary contributor of "Owing Negative CO_2" and the main force in the primary market, holding significant pricing power in the market. Additionally, government departments serve as regulators of the carbon market, promoting its stable development through the design of regulatory mechanisms.
2. All carbon-emitting organizations across the society. Essentially, this encompasses all social organizations, production sectors, management sectors, and social sectors. Any entity that utilizes energy and materials that result in carbon emissions should bear the corresponding liability for carbon reduction. Under the operation of CTMS, organizations with CEL stocks need to purchase "negative carbon" from the carbon market to settle their carbon accounts, achieving the offset of carbon stock in their carbon accounts or balancing the input and output of carbon tickets.

Many organizations that aspire to build outstanding ESG (Environmental, Social, and Governance) socially responsible brands have already announced their carbon neutrality goals. These organizations can achieve carbon neutrality by investing in carbon sequestration projects (such as afforestation, installing carbon sequestration equipment, etc.), or by purchasing "Real Negative CO_2" from the carbon market. Essentially, these organizations fund the carbon sequestration efforts of professional institutions, which fully embodies the specialization of labor in society and represents a more efficient institutional arrangement.

Some social organizations that do not produce tangible products also consume energy and generate CEL stock. These organizations have carbon ticket inflows but it is difficult to issue carbon output tickets, so they need to buy "negative carbon" from the carbon market to achieve carbon balance in their carbon accounts. As a result, with the addition of CEL expenses to their annual operational budgets, these organizations naturally tend to prioritize reductions in energy consumption and carbon emissions.

Organizations that sell products to end-consumers and receive a cash carbon fee from consumers need to purchase "negative carbon" in the carbon market to balance their carbon accounts.

All carbon-emitting organizations in the whole society must purchase the corresponding amount of "green tickets", i.e. "negative carbon" products once there is a balance of CEL, i.e. "red tickets". The red and green tickets will offset each other's liability, thus realizing the offsetting of CEL.

Therefore, once the CELM is launched, all social organizations and individuals will be integrated into the carbon market.

3. Carbon removal organizations ("negative carbon" output organizations, CCUS organizations). Carbon removal organizations are one of the key forces in achieving carbon neutrality. They produce "Real Negative CO_2", which involves removing CO_2 directly from the atmosphere. These organizations may include forestry organizations, carbon capture technology operators, and other entities that can remove carbon from the atmosphere. Recognized by the government and even internationally relevant organizations, they undergo verification by third-party institutions to periodically obtain certification of their carbon sequestration capacity. By selling "Real Negative CO_2" in the carbon market, they earn revenue. CCUS organizations may also generate income from other sources, such as using the removed carbon as a raw material for other products, such as oil repellents for the oil fields and dry ice for the food industry. With sufficient revenue, these organizations will accelerate the development of a vast CCUS industry.

   The significance of carbon removal organizations transcends mere achievement of carbon neutrality. Rather, they are instrumental in facilitating the removal of substantial carbon stocks from the atmosphere, thereby diminishing the overall carbon footprint currently present. This underscores the enduring necessity for the endeavors of such organizations in the long run.

   It is very important that carbon removal organizations should continue to upgrade their technology and scale up efforts to reduce the cost of CCUS, and when the production cost per ton of "Real Negative CO_2" reaches a cost that is acceptable to all social organizations, we will have achieved sustainable carbon neutrality.

Ecological resource regions require greater income compensation from the carbon market, which can be utilized for the maintenance and conservation of forests and grasslands, while simultaneously contributing to regional social development and enhancing the living standards of local residents, thereby realizing common prosperity. The CELM-based NCTM facilitates the implementation of the national concept that "Lucid waters and lush mountains are invaluable assets." The transfer payments between economically developed provinces and ecological resource regions are more direct and rapid, leading to better synergistic effects.

4. Carbon market investors. Carbon market investors include financial investment institutions, banks, general organizations and individuals. The carbon market encourages social capital to participate in carbon market transactions, thereby increasing capital sources for the scaled development of green finance, which will support research and development of energy-saving, emission reduction and low-carbon development technologies, and also provide a new and huge reservoir for social capital. Huang Qifan, academic advisor of the China Finance 40 Forum (CF40)[1] and former mayor of Chongqing, stated that in the process of promoting the realization of the dual carbon goals, China's energy structure and industrial structure will undergo profound adjustments, generating massive investment needs that could potentially reach 200 trillion yuan. It is impossible for the government to fully fund such a huge amount of investment, and thus it is necessary to mobilize social capital. It is crucial for the Chinese carbon market based on the CELM to complete its institutional design and construction as soon as possible, allowing institutional and individual investors to enter the market early, which is vital for advancing carbon neutrality and developing green finance.

   However, the government has to take into account the need to avoid excessive "hoarding" of carbon assets by speculative entities, which could lead to significant market fluctuations. Carbon exchanges need to continuously improve their management systems and exercise a certain degree of control. It is evident that the CELM-based carbon market is far easier to regulate than the current carbon market, being more stable and healthier than the stock market, and there is less need to worry about adverse events such as significant fluctuations and crashes.

   It should be necessary to set a certain expiration date for carbon assets (Fig. 8.2).

[1] China Finance 40 Forum (CF40), founded on April 12, 2008, is one of the most influential think tank platforms in China, focusing on policy research and exchange in the economic and financial field—a note by the translator.

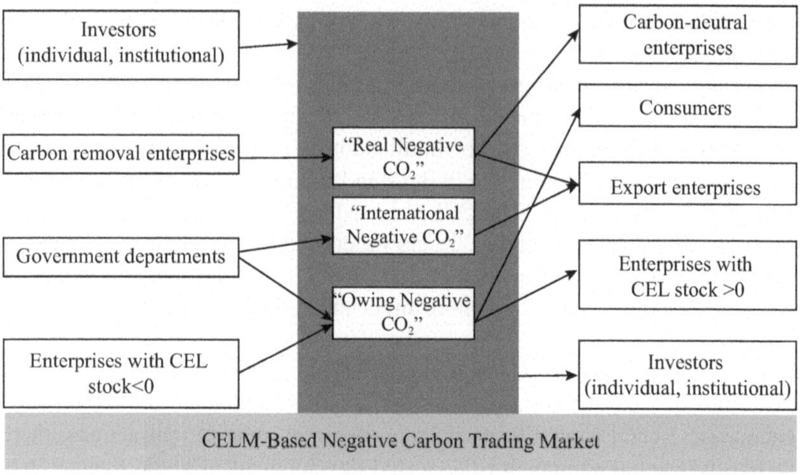

Fig. 8.2 CELM-based negative carbon trading market

8.1.5 Carbon Pricing Mechanism in the Negative Carbon Trading Market

In the CELM-based NCTM, transactions among various parties are conducted freely based on publicly disclosed trading rules. The carbon market utilizes an electronic matching system operated by the exchange to automatically facilitate transactions. Short-term and minor fluctuations in carbon prices are fully determined by market forces.

On the basis of market-based pricing, the government, as the largest provider of "Owing Negative CO_2" trading assets, leverages its oligopolistic position to exert significant influence on price, and even possesses pricing power.

Only when there are great price fluctuations in the market that affect the normal production order of the overall real economy, can the government increase the input of "Owing Negative CO_2", increase supply, or conduct repurchases to intervene in the market, forming a stable carbon asset market rather than a highly speculative one.

A normally operating CELM-based NCTM will undergo through two stages with significantly different pricing.

Phase 1: Separate pricing for each of the three trading products.

In this stage, the carbon market primarily comprises three trading products: "Real Negative CO_2," "Owing Negative CO_2," and "International Negative CO_2", each with unique pricing mechanisms that exhibit significant differences.

"Real Negative CO_2" trading prices are fully determined by the market. A segment of forward-thinking, low-carbon emission enterprises, aspiring to lead the way in carbon neutrality, will purchase "Real Negative CO_2" products to offset their CEL in their carbon accounts. This is because the enterprises using "Owing Negative CO_2" or other types of offsets cannot be considered carbon–neutral, but merely fulfilling the offset obligations mandated by the country. Only "Real Negative CO_2" genuinely removes CO_2 from the atmosphere, providing a robust scientific basis and quantifiable standard that prevents companies from easily engaging in "greenwashing." With a national-level system providing authoritative judgments, self-declared or socially declared carbon–neutral green enterprises are not acknowledged by the country. The verification process ensures that only those who genuinely contribute to carbon reduction through "Real Negative CO_2" can claim the title of carbon neutrality.

As a result, the pricing of "Real Negative CO_2" is fully determined by the transactions between the supply and demand sides.

"Owing Negative CO_2" is regulated and priced by the state based on a unified consideration of the carbon neutrality process and economic growth needs. Since the government is the sole provider of "Owing Negative CO_2" trading products, it acts as a market monopolist with absolute pricing power. The total amount of "Owing Negative CO_2" is significant, and so is the demand. The price of "Owing Negative CO_2" in the first phase is crucial, as it relates to the success or failure of the carbon market. During the trial operation phase, it can operate at zero yuan for a period of time, and after pricing commences, the price will gradually increase to accelerate the pace of decarbonation. At the same time, the affordability of economic growth and the increased costs for enterprises must be taken into account. According to estimates, the NCTM will not impose significant inflation on the overall macroeconomy in order to achieve the carbon neutrality process. In the initial stage, assuming China's total carbon emissions are 12 Gt (at 50 yuan per ton), the total cost increase would be approximately 600 billion yuan. Compared to a GDP base of over 100 trillion yuan, this increase is not significant, and there would not be significant pressure on inflation.

One of the major advantages of CELM-based NCTM is that the government has the right to control pricing. When regulating pricing, the government will definitely take into account the welfare of all people, ensuring that the fluctuation of carbon prices is within the acceptable range of the public.

"International Negative CO_2" is determined through international trade negotiations. International Negative CO_2 serves as a transmission intermediary for addressing the carbon border adjustment mechanism in international trade, aimed at resolving issues related to carbon tariffs in international trade. Typically, "International Negative CO_2" should be negotiated and determined in a multilateral framework, with phased carbon prices being established through negotiations. However, the EU's CBAM has set a poor precedent by unilaterally establishing a carbon border adjustment mechanism, and the G7 is also poised to follow suit. China and other developing countries need to adopt the CELM as soon as possible in order to avoid heavy losses.

Phase 2: Price convergence and gradual unification of the three trading products.

As the price of "Owing Negative CO_2" increases and the price of "Real Negative CO_2" gradually declines, the prices of these three "Negative CO_2" products become increasingly closer and at last converge, ultimately leaving only the "Real Negative CO_2" trading product. At this point, the international community has achieved net-zero carbon emissions, which is known as carbon neutrality. Reaching this second stage will require a relatively long period of time (Fig. 8.3).

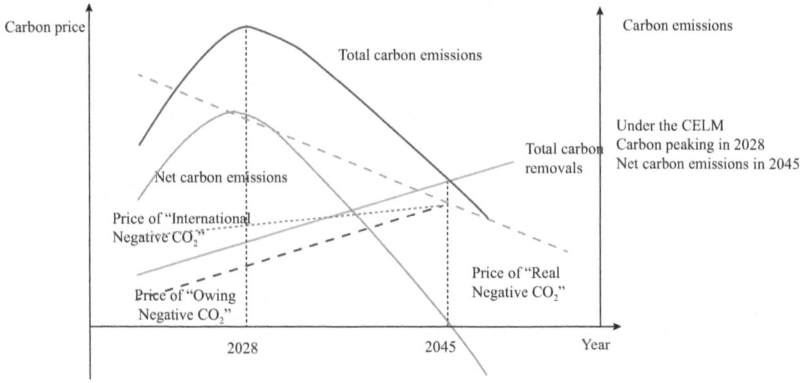

Fig. 8.3 Price trend of three "Negative CO_2" under the CELM

8.1.6 *Order Rules for the Matching of Transactions in the Trading Market*

To uphold fair market practices and ensure seamless operations, the rationale behind transaction order rules is paramount. Establishing the following key order rules for negative carbon market is imperative:

- Firstly, price is prioritized. Adhering to the universal principle of price precedence, the NCTM must also conform to this fundamental rule.
- Secondly, a strategic sequence must be established, prioritizing investors, carbon removal organizations, enterprises, and lastly, the government in a supportive role. This arrangement fosters a balanced supply–demand dynamic, stabilizes the market, and safeguards the legitimate interests of carbon market investors. The government is the ultimate carbon source owner, ultimate liability bearer for carbon neutrality, and a significant issuer of "Owing Negative CO_2". Mechanisms must be devised to incentivize all entities and individuals to reduce emissions, thereby enhancing investor confidence and mitigating risk perceptions.
- Thirdly, transactions of "Real Negative CO_2" should be prioritized over those of "Owing Negative CO_2". Funds generated from "Real Negative CO_2" transactions flow to carbon removal organizations, as they directly contribute to emission reductions. While the funds generated from "Owing Negative CO_2" flow to the government, de-emphasizing the government's role in this context.
- Fourthly, transactions with the shortest validity period should be prioritized over those with longer durations. This strategy bolsters investor enthusiasm, acts as a safeguard for investor interests, and mitigates risks associated with asset management.
- Fifthly, individual investors are prioritized over organizational investors. Policies that prioritize the interests of individual investors are deemed fitting within this context, as their engagement holds immense value in fostering a nationwide awareness towards carbon reduction.

Distinguishing itself from conventional stock markets, the carbon trading system addresses the unique challenges posed by expiration dates and the diversity of transaction objects. To accommodate these complexities, the system enables investors to place orders with enhanced reminder settings and robust investment management functionalities.

Throughout the pilot phase of the carbon market trading system, it is imperative to continuously solicit market feedback, promptly identify issues, and iteratively refine trading regulations. This approach aims to avert scenarios reminiscent of the prolonged suppression of individual investors observed in China's stock market.

8.1.7 Storage, Expiration Date, and Pre-lending of Carbon Assets

Enabling investors to acquire negative carbon products and retain and sell them until market conditions are favorable can significantly bolster investor interest, attract additional capital for carbon reduction initiatives, and foster the growth of carbon finance markets. While the extended holding period benefits investors, excessive accumulation of such assets can potentially exert a substantial market impact at a given point, posing challenges for government intervention. Consequently, establishing an expiration date for these products is crucial.

It is advisable to initially set the validity period for transaction objects at three years, aiming to prevent excessive storage and encourage investors to liquidate their holdings in a timely manner, thereby mitigating risks. This period may be adjusted based on subsequent operational performance, with a potential extension to 3–6 years once sufficient experience has been gained. Permanently extending the validity is discouraged to prevent unforeseen market disruptions.

Upon expiration of the holding period, unsold "negative carbon" products would be deemed invalid, with the transaction interpreted as the purchaser's contribution to societal carbon neutrality, that is, a testament to the investor's commitment to sequestering carbon from the atmosphere and safeguarding our planet. The carbon market investment system should incorporate a reminder feature, potentially leveraging SMS notifications, to safeguard investor interests and prevent avoidable losses.

The carbon market generally does not support such practices as pre-lending, that is, market entities realize current development by overdrawing future development potential. However, market entities may be permitted to pay market-determined rates to extend their current positions, acknowledging the need for a gradual approach to developing derivatives that support the evolution of carbon financial markets while managing risk exposure appropriately.

8.2 Carbon Futures Market

The carbon futures market holds paramount significance and is poised to assume an ever-growing role in the realm of green finance. "Real Negative CO_2" products, upon certification, necessitates no physical delivery, thereby facilitating seamless trading and aligning perfectly with the development of futures products. This market enables the discovery of forward prices, facilitating long-term hedging strategies for investments in carbon reduction endeavors. Its financial function is not only demanded by the carbon market but also constitutes a vital component in fostering the growth of green finance.

Given the protracted investment period inherent in green energy and CCUS technology industries, the carbon market must support maturity mismatches and risk management, as well. as support cross-period investments. These demands for financial derivatives underscore the necessity for a comprehensive financial system within the carbon market.

Undeniably, the government must accord paramount importance to risk prevention in the carbon futures market, as there remains possibility for excessive speculation. Historical incidents such as the 327 Treasury Bond Event,[2] "Crude Oil Treasure" episode by the Bank of China, and the recent nickel short squeeze of Tsingshan Group in the LME London Metal Exchange futures market serve as stark reminders of the potential for colossal risks in futures markets, particularly when subject to external manipulation. As a result, the government must promptly embark on a thorough examination of the potential risks unique to the carbon futures market, crafting targeted countermeasures to address them. Additionally, it is imperative to initiate top-level research and design endeavors specifically tailored to this market, with continuous refinement and optimization over time.

Overall, the dynamics of the carbon market, characterized by periods of booms and busts, are largely influenced by a limited number of factors, with government intervention playing a pivotal role. Firstly, the government holds a dominant position as a near-monopoly in the carbon market and serves as the primary exporter of carbon sources. Secondly, the comprehensive market data managed by CTMS simplifies decision-making processes. However, with the market's internationalization, it will inevitably attract international speculators, adding complexity to the landscape. Therefore, it is crucial for the government to anticipate and strategize, particularly by maintaining control over the rule-making framework.

The inevitable growth of the international carbon futures market underscores the urgency for the government to take the initiative to fight for control, including the control of the trading market, the right to make rules of the game and the right to set prices. Lessons learned from incidents like the Bank of China's "Crude Oil Treasure" episode and the nickel short squeeze of Tsingshan Group highlight the significance

[2] 327 Treasury Bond event is a very influential event in the history of China's futures market, which occurred on February 23, 1995. This event not only had a profound impact on the treasury bond futures market at that time, but also posed a severe challenge to the supervision and risk control of China's financial market—a note by the translator.

of dominating the futures market. China's carbon market, with its favorable conditions, is poised to emerge as a global leader. To achieve this, the government must possess robust theoretical and practical innovation capabilities, swiftly seizing the strategic high ground. The introduction of the CELM theory provides both theoretical underpinnings and a top-level design blueprint for the government's endeavors.

8.3 Anticipated Challenges in Carbon Market and Government Regulation Mechanism

Amidst the ongoing pursuit of the "3060" dual carbon targets, the establishment of an ideal carbon market underpinned by the CELM is expected. This ideal market envisages stability, predictability, and a robust government regulatory capacity, fostering a progressively intensified drive for carbon reduction across society. Initially, the government, as the primary holder of negative carbon resources, occupies an oligopolistic position, shaping the carbon market as a "maker". However, with the decline in the cost of "Real Negative CO_2" and the subsequent surge in market supply, the government's influence diminishes, marking the market gradually mature and stable. Nevertheless, the path to this market's development is fraught with challenges, necessitating proactive strategies, thorough planning, and preventive mechanisms. The operational challenges confronting the NCTM may arise from the following aspects:

1. In a given period, investors may purchase a large quantity of futures. Assuming that China's total carbon emissions in 2023 are 10 Gt, if the market is bullish, investors buy more than 10 Gt, or even several times this amount, meaning that the demand for "negative carbon" will greatly exceed the actual carbon emissions in the year. The actual carbon-emitting organizations have a precise requirement for "negative carbon", and if the market demand from these organizations necessitates the government's intervention to provide additional "negative carbon", the government must inject the corresponding amounts into the market. To prevent a price surge that could adversely affect the macroeconomy, the government can leverage its monopoly pricing authority to boost the supply of "negative carbon" to the market, thereby stabilizing market prices.
2. In a given period, investors may flood the market with excessive "negative carbon", which will depress the expected carbon price, undermining emission reduction efforts and inflicting losses on some investors. In such scenarios, the government can employ a buy-back mechanism at the anticipated carbon price. Given that the excess carbon was originally exported by the government and funded accordingly, this approach enables the government to maintain robust price control capabilities.
3. The futures market landscape is fraught with a myriad of unique and hazardous scenarios, ranging from notable events, such as 327 Treasury Bond Event, "Crude Oil Treasure" episode by the Bank of China, and the recent nickel short squeeze

of Tsingshan Group. These events highlight the enduring coexistence of market vulnerabilities and speculative entities. While the carbon futures market shares some inherent risks common to other futures markets, their severity is mitigated, but still deserves our attention.

A distinctive challenge in carbon futures lies in their non-deliverable nature, particularly for short positions nearing maturity. Drawing from the wisdom of other futures markets, it is imperative to manage quantity at location and margins meticulously. Additionally, reinforcing risk education and intensifying data monitoring mechanisms are vital steps towards mitigating potential exposures.

Meanwhile, it is essential to mitigate irrational short squeezes. In scenarios where carbon prices soar to irrational heights, swift and decisive measures must be in place. This includes implementing mechanisms like daily price increase caps and other regulatory tools to curb irrational and malicious market manipulations.

A notable advantage of the carbon market is the government's pivotal role as a stabilizer, offering a degree of predictability and control unparalleled in other futures markets. This advantage would be intensified if China assumes a leadership position in shaping the international carbon market.

8.4 Construction of an International Carbon Trading Market

Establishing and dominating the international carbon market should be prioritized as a pivotal national policy for China. The introduction of the CELM theory serves as a robust theoretical cornerstone for realizing this strategic ambition, emphasizing the urgency of swift and decisive action.

An international carbon market centered on "Real Negative CO_2" as its primary object is poised to encounter minimal international resistance. The CELM-based "Real Negative CO_2" represents an international standard product, with uniform content and value globally, akin to ubiquitous commodities like clothing or automobiles. Clear-cut property rights dictate who produces, who benefits, and who holds the authority to control the associated revenue, facilitating seamless international transactions. This starkly contrasts with the non-standard, non-universally recognized nature of carbon emission rights, Certified Emission Reduction (CER), and carbon tariffs, which are essentially taxes levied by Western countries on producing nations. Producers invest in pollution control, yet consumer nations impose these tariffs, lacking a robust legal foundation and posing difficulties in clarifying ownership and usage rights of the revenue from the tariffs, thereby hindering their widespread adoption.

To establish an international carbon market, China must initially expedite the global dissemination of the CELM theory and secure international consensus. This theory resonates strongly with developing nations, as it mitigates the overall welfare losses of the international community and accelerates global carbon neutrality. Additionally, the CELM theory brings development opportunities for developing nations, reduces the impact of unreasonable carbon tariff mechanism, and offers these countries a platform to earn substantial revenues from the transactions of "Real Negative CO_2", notably in carbon removal regions like Africa. Developed nations, sharing a common interest in addressing the global climate crisis, are also likely to support this initiative.

Once the CELM theory attains international consensus, foreign carbon emitters and investors will flock to China's carbon market to purchase "Real Negative CO_2", while carbon removal organizations worldwide will sell their products in this market, fostering a genuine international carbon market. The potential for further development within this market is immense. Moving forward, we envision designing and introducing innovative trading products, fostering the international futures and bond markets, and positioning China as the cornerstone of global green finance.

The establishment of China as a preeminent international carbon market, both in size and influence, will exert far-reaching significance and propel the world towards a greener, more sustainable future.

1. Enhancing China's discourse in international climate governance

Chinese academics and regulators have historically been bound by Western-defined rules and the carbon market rules. Leveraging the CELM theoretical system, China stands poised to establish a more scientifically rigorous, equitable, and efficient carbon neutrality framework, thereby garnering broader international support and recognition.

2. Pursuing the expansion of the green finance market

A study conducted by World Bank underscores the daunting task ahead, estimating that achieving global carbon neutrality over the next four decades will require investments exceeding \$200 trillion. This monumental figure underscores the urgency for China to capitalize on its potential. As the global green economy undergoes a transformation, China must strive to secure a significant international market share and exert considerable influence. To this end, the pioneering CELM-based "1+1" system, the "Carbon Ticket Management System + Negative Carbon Trading Market" model can serve as a cornerstone and facilitate the establishment of the largest and most reputable international carbon market, which will significantly bolster China's position in advancing global green finance.

8.5 National CEL Carbon Asset Registration System

The operation of the CELM-based NCTM requires a national negative Carbon Asset Registration System (CARS) as its backbone. This system serves a pivotal role in defining carbon asset ownership, facilitating transaction settlement, and ensuring rigorous verification processes. At the heart of China's carbon neutrality management framework, the national CEL CARS stands alongside the Carbon Market

Trading System (CMTS) and Carbon Ticket Management System (CTMS) as the three cornerstone data systems.

Crucially, the national negative CARS, rooted in the CELM, represents a significant departure from the national registration system for carbon emission rights that commenced in July 2021. While the earlier system focuses solely on registering carbon emission rights, the CARS is geared towards registering "negative carbon" assets, highlighting a fundamental distinction in their nature and thus, the systems themselves. Substantial resources have been dedicated to the design and establishment of these systems, emphasizing the urgency for the government to expedite the promotion and implementation of the CELM.

The main functions of the national negative CARS based on the CELM include:

1. The CARS system records the amount of "negative carbon" assets upon production, ensuring the registration and confirmation of ownership rights.

Carbon removal organizations, such as forest management entities and CCUS organizations, generate "Real Negative CO_2" that undergoes verification by internationally or nationally recognized certification bodies, which grant them a certificate of confirmation. These organizations can then access their carbon assets within the CARS system, facilitating seamless sales in the carbon market at any time.

Annually, the government injects 10 billion tons of "Owing Negative CO_2" and "International Negative CO_2" assets into the CARS system, dedicated to settling and offsetting CEL stocks acquired by emission-generating organizations. Consequently, during the initial phase, the majority of carbon assets managed by the CARS consist of government-injected assets.

When the cumulative carbon input tickets by all emission-generating organizations across society falls below the total carbon output tickets, a "negative carbon" asset is created, eligible for registration in the CARS system. This system cross-checks data with the CTMS, completing asset registration through a rigorous approval process.

2. As carbon assets enter the trading stage within the carbon market, the CARS system oversees transaction settlement and ownership transfer registration.

Owners of the three types of "negative carbon" assets can freely trade them in the market. Upon completion of a transaction, the CARS system facilitates ownership transfer registration, achieved through seamless data exchange with the CMTS system.

3. The carbon emission organizations acquire "negative carbon" assets to fulfill their obligations, thereby offsetting their emission stocks. These "negative carbon" assets need to be written off.

Quarterly, all carbon emission organizations within society undergo a settlement process in the system, where those organizations holding CEL stocks procure "negative carbon" assets from the carbon market to settle their CEL. These "negative carbon" assets are then neutralized and written off within the CARS.

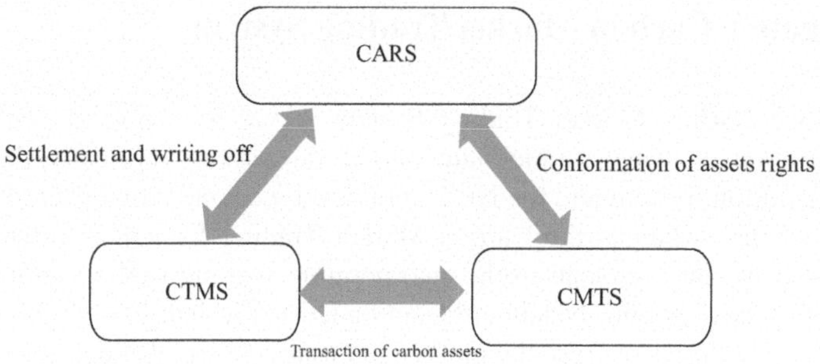

Fig. 8.4 Three core data systems for China's carbon policy instruments

The national CARS, rooted in the CELM, constitutes a pivotal big data platform within the carbon finance ecosystem. It necessitates a uniform nationwide implementation and seamless integration with both the national CMTS and the CTMS, ensuring real-time data connectivity. The system must possess high-performance capabilities, capable of supporting the real-time, high-frequency data processing demands of both the CMTS and the CTMS (Fig. 8.4).

The national CARS, the CTMS and the CMTS constitute the three core data systems of China's "1+1+1" carbon policy instruments, and stand as the most critical soft infrastructure facilitating China's journey towards carbon neutrality. Meanwhile, the world's energy Internet and renewable energy base form the complementary "1+1" hard infrastructure foundation.

The distinction of the registration system for CARS with that for CCER and that for carbon emission rights is as follows:

The registration system for CARS specializes in registering negative carbon assets, while the national registration system for carbon emission rights oversees the registration of carbon emission rights, and that for CCER handles certified emission reductions. These three systems are distinct; therefore, CARS needs to be completely rebuilt. However, under the CELM, the three are unified into one, and only the registration system for CARS is required, significantly streamlining the entire carbon asset management landscape.

The compliance cycle of carbon emission rights spans a year, with the registration system in charge of the settlement process. This paradigm contrasts sharply with the "negative carbon" offsetting process, which has prompted a redesign of CARS to cater to the unique demands of the negative carbon market.

CARS possesses three pivotal carbon assets, all conforming to standardized product specifications. The system's management focus is notably clear-cut. In comparison to the existing two registration systems, the development and operation of this system are significantly more straightforward and less complex.

8.6 Negative Carbon Market Trading System

The Negative Carbon Market Trading System serves as a pivotal platform for matching carbon exchanges to facilitate market transactions. Typically, the Carbon Asset Registration System and the NCTS are developed and administered by regulatory authorities, whereas the Carbon Market Trading System is often tailored and managed by the exchange itself, incorporating specific trading protocols like continuous trading, pricing benchmarks, and auction mechanisms. The authorities and financial regulators oversee the market and transactions, abstaining from direct management responsibilities.

For seamless integration, the Trading System must be integrated with the Carbon Asset Registration System to ensure the registration and circulation of carbon assets. Additionally, it must be integrated with banking systems to facilitate the flow of funds. Market participants in carbon trading are authorized to open accounts within the Trading System through the exchange, and must also establish accounts in the Registration System and the designated bank, as stipulated by the exchange, to effectively trade and transact.

Given the stark contrast in trading objects and rules between the NCTM and the current market for carbon emission rights, the Trading System necessitates specialized design and development efforts.

In addition to fulfilling the core functionalities of a conventional trading market system, the Negative Carbon Market Trading System necessitates the integration of specialized functional systems tailored specifically for negative carbon market transactions. These include:

1. Trading Account Management System

The breadth of users in the Negative Carbon Market Trading System encompasses virtually all social entities, including economic organizations, government agencies, diverse social groups, households, and individuals alike. Consequently, this market is poised to host the largest number of organizational accounts among existing trading systems, potentially surpassing even the stock market in terms of the number of institutional accounts. Hence, the system must possess robust user capacity and data management capabilities to accommodate diverse account management requirements efficiently.

2. Trading Matching System

The trading matching rules within this system must align seamlessly with the unique transaction order of the carbon market, which inherently differs significantly from other trading markets. The specific trading order tailored for negative carbon markets is elaborated upon in Sect. 8.1.6.

3. Carbon Asset Management and Capital Settlement System

This system ensures precise management of carbon asset data for each account, first and foremost, by aligning with trading outcomes. Secondly, it integrates seamlessly with the Carbon Asset Registration System to facilitate error-free asset registration management.

4. Transaction Management System

This system encompasses transaction compliance monitoring, management of abnormal situations, and robust safeguards against market manipulation. Its primary objective is to assist regulatory authorities in overseeing the smooth operation of the market and preventing any form of disruption or chaos.

5. Index Analysis System

As the carbon financial market continues to evolve, it is poised to emerge as a pivotal component within the broader financial landscape. Consequently, there arises a pressing societal need for comprehensive trading indicators, insightful price index analysis reports, and a diverse array of carbon market data products. To cater to this demand, the establishment of a robust index analysis system is imperative.

6. Data Security Management System

The carbon market, being a cornerstone of macroeconomic infrastructure, necessitates unparalleled levels of system security. Given its critical role, stringent measures must be in place to safeguard against potential attacks and ensure seamless disaster recovery.

Generally speaking, given the relatively straightforward nature of trading products in the negative carbon market, the complexity of developing the necessary systems remains manageable.

8.7 Integrated Carbon Pricing: Advantages of Carbon Pricing in the CELM

The academic community has been engaged in a protracted debate spanning over three decades, pondering over the optimal carbon policy instruments and methodologies for pricing carbon emissions. This discourse has yielded a vast array of research papers and reports, positioning the field as a prominent and vibrant area within climate change economics. It appears that this discourse will continue to thrive for at least another one to two decades, with no imminent resolution in sight. Furthermore, policymakers continue to grapple with the question which is the most suitable path towards carbon neutrality, a carbon tax? or a carbon market?

Among the current carbon policy instruments employed by nations, carbon taxes and carbon markets based on emission allowances stand out as the cornerstone measures, complemented by various policy add-ons. However, due to limitations in foundational theories and a lack of advanced top-level design, the application of these instruments often results in confusion, with serious policy overlapping and conflicting.

It is precisely the ongoing debate, with no definitive conclusion reached, regarding which policy instrument is more effective, that has led the international community to continually experiment with and refine decarbonation policies over the past two decades. China faces a similar situation. In practice, many Western countries have utilized either carbon taxes or trading system for carbon emission rights, or a combination of both, as their primary tools.

To date, China has yet to introduce a carbon tax policy, and the progress of its pilot carbon market has been slow, spanning over a decade with a transaction scale of less than 20 billion yuan, yielding minimal impact on carbon emission reductions. With the ambitious "3060" dual carbon targets, China must expedite the effectiveness of its policy instruments. Not only must it rely on carbon policy instruments to achieve this goal, but it also needs to address the challenges posed by mechanisms like the EU's CBAM and the G7's Climate Club.

The varying mix and intensity of application of carbon policy instruments across regions and countries have resulted in significant disparities in international carbon pricing. For instance, the current carbon price in the EU stands near 100 euros per ton, while in China, it hovers around 58 yuan per ton.

8.7.1 The CELM-Based Carbon Pricing Method

The CELM-based Integrated Carbon Pricing Strategy (CICPS) differs fundamentally from traditional approaches, such as the Pigouvian Tax method (popularized by Nordhaus and Stern), which calculates the discounted long-term social cost, and carbon market mechanisms, which centere on emission rights allocation by the governments and pricing through market transactions.

Instead, CICPS leverages the CELM-based carbon footprint big data management system to clarify the intricate carbon footprint of society at large and individual entities, scientifically quantifying the CEL of all social organizations. Aligned with the aspirations of carbon neutrality and economic growth, CICPS employs negative carbon market to regulate carbon price, aiming to achieve optimal synergy between carbon neutrality and economic growth.

Akin to the central bank's utilization of monetary interest rates to navigate the macroeconomy, CICPS presents an efficient carbon pricing strategy, albeit with two targets in mind: carbon neutrality and the need for economic growth.

As the preeminent owner of carbon output tickets, i.e., the largest exporter of "negative carbon", the government naturally assumes the role of an oligopoly in the negative carbon market. CICPS enables the government to dynamically adjust and optimize pricing by harnessing its superior pricing power in this market. This process involves modeling and analyzing the intricate relationship between the overarching carbon neutrality journey and the macroeconomy, taking into account GDP growth, exports, social welfare, regional interest balance, and other comprehensive factors. The resulting CICPS carbon pricing scheme is precise, straightforward, and implementable, with minimal negative macroeconomic impacts and substantial positive outcomes.

The government's absolute control over the "negative carbon" supply and pricing power ensures market stability and the attainment of regulatory objectives.

8.7.2 Advantages of the CELM-Based NCTM

The CELM-based negative carbon market revolutionizes the traditional approach by eschewing carbon emission rights as the object of trading. Instead, it innovatively introduces three distinct trading products: "Real Negative CO_2", "International Negative CO_2", and "Owing Negative CO_2", thereby eliminating the necessity for carbon taxes as a complementary policy instrument. "Owing Negative CO_2" serves as an effective catalyst for governments to mobilize societal efforts towards carbon reduction, mitigating the potential economic disruptions associated with such endeavors. Meanwhile, "Real Negative CO_2" and "International Negative CO_2" are positioned as flagship products, poised for direct integration into international trading platforms. The development of derivative financial instruments, such as futures and bonds, anchored on these three products, not only expands the scope and depth of the carbon market but also paves the way for the emergence of a truly global carbon market.

The CELM-based negative carbon market, underpinned by these strategic trading objects, boasts several compelling advantages.

Foremost among them is its ability to significantly expedite the journey towards carbon neutrality.

The NCTM, by directly linking "carbon emissions" with "carbon removals", possesses a potent dual-incentive mechanism that encourages both reduction and absorption. This innovative policy instrument is exceptionally efficient, as it spurs carbon mitigation efforts across society at large, transcending the limitations of targeting only a select few industries or enterprises. Consequently, the pace of decarbonization can escalate by tens of times. Should China adopt the CELM, it is anticipated to become carbon neutral by 2045.

Secondly, the macroeconomic implications are exceptionally favorable.

The CELM-driven NCTM allocates CEL equitably across every entity on all nodes of the entire social industrial chain, mitigating the risk of a disastrous concentration of burden on a node of the industrial chain. The CTMS ensures that CEL are assigned to all societal organizations in a fair, precise, and timely manner. This seamless alignment of "carbon emission" reduction with "carbon removal" enhancement fosters a positive and negative bidirectional incentive structure, promoting healthy competition and fostering high-quality economic growth across all sectors. Notably, the CEL mitigates the potentially adverse economic consequences of carbon reduction efforts, significantly amplifying their positive impacts and addressing the challenge of capital investment necessary to tackle climate change.

Thirdly, it has a high degree of standardization and marketization. Concepts such as "Real Negative CO_2", "International Negative CO_2" and "Owing Negative CO_2" are defined with clarity and precision, eliminating ambiguity and fostering national, if not international, consistency. This standardization simplifies the trading system's design, making it straightforward and efficient. The objectification and standardization of these concepts form the cornerstone for scaling up the market and fostering internationalization.

These three trading objects embody a remarkable level of marketization, as they represent asset data stemming directly from actual production processes. This distinction from government-mandated definitions ensures their authenticity and desirability as trading assets. They originate in the market, are not bestowed by the government, and can seamlessly trade and circulate within the market, making them the ideal objects for transactions.

Fourthly, the inherent potential for internationalization facilitates the ease of expanding the carbon market's scale.

The concepts of "Real Negative CO_2" and "International Negative CO_2" stand as both tangible products and pivotal policy instruments for global climate governance, offering relatively straightforward avenues for international promotion. It is foreseeable that in the foreseeable future, a myriad of enterprises worldwide will flock to China's carbon market to procure "Real Carbon CO_2" products. China, with its abundant output and cost-effective production of such products, has the potential to emerge as a magnetic international carbon market hub.

"International Negative CO_2" represents a unique carbon pricing mechanism devised by national governments to counteract carbon tariffs on exports. Its determination can be facilitated through bilateral negotiations between exporters and importers or by international trade organizations.

The NCTM harbors a substantial demand for three distinct types of carbon products, outstripping the trading volumes of carbon emission rights. As the government operates as an oligopoly within the CELM, it exerts control over the market supply of these carbon products. Consequently, the market's expansion is directly proportional to investor participation and capital inflows, capable of achieving a trillion-scale market swiftly once initiated.

This NCTM addresses the fundamental issue of the current carbon emission market's limited size and scope. The scarcity of carbon finance to support the green economy transition has significantly dampened investor enthusiasm, necessitating urgent reforms.

China's CELM-based carbon market is not solely reserved for domestic emission entities but also embraces investors, accelerating its international integration. Envisioned to become the world's largest international carbon market, China's carbon market boasts a robust theoretical foundation and substantial contributions to global climate governance, poised to garner extensive international support.

Fifthly, market accessibility for investors (both financial institutions and individual investors) is significantly enhanced.

As the CTMS built upon the CELM necessitates settlement by all organizations, the accompanying carbon market is inherently inclusive, welcoming all organizations from its inception. Given its substantial scale and government-regulated nature, this framework enables institutional and individual investors to engage with carbon assets from the outset, a stark contrast to the current carbon market, which has been in a pilot phase for over a decade yet remains inaccessible to institutional and individual investors. In light of China's urgent need for a new, large-scale, relatively stable, and capital-absorbing financial market to supplant the real estate sector, the negative carbon market emerges as an ideal candidate. Its potential far surpasses that of the market for carbon emission rights, which is inadequate for this purpose. This shift is crucial for both national and public interests.

Sixthly, it greatly incentivizes the carbon sequestration industry.

The CELM-based NCTM consciously excludes free carbon emission allowances and CCERs devoid of actual carbon sequestration. By directly integrating "carbon emissions" with "carbon removals" in its trading dynamics, it significantly bolsters incentives for research, innovation, and development within the carbon sequestration technology sector. This is especially vital for achieving carbon neutrality targets, as the carbon sequestration industry necessitates significant investments in R&D and innovation. With sufficient market incentives in place, national financial investments can be significantly reduced, fostering a virtuous cycle within the carbon sequestration technology sector.

Seventhly, it holds strategic significance to the country.

The NCTM, a pivotal component within the CELM, harmoniously aligns with the national CTMS. This synergy significantly expedites the journey towards carbon neutrality and yields remarkable macroeconomic benefits. Furthermore, it has unlocked a colossal new financial avenue for the country, generating trillions in "negative carbon" revenue, thereby serving as a potent lever for income redistribution and enhancing the progressivity of carbon reduction policies. Ultimately, the swift expansion of China's CELM-based NCTM has the potential to emerge as a global leader in terms of scale and industrial value, effortlessly garnering international recognition. This strategic move holds immense significance for the nation, positioning it favorably in addressing global challenges.

8.7.3 Comparative Evaluation of Three Policy Instruments

In conclusion, each of the three policy instruments: carbon tax, carbon market for carbon emission rights, and the CELM-based NCTM, embodies distinct characteristics. A multi-faceted structural comparison by the government reveals a clear advantage for the CELM-based NCTM (see Table 8.1). To expedite the attainment of carbon neutrality and tackle international concerns like carbon tariffs, China must prioritize the establishment and expansion of a CELM-based NCTM.

8.8 Development Trend of CELM-Based NCTM

The CELM-based NCTM, characterized by its unique "one market, two objects, three tiers, and four types of participants" framework, stands as a pivotal instrument addressing the genuine demands of global climate governance. It represents the foremost policy lever to expedite the journey towards carbon neutrality. By embracing and implementing this model, the international community can foster continuous refinement and enhancement. Expediting its pilot operations, coupled with refining

Table 8.1 Comparison of carbon tax, carbon market based on emission rights, and carbon market based on negative carbon

Policy instruments		Carbon tax	Carbon market based on emission rights	Carbon market based on negative carbon
Characteristics		A mandatory policy instrument, relying on the existing tax system, getting quick results	A quantity-oriented policy instrument, a tradable pollution permits	Market-oriented, a voluntary policy instrument for carbon neutrality
Scope		Partial	Presently about 3000 enterprises	All organizations and individuals
Reduction effect	Total emissions	Not sure	Quite sure	Quite sure
	Carbon price	Fixed price, difficult in pricing, low flexibility	Not determined, Not enough market-oriented	Relatively fixed price, easy to adjust
	Reduction speed	Relatively slow	Relatively slow	Relatively fast
	Public awareness	Relatively weak	Relatively weak	Relatively strong
	Innovation-promoting	Relatively weak	Relatively weak	Relatively strong
Internationalization		Low	Low	Relatively high
International trade conflict		Hard to solve	Hard to solve	Easy to solve
Transaction cost	MRV	Relatively low	Relatively high	Relatively low
Use of public revenue	Proportional constraint	Relatively low	Relatively high	Relatively high
	Direction	To promote equity	To focus on improving carbon reduction efficiency	To balance equity and efficiency
Market effect	Participants	Carbon emission organizations	Limited number	All organizations and individuals
	Standard	Difficult to standardize	Difficult to standardize	Easy to standardize
	Capital scale	Hard to predict	Too small in scale	Large in scale

the top-level design and operational blueprint, will position it as a cornerstone in resolving the pressing climate crisis.

Within the CELM, the government holds an absolute oligopoly, particularly in China where it provides a staggering carbon output tickets of 12 billion tons annually, exerting definitive influence on the market. As carbon neutrality progresses, the pricing for "Owing Negative CO_2" will incrementally ascend, aligning closer with the costs of "Real Negative CO_2" and real societal carbon expenses. Notably, when the prices of these two categories converge (as illustrated in Fig. 8.5), societal carbon neutrality becomes a tangible reality. At this juncture, carbon removal organizations will have amassed sufficient carbon removals to fully offset societal emissions, achieving net-zero carbon emissions for the entire society. This evolutionary process unfolds gradually and dynamically, mitigating potential macroeconomic disruptions while fostering superior economic growth amidst the green transformation.

The development of the CELM-based NCTM will exhibit the following distinct characteristics:

1. Stable Market Growth

With the entry of investors, fluctuations in supply and demand are anticipated, yet the overall market maintains a stable trajectory. This stability stems from the government's ability to dynamically adjust the supply and repurchase of trading products, thereby stabilizing carbon prices. The government could establish a "carbon neutral fund", which serves as a market stabilizer to enable the government to harness substantial revenues from the carbon market (through the sale of "negative carbon", similar to carbon tax) to form a vast fund pool. This fund can then leverage additional social capital through financial derivatives, fostering green finance operations and investments in green transformation-related industries.

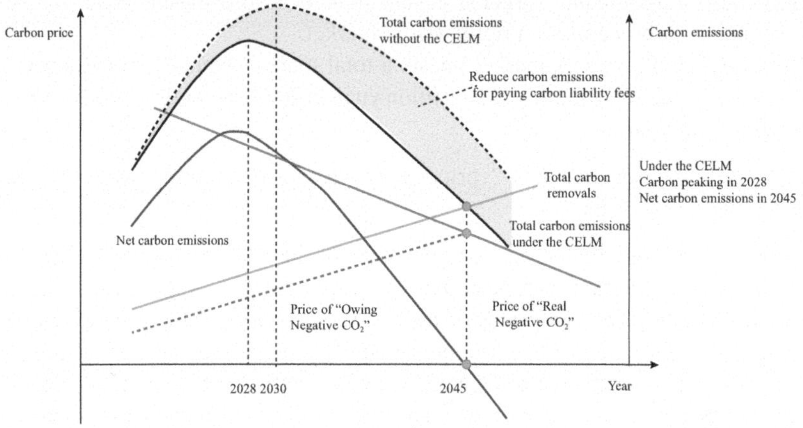

Fig. 8.5 Process of carbon neutrality in CELM scenario

Given the government's absolute pricing authority within the CELM-based NCTM, it will meticulously adjust carbon pricing in response to the carbon reduction progress and its macroeconomic implications. Even with significant influxes of social capital, the government's control remains robust, aligning with its aspirations for a well-regulated capital financial market.

2. Projected Size of China's Carbon Market

A rough estimation of the annual trading volume in the CELM-based NCTM is outlined below:

Assuming China's annual carbon emissions are A hundred million tons, with an average carbon price of P yuan/ton, the calculations are as follows:

(a) Basic Carbon Assets: A hundred million tons × P yuan/ton;
(b) Industry-Specific Positive & Negative Carbon Trading: K%;
(c) Increased Investor Holdings: B hundred million tons
(d) Turnover Rate: With an average turnover rate of N times, the total transaction volume is N × A hundred million tons
(e) International Market Volume: C hundred million tons

Thus, the annual trading volume of the CELM-based NCTM can be expressed as: $A + K \times A + B + N \times A + C = (1 + K + N) \times A + B + C$.

For instance, if $A = 100$, $K = 20$, $N = 3$, $B = 100$, $C = 30$, and $P = 100$, the annual trading volume would be $[(1 + K + N) \times A + B + C] \times P = [(1 + 0.2 + 3) \times 100 + 100 + 30] \times 100 = 5.5$ trillion yuan.

The scale of the CELM-based NCTM surpasses that of China's current carbon emission market by over a 100-fold.

This estimation excludes derivatives trading within the carbon market as well as the broader international carbon market landscape. Consequently, the CELM-based NCTM boasts a significantly larger scale and greater comprehensive value compared to the existing carbon emission rights-based market.

Currently, China's stock market boasts a total market value of 80 trillion yuan, with a total transaction volume of 257 trillion yuan in 2021, averaging a daily turnover of 925.1 billion yuan.

3. The "Owing Negative CO_2" price is progressively aligning with the "Real Negative CO_2" price

In the initial stage, the cornerstone products of the CELM-based NCTM, "Real Negative CO_2", "International Negative CO_2" and "Owing Negative CO_2", carry pivotal responsibilities. The prices of these three primary products are destined to converge, with the price of "Owing Negative CO_2" experiencing a swift upsurge. Initially, the price of "International Negative CO_2" will commence higher than that of "Owing Negative CO_2" but lower than that of "Real Negative CO_2", gradually escalating and converging towards the latter. Ultimately, the price of all three products will converge or even become equal, with the price of "Real Negative CO_2" reflecting the market CCUS cost augmented by a reasonable profit margin.

Another pivotal factor influencing the carbon pricing dynamics of the CELM-based NCTM is the interplay among the current market price for carbon emissions, social cost price, and CCUS price. While the social cost price garners government attention and serves as a crucial analytical tool for international negotiations, its practical impact may not be as profound. Ultimately, these three factors will converge, with CCUS price assuming a central role. The advancement of CCUS technology and industry will have a profound influence on this evolution.

Currently, the cost of CCUS stands at approximately 1000 yuan per ton. However, with the relentless advancement and groundbreaking achievements in carbon capture technology, coupled with the expansion of production scales, this cost is poised for a swift decline. Furthermore, the rapid evolution of CO_2 utilization technology anticipates reducing the CCUS cost to less than one-third of its present level. Consequently, the financial burden and challenges associated with achieving carbon neutrality for governments will significantly diminish. Harnessing carbon markets as a catalyst for accelerating CCUS technology advancements emerges as a pivotal objective within the realm of carbon markets.

Figure 8.3 illustrates the dynamic price trends encompassing carbon prices, CCUS costs, carbon social costs, and the price of "International Negative CO_2" within the context of the CELM scenario.

4. The carbon market stands to evolve into a pivotal monetary reservoir for China

Considering a global carbon peak of 50 billion tons annually, at a carbon price of USD 50 per ton, the annual carbon market value surpasses USD 2.5 trillion. When coupled with the projected USD 200 trillion of total green investments spanning the next three decades, the carbon market and green investments collectively constitute a colossal financial landscape. Notably, the government's robust oversight over the negative carbon market ensures stability, mitigating volatility and minimizing impacts on people's daily lives. Thus, it presents an ideal alternative to the real estate financial market as a monetary reservoir.

8.9 Policy Recommendations

In conclusion, the CELM-based NCTM, coupled with CTMS, possesses remarkable comparative advantages, offering a viable solution to nearly all challenges faced by the international community in the pursuit of carbon neutrality. Swift action is imperative.

1. Expedite the launch of the CELM-based NCTM, and discontinue the instrument of carbon tax

It is recommended that the Chinese government promptly adopt the CELM-based NCTM, discontinuing the policy instrument of carbon tax. This necessitates a comprehensive upgrade and reform of the existing carbon market, transitioning from a carbon market centered on emission rights to one centered on the CELM with

"Real Negative CO_2", "International Negative CO_2" and "Owing Negative CO_2" as primary trading objects.

2. Establish a unified carbon pricing mechanism

A unified CELM-based carbon market should be established across China, facilitating market-based carbon pricing for identical products through the carbon market's trading mechanism. Pricing must be standardized, avoiding regional, industrial, or enterprise-specific variations, because overlapping mechanism could disrupt market price signals, hinder connectivity of international carbon market, and impede the healthy development of green finance. Economic principles dictate uniform pricing. Externalities of carbon emissions are estimated based on global costs, and benefits of carbon absorption are assessed for global benefits. Moreover, reducing and absorbing 1 ton of carbon anywhere on the Earth holds equal value in addressing the global climate crisis, necessitating a unified global carbon pricing mechanism. Fiscal and industrial policies can then appropriately address industry-specific concerns.

3. Accelerate the development of a carbon market trading system

China is expected to promptly establish an international, high-standard carbon removal certification system, outlining certification standards, training professionals, and fostering powerful certification bodies to bolster the international carbon market.

Acting early and with ambition, China should strive to develop its carbon market from a premium starting point, aiming for the world's largest and most influential carbon market through top-level design. Early development should encompass a fully open carbon market, accessible to both financial institutions and individual investors, with the prompt launch of the CELM-based international carbon market as a strategic priority.

Chapter 9
Analysis of the Operation of the CELM-Based Decarbonation System

This chapter delves into the efficiency advantages of the CELM-based Decarbonation System by simulating its operation across the entire industrial chain, particularly within the construction and coal-fired power sectors. It comprehensively demonstrates the universal applicability and exceptional performance of the CELM-based system across diverse industries.

Upon the initiation of the Carbon Ticket Management System (CTMS) under the CELM, a seamless integration of input and output of carbon tickets from all participating enterprises occurs, fostering the automatic generation of comprehensive carbon ticket big data. This ensures that each enterprise's carbon footprint is accurately and promptly reflected in their carbon accounts, significantly facilitating the autonomous adjustment of industry-wide market dynamics to align with national carbon management policies. Consequently, the entire industrial chain adapts itself with the national directives, effectively propelling industries with significant carbon emissions, such as engineering construction and coal-fired power sectors, towards substantial carbon reduction.

For the effective functioning of the societal decarbonation system, it is imperative to clarify carbon neutral concepts, definitions, and standards that facilitate scientific quantification. This is necessary to assign unambiguous liability, set precise goals, and enable horizontal comparisons. Notably, concepts like carbon neutral countries, cities, enterprises, parks, and families have hitherto been ambiguous, fostering a proliferation of "greenwashing" practices that undermine the smooth progression of international carbon neutrality efforts. Therefore, Sect. 9.3 of this chapter employs the CELM to scientifically quantify and definitively clarify these pivotal concepts.

B. Yang, *The Carbon Emission Liability Mechanism*,
https://doi.org/10.1007/978-981-96-3612-9_9

9.1 Analysis of the Operation of the CELM-Based Decarbonation System in the Construction Industry

In 2022, the Chinese construction industry achieved a monumental total output value of 31.197984 trillion yuan, marking a significant 18.2% increase over 2020 figures. This sector's added value amounted to 8.33831 trillion yuan, accounting for a 6.89% share of the China's GDP, further consolidating its position as a pillar industry within the national economy.

Looking back to 2020, the construction industry's total output value stood at 26.394704 trillion yuan, accompanied by a substantial carbon footprint. Specifically, the entire construction process generated a total of 5.08 Gt of CO_2, contributing a staggering 50.9% to China's overall carbon emissions. This breakdown reveals that during the production of building materials alone, it generated 2.82 Gt of CO_2, constituting 28.2% of China's overall carbon emissions. During the construction stage, it emitted 0.1 Gt of CO_2, representing 1.0% of China's overall carbon emissions. And during the operation stage, it added another 2.16 Gt of CO_2, equivalent to 21.7% of China's total carbon emissions (as illustrated in Fig. 9.1). Given these figures, it becomes imperative to reduce carbon emissions in the construction industry, which is pivotal to achieving China's ambitious "3060" dudal carbon targets. Therefore, a thorough analysis of the functioning of the CELM-based decarbonation system within this sector holds immense significance.

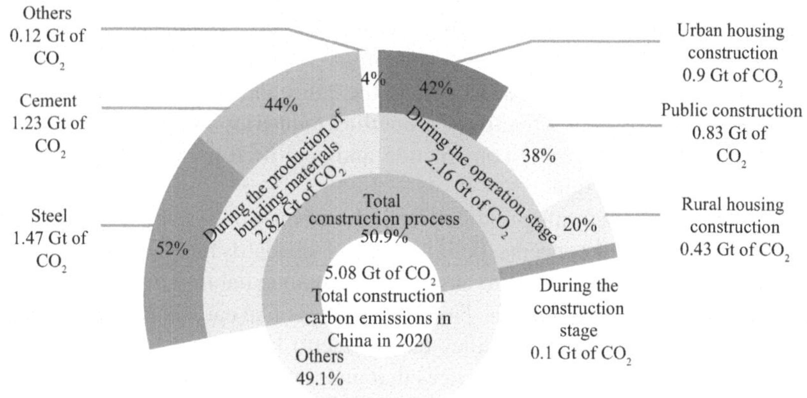

Fig. 9.1 Total construction carbon emissions in China in 2020 (*Data source* China Building Energy Consumption and Carbon Emission Research Report 2022)

9.1.1 *Transformation of Project Bidding and Settlement Regulations*

With the implementation of carbon ticket management, we can anticipate a fundamental transformation in the dynamics of project tendering and bidding. Specifically, the conventional paradigm of securing contracts through the lowest reasonable bid, primarily based on construction and installation costs, will undergo a transformation. Under the carbon ticket system, the bidding landscape will evolve to encompass:

$$\begin{aligned}\text{total bidding price} = &\ \text{total carbon emission cost} \\ &+ \text{total price of construction and installation}\end{aligned}$$

wherein:

$$\begin{aligned}\text{the total carbon emission cost} = &\ \text{the carbon emission cost of the} \\ &\ \text{engineering product} \times \text{carbon price}\end{aligned}$$

$$\begin{aligned}&\text{the carbon emission cost of the engineering product} \\ &= \text{the total CEL from consumed resources} \\ &\quad + \text{the total CEL arising from construction activities}\end{aligned}$$

This revised bidding framework instantly propels the entire industry chain towards a proactive carbon reduction mechanism, extending from downstream to upstream operations. To illustrate this concept, let's conduct a simulation analysis within the real estate sector.

Under the CELM, end-consumers directly bear the financial burden of a product's carbon footprint. For instance, a 100-square-meter residence, assuming a total CEL of 1000 tons, would incur a carbon emission cost based on the domestic carbon price of 56 yuan/ton in 2023 (for comparison, the current EU carbon price ranges from 80 to 100 euros/ton). This translates to a total carbon emission cost of 56,000 yuan, which must be factored into the overall price when it is sold. This approach underscores the principle that individuals, as ultimate consumers, are accountable for the carbon emissions associated with their purchases.

For developers, once carbon fees are collected on behalf of house buyers, they must proceed to the carbon trading market to procure "negative carbon" products to balance (neutralize) their own carbon ticket input, or invest funds in carbon reduction initiatives to secure government-certified "negative carbon" that likewise offsets their carbon ticket input. Additionally, they must maintain regular carbon account settlements for their enterprises. Notably, the carbon ticket input of developers primarily stems from the carbon ticket output issued by engineering contractors.

In the realm of real estate, integrating carbon emission costs into the overall house price underscores the growing significance of emission reduction as a core competitive advantage for enterprises. Consequently, the bidding process for construction projects is poised to undergo a fundamental shift, with the introduction of a new formula:

$$\text{the total bidding price} = \text{the total CEL} + \text{the total price of construction and installation}$$

The contractor offering the lowest total bidding price will win in the bidding process. Traditionally, total bidding price in construction projects solely encompasses the latter. Under these revised rules, construction enterprises seeking to succeed in bids must not only strive to reduce construction and installation costs but also prioritize minimizing their carbon emissions footprint. Ultimately, these novel bidding criteria will spur the construction industry towards more environmentally responsible practices and reduced carbon emissions.

Once the bidding process concludes and the winner is determined, the employer and contractor enter into an agreement based on the outcome, clearly outlining the maximum amount of carbon tickets (or total carbon fees) acceptable to the employer. The contractor then issues carbon output tickets to the employer incrementally, aligned with project progress, ensuring that the cumulative amount does not exceed the contractual limit. Upon project completion, if the contractor's total carbon output tickets surpasses its input tickets, they are eligible for "negative carbon" products, translating into financial gains; conversely, a deficit results in increased carbon emission costs.

9.1.2 Transformation of Engineering Contractors' Supply Chain Management

In light of the developer's revised bidding criteria, construction companies are compelled to innovate their supply chain systems and redefine their approach to sourcing materials and services. Specifically, the bidding and procurement rules for construction enterprises undergo a pivotal transformation:

$$\text{the total price for resource bidding and procurement} = \text{the resource's carbon emission cost} + \text{its total price.}$$

The supplier offering the lowest combined total price gains the competitive edge in the bidding process. Prior to this change, the total price for resource bidding and procurement solely included the total price of the resources. Consequently, suppliers seeking to secure contracts must concurrently strive to lower both their construction-related costs and their CEL. This supply chain bidding framework incentivizes the entire supply chain to embark on a path of carbon reduction.

Once the bidding outcome is finalized, the construction enterprise and the supplier enter into an agreement, adhering to the bidding results, to establish the total amount of carbon output tickets (or total carbon fees) deemed acceptable by the purchaser. The supplier subsequently issues carbon output tickets to the construction enterprise incrementally, in line with the progress of supplies, ensuring that the cumulative amount does not surpass the contractual limit. Upon project completion, if the supplier's total carbon input tickets falls short of its output tickets, it stands to gain from "negative carbon" incentives; otherwise, it faces increased carbon emission costs.

These rules effectively pressure suppliers to minimize carbon emissions. Material and equipment suppliers, as well as service providers, must work to reduce their overall carbon emission costs to enhance their competitiveness in the bidding process. Notably, this encompasses the total cost of all emissions generated at the upstream stages and within the supplier's own operations. Under the CELM, the burden of carbon emission costs shifts from the upstream to the consumer end, with CTMS facilitating end-to-end oversight. This approach fosters accountability across the entire industrial chain, as consumers leverage their right to know and right to choose to drive carbon reduction efforts throughout the supply chain.

9.1.3 Catalyzing Transformations in Industrial Brand Management and Qualification Management Rules

The quantified CTMS serves as both an economic incentive-disincentive mechanism and a catalyst for promoting and reinforcing corporate social green values. By quantifying both profits and social responsibility, it amplifies the incentive effect, with ESG taking on increasing significance. Under the CELM, a reverse pressure mechanism emerges across the entire supply chain of the engineering industry, motivating each participant to intensify their decarbonation efforts.

Armed with precise industry-wide carbon footprint data, government agencies can formulate more effective industrial carbon reduction policies. These policies, in turn, reinforce the push for enterprises to reduce carbon emissions, elevate their technological and operational sophistication, and ultimately diminish energy consumption and carbon emissions.

For instance, subsequent to the implementation of carbon tickets for an extended period, the government can devise policies and introduce pertinent measures, grounded in extensive operational big data, to categorize enterprises within the industry based on criteria like unit output value and carbon emission intensity per unit area. In the inaugural year, a list will be publicized, honoring enterprises with the lowest carbon emission intensity per unit and subjecting those with the highest to criticism and punitive measures. This approach, devoid of direct economic incentives for zero carbon pricing, will nonetheless significantly propel corporate carbon reduction efforts.

From the second year onwards, enterprises ranking in the top 3% of carbon emission intensity per unit may face punitive mechanisms or even the revocation of their operational licenses, thereby fostering technological advancements across the industry and intensifying carbon reduction efforts.

The CTMS, bolstered by comprehensive big data on societal carbon footprints, has elevated the scientific rigor of government regulatory policies, alleviated demands on government management capacity, and substantially reduced administrative costs. It enables the market to effectively drive the circulation of resources towards more sustainable endeavors.

9.1.4 Dual-Carbon Challenges and Management Transformation of Engineering Enterprises

Amidst the emerging CTMS, low-carbon production capabilities are poised to emerge as a cornerstone of competitiveness for engineering enterprises, marking an inevitable shift. Consequently, the integration of carbon management principles into the core foundational management mindset of these enterprises has become imperative.

To successfully confront the challenges in the dual-carbon era, enterprises must establish robust carbon management systems.

Engineering enterprises must establish comprehensive, multi-tiered carbon management systems to ensure their carbon management capabilities remain on par with industry standards. This imperative transcends mere competitiveness; it's vital for the very survival of these enterprises.

1. Enterprise-Level Carbon Management System

The system should encapsulate the holistic oversight of an enterprise's carbon emissions, carbon removals, carbon assets, and carbon trading activities. It necessitates the integration of carbon data across the entire production lifecycle, ensuring data integrity, timeliness, and precision.

Carbon Emission Management: This focuses on managing both carbon input and the emissions generated throughout the production process. Leveraging the government's CTMS, if operational, simplifies data acquisition. By integrating with the national CTMS, enterprises can analyze transactions associated with input and output of carbon tickets across all projects. Subsequently, they could design tailored carbon emission management mechanisms and make bidding and procurement rules, thereby minimizing their carbon emission costs.

In the current landscape, while energy consumption-related carbon emission data is relatively accurate, acquiring carbon emission factors for upstream raw materials and products poses a challenge, often requiring reliance on industry-standard estimates.

Carbon Removal Management: This involves the handling of the data related to carbon removal projects. For initiatives such as forestation, CCUS installations, and green energy generation, systematic data management facilitates seamless verification by regulatory bodies. Additionally, the carbon reduction achieved through technological advancements and innovative engineering planning should be under control, which offers a robust platform for providing carbon data insights and project portfolio support across the enterprise.

Carbon Asset Management: When an enterprise surpasses industry benchmarks in decarbonation, it can generate "negative carbon", which can be transformed into valuable carbon assets. By selling these "negative carbon" in the carbon market, enterprises can profitably monetize their environmental contributions. Effective carbon asset management through the carbon trading and futures markets not only mitigates their carbon emission costs but necessitates expertise to optimize returns. Consequently, carbon asset management and investment emerge as critical components of asset management portfolios for corporate finance departments.

Carbon Trading Management: As corporations strive for carbon neutrality, carbon trading becomes an integral part of their daily asset management routine. Quarterly settlement is completed through carbon trading system. To minimize future carbon emission costs and mitigate investment risks, futures trading operations will become more common.

The Enterprise-Level Carbon Management System integrates seamlessly with Park-Level and Project-Level management systems, ensuring data interconnectivity and coherence.

2. Park-Level Carbon Management System

The target of the Park-Level Carbon Management System is to oversee carbon emissions and carbon neutrality for the entire park. Amidst the widespread ambition to establish green, zero-carbon parks, it's imperative to conduct comprehensive statistical analyses of the park's total energy consumption, total carbon emissions, and carbon removals. This data foundation enables the evaluation of carbon emission levels and reduction progress, guiding strategic decisions towards low-carbon and zero-carbon goals.

3. Project-Level Carbon Management System

A comprehensive project-level carbon management system is pivotal for engineering enterprises, as their core operations revolve around engineering projects. To establish a robust foundation for corporate carbon management, engineering enterprises must implement carbon management throughout the entire lifecycle of project construction.

At the project level, carbon management encompasses three primary objectives:

First, estimation of carbon emission cost during the bidding of the project. Leveraging the execution technical blueprint of the project, enterprises meticulously calculate the carbon emission cost, incorporating industry benchmarks and internal performance metrics into the analysis.

This process involves utilizing BIM (Building Information Modeling) digital software to first quantify each project volume and material amount, subsequently applying carbon emission factors to ascertain individual and aggregate carbon emissions. While the computational methodology is straightforward, a pressing challenge lies in the inadequacy of industry-standard carbon emission factor values for diverse materials. Data gaps, inaccuracies, and a general lack of accessibility mirror the scenario of an incomplete content table in the construction cost realm. Presently, across industries, there exists a pressing need for a real-time, precise, and dynamic carbon emission factor database to underpin effective carbon management, a global challenge that underscores the urgency of collaborative efforts within the international community.

The emission factor (EF) represents the quantity of carbon emissions attributable to a specific target product within a defined system boundary. A carbon emission factor database serves as a vital index database, provided by governments or industry associations, for societal organizations engaged in program evaluation and project-level carbon emission quantification. Given current programmatic and technological constraints, constructing an accurate and comprehensive carbon emission factor database poses significant challenges, thereby fostering a pressing societal need for such a resource. Despite numerous attempts by various institutions, the pursuit of a practical, real-time, precise, and dynamic carbon emission factor database remains elusive. This endeavor consumes substantial societal resources without yielding a robust database capable of supporting comprehensive carbon emission management. However, the implementation of CTMS, grounded in the CELM, offers a seamless solution to this dilemma. Upon operation, CTMS processes and repurposes carbon footprint data from across society and all entities within its system, adhering to specific rules. This automated process within CTMS generates a foundational database of industry-specific carbon emission factors, effectively providing a near-costless, comprehensive carbon emission factor database that underpins societal carbon emission management. Furthermore, CTMS dynamically updates data, ensuring a real-time, accurate, and dynamic industry-wide carbon emission factor database, representing one of its core values for society.

Second, management of carbon emissions throughout the entire process. The selection of materials and construction plans significantly impacts carbon emissions, necessitating granular process management, real-time data control, and ensuring that actual carbon emissions remain below budgetary projections. Consequently, carbon emission management planning constitutes a vital component in the implementation of the project.

Third, estimation of carbon emissions during the operational stage. The selection of materials and equipment by contractors plays a pivotal role in determining the amount of carbon emissions during the operational phase. The emissions generated during this stage constitute a significant portion of the overall carbon footprint, and they are intimately tied to the design and execution strategies employed during the construction stage. It is imperative to abandon the reliance on industry-specific standard values in project implementation plans and instead adopt actual product-specific values. The choice of materials and suppliers directly impacts the CEL; therefore, contractors should establish their own databases for supply chain. Moreover, contractors must assume a heightened level of accountability for the carbon emission outcomes during the operational stage, under the guidance of the builder and in close coordination with the designer. The precision of the contractor's annual carbon emission data measurement for construction projects during the operational stage, coupled with efforts to minimize emissions, will serve as a valuable asset, enhancing their competitive edge and positioning them as leaders in their field.

9.1.5 Countermeasures and Strategies for Achieving Carbon Neutrality for Engineering Enterprises

Carbon neutrality represents a formidable challenge for enterprises across all industries, yet it stands as the cornerstone of corporate ESG frameworks. It also presents a strategic opportunity for enterprises to forge new competitive advantages.

1. Fostering a low-carbon mindset in enterprises

Enterprises must embark on cultivating a fresh mindset tailored for the carbon–neutral era. Carbon neutrality will inevitably evolve into a component of an enterprise's branding strategy, necessitating the issuance of an annual carbon–neutral report or an ESG report that encompasses carbon neutrality to the public. This requirement has already been stipulated by the United States Securities and Exchange Administration for listed companies, and it is poised to become the benchmark for industry leaders in the future.

As of November 2021, notable progress has been made within the United Nations Sustainable Stock Exchanges Initiative, with 26 out of 114 tracked stock exchanges issuing mandatory ESG listing criteria. Furthermore, on May 27, 2022, the State-owned Assets Supervision and Administration Commission of the State Council unveiled the *Work Plan to Improve the Quality of Listed Companies Held by Central Government*, emphasizing ESG disclosure requirements for such companies and mandating the disclosure of ESG reports from 2023 onwards.

It is crucial to underscore that the impending establishment of the CTMS by the government will usher in unprecedented transparency in the carbon footprints of organizations and their industry rankings. This increased visibility of carbon emission intensity rankings will significantly impact corporate branding. Additionally, enterprises must adopt the concept of total product pricing, which incorporates the carbon costs associated with all emissions incurred during the product's lifecycle. This approach will become the norm as all enterprise clients leverage such standards to assess product pricing in the future.

2. Positioning a dual carbon strategy as one of its fundamental strategic pillars

Formulating corporate dual carbon strategy. The top management of an enterprise should prioritize positioning a dual carbon strategy as one of its fundamental strategic pillars. This strategy transcends mere cost competitiveness and survival imperatives; it embraces corporate social responsibility and ethical principles. Given that the engineering industry contributes over 50% of total societal carbon emissions, spanning from building material production to the entire lifecycle of construction operations, it is inevitable that governmental focus will intensify on curbing these emissions.

Formulating dual carbon targets and an action roadmap. Aligned with the national "3060" dual carbon targets, enterprises must devise their own ambitious dual carbon milestones, outlining a clear path to becoming a zero-carbon entity by a specific year, ideally, well ahead of the national timeline. This endeavor necessitates strategic wisdom and a commitment to responsibility, balancing investments, efficiency gains, and market competitiveness. Rather than adopting a wait-and-see approach, proactive measures are crucial to seize emerging opportunities.

Addressing industrial front-end carbon footprint challenges. Engineering enterprises confront a significant challenge in reducing their industrial front-end carbon footprint. Achieving an overall zero-carbon enterprise is a collaborative effort, reliant not only on internal initiatives but also on transformation within upstream material production and transportation, while supply chain transformation, rooted in carbon reduction, demands substantial effort. Nevertheless, enterprises can expedite their journey towards carbon neutrality by focusing on neutralizing their own carbon increments. By breaking down targets into manageable steps and promptly crafting an action roadmap, enterprises can embark on this vital transformation.

3. Establishing a team to execute strategies

An exemplary team for dual-carbon management ought to be established within the enterprise, fostering an all-inclusive approach where top executives lead by example and engage with staff at all levels. This is pivotal not merely as a strategic imperative but also necessitates a collective effort across every project, department, and production segment. Recognizing that every aspect of the enterprise contributes to carbon emissions, a robust organizational backbone is indispensable to ensure seamless implementation.

4. Cultivating professionals and talents

Enterprises must prioritize the development of a comprehensive personnel system for carbon management. Given the broad scope and complexity of dual-carbon strategies, a single cadre of experts cannot suffice. Rather, it necessitates cultivating a versatile team equipped with the requisite professional quality, spanning from the corporate level down to individual projects.

Moreover, instilling dual-carbon awareness and technical proficiency among all employees is crucial. Each member of the organization plays a vital role in advancing the corporate dual carbon targets. By fostering not just an understanding but also practical expertise in dual carbon strategies, we empower everyone to embed eco-friendly practices into their daily routines. Be it through simple acts like saving a piece of paper or reducing electricity usage, every effort counts towards mitigating our carbon footprints.

5. Establishing a multi-tiered carbon management framework

Enterprises ought to implement a comprehensive, multi-tiered carbon management system, spanning from the corporate level down to individual projects. This system should encompass various aspects such as organizational governance, procurement strategies, technical innovations, talent nurturing, and an incentivizing reward-and-punishment mechanism. Moreover, the swift establishment of a unified guiding philosophy and a robust implementation assurance system across the organization is imperative.

6. Establishing a multi-tiered carbon management information system

Enterprises must prioritize the establishment of a multi-tiered carbon management information system capable of promptly and accurately tracking the organizational carbon footprints. This system should dynamically monitor and update the real-time carbon emission status across the entire enterprise, enabling scientific evaluations of daily emissions of every project and every program. It will furnish enterprises with vital decision-making insights and audit foundations, empowering proactive actions rather than relying on external regulatory interventions like power restrictions.

7. Revolutionizing the supply chain for sustainability

It is crucial for enterprises to promptly restructure their supplier recruitment systems and introduce a novel bidding and procurement regulation framework, that is:

$$\text{Total bidding and procurement} = \text{the carbon liability cost of the bidding object} + \text{the material price.}$$

By embracing carbon emission management among suppliers and favoring green, low-carbon building materials and equipment, enterprises can foster a more sustainable and environmentally responsible supply chain.

8. Enhancing the research and development of low-carbon processes and carbon-mitigating technologies

Engineering enterprises must intensify their endeavors towards researching and developing innovative low-carbon processes and carbon-mitigating technologies. The assessment framework for technical solutions and patented innovations should incorporate a heightened emphasis on carbon emissions, necessitating an upgrade to the evaluation system. Furthermore, the strategic prioritization of developing a comprehensive portfolio of carbon-mitigating technology patents emerges as a pivotal technical strategy for engineering enterprises.

9.2 Analysis of the Operation of the CELM-Based Decarbonation System in the Power Generation Industry

The power generation industry, particularly coal-fired power, stands as a pivotal yet not exclusively targeted sector in the current government's carbon control initiatives. The approach outlined in Sect. 11.3 misdirects focus, resulting in suboptimal carbon reduction performance, limited effectiveness, and significant macroeconomic repercussions. This section delves into a comprehensive operational analysis of the CELM carbon reduction system within the power generation domain.

9.2.1 *Carbon Control Landscape and the Nature of the Power Generation Industry Under the CELM*

The power generation industry is not the primary or sole focus of the government's carbon control efforts under the CELM. Rather, it constitutes a crucial link in the broader industrial chain. Unlike carbon source organizations, such as coal, oil, and natural gas enterprises, the power generation industry doesn't need special regulation from the government. The government employs carbon ticket input to oversee their emissions, allowing enterprises across industries to be treated equitably. Enterprises with carbon stocks can offset their emissions, and those achieving a "negative carbon" balance, where input ticket are less than output tikcets, can capitalize on the carbon market. This framework fosters competition among power generation enterprises based on their generation costs and the total cost of carbon fees.

9.2.2 *Overview of the Industry Chain of Electric Power Industry*

The electric power industry operates with distinct characteristics, necessitating a highly intricate organization across its entire industrial chain. As a public utility good, the electric power industry necessitates a harmonious blend of planning and market mechanisms. The diversity of power generation enterprises, spanning from traditional fossil energy sources, like coal, oil, and gas, to renewable alternatives such as hydropower, photovoltaic, wind, and nuclear power, underscores the vast differences in industrial chain organization among these various types.

Primary Energy Suppliers. At the forefront of this chain lies the supply of raw materials. For coal-, oil-, and gas-fired power plants, the upstream primary energy suppliers are coal mining enterprises, oil companies, and natural gas providers. These fossil fuels, when combusted, generate electricity but also contribute significantly to carbon emissions. In contrast, photovoltaic and wind power plants harness green, renewable energy sources, with nature itself serving as the primary energy supplier at no cost. This fundamental distinction translates into a substantial disparity in the carbon emission cost per kilowatt-hour between these two categories. As the costs of photovoltaic and wind power generation continue to decline, leveraging their zero-carbon emission advantage becomes crucial to achieving overall cost competitiveness per kilowatt-hour and accelerating the transition away from fossil-based electricity. Notably, coal, oil, and gas enterprises supply power plants with fossil fuels and issue carbon output tickets based on supply volumes, whereas photovoltaic and wind power plants operate without such carbon input tickets.

It is noteworthy that coal mines, oil and gas companies, and natural gas enterprises, which serve as the primary energy suppliers for coal-, oil-, and gas-fired power plants, are pivotal state-managed carbon-intensive enterprises. The state must rigorously oversee and verify their production, sales volumes, and carbon content to ensure compliance. The government's regulatory body issues carbon tickets to these enterprises, integrating them into the national CTMS.

The Power Plants: The power plants transform primary energy into secondary energy, that is, electricity. Each type of power generation employs distinct physical principles and process technology flows. Coal-, oil-, and gas-fired power plants combust fossil fuels to generate electricity, resulting in significant CO_2 emissions. Conversely, photovoltaic, wind, and hydropower harness green, renewable energy sources, converting them into electricity without emitting CO_2. Coal-, oil-, and gas-fired power plants receive numerous input tickets from their primary energy suppliers and subsequently issue sales carbon output tickets to electricity distributors based on purchase contracts. In contrast, photovoltaic, wind, and hydropower generation companies do not receive input tickets and are not obligated to issue output tickets to electricity companies.

Power Grid Enterprises: In the future, the primary function of power grid enterprises will be the transmission of electricity, with fees charged solely based on transmission volume and transmission distance. Transactions with power plants and electricity retailers will almost be zero.

Electricity Retailers: Electricity retailers acquire electricity from power plants, guided by the principle of minimizing the total cost of carbon fees and electricity charges. They receive carbon input tickets from power plants and, based on the total purchase price and total carbon tickets from each power supplier (encompassing all types of power plants), calculate and collect electricity prices and carbon fees from end users.

Power End Users: End users pay electricity prices and carbon fees to the electricity retailer, commensurate with their electricity consumption. Similarly to how water users bear drainage fees, electricity end-users ultimately bear the final cost of carbon emissions.

9.2.3 *Operation of the Electric Power Industry Under the CELM*

Take the operational mechanism of the electric power market as an example (see Fig. 9.2).

The core operation of the CELM within the power industry encompass several pivotal elements: the national management authority issues carbon output tickets to carbon-emitting organizations (including primary energy and fossil fuel enterprises),

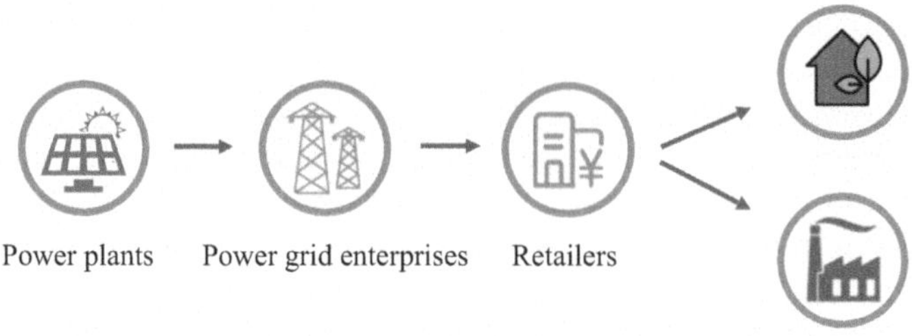

Fig. 9.2 Operational mechanism of the electric power market

which are subsequently registered into the CTMS. Electricity retailers procure electricity through bidding, factoring in both the electricity price and the associated carbon fees, and receive carbon input tickets from power plants. These retailers then sell electricity to consumers, levying both electricity and carbon fees per kilowatt-hour. Throughout this intricate industrial chain, power plants thrive and evolve amidst competition driven by the combined cost of power generation and carbon emissions. Consequently, minimizing carbon emission costs emerges as a paramount strategic imperative for enhancing their competitiveness.

Let's illustrate with the industry chain of coal-fired power plants:

In a given year (denoted as ××××), coal mining enterprises C1, C2, C3…C10, mine for varying quantities of coal (P1, P2, P3… P10 tons respectively), each with distinct carbon content (c1, c2, c3… c10 tCO_2/ton). These coal products are subsequently sold to coal-fired power plants E1, E2, E3…E10. Specifically, coal enterprise C1 supplies varying amounts of coal (CE_{11}, CE_{12}, CE_{13}…CE_{110}) to these power plants, for which corresponding carbon tickets (CT_{11}, CT_{12}, CT_{13}…CT_{110}) are issued. Similarly, coal mining enterprise C2 supplies coal (CE_{21}, CE_{22}, CE_{23}…CE_{210}) to the same power plants, accompanied by carbon tickets (CT_{21}, CT_{22}, CT_{23}…CT_{210}), and this pattern repeats for all participating mining enterprises. As for the power plants, E1, E2, E3…E10 generate electricity at varying capacities, denoted as EE1, EE2, EE3… EE10.

Coal-fired power plants E1, E2, E3…E10 supply electricity to retailers S1, S2, S3…S10. Specifically, coal-fired power plant E1 sells varying amounts of electricity (ES_{11}, ES_{12}, ES_{13}… ES_{110}) to these 10 retailers, accompanied by carbon tickets (ET_{11}, ET_{12}, ET_{13}… ET_{110}). Similarly, coal-fired power plant E2 sells electricity (ES_{21}, ES_{22}, ES_{23}… ES_{210}) to the same retailers, issuing corresponding carbon tickets (ET_{21}, ET_{22}, ET_{23}… ET_{210}), and this pattern repeats for all coal-fired power plants.

It is crucial to acknowledge that electricity retailers procure electricity from both coal-fired and green power sources (including photovoltaic, wind, hydroelectric, nuclear, and other zero-carbon sources). Coal-fired power plants must compete vigorously with green power enterprises to secure market share. Green power enterprises currently enjoy the advantages of lower power generation costs and zero carbon emissions, while coal-fired power plants rely on the stability of their power supply as their primary competitive edge.

Green power enterprises GE1, GE2, GE3...GE10 also supply electricity to retailers S1, S2, S3...S10. For instance, green power enterprise GE1 sells electricity (GS_{11}, GS_{12}, GS_{13}...GS_{110}) to these retailors, issuing no carbon tickets for each transaction. Similarly, green power enterprise GE2 sells electricity (GS_{21}, GS_{22}, GS_{23}...GS_{210}) to the same retailors, also issuing no carbon tickets, and this process repeats for all green power enterprises.

1. Carbon ticket circulation in coal purchasing for coal-fired power plants

Coal power plant E1 engages in a bidding process with coal mining enterprises C1, C2... C10 to procure its annual coal supply. This procurement is based on the coal's grade and adheres to the principle of minimizing the "total price", comprising factory price of coal raw materials plus total carbon fees.

The total carbon fees are determined by multiplying the coal's carbon content by the prevailing carbon price. In a bid to secure supply contracts, some carbon-intensive coal mining enterprises are compelled to reduce their factory price of coal raw materials, while others are forced to diminish the amount of carbon output tickets, which are offset by themselves.

In the year ××××, the actual power generation of coal-fired power plant E1 amounts to EE1, and the total annual coal purchased is calculated as follows:

$$CE_{11} + CE_{21} + CE_{31} + \cdots + CE_{101}$$

The actual CO_2 content present in the purchased coal fuel is derived as:

$$ECT_1 = CE_{11\times c1} + CE_{21\times c2} + \cdots + CE_{101\times c10}$$

Subsequently, the actual carbon content per kWh generated is computed as:

$$EC1 = ECT_1/EE1$$

It's worth noting that the actual amount of carbon tickets received by coal-fired plant E1 might be fewer than expected, given the total amount of carbon tickets received is denoted as:

$$ECT_1 = CT_{11} + CT_{21} + CT_{31} + \cdots + CT_{101}$$

These are the carbon emissions that coal-fired power plants are liable for, and the carbon ticket system serves as a mechanism to transfer the burden of this emission CEL. Consequently, the carbon liability content or the carbon ticket content per kWh is calculated as:

$$EC_1 = ECT_1/EE1$$

This formula is suitable for the calculation of similar indicators for other coal-fired power plants, including the amount purchased, the actual carbon content in their coal fuel and the amount of carbon input tickets received. In the first tier of the industrial chain, the transfer of carbon tickets is finished, essentially shifting the CEL. This pivotal link in the industrial chain is governed solely by market transactions, with the state abstaining from direct involvement in the allocation of carbon emission rights. Meanwhile, there's no need for the government to engage technical entities for accounting and monitoring, significantly reducing the demands on government management capacity and investment. This autonomy underscores one of the most vital advantages of the CELM.

2. Carbon ticket circulation in the electricity purchasing process of electricity retailors

Electricity retailors, including S1, S2, S3, ..., and S10, concurrently procure electricity from both coal-fired power plants (E1, E2, E3, ..., E10) and green power enterprises (GE1, GE2, GE3, ..., GE10).

These retailors engage in bidding for electricity based on the principle of minimizing the "on-grid price plus total carbon fees" for each period.

After the full marketization of electricity price, diverse types of electricity will spark intense competition, primarily centered around three pivotal factors: production costs, carbon costs, and time-based power supply capacity. The interplay of these core elements significantly influences electricity pricing, leading to substantial fluctuations. The carbon fee is determined by multiplying the carbon footprint of each kilowatt-hour of electricity by the prevailing carbon price.

To secure contracts, some carbon-intensive coal-fired power plants are compelled to either lower their supply price or reduce the amount of carbon tickets issued (retaining the difference to offset by themselves), thereby enhancing competitiveness by minimizing overall expenses. During peak periods for photovoltaic and wind power, the competitiveness of coal-fired power dwindles as the production and carbon cost advantages of green, renewable energy become increasingly pronounced, accelerating the transition away from fossil fuels. Conversely, coal-fired power maintains a stable generation advantage during trough periods for renewable energy output, generating high revenues and sustaining production to continuously secure investment returns.

In the year ××××, the actual electricity purchases of electricity retailor S1 amount to SE1, comprising:

$$\mathrm{SE1} = \mathrm{ES}_{11} + \mathrm{ES}_{21} + \mathrm{ES}_{31} + \cdots + \mathrm{ES}_{101} + \mathrm{GS}_{11} + \mathrm{GS}_{21} + \mathrm{GS}_{31} + \cdots + \mathrm{GS}_{101}$$

Among these purchases, the total CO_2 content reflects the cumulative carbon emissions from coal-fired power plants, while green power supplied by the green power enterprises is considered carbon–neutral. Notably, the green power enterprises may still receive carbon tickets from upstream suppliers and participate in the circulation of carbon tickets with downstream retailors, but due to their minimal contribution, they are effectively considered zero-carbon emitters for the purpose of this calculation.

The actual carbon tickets received the electricity retailor S1 stem solely from coal-fired power enterprises, totaling:

$$SCT_1 = ET_{11} + ET_{21} + ET_{31} + \cdots + ET_{101}$$

Thus, the CEL per kWh or carbon ticket content can be calculated as:

$$SC_1 = SCT_1/SE1$$

It's worth noting that S1 may also receive carbon tickets from other upstream suppliers during its operations, theoretically increasing the CEL of downstream power users. However, given their minimal impact, these transfers are not considered in the current analysis.

As for other electricity retailors, their purchase volumes, the actual carbon content, the amount of carbon tickets received, and the carbon content per kWh of electricity, are calculated in the same way. Accordingly, the transfer of carbon tickets at the second tier of the industrial chain is finished. This represents the transfer of CEL. Within this pivotal juncture of the industrial chain, the circulation of carbon tickets is solely determined by market forces and transactions. China has embarked on progressively advancing electricity trading in the market, leveraging the circulation of carbon tickets and the carbon pricing mechanism of the CELM to internalize the costs associated with electricity-generated carbon emissions. This approach negates the need for the government to intervene in the allocation of carbon emission rights or engage technical entities for accounting and monitoring, significantly minimizing administrative burdens and investment requirements. This underscores one of the most fundamental values of the CELM.

3. Electricity retailors distribute power to end consumers

When distributing electricity within their respective service territories, these retailors do not differentiate prices between coal-fired and green electricity. Instead, they allocate the total carbon tickets for a given period evenly across the total electricity supplied during that period. The retailers charge a uniform price from businesses and institutions, accompanying each charge with a carbon output ticket. For residential customers, a unified electricity price and a separate carbon fee are levied, with both charges itemized clearly on the bill.

The electricity market, particularly in China, is often characterized by non-market-oriented pricing mechanism, with the government exercising stringent control over electricity price since it is a public utility good. The government meticulously regulates adjustments to electricity prices for residents, and any losses incurred by electricity retailers are absorbed by public finances. Based on the collection of drainage fees in China and recent research findings, it is evident that households can comfortably accommodate carbon fee expenditures within their electricity bills, with the potential for gradual increases. Charging carbon fees in accordance with dynamic prices in negative carbon trading market is feasible. In 2022, carbon emission factor of power industry in China was 0.853 $kgCO_2/kWh$. Suppose the carbon price at the year was approximately 60 yuan/ton, then a carbon fee of 0.051 yuan would be added to the residential electricity price, representing less than 10% of the overall price. As the proportion of renewable energy generation rises, reducing the carbon intensity of electricity, and with the implementation of a household carbon account system enabling tiered management, low-consumption households may even receive subsidies, mitigating electricity cost increases.

The reform on pure electricity charges will be gradual and steady. Carbon fees in the electricity price in the future will either be charged separately under existing regulations or adjusted uniformly as part of a comprehensive plan.

9.2.4 *Effect Analysis*

Power generation enterprise A purchases coal, acquiring the accompanied carbon tickets, and thus assumes liability and cost for the carbon emissions represented by these tickets. When A burns coal to generate electricity and sells it to electricity retailor B, the invoice issued not only includes the electricity charges but also the carbon tickets. B, in turn, transfers these tickets to power user C, and so on.

Crucially, the carbon tickets associated with electricity sales record not the theoretical carbon emissions inherent in the product but the "CEL" to be borne by the buyer. While the actual carbon emissions originate from A, the electricity is intended for supply to B, who purchases and distributes it to power user C. Consequently, all parties involved must assume their share of CEL and cost for carbon emissions.

Due to the diverse nature of energy sources, some relying heavily on coal while others incorporating more renewable options like photovoltaics and wind, the overall cost of electricity varies significantly. Consequently, B, as an electricity retailor, opts for the lowest total cost, inadvertently placing pressure on A regarding the transfer of "liability and cost" associated with carbon emissions. Similarly, electricity user C seeks to minimize their total cost, including carbon-related expenses. This trend extends to organizations along the industrial chain, who strive to reduce carbon ticket input and increase the transfer of liability. In essence, this mechanism leverages price signals to select for lower emissions, thereby reducing the overall carbon footprint within the industrial chain. From a cost transfer perspective, imposing a carbon fee has the same function with levying a tax at the source, albeit with the added requirement of accounting for carbon emission liabilities.

9.3 Analysis of a Carbon Neutral Country, City, Park, Enterprise and Household

Currently, honor roll and black list has emerged as a pivotal tool for enhancing the image, branding, and even marketing of social organizations. As a result, numerous entities have claimed themselves carbon neutral. However, the absence of standardized green organization criteria has led to a vast playground for these organizations, fostering a prevalence of "green washing" practices that have garnered widespread societal and governmental concern.

A fundamental question arises: What constitutes the benchmark and criteria for achieving carbon neutrality among countries, cities, parks, enterprises, and households? This is crucial for the effective functioning of the international carbon reduction framework. Unfortunately, to date, there exist no scientific or quantitative standards and definitions for these carbon neutral entities, leading to a fragmented landscape of interpretations and expressions. This lack of consensus poses a significant challenge to the global pursuit of carbon neutrality. To address this issue, urgent clarification of these definitions and standards is imperative. The CELM offers a relatively straightforward path to establish scientific, quantifiable benchmarks and norms, thereby mitigating market confusion.

9.3.1 Greenwashing: The Deceptive Illusions of Profiting from Sustainable Development

Greenwashing is a tactic employed by enterprises to falsely inflate their ecological and environmental obligations and contributions through misleading, exaggerated, or outright false claims about their products, services, or business practices. As the importance of ESG principles and sustainability grows, low-carbon and environmentally friendly initiatives have gained widespread popularity. However, while leading companies genuinely strive to support sustainable development, others have resorted to greenwashing to capitalize on consumer demands and preferences. By using vague phrases like "earth-friendly", "zero-carbon emissions", and "carbon neutral", along with misleading imagery, these enterprises create an illusion of sustainability where none exists. Their products often lack any genuine sustainable advantages or features, yet they still manage to capture the attention of environmentally conscious consumers.

The European Parliament defines greenwashing as "the practices of gaining an unfair competitive advantage through the marketing of environmentally friendly financial products that do not match their actual performance". In the early 2021, the European Commission released findings from an online survey that analyzed the marketing strategies of various industries, including clothing, cosmetics, and household appliances, in the EU. Alarmingly, the survey revealed that 42% of all environmental claims made by these products were suspected of being exaggerated or deceptive.

"Greenwashing" of financial institutions has been clearly restricted by financial regulators, and the disciplinary measures are relatively strict. The Financial Conduct Authority (FCA) in the UK defines financial greenwashing as "marketing that portrays an organization's products, activities, or policies as having positive environmental outcomes when, in reality, they do not". Similarly, the U.S. Securities and Exchange Commission (SEC) describes it as "overstating or misrepresenting the ESG factors considered or incorporated into portfolio selection"

The primary motivation behind greenwashing is profit. Enterprises engage in this deceptive practice to align themselves with favorable policies, appease consumers, and meet societal expectations, all while maximizing returns and earnings. They prioritize showcasing their environmental commitments in corporate and product promotion over investing resources in actual environmental protection measures.

For instance, several listed companies intentionally veil environmental hazards, falsely asserting their exemption from environmental pollution and ESG-related issues, only to be subsequently scrutinized and penalized by environmental oversight agencies for supply chain infractions. In their ESG or sustainability reports, these companies promise drastic emission reductions that far exceed their actual accomplishments, yet fail to enact corrective measures. Additionally, some companies invest minimally in green electricity and subsequently claim to be carbon neutral. Listed companies claim to invest in carbon neutrality, but it is only a "vanity project". Such declarations by listed companies may mislead investors.

On the other hand, low-carbon transformation initiatives can unlock green credit and diminish financing expenses. Enterprises adhering to green standards can issue pertinent bonds, thereby enhancing their financing structures. Furthermore, high-performing listed companies may be included in indices, attracting domestic and international investment funds.

Amidst the dual-carbon paradigm, the ESG investment concept is progressively gaining popularity, drawing attention to green development enterprises. Consequently, companies with average financial profiles but potential to contribute to the dual-carbon targets may secure higher scores. This favorable rating can lead to a concentration of financial resources and green credit, fostering their high-quality development. However, this scenario has incentivized some companies to manipulate ESG metrics to secure additional investments.

The current state of affairs stems from the inadequate construction of ESG evaluation standards and the inherent flaws in the evaluation system. It is imperative for government regulators to expedite the refinement of these systems.

9.3.2 Defining a Carbon Neutral Country

All governments have pledged to the international community their commitment to the dual carbon targets. To fulfill their Nationally Determined Contributions (NDCs), it is crucial to establish scientific and precise national targets and implementation standards for achieving dual carbon targets.

9.3.2.1 Controversial National Dual Carbon Target Values

As China joins the international community in committing to climate action, a pivotal challenge arises: determining the precise total target value for its dual carbon goals. What is the target for total carbon emissions when carbon emissions peak? And, when carbon neutrality is achieved, what is the allowable total carbon emission limit? It's crucial to underscore that carbon neutrality for any nation doesn't equate to zero emissions but rather to achieving net zero emissions. When China achieves carbon neutrality (net zero carbon emissions), the actual carbon emissions will be considered in conjunction with the amount of carbon sequestration (forest carbon removals, CCUS, etc.). Thus, these two values form the cornerstone of China's carbon neutrality journey, yet they remain uncertain, casting ambiguity over the entire process.

There's a pressing need to clarify the exact definition of these values. Conventionally, they are understood as China's net and actual carbon emissions, respectively. However, under the CELM, this definition necessitates reevaluation and the establishment of a new international standard. The intricacies of international trade, with its vast carbon footprint, underscore the need to articulate the relationship between carbon emission imports, exports, and individual nations' carbon neutrality liability. Within the prevailing European and American-dominated discourse on climate change, the principles of "producer liability mechanism" and "whoever emits is liable" threaten to exacerbate inequities in CEL among nations.

The decades-long globalization process has reshaped the global division of labor. Developing countries often shoulder the burden of production and manufacturing, leading to higher carbon emissions. They export products with significant carbon footprints and low value-addition to developed nations while importing low-carbon, high-tech, and knowledge-intensive products and services. In contrast, developed countries adopt a consumer role, exporting low-carbon, high-tech, and knowledge-intensive products and services while importing carbon-intensive industrial products.

If each country takes liability for the actual carbon emissions within its territory, it is unfair and will not result in the Pareto optimality of carbon reduction and resource allocation in economics, because it will cause the effectiveness of the global climate economy market to fail. This is also one of the important reasons why the CELM emphasizes the "consumer liability" mechanism.

Take China for example. In 2018, the embodied CO_2 emissions of China's export products were 1.53 Gt, and the embodied CO_2 emissions of imported goods were 542 Mt. The net CO_2 emissions in China's foreign trade accounted for about 10.5% of China's total emissions. Among them, the embodied CO_2 emissions from export to the EU are 270 Mt, accounting for 17.6% of the embodied CO_2 emissions from export trade. The embodied CO_2 emissions from exports to the United States were 286 Mt, accounting for 18.7%; embodied CO_2 emissions of imported goods from the EU and the US were 31 Mt and 44 Mt, respectively, therefore, China is a net exporter of embodied CO_2 emissions.

As illustrated above, China's net export of carbon emissions is quite large. Who should bear the liability for this?

9.3.2.2 A Nation's CEL Under the CELM

Under the CELM, a nation's CEL is defined as follows:

$$\begin{aligned}\text{a nation's carbon emissions} &= \text{total actual carbon emissions}\\ &+ \text{carbon emissions imported from international sources}\\ &- \text{carbon emissions exported to other countries}\end{aligned}$$

wherein:

$$\begin{aligned}&\text{The nation's total actual carbon emissions}\\ &\quad= \text{carbon emissions from domestic fossil fuels}\\ &\quad\quad+ \text{carbon emissions from other domestic carbon sources}\\ &\quad\quad+ \text{carbon emissions attributed to imported fossil fuels}\end{aligned}$$

It is important to note that carbon emissions associated with energy imports and exports are not included in "carbon emissions imported from international sources" and "carbon emissions exported to other countries" as they are already accounted for in the "the nation's total actual carbon emissions". Notably, countries like China, which import significant amounts of energy, necessitate separate consideration for these emissions. Conversely, carbon emissions from exported energy fall under the liability of the importing nations.

As a result, China's CEL is mitigated by approximately 1 Gt annually, constituting roughly 10% of its overall emissions, a substantial figure that is poised to be a pivotal topic of discussion at future global climate forums. To this end, China should collaborate with fellow developing nations to advocate for the CELM theoretical framework and establish a novel international standard for the CEL. Upon the adoption of this new standard, China's CEL could potentially decrease by a notable 10%, marking a significant achievement.

If a universally implemented Carbon Ticket Management System connects global data, it would ensure that carbon footprint data between nations is exceptionally accurate, comprehensive, and up-to-date. Consequently, accounting for carbon emissions across countries would become relatively straightforward.

9.3.2.3 Defining a Carbon Neutral Country Based on the CELM

The question arises: What constitutes a carbon neutral country, and how can we precisely define it?

Under the CELM, a nation must assume its CEL by fully offsetting them through natural carbon removals and CCUS technologies. In essence, this means achieving net zero emissions. Specifically:

national liable carbon emissions = total national carbon removals, which translates to:

$$\begin{aligned}\text{a nation's carbon emissions} &= \text{total actual carbon emissions}\\ &\quad + \text{carbon emissions imported from international sources}\\ &\quad - \text{carbon emissions exported to other countries}\\ &= \text{carbon removal capacity of the country's natural resources}\\ &\quad + \text{CCUS carbon removal capacity.}\end{aligned}$$

When a country attains this balance, it becomes a carbon neutral nation, fulfilling its pledge towards carbon neutrality objectives.

It is important to note that the concept and implications of China's dual carbon target values, as outlined in this book, significantly differ from those prevailing in the current international perspectives and frameworks.

9.3.3 Defining a Carbon Neutral City

With China aiming for carbon neutrality by 2060, can Shanghai accelerate this timeline? To qualify as a carbon neutral city, to what degree must operations in Shanghai be devoid of carbon emissions? Does achieving carbon neutrality encompass solely energy consumption in Shanghai or must it also account for the carbon emissions embodied in all input, including electricity, materials, products, and services? This is a pivotal question.

Merely calculating direct energy-related carbon emissions in Shanghai overlooks a crucial aspect. As a major consumer hub, Shanghai relies on other provinces and cities for raw materials and electricity for its enormous construction projects and consumer goods, contributing to their carbon emissions. Thus, Shanghai bears significant liability as a provincial consumer unit. Conversely, as China's premier urban economy, Shanghai exports numerous products and services globally, exporting a substantial portion of the CEL.

Hence, the target year for achieving carbon neutrality in Shanghai and the criteria defining this status require meticulous research and precise delineation.

9.3.3.1 International Practices Regarding CEL

Currently, the CEL of nations, cities, and organizations is broadly structured based on internationally recognized Scopes 1, 2, and 3, as outlined in the *Greenhouse Gas Protocol.*

However, limiting a city's carbon neutrality target solely to Scopes 1 and 2 is scientifically flawed and inaccurate, necessitating a corrective approach (Table 9.1).

Given the complexity and vastness of emissions in Scope 3, encompassing numerous external factors, society has yet to establish a robust and comprehensive carbon footprint database capable of effectively managing this data. Consequently, organizations typically exclude emissions in Scope 3 from their carbon accounting processes, except for those with extensive carbon management expertise and stringent standards, who recognize their importance and integrate them into their management frameworks.

Hence, when an organization announces its intention to achieve carbon neutrality by a specified year without clarifying the scope of emissions covered, the goal's legitimacy becomes questionable and even risks being perceived as greenwashing.

It underscores the urgent need for an internationally recognized standard for carbon neutral organizations to ensure transparency and credibility. Merely declaring carbon neutrality to emissions in the Scope 1 and Scope 2, without addressing emissions in the Scope 3, contributes little to the emission reduction and can easily become a deceptive marketing tactic. Scenarios exist where an organization might achieve carbon neutrality in its operations (Scopes 1 and 2) yet have a higher carbon footprint in its products due to inadequate supplier management or strategic outsourcing of high-carbon processes. Such practices, coupled with the use of low-cost, high-carbon materials and accessories, undermine the genuine pursuit of carbon neutrality

Table 9.1 Operational boundaries of Scopes 1, 2, and 3

Types	Description	Explanation
Scope 1	Direct GHG emissions	Direct GHG emissions occur from sources that are owned or controlled by the company or in the city, for example, emissions from combustion in owned or controlled boilers, furnaces, vehicles, etc.; emissions from chemical production in owned or controlled process equipment
Scope 2	Indirect GHG emissions from electricity and heat	Scope 2 accounts for indirect GHG emissions from the generation of purchased electricity and heat consumed by the company or in the city
Scope 3	Other indirect GHG emissions	Scope 3 emissions are a consequence of the activities of the company or in the city, but occur from sources not owned or controlled by the company or in the city. Some examples of scope 3 activities are extraction and production of purchased materials; transportation of purchased fuels; and use of sold products and services

and mislead the public. Therefore, government authorities must closely monitor and regulate such claims to safeguard against misleading communication.

9.3.3.2 Defining a Carbon Neutral City Based on the CELM

Within the CELM, a carbon neutral city is defined by three fundamental criteria:

The primary criterion is to achieve "carbon balance". According to the principles of the CELM, a city's carbon liability is determined by the equation:

$$\text{total carbon emissions} = \text{total carbon input} - \text{total carbon output} - \text{total carbon absorption}$$

When the right side of this equation equals zero, the city is considered carbon balanced, albeit not absolutely carbon neutral. Wherein,

$$\text{total carbon input} = \text{total carbon emissions associated with all materials, goods, and services imported from other cities and consumed within the city} + \text{city's own carbon sources.}$$

$$\text{total carbon output} = \text{total carbon emissions attributed to the city for supplying materials, goods, and services to external entities out of the city.}$$

For Shanghai, achieving carbon balance and assuming the CEL at the forefront poses minimal challenge due to its dual nature as both a consumer and a creative hub. Shanghai's substantial exports of products and services, which often entail the transfer of carbon emissions to downstream entities, mitigate the overall increase in emissions. This shift necessitates a revised approach that transcends mere accounting of direct, locally generated emissions.

The second criterion is to achieve "relative carbon neutrality". This is determined by the prevailing international standards for carbon neutrality, where:

$$\text{total carbon emissions (including both Scope 1 and Scope 2)} - \text{total carbon absorption by the city} - \text{amount of "Real Negative } CO_2\text{" purchased and utilized for offset} = 0$$

Under this criterion, a city is deemed relatively carbon neutral. Notably, the total carbon emissions exclude the CEL generated by materials, goods, and services produced outside of the city (excluding purchased electricity), but include the CEL generated by electricity supplied within the city's boundaries.

For Shanghai, this standard may appear somewhat low, given its status as a service-oriented metropolis where much of the high-emitting manufacturing industry has relocated. Consequently, Shanghai's contribution to national carbon neutrality is not enough by this standard.

The third criterion is to achieve "absolute carbon neutrality".

$$\text{Total carbon input} - \text{total carbon absorption by the city} \\ - \text{amount of "Real Negative } CO_2\text{" purchased and} \\ \text{utilized for offset} = 0$$

This balance must equate to zero, signifying that the city's operational carbon emissions are fully offset through its own carbon sequestration efforts and "Real Negative CO_2". It's crucial to clarify that the "Real Negative CO_2" mentioned in this context solely refers to those procured for the purpose of mitigating the CEL and excludes any investments made.

Moreover, total carbon input includes the total carbon input of the entire Scope 1, 2 and 3, and also includes the carbon input of the carbon sources in the city. "amount of 'Real Negative CO_2' purchased and utilized for offset" encompasses both governmental and organizational contributions sourced from the national negative carbon trading market, exclusively for offsetting purposes.

Despite striving for absolute neutrality, the city may still generate carbon output that originate from its products but fall below industry standards. Provided that these emissions are accepted by external downstream consumers, the city can potentially enhance product revenue by issuing carbon output tickets, a practice sanctioned by the CELM incentive framework.

The path to becoming an absolutely carbon–neutral city, as exemplified by Shanghai's aspirations, is exceedingly challenging and may span a protracted timeline. To attain this lofty goal, the municipal government in Shanghai must devise a comprehensive and meticulous roadmap for carbon neutrality, outlining the steps necessary to achieve the highest standards of environmental responsibility.

In comparison, the second criterion appears more attainable. However, under the three criteria, the timing of Shanghai's carbon neutrality achievement presents an intriguing challenge that requires meticulous planning and execution by the municipal government. Undoubtedly, Shanghai's ultimate ambition is to transform into an absolutely carbon–neutral metropolis, a testament to its commitment to environmental sustainability (Table 9.2).

9.3.4 Defining a Carbon Neutral Enterprise

Microsoft's ambitious pledge to attain carbon neutrality by 2030 involves embracing liability for its front-end carbon emissions. Should more organizations embark on

Table 9.2 Standards for three types of carbon neutral city

Standards	Equation
A carbon balance city	total carbon emissions = total carbon input − total carbon output − total carbon absorption = 0
A relatively carbon neutral city	total carbon emissions (including both Scope 1 and Scope 2) − total carbon absorption by the city − amount of "Real Negative CO_2" purchased and utilized for offset = 0
An absolutely carbon neutral city	total carbon input − total carbon absorption by the city − amount of "Real Negative CO_2" purchased and utilized for offset = 0

this journey, the global transition towards carbon neutrality would significantly accelerate. Achieving carbon neutrality necessitates comprehensive liability for front-end emissions, a daunting task for traditional industries with high energy consumption but a feasible endeavor for high-tech enterprises that can pioneer this shift.

A notable trend within China sees leading Internet companies (like Tencent, Alibaba, and Huawei) actively embracing their social responsibilities. Tencent and Alibaba have both pledged to achieve carbon–neutral goals for their operations and supply chains no later than 2030, setting a commendable precedent for Chinese tech firms to contribute towards the national "3060" targets. This commitment underscores a commendable benchmark for carbon–neutral enterprises worldwide (Fig. 9.3).

9.3.4.1 Corporate CEL Within the CELM

The CELM underscores the pivotal role of consumers in the CEL, while concurrently emphasizing the overarching CEL of organizations from the front-end of the industrial chain. This theory assigns the financial burden of carbon emissions to consumers and mandates that each enterprise assume liability for managing the carbon emissions generated at the initial stages of the production process.

To facilitate this, the CELM-based Carbon Ticket Management System (CTMS) meticulously tracks the transfer of CEL values (carbon footprints) across all transactional parties within society. This system records exhaustive data on the CEL input and output associated with each organization's production and operational activities. Legislation will clarify the calculation for an organization's total CEL:

$$\text{total CEL} = \text{total carbon ticket input} - \text{total carbon ticket output}$$

This framework fosters a collaborative approach across the entire industrial chain, encouraging nodes to actively engage in carbon reduction efforts. Producers are incentivized to maintain a carbon emission intensity (measured as carbon emissions per unit of output) below the societal average. Achieving this benchmark exempts them from additional carbon fees and enables them to capitalize on "negative carbon"

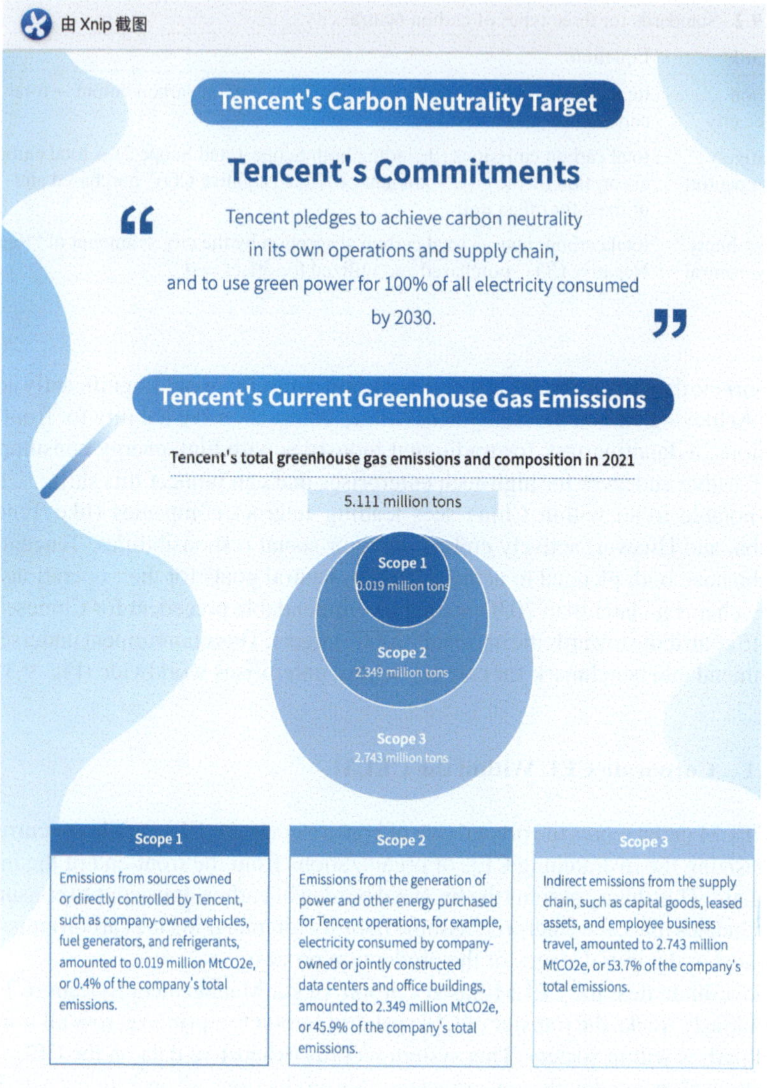

Fig. 9.3 Tencent's carbon neutrality target and commitments (*Source* Tencent Carbon Neutrality Target and Action Roadmap Report, 2022)

by earning dual rewards: financial incentives and enhanced brand premiums, thereby reinforcing their commitment to social responsibility.

Once the state establishes a carbon price through the carbon market, this price becomes an integral component of the product's overall pricing structure, ensuring that the carbon fee plays a pivotal role in shaping the commodity's total cost.

9.3.4.2 Defining a Carbon Neutral Enterprise Based on the CELM

Achieving carbon neutrality for a business is similar to the process for a carbon neutral city, encompassing three pivotal steps.

Step 1: Balancing carbon ticket input and output

The cornerstone of becoming a carbon neutral enterprise lies in maintaining a balance between carbon emissions (input) and carbon sequestration or offsetting measures (output). This balance ensures that the enterprise's carbon footprint per unit of production remains below the societal average, a fundamental prerequisite for a green and responsible business. Any imbalance necessitates the prompt purchase of "negative carbon" from the carbon market to offset.

Step 2: Zero carbon ticket output

Progressing further, the enterprise must strive to provide society with zero carbon products and services, abstaining from issuing carbon tickets to external entities. In this stage the enterprise may not fully realize absolute carbon neutrality, since it offsets carbon input with reliance on "negative carbon", that is to say, it offers relatively zero-carbon products and services, rather than absolute ones.

Step 3: Achieving absolute carbon neutrality

The ultimate goal is for the enterprise to attain absolute carbon neutrality, wherein the carbon emissions from its front-end suppliers are completely neutralized by its "Real Negative CO_2". This is achieved when

$$\begin{aligned}\text{total carbon input} &= \text{total carbon absorption}\\ &+ \text{total ``Real Negative } CO_2\text{'' purchased}\\ &\text{and utilized for offsetting purposes.}\end{aligned}$$

At this juncture, the enterprise has genuinely offset its operational CEL through self-absorption and procurement of "Real Negative CO_2" thereby achieving absolute carbon neutrality.

Moreover, absolute carbon neutral enterprises possess the capacity to export carbon output tickets to downstream entities, as their products' CEL falls below industry average level. Provided downstream buyers accept these tickets, the enterprise can generate additional revenue by issuing more carbon output tickets. This aligns with the incentives outlined in the CELM. Nevertheless, it is crucial to note that, in ESG reports and government evaluations, such enterprises should not be mislabeled as "zero carbon".

Given the stringency of these requirements, achieving absolute carbon neutrality is a formidable challenge, particularly for industries with higher emission profiles. However, low-carbon sectors stand a more favorable chance of pioneering this transformation.

9.3.4.3 Achieving Carbon Neutrality for Enterprises

Enterprises can embark on three primary pathways to attain carbon neutrality.

Firstly, they must strive to minimize the carbon footprints of their products and services. This involves adopting low-carbon raw materials, implementing eco-friendly production processes, partnering with green suppliers, and optimizing supply chain management. By collectively reducing the overall carbon emissions generated, enterprises pave the way towards carbon neutrality, though it remains a formidable challenge.

Secondly, enterprises can actively engage in carbon sequestration. They can invest in forestry projects, operate CCUS devises, and secure state-recognized "negative carbon" certificates. Some enterprises are well-positioned to adopt this approach since they have favorable conditions and abundant resources.

Thirdly, enterprises can leverage the carbon market to purchase "Real Negative CO_2" products. By acquiring the necessary amount of "Real Negative CO_2" products in the market, enterprises can offset their own CEL, effectively achieving carbon neutrality.

It is crucial to note that the current Certified Emission Reduction (CER) and China Certified Emission Reduction (CCER) should not be the offset target of enterprises seeking carbon neutrality. These indicators do not physically remove CO_2 from the atmosphere but rather represent outdated government incentives for carbon reduction technologies that may not fully contribute to genuine carbon neutrality.

Under the CELM, once the government establishes a robust carbon ticket management framework, management of organizations for carbon neutrality becomes straightforward. Within the CTMS, if an enterprise's total carbon emissions equal the sum of its carbon sequestration efforts plus the "Real Negative CO_2" purchased and utilized for offset, the organization can be officially recognized as carbon neutral. The government can then annually publish a list based on CTMS data, ensuring transparency and eliminating the potential for "greenwashing" practices in the market.

9.3.5 Defining a Carbon Neutral Park

The current trend of constructing carbon neutral (or zero-carbon) parks underscores the urgency of defining clear standards and outlining precise construction and implementation strategies. This is essential to provide accurate guidance to the market and ensure the effectiveness of such initiatives.

9.3.5.1 Defining a Carbon Neutral (Zero-Carbon) Park

Drawing from the preceding discussion, a zero-carbon park aims to neutralize all carbon emissions, including those in Scope 3, during its operational phase, achieving net-zero emissions and offering users zero-carbon products and services.

This objective necessitates a two-step approach:

Step 1: Issuing no output tickets to external enterprises and becoming a zero-carbon park.

The initial step involves refraining from allocating carbon tickets to external enterprises, thereby positioning the park as a "zero-carbon" entity. The park accomplishes this by offsetting its carbon input from upstream entities internally and offering zero-carbon products and services to its enterprises within the park. However, it's crucial to note that if the park merely offsets its CEL with "Owing Negative CO_2" purchased from the carbon market, it falls short of being a genuinely carbon–neutral park. Instead, it provides society with relatively zero-carbon offerings, not absolutely zero-carbon ones.

Step 2: Achieving real carbon neutrality and becoming "real zero-carbon park".

This step involves achieving absolute carbon neutrality, which means the CEL of the enterprise's front-end suppliers is completely neutralized by the enterprise with "Real Negative CO_2".

$$\begin{aligned}&\text{total carbon input in the park} = \text{total carbon absorbed by the park}\\&\quad + \text{total ``Real Negative } CO_2\text{'' purchased and utilized}\\&\quad \text{by the park for offsetting purposes}\end{aligned}$$

When the above equation forms, the park has attained absolute carbon neutrality. This signifies that the entire CEL associated with the park's operations is balanced through its own carbon sequestration capabilities and the purchase of "Real Negative CO_2", thereby genuinely achieving carbon neutrality.

To attain carbon neutrality within the park, we strive for green carbon sequestration and zero-carbon electricity utilization, achieving this milestone without relying on external "Real Negative CO_2" offsets from the carbon market. This endeavor signifies a high-level accomplishment, one that poses considerable challenges.

Similarly to absolute carbon neutral enterprises, real zero carbon parks may still export additional output tickets to downstream entities. This arises because the CEL associated with the park's products falls below the industrial average. Provided downstream enterprises' consent, the park can augment product revenue by issuing carbon output tickets to these enterprises.

It's crucial to underscore that the park operates under a life cycle perspective, necessitating the distinct management of carbon emissions during design, construction, and operational phases. Achieving immediate zero carbon emissions during construction phase is practically infeasible. Furthermore, with numerous existing parks in mind, this book primarily focuses on the operational phase of zero-carbon parks.

9.3.5.2 Sources of Carbon Emissions in the Park

Scope 1: Direct GHG emissions occur from sources that are within the park's physical boundaries or controlled by the park, for example, emissions from combustion in owned or controlled boilers, furnaces, vehicles, etc., excluding emissions from enterprises operating within the park.

Scope 2: Indirect GHG emissions from the generation of purchased electricity and heat consumed within the park.

Scope 3: Other indirect emissions associated with the production and operation within the park, including emissions from property management, employee commuting, and upstream/downstream products (e.g., purchased equipment, office decorations, office consumables).

Notably, emissions from transportation energy consumed by enterprises within the park and emissions from purchased products are excluded, as they fall under the category of those enterprises.

Achieving a zero-carbon park is a formidable challenge due to the necessity of managing carbon emissions from products of front-end suppliers. However, fortunately, some large parks possess the capability to establish carbon removals, thereby mitigating a portion of these emissions.

9.3.5.3 Carbon Removal Strategies Within the Park

Greening Initiatives: Tree planting not only enhances the ecological landscape of the park but also acts as a carbon removal. An adult tree absorbs over 21.8 kg of CO_2 annually from the atmosphere, a modest yet significant contribution. Some organizations embark on ambitious tree-planting endeavors in western deserts, cultivating carbon removals substantial enough to counteract their own carbon footprints.

Specialized Carbon Capture Projects: Within the park's physical boundaries, small yet potent bio-carbon sequestration projects and CCUS facilities can be launched and adopted. For instance, installing large algae bioreactors on exteriors of buildings is generates an annual alga yield of 200 kg. Each kilogram of algae consumes approximately 2 kg of CO_2, simultaneously eliminating harmful NO_2 and other exhaust gases. Furthermore, the algae are processed into a green powder, finding applications as a nutritional enhancer in cosmetics and food industries. If the park operates CCUS units, certified by a nationally recognized authority, it could acquire an amount of "negative carbon", available for carbon neutrality.

9.3.5.4 Pathways to a Zero-Carbon Park

The blueprint for zero-carbon parks necessitates a holistic, life-cycle approach, commencing with the planning and design of new parks. This offers the greatest potential for achieving carbon neutrality, facilitating the formulation of effective carbon reduction strategies and measures. To this end, the following five aspects serve as cornerstones:

1. Energy optimization: Prioritize the utilization of renewable energy sources.

The park could utilize rooftop photovoltaic systems, photovoltaic carports, and small-scale wind power installations to generate clean electricity. It could procure renewable energy for the park's operational needs. Where feasible, the park could be equipped with biogas cogeneration facilities, heat pump systems, and energy storage facilities (including power, heat, and cold storage) to satisfy the heating, cooling and power demands in the park.

2. Sustainable buildings: Strive to minimize energy consumption and elevate energy efficiency in all constructions.

The park is expected to incorporate cutting-edge energy-saving technologies, including energy-efficient insulation materials, strategic sunshades, and triple-glazed windows, ensuring that every new building is a green edifice, proudly boasting LEED Platinum certification. Additionally, smart meters are integrated into park facilities, enabling centralized control via an advanced energy management system for optimal efficiency.

3. Electrified Transportation: Use electric vehicles

The park embraces full electrification of its transportation, wherever feasible. An extensive network of electric vehicle charging stations is deployed, fostering the establishment of a rental hub for shared electric cars. These charging stations harness renewable energy sources like wind and photovoltaic power, while retired automotive batteries contribute to battery storage solutions. The charging process is intelligently controlled, adjusting charging periods and charging power as needed. Furthermore, the park could supply driverless electric vehicles, electric sightseeing vehicles, and shared bicycles, fostering eco-friendly mobility.

4. Carbon removal enhancement: Embark on ambitious carbon removal initiatives.

Extensive afforestation projects both within and surrounding the park mitigate carbon emissions. Innovative algae bioreactors adorn the exterior of building walls, augmenting natural carbon sequestration. Moreover, CCUS devices could be strategically deployed throughout the park.

5. Digitalized management: Embrace a fully digitalized, fine-grained management approach

By integrating the EcoStruxure Building Operation (EBO), EcoStruxure Power Monitoring Expert (PEM) and EcoStruxure Microgrid Advisor (EMA), the park fosters seamless collaboration among energy sources (wind, geothermal, biogas, photovoltaic power), storage solutions (large-capacity batteries, tram energy storage, heat storage), and loads (heating, cooling, electricity). This holistic approach maximizes the park's overall energy efficiency and ensures operational carbon neutrality.

By embracing the digitized, intelligent, and refined management practices within the park, the park can significantly diminish wasteful energy consumption and minimize the reliance on manual labor.

9.3.5.5 Characteristics and Challenges of Diverse Zero Carbon Parks

Zero carbon industrial parks: Given their substantial energy demands, the cornerstone of achieving zero carbon lies in ensuring that the majority of energy supply stems from renewable sources. The utilization of fossil fuels poses a significant obstacle to carbon neutrality, thus emphasizing the importance of electrifying internal operations to the fullest extent possible.

Zero carbon office parks: Office parks present a promising avenue for attaining zero-carbon goal, with a focus on renewable energy sources, digitization of green building practices, and intelligent operational management as pivotal factors.

Zero carbon residential communities: Residents contribute significantly to energy consumption. Thus, the provision of renewable energy sources and the adoption of passive building designs are crucial to reducing the carbon footprints of these communities.

9.3.5.6 Significance of Establishing a Zero Carbon Park

Beyond aligning with governmental strategic directives and serving as a societal demonstration, the construction of zero carbon parks embodies multifaceted value:

1. **Environmental protection and clean air**. Achieving high standards of environmental protection and clean air within the park enhances its quality and competitiveness, fostering a superior work and living environment for the enterprises and residents.
2. **Cost reduction for tenants**: As carbon reduction management intensifies, all carbon emissions will incur associated costs. A zero carbon park alleviates this burden for community residents, reducing their expenses and boosting the operational profitability of the park.
3. **Brand value creation**: Zero carbon parks are increasingly recognized for their brand value, attracting socially responsible enterprises seeking to rent such spaces. This trend underscores the importance of embracing sustainable practices in real estate development.

9.3.6 *Defining a Carbon Neutral Household*

For a nation to attain carbon neutrality, it necessitates not only relying on various societal organizations to curtail emissions but also emphasizing the pivotal role of demand-side (consumption-side) carbon reduction. Currently, local governments have launched numerous carbon-inclusive incentives aimed at motivating individuals and households to reduce their carbon footprints. While the existing carbon-inclusive schemes and individual carbon accounting mechanisms for residents have yet to yield substantial emission reductions, these governmental initiatives are swiftly enhancing societal awareness regarding the importance of carbon reduction.

9.3.6.1 Defining a Carbon Neutral Household

A carbon–neutral household achieves net-zero emissions by balancing its actual carbon emissions generated during production and consumption with its carbon sequestration capabilities and the purchase of "Real Negative CO_2" from the carbon market. This process involves offsetting the equivalent amount of CO_2 emitted by the household, thereby achieving net zero emissions and carbon neutrality.

Specifically, a household becomes truly carbon neutral when the following equation forms:

$$\begin{aligned} &\text{total CEL associated with all household consumption} \\ &\quad = \text{total carbon absorption} + \text{total amount of ``Real Negative } CO_2\text{''} \\ &\quad\ \ \text{purchased and utilized for offsetting purposes.} \end{aligned}$$

For environmentally conscious families eager to assume social responsibility and emerge as leading green households in the carbon neutral era, becoming a carbon–neutral household (or zero-carbon household) can be achieved through harnessing the family's carbon sequestration potential or acquiring "Real Negative CO_2" from the carbon market. This approach ensures a balance between the household's carbon emissions and its total carbon sequestration, thereby contributing to the broader goal of carbon neutrality.

9.3.6.2 Composition of Household Carbon Emissions

Virtually every aspect of household consumption contributes to carbon emissions. Any family activity, which involves the consumption of fossil fuels, generates carbon footprints and thereby incurs the CEL. These emissions fall squarely within the range of household carbon emissions.

Consequently, the composition of household carbon emissions can be categorized as follows:

1. **Carbon emissions from all purchased goods and services**: The total CEL associated with all goods and services acquired by a household constitutes the primary portion of their carbon footprint. From everyday essentials like drinking water, clothing, paper, and food to significant investments like purchasing a house, each item carries a carbon cost.
2. **Transportation-related carbon emissions**: Transportation is another significant contributor to household carbon emissions, with private gasoline-powered vehicles often accounting for the lion's share. Embracing public transportation, cycling, or even electric vehicles can significantly reduce this impact. While electric vehicles still rely heavily on coal-generated electricity, they emit comparatively less carbon. As the grid transitions towards a higher proportion of renewable energy sources, driving electric cars will become increasingly environmentally friendly.
3. **Other consumption activities.**

9.3.6.3 Composition of Household Carbon Removals

Households not only generate carbon emissions but also possess carbon removal capacity that can partially offset these emissions. In vast rural areas, many families manage land, trees, orchards, ponds, and other natural resources that possess carbon sequestration capabilities. With the establishment of a national carbon removal certification system, the carbon sequestration potential of these resources operated by households can be verified and utilized to mitigate their carbon emissions.

9.3.6.4 Establishing a Household Carbon Account

Drawing upon the CELM, a solution for managing household carbon accounts is outlined (Sect. 6.3 for details). By integrating the national Carbon Ticket Management System with the household registration system of public security departments, a dedicated household carbon account is established within the CTMS. This innovation facilitates more efficient management of household carbon emissions and incentivizes residents to adopt low-carbon lifestyles. Its objectives encompass:

1. **Totaling all carbon emissions generated by all family members**: With the ubiquitousness of electronic payment systems, totaling carbon emissions across all members of a household has become remarkably straightforward, enabling comprehensive household carbon emission summaries.
2. **Managing household carbon removals and assets**: The household account facilitates the application and registration of carbon removal certifications derived from household resources, as well as the management of carbon assets such as "Real Negative CO_2" and "Owing Negative CO_2" procured from carbon markets.
3. **Tiered management of carbon prices**: As carbon emission costs are internalized into product prices, consumers bear a portion of these costs. Households are assigned per capita CEL, priced according to varying tiers. Within the first tier,

carbon prices are set low to minimize the burden on families, and within other tiers, the prices are becoming progressively high, potentially multiplying the initial price severalfold or even more. This tiered approach would make the policy more progressive and ensure that more of the burden of carbon reduction falls on the rich.

The aforementioned carbon-inclusive mechanism, though modest in its overall impact on carbon reduction, faces challenges in establishing a comprehensive framework encompassing all household consumption links. Nonetheless, implementing a household-level carbon account offers greater manageability and fairness than individual accounts. Furthermore, absolute carbon removal capacity is considered more scientific and effective in reducing emissions compared to relative emission reduction strategies.

9.3.6.5 Strategies for Achieving a Zero Carbon Household

Carbon costs are increasingly becoming an integral part of household expenses, necessitating households to proactively consider their carbon footprint across various aspects of daily life. Here are some actionable strategies:

- **Transportation**: Opt for an electric vehicle whenever feasible and utilize public transportation for commuting.
- **Food & Beverage**: Given that meat production carries a hefty carbon footprint, controlling meat consumption can effectively lower emissions.
- **Electrification**: Transitioning to electric kitchen appliances is a substantial step towards mitigating carbon emissions.
- **Recycling**: The recycling of items such as equipment, clothing, and books plays a pivotal role in minimizing carbon emissions. Households can purchase "Real Negative CO_2" from the carbon market to offset their carbon emissions.

Many environmentally conscious individuals are eager to lead by example, investing in carbon removals to offset their family's carbon footprint and striving towards achieving zero carbon households. This is a commendable endeavor that deserves encouragement. While urban households may not directly engage in carbon sequestration projects, financially capable families can contribute by purchasing "Real Negative CO_2" from the carbon market, facilitating the widespread realization of zero-carbon households.

9.4 Summary

This chapter analyzes the whole process of the CELM-based decarbonation system, examining its application in both the construction and power generation industries. The analysis reveals that the CELM effectively fosters fair and efficient decarbonation across these sectors, generating substantial positive macroeconomic impacts. It is reasonable to deduce that the CELM holds promise for achieving favorable outcomes across various industries.

The Chinese Government could initiate by implementing the CELM-based decarbonation system within the entire power sector, anticipating notable successes.

Furthermore, this chapter employs the CELM to precisely define carbon neutral entities, including countries, cities, parks, enterprises, and households. This provides the international community with the theoretical underpinnings and methodology required to establish genuine carbon neutral organizations, thereby motivating more entities to embrace carbon neutrality.

Chapter 10
Global Carbon Neutrality Solution

Under the leadership of the United Nations, the international community has made efforts for over three decades and held 27 climate conferences in pursuit of addressing climate change. However, progress in global carbon reduction remains slow and falls significantly short of the targets set by the IPCC. The fundamental reason lies in the fact that the international community's understanding of the essence of carbon reduction remains inadequate. Without a solid theoretical foundation, top-level mechanisms are not scientifically designed. Additionally, considerations of other interests by some countries make it inevitable that progress towards global carbon neutrality is challenging.

The emergence of the CELM and its solution provides a sense of enlightenment and clarity. The CELM helps the international community identify the greatest common denominator for climate issues, effectively reducing the variables requiring negotiation and discussion to just one: the phased pricing of international "negative carbon". The CELM has identified a novel and feasible third pathway to global carbon neutrality. By leveraging the positive effects of the global economic green transition, it has the potential to comprehensively accelerate carbon reduction worldwide, achieve global carbon neutrality more quickly, and even potentially exceed the IPCC's targets (hereinafter referred to as the IPCC targets) and even accomplish them ahead of schedule.

This chapter will focus on global carbon neutrality solution based on the CELM.

B. Yang, *The Carbon Emission Liability Mechanism*,
https://doi.org/10.1007/978-981-96-3612-9_10

10.1 Major Challenges in Advancing Global Carbon Neutrality

Due to the absence of a suitable foundational theory, the international community, despite its considerable efforts and some accomplishments, has largely been groping in the dark for carbon neutrality solutions. As a result, there has been minimal substantive progress toward achieving the IPCC targets. The global carbon neutrality process currently faces the following challenges.

10.1.1 Achieving the IPCC Targets Remains Unclear Due to the Lack of a Suitable Roadmap

Under the guidance of incomplete theories, the international community has been exploring two pathways, that is, carbon emission rights and carbon taxes, yet with slow progress.

The international community has spent excessive time, resources, and substantial carbon emissions on the concept of carbon emission rights, addressing issues such as national and organizational carbon allowance distribution as well as carbon trading market schemes. Despite these efforts, the outcomes have been minimal and progress has been sluggish, with emitting substantial carbon emissions throughout the process. For over a decade or two, numerous countries and regions have embarked on implementing carbon reduction mechanisms grounded in carbon emission rights. However, the tangible progress achieved thus far underscores the formidable challenges that persist in this endeavor.

For instance, in China, the national carbon trading market has had a transaction volume of less than 10 billion yuan over the past two years, with just over 2 billion yuan in 2022. This has only impacted around 2000 coal-fired power enterprises, affecting less than 1% of China's total carbon emissions. Despite an earlier start, European and American countries have also faced limited progress due to similar theoretical foundations and mechanisms for establishing these systems.

Carbon tax, as a pivotal policy instrument, also confronts a myriad of issues and has garnered less widespread adoption compared to carbon trading mechanisms. Despite years of meticulous research on carbon tax policy tool, China still grapples with insufficient confidence, hesitating to fully implement it.

A more significant challenge is that, despite its low efficiency in carbon reduction, its macroeconomic impact has been considerable. In China, coal-fired power plants have suffered substantial losses, and there is a severe power shortage, leading to power rationing for many production enterprises. These are negative effects of the current reduction mechanism. In the EU, the carbon price has risen to 100 euros per ton, imposing a significant burden on enterprises that genuinely require allowances.

10.1.2 Technical and Cost Challenges of Multi-level Allocation of Carbon Emission Rights

In the current carbon reduction mechanism based on carbon emission rights, the technical and cost challenges of allocating carbon emission rights remain insurmountable. This could lead to the complete failure of carbon reduction system, making it unable to fulfill the crucial task of achieving global carbon neutrality on time. Allocation is a challenge, as are data verification and supervision. Implementation within a single country is difficult, and the interactions of CEL among countries are even more complex. The mechanism based on carbon emission rights has concentrated international attention on the allocation of rights, which is its major shortcoming. Since carbon emission rights are seen as essential to survival and development, it becomes difficult for countries to make concessions. The allocation schemes encompass myriad variables, rendering negotiations among nearly 200 nations an intricate endeavor. In the nuclear age, where war is not an option, this challenge persists, with negotiations stagnating for over three decades without tangible outcomes. As climate shock events become more frequent and negotiations remain deadlocked, most countries have had to set their own carbon peaking and carbon neutrality targets. Yet, these efforts still fall significantly short of the IPCC goals.

10.1.3 Free-Riding on Carbon Emissions: Carbon Leakage and Carbon Tariffs

One of the most challenging issues in the context of transboundary public goods is the problem of free-riding. Currently, the European Union implements a carbon price of approximately €80 per ton of CO_2 for carbon reduction, while most other countries have a carbon price ranging from \$1 to \$2 per ton. This discrepancy has raised concerns about the fairness of international trade and resource flows due to "carbon leakage". After failing to persuade other countries to raise their carbon prices, the EU has leveraged its national sovereignty to unilaterally introduce the Carbon Border Adjustment Mechanism (CBAM). This unilateral action by the EU has elicited a strong reaction from the international community and has had a serious impact on international trade rules and existing climate framework agreements. This move has not only provoked opposition from developing countries but has also met with strong resistance from the United States, making it a particularly thought-provoking move.

Carbon reduction is a large-scale, complex, and transboundary system that requires systemic thinking and design. While breakthroughs at specific points can have a significant positive impact, they can also lead to considerable side effects. The issue of carbon tariffs related to international trade is a key point for international coordination. It requires robust foundational theory and comprehensive system design to achieve consensus among the international community. A fair and mutually beneficial carbon tariff mechanism must address several key theoretical questions:

- The first question is whether to adopt a producer liability mechanism or a consumer liability mechanism. The emphasis of EU's CBAM on high carbon prices drives industries and capital to regions with lower carbon prices, resulting in economic losses for the EU. Meanwhile, exporting countries face the dual burden of managing pollution and emission costs while also paying carbon tariffs to importing countries. The conflict of interests between these two sides is clearly substantial.
- The second question concerns the establishment of reliable data standards. How to validate the carbon content data of imported goods and how to establish standards and systems for data formation are critical issues. This process can result in significant transaction costs and disputes.
- The third question is the carbon pricing mechanism. Should carbon tariffs be negotiated bilaterally or set by the international community? What are the theoretical basis and principles for carbon pricing? The EU's unilateral imposition of carbon prices under the CBAM has encountered strong opposition from nearly all other countries, including the United States.
- The fourth question concerns effective offset mechanisms. The exporting country must have the option to offset carbon emissions domestically, and this option mechanism must be available. But how should the standards and verification procedures for these offsets be established? How can international consensus be achieved on this matter?
- The fifth question is the allocation of carbon tariff revenues. Since these emissions primarily originate in producing nations, carbon taxes levied by importing countries, such as the EU, ought to be strategically directed towards fostering carbon reduction efforts and ensuring trade equity. Ideally, the carbon fees, which serve as a financial resource to tackle carbon pollution, should be utilized within the producing countries themselves. However, the CBAM lacks provisions for such arrangements, and instead, the revenues are intended to be a source of income for the EU, thereby raising significant concerns about fairness and equity in the global trade landscape.

10.1.4 Where Will the Substantial Funds for Carbon Neutrality Come from

The question of where the substantial funds for carbon neutrality will come from is a very practical issue and a major challenge that governments face in reconciling their carbon reduction strategies. As a result, carbon neutrality funding has become a central theme in each COP meeting, with minimal progress achieved. At the COP27 meeting held in November 2022, a significant agreement called the "Sharm El Sheikh Implementation Plan" was adopted at great cost. This agreement established the long-debated "loss and damage" fund, which became the most notable outcome of the conference. However, the sources of funding for this initiative have yet to be determined.

Given the real and pressing climate challenges facing the world, such progress is indeed far too slow.

10.1.5 How to Create a Unified Global Decarbonation System

The most effective paradigm for global decarbonation system should be identified. Countries around the world should adopt a relatively unified system to ensure efficient operations in aspects such as carbon footprint verification, carbon offsetting, and carbon pricing.

A system based on carbon emission rights is highly unreliable due to the numerous schemes for setting and allocating carbon emission rights, making it impossible to achieve a uniform approach on a global scale.

The pricing of carbon taxes is even more challenging to estimate accurately, leading to ongoing debates among economists. The choice of a discount rate becomes mired in debates lacking scientific basis and often comes down to personal opinions. Furthermore, carbon taxes lack the ability to dynamically respond to macroeconomic changes and the carbon neutrality process, resulting in inefficiency.

10.1.6 How to Organize and Implement

The current global dilemma with carbon neutrality lies not only in the lack of a clear direction but also in the slow and inefficient organization and implementation of actions. The IPCC's role is limited to assessment and research, while COP meetings primarily serve as venues for disputes over interests. Advancing global carbon neutrality and establishing a strong, legally empowered global administrative organization are urgent. Of course, the core cause is that the international community has yet to establish a scientific and consensus-based global decarbonation system.

10.2 The "1+1" Global Carbon Neutrality Solution Based on the CELM

The CELM provides a solid theoretical foundation and a viable third pathway for achieving global carbon neutrality. Based on the core principles of the CELM, a novel global carbon neutrality solution has been designed that can effectively address the aforementioned challenges. This section focuses on the CELM-based "1+1" Global

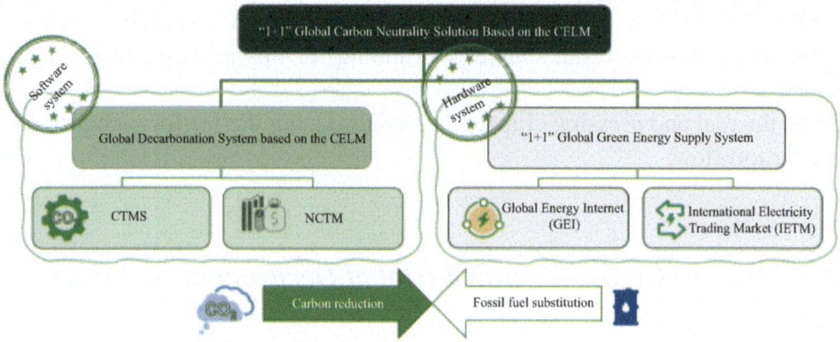

Fig. 10.1 CELM-based "1+1" global carbon neutrality solution

Carbon Neutrality Solution, which involves the establishment of a new and efficient "Global Decarbonation System + Global Green Energy Supply System". This "1+1" system will serve as a key safeguard for achieving global carbon neutrality (Fig. 10.1).

10.2.1 All Countries Establish a Global Decarbonation System Based on the CELM

This is also a "1+1" system, composed of two major subsystems: the "Carbon Ticket Management System" (CTMS) and the "Negative Carbon Trading Market" (NCTM). Together, these systems form an efficient global decarbonation framework and serve as the software infrastructure for achieving global carbon neutrality.

10.2.1.1 The Crucial Role of the CELM-Based Carbon Ticket Management System in the Global Decarbonation System

1. The CTMS supports the establishment of comprehensive, cost-effective carbon footprint big data systems for all sectors and products in each country. By delivering real-time, accurate, and complete carbon footprint data through a digital system, it provides the technical and cost feasibility for achieving societal-wide carbon reduction. Over the past two decades, China's carbon reduction mechanism based on carbon emission rights has only targeted over 2000 enterprises in the coal-fired power industry. Additionally, the timeliness and accuracy of the data could not be guaranteed due to the lack of an efficient and low-cost digital carbon footprint management system. Consequently, the marginal costs of carbon reduction have risen significantly, leading to increasingly severe impacts on the macroeconomy.

2. By leveraging market mechanisms and digital systems to efficiently and cost-effectively clarify the carbon emission liability of all organizations in society, this becomes the crucial mechanism for mobilizing societal-wide carbon reduction efforts. Based on the principle that organizations with carbon emission intensity exceeding the industry average should promptly assume their CEL (and costs), the CEL of each organization is determined by the difference between the carbon ticket input and output. This approach efficiently addresses the challenge of engaging all sectors of society in carbon reduction efforts.

10.2.1.2 The Powerful and Efficient Capabilities of the CELM-Based Negative Carbon Trading Market in the Global Decarbonation System

1. The NCTM supports all organizations within each country in conducting carbon offsetting at any time. Three types of "negative carbon" products meet the diverse needs of ordinary organizations, export enterprises, and companies that achieve carbon neutrality ahead of schedule.
2. The NCTM facilitates the establishment of a market platform for direct transactions between "carbon emissions" and "carbon removals" in each country. Enterprises with excessive carbon emission liability can purchase "negative carbon" to offset their emissions in the NCTM, while carbon removal enterprises and all organizations holding "negative carbon" can directly sell "negative carbon" products in the market. The NCTM directly facilitates both positive and negative incentives for carbon emissions. On one hand, it prompts high carbon-emitting organizations to directly pay for excess emissions costs in a short-term (on a quarterly basis), accelerating carbon reduction. On the other hand, it incentivizes carbon removal industries and low-carbon-emission enterprises to directly sell "negative carbon" products and gain revenue. Like many mature markets such as stock and futures exchanges, the NCTM can operate efficiently on its own.
3. Governments can obtain substantial carbon neutrality funds from the NCTM. The CELM-based carbon neutrality fund provides each country with ample financial resources for large-scale investments in green energy sectors. Additionally, the fund can be used for balancing interests between regions and social classes. This approach will significantly alleviate the major challenge of "climate funds" that has been a key issue at COP meetings.

10.2.2 The International Community Establishes a Global Green Energy Supply System

This is also a "1+1" system, which consists of two major subsystems: the "Global Energy Internet" + the "International Electricity Trading Market" (IETM), forming an efficient zero-carbon green energy supply system. This serves as the hardware infrastructure for achieving global carbon neutrality.

10.2.2.1 Building the Global Energy Internet

The Global Energy Internet (GEI) stands as the second pivotal global network, following in the footsteps of the World Information Internet.

The GEI is the pivotal hardware infrastructure for achieving global carbon neutrality. In essence, it is a massive system of a globalized "Smart Grid + Ultra-High Voltage Grid + Clean Energy" power Internet, which comprises three main components:

The first component is the globally distributed network of green energy production bases, also known as clean energy, including photovoltaic and wind power. The world can be divided into 3–4 regions, each covering 6 to 8 time zones, with each region possessing the capacity to simultaneously supply the world with photovoltaic and wind power.

The second component is the globally interconnected ultra-high voltage grid. It is tasked with delivering green electricity to every corner of the world. This requires the development of relevant international technical standards and significant investment, yet it remains highly cost-effective when compared to the enormous expenses associated with energy storage systems.

The third component is the smart grid system. Integrating with the global ultra-high voltage grid, the smart grid system intelligently dispatches and distributes electricity across the world based on the trading outcomes of the international electricity market. It facilitates the automatic and efficient allocation and transmission of power across the globe. These three physical hardware systems work together to constitute the perfect World Energy Internet, serving as the key infrastructure for achieving global carbon neutrality.

The establishment of this physical infrastructure demands investments amounting to tens of trillions of dollars. It calls for not only a unified framework of global technical standards and policy systems, along with coordinated efforts, but also a robust market ecosystem that encompasses demand, capital, and operational dynamics to facilitate its tangible realization.

10.2.2.2 Constructing an International Electricity Trading Market

The "Negative Carbon Trading Market + Global Energy Trading Market" will serve as a formidable financial backbone for the massive development of green power systems. Particularly, the International Electricity Trading Market (IETM) will act as a continuous funding source for global green energy supply network.

The IETM is comprised of suppliers and consumers, with the smart grid system adeptly pairing power supply with demand at every instance to enable transactions. With the backing of the GEI, the trade in electrical power can become more akin to that in the secondary market of the stock exchange, where consumers need not be concerned with the specifics of their power sources or origins.

A more advanced form of the International Electricity Trading Market should involve market makers participating in trading to regulate the electricity futures market, increase capital supply, reduce real-time supply and demand conflicts, and achieve the ability to preserve value and hedge risks.

The establishment of a market ecosystem that underpins the zero-carbon green energy supply is of paramount importance. This market has the potential to deliver substantial construction funds and enduring investment returns, while also converging global demands for green energy consumption and investment. It ensures a streamlined, global approach to the production, dispatch, consumption, investment, and management of green energy resources.

In summary, we have identified the two most critical dimensions of endeavor for the international community to achieve global carbon neutrality and ultimately address climate change: Firstly, to promote carbon emission reductions with greater efficiency and scale, while mitigating adverse effects on the macroeconomy. Secondly, to swiftly enhance the supply of zero-carbon green energy, expediting the transition away from fossil fuels. As these two endeavors progress in the same direction, the global community will be well-positioned to hasten its journey toward carbon neutrality.

The CELM-based Global Decarbonation System and the Global Green Energy Supply System are designed to ensure the effective execution of these twin strategies by the international community. The two frameworks and four subsystems of the CELM-based global carbon neutrality solution will work together to produce a cohesive and interdependent synergy, driving each other forward to forge an impeccable and ultimate resolution to the global climate challenge. Other policy instruments and solutions are crafted to support the execution and solidification of these core systems, providing refinement and supplementation.

Moreover, the global carbon neutrality system urgently requires a unique protective architecture: a governance system for carbon neutrality under the auspices of the United Nations, bolstered by the framework of the international laws. The global carbon neutrality collaboration demands harmonized technical standards, trading regulations, exchange systems, and power transmission networks, ensuring that no single sovereign power or interest group can dominate or manipulate any aspect of these integrated systems.

10.3 Establishing a Global Decarbonation System Based on the CELM

The foundational theory of the CELM represents a significant innovation on the predecessors' public goods theory, breaking through the challenges of carbon emissions as a cross-temporal, ultra-large-scale, complex mega-system public goods. It provides a solid theoretical foundation for international coordination towards global carbon neutrality. The international community can establish a new and efficient Global Decarbonation System based on the CELM.

10.3.1 Establishing an International Decarbonation Executive Organization Based on the CELM

Over the past three decades, international efforts in carbon emission reduction have struggled to achieve consensus on major policies and have failed to establish a legally empowered international decarbonation organization. This has led to numerous proposals and agreements that are difficult to implement. Currently, the most influential international organization in this area, the IPCC, is merely an academic body responsible for describing and assessing the current state of the Earth's climate and the potential crises and consequences that may arise in the future. The COP meetings are also just negotiation venues, not institutions for implementing actions.

The CELM has identified the greatest common denominator for international carbon reduction, making it relatively easier to reach a consensus. Once the conditions are in place, there is a need to establish a truly action-oriented executive organization to take the lead in implementing the following tasks:

1. Take the lead in formulating international standards for decarbonation

This encompasses the standards for carbon ticket design, data exchange protocols, CTMS system interface specifications, the definition of "negative carbon", certification standards for "Real Negative CO_2", and the pricing mechanism for "International Negative CO_2".

2. Inspect and supervise the implementation of the standards

Once a multitude of standards and mechanisms have been established, it is crucial to inspect and supervise the specific implementation to identify and resolve issues, so as to enhance the execution levels among countries, and ensure fairness and impartiality.

3. Facilitate and coordinate the establishment of Negative Carbon Trading Markets and International Carbon Trading Market across countries

The Negative Carbon Trading Market plays a critical role within the international carbon reduction framework, serving as an integral part of its smooth operation. Over the past two decades, individual countries have set up their own trading markets for carbon emission rights, and it appears that the carbon markets in most countries will need to be fundamentally overhauled. This undertaking is complex but imperative, as the existing markets for carbon emission rights are not equipped to support the global pursuit of carbon neutrality. Fortunately, the CELM-based Negative Carbon Trading Market is a highly standardized trading system. Once a prototype is established, it will be relatively straightforward for other nations to emulate.

To more effectively prompt decarbonation, it is essential for the International Carbon Trading Market to facilitate the optimal distribution of technology, resources, and "negative carbon" assets on a worldwide basis. The establishment and growth of the International Carbon Trading Market, grounded in market competition principles, is vital for providing guidance and fostering its widespread adoption.

4. Steer the pace of carbon emission reduction and the transition to global carbon neutrality

The international community must finely steer the pace of carbon emission reduction. The goal is to meet the targets for carbon neutrality while achieving favorable climate objectives and avoiding significant disruptions to global economic progress. The CELM and its Solution suggest that this is a feasible objective, and the positive economic effects of carbon reduction could be substantial. This stands in contrast to the current approach of markets for carbon emission rights, where the conflict between carbon reduction and economic growth is pronounced.

During the process, it is crucial to closely observe the interplay between carbon neutrality transition and economic growth. Should any issues arise, it will be necessary to make timely adjustments to ensure a harmonious progression.

5. Coordinate the formulation of Pricing Schemes and Phased Pricing for "International Negative CO_2"

Similar to the EU's Carbon Border Adjustment Mechanism (CBAM), which addresses carbon tariffs, carbon pricing issues are increasingly becoming significant topics in international trade. The EU's CBAM, currently a unilateral mechanism, has sparked considerable controversy and poses a significant obstacle to the development of international trade. Therefore, it is imperative to establish a more efficient multilateral coordination mechanism under the leadership of a respected international organization.

6. Promote training and organize international exchange

The establishment and operation of the Global Decarbonation System across various countries is a huge systematic project that demands a considerable team of experts. The disparities in the actual conditions of different nations necessitate targeted adjustments and designs. It is essential for the International Decarbonation Executive Organization to establish professional institutions for long-term, continuous systematic training of talents, the transfer of experiences from demonstration countries, and international research and exchange. The extensive and ongoing organizational workload requires the establishment of a dedicated institution.

7. Additional work projects

In the face of the humanity's greatest societal challenge, the range of significant work projects extends far beyond the few areas mentioned above.

The role of the International Decarbonation Executive Organization in the global carbon neutrality process is akin to the pivotal role played by the World Bank in shaping the international financial order. It will be a pivotal factor in achieving global carbon neutrality.

10.3.2 Establishing an International Decarbonation System and International Standards Based on the CELM

Over the past three decades, international efforts have primarily been directed towards implementing a system based on producer liability and carbon emission rights. Under the leadership of the International Decarbonation Executive Organization, the International Decarbonation System based on the CELM will need to be entirely reconstructed. Although it is relatively straightforward, there will still be a significant amount of work required to establish and continuously upgrade and refine various standards.

1. Establish an International Decarbonation Liability System

As previously discussed, in scenarios where the international market fails and national domestic policies also falter, the current producer liability mechanism and the carbon reduction system based on carbon emission rights are inefficient. In contrast, the carbon reduction system based on the CELM holds significant advantages.

Establishing a new international decarbonation liability mechanism and implementation mechanism according to the CELM requires international consensus and the formation of international law. In addition, extensive international coordination is necessary in the initial stages.

The core of the Decarbonation System based on the CELM theory consist of three main principles:

First, consumer liability. Consumers are accountable for the final cost of carbon emissions, with the end of the supply chain assuming overall liability for the carbon emissions of the front end.

Second, organizations with carbon emissions above the societal average must immediately bear the cost of their emissions by purchasing "negative carbon" from the Negative Carbon Trading Market for offsetting.

Third, the Negative Carbon Trading Market provides carbon offsetting products for social organizations, directly linking the supply and demand sides of "negative carbon". This market mechanism efficiently achieves positive and negative incentives in both directions.

2. Establish construction standards for Carbon Ticket Management System

Given the need for comprehensive connectivity among the CTMS across different countries, it is crucial for the international community to establish unified construction standards. Once these standards are set, they can serve as a reference for different countries, facilitating reduced construction costs and shorter timelines. Moreover, they are highly beneficial for the subsequent integration and interoperability of systems across nations.

3. Establish a data standard system for the CTMS

The establishment of a unified data standard for the CTMS will facilitate domestic decarbonation management as well as the exchange and verification of international trade data, thereby enabling efficient integration of the CTMS systems across different countries.

4. Establish an operation standard system for CTMS

The establishment of a high-level operation standard system for CTMS will facilitate the training of specialized professionals, elevate their operational efficiency across countries, and reduce the barriers to entry for effective carbon management capabilities.

5. Establish a standardized coding system for organizations and items

Given the comprehensive nature of the international carbon emission reduction system, which encompasses all organizations and items, it is essential to implement carbon labels for all items within the international community. Additionally, all organizations must clarify their liability for carbon emissions. To facilitate efficient auditing and verification of international and domestic trade, a standardized coding system for organizations and items is necessary. The current item coding systems widely used in the international market cannot fully meet the management needs of carbon labeling (carbon footprint) for all items in society. Therefore, it is necessary to develop a more comprehensive new coding standard system.

6. Establish an international standard system for carbon source (carbon content) certification

As long as carbon source data is well managed, the Decarbonation System based on the CELM will rely on market mechanisms and digital systems to operate automatically, efficiently, and precisely in the mid- and back-office. Therefore, the management of carbon sources at the front end is of paramount importance.

Carbon source management will focus on the major contributors while allowing for smaller ones to be managed more flexibly, gradually transitioning to comprehensive and detailed management. The number of major carbon-emitting enterprises is relatively small, primarily comprising entities in the fossil fuel sector, covering coal, oil, and natural gas. As decarbonation management deepens, the carbon source enterprises will be fully covered, ranging from major entities like cement plants, livestock farms, and fertilizer plants to smaller entities such as firewood factories. Any manufacturer contributing to carbon emissions will be included in the management system. The establishment of an international standard for carbon source management will provide a solid foundation for the operation of decarbonation systems in countries and across the international community.

7. Establish an international standard system for carbon removal (Real Negative CO_2) certification

Carbon removal, or "negative carbon" production, is an indispensable commodity for achieving carbon neutrality. Carbon emissions and carbon absorption are a pair of contradictory forces, and their balance leads to carbon neutrality. Encouraging massive afforestation, protecting mangroves, and developing CCUS technologies are all initiatives actively promoted by governments around the world to foster the development of carbon removals. The negative carbon industry has immense potential, and carbon removals will be a decisive force in the pursuit of global carbon neutrality.

The growth of the carbon removal industry necessitates robust mechanisms that provide strong positive incentives. The international standard system for carbon removal certification is a critical component of such a mechanism, with the NCTM being instrumental in delivering these incentives. The current CCER system has consumed a substantial quantity of government resources, yet its impact on emissions reduction has been negligible. Since CCER is a relative measure, it is unable to meet the demands of global carbon neutrality. It is therefore urgent to replace the CCER system with the international standard system for carbon removal certification. The international community must shift its focus and resources towards the development of the standard system for "International Negative CO_2" certification. Once this international standard system for carbon removal certification is implemented, it will facilitate the establishment of an internationalized negative carbon trading market. Carbon removal, or "Real Negative CO_2", is a global standard commodity that involve removing one ton of CO_2 from the atmosphere. This makes it relatively easy to establish a large "International Negative CO_2" market, significantly accelerating the development of the carbon removal industry and incentivizing activities such as afforestation, forest conservation, and the development of high-efficiency and new-type CCUS technologies.

The current CCER system does not directly correspond to carbon neutrality. For example, China has had to set a maximum offset limit of 5%, which has greatly restrained the development of the carbon removal industry. Continuing to invest heavily in the research and development of new CCER markets would be a waste of resources.

In contrast, the carbon price in the EU has reached 100 euros per ton, while the domestic CCER price in China is only between 10 to 20 yuan per ton, indicating a severe distortion in the market. Therefore, it is urgent to expedite the necessary changes to address this imbalance.

8. Establish an international standard system for offsetting CEL

Enterprises aiming to achieve carbon neutrality ahead of schedule will require their carbon emissions to be offset through "Real Negative CO_2". The standards for this are relatively simple, yet the majority of enterprises in domestic and international trade find it difficult to meet these requirements. With the prevalence of carbon border adjustment mechanisms, there is a pressing need to establish standards that facilitate efficient international trade operations.

Multilateral coordination is essential to determine the phased pricing for "International Negative CO_2" products. Additionally, a set of execution and certification standards must be developed for using these products to offset carbon emissions in international trade imports and exports.

In conclusion, the establishment of various standard systems is crucial for the construction of an efficient international carbon emission reduction system.

10.3.3 Establishing and Operating the CTMS in Each Country

Relying on the International Decarbonation System established based on the CELM, countries can establish and operate the CTMS at low cost and with high efficiency. By relying on market mechanisms and digital systems for decarbonation management, it becomes possible to clarify the CEL of all organizations in society and the carbon footprint (carbon labels) of all items in society. This will significantly accelerate the pace of decarbonation in society as a whole.

Similar to enterprise management, the key of national governance lies in the ability to obtain real-time, accurate information. With the help of the CELM-based Decarbonation System, the government's capabilities will be greatly enhanced.

10.3.4 Establishing Negative Carbon Trading Market Based on the CELM in Each Country

Under the CELM, carbon taxes and trading market for carbon emission rights are no longer considered the primary policy instruments for carbon emission reduction. The international community should embrace a third pathway: the internalization of carbon emission costs based on consumer liability mechanism and the establishment of NCTM.

The NCTM is a cornerstone of the CELM-based decarbonation system, offering a real-time operational tool for carbon offsetting for all organizations within society. Governments must allocate substantial resources to the development of the NCTM to complete the loop of their domestic decarbonation. This initiative will also greatly incentivize the growth of carbon removal industry within their respective countries.

The methodology and top-level design for constructing the NCTM are comprehensively outlined in Chap. 8.

10.3.5 Operation of the Global Decarbonation System

The domestic decarbonation primarily relies on the effective operation of the "1+1" system consisting of "Carbon Ticket Management System (CTMS) + Negative Carbon Trading Market (NCTM)". These two major systems independently drive all organizations within society to settle their carbon emissions on a quarterly basis, accelerating carbon emission reduction. The NCTM provides dual incentives for emissions. Through the NCTM, governments can obtain substantial revenue, which can be used to better invest in the national green transition. In addition, governments can also effectively control carbon pricing to regulate carbon neutrality process, aligning it with the healthy development of the macroeconomy.

The operation of the International Decarbonation System should prioritize three key aspects of work:

- First, to achieve the predetermined goals in global carbon neutrality process. This involves efficiently controlling the global carbon neutrality process through guidance on carbon pricing and organizing discussions and providing professional support to countries facing challenges.
- Second, to align with the international macroeconomic situation. Given the fragile state of the current international economy, regulating the interaction between carbon emission reduction and the macroeconomy is an important task for governments. It is anticipated that the CELM-based Carbon Emission Reduction System will have a limited negative impact on the macroeconomy and exert limited pressure.
- Third, to coordinate international carbon border adjustment mechanisms to prevent disruptions to the existing international trade system. The EU's CBAM has shown signs of unfriendly unilateralism, which has garnered global attention to how it will evolve. The CELM can effectively address the challenges associated with carbon border adjustment mechanisms.

Under the strong leadership of the International Decarbonation Executive Organization, the system can rapidly accumulate experience and continuously optimize and upgrade its operational systems. This will facilitate rapid progress in countries across the world and promote the early achievement of global carbon neutrality.

10.3.6 Carbon Border Adjustment Mechanism in International Trade

The carbon border adjustment mechanism in international trade is a double-edged sword. Properly implemented, it can accelerate the global drive towards carbon emission reduction and hasten the achievement of global carbon neutrality. However, if misused, it not only has a counterproductive effect on carbon reduction but also can hinder the development of international trade and have a detrimental impact on the global macroeconomy.

10.3.6.1 Dilemmas Encountered by Current Carbon Border Adjustment Mechanism

The EU's CBAM has dual impacts. On the one hand, it incentivizes countries to hasten the construction of their domestic carbon emission reduction frameworks to align with the carbon border adjustment mechanisms in international trade, thus contributing to global decarbonation. On the other hand, the unilateral nature of this mechanism has sparked controversy, with many nations viewing it as a form of coercion and predatory taxation by developed countries against developing nations. This has even led to skepticism about the true meaning and justice of climate change, especially considering that debates about the facts of climate change have never ceased, even within the academic and governmental circles of developed nations. The U.S. government's wavering stance on climate agreements is often attributed to the machinations of different interest groups. The estimates of carbon emission costs by successive U.S. administrations have varied widely, often driven by academic games rather than substantive policy considerations.

Therefore, it is advisable to engage in thorough communication within the existing framework of international trade rules and guided by the principles of multilateral coordination. This approach is likely to yield better results. However, in the current state of international understanding of carbon emission reduction, there is a belief that regardless of the mechanism employed, the macroeconomy will incur substantial costs. This perspective makes international coordination challenging and often leads to suboptimal outcomes. Under the current approaches of carbon taxes and carbon markets for carbon emission rights, all nations, interest groups, and individuals perceive carbon emission reduction as primarily associated with increased costs rather than opportunities. As a result, with the natural tendency to avoid risks and seek benefits, there is a general reluctance to take the lead. In contrast, within the CELM, individuals and entities are more likely to see their immediate interests outweighing the costs of investment, leading to a greater sense of urgency and motivation to take action.

10.3.6.2 Carbon Border Adjustment Mechanism Based on the CELM

The international community should promote a more positive new climate change economics theory and carbon emission reduction system, namely the CELM-based Global Decarbonation System. Once countries realize its benefits, their initiative for carbon emission reduction will be greatly enhanced. The Global Decarbonation System should not only exert pressure but also enhance the motivation of all countries.

Since the Global Carbon Neutrality Solution based on the CELM has a strong positive effect, its implementation is expected to be very promising.

Moreover, a correct international carbon border adjustment mechanism should be established. The Global Decarbonation System needs to upgrade its top-level design and introduce a more recognized, fair, and just decision-making and implementation mechanism among more countries. The current annual United Nations Climate Change Conference COP meetings resemble a battlefield rather than a platform for cooperation to jointly address the severe global challenges.

The execution plan for the Carbon Border Adjustment Mechanism based on the CELM primarily includes the following components:

1. Countries should establish their own CTMS based on international standards, and create a comprehensive national carbon footprint database that provides reliable carbon footprint data to the international community. Just like other items in society, export products are managed within the national CTMS. They follow the transaction rules to facilitate the circulation of carbon ticket input and output, thereby establishing a large dataset of carbon footprints for export products.
2. The Carbon Border Adjustment Mechanism provides credibility and verification of carbon footprints. When customs authorities in various countries verify the carbon emission data for imported products, they will access the data from the counterpart's national CTMS. Its establishment is based on national credibility and the CMTS international standards, thus eliminating possibility of false information. Of course, the management authorities should establish a supervisory mechanism to oversee the proper functioning of the CMTS in each country.
3. Exported products offset their emissions through the "International Negative CO_2" within each country's domestic carbon market. This approach to carbon offsetting upholds principles of fairness and reasonableness. When a country produces goods for consumption in another, it generates pollution domestically and bears the costs for pollution treatment. It is unfair for the exporting nation to face additional carbon taxes on these goods when they are imported by another country, which could lead to intractable international trade conflicts. However, the CELM solution elegantly resolves this dilemma.
4. It helps coordinate the phased pricing for "International Negative CO_2" through a multilateral mechanism. Based on multilateral principles and considering the varying stages of development of different countries, a multilateral coordination mechanism will provide different pricing for "International Negative CO_2" during each phase. Adjustments for the subsequent phase will be negotiated separately, ensuring that the approach keeps pace with the times.

Under the CELM, the issues of data credibility, timeliness, and verification for the carbon footprints of all organizations and items across countries have been resolved. Countries can offset their carbon emissions through the "International Negative CO_2" in their respective domestic carbon markets, keeping the carbon fees within the country, which is fair and reasonable. The remaining challenge is nearly exclusively the matter of phased carbon pricing.

10.3.6.3 International Carbon Pricing Coordination Mechanism

Under the CELM, countries offset the carbon emission of their export products within their own domestic negative carbon trading markets. By purchasing "International Negative CO_2", a specific negative carbon product, they retain the carbon emission fees within the country, which is beneficial for reducing the loss from carbon tariffs. The offset export goods become "zero-carbon products" based on "International Negative CO_2". It should be noted that at this point, these are not truly carbon neutral products. Only products neutralized (offset) with "Real Negative CO_2" can be considered truly zero-carbon products.

The pricing of "International Negative CO_2" requires recognition from both trading parties. Based on the adaptation to global carbon neutrality, it needs to consider the economic development, the stage of green economic transformation, and the macroeconomic resilience of both countries. How to quantify and analyze is a technical issue that requires further research.

The pricing mechanism for "International Negative CO_2" needs to be designed with a fairer and more efficient scheme. At the very least, it should not resemble the current unilateral mechanism of the EU's CBAM. Considerable pricing schemes for "International Negative CO_2" might include:

1. Bilateral negotiations: The pricing is determined through one-to-one negotiations between countries. As long as both parties agree and the negotiations meet their respective committed decarbonation levels, the deal is established. The downside is that the efficiency of these bilateral negotiations may be low, and the cost of negotiation can be high.
2. Joint negotiations by International Decarbonation Executive Organization and International Trade Organization: These organizations would coordinate negotiations to establish phased and categorized carbon pricing. For example, pricing could be set every two years, with three different tiers to correspond to the varying levels of development and economic resilience of different countries. This approach offers higher efficiency and ensures greater fairness in the pricing mechanism.

The "Real Negative CO_2" is a standard product that can be freely traded globally, allowing organizations that have achieved carbon neutrality to engage in transactions of "Real Negative CO_2" worldwide. The phased price for "International Negative CO_2" is lower than that of "Real Negative CO_2" but higher than that of "Owing Negative CO_2" implemented internally by developing countries. Once the price of "Real Negative CO_2" comes down to a level that all organizations can afford, the process becomes even simpler. "International Negative CO_2" can directly equal "Real

Negative CO_2" in price, eliminating the significant costs associated with international coordination. Therefore, it is crucial to vigorously develop CCUS technologies and the carbon sequestration industry.

10.3.7 Establishing the International Negative Carbon Trading Market

The establishment of an International Negative Carbon Trading Market is pivotal to advancing the global journey towards carbon neutrality. The market mechanism will strongly drive the global carbon sequestration industry and the CCUS technology industry. Primarily, it will incentivize high-carbon-emitting enterprises to bear the cost of incentives, while low-carbon-emitting enterprises that are capable of achieving carbon neutrality early may also voluntarily contribute to some of the costs. The International Negative Carbon Trading Market deals with the "Real Negative CO_2" and its derivatives, which are produced by carbon sequestration organizations and CCUS organizations. "Owing Negative CO_2" products are not allowed to trade in the International Negative Carbon Trading Market, and current CCER products are also not eligible. "Real Negative CO_2" is the product that truly removes CO_2 from the atmosphere and is a global standard product. As long as the verification system is well-established, the quantity verified by qualified institutions through legal procedures is undisputed. This makes "Real Negative CO_2" a tradable product and a storable asset without any issues.

Compared to the current trading market for carbon emission rights and the current capital market (stock market), the technical challenges of operating the International Negative Carbon Trading Market will be significantly less. Once governments recognize its necessity, the difficulty in establishing it is not overwhelming.

The International Negative Carbon Trading Market should be endorsed by national credit supervision authorities, and reviewed and authorized by international carbon emission reduction organizations.

Amount of carbon removals from carbon removal organizations and CCUS organizations around the world can enter the international carbon market, where all demand sides and institutional and individual investors can engage in trading. It is noteworthy to mention that research is needed on how to prevent and control excessive speculation, monopolization, and price hiking.

The trading products of the International Negative Carbon Trading Market will be globally valid and recognized by all countries, making them applicable for carbon offsetting in any scenarios.

10.3.8 *Event Review: History and Lessons of the EU's Carbon Tax Dispute in Aviation and Shipping Industries*

According to data from the International Air Transport Association (IATA), the carbon emissions of aviation industry currently account for 2.5% of global emissions, with a steady increase year by year. In 2019, the total CO_2 emissions from global commercial aviation reached 918 Mt, a 29% increase from 2013. If passenger traffic continues to grow at its current pace, the increase in aviation CO_2 emissions over the next three decades will be more than three times that of the period from 1990 to 2019. In response, the IATA announced in October 2021 a plan to achieve net-zero emissions for the industry by 2050. Indeed, the greatest challenge in decarbonizing the aviation industry is how to reduce its carbon footprint while passenger traffic continues to grow. The IATA estimates that by 2050, there will be 10 billion air passengers every year.

The maritime shipping industry accounts for approximately 2% of global carbon emissions, making the aviation and shipping sectors together contribute to about 4.5% of the world's total deep carbon emissions, qualifying them as significant emitters. Particularly, since the aviation and shipping industries operate transnationally, they have become a prime focus for the European Union. The EU hopes to expand its political and euro influence through the mechanism of carbon tariffs on global climate issues.

10.3.8.1 The EU's Carbon Accounting

In November 2008, the European Union's initiative to integrate international aviation into its Emission Trade System (ETS) was enacted into law by the European Parliament. As of January 1, 2012, the EU formally included international aviation within its ETS, mandating that all airlines operating routes that pass through EU airspace submit their carbon emission data and comply with the EU's designated carbon emission allowances. Airlines that exceeded these quantities were required to purchase additional allowances. This move encompassed more than 2000 airlines globally within the EU's aviation ETS framework.

At the time, it was estimated that if the EU's regulation were enforced, by 2020 the operating costs for global airlines would increase by at least 2 billion dollars. For China, in 2012, the cost increase for the civil aviation industry would be 790 million yuan, and in 2020, this cost would rise to 3.7 billion yuan. Over the 9-year period from 2012 to 2020, the total additional cost for China's civil aviation industry would amount to 17.6 billion yuan. This would have a significant impact on the global aviation industry.

10.3.8.2 Strong Countermeasures by China, Russia, the United States, and Other Countries

In response, 29 countries, including China and the United States, jointly signed a declaration opposing the EU's imposition of carbon taxes. China took a tough stance and mounted a strong counterattack. In March 2012, Airbus announced that an order for 35 A330 passenger aircraft from Chinese mainland airlines had been delayed, and an order for 10 A380 passenger aircraft from Hong Kong Airlines had been blocked, with the total value of these orders amounting to 12 billion dollars.

Russia took the lead in retaliation. In February 2012, a special meeting on the EU's aviation carbon tax was held in Moscow, where it was declared that more than 30 countries, led by Russia, were considering taking retaliatory measures against the EU for its imposition of carbon taxes on foreign airlines. Russia planned to prohibit its domestic airlines from participating in the EU's carbon trading. According to Valery Okulov, Deputy Minister, the Ministry of Transport of the Russian Federation, 29 out of the 32 countries present at the meeting had signed a document aimed at protesting the EU's aviation carbon tax. "The government's plan is to either have the EU's aviation carbon tax completely abolished or its implementation postponed," Okulov stated.

The United States forcefully retaliated. President Obama of the United States signed a bill that mandated the U.S. government to shield American airlines from the imposition of carbon taxes by the EU. The bill empowered the U.S. Secretary of Transportation with the authority to decide that if the EU enforced carbon emission taxes on U.S. airlines, the U.S. government would support the airlines in resisting such taxation. According to Reuters, the bill safeguarded the interests of American airlines. Estimates revealed that if American airlines were to pay carbon taxes to the EU, their additional expenses over the next eight years would exceed $3.1 billion. The U.S. Senate passed a bill that exempted American airlines from adhering to the EU's carbon emission regulations. Some U.S. lawmakers expressed that American airlines and passengers should not be compelled to contribute to Europe's debt reduction through an "illegal tax". Instead, these funds could be utilized to bolster job creation and economic growth within the United States.

10.3.8.3 Subsequent Progress

In the face of strong opposition from countries around the world, on November 12, 2012, the European Commission recommended suspending the EU's unilateral measures to impose carbon taxes on civil flights entering and leaving EU countries until the autumn of 2013.

In April 2013, the European Parliament and the Council of the European Union passed a decision to cease the collection of carbon taxes on non-EU international flights. It was determined that no action would be taken against international airlines that did not comply with the "EU Aviation Emission Trading Directive" before January 1, 2014.

In March 2021, the European Commission declared that the shipping industry would be integrated into the European Union's Emissions Trading System (EU ETS). To fulfill the EU's climate objectives, the costs for polluters will increase. The plan encompassed entities such as aircraft manufacturers, electricity providers, and airlines that operated within European borders, with shipping industry set to be gradually included in the carbon emissions trading framework within a span of three years. This new arrangement would encompass emissions from flights within the EU, 50% of the emissions from ships during international voyages that either arrive or depart in the EU, and emissions from ships while docked at EU ports, all falling under the existing emissions trading system.

On June 22, 2022, the revised legislative proposal to incorporate the shipping industry into the EU Emissions Trading System (EU ETS) was formally approved by the European Parliament with a vote of 438 in favor, 157 against, and 32 abstentions.

10.3.8.4 Industry Associations Are Taking Actions

The International Chamber of Shipping (ICS), a global trade association that represents the world's national shipowner associations and over 80% of the world merchant fleet, submitted a proposal to the United Nations International Maritime Organization (IMO) in September 2021. The proposal urged the adoption of internationally recognized market-based measures (MBMs) to expedite the adoption and deployment of zero-carbon fuels. The idea of imposing taxes on vessel carbon emissions globally represented a pioneering approach for any industry sector.

ICS contends that mandatory global market-based measures are preferable to any unilateral or regional international shipping market-based measures, such as the European Commission's proposal to extend the EU Emissions Trading System (ETS) to international shipping. Dispersed market-based measures, such as the EU ETS which would only apply to 7.5% of global shipping, would ultimately fail to reduce carbon emissions in global international shipping to the levels required by *The Paris Agreement*. Instead, they would complicate maritime trade.

10.3.8.5 Event Analysis: Nature of the Event, Response Strategies, and Actions

The aviation and shipping industries, which collectively contribute around 4.5% of global carbon emissions, are sectors with a unique nature that necessitates international business transactions. Consequently, they have been identified by the European Union as a strategic area for exerting its influence in international affairs, expanding the influence of the euro, and enhancing its position on climate change.

The European Union has strategically identified climate change mitigation as a means to advance its global political objectives. The EU views climate change mitigation as a domain where it can assert its international dominance. To maintain its leadership, which is under significant challenge, and to strengthen its early-mover advantage, the EU, traditionally a proponent of multilateralism, has taken the unprecedented step of imposing unilateral measures, steadfastly pushing for an aviation carbon tax. The EU seeks, through this measure, to take a dominant position and control rule-making power in global response to climate change, thereby securing a special status within the future international legal framework for climate change. Beyond the aviation carbon tax, the EU has plans to extend this approach to maritime emissions, with a broader strategic aim to strengthen its position in global negotiations on aviation emissions, to assert dominance in the global carbon finance market, to enhance the status of the euro, to mask economic promotion as environmental stewardship to boost Airbus sales and to improve the overall competitiveness of the EU's aviation sector.

In any industry, reducing carbon emissions and taking the CEL are global trends that cannot be reversed. The crucial question is how governments should understand the essence of these issues and how they should take action to avoid moral dilemmas, economic losses, and the loss of the power to set rules. It is essential to prevent the Chinese aviation and shipping industries from being significantly impacted and losing international competitiveness.

For a special industry with an international scope, a series of complex questions arise: Who assumes the CEL? Who has the right to levy carbon taxes? How should carbon taxes be applied? And the most important, who makes rules? The International Chamber of Shipping (ICS), representing the global shipping industry, has put forward a comprehensive proposal that seeks to establish industry-wide standards and rules, aiming to secure the power to set rules and collect taxes. This approach is considered both strategically astute and pragmatic, as it aligns with both the industry's rational interests and its high level of practical feasibility.

Firstly, we must understand the essence of the matter. The core essence of the carbon taxes in international aviation and shipping industries can be summarized into three points: the first is the struggle among interest groups for the right to establish rules and distribute benefits; the second is the mechanism for assuming the CEL and the rational carbon reduction strategies within the aviation and shipping industries; and the third is the issue of fair competition due to different carbon pricing policies among countries.

Based on that, we must take proactive measures while clarifying the professional and academic theoretical issues.

According to the CELM, the issue of carbon emissions in the aviation and shipping industries is straightforward. The CELM is crystal clear in its approach: carbon emissions should primarily be borne by consumers, specifically the passengers. Carbon fees should be directly added to the ticket price, collected, through the carbon trading market, by the government authorities in charge of carbon emissions in the airlines' respective countries. These carbon fees are then pooled by the countries to fund sustainable fuel development for aviation and shipping, carbon reduction technologies, and to support the green transformation of various aviation and shipping companies.

The key to international coordination here is to ensure fair competition by adopting a unified, phased pricing for "International Negative CO_2" c across different countries. As long as aviation and shipping companies from different nations have credible carbon footprint data and clear procedures for paying carbon fees to their registered countries, no other country should have the right to interfere.

Once the underlying logic of the carbon tax issue in the aviation and shipping industries is understood, the top-level design becomes theoretically simpler.

The CELM suggests that all carbon emissions contribute to the pollution of the global climate, which belongs to public goods. The carbon issues in the aviation and shipping industries are similar to those in other international trade and even to those of domestic products. All carbon emissions should be regulated and the associated costs should be borne. The argument that because your plane flies into my airspace and emits into my air, I have the right to collect carbon tax does not hold. If this logic were to be applied universally, it could lead to the absurd conclusion that if you emit carbon within your own country but the emissions drift into my airspace, I have the right to collect carbon tax from you. Such a rule would lead to chaos in the world, with war being the only method to resolve issues.

Therefore, the core issue of negotiations in the aviation and shipping industries, similar to all international trade, should be the fair competition of enterprises from different countries under different carbon pricing scenarios.

Given the nature of international trade and business operations, it is essential to establish a unified standard for carbon pricing through phased negotiations. Imposing a unilateral rule on a global business system is not a sustainable approach in the long term, and international negotiations are unlikely to be successful. It is particularly important to note that the carbon price in the carbon market must be based on the price of "Real Negative CO_2" and "International Negative CO_2", rather than that of carbon emission allowances. This approach ensures clarity in effect, consistency in standards, and the formation of an internationally unified pricing system to resolve disputes. The EU's carbon market also has its imperfections, with many free carbon allowances that could complicate international standardization. China, as a major emitter of carbon emissions, stands to suffer greater losses if it does not establish a high-standard domestic negative carbon trading market. In such a scenario, China would be at the mercy of others in setting the rules and collecting the fees. Therefore, it is imperative for China to take swift actions to shift from a reactive to a proactive stance. During the 2022 Chinese National People's Congress, Wang Changshun, a member of the National Committee of the Chinese People's Political Consultative Conference, submitted *A Proposal on Improving the Energy Consumption and Carbon Emission Management Mechanism of Aviation Transport Enterprises*. In this proposal, he suggested the Civil Aviation Administration of China should leverage its management advantages to implement comprehensive management of carbon emissions from airlines, balancing both domestic and international markets, and striving for a fair, competitive environment for Chinese aviation enterprises.

To effectively address carbon emissions within the aviation and shipping sectors, we provide the following strategic suggestions for China:

1. Initiate the establishment of the CELM-based "1+1" Decarbonation system without delay. On one side, by leveraging the CTMS, China can gather comprehensive and trustworthy carbon footprint data for all organizations and operations within the aviation and shipping industries. On the other side, carbon emissions can be offset through the purchase of "International Negative CO_2" from the CELM-based NCTM. The carbon price for "International Negative CO_2" will be determined through bilateral negotiations to ensure that carbon fees are invested domestic. Additionally, China has the opportunity to provide solutions to many countries and to promote the international development of the CELM-based NCTM.
2. Study and implement fiscal and industry policies for the aviation and shipping industries. Chinese Government should provide support in taxation and finance to reduce the total operational costs of Chinese airlines, thereby maintaining their international competitiveness.
3. Accelerate the progress of zero-carbon technologies in the aviation and shipping industries. This involves accelerating the transition to zero-carbon in the aviation and shipping industries, developing zero-carbon fuels, and advancing various carbon reduction technologies. To maintain an unassailable position in international competition, the Chinese aviation and shipping industries must excel in technology. Only by having a strong foundation in technology can the industries hope to succeed, as other methods alone will not suffice.
4. Extensively collaborate with nations worldwide to elevate China's international status. China should actively advocate for more just, equitable, and effective climate theories and solutions, striving to garner support from a greater number of allies. This approach will bolster China's discourse power and influence in global affairs, enhancing its ability to shape international norms and regulations.

10.4 Establishing a Global Green Energy Supply System Based on the CELM

To attain global carbon neutrality, a dual-pronged approach is imperative. Firstly, we must fortify our decarbonation framework, aimed at dismantling high-carbon and suboptimal production capacities, thereby expediting the decline in overall global carbon emissions. Secondly, it is vital to accelerate the development of zero-carbon green energy sources and their substitution for fossil fuels.

Leveraging cutting-edge technologies, harnessing market mechanisms to their fullest potential, and formulating an international standard system serve as cornerstone strategies for the construction of a robust Global Green Energy Supply System. This integrated approach is integral to addressing the technical intricacies, high costs, and advance hurdles inherent in cross-border transactions faced by the Global Green Energy Supply System.

The CELM-based Global Green Energy Supply System encompasses two subsystems: the Global Energy Internet and the International Electricity Trading Market. This "1+1" integrated Global Green Energy Supply System offers a comprehensive solution to the challenges faced by the international community in transitioning towards a zero-carbon green energy future. By constructing innovative transmission and distribution infrastructures, fostering innovative energy market mechanisms, and establishing new energy trading markets, we can effectively address the myriad conflicts that exist between current energy production and consumption. Notably, this framework alleviates the dilemma faced in the development of zero-carbon green energy, along with other pivotal technical hurdles.

Strategies for constructing a Global Green Energy Supply System include:

1. Overcoming the bottleneck in zero-carbon green energy advancement. Over the past decade, global green energy technologies, encompassing photovoltaic and wind power, has witnessed unprecedented strides. Manufacturing and construction costs have plummeted, translating into electricity generation expenses notably lower than those of coal-fired power, forming the most essential technological cornerstone for humanity's pursuit of global carbon neutrality. Nevertheless, despite these advancements, the influence of green energy remains limited due to challenges such as the fleeting nature of renewable generation and its inherent volatility (intermittent, fluctuating, and unpredictable), giving rise to following issues:

    - First, because of its limited total power generation capacity, green energy will still not be able to become the primary source of energy supply for an extended period of time. China, a leader in green energy development, is steadfastly expanding its investment, with data indicating that in 2022, new energy sources contributed 2.7 trillion kWh to the nation's power mix, accounting for 31.3% of total generation capacity. Yet, transforming China's new energy sector into a pivotal player necessitates a protracted period of development and refinement.
    - Secondly, traditional power grids exhibit limited adaptability in incorporating green energy sources, resulting in significant wastage of water, wind, and solar power. Therefore, the overall volume of abandoned green energy remains alarmingly high. In 2020, approximately 30.1 billion kWh of hydroelectric power untapped in major river basins across China and 16.6 billion kWh of wind power were wasted respectively. Additionally, around 5.3 billion kWh of photovoltaic energy was abandoned. All of the three amounted to a total power of 52 billion kWh. This trend persisted into 2021, with similar figures recorded. This scenario has sparked the proliferation of high-investment energy storage industries, including batteries, flywheels, air compassing equipment, pumped hydro storage, hydrogen production, and other innovative solutions. However, these advancements have significantly inflated the costs associated with green energy consumption, thereby compromising its competitiveness and widespread applicability.
    - Encouragingly, data from the National New Energy Power Incorporation Monitoring and Early Warning Centre indicates a positive shift. In 2022,

the utilization rates for wind power and photovoltaic power have increased to 96.8% and 98.3% respectively. This improvement, though achieved through substantial investment, underscores the ongoing progress towards optimizing green energy absorption.

- Thirdly, the inability to effectively deploy power resources across a broader market hinders the optimal allocation of these resources, resulting in a predicament where numerous renewable energy sources struggle to maximize their value. Even in the current power spot trading market, negative price is frequently charged by green energy suppliers. Power plants, instead of receiving payment for supplying power to the grid, are required to pay fees to the grid, severely impeding the growth and development of green energy. The root cause lies in the power grid's limitations in technologies for assimilating green energy and the absence of a unified global power supply market.
- Considering the spherical nature of our planet, wherein one hemisphere basks in sunlight while the other rests in darkness, the existence of a global low-loss transmission network would revolutionize energy distribution. Such a network could seamlessly transmit energy from the illuminated side of the globe to the night-cloaked regions, rendering energy storage a non-necessity in many instances. China's pioneering efforts in constructing and deploying its ultra-high voltage power grid demonstrate immense potential and technical feasibility for this vision. Yet, the international community lacks a tangible manifestation of this global power Internet. To expedite our journey towards carbon neutrality, it is imperative to accelerate the construction of the second Internet—the Global Energy Internet.

2. Establishing efficient and low-loss global smart network infrastructure for power transmission and distribution. The immense advantages of fostering a vast global energy market are undeniable. The fundamental physical infrastructure that must be constructed is global transmission and distribution network infrastructure featuring ultra-long-distance capabilities, low loss, high capacity, and intelligent dispatching. Only by achieving ultra-long-distance power transmission with minimal losses can the vision of a Global Energy Internet attain economic viability.
3. Crafting a global market-driven trading system for participants to ensure optimal resource allocation. The development of a vast green energy production system alongside comprehensive global supply infrastructure necessitates substantial investment, where the favorable investment return mechanism serves as a prerequisite, and the establishment of an efficient and unified International Electricity Trading Market emerges as the most crucial initiative.

10.4.1 Constructing the Global Energy Internet

The first Internet is the information Internet that transmits information and data. In contrast, the Global Energy Internet heralds a new era, transmitting electric energy on a global scale, particularly the real-time, low-loss transmission of green energy. This Internet not only addresses the challenge of storage but also enables global-scale, intelligent matching and alignment of energy supply and demand, enabling power generated anywhere can be efficiently transmitted and dispatched to the areas of greatest need. The Global Energy Internet can, moreover, underpin market-driven operations and facilitate intelligent, real-time settlements between supply and demand entities.

10.4.1.1 The Concept of Global Energy Internet

Championed by China, the Global Energy Internet embodies an ambitious vision to forge a universally interconnected grid, transcending geographical boundaries to facilitate the real-time transmission of renewable energy electricity across any two points on the globe, irrespective of the locations of power plants. This groundbreaking initiative marks the inaugural global program for concrete technology- and industry-focused collaboration within a specific domain.

The Global Energy Internet leverages cutting-edge energy, information, and communication technologies to establish global renewable energy infrastructure that fosters the efficient, clean, secure, economical, and sustainable utilization of energy resources worldwide.

The Global Energy Internet can efficiently address the global imbalance in energy consumption, enhance the efficiency of global energy utilization, and catalyze sustainable economic growth. All of the above manifests its paramount importance in the global energy transition and efforts towards carbon neutrality.

At its core, the Global Energy Internet embodies the synergy of "Smart Grid + Ultra-High Voltage Grid + Clean Energy", constituting a modern energy system that integrates cleaner energy production, wide-ranging distribution, and electrification of consumption. Moreover, it serves as a pivotal platform for the large-scale development, transmission, and utilization of clean energy.

This blueprint does not necessitate colossal investment in green energy storage. Instead, it envisions a world partitioned into three to four regions, each spanning six to eight time zones. If a desert area within one region is covered with photovoltaic panels, it can potentially meet the global demand for energy. The above describes a highly desirable global green energy blueprint.

As a part of the Global Energy Internet, the Smart Grid can achieve real-time monitoring, dynamic optimization and intelligent dispatch of the power system, and at the same time, it can also achieve collaborative operation and optimization of Distributed Energy Resources (DER) and promote the development and utilization of clean energy.

As for Ultra High Voltage (UHV) grid, it has following technical features:

- Voltage Class: 1100 kV and above.
- Transmission Current: Direct Current (DC).
- Optimal Transmission Distance: Over 2000 km.
- Line Losses: 2% to 3%.
- Merits: minimal power loss, high stability, suitability for long-distance transmission, and environmental friendliness.
- Weakness: high construction costs, a relatively novel technology, substantial investments, maintenance complexities.

China, as a global leader in UHV transmission technology, possesses a formidable technological system. This advantage positions China as the core force in the development of the world's second Internet, Global Energy Internet, establishing a pioneering edge in the global green transformation.

During thc ambitious "14th Five-Year Plan", State Grid Corporation of China (State Grid) outlines an expansive blueprint for UHV projects, envisioning the construction of "24 AC and 14 DC", (24 Ultra-High Voltage AC transmission lines and 14 Ultra-High Voltage DC transmission lines). The projects span over 30,000-km, with a transformation and conversion capacity reaching 340 million kVA, and a colossal investment of 380 billion yuan. In 2022, the State Grid intended to start the construction of 13 Ultra-High Voltage transmission lines, including 10 AC transmission lines and 3 DC transmission lines (Fig. 10.2).

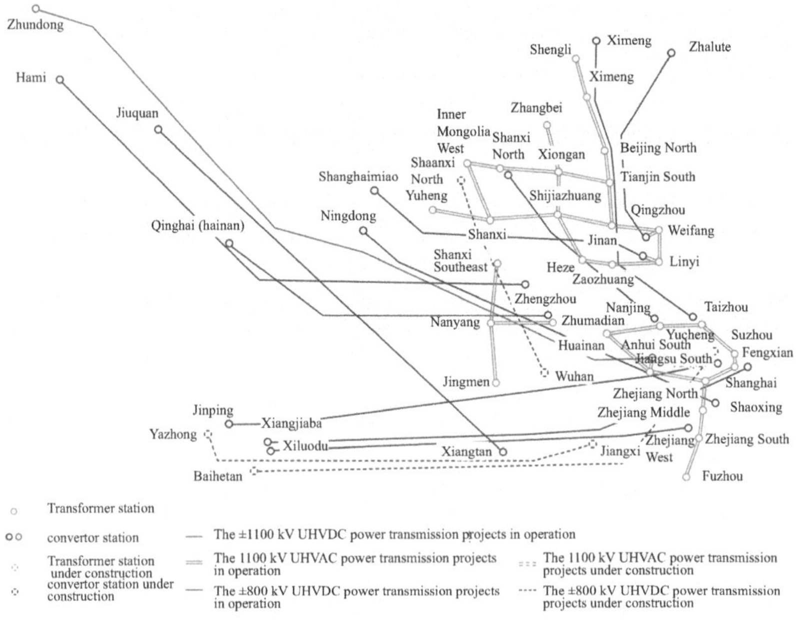

Fig. 10.2 The current status of UHV construction in China (2020)

The establishment of the Global Energy Internet holds immense potential to expedite the realization of "Three Transitions", meaning a transition in production towards clean energy, a transition in energy distribution to wide areas, and a transition in energy consumption towards heightened efficiency and environmental friendliness. Collectively, these three transitions serve as a potent catalyst for the extensive development and utilization of global clean energy resources, offering a viable blueprint for accelerating global energy transition and mitigating carbon emissions.

The Global Energy Internet not only draws upon China's domestic rich experience and strategic opportunities, but also follow the trend of green and low-carbon development worldwide. In the future, China will remain steadfast in providing its unique approaches and efforts for the construction of the Global Energy Internet.

10.4.1.2 Progress of the Global Energy Internet

In March 2016, Beijing witnessed a landmark moment, the birth of the Global Energy Internet Development and Cooperation Organization (GEIDCO), which is the first international organization in the energy sector spearheaded by China. Over the subsequent years, the GEIDCO has blazed a trail of innovative development for international organizations, imbued with distinct Chinese characteristics, as it has actively championed the construction of the Global Energy Internet.

The GEIDCO has been vigorously championing the advancement of the Global Energy Internet, embarking on profound interdisciplinary research covering energy, climate, and the environment. It has published over 80 groundbreaking achievements, including the book *Cracking the Crisis* sponsored by the GEIDCO, and established a global collaborative platform featuring in wide consultation, joint contribution and shared benefits. What's more, it has also enhanced significant advancements in numerous clean energy and grid Internet projects. These efforts have made substantial contributions to fostering international cooperation in energy and advancing green and low-carbon development. As the initiator of the organization, the State Grid Corporation of China has diligently pursued the development of the Energy Internet in recent years, constructing a power grid that boasts the world's highest voltage class, unparalleled capacity for energy resource allocation, and the largest-scale integration of renewable energy, with 580 million kilowatts of renewable energy installed. Furthermore, it has successfully completed 30 Ultra-High Voltage transmission projects, which transmitted 525 billion kilowatt-hours of clean energy in 2021, equivalent to reducing CO_2 emissions by 440 Mt, significantly facilitating the China's energy transition and carbon emission reduction.

The Global Energy Internet has been incorporated into the framework of implementing *The 2030 Agenda for Sustainable Development*, promoting the implementation of *The Paris Agreement*, advancing global environmental governance, and addressing the challenges of electricity scarcity, poverty, and health issues. Meanwhile, it has been included in the outcomes of the policy recommendations of the United Nations High-level Political Forum for three consecutive years.

In conclusion, the establishment of a Global Energy Internet, becoming both a domestic program with Chinese characteristics and an international action with global endeavors, will stand as one of the most vital initiatives aimed at achieving global carbon neutrality and completely resolving the pressing climate crisis facing the humanity.

10.4.1.3 Essential Technologies Driving the Construction of the Global Energy Internet

1. Smart Grid Technology

Smart grid is a power system that harnesses the information and communication technologies to realize intelligent control and management of power system, thereby enhancing its reliability, sustainability, and economic efficiency. Besides enabling real-time monitoring, dynamic optimization, and intelligent scheduling, smart grid can also facilitate collaborative operation and optimization of distributed energy resources, thereby fostering the widespread development and utilization of clean energy.

Crucially, smart grid technology fosters cooperative operation and optimization of distributed energy resources, such as wind and photovoltaic power, and effectively integrates these resources with the peak shaving and valley filling strategy, contributing to meeting the intensive and variable electricity demand for power.

2. Peak Shaving and Valley Filling Strategy.

The peak shaving and valley filling strategy holds paramount significance in the following aspects.

Firstly, significantly diminishing the peak-to-valley disparity within the power system. The strategy can minimize load fluctuations, enhance load utilization efficiency, and bolster the cost-effectiveness of the power system.

Secondly, fostering the development of clean energy sources. By integrating clean energy with advanced energy storage technologies, it facilitates the optimal utilization of renewable resources, ultimately accelerating their development.

Thirdly, enhancing the reliability and stability of the power system. Leveraging energy storage and intelligent control mechanisms, it dynamically adjusts and optimizes the power system, enhancing its reliability and stability.

3. New Power System

The new power system refers to the system featuring in greater efficiency, flexibility, intelligence, and environmental friendliness, which is based on smart grids and constructed with cutting-edge technologies, innovative modes of operation, and forward-thinking business models. This new system embodies a synergy of distributed energy resources, the Energy Internet, electrification, digitization, and artificial intelligence, collectively forging a brand new and future-oriented power system.

Major characteristics of this new power system include:

- Distributed Energy: The new power system transforms the traditional centralized power system into a decentralized one through the application of distributed energy, thereby enhancing the reliability and stability of the power system.
- Energy Internet: By leveraging the Energy Internet, the new power system enables seamless interconnectivity across diverse energy sources, significantly boosting energy utilization efficiency and cost-effectiveness.
- Electrification: By harnessing the electrification, the new power system fosters its profound integration with various sectors, enabling the joint development of power, transportation, construction, industry, and beyond.
- Digitalization: The new power system embraces digitalization, enabling comprehensive monitoring and intelligent dispatching. This transformation not only boosts operational efficiency but also enhances the system's sustainability.
- Intelligence: Infused with intelligence, the new power system achieves unparalleled levels of self-adaptation, self-organization, and self-healing, fortifying its resilience against disasters and further elevating its reliability.

4. Virtual Power Plant (VPP)

The Virtual Power Plant refers to an integrated power system, embracing a diverse array of distributed energy resources, such as solar, wind, and energy storage. It leverages intelligent control and management to conduct collaborative operation and optimization of the power system.

To actively participate in grid peak shaving and valley filling, the VPP employs several strategic methods:

- Energy Storage System: The VPP harnesses energy storage systems (such as batteries and supercapacitors) to store excess electricity. When in need, the stored energy is released, effectively bridging the peak-to-valley gap of the power system.
- Flexible Load: Through controlling flexible load, the VPP adjusts power consumption patterns in real-time. During peak hours, it reduces loads to alleviate grid stress, while during off-peak periods, it increases loads to increase the available capacity, thereby contributing to both peak shaving and valley filling.
- Virtual Power Generation: By the collaborative operation and optimization of multiple distributed energy resources (DERs), the VPP can generate electricity virtually, injecting surplus power into the grid, precisely to bridge the peak-to-valley gap.

10.4.1.4 Challenges in Establishing the Global Energy Internet

To establish a Global Energy Internet, Ultra-High Voltage (UHV) and Extra-High Voltage (EHV) technologies stand pivotal and can facilitate transnational and transcontinental long-distance transmission of secondary energy resources and conduct power trading. Nevertheless, this potential also confronts some technical and financial hurdles, notably including following aspects:

- Prohibitive Construction Costs: The establishment of UHV and EHV transmission lines necessitates significant capital investment and sophisticated technological expertise. Notably, the need for constructing numerous transformer stations and extensive transmission networks incurs substantial expenses, posing a formidable challenge.
- Intricate Technical Complexity: Constructing UHV and EHV transmission lines necessitates overcoming intricate meteorological and geological landscapes. Therefore, it needs to address safety and stability issues, leading to extreme technical difficulties.
- Cross-Border Coordination Challenges: The establishment of the Global Energy Internet necessitates harmonizing diverse legal frameworks, policies, and conflicting interests across multiple countries and regions, which is inherently complex.

Notwithstanding these challenges, the Global Energy Internet, along with the rapid development and application of global renewable energy, will become a pivotal technical tool for driving towards the clean energy transition worldwide. Furthermore, it emerges as vital energy infrastructure integral to achieving global carbon neutrality and fostering the sustainable growth of the world economy.

10.4.1.5 China's Opportunities in Establishing the Global Energy Internet

Since China has emerged as a front-runner in the widespread adoption and promotion of Ultra-High Voltage (UHV) and Extra-High Voltage (EHV) technologies, it can offer cutting-edge technologies and expertise to underpin the construction of the Global Energy Internet. At the same time, China is vigorously enhancing the development and application of renewable energy sources, moreover, the construction of the Global Energy Internet also aligns with its strategies of fostering economic transition and carbon neutrality. Consequently, the establishment of the Global Energy Internet through UHV and EHV technologies presents China with a momentous opportunity of unparalleled importance.

This endeavor will not only facilitate the efficient transmission of secondary energy across vast distances, transcending national borders and continents, but also facilitate international power trading, thereby optimizing global energy consumption patterns and accelerating the reduction of carbon emissions. Furthermore, the integration of this global energy infrastructure with other sectors like electric vehicle charging networks and smart grids holds immense potential to provide the technological backbone and innovative solutions required to propel the global carbon neutrality forward.

10.4.2 Development Status and Experience of European Power Market

Today, the marketization of some international power markets, such as those in the European Union and the United Kingdom, has significantly surpassed that of China's power market. Their expertise in cross-border power trading, robust transmission and distribution capabilities, along with extensive experience, offer invaluable insights for China to emulate and research.

10.4.2.1 Overview of the European Power Market

The European power spot trading market stands as a unified platform, encompassing power markets from diverse countries, united in the pursuit of optimal power resource allocation and maximizing economic benefits through cross-border transactions. This integrated market spans across European Union member states and extends to select non-EU nations. Furthermore, it allows bilateral agreements and exchange trading of power among generators, suppliers, traders, and end-users, exemplifying a high degree of liberalization, competitiveness, and regional integration.

1. General market landscape

Within the vibrant European power landscape, several prominent spot trading markets thrive, with the European Power Exchange (EPEX) and the Intercontinental Exchange (ICE) leading the way. These platforms offer a diverse array of trading options, including day-ahead markets, intraday markets, power distribution markets, and derivatives markets.

Through a multitude of mechanisms, European power markets are intricately synchronized and coupled, with the pinnacle of these forces being the Single Day-Ahead Coupling (SDAC). As Europe's premier spot market for power, the SDAC encompasses a broad spectrum of 20 markets, stretching from Portugal to Finland and from Ireland to Poland. At noon each day, the SDAC conducts a pan-European auction, determining the price and volume of electricity to be traded for the 24 h of tomorrow. The trading rules of the SDAC are set and enforced by the Nominated Electricity Market Operators (NEMOs) in each country or region, which are usually power exchanges or other relevant bodies responsible for organizing day-ahead market bidding and settlement within their own markets and coordinating with other NEMOs for cross-border transactions.

2 Regional markets and cross-border transactions

Europe boasts several prominent regional power spot exchanges, including the Nord Pool, the EPEX SPOT, and the GME. These regional markets, each comprising power markets from multiple countries, have integrated into a unified European power market. Currently, the regional power markets in Europe can be categorized into several distinct regions, including:

- Central Trading Region (CTR): Covering Belgium, the Netherlands, Austria, and parts of Germany.
- Nordic Trading Region (NTR): Covering Sweden, Norway, Denmark, Finland, and so on.
- United Kingdom Trading Region (UTR): Spanning England, Wales, Scotland, and so on.
- French Trading Region (FTR): Including France and its neighboring areas.
- South Eastern European Trading Region (SEETR): Encompassing portions of Croatia, Bosnia and Herzegovina, Serbia, Macedonia, Greece, Bulgaria, Romania, and other countries.

Despite differences among regional markets, they share numerous commonalities. To foster harmonization and interconnection, the European Network of Transmission System Operators for Electricity (ENTSO-E) plays a leading role. As the governing body responsible for coordinating the operation and planning of national electricity grids in Europe, the ENTSO-E ensures the reliability and stability of the European power system. To uphold the unified European power market, the ENTSO-E manages and operates grid interconnection through following key strategies:

(a) Developing and promoting pan-European power rules and standards, thereby ensuring interoperability and seamless interconnection among national power systems.
(b) Coordinating the operational and planning of national power systems, ensuring the overall reliability and stability of the European power system.
(c) Facilitating cross-border power trading by enabling the formidable interoperability of national power markets in the Europe.
(d) Enhancing the construction of cross-border electricity transmission lines across European nations, thereby striking the balance between energy demand and supply.
(e) Promoting the smart grid technology and power market trading systems, aimed at enhancing the efficiency and reliability of the European power system.

Through these comprehensive measures, the ENTSO-E is dedicated to managing and operating the European grid interconnection, ensuring the stable and optimal functioning of the unified European power market. In terms of grids, the Europe has implemented synchronous interconnection with different frequencies (50Hertz and 60Hertz) and High-Voltage Direct Current (HVDC) interconnection to seamlessly interconnect national grids.

In the current European power spot trading market, cross-border transactions stand as a prevalent and pivotal trading modality. This approach fosters mutual complementation and exchange of power resources among nations, facilitating their optimal allocation across borders. To enable smooth cross-border trading, ample power transmission capacity is imperative, thereby driving the European power spot trading market's commitment to developing robust cross-border electricity transmission networks to enhance these transactions. Participants can access cross-border transmission through various allocation mechanisms, including auctions and sealed-bid auctions. Moreover, unified or compatible market rules and mechanisms, coupled with effective coordination and cooperation, are indispensable for cross-border power trading. Under this context, the International Grid Control Cooperation (IGCC) was established in 2010, offering a dedicated trading platform for European nations to achieve cross-border balancing. At the same time, the EU has enacted a comprehensive suite of legal frameworks, notably *The European Third Energy Package* and *The EU Electricity Network Codes and Guidelines*, aimed at fostering deeper market integration and greater interconnection among member states. Cross-border electricity trading and transmission in the European power spot market not only bolster the market's integration and optimization but also enhance the reliability and cost-effectiveness of the power supply, and contribute significantly to advancing the continent's energy transition and achieving ambitious decarbonation targets.

3. Regulation of the European power markets

The governance of the European power spot market is entrusted to National Regulatory Authorities (NRAs) in countries and regions, the Agency for the Cooperation of Energy Regulators (ACER), and the Association of Issuing Bodies (AIB). The ACER, as a pan-European regulatory body, bears the mandate to oversee cross-border trade in both electricity and natural gas markets, while the AIB issues Green Energy Guarantees of Origins (GOs) that are interconnected in the Europe. These GOs provide proof that a given share or quantity of energy was produced from renewable sources. The NRAs, on the other hand, vigilantly supervise national or regional power market operators and participants, ensuring their compliance with pertinent laws and regulations. The ACER, in its pivotal role, coordinates the collaboration among NRAs and fosters both integration and competition within the European power market.

Network integration and marketization of European power significantly ensures its stable supply and bolsters the resilience of power grids, emerging as a vital pillar for Europe to navigate risks associated with electricity supply disruptions and the potential threat of war-related energy crises.

Germany announced to phase out nuclear power in 2011, but due to its challenges in the development of renewable energy sources, it, during its energy transition, still needs to rely on energy supply from other countries. However, cross-border transactions enable Germany to procure nuclear power from France and other countries to compensate for deficits in domestic renewable energy. In turn, by exporting its surplus renewable energy, Germany fulfills the optimal allocation of energy resources and maximizes economic profits.

10.4.2.2 Interconnection Among the Europe and North Africa, West Asia, and Russia and Their Transnational and Transcontinental Electricity Transmission

European grids stand as one of the most large-scale transnational electricity grids, thereby playing a significant role in fostering interconnections with adjacent nations and regions. In the Europe, there are many pivotal transnational power interconnection systems, notably the West–East Power Corridor, the Mediterranean Electricity Transmission System (Med-TSO) bridging North Africa and Europe, and the Baltic Energy Market Interconnection Plan (BEMIP).

North Africa: The electricity Internet between North Africa and Europe relies mainly on submarine cables, such as the SEA-ME-WE 3 cable connecting Italy and Tunisia, and the MAR-NED cable spanning between Italy and Morocco.

West Asia: The electricity Internet between Europe and West Asia is anchored by Turkey, a pivotal energy hub linking the two continents. There is an array of power transmission lines between Europe and Turkey, especially those linking Turkey with Greece and those linking Turkey with Bulgaria.

Russia: The electricity Internet between Europe and Russia, traditionally relying on transmission lines like lines connecting Russia to Finland and Norway respectively, have undergone significant changes in the wake of the Russia-Ukraine conflict. Nonetheless, the existing Internet infrastructure remains instrumental for Europe in handling cross-border energy supply and consumption, and contributes to economic development and environmental conservation of the continent and neighboring regions. Going forward, Europe will adhere to its commitment to cooperation with neighboring countries and regions on the rules and scale of cross-border electricity transmission transactions, in order to better cope with the challenges in the power market.

10.4.2.3 Trading Rules in the European Power Spot Market

The European power spot market distinguishes itself by its ability to accommodate diverse sets of trading rules, facilitating efficient, cross-border power transactions as well as transmission and distribution. These reflect European grids' robust adaptability to market dynamics and underscore the synergy achieved within the power market, therefore, the market has attained a remarkable level of maturity.

1. European trading system and rules

Since the nineteenth century, Europe has embarked on an ambitious journey to the construction of interconnected power grids, as a result, five regional power grids have been running now. In terms of operation, the day-ahead market is operating in a unified manner, while the intraday market is still in the process of coupling. When it comes to participant entities, power exchanges are responsible for matching supply with demand, while power transmission, distribution, and interconnection are delegated to TSOs (Transmission System Operators), DSOs (Distribution System Operators), and ITOs (Interconnection Transmission Operators) respectively.

The harmonization of the market is achieved through power market coupling, a pivotal mechanism that brings together three key players: transmission grid operators, power spot exchanges, and power clearing houses. In addition to being responsible for operating their own national transmission grids, transmission grid operators also need to coordinate with their counterparts in other countries to calculate the amount of electricity transmission across national borders. Meanwhile, power spot exchanges take charge of the power market coupling, which is in essence an algorithm designed to minimize overall electricity costs across Europe.

The coupling of the import and export markets for electricity operates under the fundamental principle that electricity prices are inherently lower in export markets and higher in import markets. This mechanism ensures the flow of electricity from regions with lower prices to those with higher prices. In the case of the export market, a surge in demand prompts a rightward shift in the price curve, leading to an increase in electricity prices. Conversely, in the import market, as supply initially rises, prices subsequently decrease, contributing to a gradual convergence of electricity prices across both markets. This phenomenon is referred to as electricity price convergence after market coupling.

Furthermore, the comprehensive market coupling bolsters resilience by enabling Europe to function as a vast buffer, absorbing and mitigating the impact of significant events that might otherwise disrupt individual countries. Examples include financial crises such as the subprime and banking crises, extreme weather conditions like cold snap or heat wave, and the adverse effects stemming from excessive power installations. These challenges are distributed evenly across Europe, minimizing their localized impact.

The European power market's coupling process has witnessed two projects, day-ahead market coupling and intraday market coupling. Initially, day-ahead market coupling was simply the pilot project that operators of power transmission grids voluntarily participated in. As the operational benefits became evident, participants' enthusiasm grew, prompting the EU to formalize these two projects into regulations, mandating market coupling.

The European power market incorporates various types of markets, characterized by its decentralized nature and reliance on medium- to long-term physical contracts as its foundation. Electricity generators and consumers independently determine the daily generation and consumption curves at the day-ahead stage, with any deviation in electricity volume adjusted through day-ahead and real-time balancing transactions.

The European power market can be divided into wholesale market and system market in terms of the overall structure, and the former is divided into floor trading market and over-the-counter market. Furthermore, the floor trading market can be divided into two pieces: derivative market and spot market. The latter market is further divided into day-ahead market and intraday market, both of which are handled by spot exchanges, while the real-time balancing of the intraday market, which is the next level down, is handled by grid operators.

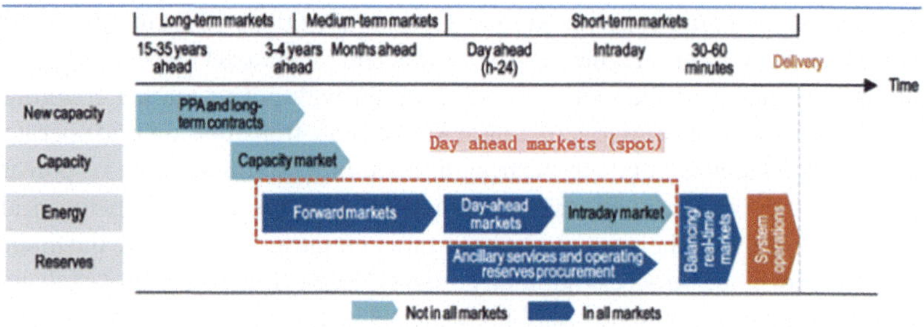

Fig. 10.3 Short-term, medium-term, long-term, day-ahead, intraday, real-time, and ancillary services markets (*Source* CSC Financial Co., LTD)

The day-ahead market and the intraday market are designed with different objectives that complement each other. The day-ahead market is a one-time bidding market that can trade products with hourly prices, while the intraday market is a listing process with continuous transaction, allowing these traders to manage open positions in terms of seconds, minutes, and hours, with the goal of profiting from price fluctuations.

The day-ahead market seeks to maximize market liquidity, and this maximization should cover the maximum amount of information in the entire market, thereby its price index can be used as a price benchmark for the entire market. However, the intraday market is designed to leave market entities the opportunity to correct the position of the last, such as the observation of the transaction volume to make the last deviation adjustment. The price in the day-ahead market is a common index for financial derivatives, while the price index in the intraday market is closer to that of the balancing market (Fig. 10.3).

Trading agencies operate independently from the transmission and distribution system. Trading agencies must uphold principles of neutrality and equity, fostering trust among all market participants, while system dispatching agencies need to secure contract execution at their best and maintains the power balancing dispatch.

Ensuring anonymity in trading entities is crucial. When numerous trading entities engage in open market transactions, the system generates orders solely for record-keeping purposes, ensuring that the two parties remain unaware of each other's identities.

The guarantee system is a significant principle of market operation, dictating that the market itself provides assurances. This means that for every transaction concluded within the market, participants can transact with confidence, without the worry of counterparty default. In the event of a default, the exchange imposes penalties on the offending market participant, rather than relying on individual action. Such a system ensures more effective and equitable penalties for breaches of contract.

Transparency is an indispensable attribute of the power market. The exchange must disclose transaction volumes and prices, fostering a clear and equitable trading landscape. Furthermore, the public availability of transaction data serves as a vital foundation for energy regulators to oversee and govern the entire power market effectively.

The marginal pricing system is imperative. The European power spot market uses this mechanism to determine electricity prices. Therefore, the electricity price is tied to soaring natural gas prices. In spot power trading, the "marginal price" serves as a pivotal pricing instrument for wholesale electricity transactions. Transactions are concluded sequentially from the lowest to the highest offer, and the last supplier's offer that enables sold power meeting the load demand is named the system price, known as the marginal price. Any generating unit offering above this threshold (i.e., system price) finds its power unsold, resulting in a failed bid. Conversely, generating units' bidding below the marginal price does not settle their spot power based on their individual offers but rather align with the system's marginal price.

Residential electricity price is primarily composed of energy costs, grid access fees, and related taxes and fees, among which energy costs (i.e., the on-grid electricity price of power plants) account for only one-third of the consumption costs for end users.

Specialized policy intervention in response to energy crises is crucial. Facing pressing energy crises, the EU has put forth a series of proposals aimed at mitigating soaring energy prices. On September 14, 2022, the European Commission put forward a comprehensive set of emergency intervention measures tailored specifically for the European energy market. These interventions aim at mitigating the escalation of electricity prices, a direct consequence of the profound imbalance between gas supply and demand caused by the Russia-Ukraine conflict. These measures primarily aim to decrease electricity prices by curbing natural gas-fired power generation through reducing special demand and limiting the profits of non-gas-fired power generation enterprises. Furthermore, financial subsidies are provided to vulnerable end-users through the imposition of a "windfall profit tax" on non-gas-fired power generation enterprises and energy companies, with the revenues also being utilized for investment in renewable energy generation.

The European energy crisis has compelled the European Union to take decisive action in regulating energy prices. The innovative proposal, centered on repurposing excess earnings generated by power generators to subsidize consumers. This strategic shift is poised to ignite a surge in demand for the European user energy storage market, fostering its growth and development.

2. Trading system and rules in the United Kingdom

The power spot trading landscape in the United Kingdom showcases a liberalized market characterized by robust competition. This framework encourages bilateral contracts and exchange trading among generators, suppliers, traders, and users. Currently, there are two exchanges focusing on power spot trading in the UK, the N2EX and the APX.

N2EX, a fully-owned subsidiary of Nord Pool Spot, is dedicated to operating within the UK's energy landscape, specializing in day-ahead and real-time power spot trading service. The day-ahead market necessitates the submission of electricity generation or consumption offers the day prior to trading, with prices and dispatch schedules for each hour of the subsequent day determined based on anticipated demand and supply. In contrast, the real-time market dynamically adjusts prices and schedules every half-hour on the day of trading, responding to actual demand and supply conditions. Additionally, the N2EX offers the physical notification service, enabling bilateral contract participants to seamlessly communicate their contract information to the National Grid, the system operator.

Contrarily, APX, with its operation spanning the UK, Netherlands, and Belgium, boasts over 70 participating members and offers comprehensive service parallel to N2EX, including day-ahead and real-time electricity spot trading, along with physical notification service. The APX further distinguishes itself by providing cross-border capacity auctions, creating a platform where participants can bid for transmission capacity across regional borders.

The power spot trading system in the UK operates on the bidding principle, whereby supply and demand parties submit their prices and quantities, with the market automatically matching these to conclude deals. The bidding principle aims to secure the development of renewable energy from the following aspects:

- Preferential treatment: The British power market has put forward various incentives for bolstering development and investment of new energy, such as subsidies and tax reduction and exemption.
- Green certificates: The power market in the UK has embraced the innovative green certificate system, issuing corresponding certificates for electricity generated by renewable energy resources. These certificates are tradable assets in the market, generating additional revenue streams for producers, furthermore enhancing the economic profits of renewable energy power generation.
- Pricing mechanism: The British power market operates under the marginal pricing system, where the market price is pegged to the cost incurred by the producer paying most for production. This approach ensures that new energy power generation is competitive in the market, as well as motivating electricity producers to embrace more sustainable and cost-effective generation methods.

In summary, the bidding principle of the UK's power spot trading implements a blend of strategic measures aimed at nurturing the development of new energy sources. These measures not only spur investments and advancements in renewable energy but also uphold the principles of fairness and vigorous competition within the market.

10.4.2.4 Coupling of the European Power Market with the Carbon Market

The carbon market in Europe, known as the European Union Emissions Trading System (EU ETS), serves as a vital tool for many countries in their efforts to reduce carbon emissions and achieve carbon neutrality. Power generation is the primary source of emissions, thus fostering a close relationship between the power market and the carbon market.

The EU ETS employs a "cap-and-trade" mechanism. Specifically, the EU first sets an annual cap on the total amount of CO_2 emissions, and then allocates emission allowances to individual companies. Companies can emit carbon as long as they hold sufficient trading allowances. If they do not have enough allowances, they need to purchase more from the market.

Currently, the EU ETS is the largest carbon trading market globally, with approximately 110,000 factories and airlines participating. It covers the energy industry and heavy industrial sectors, accounting for around 40% of the EU's total CO_2 emissions.

The EU ETS primarily influences the power market through carbon pricing signals. On one hand, power plants need to purchase carbon emission allowances, and an increase in carbon prices raises their production costs, leading to a corresponding increase in electricity prices. On the other hand, high carbon prices incentivize the moderate substitution of low-carbon energy sources (such as wind, solar, and nuclear power) for high-carbon energy sources (like thermal power), thereby affecting supply–demand relationships and electricity prices. The EU ETS utilizes market-based mechanisms to limit CO_2 emissions and, by influencing industrial costs and electricity prices, encourages the substitution of low-carbon energy for high-carbon energy, contributing to the EU's achievement of carbon reduction targets. Participants in power exchanges must simultaneously hold emission permits in the carbon market to ensure that their electricity production does not exceed their allocated allowances. Due to the close linkage between these markets, changes in carbon prices have an impact on electricity prices, further motivating the electricity sector to align with carbon reduction targets.

10.4.2.5 Enhancing the Absorption of Renewable Energy Power

As more and more renewable energy is put into the European power market, how to absorb the new energy and make them provide electricity for Europe more effectively has also become a very important issue.

In order to improve the capacity of absorbing renewable energy power, Europe is promoting a series of policies, regulations, and measures to better integrate renewable energy. For example, Europe is advancing the "Clean Energy Package" plan, which aims to create a better market and investment environment for renewable energy, helping more clean energy to flow into the European power system.

Market-based support mechanisms for renewable energy are encouraged. European countries have established various support mechanisms for renewable energy, such as subsidies, priority purchasing, and feed-in tariffs, to encourage the development of renewable energy. These mechanisms are typically implemented in a market-oriented manner, with the acquisition price of renewable energy determined through bidding or other methods to ensure its competitiveness in the market.

The power market in Europe is flexible, enabling it to adapt to the volatility and uncertainty of renewable energy. For instance, when the supply of renewable energy sources, such as wind and solar power, is insufficient, the power market can adjust prices to attract supplies from other generation methods, thereby satisfying market demand.

Cross-border power trading is another available choice. The power spot market in Europe can balance the supply and demand of renewable energy through cross-border trading. For example, if a country has a surplus of wind energy supply, it can export the excess electricity to other countries to generate revenue. Conversely, if renewable energy supply in a country is insufficient, it can import electricity from other countries to meet its demand.

Smart grid technologies could provide a solution. The power spot market in Europe is adopting smart grid technologies, such as smart meters, energy storage, and power forecasting, to enhance the absorption capacity of renewable energy. These technologies can assist the power system in better predicting and managing the volatility and uncertainty of renewable energy, thereby achieving more efficient energy utilization.

10.4.2.6 Carbon Leakage Risks and Carbon Cost Offset and Sharing

Many European countries import a significant amount of electricity from other nations annually, including those with higher carbon emissions. This trend can incentivize these countries to rely on cheaper and more accessible fuels, potentially leading to carbon leakage and other environmental issues.

The imported electricity may be generated using high-carbon energy sources such as oil and coal, increasing the indirect carbon footprint of importing countries. Even if a portion of the imported electricity is produced using renewable energy, the producing country may still have excess fossil fuel capacity. Importing renewable electricity does not necessarily lead to a net global reduction in carbon emissions. To mitigate this issue, Europe is taking measures to reduce the carbon emissions associated with imported electricity. These measures include adopting more efficient energy technologies, launching more renewable energy projects, and introducing carbon emission taxes to reduce the economic cost of importing electricity from countries with lower carbon emissions while diminishing the competitive advantage of importing electricity from countries with higher emissions. Importers and exporters should negotiate the sharing of carbon costs to avoid situations where the exporter benefits while the importer bears the environmental costs.

The importer pays a subsidy for the carbon price difference. Taking into account the energy mix used to produce and export electricity and the difference in carbon prices, the importer pays a corresponding price premium to the exporter.

It is essential to jointly deploy emission reduction technologies, such as Carbon Capture and Storage (CCS) technology, to share costs and improve the overall emission reduction efficiency of the power system.

Additional "renewable energy substitution" transaction can be implemented, where the exporter provides renewable energy certificates equivalent to the amount of imported electricity to offset the indirect emissions of the importer.

Carbon trading could be initiated, where the importer purchases an equivalent amount of emission reduction credits from the exporter to compensate for the increase in its carbon footprint. Overall, ensuring fair and reasonable carbon cost sharing and implementing carbon offsets in cross-border power transactions are conducive to promoting global emission reduction and sustainable energy development. Relevant policies require negotiations between producers and consumers.

10.4.2.7 Impact of Brexit and the Russia-Ukraine Conflict

After the United Kingdom's withdrawal from the European Union, the UK will cease to be a part of the EU, implying that the Union will lose its influence and role in the power market of the UK. Additionally, potential changes in trade relations and policy frameworks between the UK and the EU may impact the liquidity and stability of the European power trading market.

The conflict between Russia and Ukraine has brought many influences to the European power trading market.

Price fluctuations: The demand for electricity during peak hours has led to a rise in electricity prices in some European countries. Additionally, the escalating situation in the Russia-Ukraine conflict has resulted in the suspension of Russian gas exports, causing a subsequent increase in gas prices. These high energy costs have put pressure on businesses in some countries to face increased production costs.

Energy security: Russia is one of crucial energy suppliers in Europe. The risks to energy supply triggered by the war have raised concerns about Europe's energy security. European countries have had to seek alternative energy sources to ensure a stable energy supply.

Power trade: As Ukraine serves as a pivotal transmission hub for Europe's electricity, the impact of the war on Europe's power market is evident.

European market unity: Russia ranks first among Europe's major energy trading partners. The war has had a negative impact on the relationship between Russia and the European Union, which could potentially make the unity of the European market more difficult to maintain.

The Russia-Ukraine conflict has had a profound impact on the European power trading market, including price increases, energy security, power trade and European market unity. Europe's energy and power supply chains need to be reassessed for a more stable and sustainable future.

10.4.3 Overview of the Power Markets in the United States, Canada, and Japan

While there exists a discernible disparity in the levels of marketization and grid sophistication between the United States, Canada, Japan, and Europe, there are still many aspects worth learning by China's power market during its transformation.

10.4.3.1 The United States

The US power spot trading market encompass several key regions, including ISO-NE (covering the New England area), NYISO (covering New York State and parts of neighboring regions), PJM (spanning 13 states and Washington District of Columbia), MISO (encompassing the Midwest and South), and ERCOT (covering the state of Texas). These power markets operate on a bidding principle, that is, both the supply and demand sides submit prices and quantities, and the market automatically matches and promotes transactions. Market participants in these markets include electricity generators, traders, distributors, large consumers, as well as power exchanges.

In the U.S. power spot trading markets, the RTO (Regional Transmission Organization) is a crucial institution, primarily responsible for managing and operating the power transmission system.

The RTO is a nonprofit organization established with the approval of the Federal Energy Regulatory Commission (FERC). Its membership comprises electricity producers, traders, distributors, large consumers, and others. The RTO is responsible for managing and operating the power transmission system, including activities such as monitoring electric load, dispatching power generation units, coordinating electricity transactions, and maintaining power transmission facilities. These efforts aim to ensure the reliability and safety of electricity supply. Additionally, the RTO oversees the coordination of power transactions, ensuring fairness, transparency, and stable operation of the market. It matches the electricity demand of suppliers with that of consumers, thereby optimizing the allocation of power resources and maximizing economic benefits.

The U.S. power spot trading markets are subject to regulation and oversight by both federal and state governments, with the goal of ensuring fairness, transparency, and stable operation of the markets. Furthermore, to guarantee its stable functioning, the power market is expected to collaborate with regional grid operators, who are responsible for managing and operating the power system, encompassing activities like monitoring electric load, dispatching power generation units, and maintaining power transmission facilities. This ensures harmony between the transactions in the power market and the operations of the power system.

10.4.3.2 Canada

The power spot trading markets in Canada primarily cover several regions, such as the Ontario, Quebec, and British Columbia power markets. These markets operate on a bidding principle, where both suppliers and demanders of electricity submit prices and quantities, which are then automatically matched and traded by the market.

The power spot trading markets in Canada and the United States exhibit a significant degree of interconnection and mutual trading activities. This integration is facilitated by an extensive network of cross-border transmission lines between Canada and the United States, such as the Quebec-New England and Ontario-Northeastern

United States lines, which serve as the backbone infrastructure enabling electricity trading between the two nations.

Additionally, Canada and the United States work together to launch some transnational power trading projects, such as the "New England-Quebec Transmission Line" project between Quebec in Canada and Massachusetts in the United States, which aims to transmit electricity generated by hydropower stations in Quebec to the Northeastern region of the United States.

10.4.3.3 Japan

The power system in Japan is divided into two main grids: the Kanto Grid and the Kansai Grid. The Kanto Grid covers Tokyo and its surrounding areas, Hokkaido, the Tohoku region, and the Chubu region, and operates at a frequency of 50 Hz. The Kansai Grid, on the other hand, covers Osaka, Kyoto, Kobe, and their surrounding areas, and operates at a frequency of 60 Hz.

The Japan Electric Power Exchange (JEPX) is largest power spot trading market in Japan, established in 2005. Market participants include power generators, traders, distributors, and large consumers. Its bidding rules employ a bidding and hedging principle, where both suppliers and demanders of electricity submit prices and quantities, which are then automatically matched and traded by the market. Trading takes place in two sessions: the "Intraday Market" for the current day and the "Day-Ahead Market" for the next day.

The power trading market of the Tokyo Electric Power Company (TEPCO) is operated by itself and primarily serves Tokyo and its surrounding areas. Market participants include power generators, traders, distributors, and large consumers. Its bidding rules also adhere to the bidding and hedging principle, where both suppliers and demanders of electricity submit prices and quantities, which are then automatically matched and traded by the market. Trading takes place in three sessions: the "Intraday Market" for the current day, the "Day-Ahead Market" for the next day and the "Month-Ahead Market" for the upcoming month.

10.4.4 Exploration and Practice of Market-Oriented Reforms in China's Power Sector

After more than two decades of efforts, China's power market system has undergone a significant transformation, shifting from a heavily planned economy model to a more market-driven system, characterized by a growing integration of market-based elements. Nevertheless, this transition has been fraught with challenges, resulting in a pronounced imbalance in the pace and extent of marketization across the entire industry chain. Despite these advancements, there remains a substantial gap towards achieving full marketization, underscoring the significant potential for further reforms and improvements.

The diverse segments within the entire electricity market landscape, spanning generation, storage, transmission, distribution, sales, and end-users, display varying levels of marketization. For instance, the power generation segment boasts numerous market participants and is generally well-established in its market-oriented nature. Conversely, the rapid advancements in energy storage, pivotal to supporting the growth of renewable energy, involve a complex interplay of diverse market actors, planning mechanism and market mechanism. Notably, the backbone transmission grid remains inherently monopolistic, posing a formidable obstacle to the overall marketization of China's electricity sector. While the liberalization of the electricity retail market has effectively expanded the pool of market participants, the issue of cross-subsidy reform within the user market continues to be a vexing challenge, with the path forward remaining uncertain and difficult to navigate.

10.4.4.1 Goals of Reform in China's Power Market

The core objective of power reform endeavors is to stimulate the vitality of power generation and consumption by supply-side reform, thereby propelling the overall transformation of the energy structure. This is accomplished through harnessing the power market as a catalyst, with the ultimate goal of attaining a substantial proportion of clean energy in the energy mix. The recent reform initiatives undertaken in China's power market are precisely targeted at addressing the following pressing challenges:

1. The absence of a robust market trading mechanism and the subsequent inefficiencies in resource allocation have contributed to suboptimal utilization rates. The absence of an effective competitive framework on the supply side has hindered the free flow of market transactions between power generation enterprises and end-users, thereby impeding the market's capacity to play a pivotal role in determining resource allocation. Consequently, energy-efficient, high-performance, and eco-friendly units struggle to achieve their full potential, with instances of curtailed renewable energy generation (such as hydro, wind, and solar) arising periodically. Moreover, in certain regions, a paradoxical situation arises where both power surpluses and shortages coexist simultaneously.
2. The pricing structure remains irrational, with the establishment of a fully market-driven pricing mechanism still pending. The current electricity pricing framework is heavily influenced by government regulation, resulting in price adjustments that often trail behind cost fluctuations. This delay hinders the timely and reasonable reflection of electricity usage costs, market supply–demand dynamics, resource scarcity, and environmental protection expenses.
3. The transformation of government functions is incomplete, and the coordination mechanisms for various planning initiatives are flawed. Significant discrepancies

exist between the planning and actual implementation of specialized development plans. Market development efforts are insufficient, and planning capabilities are inadequate to keep pace with evolving needs and changes in the external environment.

4. The development framework is inadequate, posing challenges for the advancement and utilization of new and renewable energy sources. The production capacity of equipment in new energy sectors, such as photovoltaic power generation, is misaligned with construction, operation, and consumer demands, failing to foster a mutually reinforcing cycle between research, production, and utilization. The issues surrounding non-discriminatory and seamless grid integration for new and renewable energy generation remain unresolved.
5. Legislative and regulatory updates lag behind, impeding the marketization and sustainable development of the power market. The market-oriented reform of the energy supply system is a complex macroeconomic endeavor that spans multiple facets and encounters substantial hurdles. Consequently, the reinforcement and support of a robust legal framework are imperative for its success.

10.4.4.2 Practice of Market-Oriented Reform in China's Power Industry

The four major steps initially determined for the reform of the electric power system were "separating power plants from power grids, separating core business from non-core businesses, separating transmission from distribution, and implementing competitive bidding for power grid access." In 2002, China embarked on a transformative journey, prioritizing the separation of power plants and grids, along with distinguishing core and non-core business operations. This endeavor led to the State Council restructuring the assets of the State Power Corporation, birthing two prominent grid companies, five major power generation enterprises, and four supporting organizations, with the oversight of the State Electricity Regulatory Commission ensuring regulatory compliance. These reforms at the heart of electricity supply catalyzed a diversification of market participants on the generation front, fostering a competitive landscape for grid access through bidding processes. Advancing to 2021, within the framework of the new-type power system, China has evolved into a power sector architecture distinguished by its "Two Grids, Five Majors, and Six Minors"[1] configuration.

1. Progress of China's power trading market

The groundbreaking market-oriented reform, initiated in October 2021, aimed at widening the scope of electricity price fluctuations, paved the way for heightened market anticipation regarding the development of novel power systems and

[1] This refers to two grids, five major power generation groups and six power investment enterprises in China—a note by the translator.

the construction of robust power markets. Notably, embracing market-driven mechanisms has the potential to significantly mitigate the costs associated with the ongoing structural transformation of the energy sector.

The construction of China's electricity market accelerated significantly in 2022, with the proportion of market-oriented transactions soaring by 39% year-on-year to 5.25 trillion kWh, exceeding seven times that of 2015. The share of market-traded electricity in total electricity consumption across the society exceeded 60%, an increase of 15.4 percentage points year-on-year.

The construction of the power market in 2022 was noteworthy, with remarkable advancements. Beyond the 14 state-designated pilot provinces actively engaging in spot power trading, many non-pilot provinces also successively embarked on trial operations. From a policy perspective, on November 25, 2022, the National Energy Administration issued the *Basic Rules for Power Spot Market (Draft for Consultation)*", marking a milestone as the first comprehensive national-level guidance for establishing a power spot market. Throughout 2022, various regions witnessed a proliferation of medium- to long-term electricity trading products, characterized by increased frequency, shorter cycles, and finer time intervals. This evolution met the diverse needs of entities seeking flexible adjustments to their medium- to long-term contracts, effectively contributing to the balancing of electricity supply and demand. Despite promising growth in the transaction scale, the trading volume in power market holds significant potential for expansion. With society's total electricity consumption reaching 8.64 trillion kWh, a 3.6% year-on-year increase, and the secondary and tertiary industries collectively accounting for approximately 83% of this total, estimates suggest that the share of power market transactions could soar to 80%. Nevertheless, the path to constructing and transforming the power market has not been without challenges, and numerous challenges still lie ahead.

The first challenge is how to rationalize the electricity pricing system. A large number of power generation enterprises and users are still within the "planned" scope and have not been incorporated into the market, making it difficult to find solutions to the issue of "cross-subsidies".

The second pivotal challenge revolves around how to substantially bolster inter-provincial transmission and distribution capabilities, mitigate the surge in negative pricing for renewable energy, and diminish the dependency on fresh installations solely for addressing peak power demands. The current constraints in these inter-provincial capabilities, stemming from factors including technical limitations of transmission grids, ineffectual transmission and distribution mechanisms, complexities in cross-provincial electricity trading, and a limited market scope, have resulted in a comparatively low efficiency in the nationwide allocation of power resources.

The third challenge concerns how to minimize the extensive losses incurred by coal-fired power enterprises. The inadequate proportion of spot trading in the power market, coupled with the substantial delay in medium- to long-term transactions responding to electricity price fluctuations, has hindered the timely reflection of genuine market supply and demand dynamics. This inability to adapt promptly has failed to alleviate the spiraling costs of coal-fired power generation, consequently leading to substantial losses for these enterprises. Since the latter half of 2021, coal prices have experienced a remarkable surge. As estimated by the China Electricity Council, this surge translated into an additional 600 billion yuan in coal procurement costs for coal-fired power enterprises nationwide in 2021. Notably, from August to November, some coal-fired power sectors within the industry experienced a staggering 100% loss rate, with the cumulative loss rate for the entire year hovering around 80%.

The fourth challenge entails developing a robust spot power market, enhancing transmission and distribution capabilities of power grids, rationalizing the electricity market mechanism, and harmonizing it with carbon emission reduction strategies. Meanwhile, it is essential to balance the interests of coal-fired power enterprises and significantly enhance the integration of renewable energy into the grids, thereby accelerating the transition from fossil fuels. Key to this endeavor is capitalizing on the three pivotal advantages of the spot market: Firstly, its high-frequency (7×24 h continuous trading) and short-cycle (hourly/15-min intervals) nature aligns perfectly with the volatile and unpredictable characteristics of renewable energy. Secondly, within a level playing field of market competition, renewable energy generation boasts lower marginal costs, while the global energy crisis, elevating primary energy prices, renders thermal power's marginal costs comparatively higher, thus enabling renewable energy to automatically secure priority dispatch in the market. Lastly, spot trading fosters peak-to-trough price differentials, creating lucrative opportunities for third-party market entities like energy storage, and incentivizing flexible resources to bolster renewable energy consumption. Currently, the positive impact of spot power market on promoting the consumption of renewable energy is becoming increasingly evident. Statistics from the State Grid Corporation of China reveal that cross-regional and inter-provincial trading of surplus renewable energy has reduced renewable energy curtailment by over 23 billion kWh in the past four years.

The fifth challenge revolves around harnessing the power market reform as a catalyst to bolster the government's investment attraction capabilities. In the context of tightened electricity supply and demand, certain local governments are hesitant to embrace full-fledged electricity marketization, primarily due to concerns that increased electricity prices will impose additional burdens on enterprises, thereby potentially eroding the allure of local investment prospects (Fig. 10.4).

2. Power generation

Over the past four decades, China's unwavering commitment to reform and opening-up policies has resulted in remarkable economic growth, spurring a surge in electricity demand that, in turn, necessitated massive investments in power generation. This progress has been fueled by collaborative efforts from the state, local governments, and private enterprises, particularly in the realm of new energy sources, achieving an astonishing growth rate. A diverse energy mix now thrives, comprising coal-fired, hydro, nuclear, photovoltaic and wind power, among others. Coal-fired power enterprises exceed 2000 in number, with countless other types of power generation ventures also contributing significantly. The insatiable appetite for economic

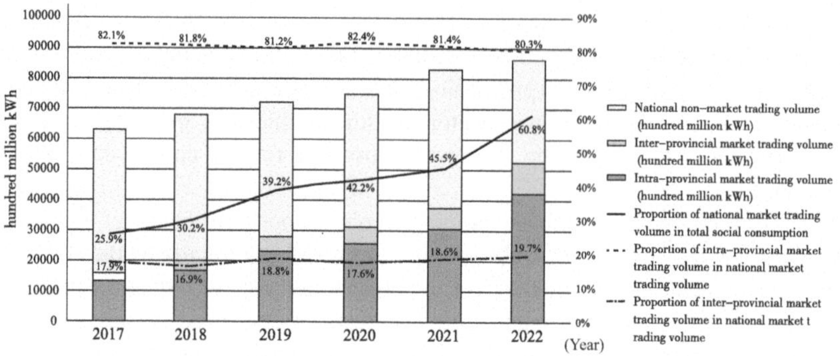

Fig. 10.4 National electricity consumption and trends in market-based transactions from 2017 to 2022 (Including Intra-provincial and Inter-provincial Data) (*Note* The intra-provincial and inter-provincial transaction data in 2018 excludes transactions of electricity generation rights. *Data Source* China Electricity Council, Beijixing Electricity Sales Network, compiled by Energy Foundation China)

expansion has prompted the government to progressively ease investment restrictions, fostering a fully market-oriented power generation sector where both state-owned and private capital in new energy fields compete vigorously. Remarkably, the Ministry of Finance estimates reveal that within the last decade, the costs associated with onshore wind and photovoltaic power generation have plummeted by approximately 30% and 75%, respectively. This cost reduction has translated into a substantial increase in power generation capacity, soaring from 1.167 trillion kWh in 1998 to an impressive 8.38863 trillion kWh in 2021. Notably, renewable energy now accounts for 31.6% of this total capacity, as depicted in Fig. 10.5.

If the transmission, distribution, and power trading systems are fully embraced by market forces, there remains considerable untapped potential for unleashing the investment momentum within the power generation sector.

3. Power storage

As the new energy market expands in size and significance, energy storage has emerged as a pivotal element, driving rapid growth in both investment scale and project numbers. However, the current landscape, characterized by uncertain market returns, necessitates a heavy government involvement in energy storage market investment mechanisms. This deep entanglement with power transmission and distribution adds layers of complexity to the overall marketization of the power sector, potentially hindering the subsequent advancement of the energy storage industry.

According to statistics from the CNESA DataLink Global Energy Storage Database, by the end of 2022, the cumulative installed capacity of electrical energy storage projects commissioned worldwide was 237.2GW, with an annual growth rate of 14.9% (Fig. 10.6). The cumulative installed capacity of pumped hydro storage fell below 80% for the first time, down by 6.8 percentage points compared to the same period in 2021. The cumulative installed capacity of new energy storage reached 45.7GW, with an annual growth rate of 79.9%, and lithium-ion batteries continued

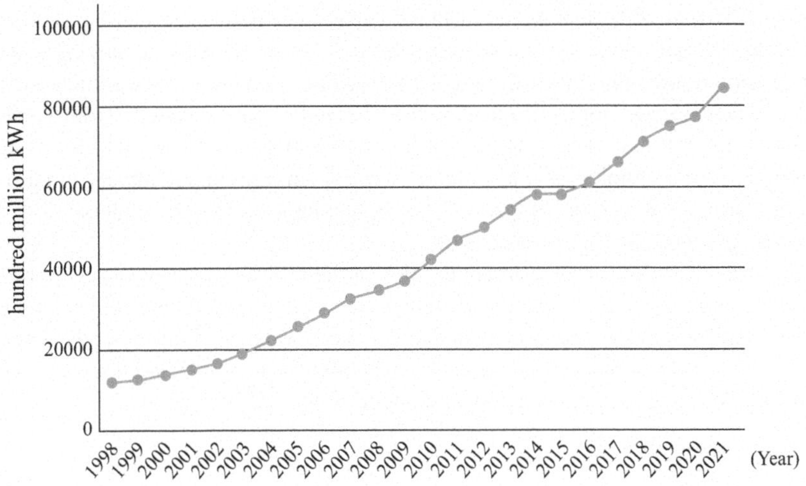

Fig. 10.5 Change of power generation in China from 1998 to 2001 (*Source* National Bureau of Statistics)

to occupy a dominant position, with a market share of 94.4%, increasing by 3.5 percentage points compared to the same period in 2021.

According to incomplete statistics from global energy storage project database of the (CNESA) located in Zhongguancun, Beijing, by the close of 2022, the world's cumulative installed capacity of electric energy storage projects reached 237.2GW, marking a 14.9% increase. Notably, for the first time, cumulative installed capacity of pumped storage fell below 80%, a 6.8 percentage point decline from 2021 levels. Conversely, new energy storage capacity surged, reaching 45.7GW, a remarkable 79.9% increase, with lithium-ion batteries dominating the market with a 94.4% share, up 3.5 percentage points.

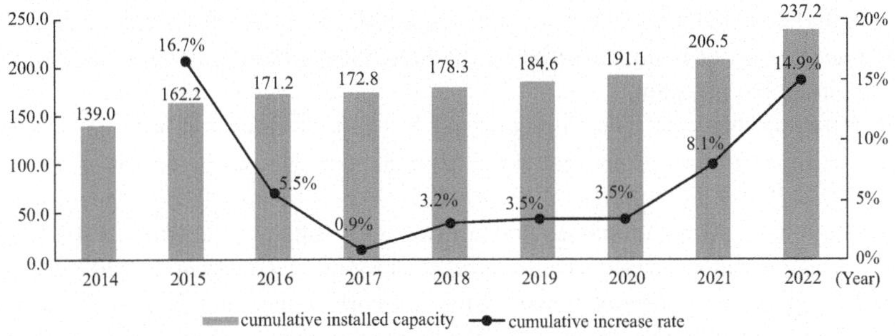

Fig. 10.6 Cumulative installed capacity of energy storage worldwide from 2014 to 2022 (*Source* Prospective Industry Research Institute, China Magisterial Energy Network, http://www.eco.gov.cn, CNESA, Great Wall Glory Securities)

From 2016 to 2022, the annual installed capacity of new energy storage projects within the global power system soared from 0.7GW to 20.4GW, achieving a staggering compound annual growth rate of 75.4%. This translates to a significant jump in the of new energy storage projects within the global power system, from 1.2% to 19.3% of total global energy storage projects. While the installed capacity of new energy storage technologies within the power system remains relatively modest at this juncture, the development growth rate is accelerating rapidly, underscoring the immense potential for future expansion.

Despite the variety of investment entities in the realm of energy storage, private endeavors find themselves at a disadvantage due to their significant reliance on the market size of power grid access and associated services. Consequently, energy storage and power transmission operate independently, guaranteeing a level playing field for diverse market participants to compete fully and fairly.

4. Power transmission

Currently, China's power transmission landscape is dominated by two national grids: the State Grid Corporation and the Southern Power Grid, with the pace of reform lagging behind the global pursuit of carbon neutrality and China's dual carbon targets. The decades-long monopoly in transmission grids has remained largely unchanged, hindering the overall reform of China's power market and discouraging investment from various stakeholders.

There is an urgent necessity for a groundbreaking and visionary blueprint for the transmission market, one that draws inspiration from the proven success stories of power market models across various countries and regions. This innovative design ought to seamlessly integrate internet and digital thinking, shatter conventional paradigms, and accelerate the transformation of the transmission sector towards unprecedented heights.

5. Power distribution

Incremental distribution stands as a pivotal area in China's ongoing reform efforts, yet the outcomes have been underwhelming. While numerous projects have been greenlit and initiated in recent years, only a handful have yielded satisfactory results, with many failing or being acquired by the State Grid, effectively being assimilated into the monopoly system.

In 2016, the National Development and Reform Commission and the National Energy Administration promulgated the *Management Measures for Orderly Liberalization of Power Distribution Network Business*, clarifying that the incremental distribution network encompasses power grids with voltage levels up to 110 kV and local grids like industrial parks (Economic Development Zones) up to 220 (330) kV, excluding the construction of transmission networks exceeding 220 kV. Additionally, this business extends to stock distribution networks invested, constructed, and operated by other enterprises, such as local power grids. Subsequently, the nation has initiated five rounds of pilot projects for incremental power distribution, totaling 459 projects, yet only a handful have been recognized as successful.

Zhengzhou Airport incremental power distribution project operated by Xinggang Power, one of the first batch of reform pilot projects, aimed to foster a competitive distribution network within the licensed supply area in competition with State Grid Henan, thereby bolstering local investment with more favorable energy conditions. However, in mid-March 2023, a setback occurred when the Airport Area Management Committee, Xinggang Power's controlling entity, directed the sale of all distribution network assets to State Grid Henan, effectively signaling the failure of the pilot project.

Amidst the setback in the incremental power distribution reform, the announcement of the first round of transmission and distribution price supervision underscored the policymakers' unwavering commitment to advancing reforms of power system and mechanisms, reigniting hope within the incremental power distribution industry.

On May 15, 2023, the National Development and Reform Commission promulgated the *Notice on Provincial Power Grid Transmission and Distribution Pricing and Related Matters for the Third Regulatory Cycle* (hereinafter referred to as No. 526), marking a historic milestone by introducing, for the first time, capacity (demand)-based electricity charges differentiated by voltage levels. This reform enables incremental power distribution projects to legally tap into a portion of the revenue generated from users' capacity (demand) charges. Experts applaud No. 526 as a groundbreaking reform that addresses the long-standing challenge of incremental distribution networks struggling to secure capacity electricity charges.

However, the inherent complexities and obstacles within the incremental distribution reform persist, necessitating further deepening of the reform measures.

Despite eight years of reform efforts and seven years of pilot implementation, the incremental distribution network remains but a fraction compared to the sprawling main power grid in terms of scale. Nevertheless, the implications of this minor yet significant sector merit our profound examination. A Zhejiang-based incremental distribution network owner shared with a financial reporter that while the costs associated with the construction of distribution network are largely unclear beyond the State Grid, the establishment of benchmarks threatens to disrupt the substantial interests of the grid companies. For instance, substation construction projects are often awarded to the tertiary companies of the Grid, which subsequently subcontracts to private firms, yielding intermediary margins that can soar up to 20% of the total project fund.

Beyond cost benchmarking, in the context of achieving the dual carbon goals, the construction of a new type of power system centered around new energy, specifically, an active distribution network incorporating distributed power sources, has become a central focus of market attention. Looking ahead, will China continue with its "unified national grid" model, or will it pursue the development of distributed microgrids more actively? A silent struggle is already underway.

Moreover, the market-driven development of city-level and urban regional distribution networks faces immense hurdles, primarily due to the exclusive monopoly held by transmission backbone networks. The success of power distribution reform hinges critically on the State's unwavering commitment and a well-conceived, rational top-level design.

6. Power sales

Since the release of *Opinions on Further Deepening the Reform of Electricity* (commonly referred to as No. 9 Document) in 2015, the number of diversified power sales companies has been rapidly increasing. According to the latest data from Qichamao,[2] as of October 17, 2022, the electricity sales sector boasts an impressive tally of 15,328 enterprises. This exponential growth, particularly between 2015 and 2017, saw a surge in the number of new enterprises, peaking at an astounding 4068 in 2017. However, starting from 2018, the number of new enterprises has declined, with 612 new enterprises in 2021. As of October 17, 2022, the number of new enterprises in 2022 is 211.

From a corporate structure standpoint, the power market has embraced full market competition, with the majority of players now operating under a market-driven framework. Nevertheless, the operational landscape remains encumbered by the planning systems that govern power generation, transmission, and user ends. Achieving a fully market-oriented system remains a formidable challenge and there is a long way to go.

10.4.4.3 China's Power Market Reform: A Work in Progress

The unveiling of the *Opinions on Further Deepening the Reform of Electricity* in 2015 marked a pivotal moment in China's power sector. This landmark reform, advocating the framework of "allowing for more competition in electricity generation, sales and consumption while tightening government regulation of power grid, transmission and distribution", has promoted significant policy initiatives and actions. While notable changes have occurred across generation, storage, distribution and sales sectors (excluding transmission sector), the outcomes have yet to fully meet the initial aspirations, standing in stark contrast to the ongoing efforts towards global carbon neutrality and China's dual carbon goals.

More recently, China's proposal to establish a national unified large market represents a strategic move. This initiative aims to leverage market pricing mechanisms to determine the floating trading prices of clean energy sources like hydropower, wind power, and photovoltaic energy in exporting provinces and regions. The resulting floating value-added component could serve as a catalyst for economic growth within these exporting regions.

China boasts a substantial electricity market, characterized by immense total power capacity and UHV transmission lines that are unparalleled in scale and reach globally. Should power market reform in China prove successful, its implementation will serve as a pivotal source of invaluable insights for the development of the international power market.

This book holds the belief that the cornerstone challenges hindering China's long-term progress in power reform stem from an ambiguous foundational theory of

[2] It is a business support tool that can query the basic business information and surrounding information of enterprises—a note by the translator.

reform, a lagging top-level design for comprehensive power reform, and inadequate competition within the transmission network market. The strategy of "allowing for more competition in electricity generation, sales and consumption while tightening government regulation of power grid, transmission and distribution" falls short of ensuring the success of power reform endeavors in China. Furthermore, issues such as disorganized subsidy policies at the power generation end, an unjustified carbon emission cost mechanism, and the persistent cross-subsidy mechanism challenges at the power end, all pose significant barriers to advancing power reform in China.

Hence, the time has come to unequivocally endorse a robust economic theory underpinning power reform and embark on a comprehensive overhaul and enhancement of the top-level design for power reform. This endeavor is imperative to achieving a pivotal breakthrough in the realm of power reform.

10.4.5 Comprehensive Blueprint for the International Electricity Trading Market

To forge a green energy landscape for the global community, we must strive towards the following visionary goals: Firstly, we target at fostering global green energy production and achieving real-time, optimal allocation and distribution of electricity worldwide. This means that zero-carbon green energy generated anywhere can seamlessly flow across borders, ensuring real-time accessibility globally. Secondly, mirroring the resilience of the information Internet, the International Electricity Trading Market must possess robust system architecture where localized network disruptions do not impede the overall transmission of electricity. The energy supply at any given point must be accessible through multi-directional transmission lines, ensuring continuity and reliability. Thirdly, we aspire to establish a spot market where electricity generated at any time, from any location, can be traded instantly between supply and demand. The transaction data must be seamlessly transmitted and integrated into smart power dispatching systems. Lastly, we aim for an electricity market that offers efficient, fair pricing for each bidding period, underpinned by a comprehensive and transparent market mechanism. This will ensure optimal resource allocation, while safeguarding basic electricity consumption for residents at affordable rates, with pricing and consumption protections enforced through robust mechanisms.

Realizing this ambitious vision necessitates the development of a novel global power system, which incorporates not just a robust hardware infrastructure, including advanced transmission networks, intelligent power dispatching systems, and a real-time international power trading platform, but also a set of software infrastructure, including meticulously crafted trading rules, software systems, a robust international legal framework, complemented by an effective executive organization system and operational implementation mechanisms, covering treatment plans, emergency response and supplementary measures.

10.4.5.1 Entities of the International Electricity Trading Market

The construction of the International Electricity Trading Market entities revolves around fully activating the market, fostering fair competition, catering to users' needs, and enhancing market efficiency. This effort endeavors to minimize government intervention through the utilization of market mechanisms, with each entity's functions and liability clearly defined. The primary entities in this market landscape include:

1. Power generation and storage enterprises: These qualified entities are empowered to sell their power generation and storage capacity in the market. Power enterprises that meet specific production capacity and standards and offer zero-carbon electricity offset by "International Negative CO_2", can apply for trading entity status. Their revenue model revolves around selling electricity and generating profits based on the kilowatt-hour price. Their core competitiveness stems from comprehensive cost management and power supply adaptability.
2. Electricity retailers: These enterprises purchase electricity from generation companies and resell it to end-users. They play a pivotal role in working out electricity consumption plans and serving customers, contributing significantly to peak shaving and valley filling in the whole system. Their income model involves earning through the price difference between buying and selling electricity. They aim to procure electricity at the lowest possible cost and sell it to customers with a markup. Being both market-driven enterprises and responsible for optimizing market resource allocation, they also undertake the vital function of ensuring the livelihood of people, therefore, they are predominantly state-controlled.
3. Transmission and distribution enterprises: These entities are tasked with transmitting electricity and intelligently configuring transmission based on demand (as determined by transaction outcomes). They adopt a toll-based revenue model, deriving income from electricity transmission fees rather than price differences. Similar to the model of highway operating companies, they provide nondiscriminatory services to all types of power generation enterprises. To facilitate system operations, they maintain a relatively stable periodic quotation system.
4. Power users: Power users have the option to procure electricity from power retailors or directly from generation and storage enterprises. They are charged usage fees accordingly.
5. Trading centers: The trading center serves as the hub of the power trading market, encompassing critical functions such as transaction matching, settlement, and managing the qualifications of trading participants. It operates independently from the government, grid operators, and other power market entities to ensure their compliance.
6. Clearing centers: As an impartial organization, the clearing center oversees the liquidation of transactions between parties. After getting final transaction data, it facilitates financial settlements among parties, and ensures the timely availability of funds.

7. Financial institutions: Collaborating with trading centers and clearing centers, financial institutions are responsible for efficiently settling and clearing transactions within the power market.
8. Decision-making and regulatory authorities: These bodies are tasked with crafting power market trading regulations, overseeing the transaction process, reviewing and approving significant matters, and ensuring that relevant government departments shoulder their respective costs.

10.4.5.2 Trading Objects of the International Power Market

The international power market revolves around "International Negative CO_2"-based "zero-carbon power" as its core trading object.

Zero-carbon power encompasses not just carbon-free renewable energy, like photovoltaic and wind energy, but also coal-fired power that has fulfilled carbon offset obligations. These offsets could be "International Negative CO_2", not necessarily "Real Negative CO_2". "International Negative CO_2" can be sourced from globally recognized domestic or international carbon markets. The pricing for "International Negative CO_2" is established through multilateral collaboration.

As the market evolves, the international power market will broaden its trading portfolio to include various energy products and derivatives.

10.4.5.3 Transaction Model

The International Electricity Trading Market operates as a global, professional platform for the trading and global delivery of electricity products, entirely grounded in market mechanisms. Leveraging a digital trading system and bound by the legal framework of trading rules, the market's trading system automatically matches offers and bids from participants, facilitating seamless settlement and clearing processes.

Trading centers and international regulatory authorities collaborate to oversee the delivery process and safeguard the sustainable operation of the international power market. This robust framework ensures that the outcomes of transactions within the market are reliably guaranteed (Fig. 10.7).

10.4.5.4 Trading Rules

Trading mechanism: The design of the trading mechanism necessitates clarity on several fundamental principles. Firstly, the price principle takes precedence, where buyers offering higher prices are prioritized, and sellers offering lower prices are served first. Secondly, the time principle comes into play, where in cases of identical prices, transactions are processed on a "first-come, first-served" basis. To enhance the effectiveness of these rules, we can draw upon the extensive experience of both the Chinese and EU markets for establishing additional necessary trading rules.

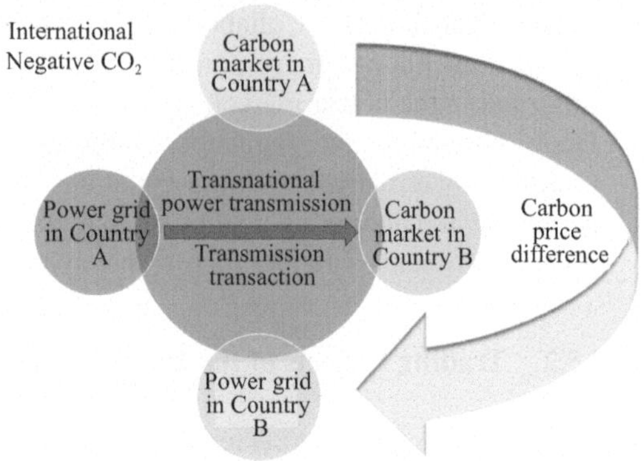

Fig. 10.7 Transaction logic diagram of international power market

Price mechanism: The cornerstone of our pricing framework lies in the principle of zero-carbon electricity quotation, which aims to internalize carbon emission costs. This approach ensures that all types of electricity compete on an equal footing, allowing zero-carbon green energy to showcase its inherent competitive advantage while acknowledging the critical role of traditional coal-fired power in ensuring supply security.

Distinct from domestic power markets, international power trading ought to forgo the use of carbon tickets and instead embrace "zero-carbon" electricity prices, offset by "International Negative CO_2". This shift can significantly enhance transaction efficiency. In contrast, the domestic power trading market, in view of minimizing the upfront concentration of costs to mitigate macroeconomic impacts, adopts a total price bidding system that incorporates carbon tickets, with transaction settlements occurring through a "cash + carbon tickets" model.

10.4.5.5 Clearing

Power trading markets differ significantly from capital markets in the stock industry, particularly in its post-transaction settlement process. The potential for non-settlement underscores the importance of establishing robust mechanisms to address such contingencies.

Firstly, establishing a margin account system is paramount to ensuring performance and facilitating large-scale transactions. This involves setting transaction settlement ratios, defining settlement procedures, and standardizing the handling of non-delivery scenarios. Furthermore, incorporating national sovereign credit guarantees can bolster creditworthiness and ensure the long-term sustainability of transactions.

Secondly, addressing carbon offset (carbon ticket) processing is crucial. In international power trade, the object is the "pure zero-carbon" electricity, offset by "International Negative CO_2", thereby eliminating the need for complex carbon ticket processing.

Thirdly, the cost of grid transportation must be considered. The purchaser bears the liability for grid transmission costs. The trading system provides a comprehensive terminal price for each product, encompassing pure electricity, carbon offsets, grid transmission, and transaction fees. This mechanism streamlines settlement processes and enhances efficiency.

The trading centers, in collaboration with financial institutions, implement the entire settlement and clearing process, including physical delivery. Drawing from the extensive experience of the international futures market, this process is well-established and unlikely to encounter significant obstacles.

10.4.5.6 Establishing an Operational System for International Electricity Trading Market

To fully realize the potential of the International Electricity Trading Market, it is imperative to establish a comprehensive set of international standards, encompassing technical agreements, rules, management regulations, and legal provisions governing transactions. This is a complex, systematic endeavor that necessitates a robust operational system and organizational framework based on these standards to ensure the system's sustainable operation.

Fortunately, the international community boasts a rich history of constructing successful international trading systems for stocks, futures, and bulk commodities. With a well-conceived top-level design for the International Electricity Trading Market, the overall system design and operational implementation should proceed smoothly.

10.4.6 Integration Between the International Power Trading System and the Global Energy Internet

The International Electricity Trading Market must be seamlessly integrated with the smart grid operating system within the Global Energy Internet, ensuring that all trading outcomes are promptly fed into the smart grid's operational framework. This integration allows the smart grid operating system to intelligently link various power supply organizations with the Global Energy Internet, conducting the transmission of power resources and efficiently managing the transmission and distribution of all transactions.

To govern the Global Energy Internet and smart grid system effectively, a comprehensive set of systems must be developed, addressing issues such as authority establishment and power distribution attribution. These systems must ensure fair and secure operations, adhering to international legal constraints and guarantees.

10.4.7 Value Analysis of the Global Green Energy Supply System

The Global Green Energy Supply System, as one of the two pivotal systems for achieving carbon neutrality, holds immense value for the international community. This vast global market for green energy brings forth several crucial benefits:

1. Energy independence and sustainability: Global development is liberated from energy constraints, with clean and sustainable energy production readily available. This upgrade in energy production accelerates the transition towards zero-carbon green energy, further displacing fossil fuels. Consequently, energy supply capabilities are enhanced, and energy shortages in underdeveloped regions are mitigated.
2. Optimal allocation of electricity across time and space: The system breaks down barriers, enabling the optimal allocation of electricity globally. It overcomes the intermittency and volatility of renewable energy sources like wind and photovoltaic energy, significantly reducing energy storage investments and mitigating carbon emissions. This, in turn, lowers the cost of global energy consumption.
3. Market expansion and industry incentives: Market expansion strengthens positive incentives within the energy industry, fostering the rapid deployment of new energy capacities. As zero-carbon green energy gains a substantial boost in supply capacity, it attracts better returns, significantly alleviating funding shortages for the global carbon neutrality transition. This acceleration propels the replacement of fossil fuels.
4. Reduced investment in green energy storage: The current investment in energy storage is enormous. The establishment of a global green energy supply system further reduces green energy costs and enhances its competitiveness.
5. Abundant supply of clean energy: This plays a pivotal role in advancing global economic development. By addressing power shortages worldwide, not only will affected regions and developing countries experience enhanced economic growth and societal well-being, but it can also significantly lower electricity prices, thereby alleviating the financial burden on consumers.

10.5 Treatment Plan for Historical Carbon Stock

To achieve global carbon neutrality and ultimately resolve the pressing climate crisis, the international community must pursue two parallel yet complementary paths. Firstly, there is an urgent need to prioritize accelerating the ongoing reduction of carbon emissions, expedite the transition to zero-carbon green energy sources, curb the tide of emissions growth, and swiftly progress towards a global carbon peak, ultimately leading to carbon neutrality. Secondly, concerted global efforts must be made to address historical CEL and provide substantial financial support to developing nations for their green transformation endeavors.

These two paths do not clash but rather reinforce each other, forming the cornerstone for humanity's survival. Even amidst debates over historical liability, governments should maintain their momentum in accelerating carbon reductions, as is currently being done. On the basis of voluntary reduction, more efforts could be made. This necessitates improved theoretical frameworks and well-designed carbon reduction programs that clearly articulate both the benefits and true costs. Currently, the fear of costs and perceived inadequate benefits has led the international community to prioritize allowance negotiations and free-riding strategies, rather than addressing the root of the issue.

10.5.1 Carbon Reduction Could Make Positive Impact on National Macroeconomies

The flawed analyses of some influential institutions, including the IMF, have hindered progress in the climate agenda. At COP27, Kristalina Georgieva, Managing Director of the International Monetary Fund (IMF), emphasized that to achieve the carbon reduction targets by 2030, the average global carbon price must reach 75 per ton. She stated, "Unless we price carbon predictably on a trajectory that gets us at least to $75 average price per ton of carbon in 2030, we simply don't create the incentive for businesses and consumers to shift." However, the current global carbon price stands at approximately $5 per ton, a significant gap primarily due to concerns over the impact on industrial competitiveness and uncertainty surrounding other nations' policies, discouraging unilateral price hikes.

It is crucial to understand that the carbon price should accurately reflect the price assigned to each ton of CO_2 actually emitted. However, the prevalent carbon pricing mechanism merely captures the transactions occurring outside the free allowances, disregarding the broader emissions landscape. For instance, if China's current carbon price stands at 56 yuan/ton, yet the emissions entering the market in 2022 represent a mere 0.4% of total emissions, the actual effective carbon price dwindles to approximately 0.23 yuan/ton.

The IMF's overly high estimate significantly distorts the global perception of the true cost of carbon emission reduction, fostering reluctance among nations and exacerbating the pace of remedial actions. This stems from an erroneous theoretical extrapolation.

Under the CELM-based top-level design for decarbonation, the unit cost of reducing emissions can be drastically minimized, accelerating the rate of decarbonization by two orders of magnitude. Furthermore, carbon reduction efforts can bolster a country's macroeconomic health, fostering a shift in attitudes towards carbon reduction.

10.5.2 Stockpile Disposal Proposals

To facilitate the green transition, particularly in developing nations, a modest baseline carbon price should be established for historical emissions, ensuring it meets the minimum investment requirements for global societal transformation. Each country's liability cost should be calculated against this price, establishing a clear financial obligation.

Concurrently, it is essential to craft and execute an international green transformation investment plan and governments need to find a scientific, equitable, and reasonable distribution principle. When funds are allocated to a country, the discrepancy between its allotment and liability cost represents its net liability. Countries with a positive balance can expect financial support, while those with a negative balance must contribute a corresponding amount to the international community.

Global Carbon Neutrality Solution grounded in the CELM offers a significant advantage in tackling the historical emission stockpile. By resolving the intricate issues surrounding the sourcing and returns of investment funds, contributing nations stand to gain substantial positive returns, thereby facilitating smoother collaboration among countries and diverse interest groups. The COP 27 conference, which grappled with nearly two decades of financing discussions yet yielded limited tangible outcomes, underscores the daunting challenge of securing the investments necessary for a global green transition. The intractability of this endeavor, if left unresolved, portends an insurmountable obstacle. However, the CELM and its accompanying Solution present a comprehensive solution to this challenge.

10.6 Financing for Green Transition in Developing Countries

Currently, developing nations bear the brunt of the climate crisis and confront the most formidable financial hurdles in pursuing a green transition. The financing gap for green transition in these countries has emerged as a paramount challenge for the international community striving for global carbon neutrality. This issue has dominated recent COP conferences, consuming significant attention and resources, yet it remains a pressing matter that demands urgent attention.

The deployment of CELM-based Global Carbon Neutrality Solution holds the promise of substantially easing the immense financing gap for green transition in developing countries. Firstly, it drastically cuts the cost of achieving a green transition. Previously, the lack of cost-effective solutions hindered progress in developing countries. Now, the CELM-based Solution slashes costs by two orders of magnitude, significantly reducing the challenges. Secondly, it significantly enhances the return on green investments. Without attractive returns, securing capital for green initiatives remains arduous. However, high returns from green investments will spawn abundant financing sources for the green transition in developing countries. CELM-based Global Carbon Neutrality Solution internalizes carbon reduction costs, bolstering the competitiveness of low-carbon energy and products, thereby naturally attracting investments. Furthermore, the CELM-driven Negative Carbon Trading Market fosters a more direct and real-time cashability of low-carbon energy and products, transforming capital from a constraint into a sought-after investment opportunity.

10.7 Effect Analysis of the CELM-Based Global Carbon Neutrality Solution

The Global Carbon Neutrality Solution grounded in the CELM illuminates a highly efficient and cost-effective path for humanity to achieve the aspiration of global carbon neutrality, thereby definitively addressing the pressing climate crisis. This breakthrough paves a smooth way for the international community towards a carbon–neutral future. Embracing CELM-based Solution will foster numerous positive societal effects:

1. Resolving the climate challenge efficiently and feasibly: It offers an efficacious and viable alternative to the past challenges of conflicting interests, coordination hurdles, soaring costs, sluggish carbon reduction rates, and funding shortfalls. The CELM emerges as a third pathway, demonstrating both practicality and efficiency in pursuing global carbon neutrality.
2. Accelerating the pace of global carbon neutrality: Early adoption and implementation of CELM-driven solution expedite societal-wide decarbonation and hasten the transition from fossil fuels. This momentum aligns with the IPCC's ambitious target of limiting global average temperature increase to 1.5 °C above pre-industrial levels, instilling renewed hope amidst current despair.
3. Optimizing the economic impact of carbon reduction: It enhances the positive macroeconomic effects of carbon reduction while significantly mitigating its negative consequences. By doing so, it drastically lowers the financial burden associated with emissions reduction efforts, contrasting sharply with the dire macroeconomic forecasts of current carbon reduction mechanisms. This optimism stems from the discovery of an apt theoretical foundation and practical solution.
4. Catalyzing new industries and job opportunities: The green economic transition, with its favorable macroeconomic implications, will spur substantial investments and employment prospects, thereby propelling high-quality economic growth.
5. Addressing the issue of international carbon tariffs: It effectively mitigates international trade frictions arising from CBAM implementations.
6. Providing funds: It meets the financial demands of the international community, particularly those of developing nations, for green transition. Financial instruments such as the CELM-based NCTM, International Carbon Trading

Market, and International Electricity Trading Market, pave the way for governments to access substantial funding avenues, ensuring ample resources for green initiatives.

7. Enhancing the equity in carbon emission reduction efforts among nations. By circumventing the allocation of carbon emission rights and augmenting revenue streams from green transition investments, the CELM diminishes concerns over fairness in carbon reduction endeavors.
8. Bolstering international security and relation. The climate crisis has long been a significant source of tension within the global community, often trapped in a zero-sum or negative-sum game. However, the recognition and adoption of the CELM by nations worldwide can rapidly catalyze global cooperation. This collaborative framework fosters a shared understanding of the benefits of win–win cooperation, thereby diminishing the risks of conflict and division.

Furthermore, the execution of the CELM and its corresponding Global Carbon Neutrality Solution, along with its innovative ideas and methodologies, offers a roadmap for resolving numerous global public goods challenges, setting a precedent for future collaborative endeavors.

10.8 The Urgent Tasks of the International Community

With the emergence of the CELM and its comprehensive approach to achieving global carbon neutrality, a grand vision for addressing the climate crisis has been unveiled. The pivotal task now lies in the hands of the international community to translate this vision into action. We must expedite the following crucial endeavors:

1. Foster a profound understanding, refinement, harmonization, and promotion of the CELM and its Global Carbon Neutrality Solution among nations. Achieving a unified consensus on proactive measures is imperative, as this represents the most viable and promising pathway towards global carbon neutrality discovered thus far. It also lays a solid theoretical foundation for comprehensively tackling the global climate challenge.
2. Expedite the organization of international forums and seminars centered on diverse aspects of the CELM and its Global Carbon Neutrality Solution. These platforms will facilitate learning, comprehension, and enhancement of the CELM, thereby fostering a unified global understanding of climate issues and carbon neutrality pathways.
3 Establish an efficient global action organization to spearhead progress. Given the sluggish pace of global carbon neutrality efforts, an effective global entity is necessary to coordinate initiatives, expedite the transition towards the right path, and implement meaningful actions.

Among the most influential international bodies currently engaged in climate change, the Intergovernmental Panel on Climate Change (IPCC) and the United Nations Climate Change Conference stand out.

The IPCC, jointly established in 1988 by the World Meteorological Organization (WMO) and the United Nations Environment Programme (UNEP), shares a Nobel Peace Prize with former US Vice President Al Gore in 2007. Its primary function is to assess the current scientific understanding of climate change, its potential societal and economic impacts, and potential adaptation and mitigation strategies. However, it functions as a research assessment body without legal authority to enforce actions. Despite issuing six influential assessment reports, the IPCC has yet to translate its findings into tangible actions.

Another organization with profound impact is the United Nations Climate Change Conference, commonly referred to as the COP. The COP, an acronym for "Conference of the Parties", annually brings together nations that are part of the United Nations Framework Convention on Climate Change (UNFCCC) to collaboratively discuss and address the global climate challenge. Despite 27 years of negotiations and competing interests among nations worldwide, the outcomes in terms of advancing carbon neutrality have been less than satisfactory.

The Sharm el-Sheikh Implementation Plan, unveiled at the conclusion of COP27 following multiple rounds of intense negotiations, outlines a framework for a loss and damage fund. While the establishment of such a fund is a step forward, the absence of a concrete funding source remains a critical unresolved issue.

To truly embark on substantial actions to tackle the global climate crisis, it is imperative that the international community promptly addresses the current dilemma of lacking a robust organization dedicated to climate change. This organization must legally address issues of authorization, establish an effective decision-making mechanism, and maintain a standing working committee to ensure swift and orderly progress across all fronts.

While existing professional committees, such as the World Energy Internet Organization initiated by China, have undertaken valuable technical work, their impact is limited by the absence of legal authorization and administrative authority.

To advance critical practical work, specialized committees should be established, each with distinct functions. These could include a Committee on Emission Reduction Mechanisms, a Committee for Emission Reduction Standards, an Energy Internet Professional Committee, a Carbon Tariff Professional Committee, a Technical Committee for Emission Reduction, and a Publicity and Education Committee. Together, these committees can drive forward meaningful progress towards addressing global climate change.

1. Expedite the completion of the top-level design for a carbon neutrality solution grounded in the CELM. This blueprint outlines the challenges we confront, the theoretical underpinnings, guiding principles, roadmap, and vision for a novel international social order centered on global carbon neutrality. Authorized bodies within the international community should spearhead the swift formulation of the architectural blueprint for this path, facilitating its execution.
2. Foster the swift establishment and operation of the "1+1" Global Decarbonation System based on the CELM. This entails encouraging nations to establish CELM-based Carbon Ticket Management System and Negative Carbon Trading Market,

thereby bolstering the efficiency of national carbon reduction efforts. Gradually, we aim to interconnect CTMS globally, forge an international negative carbon market, and ultimately establish a comprehensive global carbon reduction system.

3. Intensify efforts to develop a "1+1" Global Green Energy Supply System, encompassing a Global Energy Internet and an International Electricity Trading Market, and accelerate the deployment of zero-carbon green energy sources and expedite the transition from fossil fuels. This will not only furnish ample zero-carbon energy for global development but also serve as a potent catalyst for global economic growth.
4. Establish an international negative carbon pricing coordination mechanism to mitigate the adverse trade impacts of carbon reduction and amplify its positive momentum. Amid accelerated carbon reduction efforts, this multilateral mechanism will ensure smooth international trade, enhancing overall quality and global welfare.
5. Continuously upgrade and optimize the CELM-based Global Carbon Neutrality Solution, striving for global carbon neutrality at the earliest. This comprehensive approach aims to fundamentally address the climate crisis while fostering global economic development. The CELM-based Solution holds vast potential for in-depth exploration, ample room for improvement, and ongoing enhancement during implementation, ultimately yielding a more favorable global macroeconomic outcome.

10.9 Global Carbon Neutrality: A Vision for the Future

The 2023 Chinese Spring Festival witnessed the remarkable premiere of "Wandering Earth II", a cinematic masterpiece that once again captivated audiences worldwide. This film poignantly depicts how diverse nations, factions, interest groups, and communities with varying values unite in the face of a catastrophic planetary threat. Amidst fierce conflicts that nearly jeopardized humanity's survival, they ultimately forged a common front, securing a glimmer of hope for mankind's survival.

A sentence uttered by the protagonist, acted by Wu Jing, resonates deeply: "Can we survive?".

This question elicits a harsh reality: the paramount crisis facing our planet is not a fictional solar calamity but the very real threat of climate disaster.

The over three-decade journey of international climate cooperation, mirrored in the annual UN climate conferences attended by approximately 50,000 participants, has been fraught with challenges. Progress has been painfully slow, with a murky path forward, elusive consensus on liability, and a dearth of concerted actions. As depicted in the film, Zhou Zhezhi, China's top representative in the fictional UEG (Earth Coalition Government), laments, "Humans have harnessed the most intricate and advanced technologies to create weapons that turn against each other," a tragic irony and a stark reminder of the profound challenges we face.

However, humanity also possesses another trait, as eloquently articulated by Zhou Zhezhi, "In the face of crisis, only liability prevails." This sentiment is deeply inspiring and exerts a profound influence on all, emphasizing the urgency and necessity of our collective endeavor. The word "only" underscores the absence of alternative paths. We are compelled to devote ourselves fully to resolving this crisis, embracing our liability, and striving for the continuity of humanity. When one individual rises to the occasion, others will follow suit.

Currently, humanity has witnessed remarkable advancements in green energy, the energy Internet, CCUS technologies, robotics, and intelligent technologies. Technologically speaking, we are poised at a juncture where solving the climate problem is within our grasp. Nevertheless, the challenge lies in fostering international consensus and solidarity, as well as devising a comprehensive social governance and operational framework. Here, sociology and economics research play a pivotal role in guiding our way forward.

The emergence of the CELM has illuminated a clear path for humanity to tackle the climate crisis. It is urgent for responsible groups to continually propel the international community towards heightened awareness and concerted action.

We are convinced that the eventual resolution of the climate problem is not merely a distant dream but a theoretically feasible endeavor. Through relentless efforts and collective actions, the international community can achieve global carbon neutrality on schedule, comprehensively address the human-induced climate challenge, and leave behind a legacy of invaluable lessons for humanity in tackling shared global issues.

Chapter 11
Macro-level Impacts of Implementation of the CELM: An Insightful Case Study from China

China, akin to other global economies, has proposed ambitious dual carbon targets, transcending mere carbon neutrality aspirations. At its core, this dual carbon effort endeavors to propel China to transform in three aspects, including economic growth models, societal lifestyles, and energy supply systems, all vital components of national rejuvenation. Recognizing the intricacies, the Chinese Government has identified four pivotal relationships to navigate: balancing international and domestic considerations, harmonizing development with emission reduction, ensuring transformation without compromising security, and striking a chord between short-term gains and long-term sustainability. This poses a formidable challenge to the strategic framing of carbon neutral targets, necessitating a thorough understanding of its impacts on macroeconomy, consumption upgrades, development pace, international trade dynamics, and regional economic shifts. The design of policy instruments must be precise, neither lagging nor rash, underpinned by a profound comprehension of the underlying logic of carbon neutrality and wisdom of top-level design.

With the implementation of the CELM, a meticulous examination of its multifaceted implications becomes paramount. It is plausible to anticipate that the CELM will not merely facilitate China's progress towards carbon neutrality but also exert transformative, positive impacts on the macroeconomic landscape, including economic restructuring, green financial markets, international trade patterns, and people's livelihoods.

11.1 Impacts on Government Carbon Control Policies

For an extended period, the government's carbon reduction policy framework has suffered from inadequate top-level design support, resulting in sluggish and inefficient progress. The Central government's vision of advancing towards carbon peaking and neutrality underscores the importance of striking a balance between ambition

B. Yang, *The Carbon Emission Liability Mechanism*,
https://doi.org/10.1007/978-981-96-3612-9_11

and economic feasibility, advocating a measured approach that neither overburdens the macroeconomy nor procrastinates. Amidst this delicate balance, the challenge lies in how to swiftly navigate towards carbon neutrality through the most equitable and efficient path. Unfortunately, the theoretical and practical advancements in carbon emission reduction over the past two decades have been sluggish, until the introduction of the CELM, which has significantly altered this stagnant landscape.

11.1.1 Enhancing the Design of Carbon Emission Policy Instruments with Robust Academic Theories

Currently, policy instruments aimed at reducing carbon emissions encompass a range of measures, including supply-side interventions like taxing traditional fossil fuels to restrict their supply, subsidizing and tax-exempting green energy to boost renewable energy sources, as well as demand-side incentives like granting carbon allowances and controlling emissions for major energy consumers. However, these policies encounter numerous challenges during formulation and implementation, including a dearth of data-driven insights, arbitrary decision-making, inequitable distribution among enterprises, market-driven rent-seeking behaviors and challenges in ensuring fairness across regions and consumers.

The advent of the CELM has illuminated the fundamental principles and operational mechanisms underlying carbon emissions, marking a significant breakthrough in climate change economics. By grounding policy instrument selection and top-level design in robust economic theories, the government has been able to streamline the policy formulation process. This foundation has provided clarity on critical aspects of carbon management, such as carbon data verification and carbon market design, offering a more precise roadmap from theory to practical implementation.

11.1.2 Streamlining and Optimizing Carbon Control Policies, Enhancing Efficiency

The CELM empowers the government with robust decision-making capabilities and administrative controls, enabling a shift away from inefficient instruments like carbon taxes, subsidies, and allowance systems. By harnessing the strengths of the CELM theory and framework, the government can adopt a market-oriented approach to devise policy instruments that are more efficient, equitable, and cost-effective.

The current landscape of carbon emission rights, CCERs, green power, green certificates, carbon-inclusive mechanisms, and financial subsidies is fraught with complexity, overlap, conflict, unfairness, and high implementation costs. The CELM presents an opportunity to eliminate these redundant, conflicting, and inefficient carbon reduction mechanisms. With the internalization of carbon emission costs, many of these mechanisms become obsolete, facilitating a substantial streamlining and optimization of the government's carbon control policies.

11.1.3 Significantly Curtailing the Cost of Government Regulation and Enforcement Across Society

The monitoring, reporting, and verification (MRV) mechanism is a crucial aspect of the carbon trading system. In instances like Beijing carbon trading market, the Beijing Municipal Development and Reform Commission oversees the design and supervision of this mechanism. In accordance with the requirements of MRV mechanism, the authorities responsible shall carry out targeted verification on the emission reports submitted by the emission control enterprises. Shanghai carbon trading market has introduced an additional layer of verification by establishing a fourth verification entity. This intricate process requires that the annual emission reports submitted by emission control enterprises undergo rigorous scrutiny by a third-party institution. Subsequently, the fourth-party verifier conducts spot checks on the third-party's verification report, aiming to uphold the utmost authenticity of the emission and verification report data. Nevertheless, despite these measures, the quality of carbon verification data has continued to pose a significant challenge in recent years.

The shortcomings in cost, efficiency, and fairness of these verification and supervision mechanisms are evident.

The CELM, on the other hand, guarantees the government access to a highly reliable, real-time, accurate, and comprehensive carbon footprint database for all goods across society at minimal cost, thereby significantly reducing the burden on enterprises.

11.2 Impacts on Macroeconomy

The international community faces significant pressure in designing carbon emission reduction policies, primarily stemming from the integration of carbon emissions' external costs into the overall energy price through carbon taxes or trading fees. This integration threatens to induce macroeconomic inflation, potentially hindering economic development and compromising people's well-being.

However, a comprehensive assessment of the CELM program reveals a promising outlook for the macroeconomic impacts of carbon reduction. If the policy is crafted meticulously, its positive effects on the macroeconomy can surpass potential challenges. The Achilles' heel in current policy mechanisms lies in the front-end placement of all carbon costs within the industrial chain, intensifying the pressure on the highest marginal cost segments, thereby undermining economic growth. This concentrated burden on upstream enterprises, like power producers, disrupts power supply, restricts production, and adversely affects the operations of the entire industrial chain. Moreover, without a sufficient increase in carbon prices, societal emission reductions stagnate, as the downstream consumption-side fails to perceive the pressure from carbon costs, hindering consumer-driven emission reductions. Consequently, carbon reduction policies lag behind their intended implementation timelines.

11.2.1 Analysis of Burden on Macroeconomy

Considering China's economic landscape in 2022, with a GDP of 121 trillion yuan and carbon emissions totaling 12.1 Gt, imposing a carbon fee of 50 yuan per ton would result in a total fee of approximately 605 billion yuan, accounting for a mere 0.5% of GDP. This proportion is negligible, unlikely to spark significant inflationary pressures, and far less than the inflation levels witnessed in recent years due to monetary easing measures. With effective public communication, the public would accept this fee naturally.

Furthermore, the performance of the trading markets for carbon emission rights in 2022, with only 179 million tons transacted and a total carbon fee of less than 8 billion yuan, underscores the market's current limitations in driving meaningful carbon emission reductions. Both the volume of traded emissions and the total carbon fee remain too small to exert a substantial impact on emission reduction efforts.

Assuming that by 2030, even if China's carbon price aligns with the current EU level of 80 euros per ton, equivalent to approximately 600 yuan per ton, China's GDP is projected to grow at an average annual rate of 4%, reaching a staggering 165 trillion yuan in 2030 (adjusted from the prices in 2022). In line with the ambition to peak carbon emissions, a 65% reduction in carbon intensity from 2005 levels is anticipated. The total carbon fee is estimated to reach approximately 7.7 trillion yuan in 2030, constituting 4.6% of GDP, with the ensuing inflation levels remaining manageable overall.

This scenario arises from the fact that the substantial carbon fees China incurs does not represent a net burden on the national economy but rather a redistribution of economic welfare. The government intends to utilize these carbon revenues to procure "Real Negative CO_2" products from carbon removal enterprises, finance green energy initiatives, and bolster carbon-reduction technology industries, thereby generating substantial job opportunities and augmenting citizens' incomes. This aligns with the dual dividend concept often associated with environmental taxation.

However, a prevailing challenge lies in China's immense macroeconomic scale, where mere billions of yuan annually in carbon fees have a limited impact on emissions reduction while inadvertently disrupting economic operations. Governments at various levels grapple with allocating carbon emission allowances and energy usage rights, inadvertently impeding regular production processes.

The CELM addresses this dilemma thoroughly. Its core principle for mitigating adverse macroeconomic impacts revolves around two key strategies:

- Firstly, it distributes the cost or the CEL evenly across the entire industrial chain, avoiding a disproportionate burden on any single link. This ensures that the carbon cost is not solely imposed on the upstream or downstream segments but is shared among organizations and consumers whose carbon intensity surpasses the industry average. By spreading the cost evenly, the CELM minimizes disruptions to the macroeconomy.
- Secondly, it optimizes resource allocation within the carbon reduction market. Contrary to the prevailing carbon allowance mechanisms, the CELM avoids significant disruptions to critical industrial chain segments, instead facilitating optimal allocation of market resources through the following three primary aspects:

  1. Each segment within the macroeconomic industrial chain will undergo natural selection, ensuring the survival of the fittest and fostering high-quality development. The CELM empowers low-carbon, high-quality enterprises across the industrial chain to reap the benefits of carbon emission reductions and cost savings, thereby enhancing their market share, scaling up their operations and profits, and significantly contributing to the high-quality progression of every industry. Conversely, high-carbon, low-quality enterprises will be phased out, vastly improving the overall quality of the macroeconomy.
  2. The optimization of resource allocation is automatically narrowed down to the minimum product unit. Under the CELM, carbon reduction granularity extends beyond generic product types to encompass specific products tailored for distinct user groups. This approach, within the smallest competitive market unit, encourages the gradual elimination of inefficient, high-carbon production capabilities, as manufacturers compete based on total cost advantages in both production and emissions. Meanwhile, enterprises with a competitive edge reap low-carbon incentives, lowering their overall costs and driving societal-wide high-quality development.
  3. It helps enlarge the optimization scope of resource allocation to encompass the global arena. If the production cost of a specific segment within the domestic industrial chain surpasses a certain threshold, it becomes economically viable to substitute those products with imports, thereby relocating production capacity and associated carbon emissions to foreign shores. This strategic shift in resource allocation optimizes the domestic economy by reducing costs and mitigating local emissions, while simultaneously transferring the production burden and emissions to international partners (Fig. 11.1).

- Thirdly, it mitigates the macroeconomic impacts of rising carbon emission costs on consumers. Under the CELM, while the government generates revenue through Negative Carbon Trading Market, consumers inevitably face increased expenses. To counteract the potential reduction in consumer purchasing power and its subsequent impact on consumption, the government can strategically utilize the garnered carbon fees to subsidize consumers in various forms, such as coordinating with individual income adjustment tax policies to improve tax thresholds. Furthermore, by enhancing the progressivity of policies through the household

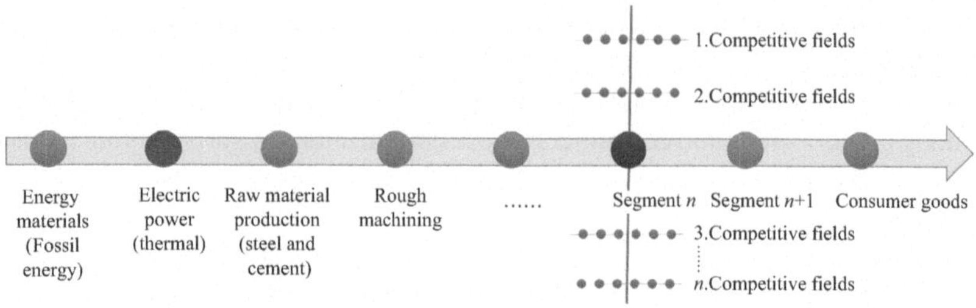

Fig. 11.1 Difference of impacts of the CELM and carbon allowance mechanism on industrial chain

carbon account mechanism, the financial burden on low-income households can be significantly alleviated.

11.2.2 Impacts on Investment

The impacts of carbon reduction policy instruments on investment represent a pivotal aspect of their macroeconomic implications.

If the carbon tax is implemented as a policy instrument, it is projected that with a tax rate of 200 yuan/ton, investments across various sectors will experience more pronounced declines. Specifically, the construction sector may see a 5.64% reduction in investment, the metal mining sector a 4.94% decrease, and the chemicals sector a 3.17% dip. Notably, as the carbon tax rate escalates, there exists a negative linear relationship with the rate of investment change, indicating a direct and substantial impact.

However, adopting a CELM-based approach could moderate these effects.

Firstly, under the CELM, heavy industrial sectors at the front-end of investment do not bear direct carbon fees as long as they are capable of issuing carbon output tickets. This approach fosters a competitive environment where inefficient producers are naturally phased out, while competitive enterprises reap the benefits of low-carbon incentives and cost reductions.

Secondly, the substantial carbon fees generated by the government through the sale of negative carbon products are channeled into green and economic transformation investments, effectively augmenting the overall investment landscape. It is estimated that over the next three decades, carbon neutrality endeavors in China will necessitate investments totaling 200 trillion yuan, a colossal figure that underscores the significance of strategic investment allocation.

Lastly, it is crucial to undertake detailed input–output mathematical modeling based on the CELM in the future, conducting rigorous quantitative analyses to facilitate more precise projections and informed decision-making.

11.2.3 Impacts on GDP

When implementing the carbon tax policy with a rate of 200 yuan/ton, China's GDP is projected to experience a decline exceeding 2%.

However, under the CELM, the initial impact on upstream industries remains minimal, as long as enterprises issue carbon output tickets, without incurring additional costs. Consequently, these core enterprises face negligible pressure. Furthermore, the modest revenue generated from carbon fees can be strategically utilized by the government to foster economic advancement, technological advancements, and investments in carbon reduction initiatives, thereby fostering new GDP growth and enhancing household incomes. As a result, the overall impact on end-consumer spending remains limited, indicating that the CELM exerts a relatively small negative influence on GDP while fostering significant positive outcomes.

11.2.4 Positive Macroeconomic Impacts of the CELM

The CELM fosters economic transformation and enhances economic quality by imposing significant pressure on enterprises with outdated technology and high carbon emissions. Conversely, it incentivizes enterprises with low carbon emissions, fostering a market environment where superior enterprises thrive, ultimately benefiting the overall economic quality.

Moreover, the CELM bolsters the international export earnings of carbon negative industries. The pursuit of carbon neutrality fosters the emergence of numerous novel industries, increasing the international export of negative carbon products and spurring the development of green finance.

Lastly, the CELM drives substantial investment. China's commitment to green transformation, involving investments totaling nearly 100 trillion yuan, serves as a formidable catalyst for economic growth.

11.3 Impacts on Energy Policy

The transition towards carbon neutrality necessitates a pivotal shift in the energy landscape, replacing fossil fuels with green, renewable sources like wind, photovoltaic and bio energy. This transformation poses a formidable challenge for policymakers, as it involves intricate technical and economic considerations. Balancing short-term and long-term objectives, managing investments in both fossil fuel projects and emerging green energy initiatives, and reconciling economic growth with carbon neutrality goals, are all crucial yet complex endeavors. Coal-fired power plants in China, with significant long payback periods, further complicate the picture, requiring the government to delicately weigh the interests of original investors against the broader economic and environmental implications. These complexities hinder the effective implementation of policy instruments like carbon taxes and emissions trading markets, as high prices could stifle economic growth and pose challenges for the government.

Currently, China's energy policy framework faces numerous hurdles, with policies on carbon emissions, energy usage rights, new energy subsidies, coal price deregulation, and electricity price controls overlapping and leaving gaps, resulting in suboptimal overall efficiency and significant macroeconomic impacts. It's time to clarify these policies.

11.3.1 Redefining Decarbonation Strategies

Do coal-fired power plants bear the brunt of China's carbon reduction efforts? Can their decarbonization accelerate China's pace to carbon neutrality? Should China emulate Western models for the design of top-level carbon reduction policy?

The CELM offers a resounding "no" to these questions.

Based on the data from the China Electricity Union, China's total CO_2 emissions in 2019 amounted to approximately 10.2 billion tons, with thermal power generation (predominantly coal-fired) contributing roughly 4.2 billion tons, constituting a significant 41% of China's overall carbon footprint, marking it as a primary emitter.

A prevalent misconception among dual carbon experts and leaders is that solely focusing on reducing emissions from coal-fired power enterprises will inherently lead to comprehensive emissions reductions and expedite national carbon neutrality. They believe that once the coal-fired power enterprises curb their emissions, the total carbon emissions are controlled. Consequently, the national carbon trading market is widely referred to as the trading market for carbon emission rights.

In the national carbon trading market launched in 2021, the power generation sector, comprising 2225 power generation enterprises and self-generation power plants, was among the first batch subjected to national management. Collectively, these entities emit approximately 4 Gt of CO_2 annually, constituting a staggering 40% of China's total annual carbon emissions. Currently, thermal power holds a dominant position in China's power generation mix, with installed capacity exceeding 55% and annual power generation accounting for over 75% of the total. As a result, coal-fired power enterprises will inevitably serve as the backbone of the national carbon market, with over 90% of them embarking on carbon market participation for the very first time. Notably, 186 of these enterprises have already participated in regional pilot carbon markets.

Yet, it is imperative to recognize that this perspective falls short of comprehending the full extent of carbon emissions across society.

This simplistic mindset fundamentally misrepresents the intricate operational dynamics and impact mechanisms of carbon emissions within society, offering but a superficial glimpse of the issue. Regrettably, our strategy for carbon reduction has been rooted in this flawed perception for over two decades. Despite being operational for a decade, the carbon market has witnessed a total trading volume of less than 20 billion yuan, with some trading days witnessing transactions as low as a few thousand yuan, hardly sufficient to cover even the daily electricity and carbon emission costs. It is inconceivable that such a carbon market can significantly contribute to the nation's aspiration for carbon neutrality.

Coal-fired power plants have suffered most. Lately, escalating coal prices have plunged these enterprises into widespread financial losses. Amidst national carbon control and reduction efforts, production capacities of coal-fired power plants are constrained by carbon quotas, significantly inflating costs and exacerbating their financial losses. Some enterprises even. have resorted to misreporting their carbon emissions merely to survive.

Further confounding the situation, certain provinces, in pursuit of carbon emission control, have imposed restrictions on power plants' output and enthusiasm, inevitably limiting the power supply to manufacturing enterprises. This approach is highly detrimental to the macroeconomy.

The administrative measures aimed at carbon emission reduction have had profound disruptions on the smooth functioning of the entire market. There is no robust top-level design theory and framework, and the specific policies are impractical, leading to low implementation efficiency and unjust treatment of coal-fired power enterprises. After all, coal-fired power enterprises remain vital suppliers of energy for current economic growth, and the existing top-level carbon reduction mechanism has significantly hampered the normal operations of the macroeconomy.

This state of affairs has persisted for years and necessitates urgent adjustment. Fundamentally, it is imperative to clarify the essence of the carbon challenge.

11.3.2 Beyond Coal and Electricity: A Comprehensive Approach to Decarbonation

It is crucial to recognize that solely focusing on reducing carbon emissions from coal-fired and electricity enterprises is a limited perspective. The notion that "controlling the emissions from coal-fired power enterprises equates to controlling national carbon emissions" stems from a misconception about the intricate dynamics within the carbon reduction mechanism.

11.3.2.1 Dissecting the Carbon Challenge

Firstly, let's dissect the carbon emissions. It's true that the coal-fired power sector contributes a substantial 41% to overall societal carbon emissions. However, the electricity generated by these plants fuels the entire society's energy needs. Consequently, the direct emission reduction efforts undertaken by coal-fired power enterprises are estimated to have a modest 20% impact on the sector's overall carbon footprint (this figure is likely an overestimate, without specific studies). When considering the broader context, the actual influence of reduction efforts from these enterprises on the total carbon emissions in the industry amounts to roughly 8% (41% * 20%). Thus, even if the coal-fired power industry achieves remarkable emission reductions, it can only account for 8% of the societal demand for carbon mitigation. The remaining 92% of the carbon reduction potential remains largely untapped, highlighting the need for a more comprehensive strategy.

From a different analytical angle, we gain further insight into the complexity of the issue. The total carbon emissions (Q) of the coal-fired power industry are intricately linked to several key factors:

$$\begin{aligned} Q = &\text{coal-fired power generation} \\ &\times \text{ carbon emission intensity of the industry} \end{aligned}$$

Or, alternatively,

$$\begin{aligned} Q = &\text{total national electricity demand} \\ &\times \text{ proportion of coal-fired power generation} \\ &\times \text{ coal consumption per unit of electricity} \\ &\times \text{ unit carbon emissions of coal} \end{aligned}$$

wherein, the total national electricity demand is driven by the country's economic growth. Unless there is a significant improvement in overall energy efficiency across industries, economic expansion will inevitably spur an increase in electricity demand.

The proportion of coal-generated power is dictated by the prevailing transmission capacities of coal-fired, photoelectric, and wind power sources, as well as the technical constraints of the grid. Given the significant limitations in the current transmission capacity of photoelectric and wind power, coupled with their inherent volatility and intermittency, enhancing these capacities is a protracted endeavor. Consequently, coal-fired electricity remains the backbone of the grid, accounting for 60% of the electricity supply, a status that is unlikely to shift drastically in the foreseeable future.

Coal consumption per kilowatt-hour in China has been steadily declining, reaching 305 g in 2021, outperforming America and Germany and only second to Japan. However, the scope for further improvement is narrow, and the marginal cost associated with reductions is high.

The carbon emissions per unit of coal are fundamentally governed by chemical reactions, where burning 1 ton of standard coal in the air equates to the combustion of 0.67 tons of carbon, releasing 2.46 tons of CO_2. This inherent process cannot be altered by advancements in enterprise or industry technology.

It is imperative to acknowledge that the carbon emissions from the coal-fired power industry are inherently tied to overall electricity demand and the chemical processes involved, rendering them impervious to changes caused by industry-specific emission reduction technologies or current policy mechanisms. Regrettably, this crucial insight has been overlooked by academia and policymakers for over two decades.

Therefore, the current focus on decarbonation within the coal-fired power industry misses the mark, targeting links with the least significant impact. Surveys of coal-fired power enterprises reveal that after years of technological advancements, their energy consumption per kilowatt-hour has already reached international benchmarks, limiting the potential for substantial carbon emission reductions. Moreover, the relentless pursuit of emission reductions and continuous technological upgrades have pushed up the marginal cost, diminishing the marginal benefits achieved. Consequently, the escalating costs of carbon emissions and management have imposed significant burdens on coal-fired power enterprises, which, in turn, have broader negative impacts on the macroeconomy.

11.3.2.2 Challenges and Difficulties Surrounding Decarbonation in the Coal-Fired Power Industry

1. Carbon trading dilemma for power generation enterprises

Power generation enterprises confront a daunting dual challenge: maintaining growth while simultaneously slashing carbon emissions. This balancing act poses a significant burden, as the escalating demand for electricity complicates efforts to decarbonize. Over the past decade, China's GDP has grown at an average annual rate of approximately 6%, paralleled by a 5.7% surge in electricity consumption nationwide. While economic development has entered a new era characterized by slower growth rates and optimized consumption patterns, the power sector must still contend with surging demand as the country's economy continues to expand. Notably, thermal power remains a cornerstone of China's energy supply for the foreseeable future.

2. Untapped carbon reduction potential in the power generation sector

Decades of reform and opening up, particularly in the last decade, have yielded notable improvements in power generation efficiency and carbon mitigation through renewable energy technologies.

The *Annual Development Report of China's Power Industry (2022)* indicates that CO_2 emissions of thermal power generation decreased by 21% from the 2005 level, reaching approximately 828 g/kWh in 2021. However, further exploring technical avenues for carbon reduction in the sector has become increasingly arduous, and mandatory technical standards alone are no longer viable for achieving deeper decarbonization. China's rigorous standards for emissions in power sector, coal consumption of generation units, and grid losses are now at or nearing international benchmarks, leaving limited room for further energy savings and emission reductions. Consequently, advancing clean energy and low-carbon technologies is imperative, yet these efforts are hindered by technological uncertainty, a lack of core competencies, and high costs. Therefore, sole reliance on low-carbon technologies to reduce emissions in the short term is impractical, necessitating a holistic approach that considers the entire emission reduction potential in the industry and sets achievable cap-and-trade targets.

3. Current status and challenges of decarbonation in the power industry

Power generation enterprises are currently confronted with an imminent surge in operational costs, particularly in the short term, following their integration into the national carbon market. The escalating demand for electricity inevitably translates into heightened CO_2 emissions. To adhere to government-mandated carbon emission allowances while ensuring uninterrupted power supply, these enterprises must resort to strategies such as upgrading power plant technology, embracing clean energy generation methods, implementing carbon capture technologies, or engaging in carbon trading. These measures, while crucial for achieving emission reduction targets, inevitably inflate operational expenses.

A notable estimation suggests that when coal-fired power enterprises allocate 3% of their total carbon emissions to purchased allowances at a carbon price of 50 yuan/ton, their profits diminish by a substantial 2.8%. This significant impact on the financial health of coal-powered enterprises underscores the gravity of the situation, yet it fails to yield tangible results in carbon reduction. Should the proportion of carbon emissions requiring purchase by coal-fired companies escalate, the consequences could be dire. After all, coal-fired power continues to underpin China's macroeconomic stability for the foreseeable future.

Thermal power enterprises, a pivotal segment within the power generation sector, are already grappling with high debt levels and financial losses. The rise in costs will further exacerbate their production burdens. The volatility of carbon allowance prices, coupled with stricter allowance allocations and an increasing reliance on purchased allowances, will steadily intensify their operational pressures. For these enterprises, carbon emission costs are gradually transforming into a pivotal component of their overall production expenses. However, the limited marketization of the power industry hinders the seamless transfer of these costs to downstream entities.

Moreover, power generation enterprises face challenges in effectively transmitting carbon prices and managing their generation output. In most regions of China, the on-grid electricity price and selling price are still subject to government approval, rather than being fully determined by market forces. Consequently, the electricity price fails to accurately reflect the carbon price or the disparities in emission reduction technology levels and associated costs among different units. Additionally, power generation plans are formulated by the government, limiting the ability of enterprises to fully align their generation output with market demands. Given the intermittent nature of other renewable energy sources and their transmission capacity constraints, thermal power generation will continue to play a vital role in ensuring the secure supply of electricity for the foreseeable future.

The power generation sector is among the first batch included in the carbon trading, with the baseline method being employed in accordance with allowance setting and allocation plan approved by the State Council. Within this baseline allocation framework, power generation enterprises that excel in management and maintain lower emission intensities per unit product than the established baseline are poised to accrue surplus allowances. As the carbon market matures, companies generating greater volumes of electricity will receive proportionately more allowances, further amplifying their competitive edge. Moreover, the ongoing reforms in the electric power system are expanding the market landscape for generation opportunities. Conversely, enterprises with suboptimal management, less advanced technical equipment, and higher emission intensities per unit product compared to the baseline will likely face a shortage of allowances, potentially compromising their future market competitiveness. However, an intricate paradox arises due to the government-mandated power generation plans: enterprises with surplus allowances may be constrained from increasing output, while those without surpluses are obligated to meet their generation targets.

Currently, China's electricity market reform is progressing steadily, with the government advocating the gradual phase-out of power generation plans and the acceleration of market-oriented pricing for both the generation and sales sides of electricity. Nevertheless, the full realization of these reforms necessitates a gradual process.

4. Undue control of the coal-fired power industry may spark financial risks, adversely impacting the macroeconomic landscape

Ma Jun, a former member from the Monetary Policy Committee of People's Bank of China, cautioned during a Boao Forum briefing that if high-emitting enterprises and industries fail to cut their carbon footprint within the next three decades, they will have to be phased out, potentially triggering financial risks.

While this perspective invites scrutiny, Ma's rationale stems from the assumption that the transition to clean energy will diminish revenues for heavily polluting sectors, fostering a surge in non-performing loans. His team forecasts a dramatic rise in coal loan default rates of coal-fired power companies, from 3% today to an alarming 22% by 2030, posing a formidable challenge for the financial system.

In fact, numerous coal-fired power projects in China are still in their investment recoupment phase, amidst escalating electricity demand. Imposing stringent carbon reduction mandates on this sector could render decades of investments unviable, squandering trillions in capital with minimal return on investment and fostering high levels of bad debt, ultimately harming the macroeconomy.

China has the potential to strike a more harmonious balance. It can achieve carbon neutrality swifter, without jeopardizing the coal-fired power industry or the macroeconomy, by embarking on profound reforms in academic theories, policy frameworks, and carbon reduction mechanisms. Such endeavors necessitate groundbreaking innovations and advancements.

5. The lion's share of China's carbon reduction efforts lies beyond the coal-fired power sector

It is intriguing to note that despite the non-coal power industry's significant impact (80% weight) on carbon reductions of the coal-fired power sector and impact (90% weight) on carbon reductions of the whole society, it often escapes the spotlight in public discourse on carbon emissions. This underscores the inadequacy of our current scope in addressing carbon reduction.

As evidenced by the correlation analysis in Sect. 11.3.2.1, the non-coal sector's pivotal role in mitigating carbon emissions is undeniable. From a different vantage point, power generation serves as the cornerstone for production and macroeconomic development, with power generation enterprises assuming the pivotal role of ensuring the energy supply for the entire society. Furthermore, focusing solely on reducing electricity consumption to curb emissions, particularly through limiting GDP growth, could lead China into a trap set by developed nations. Conversely, if societal production enterprises can generate twice the GDP using the same amount of electricity, effectively halving the emission intensity per unit of GDP, this avenue for carbon reduction is more feasible and cost-effective than striving for a 50% reduction in emissions per unit of power generation. Similarly, if the same GDP is achieved with just half the electricity consumed previously, the power industry's output and emissions would correspondingly decrease by 50%. By embracing economic transition, fostering the digital economy and service sectors, we can significantly lower the carbon emission intensity per unit of GDP compared to that of traditional industries like construction, cement, and steel industries.

As previously mentioned, the technical potential for carbon reduction per unit of electricity generated in the power sector, as well as the cost-effectiveness of such reductions, are currently constrained. Nonetheless, there remains ample opportunity to diminish the carbon emission intensity per unit of GDP within social production enterprises. Notably, Chin's carbon emission intensity per unit of GDP stands at 2.3 times that of the United States and 3.5 times that of Europe.

Despite the intense focus on the domestic dual carbon agenda, the reality is that coal-fired power enterprises are already under immense strain, while organizations and individuals at large remain largely unburdened by direct pressure. This disparity constitutes a significant challenge in the ongoing pursuit of carbon neutrality.

It is crucial to recognize that carbon emission reduction efforts in the power sector cannot be isolated from the broader economic context. Carbon footprints of the power industry are intimately tied to the input–output levels and carbon intensity of various industries, highlighting the need for a holistic and dynamic approach to addressing emissions. A segmented or static perspective risks misdirecting our efforts and undermining progress towards a sustainable future.

The utilization of energy and the associated carbon emissions embody a comprehensive, chain-wide concept that transcends individual industries. Thus, carbon emissions should be holistically evaluated and distributed across the entire societal industrial chain. Designing an isolated carbon reduction policy solely for a pivotal sector within the broader macroeconomy would be misguided. Carbon reduction is a complex, systemic endeavor that cannot be tackled effectively by focusing solely on one link in the chain. China currently faces a predicament: achieving significant carbon reductions in the coal-fired power sector, which has limited room for improvement, necessitates accepting the potential consequences of stagnant economic growth and a decline in living standards.

China's carbon reduction efforts in the past two decades have proven this point. To address this challenge, a global and comprehensive mindset must guide the research and formulation of top-level strategies that effectively tackle the issue and accelerate China's progress towards carbon neutrality. However, the current top-level design and carbon reduction initiatives are misguided, characterized by enormous challenges, high costs, low efficiency, and substantial harm to the macroeconomy. Urgent changes are needed. Instead, we must embrace a strategy that promotes carbon reduction across entire industries, recognizing that such an approach can influence up to 80% or even more than 90% of overall carbon emissions. This holistic approach must be implemented efficiently and cost-effectively.

Therefore, it is imperative to recognize that focusing solely on carbon reductions in the coal-fired power sector addresses less than 8%, or even less than 5%, of society's total carbon emissions. In contrast, implementing carbon reduction measures across society and all industries is more cost-effective and has the potential to impact over 90% of emissions. Consequently, we must swiftly reevaluate and restructure our current carbon reduction policy framework.

11.3.3 Carbon Market Limited to Coal-Fired Power Industry Can't Achieve Optimal Resource Allocation

The essence of the market mechanism lies in its ability to harness the invisible hand to efficiently balance and allocate social resources, often resulting in an effective distribution of market resources. However, in instances where market operations fail, the government intervention, albeit minimal, becomes necessary. This may involve formulating rules, defining initial rights and responsibilities, establishing markets, and overseeing operations. Yet, the government's capacity to artificially construct markets should not be overstated.

The carbon market is envisioned to drive carbon reduction from the most cost-effective sectors, as opposed to focusing solely on the most expensive ones like thermal power. This approach minimizes the loss of social welfare during the decarbonization process. Currently, the carbon market primarily engages the coal-fired power industry, a strategy that promotes carbon reduction at a disproportionately high cost, leading to significant macroeconomic and social welfare losses, and an imbalanced input–output ratio.

The impact of carbon market on resource allocation within the coal-fired power industry alone is limited, with the actual costs far outweighing the benefits. For the carbon market to truly flourish, it must adopt an efficient and cost-effective method of involving social organizations and individuals, thereby achieving superior outcomes. Unfortunately, due to limitations in the current foundational theories of carbon emission reduction and issues within the top-level design, the current mechanism fails to accurately trace the carbon footprints of numerous industries and enterprises, hindering the expansion of carbon reduction efforts. Consequently, the current carbon market mechanism struggles to fulfill its potential.

Currently, the trading markets for carbon emission rights, involving around only the coal-fired power industry, are largely artificial constructs based on a misguided and simplistic interpretation of Coase Theorem.

While the Coase Theorem holds immense value in suggesting that markets with clearly defined property rights and low transaction costs can surpass government taxation in achieving optimal resource allocation. The core essence of Coase Theorem remains pivotal in guiding government policies aimed at carbon reduction, serving as the cornerstone of such initiatives.

However, when it comes to decarbonation, the straightforward application of the Coase Theorem is inadequate. In the context of climate change, the notion of "property rights" within this theory cannot be equated solely with "carbon emission rights". Similarly, the concept of an "effective low-cost market" does not automatically translate to a singular carbon market focused solely on the coal-fired power industry. Coase Theorem, while insightful, did not anticipate the intricacies of regulating carbon emissions. Regarding carbon emission public goods, some experts erroneously equate property rights with carbon emission rights and envision a carbon market confined to a single or a few industries. This is a superficial understanding that fails to grasp the full potential and complexity of carbon markets.

It is crucial to acknowledge that the theoretical foundation for establishing carbon markets stems from the Coase Theorem, which advocates for the efficient allocation of social resources through the clarification of property rights and low-cost market transactions. Carbon markets are designed to minimize the impacts on macroeconomy and social welfare while achieving cost-effective carbon reduction through pricing and trading mechanisms.

Unfortunately, China's current carbon market operates contrary to its intended purpose.

The dominance of planned economy in China's electricity pricing system hinders the effectiveness of carbon market in the industrial front end. In contrast, the market-oriented power markets in Europe and the US enable carbon pricing to drive social carbon reduction through market mechanisms. Currently, the carbon markets in China not only undermine the macroeconomy but also contradict the original intentions of the government.

Given China's unique circumstances and the characteristics of the carbon market, addressing the social cost of carbon emissions through the backend industrial chain and consumer side would be more efficient, be it through carbon taxes or carbon markets. While the book advocates for carbon markets over carbon taxes, it suggests transitioning from a coal-industry-focused carbon market to a comprehensive "negative carbon" market encompassing the entire society and industry.

Carbon emission is a public good that transcends time, space, and is inherently large-scale and complex. Neither Pigou nor Coase, in their time, fully anticipated the scale and intricacies of carbon emissions. Governments must build upon their legacies and innovate to tackle the pressing issues of emissions and climate change.

11.3.4 Decarbonation Strategy for the Coal-Fired Power Sector Within the CELM

Within the CELM, coal-fired power enterprises, unlike those in carbon-intensive industries like coal mining, oil, and natural gas, are not the primary targets of carbon mitigation efforts. Instead, they are just a link in the industrial chain, necessitating neither dedicated government resources for specific regulation nor the establishment of a standalone carbon market.

By integrating carbon emission costs into their power products through the CELM-based carbon ticketing mechanism, coal-fired power enterprises engage in free-market bidding alongside green energy sources like photovoltaic and wind power, adhering to the principles of free competition. This approach emancipates coal-fired power from the shackles of planned carbon emission controls and lifecycle management, allowing its market life to be solely dictated by demand dynamics and competitiveness after bearing carbon costs. Amidst the current challenges posed by carbon reduction policies across the power generation landscape, the CELM-based carbon liability framework thoroughly liberates the coal-fired power sector, enabling it to sustainably contribute to national economic growth, enhance industry returns, and optimize market resource allocation for societal welfare gains.

It is crucial to recognize that the CELM does not alleviate the carbon reduction pressures from the sector. Rather, it intensifies them amidst the competitive landscape shaped by zero-carbon-cost green energy sources.

The CELM-based "1+1" system introduces carbon emission costs into power products in a measured fashion, distributing these costs across the entire industrial chain. This strategy gradually alleviates the burden on fossil fuels and provides coal-fired power enterprises with an extended adjustment period. In contrast to carbon emission right systems, which can introduce market disruptions and confusion, the CELM approach ensures a smoother transition.

Moreover, the CELM "1+" system, without the implementation of subsidy policies, strengthens the price advantage of green, renewable energy sources, thereby accelerating the natural substitution of fossil fuels. This process unfolds gradually, avoiding abrupt energy transitions and revolutionizing the energy landscape with a high degree of marketization. Notably, this approach minimizes administrative intervention, reduces the management burden on the government, and mitigates decision-making risks and corruption concerns within policy implementation bodies.

11.4 Impacts on Imports and Exports

The varying carbon emission reduction mechanisms and the substantial disparities in carbon pricing and tax policies across nations significantly influence the global import and export landscape.

1. Effect of domestic carbon tax or carbon pricing on exports

Experts contend that if China were to implement a carbon tax policy, its consequences on exports would be profound. For instance, at a carbon tax rate of 200 yuan/ton, the power sector would experience an export change rate of -13.88%, while the construction sector would witness an export change rate of -5.64%, particularly impacting steel and aluminum products drastically. Other industrial sectors would also be affected to varying degrees, with huge overall impact. Furthermore, as the carbon tax rate escalates, the total export change rate steadily diminishes, showing a negative linear correlation. The calculations reveal that a carbon tax in China would have a severe negative effect on economic growth, presenting an unfavorable policy framework. This, coupled with other factors, explains why China, like many other nations, has yet to adopt a carbon tax policy.

2. The EU CBAM's Impacts on Imports and Exports

Chinese enterprises are poised to confront challenges akin to the European Union's CBAM, which is set to commence operations in 2023. This mechanism stipulates that products from nations lacking a comparable carbon price and aiming to export to the EU will be levied at the prevailing price of EU carbon market. Currently, the price in EU carbon market is approximately tenfold higher than China's, underscoring the potential severity of the impact if the Chinese government and exporters are unprepared. International carbon tariffs are poised to become a pivotal factor influencing China's exports in the future, with the US *Clean Competition Act* already signaling a similar trajectory.

Nonetheless, the EU's CBAM is not an insurmountable challenge. By anticipating and responding appropriately in line with the CELM, China, as a major exporting nation, stands to benefit.

3. Impacts of China's carbon tariffs on imports

China's substantial import volumes, particularly of fossil fuels like oil, natural gas, and coal, contribute significantly to carbon emissions, thereby impacting its journey towards carbon neutrality. In the context of the accelerated process of the EU CBAM and the G7 Climate Club mechanism, China must prioritize developing its own carbon tariff scheme. Adhering to the CELM principles, the achievement of carbon neutrality within a nation is intimately tied to the management of carbon emissions associated with the import and export of goods. Hence, China necessitates the establishment of a comprehensive carbon emission management system and an import–export carbon tariff regime to bolster its carbon neutrality aspirations and mitigate losses stemming from carbon leakage.

11.4.1 Impacts on China's Exports

The combined influence of domestic CELM-based Decarbonation System and the EU CBAM mechanism significantly impacts export trade. In the realm of carbon reduction, export enterprises and their products must adhere to the stringent standards of both frameworks, encompassing CEL data and offset requirements. This poses heightened challenges for exporters. Fortunately, the CELM offers robust support in managing CEL data and offsets, empowering Chinese export enterprises to transform potential pressures into growth opportunities.

11.4.1.1 Addressing the EU CBAM

The EU CBAM mechanism mandates that imported goods carry the carbon emission cost equivalent to the price level in the EU carbon market (ranging from 80 to 100 euros per ton), contingent upon the provision of credible carbon footprint data. Without an adequate domestic system in place, China's exports to the EU risk significant disruption.

The timely implementation of the CELM emerges as a pivotal strategy for Chinese exporters to navigate the EU CBAM. It not only serves as an effective countermeasure but also enhances the international competitiveness of Chinese exports.

A cornerstone of this strategy is leveraging the CTMS to furnish reliable carbon footprint data. By offering authoritative and accurate carbon footprint information provided by the CTMS, Chinese exporters can mitigate potential non-tariff barriers. Notably, China's current system in this area is inadequate and costly, highlighting the urgency for improvement. The accounting of carbon footprint data is related to the scope of carbon emissions of the product. The CTMS coverage, spanning Scope 1 to Scope 3 of the *Greenhouse Gas Protocol*, ensures the provision of precise and comprehensive data, thereby strengthening China's position in the global export market.

Secondly, China's export products offset their emissions domestically. Chinese export enterprises can adopt the role of end consumers or retailers, acquiring "International Negative CO_2" to mitigate their emissions in the CNTM, thereby aligning with internationally recognized carbon pricing standards and transforming their products into "zero-carbon products". In this way, there is no loss of domestic GDP. China's exports have achieved carbon offsetting at home, and carbon tariffs on Chinese exports cannot be charged twice according to the EU CBAM. Furthermore, paying for carbon emissions in China is of course more conducive to enhancing the wellbeing of the Chinese people.

The EU CBAM adheres to three fundamental principles for carbon border regulation:

1. Uniform treatment for all imported goods under the CBAM framework.
2. Exemption from carbon levies if the required carbon price is already paid in the exporting country.
3. Ensuring that no product is subjected to multiple carbon emission charges in international trade.

China's CTMS can furnish reliable carbon footprint data. By offsetting the CBAM-compliant carbon emissions within the domestic NCTM, exported products can then enter the EU market without facing additional carbon tariffs.

The stringent and arguably unjust carbon pricing rules under the EU CBAM necessitate bilateral negotiations or multilateral discussions facilitated by the International Trade Organization. In contrast, the "International Negative CO_2" pricing mechanism under the CELM presents a more equitable alternative.

Undeniably, mechanisms akin to CBAM pose challenges to the cost competitiveness of Chinese exports. To mitigate the impact of carbon fees (or tariffs) on the competitiveness of our exports, the following initiatives are crucial:

Firstly, enterprises must expedite the innovation of decarbonation technologies to minimize carbon intensity. For instance, Turkey's steel products boast a carbon content less than half of China's, necessitating China's swift catch-up. It is imperative for Chinese enterprises to align their carbon intensity per unit output with international benchmarks as soon as possible, given that high-carbon products and industries are swiftly being phased out, and this trend is only intensifying. As a manufacturing giant, China still has a long journey ahead, and the Chinese people must strengthen their efforts. A lower carbon content per unit for each product will increasingly emerge as a hallmark of manufacturing powers.

Secondly, efforts to reduce carbon emissions must encompass the entire supply chain, adopting a holistic approach rather than focusing on isolated links. Currently, domestic carbon emissions monitoring primarily covers around 2000 coal-fired power enterprises, which is inadequate for fostering a low-carbon industrial chain as a whole. The CELM offers a valuable policy instrument that can propel the entire industrial chain towards accelerated carbon reduction.

Thirdly, the government must provide robust policy support. Leveraging the carbon fees collected, the government can offer preferential value-added tax and income tax rates, thereby minimizing the total cost of domestic export products.

11.4.1.2 Redefining the International Carbon Tariff Landscape

Amidst the impending universalization of carbon tariffs, if the CELM, which advocates "consumer liability", gains global acceptance, if China's industrial production technology progresses rapidly, advancing the carbon emission intensity of various industries globally, and if the international community generally raises the international carbon price and improves the internalized emission cost of products, imposing and raising carbon tariffs is beneficial to China. As a significant manufacturer and net exporter of carbon emissions, China issues numerous carbon output tickets, enabling it to collect substantial carbon fees from foreign consumers, significantly augmenting fiscal revenue.

Scholarly estimates reveal that China is a net exporter of "carbon emissions" in international trade. In 2018, China's exported products generated 1.53 Gt of embodied CO_2 emissions, while imports accounted for 542 Mt, with net foreign trade CO_2 emissions comprising approximately 10.5% of the country's total. Notably, exports to the EU contributed 270 Mt of CO_2 emissions, representing 17.6% of China's total export carbon emissions, while the embodied CO_2 emissions of goods imported from the EU are 31 Mt.

In response to the EU's CBAM, which aims to impose carbon tariffs on imported products, it is evident that Chinese government departments and academia have yet to grasp its principles, leading to opposition and even legal prosecutions at the International Trade Organization. Rather than resisting, China should harness CBAM to increase revenue figuring out how it works.

China, as a prominent production exporter, imposes carbon fees on consumer nations, distinguishing its approach from the EU's CBAM, which levies carbon tariffs. This constitutes two distinct logical frameworks. China's rationale, rooted in the CELM theory, claims that consumers shoulder not only the production costs but also the associated carbon emission costs of goods. Usually, the costs are charged by the producing country in accordance with the market mechanism. In contrast, the EU's logic stems from the premise that its high carbon pricing triggers "carbon leakage", resulting in regional investment and tax spillovers. Consequently, the CBAM aims to recover losses by collecting carbon fees from countries with lower carbon prices, thereby incentivizing them to hike their carbon pricing and intensify emission reduction efforts. Notably, the EU CBAM exempts imports that already bear equivalent carbon costs in their country of origin, offering China an opportunity to safeguard its export interests through strategic arrangements.

If China were to implement the CELM, ensuring that all exports have undergone offsetting by "International Negative CO_2" at a specified price level within China and exporters could provide comprehensive, precise, real-time carbon footprint data through the CTMS, the EU would be unable to levy taxes on Chinese exports. Moreover, since the EU CBAM treats imports uniformly regardless of origin, the competitiveness of Chinese products remains the same, enhancing both government and exporter profits while EU consumers ultimately bear the carbon costs. However, it's crucial to acknowledge that if China's export products exhibit higher carbon emission intensities than global standards, necessitating steeper internal carbon costs than competitors, this could erode our price competitiveness, potentially leading to market exclusion. This underscores the need for strong low-carbon capabilities in the export sector, as the new green and low-carbon market mechanism swiftly eliminates those with intensive carbon.

Therefore, the Chinese Government, businesses, and academia must thoroughly figure out the underpinnings of international carbon liability and border regulation mechanisms, crafting proactive responses. Amidst a global push for intensified carbon reduction and early achievement of carbon neutrality, China, as a significant net carbon emitter, stands poised to capitalize on rising international carbon prices. Urgent priorities include: firstly, establishing a robust CELM-based decarbonation system aligned with global climate solution; and secondly, bolstering industrial technological capacities to drastically reduce carbon intensity and forge new competitive edges.

In summary, it is profoundly unjust for manufacturing nations involved in international trade to solely shoulder the environmental consequences and governance expenses associated with carbon emissions, while also being compelled to pay carbon taxes to importing countries. The CBAM, which imposes carbon tariffs under the pretext of preventing carbon leakage and ensuring fair competition, falls short in transparency regarding the utilization of carbon tariffs and fund ownership, thereby compromising its purity. By including certain private purposes, the CBAM risks being misinterpreted by the global community as a measure aimed at safeguarding cost competitiveness of domestic enterprises rather than genuinely reducing carbon emissions. This deviation from the core objectives and scope of carbon reduction efforts has led to perceptions of trade protectionism. Ideally, revenues generated from CBAM-like mechanisms ought to be exclusively invested in carbon reduction initiatives within exporting nations, rather than being treated as standard tariff revenue, as is currently the case.

The CELM, a consumer liability mechanism, advocates for a more equitable distribution of the CEL, where Western consumer nations assume a proportionate share for imported products. By adopting the CELM, a fair and reasonable mechanism for addressing carbon emissions in international trade can be established, thereby enhancing global efforts to reduce emissions. This transition necessitates a substantial increase in China's influence on climate-related issues and a proactive role in shaping the rules of the carbon economy. China should leverage legal arguments, actively promote the concept of consumer liability, and rally developing nations to advocate for the establishment of a more equitable CEL mechanism.

Given the evolving landscape of a global carbon pricing system, developing nations will inevitably face a heavier burden in reducing carbon emissions. Consequently, a mechanism for transfer payments to these countries, facilitated by the United Nations or the World Trade Organization, is imperative. While previous initiatives like the US$10 trillion Climate Finance Fund have failed to deliver tangible results due to their reliance on donations, the modest progress made at COP27 underscores the need for more effective solutions. A system where developed nations invest in green projects in exporting countries, based on imported carbon emissions and international carbon prices, could address inter-country financial transfers, incentivize developing nations to reduce emissions, and serve as compensation for historical over-emissions of developed nations. This innovative mechanism holds immense potential and merits serious consideration by the United Nations and the World Trade Organization.

11.4.1.3 China's Exports and Carbon Neutrality

Approximately 10% of China's total carbon emissions are embodied in its exported goods, underscoring the significance of international carbon neutrality standards, domestic carbon reduction systems, and foreign carbon tariff mechanisms on China's pursuit of carbon neutrality.

In the long term, China's exports will confront three distinct scenarios in importing countries.

The first scenario envisions a scenario where the EU and G7 nations impose stringent carbon tariff thresholds, complemented by comprehensive carbon emission reduction frameworks. In this context, Chinese export enterprises leverage the CELM system to facilitate carbon offsetting within the domestic carbon market, effectively transferring the burden of carbon emission costs to consumers in importing countries. Given the current EU carbon pricing, "Real Negative CO_2" offsets suffice, genuinely neutralizing the carbon footprint of exported products. This not only aligns with China's pursuit of overall carbon neutrality but also implies that consumers in the importing country primarily shoulder the liability for China's export-related emissions.

For Chinese exporters, a competitive edge in carbon emission intensity compared with that of international suppliers can bolster product competitiveness and export volumes, thereby enhancing China's overall export performance. Conversely, a lack of such advantage may lead to market exclusion due to high costs, curbing export volumes. The future landscape of export competition increasingly revolves around low-carbon, green, and high-quality standards.

The second scenario features a reduced carbon tariff coupled with an enhanced decarbonation mechanism. Here, exporters could purchase "International Negative CO_2" domestically for offsetting purposes, ensuring that the CEL does not shift to importing countries. This approach intensifies domestic carbon neutrality challenges while still involving consumers in the importing country in emission cost-sharing.

In the absence of a carbon tariff system and effective reduction mechanisms (third scenario), China faces two strategic options if an international CEL mechanism is established based on the CELM system: One is to adopt a rigorous standard, offsetting all exports by purchasing "Owing Negative CO_2" domestically, thereby retaining the CEL within China and augmenting domestic carbon neutrality efforts. This approach capitalizes on China's robust and unified CELM, simplifying operations and underscoring its climate commitment. Alternatively, China may choose not to domestically offset emissions from exports, but to transfer carbon liability to importing countries, reducing total costs of the exports but compromising on climate liability and complicating domestic CELM operations, potentially hindering the effective implementation of carbon reduction measures.

The book advises that all domestic exports should at least offset their emissions by purchasing "Owing Negative CO_2" domestically.

11.4.1.4 Impacts of the CELM and Carbon Tariffs on China's Export Landscape

Amidst the global push for carbon neutrality, fueled by the EU's CBAM and the G7 Climate Club initiatives, an international carbon tariff system in trade is poised to take shape. This mutual influence of China's domestic CELM with the international carbon tariff mechanism will profoundly shape the trend of China's export landscape, exhibiting the following distinct features.

Firstly, the advent of an international carbon tariff system exerts a neutral yet decisive influence on China's export performance, contingent upon the quality and sustainability of its export industry. Low-carbon, cost-efficient, and high-quality exporters will gain a competitive edge, enhancing profitability and expanding market share. Conversely, those with high carbon footprints and cost disadvantages may experience a decline in exports or even market exit.

Secondly, China stands to generate significant carbon fee revenues from exported goods. It is imperative that these funds be wisely invested in bolstering high-quality industrial development and fostering competitive advantages, while meticulously avoiding simplistic subsidies that could attract international trade sanctions.

Thirdly, the structural transformation of China's export sector will be pronounced. A surge in exports from low-carbon, high-quality industries will be anticipated, while high-carbon, low-quality sectors will witness a notable decline in total exports. This will necessitate a substantial readjustment of China's overall export portfolio. Both the Chinese government and exporters must act swiftly to accelerate the transition towards low-carbon, green, and high-quality development.

11.4.2 Impacts on China's Imports

The implementation of the CELM will profoundly reshape China's import landscape, facilitating a more balanced mix of imported goods and accelerating progress towards carbon neutrality goals.

11.4.2.1 CEL in Imported Products

With the implementation of the CELM, regulatory authorities and customs must view all imported products as potential carbon emitters and meticulously process their CEL data. This approach is vital for mitigating the impact of imported goods on China's carbon neutrality.

1. China takes the lead in implementing the CELM. In cases where the exporting enterprise can furnish credible carbon footprint data, this information will be incorporated into the CTMS. Conversely, if reliable data is unavailable, the CTMS

standards will be applied, with gradually escalating controls to prevent significant carbon leakage.

2. When both parties establish a mutually trustworthy CTMS framework grounded in CELM principles, they can directly share dynamic and precise product carbon footprint data.

This enables regulatory authorities to compare and analyze carbon footprints of imported versus domestic products, promptly addressing any discrepancies or anomalies.

11.4.2.2 Implementing Carbon Tariff Measures

Amidst the global push for carbon neutrality, mechanisms like the CBAM in the EU and the G7 Climate Club are poised to become prevalent trends. China should promptly follow suit by establishing a comprehensive carbon tariff system, which will serve the following pivotal roles:

1. Mitigating and controlling imported CEL: By levying carbon tariffs, we can ensure that imported products shoulder a fair share of carbon emission costs, commensurate with domestic products. This strategy effectively curtails the overall liability of imported carbon emissions, thereby fostering a more eco-friendly and low-carbon import portfolio.
2. Ensuring fair competition and shielding domestic industries: One cornerstone of CBAM legislation is preventing carbon leakage, safeguarding equitable competition for domestic enterprises, and mitigating business and tax outflows.
3. Generating revenues and increasing consumer expenditure: While the government's tariff revenue will increase, the carbon tariff will inevitably be factored into the total cost of goods, leading to a rise in consumer prices for imported items. Notably, given the high energy consumption and discretionary nature of imported products, their impact on low-income households is relatively muted. Over time, as the CELM and carbon tariff mechanisms are globally adopted, a new equilibrium will emerge between national carbon tariff revenues and residents' carbon emission costs.

11.4.2.3 China's Imports and the Pursuit of Carbon Neutrality

China's imports are not only substantial but also characterized by a high carbon footprint, particularly in the realm of fossil fuels such as coal, oil, and natural gas. In 2022, China imported 508 million tons of crude oil, with an import dependency rate of 71.2%, and 152.07 billion cubic meters of natural gas, amounting to a 40.2% import dependency. Moreover, in 2018, the embodied CO_2 emissions from China's imports totaled 542 million tons, accounting for 5.7% of the overall carbon emissions that year.

Drawing on the consumer liability principle inherent in the CELM and the criteria for a carbon–neutral nation (detailed in Sect. 9.3.2), China will shoulder the CEL for its imports. Consequently, controlling the carbon footprint of imported products is a vital component of the national carbon reduction strategy, warranting heightened attention.

By implementing the CELM and carbon tariff measures, China can effectively mitigate and manage the CEL associated with imported carbon emissions, thereby advancing its ambition towards achieving carbon neutrality.

11.4.2.4 Impacts of the CELM and Carbon Tariffs on Chinese Imports

Amidst the global push towards carbon neutrality, propelled by the EU's CBAM and the G7 Climate Club initiatives, an international carbon tariff system for trade will be established. When coupled with China's domestic CELM carbon emission reduction framework, this dual force will reshape China's import landscape in profound ways.

Firstly, the combined influence of the CELM and the carbon tariff mechanism will significantly mitigate China's import-related carbon footprint, aligning with its aspirations for carbon neutrality. As China surpasses the middle-income trap and consumption levels continues to rise, the potential for import growth remains substantial. Effectively managing the transfer of the CEL associated with imported goods will not only bolster China's domestic efforts but also contribute significantly to global carbon neutrality efforts.

Secondly, the Chinese government will garner additional revenue through carbon taxes imposed on imported products. This revenue stream should be allocated strategically:

1. Revenues from developed countries: The carbon tariffs levied on imports from developed nations can be directed towards funding green transformation initiatives within China. Given their higher liability for emission reduction, there is no rationale for returning these tariffs to their source countries.
2. Revenues from developing countries: In accordance with the consumer liability principle in the CELM, these revenues should be invested in their green transitions. This approach underscores China's commitment to equity and underscores its significant role in addressing climate change.

Thirdly, China's import structure will undergo marked adjustments. Imports of low-carbon, high-quality products will surge, while those of high-carbon, low-quality products will dwindle considerably. This transformation will profoundly reshape China's overall import industry.

Moreover, the implementation of the CELM and carbon tariff systems will significantly accelerate the transition from fossil fuels to renewable energy sources. This will lead to a substantial reduction in the import of fossil fuels (oil and natural gas), curbing significant foreign exchange outflows and significantly enhancing China's energy self-sufficiency. Ultimately, these measures are of strategic importance for China's energy security.

11.5 Impacts on Finance

Green finance, particularly carbon finance centered around carbon assets, has emerged as a pivotal area in contemporary finance. Despite encountering some setbacks in recent years due to the complexities of the carbon trading market, carbon finance remains a highly anticipated event within the financial landscape. The colossal investments, measured in trillions of dollars, necessary for green transformation, coupled with the vast financial assets, are undeniably alluring. However, until now, these aspirations have largely remained theoretical, akin to gazing at reflections in a mirror.

"Carbon finance" is rooted in the evolving international climate policies. Its objective is to harness financial capital as a catalyst for enhancing environmental rights and interests. By leveraging financial instruments and methodologies, it facilitates the trading and circulation of carbon-related financial products and their derivatives on market-driven platforms, ultimately striving for low-carbon, green, and sustainable development.

Currently, the advancement of green and carbon finance faces significant hurdles, including the absence of an internationally recognized, credible standard asset, the intricacies involved in the creation and management of underlying assets, and the challenge of reconciling with macroeconomic conflicts.

The CELM presents a transformative solution, poised to alter the current predicament faced by green and carbon finance, ushering in a new era. By offering a novel, top-level design for the carbon market, robust data and institutional backing, and more refined product designs, the CELM lays the groundwork for the growth of green finance.

Should the CELM-based carbon unit system mature and successfully undergo pilot testing, it stands to revolutionize not only the entire financial industry but also global economic development and world peace, opening up unprecedented avenues for progress.

11.5.1 The CELM: Navigating the Financial Predicament

With China's financial assets totaling nearly 400 trillion yuan, the pursuit of the dual-carbon goal necessitates the reassessment of assets across industries and enterprises, while simultaneously leveraging green finance to explore new business horizons. The CELM emerges as a vital tool, capable of assisting international finance in overcoming its current predicament and forging new paths for development.

1. The CELM facilitates repricing and risk management of traditional finance

The CELM provides a framework that enables traditional financial institutions to effectively reprice assets and enhance risk management strategies, aligning with the evolving demands of the green economy.

The financial industry, as a pivotal sector supporting the real economy, is swiftly evolving by integrating the ESG framework and adapting to industrial shifts. This evolution aims to deliver more tailored, precisely priced, and financial services that align returns with risks.

The CELM emerges as a comprehensive, scientific, and quantitative assessment tool tailored for traditional finance. It meticulously captures changes in management quality, including cost change, competitiveness change, within traditional industries, empowering risk mitigation and value assessment for conventional business endeavors.

2. The CELM-based carbon market fosters the growth of green and carbon finance.

Witnessing an annual expansion, the trading volume of this negative carbon market is poised to reach substantial heights, ultimately tapering off as global carbon neutrality is achieved over approximately four decades. This transition period promises to significantly augment traditional finance through two primary avenues:

- Firstly, it introduces new increments, that is, increments of carbon asset trading and new increments of carbon finance. Currently valued in billions annually, the transition to a negative carbon market anticipates a leap into the trillions, unlocking vast potential for spot trading, carbon asset management, derivatives trading, and associated services.
- Secondly, it addresses the green financing needs arising from the transformation of traditional industries. Carbon neutrality and reduction efforts permeate every sector, organization, and household, necessitating a comprehensive green transformation of society. Traditional industries and enterprises, thus, require massive green finance support, creating immense opportunities for green financial interventions.

In conclusion, the early adoption of the CELM presents the international financial market with fresh opportunities and expansive development horizons. Urgent action by the global community is imperative to harness these benefits.

11.6 Impacts on Markets and Enterprises

The CELM fundamentally reshapes the competitive landscape of the market, ensuring that the carbon footprint of every enterprise becomes transparent and every enterprise is inseparable from the broader carbon reduction framework. This system strongly incentivizes enterprises to embark on carbon reduction efforts, leading to a profound transformation of both market and enterprise ecosystems, centered around the targets of carbon reduction and high-quality development.

Enterprises must adapt their business strategies and rebuild their core competencies to align with the new market dynamics, with green and low-carbon capabilities emerging as crucial differentiators. Failure to do so could result in elimination due to escalating costs and heightened ESG scrutiny.

11.6.1 Corporate CEL Data

Currently, several key emission-intensive enterprises find themselves constrained by the dual-carbon policy and carbon emission allowance system, where expansion is contingent upon carbon emission allowances. Consequently, they are reluctant to disclose operational carbon emission data to evade verification, resulting in three prominent issues: lack of initiative, inadequacy, and non-standardization in reporting. These issues, in turn, manifest as four key challenges: insufficient motivation for disclosure, preference for confidentiality due to regulatory concerns, absence of uniform disclosure rules and standards, and lack of carbon data auditing mechanism. However, the current system offers no viable solutions to rectify this situation.

The introduction of the CTMS based on the CELM represents a significant breakthrough. It enables the government to capture, analyze, and make transparent the carbon footprint of the entire society in real-time, accurately, and dynamically, all at minimal cost. This "System + Technology" approach presents a genuine and effective path forward.

Under the CELM, the government's regulatory focus shifts, with non-carbon-source enterprises, like coal-fired power and steel enterprises, receiving less attention, while carbon-intensive enterprises, such as coal, oil, and natural gas, become the primary target of regulation.

By implementing the CELM-based CTMS, organizations and stakeholders could gain access to comprehensive, dynamic, and real-time information on the carbon footprints of each material, product, and service, at low cost and with a high degree of fairness. This facilitates the rapid establishment of a societal system where all parties mutually supervise and drive carbon reduction efforts.

Within the CELM, carbon footprint data of enterprises is objective and real, which eliminates the need for enterprises to costly process and declare. Instead, they can focus their energies on enhancing management, reducing carbon emissions, and pursuing higher quality development.

11.6.2 Restructuring Enterprise Competitiveness

Within the CELM, fostering low-carbon practices emerges as the cornerstone of every enterprise's competitive edge.

Primarily, the cost factor comes into play, where carbon reduction translates into cost savings. Low-carbon enterprises under this framework can reap profits from selling "negative carbon", while high-carbon enterprises incur carbon offset expenses, creating a significant cost disparity. As carbon prices escalate, this cost gap widens, intensifying the pressure on high-carbon enterprises' survival.

Furthermore, the ethical imperative and brand enhancement derived from ESG reporting and societal transparency contribute significantly. In the pursuit of global carbon neutrality, successful ESG performance is vital for enterprises' growth, with ESG brand recognition becoming a crucial survival tactic. The CTMS provides real-time, precise, and dynamic carbon emission data, which significantly impacts market dynamics, augmenting the cost and ethical burdens on high-carbon emitters.

Thus, enterprises under the CELM must relentlessly pursue carbon reduction through management refinement, supply chain optimization, and technological innovations, aiming to attain the pinnacle of low-carbon industry standards to avoid market exclusion.

11.6.3 Reshaping the Market Ecosystem

The CELM establishes an unparalleled level playing field, grounded in objective and verifiable data, devoid of corporate manipulation. Enterprises no longer need to invest heavily in carbon footprint data or grapple with data integrity concerns. ESG reports in the future will rely solely on the CTMS-generated data, precluding arbitrary fabrication. Carbon neutrality status is solely determined by the system and data, unaffected by corporate self-promotion or industry associations.

This shift enhances the business environment for virtuous companies, which are granted unrestrained access to energy resources and freed them from carbon allowance constraints and power supply anxieties. The role of the government evolves from allocating allowances to leveraging market mechanisms to eliminate high-carbon capacities, fostering high-quality development.

Under the CELM, the government only needs to pay minimal regulatory expenses, and a healthier and more robust market ecosystem will emerge, thereby nurturing a superior institutional environment for high-quality economic growth.

11.7 Impacts on People's Livelihood: Household Income and Consumption

The government's paramount concern encompasses not only the macroeconomic implications but also the profound impact of carbon neutrality efforts on people's daily lives. In view of this dual consideration, the government tends to take cautious approaches when formulating policies, which results in the gradual pace of carbon reduction initiatives. While academic discourse might exaggerate certain pressures, it is prudent to acknowledge that the modest scale of current carbon reduction policies and their limited societal impact may fail to make residents perceive the influence on their income levels.

Given China's vast population of 1.4 billion, with total carbon emissions reaching 12.1 billion tons in 2022, an analysis reveals insightful figures. According to statistics from developed countries, residential consumption accounts for 80% of emissions, and then carbon footprint of each resident will be approximately 6.9 tons annually: $121 \times 80\%\ 14 = 6.9$ ton/person. Applying domestic and international carbon prices, 50 yuan/ton domestically and 80 euros/ton in the EU, yields a range of potential carbon fees per person, from 345 yuan to over 4000 yuan, respectively. Even if China's carbon price escalates to 200 yuan/ton, as some scholars predict, the annual carbon cost per person would still be manageable at 1380 yuan, representing a median figure within affordability thresholds.

For a family of four, this translates into an annual carbon cost ranging from 1380 yuan to over 16,400 yuan, based on extreme scenarios. It is clear that the EU carbon price estimate is too high, and China does not need such a high carbon price to achieve carbon neutrality. Instead, a more feasible scenario based on a 200 yuan/ton carbon price suggests an annual household expenditure of approximately 5520 yuan. Importantly, this estimation overlooks potential favorable factors like accelerated green energy adoption and reduced CCUS costs, suggesting that the actual impact on household consumption and real incomes may be more tolerable. For low-income households, this estimated burden could pose challenges, necessitating complementary measures. Strategies such as enhancing tax systems, adjusting the distribution of household carbon allowances, and implementing progressive carbon pricing (as outlined in Sect. 6.3) with subsidies for per capita emissions below benchmarks, can help alleviate the financial strain while fostering equitable transition towards carbon neutrality.

The expenditure incurred by residents through the carbon fees, as analyzed previously, can be viewed as a vital input that significantly enhances the quality of life, yielding profound benefits. It not only improves air quality but also upgrades the overall standard of living and reduces the incidence of illnesses. Importantly, the carbon fees collected by the state are not solely a financial burden; a substantial portion of these funds is reinvested in the community through carbon markets and transfer payments, thereby enabling rural families in carbon removal provinces to augment their incomes. Furthermore, national green investments foster an increase in household incomes and job opportunities.

However, there remains a pervasive concern among individuals regarding the abrupt imposition of carbon fees and the sensitivity of such policies, fearing that they may elicit public resistance. To address this, some suggest offering free carbon tickets akin to clothes tickets, or food tickets in the past, only charging for exceeding a specified threshold. This approach is rational, and China must ensure that policies are implemented in a gradual and equitable manner.

11.7.1 Implementing a Household Carbon Account Mechanism to Mitigate the Impacts of Carbon Emission Reduction on Household Income

The government introduces a household carbon account mechanism within the CTMS, designed to meticulously track and record the carbon emissions of each household. This following two approaches aim to optimize carbon-related costs and benefits for residents, fostering a more compassionate and public-friendly policy framework that not only garners widespread support but also heightens awareness around carbon reduction efforts.

Firstly, a standard household carbon emission fee is imposed, accompanied by a tax rebate mechanism to mitigate the financial burden on households. By specifying the amount of carbon fee refunds per individual, this system incentivizes low-carbon lifestyles, potentially boosting the income of eco-conscious families.

Secondly, a tiered household carbon fee structure is established to discourage excessive consumption and generate additional revenue for carbon reduction initiatives. This mechanism comprises three tiers, with the base tier applying standard pricing. As per capita carbon emissions escalate into the second tier, the carbon fee doubles, and into the third tier, it multiplies severalfold or even exponentially.

The entire mechanism operates seamlessly within the CTMS, with annual settlement of household carbon account, similar to that of personal income tax.

The significance of the household carbon account mechanism transcends that of carbon-inclusive policies. Therefore, the government should prioritize its planning and development, as detailed in Sect. 6.3.

11.7.2 Case Study: Household Carbon Fee

Two retired professors from Tongji University, who now reside by their own, measured their household's annual carbon emissions. Their findings revealed that, inclusive of emissions from respiration, the total carbon footprint of their two-person household amounted to approximately 7.5 tons. This figure is notably below the societal average, attributable to their reduced activity levels and modest consumption habits.

When applying the domestic carbon pricing rate of 56 yuan per ton prevalent in 2022, the resulting annual carbon fee for the entire household calculates to 420 yuan. This amount poses a negligible impact on the living standards of these two educators (Table 11.1).

Table 11.1 Annual carbon emissions of a professor's household in Tongji University

Items	Carbon emissions
Electricity	3200 kg
Natural gas	500 kg
Breathing	1650 kg
Diet	1000 kg
Others	1000 kg
Total	Approximately 7.5 ton (daily emissions)

11.7.3 Summary

The CELM-based carbon fee system demonstrates a minimal negative impact on residents' welfare while fostering positive outcomes, thereby ensuring the policy's progressiveness. Consequently, the government's burden remains manageable, yet the intricate design of policy tools holds the key to its success, rendering it paramount. A shift in the mindset when devising current top-level design is imperative, advocating for the establishment of a CELM-based household carbon account mechanism that harnesses digital technologies for optimal results.

11.8 Impacts on Individual Consumption Habits

Central to the CELM lies the principle of consumer liability, whereby the end-user bears the financial burden. This framework anticipates a future where product pricing incorporates carbon emissions and associated fees, prompting a positive shift in consumer awareness and fostering proactive carbon reduction behaviors.

Acknowledging that consumption drives production, curbing excessive indulgence in energy-intensive products becomes paramount. Speculative investment in real estate sector contributes to the phenomenon of ghost cities, exacerbating both economic and environmental burdens. Multiple property ownership not only strains resources but also generates double carbon emissions: initially from construction materials and construction processes, and subsequently from operational activities.

Embedding carbon fees within product costs and transparently disclosing carbon footprints will impose both economic and moral restraints on consumers, guiding them towards more sustainable choices.

In the future, the price of all consumer goods will consist of three components: direct product prices, taxes and fees, and carbon fees. Manufacturers retain direct product prices to cover costs and generate profits, while the state collects taxes and fees to fund public services. Carbon fees are uniformly administered by national financial departments and invested in carbon reduction initiatives by environmental authorities. Given equivalent quality and specifications, consumers will tend to choose products with the lowest overall price, allowing the invisible hand of the market to propel a nationwide carbon reduction movement. This dynamic will encourage both consumers and manufacturers to pay close attention to daily carbon pricing, fostering a collective commitment to carbon reduction.

Raising public consciousness about low-carbon lifestyles is paramount for China to attain its dual carbon targets. Introducing household carbon accounts grounded in the CELM system represents a pivotal and efficient measure that reinforces consumption constraints, both financially and morally.

Currently, China's domestic carbon market revolves around the trading of carbon emission allowances, with the government allocating these allowances freely. By 2022, the trading price hovered around 56 yuan per ton, marking a stark contrast to the price range of 80 to 100 euros per ton in EU carbon markets, which is nearly tenfold higher. The prevailing domestic carbon price remains inadequately low, exacerbated by market inefficiencies such as the planned electricity pricing. Consequently, carbon emission cost can't be transmitted effectively, rendering that the front-end enterprises are heavily burdened with carbon emission costs yet plagued by instances of data manipulation, while back-end consumers remain largely unaffected. The carbon price fails to be included in the overall product cost, impeding its ability to effectively modulate consumer demand and foster a competitive environment on the supply side. In light of the "3060" dual carbon targets, it is imperative for the government to progressively align the "negative carbon" price with the actual cost of CCUS until they are equal.

11.9 Impacts on National Security and Taiwan Strait Situation

China's carbon neutrality goal not only has strategic significance for sustainable economic development and ecological optimization, but also for national security and Taiwan Strait situation.

11.9.1 Energy Self-Sufficiency: A Crucial Capability in Navigating Regional Wars

A pivotal insight concluded from the ongoing conflict between Russia and Ukraine underscores the paramount importance of energy and food security as the cornerstone for initiating and managing large-scale, modern regional wars. At the heart of this necessity lies the self-sufficiency rate, which emerges as the most vital factor. In the absence of robust energy and food security, no nation, regardless of its strength, wealth, or military capacities, can sustainably confront the challenges posed by a large-scale regional conflict.

Russia, despite its weakened economic position with a GDP of $2.25 trillion in 2022, which, in comparison to that of China, was merely one-eighth of its size and equivalent to that of Guangdong Province, has demonstrated a remarkable resilience in the face of adversity. While its military prowess, including weaponry and armed forces, may not be as formidable as in the past, Russia's response to the concerted hostility of the United States, NATO, and the G7 in the Russia-Ukraine conflict has been relatively calm. Furthermore, its domestic stock market has witnessed a notable upswing over the past year, attributable primarily to Russia's achievement of self-sufficiency in energy and food production.

11.9.2 The Significant Implications of the Russia-Ukraine Conflict

Over a year since the onset of the conflict between Russia and Ukraine, numerous domestic experts and government officials hold the belief that the EU's large-scale reversion to coal-fired power represents a departure from its commitment to carbon neutrality. They argue that the EU's previously radical stance on climate issues and carbon emission reductions was a strategy to mislead developing nations like China. Such reductions serve merely as a tool to suppress these countries.

This perspective, however, is short-sighted. Indeed, the primary lesson derived from the conflict for the international community and the European Union is the pursuit of enhanced competitive advantages and control over their circumstances, which includes exerting greater pressure on Russia. Most crucially, it underscores the importance of reducing dependency on Russian energy, specifically oil and gas, thus freeing the EU from its reliance on fossil fuels. Similarly, the EU's endeavors to bolster energy security align seamlessly with its aim of achieving carbon neutrality.

Following the onset of the conflict, while the EU temporarily revived coal-fired power plants to address immediate energy shortages, it simultaneously intensified its efforts to transition towards renewable energy sources and stepped up its carbon emission reduction initiatives. The EU's carbon price, which had plummeted to €25 per ton at the start of the conflict, has since rebounded to between €80 and €100 per ton. Moreover, the EU's CBAM has been legislated and implemented.

In reality, the Russia-Ukraine conflict has not weakened but rather bolstered the EU's resolve to reduce carbon emissions. It is essential to understand the core issues rather than being misled by short-term phenomena.

Furthermore, the Russia-Ukraine conflict has imparted significant lessons regarding energy security and national security to the global community.

Firstly, energy continues to be the central cause and instrument of regional conflicts. Given the substantial economic stakes involved, energy wields considerable influence over regional and national security dynamics. This paradigm of international competition has persisted for almost a century and remains relevant today. Concerning a nation's strategic security, energy independence and control are paramount. Without addressing energy security, regional conflicts cannot be effectively resolved through military means alone.

Secondly, the options for resolving conflicts among major powers remain entirely open, without any taboo areas. This situation poses the greatest uncontrollable risk to the international community since World War II.

Thirdly, solutions to energy security can be synergized with strategies aimed at achieving carbon neutrality. The shift away from fossil fuels required for carbon neutrality can significantly diminish the demand for imported fossil energy, thereby enhancing energy autonomy and control, ultimately improving the security of energy strategies.

11.9.3 The Second Front of the Russia-Ukraine Conflict: The Energy War

When the conflict between Russia and Ukraine commenced, there were two principal fronts: the main battlefield involving Russia and Ukraine, and the energy warfare front pitting Russia against the United States. At the outset of the conflict, Europe and the United States imposed joint sanctions on Russia, which included the seizure of Russian overseas assets, exclusion from the SWIFT banking system, and the closure of airspace routes.

Russia responded by leveraging its energy supplies to undermine the EU, compelling the EU to pay higher prices for oil and gas. This, in turn, initially benefited the Russian economy and led to positive performances in its stock markets. The United States seized this opportunity to supply oil and gas resources to the EU at prices several times higher than normal, inflicting political, economic, and military damage on Europe. This move also diminished the threat posed by the euro to the dollar and forced a substantial migration of European businesses and capital toward the United States.

11.9.4 Pressure of Energy Security on National Security

China faces greater threats to its energy security compared to the European Union. The situation across the Taiwan Strait exemplifies such challenges, where energy and food security stand out as the two most significant vulnerabilities. In 2022, China imported approximately 508 million tons of crude oil, representing a 1% year-on-year decrease, yet the level of external dependence rate remained high at 71.2%. Despite a decline in natural gas imports by 10.4% to 152.07 billion cubic meters in 2022, the external dependence rate still stood at 40.2%. These figures indicate that China's oil and gas resources are insufficient to sustain the continued economic growth, with crude oil import dependence surpassing the internationally recognized warning threshold of 60%.

China possesses coal reserves estimated at around 200 billion tons. Based on the current annual consumption rate of approximately 4 billion tons, these reserves offer roughly 50 years of recoverable capacity. When compared to the coal mining potential in the United States (240 years) and Russia (470 years), China's coal energy security reserves appear less favorable.

High dependence on fossil fuels poses significant threats to China's energy security, including supply shortages and risks of being controlled, unaffordable predatory pricing, and the logistical challenges associated with transporting large volumes of fossil fuels over extremely long distances. The strategic vulnerability known as the "Malacca Dilemma", along with current countermeasures taken by China, warrants deeper exploration.

11.9.4.1 The Malacca Dilemma and Chinese Actions

The Malacca Dilemma refers to the strategic vulnerability associated with the heavy reliance on the Strait of Malacca for maritime trade. The number of oil tankers passing through the Strait of Malacca to South China Sea (from Singapore to near Taiwan, China), is three times that of the Suez Canal and five times that of the Panama Canal. Consequently, any disruptions in these vital waterways could lead to short-term global or regional supply interruptions. The Strait of Malacca serves as China's "maritime lifeline". Any incident could severely impact China's energy security, creating what is known as the Straits Dilemma.

Currently, over 80% of China's oil imports transit through the Indian Ocean and the Strait of Malacca. With the continuous rise in China's crude oil consumption, the International Energy Agency (IEA) projects that by 2030, 80% of crude oil in China is dependent on imports. The scarcity of domestic oil and gas resources, coupled with the vulnerabilities inherent in these transportation channels, pose significant risks to China's economic, political, and military security. In recent years, these risks have grown, necessitating that China develop and implement long-term solutions to ensure energy security.

The onset of the conflict between Russia and Ukraine has heightened the urgency of the Malacca Dilemma, requiring the Chinese government to address energy security with utmost seriousness.

To mitigate the challenges posed by the Malacca Dilemma, the Chinese government has undertaken proactive measures. These include promoting the construction of the China-Myanmar oil and gas pipeline, the development of Gwadar Port project in Pakistan, and exploring projects such as the China-Russia-Kazakhstan canal initiative.

11.9.4.2 Reflections on China's Response to the Malacca Dilemma

China's various initiatives to address the challenges posed by the Malacca Dilemma will undoubtedly yield some positive outcomes. However, the extent to which these efforts will swiftly resolve the underlying issues demands significant investment and a prolonged period of observation.

Given China's current energy consumption structure, none of the aforementioned measures alone can fundamentally enhance China's energy security according to the traditional concepts of sufficient supply, secure transportation routes, and stable prices.

While diversifying transportation channels and constructing oil and gas pipelines can contribute to improved energy security, these solutions are not the most resilient, prone to disruption and reduced effectiveness. Nonetheless, these projects are still necessary steps considering the interplay of political considerations, regional economic impacts, and the direct costs and benefits of each endeavor. However, they must transcend mere energy transportation concerns and address the Malacca challenge holistically.

To better control energy security within its own hands, China faces challenges similar to those of the EU. The solution involves accelerating the transition from fossil fuels to renewable energy sources, significantly reducing the overall demand for fossil fuels. Additionally, expediting the construction of an energy Internet would help to mitigate the vulnerabilities associated with fossil fuel supply routes.

11.9.5 The CELM Significantly Enhances China's Energy Strategic Security

It is imperative for China to swiftly adopt the CELM to achieve a definitive shift from fossil fuels to renewable energy sources and the absolute replacement of oil and gas transmission with electricity via the Energy Internet. The security of China's energy strategy can be markedly improved in the following ways:

1. Significant reduction in fossil fuel demand

The deployment of the CELM will precipitously reduce the overall consumption of fossil fuels through an exceptionally efficient decarbonation framework.

First, the CELM integrates all organizations and households into the carbon emission reduction scheme, driving down the consumption of fossil fuels. A bidirectional incentive mechanism will motivate widespread participation in carbon reduction efforts, fostering high-quality development across industries, phasing out high-carbon emission products and enterprises, and encouraging a shift towards green energy among organizations and households.

Second, the CELM will effectively catalyze the growth of renewable energy. Under the CELM, the environmental costs of fossil fuel emissions are internalized. As carbon prices rise, the environmental and economic advantages of renewable energy will become increasingly apparent, accelerating the transition from fossil fuels to renewables. Much of the renewable energy production is situated in domestic deserts, barren lands, and neighboring countries, which limits the scope of control, shortens supply chains, and enhances security.

The synergistic effects of these two aspects will reinforce each other, ultimately reducing fossil fuel usage to less than 20% of total energy consumption.

By significantly diminishing China's total demand for fossil fuels, its reliance on foreign sources will decrease, thereby bolstering China's energy strategic security.

2. Replacing oil and gas transmission with electricity via the Energy Internet

The transportation of fossil energy relies on methods such as tankers, trains, and oil and gas pipelines, often spanning thousands to tens of thousands of kilometers. These modes of transport present large, visible targets and rely on singular pathways, making them highly susceptible to attacks, control, and sabotage both at sea and on land, thus compromising their safety and controllability.

In contrast, the Energy Internet utilizes Ultra-High Voltage (UHV) transmission lines to convey electricity. These lines are aerial, neither traversing seas nor buried underground, and can be monitored regularly using satellites and drones, offering convenience and low operational costs while significantly enhancing security.

3. Leveraging the Energy Internet to enhance energy security resilience

The Energy Internet employs a grid-based transmission system, enabling any region to be interconnected in all directions. Within this network, even if multiple nodes are compromised, ensuring the uninterrupted power supply to any area remains feasible. This resilience is analogous to the robustness observed in the information Internet, where network connectivity is the most secure and adaptable. Amidst an increasingly complex international landscape, transforming the power grid into an Energy Internet holds significant security and strategic value.

11.10 Impacts on China's Total CEL Accounting

Since China committed to its dual carbon goals to the international community, determining the specific target values for these goals has presented a significant challenge. What should be the peak carbon emission target? And what is the permissible total carbon emissions during the carbon–neutral era? Achieving carbon neutrality means reaching net-zero emissions rather than absolute zero. When China achieves carbon neutrality (net-zero emissions), actual emissions will need to be balanced with CCUS capacities. Thus, these two values are fundamental components of China's journey to carbon neutrality, yet there remains a lack of clear, authoritative international standards defining them. The ambiguity around these values is equivalent to lacking definitive goals for China's carbon–neutral process, underscoring their critical importance.

How precisely should these two values be defined? Currently, it is assumed that they represent China's net carbon emissions and actual total emissions at the time of achieving these targets. According to the CELM theory, these definitions require re-evaluation, and a new international standard should be established. Given that international trade involves significant flows of embodied carbon emissions, the relationship between these flows and carbon neutrality liability of each country must be clarified. In the current context, where European and American leadership shapes international climate policies, the "producer liability" system assigns liability based on the entity causing the emissions. However, due to the international division of labor fostered by globalization over the past decades, developing countries have largely assumed the role of producers and manufacturers. This means they bear a larger share of carbon emissions, exporting high-carbon, low-value-added goods to developed countries, and importing low-carbon, high-value-added products such as high-tech, knowledge-intensive, and financial services. While developed countries are consumer countries, exporting low-carbon, high-value-added products such as high-tech, knowledge-intensive, and financial services and importing high-carbon, low-value-added goods.

Imposing liability for territorial carbon emissions alone is inequitable. Such an approach also leads to suboptimal resource allocation from an economic standpoint, undermining global efforts to reduce carbon emissions and achieve macroeconomic Pareto optimality. This is because such a logic could result in market failures within the global climate economy. This is one of the key reasons why the CELM emphasizes a "consumer liability" mechanism.

As stated in Sect. 9.3.2.2, carbon emissions that a nation is liable for should be:

$$\begin{aligned} \text{a nation's CEL} &= \text{total actual CEL} \\ &\quad + \text{CEL imported from international sources} \\ &\quad - \text{CEL exported to other countries} \end{aligned}$$

wherein, the CEL associated with energy imports and exports are included in "CEL imported from international sources" and "CEL exported to other countries".

Once new international standards are established and implemented through the consumer liability mechanism, China's CEL could be reduced by approximately 1 billion tons annually, accounting for roughly 10% of the total, a comparatively large figure.

Current international rules attribute liability to producers, meaning Europe and the United States may be reluctant to accept a consumer liability framework. This presents a critical issue for future negotiations in the global climate forums. China should collaborate with other developing nations to advocate for the CELM and work towards establishing a new international standard for the CEL.

If the CTMS based on the CELM is established globally and its data interconnected, the accuracy, completeness, and timeliness of carbon footprint data exchanged between countries would be vastly improved, simplifying the settlement of carbon emissions among countries.

According to the CELM theory, a carbon–neutral country is one whose carbon emissions are fully offset through natural carbon removals and CCUS technologies, thereby attaining net-zero emissions. Nations achieving this status would fulfill their commitments to carbon neutrality.

11.11 Quantitative Analysis of the Economic Effects of the CELM

The use of computable general equilibrium (CGE) models to analyze the impact of carbon taxes and carbon prices has yielded numerous studies on the quantitative effects on the macroeconomy. However, the accuracy of these analysis methods remains limited. The global climate issue encompasses a multitude of influencing variables. Beyond the crucial factor of carbon pricing, there are numerous additional influencing factors, such as technological advancements, international carbon tariffs, CCUS costs, shifts in consumption preferences, and changes to the supply chain driven by events like pandemics. The multivariate correlations within complex systems are challenging to capture by using relatively simplistic modeling techniques, which fail to accurately reflect the intricacies of the real world. Each variable exerts a non-linear influence, and parameters often do not align with reality. As a result, the outcomes derived from traditional equilibrium model algorithms are seldom utilized in the design of policy instruments and can only be considered a quantified qualitative analysis that broadly aligns with the current state of affairs. This leads to a dearth of practical solutions offered by the economic academic community to policymakers.

Quantitative analysis of the impact of the CELM on various aspects of the macroeconomy is crucial, and there should be significant innovations to provide government decision-makers with more robust quantitative model support. Presently, the conditions for such innovations are gradually maturing.

In the era of big data and artificial intelligence, provided there is sufficient big data and macroeconomic data, we can bypass traditional economic modeling methods. By leveraging historical decarbonation and macroeconomic big data, advanced modeling techniques can be employed to analyze the correlations among various variables, predicting future trends with reduced modeling complexity. Advances in big data, machine learning, and neural network technologies might bring substantial changes to macroeconomic effect analysis.

Once such a system is established and operates continuously, government authorities will gain access to comprehensive, complete, and precise data. As years pass and big data accumulates, the challenges associated with analyzing the macroeconomic impacts of the CELM will differ markedly from the past. It will enable the full utilization of big data, machine learning, and neural network algorithms to conduct more accurate analyses of macroeconomic big data, such as evaluating the impacts of various factors on macro inflation, consumer interests, carbon tariffs, and regional interest adjustments.

With the implementation of the CELM, complemented by the CTMS, CARS, and CMTS which collectively form the "1+1+1" trio of big data systems, the analysis of the climate economy becomes far more manageable. These systems allow for daily data accumulation, providing a vast dataset that integrates the comprehensive impact of various factors. Results derived from time-series analysis become more realistic and can be fully utilized in the day-to-day management and application of policy instruments. Algorithmic tools based on these principles, supported by the CELM and other policy instruments, enable increasingly accurate big data model analyses and the integration of carbon pricing methodologies. Carbon price adjustments can thus be strategically deployed to achieve a balance among decarbonation progress, macroeconomic stability, consumer tolerance, and export trade dynamics. This allows data and systems to genuinely support macro-level decision-making, giving the government robust control over the decision-making process.

While the CELM does not prescribe explicit quantitative controls, it leverages carbon pricing to gently influence the broader economic system. Through the collection of extensive empirical data, the theory aims to progressively consider all aspects of the situation, thereby achieving carbon neutrality. Control over the carbon–neutral process will be strengthened as a result. Over the next four decades, as the accumulation of carbon footprint and related data grows, governments will be able to utilize a single carbon price to manage the transition to carbon neutrality, making increasingly accurate forecasts of macro impacts and enhancing control capabilities.

11.12 Climate Change and Current Economic Situation

Addressing the climate crisis is a paramount task for humanity today, one that requires the concerted effort of all nations and individuals, a true embodiment of a shared future for mankind.

Achieving carbon neutrality and resolving the climate crisis represents the greatest challenge and the most significant strategic opportunity for human society, and for China in particular. The global green transformation aimed at tackling climate change and achieving carbon neutrality is poised to become the world's largest emerging market. To become a central player in this transformative event is vital for China to seize the initiative.

Any organization or country that can lead humanity toward a genuine resolution of the climate crisis is destined to become a future global leader and wield considerable influence within the international community.

Fortunately, China holds a favorable card in the global climate game. Its photovoltaic, wind power, and other renewable energy industries boast absolute capacity and technological advantages. Moreover, China's expertise in Ultra-High Voltage (UHV) transmission technology, essential for constructing the Global Energy Internet, places it at the forefront of innovation.

Leveraging these green transformation strengths, as China progresses in solving climate issues and achieving global carbon neutrality, it should be guided by the principles of the CELM. The CELM-based Global Carbon Neutrality Solution must serve as the blueprint, requiring China to articulate its climate ambitions more prominently and boldly. This will garner the support and recognition from more countries, positioning China as a leader in the global effort to combat climate change.

11.13 Summary

In conclusion, the CELM exerts positive impacts on the macroeconomy, consumer ends, enterprises, import and export activities, and energy policies, demonstrating significant advantages over traditional policy instruments, such as carbon taxes, carbon emission rights, and carbon market.

From the analysis conducted throughout the preceding chapters, it is evident that the principles of the CELM are straightforward, and easy to be explained and understood. The international community stands to fully recognize the CELM for its fairness and efficiency in carbon reduction.

For instance, consider the ongoing reform of residential electricity policies. In 2022, the price was 0.6 yuan per kWh. The carbon emission factor of power industry in China was 0.853 kg CO_2 per kWh. If calculated based on the price of approximately 60 yuan per ton of CO_2 in the current carbon market, the carbon fee would add 0.051 yuan per kWh, representing an 8.5% increase on residential electricity costs. However, most households would receive rebates that would not increase their total annual expenditure. Adding a separate item that residents can afford would significantly enhance public awareness of carbon emission reduction. Power grid companies would be incentivized to procure the electricity with lowest costs (the sum of carbon tickets with generation costs). This would drive power plants to minimize their carbon costs when generating electricity, absorb carbon, or switch to renewable energy sources. Steel mills would similarly opt for low-carbon and low-cost power supplies, reducing emissions during steel production and potentially selling surplus carbon tickets. Consequently, car manufacturers purchasing steel plates would naturally seek qualified products at lower costs (inclusive of carbon fees). Carbon reduction across the entire industry chain can thus be effectively driven.

By adjusting the negative carbon price at the source, the government can mobilize society to reduce carbon emissions in the most effective manner and at a reasonable scale, contributing to carbon neutrality while the macroeconomy benefits positively. The CELM enables the government to leverage market mechanisms to reduce carbon emissions as much as possible, reducing reliance on subjective administrative planning, thus saving resources and effort.

China should intensify its efforts to promote the implementation of the CELM, fostering a shift towards a green and low-carbon economic growth model, encouraging a simpler and greener lifestyle, and promoting cleaner and more renewable energy consumption.

Chapter 12
The Necessity, Feasibility and Urgency of Implementing the CELM

The year 2021 marked the beginning of China's endeavor to meet the "3060" dual carbon targets. These targets are ambitious, challenging, and come with a tight deadline, particularly the "3060" carbon neutrality goal, which places increasing pressure on China. It is imperative for China to identify and expedite the implementation of an effective carbon reduction roadmap. In pursuing the "3060" dual carbon targets, the most critical element is the efficient design of top-level mechanisms. With a sound carbon reduction framework in place, the awareness of carbon reduction, the advancement of carbon reduction technologies, and the mobilization of substantial green transformation funds will naturally follow.

The CELM stands out among the various proposed climate policy instruments for its advantages in fairness, effectiveness, and international development potential. China should take the lead in refining the theoretical basis, optimizing the implementation plans, and accelerating the deployment and execution of the CELM.

12.1 Top Ten Breakthroughs in the CELM

The CELM and the Global Carbon Neutrality Solution represent a novel approach toward achieving global carbon neutrality. These developments hold significant breakthrough potential in multiple areas and offer renewed hope for attaining the optimal scenario of limiting global temperature rise to 1.5 °C by the end of the twenty-first century, as proposed by the IPCC.

Breakthrough 1 Reconstructing the fundamental theory of climate change economics and global carbon neutrality solution

Presently, the foundational theories employed by the international community to address climate change are rooted in traditional economic theories of external public goods. The theoretical framework guiding the design of carbon emission policy instruments largely hinges on the principles of the Pigouvian Tax and the Coase

B. Yang, *The Carbon Emission Liability Mechanism*,
https://doi.org/10.1007/978-981-96-3612-9_12

Theorem, leading to the derivation of two primary policy instruments, carbon taxes and carbon emission allowances, along with their various iterations. Given the evolution of carbon reduction practices over the past three decades, it is clear that these efforts have fallen short. The United Nations Climate Change Conferences (COP) have spanned nearly three decades yet remain fraught with challenges. Meeting the IPCC's goal of keeping global warming below 1.5 °C seems increasingly difficult.

The CELM accurately identifies the essence of the issue regarding carbon emission as a public good: carbon emissions constitute large-scale, complex public goods with negative externalities that span both time and space. These externalities can persist for periods ranging from decades to centuries, affecting populations globally rather than locally. The liabilities and impacts of carbon emissions encompass all societal organizations and individuals. The intricate mechanisms involved in reducing carbon emissions necessitate sophisticated mathematical modeling and computation. Consequently, traditional public goods theories (such as the Pigouvian Tax and the Coase Theorem) are inadequate for addressing contemporary carbon emission problems. The academic community must build upon the work of its predecessors to innovate new foundational theories.

The CELM posits that, following over three decades of international climate-related negotiations and collaborations, the current economic proposition concerning global climate change has evolved. Specifically, under clearly defined carbon emission reduction targets, based on the constraints of total carbon emissions (500 Gt after 2020) and the timeline for reaching net-zero emissions (by 2050) stipulated by the IPCC, the objective is to realize the dual carbon commitments of major nations. This necessitates seeking suitable pathways for decarbonation that optimize resource allocation and strike a balance between overall and partial benefits as well as a balance between efficiency and equity.

The CELM delves into the fundamental nature of carbon emissions as a public good (First Principles), proposing two postulates, seven consensuses, and deducing two assumptions along with three principles of carbon reduction management for society as a whole. This forms the solid foundation for constructing a new Global Carbon Neutrality Solution.

To tackle the genuine proposition of the climate challenge, based on the three principles of the CELM, we advocate for the implementation of a highly market-oriented global carbon neutrality solution, which represents the third way to address the global climate issue. This involves setting up two systems, the Global Decarbonation System and the Global Green Energy Supply System, and encompassing four sub-systems: the Carbon Ticket Management System (CTMS), the Negative Carbon Trading Market (NCTM), the Global Energy Internet (GEI), and the International Energy Trading Market (IETM). The aim of the Global Decarbonation System is to establish a mechanism of consumer liability, where the downstream entities of the industrial chain take comprehensive liability for the upstream entities. Utilizing digital technology capabilities, this system aims to create a comprehensive database for carbon footprints. By setting up a carbon market based on negative carbon, it offers negative carbon offsets to entities bearing the CEL. Furthermore, through the integration of carbon pricing, the societal cost of actual carbon emissions will be progressively internalized, thereby driving decarbonation across society and stimulating green technological innovation. The goal of the Global Green Energy Supply System is to establish a Global Energy Internet capable of deploying zero-carbon green energy on a 24-h basis worldwide. Through the International Energy Trading Market, all "zero carbon" green energy (offset by "International Negative CO_2") can be freely traded, achieving optimal resource allocation. The Global Decarbonation System accelerates the carbon reduction efforts of the international community, while the Global Green Energy Supply System expedites the substitution of fossil fuels. Both systems work in concert to speed up the realization of global carbon neutrality. This is the core idea of the CELM.

The CELM highlights the inherent flaws in the long-standing "polluter pays" principle pursued by the international community and underscores the necessity of implementing a "consumer pays" mechanism on a global scale. The CELM provides the most efficient and equitable methodological framework for addressing numerous critical issues surrounding global carbon neutrality.

Building on the CELM, we construct the most effective global carbon neutrality solution, a "1+1" system comprising the "Global Decarbonation System + Global Green Energy Supply System". These two systems complement each other as two facets of carbon neutrality. The former accelerates carbon reduction throughout society via a "purely soft" mechanism design, while the latter utilizes "core hard" infrastructure related to the Energy Internet to facilitate the efficient global supply of green energy and accelerate the phasing out of fossil fuels. This approach provides the international community with a genuine third pathway to global carbon neutrality that can achieve the target of limiting temperature rise to 1.5 °C set by the IPCC.

Breakthrough 2 Establishing a comprehensive, accurate, and dynamic database of the carbon footprint for the entire society

Currently, the international community faces three primary challenges in carbon emission reduction management:

1. Lack of a complete, accurate, and dynamic database for carbon emission factors of all product: There is no dynamic database for carbon emission factors across various industries, making program evaluation and policy instrument design challenging. Although numerous R&D teams are working on creating such databases, they lack effective methods and face issues such as high R&D costs, low-quality data, and impractical applications. Some rely on outdated data, while others merely replicate existing information domestically and internationally. Attempts to use blockchain for data management have encountered problems like data omissions, overlaps, and insufficient data volumes, failing to provide substantial value to society.
2. High costs and poor quality of carbon emission data inventory: Organizations emitting carbon face high accounting costs and poor data quality, making it difficult to prevent fraudulent activities. For coal-fired power plants entering the carbon market, repeated rounds of carbon verification add up to unsustainable implementation costs. Currently, despite the carbon market being relatively small, the industries of carbon inventory, carbon verification, and carbon reduction

certification consulting have grown significantly. Some institutions claim that it is necessary to train 200,000 talents for carbon inventories, with annual costs per person estimated around 200,000 yuan. This implies that labor costs alone would reach approximately 40 billion yuan annually, far exceeding the current trading volume of just a few billion yuan in the national carbon market. Such a market structure is unhealthy, imposing excessive social costs and potentially leading to significant welfare losses.

3. Challenges in obtaining carbon emission data and slow expansion of management scope: Despite China's nearly two-decade-long efforts to promote carbon emission reduction, only one sector (coal-fired power sector) has been integrated into the national management, primarily due to the difficulty in verifying corporate carbon emission data.

The CTMS based on the CELM can effectively resolve these three challenges. Supported by the self-operating and self-regulating CTMS, governmental authorities would only need to keep the carbon source organizations and carbon source data under control. Without requiring substantial governmental investment in supervision, a large database of digital carbon footprints could be established, featuring high data accuracy, coverage of all goods and services across society, and real-time dynamic updates.

With a carbon–neutral digital infrastructure like the CTMS, most of the challenges associated with governmental carbon management could be efficiently addressed.

Breakthrough 3 Proposing a new top-level design for the carbon market

The journey towards carbon neutrality and the current state of the carbon market are compelling a change of top-level design.

July 16, 2022 marked the first anniversary of the launch of the national carbon emission trading market. By July 15, 2022, the cumulative turnover reached nearly 200 million tons, with a cumulative transaction value of nearly 8.5 billion yuan. By the end of 2022, the national carbon market had seen a cumulative turnover of 230 million tons, amounting to a total value of 10.475 billion yuan. However, the trading volume, vitality, and incentive effects of the carbon markets have remained suboptimal.

Since the inception of the national carbon trading market, four significant issues have emerged: a lack of diverse participants, insufficient liquidity, an immature price transmission mechanism, and limited utilization of financial instruments.

The CELM aims to reconstruct the top-level design of China's carbon market:

The CELM introduces a novel top-level design scheme for the carbon market, constructing a negative carbon market framework that encompasses a unified national carbon market, two core trading objects (Real Negative CO_2 and Owing Negative CO_2), three market tiers, and four trading participants.

1. Transforming Carbon Emission Rights and CCER Markets into Negative Carbon Markets: This entails a fundamental redefinition of the nature of carbon markets.

2. Establishing a unified national carbon market: According to the CELM, it is essential to consolidate the carbon markets rather than decentralize them. Provincial and municipal carbon markets should merge into one national carbon market. The CCER carbon market does not need to be reconstructed.
3. Proposing two core trading objects: These include "Real Negative CO_2", "Owing Negative CO_2" and "International Negative CO_2" in special phases. The CELM could meet the offset requirements of carbon–neutral organizations, exporting entities, and carbon-emitting entities, including the investment needs of carbon assets.
4. Proposing pathway for constructing International Carbon Market: Developing a large-scale international carbon market presents a strategic opportunity for China. For the international carbon market to thrive, the trading objects must adhere to a uniform international standard. The "Real Negative CO_2" standard products proposed by the CELM provide the feasibility for swiftly building a vibrant international carbon market.

Through collaboration with the CTMS, the top-level design of the carbon market based on the CELM addresses current issues such as the market's small scale, insufficient liquidity, and the difficulty of verifying carbon data. The CELM can rapidly expand the scale of annual transactions from less than 10 billion yuan to trillions of yuan in transactions, a 100-fold increase. This enables all social organizations, individuals, and investors to engage with the carbon market from the outset.

Breakthrough 4 Establishing a more scientific and efficient method for carbon pricing

Internalizing the social costs of carbon emissions in a scientific and reasonable manner is paramount to addressing the temporal and spatial externalities associated with carbon emissions. The current carbon pricing method, based on social cost and carbon emission rights, is rooted in traditional economic models designed for simpler public goods, presenting numerous shortcomings and failing to address the myriad challenges of carbon pricing.

The CELM proposes a new Integrated Carbon Pricing Strategy (ICPS): Anchored in the objective of carbon neutrality, this strategy relies on comprehensive market information, leveraging market mechanisms as its primary tool. Utilizing complete carbon footprint big data and macroeconomic dynamic data, combined with the carbon neutrality process and macroeconomic carrying capacity, ICPS employs a big data modeling and intelligent analysis system to achieve more precise pricing. This innovative approach establishes a new methodology for pricing the external costs of large-scale, complex public goods with temporal and spatial externalities. The integrated carbon pricing strategy mitigates many drawbacks of traditional external cost pricing methods for public goods and introduces multiple advantages (see Sect. 8. 7 for detailed discussion).

Breakthrough 5 Solving the issue of carbon border adjustment mechanism for the international trade

International coordination on climate change stands as the greatest challenge to achieving global carbon neutrality. The traditional theoretical underpinning of "emitter pays" has significant flaws, skewing the direction of negotiations at the United Nations Climate Conferences towards competition over cooperation, yielding suboptimal results.

The CELM elucidates the internal logic of the CEL among nations. Grounded in the principle of a "consumer liability" mechanism, the Global Decarbonation System based on the CELM can adeptly address the issue of carbon tariffs between countries, providing a reliable framework for carbon data and emission cost-bearing plans. This can be achieved through regular negotiations on the "International Negative CO_2" price. The solution is straightforward, fair, efficient, and effective.

Breakthrough 6 Achieving positive macroeconomic effects through carbon emission reduction

The CELM internalizes the cost of every ton of carbon emitted, ensuring high fairness and significant emission reduction effects. The entire mechanism distributes carbon emission costs evenly across society, minimizing the competitive impact on businesses while rewarding high-quality production capacities with lower carbon emission intensities. This reduces overall costs, thus having minimal impact on the macroeconomy and social welfare. Notably, the effect of decarbonation on the coal-fired power industry is nearly neutralized, which is highly beneficial to the macroeconomy.

Under the CELM, organizations exceeding the industry average carbon intensity face increased pressure on their emissions costs, with immediate enforcement. Entities surpassing the average carbon intensity incur progressively higher carbon emission costs, effectively promoting the displacement of inefficient practices with superior ones, thereby fostering high-quality macroeconomic development.

Additionally, the revenue generated from carbon fees can be allocated to carbon emission reduction projects and carbon removal initiatives, as well as income redistribution to assist low-income groups. This would substantially enhance social welfare and yield better dual dividends. If these investments are directed towards energy and carbon removal provinces, inter-regional transfers could also be optimized.

Breakthrough 7 Mobilizing society-wide carbon reduction efforts

Achieving China's "3060" dual carbon targets requires the participation of all social organizations and residents in carbon reduction efforts. The focus on carbon emission reduction solely in key industries, prioritizing the large over the small, is fundamentally flawed and makes it difficult to achieve carbon neutrality by controlling only the larger contributors.

Within the CELM-based "1+1" top-level design, the entire social organizations and individuals are incorporated into the decarbonation system from the outset. This mobilizes all societal forces towards carbon reduction, achieving optimal resource allocation across society. This approach will significantly expedite global decarbonation, enhance social welfare, forge a new landscape for global carbon neutrality, and transform the current situation where the whole society has labored for over a decade yet managed to promote decarbonation only within the coal-fired power industry.

Breakthrough 8 Unveiling a new trillion-level source of government fiscal revenue

One of the paramount challenges facing the international community in addressing climate change and transitioning to a green economy is the scarcity of financial resources. Research from the World Bank reports that an estimated $250 trillion in investment is needed globally to achieve carbon neutrality and facilitate a shift towards a sustainable economy. However, the sources of this substantial funding remain largely unidentified. After a decade of contentious debate, the COP 27 conference managed to agree on the intent to establish a $100 billion fund aimed at compensating developing nations for "loss and damage" due to climate change impacts. This was nearly the sole significant outcome of the COP 27 conference, highlighting the financial hurdles the international community faces in achieving a green economic transformation.

According to CICC (China International Capital Corporation), by 2060, China's total demand for green investment is projected to reach 139 trillion yuan. Given the massive scale of these funds, it is clear that the government alone cannot shoulder this responsibility. The CELM presents a new trillion-level source of fiscal revenue for the nation, comparable to the current aggregate of individual tax revenues, signifying its importance. This revenue promises several key advantages:

1. Mitigating regional development disparities: The economic structure between eastern and western regions, as well as between energy-carbon removal provinces and energy-consuming provinces, stands to be enhanced. The widening gap between wealthier and poorer areas could be narrowed as the western regions, energy-carbon removal provinces, autonomous regions, and municipalities receive substantial investments in carbon emission reduction projects, thereby stimulating local economies and improving the ecological environment.
2. Enhancing resident tax structures and increasing progressivity of tax policies: This can be integrated with broader tax reforms, such as substantially raising the personal income tax threshold and lowering corporate income taxes, which would contribute to increased social welfare. The redistribution of income through the household carbon account mechanism and household tiered carbon fees supports the goal of shared prosperity.
3. Enhancing ecological environment and welfare: By decreasing carbon emissions and pollution, there is potential for a significant improvement in social welfare, reduced healthcare costs, and an enhanced sense of well-being among the public.

Breakthrough 9 Elevating the Global Energy Internet

The Global Energy Internet initiative, a significant contribution from China to address global climate issues, has been operational for some time and holds considerable promise for advancing global carbon neutrality and the transition to a green economy. However, to expedite progress, certain pivotal challenges need to be resolved.

The CELM proposes enhancements to the top-level design of the International Energy Trading Market, facilitating international negative carbon offsets. This would integrate traditional power and renewable energy across different countries and regions into a unified "zero-carbon electricity" grid, ensuring fair trading on a level playing field and opening new avenues for the expansion and enhancement of the International Energy Trading Market.

Under the CELM, the power market must undergo a thorough market-oriented transformation along the entire industrial chain, ensuring complete and equal competition in every sector. Policies should be designed separately in areas requiring ongoing support, while minimizing all forms of market coupling and cross-subsidies.

The CELM-based electricity reform introduces a household electricity account mechanism, which significantly amplifies the reform momentum within the power market, improves the distribution among different income groups, enhances policy progressivity, and promotes energy conservation.

Breakthrough 10 Accelerating the global carbon neutrality process and achieving the IPCC target

Through the following three strategies, the CELM aims to accelerate the global journey towards carbon neutrality, potentially aligning with the optimal temperature control target set by the IPCC:

1. Initiating comprehensive emission reductions: Unlike traditional schemes where over 90% of carbon emissions from key industries, particularly coal-fired power plants, are beyond their direct control, the CELM-based Decarbonation System engages the entire society and all organizations in concerted emission reduction efforts, enhancing the efficiency of resource allocation.
2. Simplified, equitable, and efficient international coordination: Under the consumer liability mechanism, achieving international coordination becomes more straightforward. Challenges like carbon exports, carbon leakage, and carbon tariffs in traditional mechanisms are significantly mitigated.
3. Substantial reduction in global investment for carbon neutrality: By mobilizing widespread participation in carbon reduction, governments can garner substantial carbon fee revenues, thereby visibly reducing the national burden of achieving carbon neutrality.

In summary, the CELM offers renewed hope for addressing humanity's climate challenges

Observations from COP 27 highlight the ongoing urgency in addressing humanity's climate crisis. Despite decades of dedicated research and exploration by countless scholars across diverse disciplines, both governmental bodies and academic institutions continue to navigate their paths toward solutions.

The CELM and the associated Global cCarbon Neutrality Solution have identified a novel approach that promises fairness and efficiency for the international community. This framework provides robust theoretical support and institutional safeguards necessary for realizing the IPCC's optimal plans for climate stabilization.

Moreover, the CELM's principles and methodologies offer a scientific and efficient model not only for achieving global carbon neutrality but also for tackling the emission issues of other GHGs, such as methane and nitrous oxide. This approach can also serve as a blueprint for the design of other environmental public goods systems, marking a significant contribution from today's economic academia to the international community.

At its core, the CELM leverages the strengths of interdisciplinary integrated research and harnesses the power of digital capabilities to obtain comprehensive data at lower costs. Furthermore, it employs market mechanisms to resolve various issues, achieves optimal resource allocation, and establishes a fair and efficient system.

China should expedite the implementation of the CELM program, leveraging its strengths in green energy industry to demonstrate greater climate ambition to the international community. By assuming a larger role in global carbon neutrality efforts, China can achieve leadership in the fight against climate change, contributing significantly to worldwide sustainability efforts.

12.2 The Necessity of Implementing the CELM

The implementation of the CELM can provide a powerful impetus toward achieving China's "3060" dual carbon targets, and deliver numerous benefits, underscoring its significant national strategic importance. Therefore, accelerating its implementation is essential for our country.

12.2.1 The Value of Implementing the CELM

The operation of "1+1" system based on the CELM can bring substantial value to governments, enterprises, and the international community.

1. Self-operation, strong drive, high efficiency

Once the country secures and manages the carbon sources, that is to say, after carbon source organizations (such as energy companies, importers, and carbon-producing entities) accurately measure and verify their emissions, the generated data is integrated into the CTMS. This allows the system to function autonomously without procedural issues. The operating costs and regulatory (MRV) expenses of the CTMS process are minimized. Consequently, the drive for carbon reduction among all societal organizations and individuals is significantly strengthened. Utilizing market price signals, the entire society can be mobilized to participate in carbon reduction efforts. Leveraging the position of being the largest carbon source exporter and negative carbon exporter, the government can precisely regulate the carbon reduction process in the market, accelerate the pace of carbon reduction, and have minimal impact on the macro-economy, achieving an optimal input–output ratio.

2. Accelerating carbon emission reduction across society and industries, and achieving carbon neutrality more than a decade ahead of schedule

All carbon footprints are accurately recorded from their origin, and the diffusion and aggregation of carbon sources are precisely measured and summarized in real-time. The carbon emission liability and costs of all industries are clearly defined, making it easier to design the "1+N" policy framework for the national dual carbon targets, thus driving carbon emission reductions more efficiently. Under the CELM, carbon reduction becomes a core competitive element for organizations in terms of both product cost and social responsibility, and even a baseline for survival.

A notable value of the CELM is its ability to drive participation of all industries and the whole society in carbon emission reduction from both economic and social responsibility (brand effect) perspectives, with low costs and high efficiency. Unlike the current situation where only a few thousand coal-fired power plants participate, the CELM will play a pivotal role in achieving carbon neutrality in China.

Calculations suggest that if the CELM were operational, the "3060" dual carbon targets could be met well in advance, with China reaching its carbon peak 2 to 3 years earlier and achieving carbon neutrality more than a decade sooner.

3. Robust self-correction ability, flexibility, and precise macro-economic impact control

Currently, the implementation of decarbonation policies faces significant challenges and progresses slowly, primarily due to the worry of its substantial impacts on the macro-economy. Numerous research teams, employing mathematical models, have concluded that these effects are notably adverse. Given China's annual carbon emissions of approximately 12 billion tons and a projected future CCUS cost of 200 yuan per ton (with the carbon price in domestic carbon market around 56 yuan per ton in 2022), the total carbon cost amounts to 2.4 trillion yuan. Relative to China's GDP of 121 trillion yuan in 2022, this represents 1.9% of GDP, which falls within acceptable range. We believe that the impact of carbon pricing has been overstated. The key of the issue lies in the absence of an effective method to expedite carbon reduction with minimal macro-economic disruption. The CELM offers a viable solution for the government.

Through the "CTMS + NCTM" framework grounded in the CELM, the government gains visibility into the impact of carbon reduction on the macro-economy, market dynamics, and business fundamentals. With precise regulation and control of negative carbon prices in the carbon trading system, the government can make adjustments promptly, enhancing government oversight.

4. Elimination of carbon leakage

The CTMS ensures low-cost operations and precise statistical analysis of the carbon footprints of the entire society, effectively eliminating "carbon leakage". The data is comprehensive and accurate, ensuring no omissions or miscounts within the entire industrial chain. Ultimately, accountability is maintained as the total carbon tickets issued by the government to carbon source organizations align with the total negative carbon sold in the market.

5. Significant reduction in national carbon regulation costs

The regulatory costs and integrity challenges associated with carbon management can be mitigated. Presently, high MRV costs related to the allocation of carbon emission rights and market clearing result in elevated transaction costs. Incidents of carbon data fraud (even some series cases) have also surfaced, prompting some research institutions to recommend carbon tax schemes. However, the CELM and its approach are deemed more efficient and equitable than a carbon tax.

6. Relieving pressure from international carbon tariffs

Facing imminent international carbon tariffs, Chinese enterprises require strategies to maintain competitiveness. By upgrading domestic exports to zero-carbon products via offsets by "Real Negative CO_2" or "International Negative CO_2", they can cope with the tariff mechanism like EU's CBAM, avoiding the passive scenario where they suffer increased carbon reduction costs and environmental costs at home while being levied tariffs at abroad.

7. Establishment of a leading international carbon market

The CELM furnishes theoretical support and practical implementation plans for China to establish a leading international carbon market, supporting the creation of the world's largest unified carbon market.

8. Creation of a substantial green fiscal revenue stream

With an estimated $200 trillion needed for carbon–neutral investments over the next three decades, governments require efficient financing channels that do not disrupt the macro-economy. The revenue derived from the CELM, adjusted for negative carbon contributions, is scientifically and legally sound. Through the CELM-based "1+1" system, governments can secure significant revenues from the carbon market.

9. Continuous expansion of big data on societal carbon footprints

The CTMS automatically generates a vast database for carbon emissions, providing granular insights into the carbon footprints of all resources, products, and services. This enables the easy analysis of the average carbon emissions of each product category (carbon emission factor database), offering robust data and computational support for carbon reduction initiatives across industries.

Utilizing CTMS data, policymakers can formulate systematic guidelines, such as industry emission standards and criteria for phasing out outdated production capacities, backed by precise big data ensuring alignment and accuracy.

The CTMS big data can be harnessed to develop various types of data products, forming a value-added carbon data industry that supports sustainable practices and innovation.

12.2.2 The Significance of Implementing the CELM

1. Shifting China's passive position in the global climate game

For over three decades, the international discourse on climate change has been largely framed within rules set by Europe and the United States. As a major carbon emitter, China has often found itself in a passive position. By promoting the "consumer liability" principle and carbon market rules embedded in the CELM, China can significantly elevate its standing in the international carbon arena and garner support from a broader coalition of nations. A cornerstone of the CELM is the principle of "consumer liability" rather than "producer liability", meaning that the liability for carbon fees should reflect the efforts of the producing country to reduce emissions and eliminate production-related pollution.

Additionally, the integration of the CELM "1+1" system with China's advanced green energy industry and energy Internet technologies transforms China from a follower to a leader in global climate initiatives.

2. Accelerating achievement of national dual carbon targets

Implementing the CELM could enable China to reach its carbon peaking target 2–3 years ahead of schedule and achieve carbon neutrality over a decade earlier than currently projected under existing policy frameworks.

3. Delivering a double dividend effect

The CELM offers a dual dividend effect in increasing social welfare. Firstly, it incentivizes carbon emission reduction, strengthens pollution control, and improves environmental quality through a two-pronged approach. Secondly, the net economic benefits derived from negative carbon revenues can be reinvested into carbon reduction projects and technology development, fostering additional social employment, personal wealth, and sustained GDP growth. Leveraging economic growth to balance income distribution is a rational strategy for achieving shared prosperity.

Various studies indicate that achieving carbon neutrality will require at least 200 trillion yuan in investment over the next three decades. The CELM can effectively mobilize society-wide efforts towards emission reduction, significantly lowering overall investment and costs. It is projected to save more than 50% of the required investment, equating to over 100 trillion yuan, and reduce costs by over 80%. Additionally, it would mitigate the hundreds of billions of dollars in carbon tariffs currently paid to the United States and Europe.

4. Enhancing public awareness of low-carbon living

The "consumer liability" principle under the CTMS, facilitated by the implementation of the CELM-based carbon emission reduction system, can rapidly permeate throughout society. This would engage organizations and individuals in carbon reduction actions, quantifying their liabilities and allowing for the calculation of carbon neutral costs. Meanwhile, the mechanism, in turn, would elevate public awareness regarding carbon emission reduction and environmental protection.

5. Providing reference for other environmental tax policies

In the era of big data and AI, economic theories can leverage these technologies to design high-precision, low-cost policy instruments. The CTMS can provide big data support for other environmental taxes and offer insights for environmental policy design in various sectors.

12.3 The Feasibility of Implementing the CELM

One of the four critical components of the CELM, the Carbon Ticket Management System (CTMS), encompasses a comprehensive carbon footprint data for all organizations, goods, and services within the country. The implementation of the CTMS is intricate and extensive, involving not just software development but also the establishment of supporting infrastructure and operational frameworks. As a novel system, CTMS poses unique challenges compared to setting up a Negative Carbon Trading Market or International Energy Trading Market. However, if the CTMS is successfully implemented, the deployment of other CELM systems would be considerably smoother.

Despite its complexity, the CTMS is highly feasible compared to current carbon reduction systems, with lower levels of difficulty and investment required.

1. Drawing from experience in large-scale financial systems

China possesses substantial experience in developing large-scale financial systems, from which CTMS can draw valuable lessons. The nation's Golden Tax Project exemplifies this expertise, representing the world's most robust national value-added tax (VAT) system. Evolved to its fourth phase, the Golden Tax Project has operated for many years, amassing extensive experience in constructing large-scale national financial systems. While VAT systems manage varying tax rates across industries, along with distinctions between local and national taxes, requiring annual adjustments and complex settlement procedures, the CTMS is relatively straightforward. It primarily records carbon emission liability data without engaging in rate and fee calculations. Settlements are simple, adhering to the principle of balancing inputs and outputs. Once governmental policies are set in motion, the CTMS can be established relatively swiftly.

2. Overcoming technical challenges

The CTMS presents new challenges, yet these are manageable. Common technical challenges include handling large volumes of data, ensuring robust anti-fraud mechanisms, maintaining security, and developing a dynamic intelligent coding system encompassing all materials, goods, and services. However, with dedicated research and development efforts, it is feasible for government agencies to devise a coding system capable of tracking and analyzing the carbon footprint data of every commodity and commodity type.

3. Legal support system for CTMS operations

Effective CTMS operation necessitates a robust legal support structure. Given the global significance of carbon emissions, legislative groundwork in China and worldwide is well-established. Understanding the theoretical framework of the CELM and its value will facilitate legislative processes without significant obstacles. The legal and economic logic underlying the CTMS is relatively straightforward, simplifying legislative technicalities and avoiding the complexities inherent in accommodating diverse stakeholder interests. Compared to the instrument of carbon taxes proposed by many experts, CTMS legislation is simpler and more straightforward.

4. Establishing operational framework for the CTMS

CTMS operations encompass multiple facets, including system and data operations, regular settlement of organizational carbon accounts, carbon emission management for carbon source enterprises, and decision-making systems based on big data. Drawing parallels with the established experience of VAT systems, these frameworks can be effectively implemented. Currently, the Ministry of Ecology and Environment oversees climate change, and the central government will designate the specific department responsible for CTMS operations. Integrating CTMS within the financial sector may offer logistical advantages, whereas the Ministry of Ecology and Environment could be responsible for the operations of the negative carbon market. Overall, China's carbon emission reduction system is strategically managed by the Ministry of Ecology and Environment, aligning with national governance requirements.

5. Minimal investment required for CTMS infrastructure

As a national big data platform, the CTMS involves one-time development and construction yet is applicable across all industries, enabling intensive application and maintenance. The construction and operational costs are modest. And the investment required is negligible relative to the socio-economic benefits it generates, thereby imposing no undue burden on the government. In fact, a government-operated system based on the CTMS would significantly reduce costs compared to the current MRV expenses associated with carbon emission allowances, warranting swift acceleration.

6. Alignment with national policies

Digital transformation is a cornerstone of China's national strategy. The CTMS addresses the challenge of recording carbon footprint data efficiently and at low cost through digital technology, serving as crucial infrastructure to achieve China's dual-carbon targets. By facilitating a fully paperless big data management and operation system, the CTMS embodies the lowest carbon solution. In contrast, the current carbon emission allowance system is cumbersome and resource-intensive. Thus, the operation of the CTMS is more aligned with national policies, positioning the "Golden Carbon Project" as a pioneering initiative that could spearhead China's digital transformation and set a global precedent.

7. No technical obstacles in reforming China's carbon market

Grounded in the principles of the CELM, the top-level design of the negative carbon market has largely taken shape. The technical obstacles associated with reforming China's carbon market have been largely overcome. The primary challenge now lies in reconciling the interests of various stakeholders. Achieving the "3060" dual carbon targets is paramount to national prosperity and international competitiveness. Therefore, any interest groups must yield to the overarching reform agenda, which necessitates high-level national commitment and coordination to ensure successful implementation.

12.4 The Urgency of Implementing the CELM

Both the "3060" dual carbon target and the international climate imperative underscore the urgency of accelerating the implementation of the CELM system. Whether considering domestic efforts toward carbon neutrality or the evolving international landscape, there is a pressing need to expedite the adoption of the CELM.

1. Tight timeline for achieving dual-carbon targets

China faces a formidable task in meeting its dual-carbon targets given its status as the world's largest carbon emitter, contributing approximately one-third of global emissions. The ongoing reliance on coal-fired power plants and the limited efficacy of the existing carbon reduction measures make it challenging to meet the "3060" targets under the current system.

To realize the dual carbon targets, China's greatest opportunity does not rest solely on expanding the green energy sector, making massive financial investments, or increasing R&D expenditures on low-carbon technologies. Instead, the key lies in identifying the most accurate guiding theory and establishing a fair and effective carbon–neutral top-level design. If the foundational framework is robust and the incentives for carbon emissions are appropriately structured, all resources and technologies will align naturally toward carbon neutrality. Government focus should pivot from the allocation and trading of carbon emission rights and CCER certifications to this foundational aspect.

2. Redundancy of high-cost carbon emission management systems

Lacking a sophisticated theoretical framework for climate economics, the government has resorted to numerous inefficient policy instruments to construct complex carbon management systems aimed at reducing emissions. These systems are costly and inefficient, encompassing activities such as allowance allocation, carbon emission verification, and carbon trading markets, among others. Over time, various entrenched interest patterns have emerged, complicating reforms. For instance, the

CCER system has proliferated into over 200 methodologies, and the Ministry of Ecology and Environment continues to solicit new ones. Efforts like Beijing's reconstruction of the CCER market and Guangzhou and Hainan's plans to establish an international carbon trading market exemplify this trend.

There is an industry-wide misconception that carbon neutrality represents a lucrative opportunity, leading to a rush to stake claims without a clear understanding of the underlying principles. This hasty expansion is unsustainable and results in significant social waste, high costs, and inefficiencies. Transitioning to a new, efficient system necessitates overcoming the inertia of these established but ineffective structures, underscoring the need to expedite the validation, refinement, and implementation of the CELM. Doing so will substantially lower the societal costs of carbon reduction and simplify the system.

3. Enormous impact of current carbon emission reduction system on the macroeconomy

The current carbon emission reduction system, centered around carbon emission rights, lacks efficiency in carbon reduction and progresses slowly toward carbon neutrality, yet exerts a notable impact on the macroeconomy. Coal-fired power sector, for example, suffers considerable losses, dampening the enthusiasm for power generation and extending the payback period for its massive investments. Seasonal power shortages have disrupted industrial production and caused severe economic losses.

This scenario demonstrates that the current system is insufficiently effective in reducing emissions while imposing excessive negative impacts on the macroeconomy. Urgent changes are needed. The CELM promises to increase the rate of carbon reduction by more than 100 times initially, positively impacting the macroeconomy and warranting prompt implementation.

4. Response to the launch of international carbon tariffs

Implementing the CELM at an early stage will equip China to address mechanisms similar to the EU's CBAM. The CELM can tackle two critical issues: providing reliable carbon emission data and offsetting carbon emission liability. The CTMS can furnish verifiable carbon footprint data for export products, while the NCTM can offset the carbon emission liability of these exports.

As international carbon emission regulations multiply, they will increasingly impact China's international trade and capital markets. For instance, the U.S. Securities and Exchange Commission (SEC) has introduced new rules for climate information disclosure, placing stricter reporting requirements on the carbon emissions of products and services offered by U.S.-listed companies. Consequently, Chinese enterprises seeking to enter international markets will require credible carbon footprint reporting and low-carbon products.

5. Challenges and costs of national carbon emissions regulation

On March 14, 2022, the Ministry of Ecology and Environment reported several instances of fraudulent carbon emission data reports.

Four intermediary verification agencies were disclosed, their primary role being to issue carbon verification and testing reports for enterprises. Issues included false reports and inadequate verification procedures. The authenticity of carbon emission data is fundamental to the integrity of the carbon market and directly influences the supply and demand dynamics of carbon allowances. Currently, the market hosts a multitude of carbon-related service and consultancy firms of varying professional standards. Ensuring the accuracy of carbon emissions data relies heavily on a robust Monitoring, Reporting, and Verification (MRV) system, with third-party verification playing a crucial role in maintaining data quality.

The existing MRV system for the supervision of carbon trading market entails significant investment and faces operational challenges. A vast infrastructure is required to support the system, and the costs are substantial. The current carbon trading based on emission rights allowances necessitates continuous oversight of each enterprise's emission processes and levels. This approach offers limited control and monitoring, typically restricted to specific industries and large enterprises. Given the holistic nature of carbon emission reduction, which involves all businesses and residents, the existing mechanisms and technical capabilities can regulate only a fraction of enterprises, thereby slowing the pace of nationwide carbon reduction efforts.

The CELM is designed to mitigate these issues. As a self-operating and self-regulating framework, effective management of carbon sources would significantly reduce the regulatory costs associated with monitoring the carbon footprints of the entire industry chain.

6. Urgency of reforming carbon trading market

The current carbon market, based on emission rights, has not played a pivotal role in advancing China's path to carbon neutrality. Its scale remains limited, and the its financial functions have yet to be fully realized, despite the considerable negative effects. China must expedite the reform process and transition to the CELM-based negative carbon market model. This shift would position China's carbon market as a global leader and a vital driver towards achieving the "3060" dual carbon targets.

Chapter 13
Dual Carbon Policies and Action Plans

With the establishment of the CELM, China will gain an efficient tool for achieving carbon neutrality, enhancing policy equity and enabling targeted measures across various sectors to attain the dual carbon targets. The previously complex policy instruments, such as carbon emission allowance system, reduction targets, allocation of energy usage rights, and dual-control indicators, can now be significantly streamlined, with some instruments potentially phased out entirely.

Given the current international climate pressures and China's commitment to carbon neutrality, it is imperative that China upgrade its top-level design for dual-carbon policies and implement effective measures promptly. Guided by clear theoretical frameworks and strategic programs, China's dual carbon initiatives can be systematically planned, dismantling outdated practices where necessary, and promoting rapid, orderly, and efficient progress.

13.1 Accelerating the Establishment of CELM in China

We should proceed with caution, taking a holistic approach. Accelerating the establishment of the CELM and prudently advancing decarbonation can prevent the current issues of arbitrary carbon charges and sporadic carbon reduction efforts.

Once the CELM Decarbonation System is in place, government authorities will be able to precisely control carbon footprint data, design comprehensive strategies, and optimize overall performance. Through the calibrated control of several variables, the overall rhythm can be managed to amplify positive effects while mitigating adverse impacts on the macro-economy.

B. Yang, *The Carbon Emission Liability Mechanism*,
https://doi.org/10.1007/978-981-96-3612-9_13

By employing a combination of approaches, including total carbon source regulation, carbon price adjustments, "Owing Negative CO_2" inputs, and "Real Negative CO_2" production, the process towards peaking emissions and achieving carbon neutrality can be regulated effectively. This market-driven mechanism will enable macroeconomic optimization and development. Rolling blackouts and other ad hoc carbon reduction measures can thus be phased out entirely. With a coordinated national strategy, regional and industrial policies are unnecessary, improving nationwide carbon reduction efficiency.

The current allowance system for carbon emission rights should be discontinued as soon as practicable, since no existing method of allocating carbon emission rights achieves optimal efficiency. Under the CELM, given current technological conditions, the allocation and enforcement of carbon allowances is no longer an unavoidable aspect of decarbonation in any country. Based on global carbon footprint data, every economic entity should bear financial liability for its carbon emissions. Carbon emission pricing should be determined through objective data on carbon emission inventories and market transactions, thereby achieving optimal societal efficiency and enabling flexible control over China's carbon neutrality process.

China should refrain from reconsidering the use of carbon taxes. Carbon tax instrument exhibits numerous shortcomings in decarbonation effectiveness and lacks the advantages of practical implementation; therefore, it is inappropriate to continue studying the pricing and operational systems of carbon taxes.

13.2 Achieving a Unified National Negative Carbon Trading Market

The provincial-level pilot markets for carbon emissions rights have lagged behind expectations. Over a decade of experimentation has confirmed that China's carbon market construction should be promptly upgraded to a national unified Negative Carbon Trading Market and integrated into the international carbon market based on the CELM. This will accelerate China's capture of the strategic high ground in the international carbon market.

CER/CCER incentives should be phased out. It is suggested to terminate the incentives for relative emission reduction and instead to bolster the development of "Real Negative CO_2" industries that offer greater growth potential and international competitiveness. Once the carbon emission costs are fully internalized, the original incentives such as CER/CCER projects can be adjusted to supplementary measures like tax reductions (including VAT and income tax) and financial policies, rather than serving as core policies. Fiscal policies should be applied judiciously.

13.3 Implementing Precise Carbon Reduction Policies to Drive Out Inefficient Practices

To achieve the "3060" dual carbon targets, the Chinese Government has formulated a comprehensive "1+N" policy framework for carbon peaking and neutrality. The "1" in "1+N" refers to the *Working Guidance for Carbon Dioxide Peaking and Carbon Neutrality in Full and Faithful Implementation of the New Development Philosophy*, along with the *Action Plan for Carbon Dioxide Peaking Before 2030*. The "N" encompasses policy measures and actions in each key sector and industry, as well as in each province and city.

Upon the completion and operation of the CTMS based on the CELM, a comprehensive understanding of global carbon footprint data will be achieved, significantly simplifying the formulation of the government's "1+N" policies and enhancing the efficiency of policy instrument design. A key indicator for the high-quality development of industries is carbon emission intensity, or carbon emissions per unit of GDP, which should be incorporated into the evaluation of the management performance of local governments, central enterprise, and state-owned enterprises.

For example, within the construction industry, there are approximately 100,000 construction firms, with significant variations in carbon consumption per unit of output value and per unit of building area. Leveraging CTMS big data, it becomes feasible to rank all enterprises in real-time based on these two carbon emission intensity metrics (hereinafter referred to as "dual rankings"), make a "red and black list",[1] and design policies that promote good practices over poor ones. In the first year, a "red and black" list is made to leverage social and brand influence on the enterprises. In the second year, additional fees are charged to the top 3% of enterprises in the dual rankings for excess emissions. And in the third year, the qualification of 3% of the enterprises with the highest carbon intensities will be suspended. Carbon reduction policies can be incrementally strengthened to foster market quality and orderly phase-out of high-energy-consuming and low-quality production capacities.

Similarly, other industries can exert pressure on high-emission, backward production capacity enterprises by controlling both output value and carbon emissions per unit of output, compelling them to improve their development quality or gradually exit the market.

[1] Red and black list is a mechanism which aims to reward the enterprises on the red list for their contributions while punish those on the black list for their dishonest behaviors—a note by the translator.

13.4 Launch of the Carbon Market and Adjustment of Tax Burden Structure

Upon the initial rollout of the CELM-based NCTM, the nation can adopt a zero-carbon price during the pilot phase. Once the market officially commences operations, the price of "Owing Negative CO_2" can start from the current price for carbon emission right. This approach is more comprehensible and acceptable to the market and allows for testing the macroeconomic responses.

Based on the current carbon price of 60 yuan per ton for 12 billion tons of carbon emissions, the market would incur an additional cost of approximately 720 billion yuan. Relative to China's total GDP of 120 trillion yuan, this pressure is manageable. If it is observed that the increased costs of market consumer goods, including electricity prices, do not effectively compel producers to change their behaviors, then accelerating the rise in carbon prices may be necessary.

Simultaneously, the government should implement fiscal linkage measures, adjust the tax structure, and reduce the tax burden on certain corporate taxes. This includes significantly raising the tax threshold to avoid the regressive effects of carbon fees.

13.5 Arrangements for Carbon Fee Revenue

With the CELM in place, the government can swiftly generate substantial carbon fee revenue through the CTMS and the NCTM. Assuming China's total annual carbon emissions are 12 billion tons of CO_2, and using the current average price of carbon emission rights, the government would collect approximately 720 billion yuan annually. Carbon prices in Europe and the United States are already around 80 euros per ton. When the domestic carbon price reaches 100 yuan per ton, the government would accrue roughly 1.2 trillion yuan annually.

This revenue, derived from increased costs passed onto consumers and enterprises, should be entirely dedicated to initiatives supporting the dual carbon targets, such as livelihood development projects in carbon removal areas and subsidies for low-income groups. The government must clearly define the authorities responsible for collecting and utilizing these revenue streams effectively, ensuring that the costs borne by consumers contribute positively to the decarbonation efforts.

In funding dual-carbon target projects, the efficiency of these investments varies widely, and priority should be given to those that are most efficient and suitable for investment:

1. Directly Purchasing "Real Negative CO_2": Directly purchasing "Real Negative CO_2" from the market provides immediate incentives for carbon removal enterprises. A fair and effective market mechanism can significantly boost the development of the carbon removal industry. "Real Negative CO_2" is a huge industry, and the government should strive to lead the world in this industry. Being a major exporter of "Real Negative CO_2", China can earn substantial

foreign exchange and contribute to shaping the international carbon market. After social organizations procure "Real Negative CO_2", if there remains a surplus, the government should purchase the remainder to sustain the industry's development momentum.

2. Establishing a "National Carbon Neutral Fund": A fund is expected to set up to invest in projects across various sectors that align with the dual carbon targets, pooling resources for impactful initiatives. The fund will serve as a stabilizer in the carbon market, conducting buyback and release operations to ensure its vitality and stability. Investments should also support the green economic transformation under the Belt and Road Initiative, aiding partner countries and regions in developing green energy and carbon–neutral systems.
3. Investment in green and renewable energy projects: To accelerate the transition from fossil fuels, interest concessions and guarantees for green energy projects should be offered. These investments should adhere strictly to market principles, focusing on returns rather than policy-driven investments without considering output.
4. Providing financial support to the Global Energy Internet projects: Global Energy Internet is essential for addressing the intermittency of green energy and maximizing the utilization of solar resources. China is expected to strengthen R&D in related technologies and ensure adequate funding to maintain China's leadership in this field.
5. Investment in carbon neutral projects in energy-rich provinces and carbon removal provinces: The funds could assist these regions in transforming their industries, boosting their economies, creating jobs, as well as improving living standards and achieving balanced inter-regional transfers.
6. Providing loans and interest subsidies for carbon reduction and carbon removal projects: Projects involving energy use and conversion often suffer from a lack of funding; the National Carbon Neutral Fund can provide credit support following a rigorous evaluation process. Loans to enterprises aimed at innovating carbon reduction technologies should be concessional but not interest-free to avoid inefficiencies and governance issues. Carbon sequestration projects, whether ecological or technological, should also receive preferential loan support.
7. Equity investment in enterprises with key dual-carbon technologies: It is suggested to increase equity investment in domestic and international enterprises with dual carbon innovative technologies, particularly those specializing in CCUS technologies and R&D of CO_2 resource utilization. Technological innovation should be incentivized through market mechanisms rather than direct grants. Equity investments are made through multiple funds, and the management rights of underperforming funds should be reclaimed. Meanwhile, the government should perform comparative analyses across portfolios and select cooperative investment institutions demonstrating superior performance.
8. Investment in high-value dual-carbon soft research projects. Soft research projects do not yield direct market returns, yet they are indispensable for

China to construct a robust dual carbon system and enhance its influence on global climate issues, necessitating national funding support. Reflecting on the past three decades of dual-carbon research, the ratio of input to output in soft research projects has been relatively low, a situation that warrants serious attention and introspection. The government must address the current state of dual-carbon research where capital investment and output are disproportionately low compared to carbon emissions.

9. Enhanced efforts to train dual-carbon talents. If the government were to organize a unified certification program for dual-carbon talents, relevant personnel could obtain certificates upon passing an examination, and training institutions could receive subsidies based on the number of certified professionals they produce. Currently, the dual-carbon education and training sector is emerging, and efforts to promote its development should be intensified. Standards for individual and enterprise qualifications should be established promptly, and the construction of the certification system should be expedited and gradually standardized. Many current dual-carbon educational programs are flawed and may be counterproductive. The field is somewhat skewed due to systemic issues and the need for updating the existing knowledge base.
10. Construction of carbon neutral market mechanisms and systems. In the journey toward carbon neutrality, the establishment of a "1+N" policy framework, encompassing the development and maintenance of various CELM systems, demands extensive research and design. This policy framework is vast, impacting all facets of society. Ensuring the efficiency of policy tools is a task for academics, and the government must allocate sufficient resources. To guarantee the effectiveness of these inputs, the scientific and rational setup of projects is crucial to ensure that China's dual-carbon research is progressing in the correct direction.
11. Policy guidance to promote green consumption behaviors and lifestyles. A pressing issue in climate governance is how to influence human consumption choices, instill green consumption concepts, and foster eco-friendly living habits. For instance, despite the affordability of photovoltaic power generation, are businesses and households motivated to install solar panels? With advancements in electric vehicle technology, will there be a willingness among people to switch to electric cars? Numerous social surveys indicate that changing consumption habits and lifestyles is challenging.

In real human behavior decision-making, cost is only one dimension of decision making. In fact, with limited attention and action, people don't always make the best choices financially.

A classic example is the "Energy Efficiency Gap". For example, even if simple decoration and enhanced building insulation can greatly reduce heating costs, many qualified families are still unwilling to renovate old houses. Many people buy less efficient refrigerators, air conditioners and washing machines, for example, even though energy-efficient appliances are cheaper in the long run. What's more, when people buy a car, they do not consider the displacement, only to find that they spend a lot on oil.

These less rational choices may simply be due to the inertia of consumption, or simply not paying attention to their energy consumption, or not knowing that there are more energy-efficient and less expensive options, so climate policy often needs to focus on behavior change. These policies can be simple. Many studies have shown that simply getting consumers to pay attention to their energy consumption can promote green behaviors. For example, some experiments have found that the installation of real-time electricity meters or timely delivery of user electricity information can promote the reduction of household electricity consumption by 3% to 15%.

Of course, the fact that you are aware of it does not necessarily mean that you will act. A British experiment randomly divided hundreds of families into two groups. The experimental group of families participated in carbon footprint calculation lectures, and experts calculated the annual carbon emissions of these families and pointed out specific ways to reduce emissions. However, the tracking results showed that compared with the control group, the experimental group of households did not differ in their actual actions: household energy consumption did not decrease and transportation modes did not change. Most people said they had done their best to be environmentally friendly, and the remaining low-carbon actions were too troublesome. We should study how to change habits social groups from a sociological perspective.

Anyway, to change a society's consumption theory and establish new green living habits, the government needs a lot of input:

First, greater efforts should be made to publicize and promote educational work, and it should be effective. The governments are expected to try, observe and practice to find a more effective method, and promote it worldwide under the leadership of the United Nations.

Secondly, combining economic incentives with moral encouragement can be highly effective. The household carbon account mechanism based on the CELM is a promising strategy. Building on this foundation, both positive and negative incentives for household carbon emission reduction should be utilized, integrating both material and moral incentives effectively.

In terms of material incentives, households whose per capita carbon emissions fall below a standard threshold should receive economic rewards, while the carbon fees should progressively decrease from a low base to even exemption. Conversely, households exceeding the standard will face a tiered pricing scheme, bearing a higher multiple of the cost. Larger homes, oversized air conditioners, and vehicles with significant engine displacements should face escalating costs, thereby enhancing the material disincentives for excessive emissions.

Regarding moral incentives, leveraging the data from household carbon accounts can be instrumental. By ranking household carbon emissions on the family's settlement information page and clarifying each household's position within the broader societal context, the government can foster a sense of responsibility. Households with low per capita carbon emissions should be recognized with gratitude, praise, and encouragement in their carbon emission statements. Conversely, households with high emissions should be alerted to their status. This approach incurs no monetary cost but can have a profound impact on public behaviors.

If the government possesses comprehensive data on the entire society's carbon footprint, it could implement even more targeted and effective measures.

It is worth noting that while local governments currently devote significant attention and resources to implementing carbon-inclusive mechanisms, the outcomes have been minimal. Therefore, local policies should avoid consuming excessive resources.

The scale of investment required to achieve carbon neutrality is immense, and governments must be vigilant about the efficient use of funds. Two categories of inefficient spending deserve particular attention:

1. Subsidizing enterprise R&D projects without compensation

Subsidizing enterprise R&D projects without compensation can lead to inefficiencies and integrity issues, as such projects may become relationship-driven or personalized initiatives. The selection of R&D projects should be guided by market forces and informed by market demand. A more effective way to support technological innovation is through tax reductions and equity investments. Increasing investment in equity funds that excel in the dual-carbon field would be more efficient and yield better returns.

2. Addressing ineffective soft research

Considerable research has been conducted in the dual-carbon field, yet the input-to-output ratio has been unsatisfactory, and the resultant carbon emissions have been significant. While funding soft research is vital, it should focus on the projects that make breakthroughs and bring genuine practical value. Studies that are misdirected or impractical should be minimized. Examples include research on carbon emission quota schemes, the CCER system, methodologies for CCER certification, and macroeconomic model calculations. Despite the extensive study of climate macroeconomic models, the number and complexity of real-world variables often exceed the assumptions of these models, rendering their findings shelved and seldom adopted by governmental authorities. Additionally, research focused on carbon markets for emission rights should be shifted towards negative carbon trading mechanisms.

13.6 Compensation and Transfer Payments for Energy Resource Provinces and Carbon Removal Provinces

Achieving global carbon neutrality requires international cooperation; similarly, China's carbon neutrality must be a nationwide effort.

Recognizing this, the government acknowledges that carbon neutrality must be supported by a national plan where regional interests are balanced fairly to ensure success. Critical questions remain regarding the arrangement of liability and rights among energy resource provinces, carbon removal provinces, and economically developed regions. How to facilitate the development of these regions under the dual carbon targets is an essential challenge. However, current policy designs are somewhat awkward due to theoretical confusion about the roles and liability of different regions concerning carbon emissions.

Energy and resource-rich provinces provide essential energy production and supply to economically developed regions while investing in environmental governance and industrial transformation. Without a solid theoretical basis, there is no fundamental solution to quantifying the liability and rights of these regions during the transition to carbon neutrality. As a consequence, economically developed regions are not sufficiently motivated to assume liability for the carbon emissions generated by energy and resource provinces, and the latter, too, lack adequate incentives to reduce their own emissions. The carbon allowance mechanism, which employs a planned economy model to enforce emission reduction targets, lacks clarity and efficiency, remaining a subject of prolonged debate. This undermines the enthusiasm of both types of regions to shoulder their liability and implement the dual carbon strategy, significantly affecting China's progress toward carbon neutrality.

China's carbon market pilots have struggled for over a decade and have been unable to provide a source of funds to address regional disparities, which is a major limitation of the market for carbon emission rights.

The CELM theory addresses the liabilities and rights of all parties involved in carbon neutrality from both a legal and economic standpoint. Based on the CELM, the liabilities and interests among regions in China, particularly energy resource provinces, carbon removal provinces, and developed areas, will be clearly defined, allowing for smoother inter-regional compensation schemes, transfer payments, and associated market operations.

Through the operation of the CELM, the substantial funds collected annually by the government from the sale of "Owing Negative CO_2" in the carbon market should primarily be invested in the construction of projects for "3060" dual carbon targets in energy resource provinces and carbon removal provinces. This would aid in the economic transformation and social development of these regions and improve the standard of living for their residents.

Given the special transfer payment funds for energy resource provinces and carbon removal provinces, it is recommended that, in principle, the amount of transfer payments be estimated using the following formula:

$$\begin{aligned}&\text{amount of transfer payment from the State to energy resource provinces}\\&\quad=\text{approved amount of provincial energy carbon sources}\\&\qquad\times\ \text{carbon price}-\text{carbon fees paid by consumers}\\&\qquad\text{(including organizations) in the province}\end{aligned}$$

Within this framework, a carbon balance formula grounded in the CELM would be:

$$\begin{aligned}&\text{approved amount of provincial energy carbon sources}\\&\quad+\ \text{carbon ticket input from other provinces}=\text{carbon ticket output}\\&\quad\text{to other provinces amount of carbon consumed by consumers}\\&\quad\text{(including organizations) in the province}\end{aligned}$$

Thus, the carbon emissions that should be attributed to the province are the carbon consumed by consumers (including organizations) in the province.

$$\begin{aligned}&\text{carbon emissions attributed to the province}\\&\quad=\text{approved amount of provincial energy carbon sources}\\&\qquad+\ \text{carbon ticket input from other provinces}\\&\qquad-\ \text{carbon ticket output to other provinces}\\&\qquad-\ \text{total amount of carbon sequestration in the province}\end{aligned}$$

Carbon removal provinces can also directly benefit from the carbon market by selling "Real Negative CO_2", reaping tangible benefits. Initially, the total benefit may be modest, but the "National Carbon Neutral Fund" can reinvest these proceeds. If the demand in the market for "Real Negative CO_2" is insufficient, the "National Carbon Neutral Fund" should directly purchase the surplus "Real Negative CO_2" from the market, ensuring that carbon removal provinces realize their profits promptly. This approach underscores our commitment to the principle that "clear waters and lush mountains invaluable assets", as emphasized by President Xi Jinping. By ensuring that carbon removal provinces have the enthusiasm and financial resources to build and protect forests and undertake carbon removal projects, we lay the groundwork for sustainable development. On the foundation of environmental protection, we aim to foster economic growth and enhance the living standards of the populace.

Establishing a system of carbon neutral compensation and transfer payments for these two types of regions will significantly accelerate the national carbon neutrality process. It is imperative to establish a new interregional liability mechanism and special transfer payment system based on the CELM.

Furthermore, the National Carbon Neutral Fund should prioritize investing in green projects within these two types of regions to stimulate their development. Internationally, and within the context of the "Belt and Road Initiative", China should lead by investing in green projects in developing countries and promoting global coordination on carbon reduction efforts.

13.7 Increasing Incentive Policies for the Circular Economy

The circular economy plays a pivotal role in both resource reuse and decarbonation, and thus deserves vigorous promotion. Models such as the recycling industry and used goods sharing platforms are critical components of a circular economy and should be actively developed. Currently, the development of the domestic recycling industry is insufficient, necessitating the design of more robust incentive policies.

Given China's scarcity of per capita resources, the circular economy can meet a significant portion of these needs efficiently. Platforms such as Aihuishou (www.aihuishou.com) have made commendable strides in extending the lifecycle of goods, conserving resources, and reducing carbon emissions. The government should provide strong support to these initiatives.

To intensify policy efforts, we recommend the following two key areas of focus:

1. Tax reductions: Implement Value-Added Tax (VAT) and corporate income tax reductions to bolster the industry through favorable tax policies.
2. Support for stock market listings: Facilitate the A-share listings of enterprises engaging in circular economy to provide them with additional capital and market recognition.

13.8 Nine Recommendations for Actions

Based on the analysis of the necessity, feasibility, and urgency of establishing the CELM outlined in Chap. 12, its implementation is imperative given the clarity and ongoing promotion of the national "3060" dual carbon targets. The CELM promises significant advantages and strategic significance in addressing both domestic and international challenges during the journey towards carbon neutrality. To expedite this process, we recommend the following actions:

1. Organization and implementation

Establish a specialized team at the central government level to lead the deepening research and implementation of the CELM. This team should spearhead the top-level design and construction of the CELM-based NCTM. Strengthen central leadership to break through existing interest patterns and prioritize the overall national interest.

2. Further refinement of the CELM theoretical system

Conduct comprehensive validation of the CELM theoretical system to demonstrate its correctness and advantages, as well as its impact on carbon emission reduction processes and macroeconomic aspects. Continue to refine and improve the system.

3. Accelerating the implementation plan for the CTMS

Optimize the implementation plan for the CTMS, identify and resolve issues encountered during implementation, and formulate corresponding solutions.

4. Top-level design and construction of the NCTM

Develop a top-level design for the reform and upgrade of the carbon market. Accelerate the market-oriented and international development of China's carbon market.

5. Research and design of supporting policies for the CELM theoretical system

Identify the necessary supporting policies for the operation of the CELM. Accelerate the implementation of these policies and create conditions for the early operation of the CELM.

It is essential to review and eliminate existing decarbonation policies that do not align with current developmental needs. The current policy system is complex, inefficient, and impractical. Many stakeholders will be involved in the process of streamlining and reform. The central government should resolutely implement these measures. This is a pivotal effort for national rejuvenation, and the government must act swiftly to overcome any resistance and stay ahead of the timeline.

6. Supporting legislation for the operation of the CELM

Initiate legislative work promptly, considering its lengthy cycle. The legislative process for China's carbon neutral system is a systematic project requiring long-term and persistent efforts. Proper top-level design is essential to prevent unnecessary reconstruction.

7. Development and trial operation of the CTMS

Draw upon the experience of the Golden Tax Project to accelerate the research and development of the CTMS and its supporting subsystems. Design and promote comprehensive trial operations throughout the entire power industry chain to gain experience and lay the foundation for national and global promotion.

8. Research and design of the CTMS operational system

Implementing the CTMS nationwide requires an operational management system from the central to the local levels. Designing an efficient, clean, and low-cost operational organization is crucial. Clearly define the responsible entities, build the operational system, and continuously optimize it for long-term operation.

9. Trial operation and comprehensive promotion

Conduct trial operations to observe data accuracy, optimize and adjust the software system and operational control system, and prepare for comprehensive promotion.

13.9 China's Climate Ambitions and Global Contributions

When the initial draft of this chapter was written, the global novel coronavirus pandemic had persisted for three years, and Shanghai was grappling with the severe impacts of the Omicron variant. The pressures on Shanghai were unprecedented, with far-reaching implications for the entire country. Simultaneously, the conflict between Russia and Ukraine erupted on February 24, 2022, and remained unresolved, causing serious instability worldwide, dividing the international community, and threatening global peace and security. Relations between China and the United States, which have significantly influenced international security and cooperation, continued to face challenges, placing substantial strain on the normal functioning of the international community.

However, the greatest challenge facing humanity in the coming decade is the looming climate catastrophe, and it is urgent in timeline. The climate crisis poses a more significant and long-term threat than the novel coronavirus, requiring greater sacrifices. Consider the potential devastation to coastal cities globally if temperatures rise and the ice caps of the Arctic and Antarctic melt, causing sea levels to rise by four meters.

The "3060" dual carbon targets pledged by the Chinese government at the UN conference exemplifies the responsibility of a major nation and demonstrates a profound commitment to building a community with a shared future for mankind. This is indeed reflective of China's role as a global leader.

Currently, China accounts for approximately one-third of global carbon emissions. Achieving carbon neutrality sooner rather than later is crucial for addressing the global climate issue. It is essential that China's theoretical framework and technical pathways to carbon neutrality be validated, serving as a successful practical model for the world. China is expected to lead the way towards successful carbon neutrality, ultimately contributing to solving the global climate crisis.

China's commitment to the "3060" dual carbon targets reflects the government's considerable confidence. Although many significant challenges remain unaddressed, the government is committed to finding more effective solutions in the future.

Considering China's journey towards carbon neutrality comprehensively, the nation is already at the forefront of the world in green energy technology, green energy production, energy Internet, and green finance. However, it lags behind in carbon emission governance theory, policy instrument design, environmental governance, carbon market operations, and carbon sequestration technologies. The government needs to advance in these areas to fulfill China's climate ambitions and make a substantial contribution to resolving the global climate issue.

13.9.1 Solutions and Support Systems for China's Climate Ambitions

The emergence of the CELM presents an opportunity to transform the foundational landscape of climate economics in China. With the CELM as a guiding principle, China's carbon emission governance system, carbon market development, and carbon sequestration technology and industry stand to achieve significant breakthroughs, positioning the country at the forefront of these fields.

Guided by the CELM and focused on the CELM global carbon neutral solution, China should invest in the development of technologies and industries associated with two core systems (the Global Decarbonation System and the Global Green Energy Supply System) and four subsystems (the CTMS, the NCTM, the GEI, and the IETM). Efforts should include active investment in both the soft and hard infrastructure required to support these systems, promoting the establishment of a carbon currency system, and taking a leading role to secure a larger market share and enhanced international influence in the green transformation of the global community. It is particularly important to integrate related industries and software system construction organically to achieve a greater overall advantage. The Chinese government has a real opportunity to attain global climate leadership within the next four decades (Fig. 13.1).

Through the organic integration of various subsystems, China can build a robust architecture to support its climate ambitions. By actively piloting the framework domestically, once mature, it can be rapidly introduced to the international market, contributing to global carbon neutrality. If specific breakthroughs are achieved in each subsystem, the synergistic advantages will amplify, bringing China closer to realizing its climate aspirations and enhancing its global contributions. In turn, this will bolster China's international influence and discourse power.

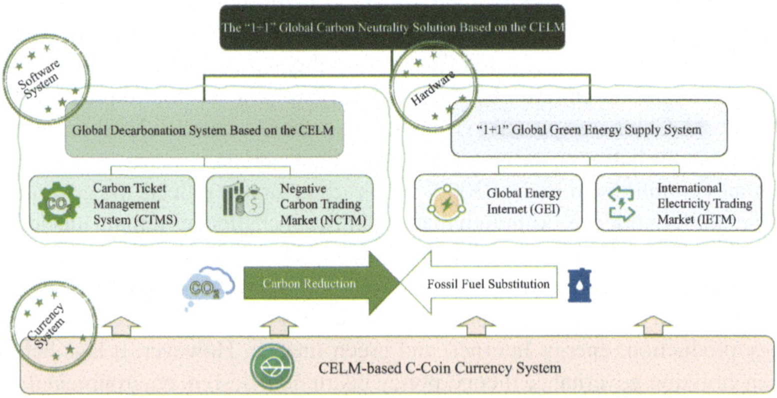

Fig. 13.1 An architecture to support China's climate ambitions

13.9.2 Key Breakthroughs in the Support Systems

China has a solid foundation for achieving its global climate ambitions and establishing major subsystems. It is imperative to race against time to improve and promote these support systems. Firstly, progress on global climate issues cannot be delayed; secondly, in the competition for influence, technology, industry, and finance, the Chinese government must remain vigilant and proactive.

1. Continually improving the theoretical system of climate governance based on the CELM

To achieve its climate ambitions, China must lead academically in global climate governance, securing the commanding heights in academic and theoretical exploration, and increasing its influence in setting rules and standards for global climate governance. Academic research should focus on top-level design, problem-solving, and practical applications, while controlling the number of purely academic studies aimed at publishing papers and securing funding. The research capabilities in sociology, law, and economics need enhancement, and China should strive for prominence in international academic organizations that set standards. In the past three decades, China has faced challenges in this regard, and this must change. The introduction of the CELM represents a breakthrough. Domestic dual carbon research forces should strengthen integration and collaboration, accelerate the refinement of relevant theoretical systems, and support the continuous improvement of implementation plans. Meanwhile, they are expected to consistently address practical issues, and exert positive influence on the international community. This will enable more countries to recognize and support the solutions proposed by Chinese government.

2. Accelerating the construction of an internationally-oriented CTMS

The government should expedite the launch of the CTMS to quickly gain application effects and experience. The deployment of the CTMS will mobilize all societal organizations and individuals to participate in carbon emission reduction, beyond the current scope of about 2,000 enterprises.

Upon gaining experience, the system should be rapidly promoted globally. This will not only expand the influence of Chinese solutions but also establish a China-led international standard for carbon footprint data. Additionally, it will lay a solid foundation for data interoperability and the development of an international carbon market.

3. Building an internationally-oriented NCTM Based on the CELM

Presently, Guangzhou and Hainan are actively constructing an international carbon market. To achieve a breakthrough, it is essential to shift from a carbon emission rights-based approach to the CELM-based negative carbon market framework. This will allow for the rapid accumulation of practical experience and subsequent expansion to the global stage.

4. Accelerating the construction of a Global Energy Internet

The Global Energy Internet is likely one of the greatest inventions since the Information Internet and is a critical infrastructure for achieving carbon neutrality. It is capable of transmitting energy over thousands of kilometers with less than 2% loss. Establishing a large photovoltaic energy base across the deserts of the Earth's in three major regions could provide a reliable supply of photovoltaic clean energy, meeting the global demand for round-the-clock clean energy, a vision of limitless potential. China should leverage its technical expertise in UHV power grids, accelerate their construction and application domestically, and promote them globally through the United Nations after achieving successful outcomes, thus leading the development of the Global Energy Internet.

Additionally, China is expected to accelerate the advancement of smart grid technology, support the construction and operation of International Energy Trading Market, and gain greater influence over the transmission and distribution of the Global Energy Internet.

5. Building a large-scale, low-cost green energy production network

China should accelerate the construction of green renewable energy production bases primarily using photovoltaic and wind power, and capitalize on the scale and technological advantages of China's green energy industry to hasten the substitution of fossil fuel power generation domestically. Meanwhile, China should expand this scale advantage to supply power to the world via the energy Internet, thereby securing a larger share of the global green power supply market.

6. Accelerating the development of manufacturing sector for green energy industries

In the equipment manufacturing sector for photovoltaic and wind power industries, China has achieved leading positions in technology, quality, and cost-efficiency. To maintain this lead and secure market share, China needs to stay ahead in technology, raw materials, quality assurance, and manufacturing costs. Under the guidance of sound governmental policies, China's manufacturing sector for green energy industries has made enormous success, gained international recognition, and paid a high price, too. Efforts must continue to accelerate development and sustain these advantages.

7. Increasing incentives for carbon sequestration technology and manufacturing industries

Carbon sequestration technologies, including CCUS technologies and CO_2 development and utilization technologies, have vast potential for growth. CO_2 might become a resource and material utilized across various industries. Presently, CO_2 has already been employed in oil recovery and new power generation media, and further breakthroughs are imminent. The government should leverage the market scale and financial benefits of the carbon market to strongly support the R&D of diverse carbon sequestration technologies, offer ample incentives for innovations that utilize CO_2 as a production resource, and foster the international competitiveness of these technologies.

8. Developing carbon removal (negative carbon) industry

With advanced carbon sequestration technology, the carbon removal industry can be vigorously developed to produce a significant amount of "Real Negative CO_2". Trading these assets in the international carbon market can generate foreign exchange earnings, aiding China in accelerating its carbon neutrality goals and contributing to the global market. The carbon removal industry will play a pivotal role in solving global climate issues, with enormous potential and worth pursuing. Large-scale afforestation, protection of marine mangroves, and preservation of wetlands are also key directions for the carbon removal industry, generating carbon removals while improving the environment.

9. Developing green finance and green international investment

Green finance serves as the driving force and accelerator for carbon neutrality, since decarbonation projects, technology R&D, and other initiatives require comprehensive financial support. With over $200 trillion in global investment needed for carbon neutrality, if China's solutions play to their strengths, China's capital advantage can exert greater influence. It is worth noting that China's progress toward carbon neutrality and its contributions to addressing global climate issues not only require the support of China's green finance but will, in turn, foster the development of green finance within China and accelerate the internationalization of the Chinese currency.

The Chinese government needs to formulate a detailed green finance development plan, prioritizing the development of an international NCTM. For instance, leading investments in green projects in underdeveloped and developing countries and regions, such as renewable energy production bases and carbon removal initiatives, will increase China's positive influence in these areas.

13.9.3 Outlook

In summary, the journey toward carbon neutrality presents both challenges and opportunities, entailing a profound transformation of the economy and society, impacting a wide array of fields. The principle of "ideas take the lead and technologies play the pivotal role" will be prominently displayed throughout this process. For China to secure a leading edge in the new round of international competition where climate issues serve as the core carrier, the country must engage in proactive research and planning, strategic top-level design, and systematic layout. Through advancements in ideological theory and technology, China aims to gain industrial dominance, making global carbon neutrality a key driver of its national rejuvenation.

China has laid a solid foundation to achieve the "3060" dual carbon targets. Under the strong leadership of the Communist Party of China (CPC), the government will leverage the advantages of the Chinese system and mobilize the talents across various fields. Supported by world-leading theories and technologies, the government is well-equipped to create a comprehensive solution to global climate issues, positioning itself as a leader in academic, technical, and financial aspects of climate change to lead all countries toward significant early achievements in carbon neutrality. In short, China aims to make the greatest contribution to protecting the Earth and fostering the sustainable development of a community with a shared future for mankind.

Chapter 14
New Principles for Public Goods

Through a comprehensive review and analysis of theoretical exploration and governance practices related to global climate change in the past three decades, this book identifies existing problems within the current economic theory of climate change and the implementation of decarbonation strategies. It introduces a novel framework, from foundational theory to practical solutions. The CELM offers a fresh theoretical framework and innovative perspectives for the economics of climate change, providing enhanced opportunities to address the global climate challenges effectively. In the realm of governing large-scale complex public goods characterized by spatial and temporal externalities, the CELM surpasses the limitations of traditional frameworks such as the Pigouvian Tax principle, the Coase Theorem, and Nordhaus' climate economic models, introducing significant innovations and advancements to the foundational theories of global climate governance.

The CELM reveals the core and essence of current global climate change (First Principles), establishing a new top-level theory for global climate governance. It lays the groundwork for the international community to overcome the challenges in climate governance and build a fair and efficient global climate governance system. By integrating the concept of a shared future for humanity, the CELM transcends the limitations of traditional climate economics theories. It shifts the focus from calculating long-term carbon emissions to carbon pricing based on total emissions target and net-zero emission time target. Utilizing intelligent analysis of the macroeconomic impacts of carbon footprint data and carbon prices, the theory promotes efficient and precise market-based integrated carbon pricing. Moreover, by regulating the entire carbon–neutral process through a unified carbon price factor, it aims to balance macroeconomic factors, the international trade, regional development, and consumer interests, thereby achieving optimal global efficiency and meeting carbon reduction goals. This approach seeks to establish a fairer and more effective policy framework, contributing to the goal of limiting global average temperature increase to 1.5 °C, as set by the IPCC.

B. Yang, *The Carbon Emission Liability Mechanism*,
https://doi.org/10.1007/978-981-96-3612-9_14

The CELM holds the potential to expedite the achievement of carbon neutrality by a decade and save trillions of dollars in investments. This could clarify the path towards resolving the pressing issue of global climate change.

Moreover, the CELM, which has demonstrated significant utility in climate governance, can be adapted for application to other large-scale complex public goods, evolving into a more universal principle for public goods.

14.1 Innovations in Climate Change Economics

In the field of climate change economics, the CELM introduces significant innovations in several key areas.

14.1.1 Redefining Climate Change Economics

As the saying goes, a problem well stated is a problem half solved. For over three decades, the dilemma in climate change economics has stemmed from differing definitions of the problem across various schools of thought, leading governments astray. Many have relied on the Pigouvian Tax principle, specifically, the carbon tax method, to address the externality of carbon emissions. Their approach lies in how to accurately calculate long-term social costs and apply appropriate discount rates. This has resulted in inconsistent approaches, exemplified by the varying carbon prices calculated by three US administrations according to their political needs. Even renowned economists like William Nordhaus and Sir Nicholas Stern have highlighted substantial discrepancies in carbon pricing, leaving policymakers uncertain about how to proceed.

The carbon trading scheme based on the Coase Theorem, which focuses on the allocation of carbon emission rights, has also led to misguided efforts both internationally and domestically. These missteps are not due to flaws in the original theories proposed by Pigou and Coase but rather to their subsequent misapplication. Their ideas remain crucial components for addressing climate issues. However, they were formulated during an era that did not grapple with the complexities of super-complex public goods like carbon emissions. Instead, they addressed simpler public goods scenarios, such as conflicts between farms and ranches, or between factory emissions and local residents. We could not simply apply the theories of our predecessors to solve global climate change, which is quite different from these simple public goods.

Global climate change we face involves the governance of large-scale and complex public goods with spatial and temporal externalities. Significant theoretical and policy innovations are required to effectively tackle these challenges. Notably, Coase criticized modern economists for engaging in "blackboard economics" and emphasized the importance of empirical investigation and deriving solutions from real-world practices rather than merely replicating existing economic theories.

The CELM clarifies the confusion in climate change economics and redefines the true proposition of this field.

Firstly, it presents a new understanding of global climate change as public goods. Global climate change is a complex and large-scale system that possesses complexities not found in ordinary public goods. One distinctive feature is its spatial and temporal nature. Over the long term, carbon emissions from coal burning anywhere on the planet can affect the entire globe. If temperatures rise by 2 °C, some areas might flood, while others could see increased food production. Another feature is the vast number of stakeholders involved. Global climate change affects all countries, regions, non-productive organizations, businesses, and individuals indiscriminately, making the coordination of interests due to policy settings more challenging than ever. The third feature is the high level of systemic complexity. While carbon emission reduction benefits all countries, organizations, and individuals, determining who bears the cost and how liabilities are allocated pose a significant challenge.

The CELM proposes a new understanding that carbon emissions constitute large-scale, complex public good with temporal and spatial externalities. It integrates knowledge and technology from multiple disciplines, breaks through previous theories, and seeks appropriate solutions to better achieve fairness and enhance efficiency.

Secondly, it offers a new definition of the key tasks for global carbon neutrality solutions. The key tasks for global carbon neutrality are not about calculating the long-term social costs of carbon emissions, nor setting carbon tariffs, or allocating carbon emission rights. Rather, they are about achieving the IPCC's optimal temperature control goals, simplifying international coordination, maximizing the benefits of input and output, minimizing the impacts on the macroeconomy, and reducing the loss of social welfare. Based on this, the CELM posits that the key tasks of the global carbon neutrality solution include: addressing the spatial and temporal externalities and large-scale complexity of carbon emissions, clarifying the responsibility system and the comprehensive big data of the global carbon footprint, realizing market-based integrated carbon pricing, formulating fair and efficient policies, and effectively coordinating the interests among international stakeholders, to achieve the goal of global carbon neutrality.

14.1.2 Insight into the Importance of Consumer Liability Mechanism on Climate Change

The CELM introduces the consumer liability mechanism, which can more efficiently and equitably address the challenges of international coordination and regional interest alignment in climate issues. The CELM conducted credible research and analysis, concluding that the selection of liability mechanism had either been neglected or deliberately avoided in previous studies, which is exactly the critical point.

14.1.3 Designing an Efficient and Low-Cost Method to Obtain Comprehensive Carbon Footprint Data

Only by breaking through the barriers of comprehensive carbon footprint data and conducting top-level design for a new decarbonation management system can the CELM achieve significant improvements in overall efficiency. In the current digital age, particularly drawing upon China's extensive experience from the "Golden Tax Project", there exists a viable solution for managing carbon footprint data. By processing the input and output of carbon tickets, a large database for the carbon footprint can be established efficiently and at low cost, spanning from individual organizations to the entire social industrial chain. Using big data and algorithms, this approach can automatically generate and frequently update a dynamic, accurate, and complete database for societal carbon emission factors.

14.1.4 New Schemes for Integrated Carbon Pricing

To address the spatial and temporal externalities of carbon emissions, social costs must be internalized in a structured manner. Current carbon pricing methods based on social costs (such as carbon taxes, also known as "price coordination mechanism") and those based on carbon emission rights (such as carbon markets, also known as "quantitative mechanism") are rooted in traditional economic models for simple public goods, which have numerous shortcomings and fail to resolve the issue of carbon emission pricing. The CELM proposes a goal-oriented and market-driven solution leveraging comprehensive carbon footprint data, carbon neutrality processes, and macroeconomic dynamics. The CELM-based Integrated Carbon Pricing Strategy (CICPS) is systematically implemented through machine learning and artificial neural network intelligent analysis. CICPS, grounded in the CELM, is a novel approach to pricing the external costs of large-scale, complex public goods with spatial and temporal nature. This new integrated scheme avoids many drawbacks of traditional pricing methods for external costs of public goods and offers numerous advantages.

For a long time, the economic community has not adequately explored the possibility of building a comprehensive big data system for the carbon footprint of society, nor has it sufficiently leveraged the capacities of digital information systems, big data, and intelligent analysis systems. These three factors are increasingly influencing economics. Economists alone, relying solely on economic theories, find it challenging to solve challenges associated with large-scale and complex public goods. The economic community should place greater emphasis on the integration and application of theories, tools, and methodologies from diverse disciplines.

Leveraging carbon footprint big data and macro operational data and harnessing the significant capabilities of machine learning and intelligent analysis systems are far more potent than the macroeconomic analysis models currently employed by governments. As time goes by, the data will accumulate significantly, algorithms will become more mature, and the analysis results from intelligent systems will become more accurate and effective. Consequently, policy instrument based on comprehensive market-oriented carbon pricing will become increasingly practical.

This is akin to the current use of single currency interest rates as a primary control tool in macroeconomics. For instance, the People's Bank of China and the Federal Reserve can effectively intervene and adjust the macroeconomy by using interest rate as the main instrument alongside supportive fiscal and monetary policies.

14.1.5 Driving Carbon Emission Reduction Across Society

The CELM ingeniously utilizes the operations of the CTMS and the organizational and household carbon account system to efficiently and cost-effectively mobilize all organizations and individuals to actively reduce carbon emissions. By harnessing the power of the system, it fosters a culture of low-carbon consumption. This is an efficient method that has not yet been discovered elsewhere in the world.

The innovations of the CELM are crucial for breaking through the current climate dilemma. Continuous refinement and application are required by the international community.

14.2 Innovations in Climate Governance Policy Instruments

Currently, a wide array of policy instruments for carbon emission reduction have been implemented both domestically and internationally, yet the outcomes have been disappointing. The Global Carbon Neutrality Solution based on the CELM embodies multifaceted innovations and promising feasibility.

14.2.1 Addressing Most Challenges of Current Climate Policy Design

The CELM meticulously incorporates considerations such as carbon neutrality process, international trade dynamics, macroeconomic impacts, potential losses to social welfare, incentives for the adoption of carbon-reducing technologies, and secure funding avenues for emission reductions. This holistic approach mitigates significant risks and significantly reduces the complexity of coordinating diverse stakeholder interests.

14.2.2 Significantly Reducing the Coordination Difficulties of Almost All International Interest Groups

Through the consumer liability mechanism and the CTMS, the challenges associated with carbon tariffs in international trade can be addressed in a straightforward and quantitative manner. This approach addresses the credibility of carbon footprint data and greatly reduces the difficulty of international coordination. Approaches such as Nordhaus' carbon tax harmonization and the allocation of carbon emission rights based on different principles have proven to be nearly ineffective. Under the CELM, international coordination is simplified to negotiating the price of "International Negative CO_2" and implementing phased pricing, marking a significant breakthrough after more than three decades of international decarbonation coordination.

14.2.3 Providing the Government with a Simple, Controllable, and Powerful Intelligent Control System for Decarbonation

By correlating carbon prices with macroeconomic data, an intelligent control system for decarbonation based on carbon pricing is modelled and established. Through the accumulation of big data and annual machine learning of intelligent systems, the carbon neutrality process can be controlled with increasing accuracy, optimizing macroeconomic effects and the efficiency of the entire society and the whole world. The government can effectively manage the overall carbon neutrality process through a single element, the carbon price, more effectively than it regulates the macroeconomy through monetary interest rates.

14.2.4 Fundamentally Improving the Fairness and Efficiency of Policy Instruments

Decarbonation policies often tend to result in regressive effects. The CELM can better improve social equity through mechanisms, such as consumer liability and household carbon account management, and it is relatively easy to adjust policies.

14.2.5 Execution and Implementation of the CELM

Contrary to conventional governance instruments like carbon taxes and emission rights, the CELM presents a holistic, streamlined, and highly effective alternative. It excels in practical implementation, boasting low costs, minimal state intervention, and a heightened level of market integration. Nevertheless, to ensure optimal carbon reduction and pricing, robust central government oversight is crucial. Thanks to its advanced marketization, government agencies face reduced administrative burdens, thereby mitigating the risk of corruption.

14.3 The CELM: Future Research Projects

The introduction of the CELM paves the way for a paradigm shift in achieving global carbon neutrality, offering a more efficacious and equitable approach to mitigating carbon emissions on both international and regional scales. This framework endeavors to minimize negative economic impacts while amplifying positive impacts. Given its nascent stage, comprehensive research across various disciplines is imperative to refine its theoretical underpinnings and practical implementation plans, ultimately translating the CELM into a groundbreaking Chinese solution to the global climate change.

The research landscape for the CELM is vast and multifaceted:

14.3.1 Sociological, Legal, and Governance Dimensions of Global Climate Challenges

Direction 1: Proposing an international legal framework for global climate change.

Sort out the current international legal framework governing global climate issues, conduct an in-depth analysis of the core issues and underlying causes, assess and build upon existing achievements, and propose a new international legal framework according to an advanced theoretical system.

Direction 2: Addressing fairness challenges in global climate action

Focus on fairness challenges among interest groups, nations, domestic regions, and communities. Through meticulous analysis of the current landscape, strive to develop targeted solutions.

Direction 3: Resolving the "Impossible Trinity" in global climate governance

Conduct an in-depth analysis of the intricate relationship between the CELM and the "Impossible Trinity" that often confronts global climate governance: balancing global synergy, fairness and efficiency, and national interests. Unlock innovative solutions and innovate governance theories and operational blueprints for global public goods.

14.3.2 *Economics of Climate Change*

Direction 4: New perspectives of Economics of Climate Change

Global carbon neutrality presents a challenge to the neoclassical economics that has dominated for the past four decades. For spillover effects that span time and space, such as climate change, merely accounting for externalities is insufficient to reflect the environmental constraints on economic development within the basic assumptions of neoclassical economics: complete information, certainty, and perfect competition. The single metric of carbon emissions will become a unified constraint on global economic and social development, necessitating an analysis of their impacts on economic growth. How will the interplay among public policy, social governance, and market mechanisms evolve during the transition to carbon neutrality?

These questions will be answered by time. The progress towards carbon neutrality will prompt exploration into bridging the gap between the real market economy and the idealized neoclassical market economy.

Direction 5: Impact of global implementation of the CELM on the interests of different groups

The externalities of carbon emissions are global, and coordinated worldwide action to reduce emissions is extremely challenging. Historically, carbon emission rights have been equated with carbon development rights, and the impact of implementing a new mechanism on the interests of countries, regions, and stakeholder groups will draw significant international attention. Establishing new rules for the carbon emissions is key, and shifting from "producer liability" to "consumer liability" will entail substantial adjustments in the interests of the involved parties. The international community must exert considerable effort to construct a new discourse and governance coordination system.

14.3.3 *Carbon Emission Liability Mechanism (CELM)*

Direction 6: Macroeconomic impact of implementing the CELM

From a price of zero yuan to the actual cost of carbon neutrality, how will negative carbon affect the macroeconomy?

The CELM is a holistic framework influencing economic organizations at various levels. For over two decades, governments have been cautious about introducing decarbonation policies like carbon taxes and emission allowances, primarily due to concerns about their macroeconomic impacts. The CELM advocates for a relatively uniform carbon reduction policy across industries, and how will this affect the macroeconomy and specific sectors? Additionally, it is necessary to consider the design and effect analysis of policy instruments tailored to each industry segment.

Direction 7: In-depth study of the CELM effects

Fairness and effectiveness are key criteria for evaluating the quality of policy instruments. Carbon taxes have regressive effects, and what is the impact of carbon tickets? Are farmers paying more? Do the poor pay more? Does it benefit developed regions more? How should the government cope with that? Current research suggests it exerts a positive effect, but more in-depth quantitative research is needed.

If issues arise, how can they be coordinated with fiscal and tax policies to make adjustments?

Direction 8: Impacts of the implementation of the CELM on international competitiveness of Chinese products

The launch of international carbon tariffs is imminent, with the CBAM prepared for implementation, and the climate club of developed countries is closely watching. China takes the lead in implementing the CTMS and the NCTM based on the CELM, aiming to raise the carbon price to a reasonable level as soon as possible and accelerate convergence towards the CCUS market price. This is the only viable path to expedite the realization of carbon neutrality. What will be the impact on the cost of China's exports during this transition? How significant will the effect on competitiveness be? Will exports increase or decrease? These are critical questions. The preliminary judgment of this book is that once Western countries implement the CBAM carbon tariff policy, if China initiates the CELM first, it will be highly beneficial to China's export trade.

Direction 9: Government control over the carbon market and macroeconomy through integrated carbon pricing

The government controls two key elements of the carbon trading market: the quantity of imported carbon sources (negative carbon) and the negative carbon price. By adjusting the supply, the government modulates the price in carbon market and regulates the impacts of decarbonation on the macroeconomy.

Utilizing comparative analysis of macroeconomic models and historical data via AI neural network algorithms, better algorithmic tools are identified and more effective regulatory strategies are developed.

Direction 10: Impacts of the CELM on regional economies

It is anticipated that the CELM will be highly beneficial to less developed areas. How will the CELM affect the economic interactions among energy-producing regions, carbon sink regions, and developed regions? Further quantitive analysis of the interactions between carbon footprints and carbon cost compensation among regions is required. The national carbon–neutral fund will foster a more balanced and healthy national development.

Based on model simulations, the effects of different parameter settings can be predicted to identify the relatively optimal solutions.

Direction 11: Analysis of the impacts of the CELM on resident groups

The regressive nature of the policy is unfavorable for ordinary people. After the implementation of the CELM, the unfairness derived from the consumer liability mechanism may exist, therefore, the differential effects between rich and poor, urban and rural areas, need to be further quantified and analyzed. Better adjustment policy instruments should be designed to mitigate any adverse impacts.

14.3.4 Carbon Ticket Management System (CTMS)

Direction 12: Deepening the design of the implementation plan for the CTMS

There are numerous details within the CTMS implementation plan that require thorough study and verification. To develop a complete and reliable implementation plan, many supporting laws, technologies, data standards, and operational plans must be feasible. Extensive research and development of each subsystem are necessary.

Direction 13: International operation of the CTMS

Bringing the CTMS to the global stage and establishing international standards holds significant value for achieving global carbon neutrality. As a standardized commodity, negative carbon can be traded globally, ensuring that resources flow to countries where the cost of negative carbon is lowest, thus maximizing fairness and social welfare. Building on the experience gained in one country, more design work is needed to promote the acceptance of the CTMS within the international community.

Direction 14: A coding system covering all materials, products, and services across society

The coding system represents a critical aspect of digital management for the entire society. An efficient, comprehensive, and intelligent new commodity coding system is needed, one that supports both extremely granular mass category analysis and the daily proliferation of objects, products, and services.

Whether the current international standard GS1 can meet the needs of the CTMS is questionable. Given the current international landscape, it is worth exploring in depth whether China needs a set of coding standards that it can control.

14.3.5 CELM-Based NCTM and Green Finance

Direction 15: In-depth study on the top-level design of the CELM-based NCTM

With carbon neutrality as the goal, the CELM-based NCTM aims to trade "negative carbon", envisioning a global unified carbon market while also meeting the challenges posed by international carbon tariffs. Therefore, many schemes need designing for the NCTM, including:

1. Detailed design of the promotion path for a global unified NCTM.
2. Research on solutions for the NCTM in relation to international carbon tariffs.

Direction 16: Research on the development of the international carbon market and the evolution of the global financial landscape

How can China promote the construction of an international carbon market and transition from the current market for carbon emission rights to a negative carbon market? The impact of the international carbon market on the global financial landscape remains a topic for further study.

14.3.6 Government Carbon Neutrality Policy and Industry Policy Based on the CELM

Direction 17: Comparative analysis of the advantages and disadvantages of the CELM versus existing carbon reduction policy instruments

Current government policy instruments include carbon taxes, carbon allowances, trading carbon emission rights, government subsidies, energy taxes, environmental taxes, and other carbon reduction policy instruments. It is necessary to compare and analyze the advantages and disadvantages of the CELM versus existing policy instruments, focusing particularly on equity and efficiency, rent-seeking issues, double taxation, and the effects on global governance.

Direction 18: Research on the CELM-based "1+N" policy design

The CELM framework serves as the "1" to achieve carbon neutrality, while the industry policies and fiscal policies designed according to this framework represent the "N", forming a policy matrix that will better accelerate carbon reduction. After the top-level policy instrument is established, the policy design for various industries remains crucial, as sound policy design can play a significant role.

Direction 19: Research on innovation incentive mechanisms and subsidy policy design for various green transformation industries

Within the entire industrial system aimed at carbon neutrality, there are many segments. How can we incentivize their innovation and industry development, and how can we design subsidy policies to support them? In recent years, the annual scale of fraudulent subsidies for new energy vehicles has reached tens of billions of yuan, a long-standing issue remaining unsolved, suggesting potential loopholes and problems in the top-level design of the policy system.

Industrial subsidy policies are generally prone to serious negative effects, such as fraud, high regulatory costs, and corruption in approvals. In designing the incentive mechanism, external costs should be internalized as much as possible to reflect the actual product cost, highlighting the cost advantages of new technologies and brand value advantages, minimizing direct subsidies for new technologies and large-scale free funding for projects. Policies like tax preferences and low-interest loans may be more suitable. Of course, the circumstances of each technological segment are quite different, requiring specialized research and policy design.

14.3.7 Management of Other GHG Emissions

Direction 20: Schemes for other GHG emissions

The CELM effectively addresses the challenges associated with carbon emissions and sets a good example for solving problems related to other GHG and environmental public goods. The international community can leverage and adapt the CELM to tackle GHG control issues, such as methane (CH_4) and nitrous oxide (N_2O), given that the greenhouse effect of CH_4 is 20 times stronger than that of CO_2, and the greenhouse effect of N_2O is 300 times stronger than that of CO_2.

Furthermore, the CELM provides a model and reference for addressing other environmental public goods issues.

14.3.8 Global Energy Internet and International Energy Trading Market

Direction 21: Construction scheme for the Global Energy Internet

Research focuses on the three main mechanisms of the GEI: First, the hardware network connection mechanism, including technical objectives, technical mechanisms, and implementation plans. Second, the market mechanism, involving the allocation of responsibilities and investment distribution among participants, and how to secure investment returns and sufficient incentives. Third, the legal protection mechanism, such as how to enforce technical standards and market norms through legal systems to protect the interests of both large and small countries.

Direction 22: Construction and operation plan for the IETM

The IETM is a cornerstone of the Green Energy Supply System.

The top-level design, pricing mechanism, carbon cost treatment mechanism, trading rules, operational management systems, and many other aspects of the IETM need to be researched and designed.

Direction 23: Top-level design of China's power market reform

Summarize the successes and failures of China's reforms over the past two decades. The current top-level design reform under existing technical conditions and market environments encompasses the management system, technical architecture, and market system, and explores how to eliminate monopolies, enhance efficiency, and reduce costs.

Direction 24: Transmission network construction scheme for China

Designing the optimal technical and market mechanism architecture for China's Energy Interconnection ensures safe operations while breaking natural monopolies, fostering a more competitive market environment where investment efficiency is improved and overall transmission costs are reduced.

Direction 25: Reform plan for China's electricity pricing mechanism

Seek the most efficient pricing mechanism for allocating power resources in China, eliminating cross-subsidies and reducing fiscal subsidies. Use the pricing mechanism to promote the development of new energy sources and accelerate the phase-out of fossil fuels. Conduct an in-depth analysis of the household electricity account mechanism to ensure that the welfare of residents is minimally impacted by carbon emission costs and electricity price reforms, thereby enhancing their perceived gains from electricity market reforms.

14.3.9 China's Discourse Power and Influence in International Climate Cooperation

Direction 26: Achievements, problems, challenges, and strategies in new stage of the research on carbon neutrality solutions in China

Currently, China faces a significant shortfall in academic discourse power within the context of international climate cooperation. For instance, despite a notable increase in citations and a significant rise in proportion, Chinese literature accounts for only 6.1%, 2.6%, and 3.0% of the total citations in the fields of climate change science, impact adaptation, and mitigation, respectively, as reported in the Sixth Assessment Report of the IPCC. This disparity is starkly inconsistent with China's carbon neutral industrial capabilities and its national standing. To some extent, this has constrained the influence of "China's voice" in global climate governance. China should accelerate innovations in carbon reduction technology, green energy, carbon-neutral economics, and policy instruments to elevate its international status.

Direction 27: Strategies for Chinese academics to exert influence on global climate issues

Over the past three decades, China has dedicated substantial research resources to carbon neutrality. However, how can Chinese academics exert greater influence and have a stronger discourse power in the global climate forum and standard-setting processes? This requires strategic planning, organization, and effective action by the government; investment alone is insufficient.

14.4 Analysis of New Principles for Public Goods

Following a comprehensive review of the current global carbon neutrality system, it is clear that the CELM and its Solution will play a pivotal role in addressing climate issues. This represents humanity's hope for solving the global climate crisis. It is expected that the international community will transition from a carbon emission reduction pathway based on producer liability and carbon emission rights to a CELM decarbonation pathway centered on consumer liability and negative carbon products.

Furthermore, the CELM, originating from the governance of carbon emissions, exhibits stronger universality and can be abstracted and upgraded into a governance theory for general public goods. Compared to the traditional Pigouvian Tax principle and the Coase Theorem, which address public goods issues, the CELM is more practical and applicable.

By further abstracting and upgrading the CELM proposed in this book, we can derive New Principles for Public Goods (PPG): If the negative external liability of public goods can be clearly defined, the amount of liability can be measured by certain methods or confirmed through transaction negotiations, and there are corresponding offsetting goods, then a specific liability mechanism can be designed and a trading market for these offsetting goods can be created. This would improve the efficiency of the allocation of social resources and achieve Pareto improvement.

The PPG is anticipated to become a more significant application theory for public goods following the Pigouvian Tax principle and the Coase Theorem.

14.4.1 Characteristics of New Principles for Public Goods

Unlike the Coase Theorem, which takes the right as the starting point to solve the problem, the CELM begins with liability to address the issues associated with carbon emissions. This approach aligns with the Pigouvian tax principle, which also starts from the external liability of public goods.

The PPG establishes a market for liability offsets by clarifying liability and identifying suitable liability offsets, thus creating a fully compatible and effective market for liability hedging. Through the successful construction of a market mechanism for resolving the negative externalities of public goods and establishing an effective market for offsetting goods, the PPG enhances the efficiency of the allocation of social resources. This breaks the limitations of the market mechanism in the Coase Theorem, which can only be applied to the field of simple and large-scale or complex but small-scale public goods.

For large-scale public goods, the government's design of trading markets based on negative externalities often fails to establish a fully compatible and effective market, making it difficult to achieve optimal resource allocation. It can even lead to adverse outcomes, such as the overall loss and elimination of an industry, causing collective losses throughout the entire industrial chain. In such cases, the trading market deals only with the trading of rights, lacking a trading mechanism for liability offsets, meaning no one would spend money to purchase liability offsets to counteract the externalities of public goods.

The Coase Theorem primarily relies on the market mechanism to solve problems and is widely respected. Beyond the ETS, is there another way for the market mechanism to address public goods issues? The PPG offers a feasible path toward marketization.

The Pigouvian Tax principle depends on government pricing and administrative enforcement. While society generally disapproves of tax increases, the Pigouvian

Table 14.1 Comparison of problem-solving approaches among three public goods theories

Public goods theory	Solutions	Problem-solving
The Pigouvian Tax principle	tax	Liability → the amount of liability → tax → assuming liability
The Coase Theorem	Trading market for rights	Rights → determining rights → trading of rights → paying the cost
The PPG	Liability offset market	Liability → the amount of liability → trading of offset → liability offsetting

Tax principle has its advantages: it starts from liability and internalizes the social costs into the product, bringing the total social cost closer to the total private cost. The PPG fully integrates and absorbs these two advantages of the Pigouvian Tax principle. The amount of liability for all organizations is effectively determined through the circulation of carbon tickets, and the liability is offset by the trading of negative carbon, ingeniously achieving the internalization of carbon emission costs and solving the problem through the market mechanism.

In summary, the PPG combines the strengths of both the Pigouvian Tax principle and the Coase Theorem while avoiding their weaknesses, representing a significant advancement in the theory of public goods governance (see Table 14.1).

14.4.2 Examples of Application of the New Principles for Public Goods

The PPG not only can play a significant role in the field of carbon emissions through the establishment of the CELM but also can be applied to numerous current environmental pollution fields to enhance current governance policies.

In chemical industry pollution control, the government typically mandates that manufacturers install accompanying pollution treatment facilities. The operational costs of these facilities are high, significantly increasing product costs, and there is considerable possibility for manufacturers to discharge pollutants without using the treatment facilities. Pollution treatment devices are often not operational, only being turned on during inspections by regulatory authorities, leading to "gray area" supervision issues. Since pollution treatment and discharge are intertwined, government oversight is challenging, requiring surprise inspections and imposing high demands on governmental supervision capacity and costs.

The offsetting of pollution discharge involves treating pollutants and discharging them after treatment. If the system design separates pollution treatment from discharging, managed by a third party, a liability offset product market, or even a competitive market in some large industrial zones, can be established, improving service quality and reducing costs. Government oversight would be greatly simplified, requiring merely verification of upstream and downstream trading contracts, equipment power consumption, and raw material usage.

There are numerous scenarios for managing public goods with negative externalities like carbon emissions and pollution discharge, and governmental decision-making bodies should prioritize the PPG when designing governance plans.

14.4.3 Differences Between the New Principles for Public Goods and the Coase Theorem in the Application of Carbon Emission Governance

Coase made a very important observation that if market transaction costs are sufficiently low, regardless of how initial property rights are defined, market transactions can facilitate the optimal allocation of resources. This is the most valuable contribution of Coase Theorem. Coase Theorem highlights two critical social truths: First, the definition of property rights is crucial. Individuals with permanent property rights are persistent, and clearly defined property rights encourage people to strive to maximize the value of those rights. The importance of property rights cannot be overstated. A society where property rights are not protected will find it very difficult to grow its total wealth. Second, the government should intervene as less as possible in areas where the market can effectively allocate resources, as free trade in the market enhances the efficiency of the allocation of social resources. Coase Theorem is particularly important and effective in the field with simple large-scale externalities and complex small-scale externalities, serving as the cornerstone theory for many social policy-making frameworks.

However, the effective application of the Coase Theorem has several prerequisites: First, property rights must be fully defined; second, transaction costs should be minimal; third, free trade must be feasible. Given the high requirements for its application scenarios, the Coase Theorem is challenging to apply directly to large-scale public goods. Instead, it offers a conceptual framework rather than a direct solution. Today, economists and policymakers in the realm of public goods tend to apply the theorem directly as a solution, resulting in rushed initial grants of power to governments to allocate public goods, which may not be ideal.

In dealing with large-scale, complex public goods, the Coase Theorem is limited due to its inherent constraints. The Coase Theorem cannot adequately address the incompatibility of interests of stakeholders in large public goods. Defining property rights can be either extremely difficult or costly, and the results of transactions in incompletely compatible markets can lead to poor allocation of social resources. The trading outcomes of a few or a small number of traders do not benefit other stakeholders and may even cause harm.

Theoretically, applying the Coase Theorem to address the problems of carbon emissions, specifically in terms of allocation and trading of carbon emission rights, has significant flaws and shortcomings.

Firstly, the initial allocation of carbon emission rights is extremely challenging, even with very high investment costs. Over the past three decades, despite efforts of 27 COP conferences, there has been no satisfactory resolution on the allocation of carbon emission rights among countries, and conflicts between nations have escalated, ultimately leading to a shift towards the Intended Nationally Determined Contributions (NDC) method. Similarly, the allocation of carbon emission rights within a nation is also fraught with difficulties and should be reconsidered. Although the national government holds absolute authority to impose distributions, it cannot achieve the desired outcome.

Secondly, there is another significant issue: the trading results of the carbon market for emission rights do not lead to the optimal allocation of social resources, and the associated social costs are excessively high, which is clearly unreasonable. China's carbon market has been nearly detrimental, causing widespread power outages that have significantly hampered economic growth.

The reason lies in the orientation of trading results, where organizations with higher marginal income per unit of carbon emission rights increase their purchases and expand their usage, while enterprises with lower marginal returns per unit of carbon emission rights reduce production and may eventually be phased out. As carbon prices continue to rise, entire industries might be eliminated, including the coal-fired power sector. Ultimately, the directive to cut power generation is highly detrimental to the macro-economy, resulting in substantial social welfare losses and extremely poor efficiency in social resource allocation.

The loss or elimination of entire industries is very detrimental to economic growth. Even though the coal-fired power industry is the highest emitter of carbon, we still do not recommend that the coal-fired power industry incur losses and shut down. If the entire coal-fired power industry were to cease operations, it would deal a severe blow to China's economy, potentially bringing the country's total GDP close to zero. The focus of carbon emission reduction only on sectors like coal-fired power, steel, and cement represents one of the greatest theoretical fallacies in the pursuit of global carbon neutrality, and the international community has paid a very high price for its persistent global promotion with high cost and low efficiency.

If the decarbonation mechanism were designed based on carbon emission liability, further grounded in consumer liability, and trading of negative carbon assets were conducted through a negative carbon market, enterprises and products with lower marginal costs of carbon emission reduction would reduce their emissions first, while enterprises with higher marginal costs would reduce their emissions later. But once the cost of carbon emissions is internalized, their production would decrease, thereby improving the efficiency of the allocation of social resources. If the cost of carbon emissions is reduced, social welfare can be enhanced. Furthermore, under the implementation of the CELM, carbon-intensive enterprises could receive greater rewards if they perform below the average level of their industry. Competitive units within all industries would only eliminate the worst enterprises and products with high-carbon emission intensity at the smallest possible scale, minimizing the scope of natural selection to the smallest competitive unit, ensuring the industrial chain remains unharmed and keeping the social cost of carbon emission reduction to a minimum. This would maximize social welfare and achieve optimal resource allocation. Natural selection based on the carbon emission intensity of the smallest competitive unit within the industry is very conducive to high-quality development and economic growth.

In summary, although both the Coase Theorem and the CELM embrace market mechanisms, their effects differ significantly. China should reconsider the market mechanism for carbon emission rights currently being implemented.

14.5 Outlook

The climate problem continues to worsen, and human self-rescue efforts have not yet succeeded; therefore, continued hard work is required!

The CELM has established a comprehensive suite of global carbon neutral solutions, ranging from theory to decarbonation governance policies, which markedly differs from the current system formed over more than three decades. It boasts higher decarbonation efficiency, lower social costs, and better social welfare benefits, and its implementation needs to be accelerated urgently.

While the current system is inefficient, carries high macroeconomic costs, and is challenging to coordinate both internationally and domestically, falling far short of governmental objectives, transitioning to a new system will also encounter numerous difficulties. Presently, many existing systems would require significant changes, or even be dismantled entirely, which would face significant conflicts of interest and substantial resistance. However, the current system falls short of meeting the targets set by the IPCC, and governments will have to accept the reality.

According to the IPCC report, humanity has only one last chance. In light of this urgency, we must strive to promote reforms within the global climate governance landscape. Firstly, the reform of the international regulatory framework is essential. We need to promote China's vision of "building a community with a shared future for mankind," advocate for the "consumer liability" mechanism, and establish an international unified negative carbon trading market based on the CELM. Secondly, the reform of the domestic decarbonation governance system is necessary. Aligning with the aspiration of carbon neutrality, while prioritizing equity and efficiency, we need to establish a system of policy instruments with high input–output ratios. Under the new theoretical framework, we should develop governance rules and relevant regulations, establish a national CTMS, and create a new NCTM, thereby formulating a "1+N" policy architecture.

Transitioning from the outdated to the innovative necessitates recognition and steadfast commitment at the national policy-making level. If China's CELM prove to be a pioneering success, it will have a transformative impact on China's development and national property in the forthcoming era. It is expected that CELM and its solutions will empower China to meet its "3060" dual carbon targets, actualize its climate aspirations, and serve as a global exemplar for carbon neutrality.

Of course, the CELM is novel and requires improvements in many aspects.

Chapter 15
The CELM and Its Solution: FAQ

Since the introduction of the CELM and the Global Carbon Neutrality Solution, numerous questions have been raised by experts within the industry, which is very beneficial for clarifying its theoretical framework. Here, we sort out these pertinent questions to facilitate a better understanding.

15.1 Basic Concept of Carbon Tickets

Q1: Is there any difference between the carbon tickets mentioned in the CELM and the forestry carbon tickets currently being explored by some provinces and cities in China?

A: The carbon ticket referred to in the CELM is a document that records the circulation of the CEL of goods (or services), also known as a carbon footprint record.

The ticket issued by the supplier is called an output ticket, while the ticket received by the purchasing party is termed an input ticket. This is analogous to the input and output tickets in China's value-added tax system.

Currently, some provinces and cities in China, such as Fujian and Zhejiang, are exploring the application of carbon tickets, which refer to the certification of carbon sequestration quantities from forestry carbon removal projects. This is part of the current CCER system and is used to purchase carbon allowances to offset a portion of carbon emissions. Its significance is quite different from the concept of "carbon ticket" in the CELM.

The pilot forestry carbon tickets in these provinces and cities are what the CELM calls quantity certificates of "negative carbon". After verification by the carbon removal certification system, they should be registered in the national unified "negative carbon" registration system and can then enter the carbon market for trading.

B. Yang, *The Carbon Emission Liability Mechanism*,
https://doi.org/10.1007/978-981-96-3612-9_15

Q2: Is the Carbon Emission Liability Mechanism (CELM) independently constructed? How does it compare with the "carbon ticket" concept proposed by Mr. Wang Yusuo, Chairman of ENN Group, and Professor Zhong Maochu of Nankai University during the 2022 Two Sessions[1]?

A: The CELM is an innovative theory in climate change economics and a global carbon neutrality solution proposed by a research team led by Dr. Yang Baoming of Tongji University, building upon the previous accomplishments in international climate change economics.

The "carbon ticket" concept, proposed by Mr. Wang Yusuo, Chairman of ENN Group, and Professor Zhong Maochu of Nankai University, refers to a certificate of carbon emission consumption rights, similar to the use of food tickets and cloth tickets in the planned economy era. However, in the digital era, such a scheme is inefficient. Moreover, it is difficult to formulate the allocation policy of carbon consumption rights. For individuals, they can be allocated evenly (which is also unreasonable in fact), but for different businesses and social organizations, there is no solution provided. These so-called carbon ticket schemes remain conceptual and are less feasible and more difficult to implement.

Q3: What exactly is the amount contained in the carbon ticket? Is it the "carbon content" or the amount of "transferred carbon liability" embodied in the commodity?

A: The amount contained in the carbon ticket can be defined as the amount of the CEL undertaken by both parties involved in the commodity transaction, which is also the amount of transferred carbon liability. It can also be viewed as the carbon emissions embodied within the commodity that are not offset. If the intermediary organizations do not conduct carbon offset procedures, it equates to undertaking the full CEL for the commodity's carbon footprint.

Under the CELM, producers are permitted to purchase negative carbon assets for carbon offsets, meaning the input tickets received at a certain production stage may not represent the actual carbon content of the commodity but rather the amount of transferred CEL.

Q4: Can carbon tickets be integrated with VAT invoices?

A: The carbon ticket is closely linked to the VAT invoice, but the two should operate independently to avoid complicating business transactions. The data from both systems should be interconnected, allowing for cross-verification. While the purpose and treatment principles of the two share some similarities, the differences are significant. From the outset, the carbon ticket should fully adopt digital form and there is no need to go through the process of paper bills.

Q5: Can carbon tickets be integrated with electricity, gas, fuel, and heating charges?

---

[1] The two sessions, China's biggest annual political event, refer to the annual sessions of the National People's Congress, the nation's top legislature, and the National Committee of the Chinese People's Political Consultative Conference, the country's top political advisory body.

A: A carbon ticket is circulated through an independent national CTMS, with each social organization responsible for offsetting their CEL on a regular basis. At the consumer end, the carbon fee can be flexibly designed according to the specific circumstances of different products and industries. The carbon fee in electricity, gas, fuel, and heating bills can be added in the current receipt format as an independent item, much like how drainage charges are currently levied.

Q6: What is the specific meaning of the red ticket and green ticket mentioned in the CELM-based carbon management system? What is their difference?

A: The CEL of each organization is confirmed through the transfer of carbon tickets. Here, the transfer of carbon tickets signifies the transfer of the CEL, which is a negative asset for the organization, also known as red tickets. The CTMS uses carbon tickets to record the accumulation and transfer of the CEL from carbon sources to various products or services throughout the entire industry chain of all organizations.

Warrants for various types of negative carbon assets can be called green tickets. Green tickets are positive assets that can generate income in the national carbon market. There is a hedging offset relationship between red and green tickets.

Every quarter, all organizations are required to settle their CEL. Organizations with a surplus CEL after deducting carbon inputs and outputs need to purchase negative carbon products in the national carbon market, i.e., obtaining green tickets, to achieve a red-green offset, thus assuming the corresponding carbon liability.

15.2 Liability and Commitment for Carbon Emissions

Q7: Approximately 60–70% of the carbon emissions associated with products of chemical companies originate from upstream energy enterprises and large chemical processes. Moreover, as for the downstream enterprises, their contribution to the products' carbon footprint is relatively lower. Therefore, the role of enterprises at the back end of the industrial chain in reducing carbon emissions is diminished. Given the consideration of focusing on major contributors while relaxing control over small ones, wouldn't it be simpler and more effective to concentrate on regulating the large upstream enterprises?

A: That's an insightful question, but from the theoretical and empirical perspectives of international and domestic carbon reduction efforts over the past two decades, the reality is quite the opposite. Focusing solely on major emitters and relaxing control over smaller contributors is a significant misconception in the realm of carbon emission reduction.

Historically, both international and domestic carbon reduction strategies have prioritized large emitters, particularly those in the coal-fired power, steel, and cement industries, due to a lack of robust theoretical frameworks and efficient programs. The results have been disappointing.

Research indicates that while coal-fired power, steel, and cement producers in the upstream supply chain are substantial emitters, their emissions are heavily influenced by the resource demand (which impacts total demand) driven by the downstream industry chain and the chemical reactions (which affect unit carbon emissions). This underscores the First Principles of societal carbon reduction. These factors are not determined by the upstream enterprises themselves. Instead, the primary impact of these industries on sector-wide carbon emissions lies in process improvements. Under the pressure of dual carbon targets, these industries have been promoting technological transformations for years, reducing their impact on sector-wide emissions to less than 5%. In other words, even if the total carbon emissions of these industries account for 90% of the whole society, the impact of their technological transformations on the carbon emission reduction of the whole society will not exceed 5%. To achieve carbon neutrality, controlling just 5% of emissions is insufficient; we need to control the entirety of societal emissions to drive overall reductions and meet China's "3060" targets on time.

Many scholars and executives believe that China's carbon neutrality can be achieved by focusing exclusively on large emitters, which is an unrealistic assumption and reflects a lack of understanding of the nature of carbon neutrality.

China must adjust its approach and align with the CELM concept and the "1+N" decarbonation framework to promote nationwide carbon emission reduction and achieve the "3060" dual carbon targets.

Moreover, economic theory clearly states that the choices made by downstream enterprises significantly impact upstream suppliers: this is the power of the market. In designing carbon reduction policies, it is crucial to leverage market forces. The CELM emphasizes that each node in the industrial chain should be accountable for the total carbon emissions of their upstream suppliers, thereby driving the entire chain towards lower emissions.

Some enterprises within the industrial chain may contribute minimally to the carbon footprint of their products and might believe their role in industry-wide carbon reduction is negligible. This underestimates the impact and liability of these enterprises. In practice, your decisions are connected with the survival and development of upstream entities, therefore, your choices largely determine the carbon content of the final product to a large extent. Although your direct emissions may be minimal, selecting low-cost, high-carbon materials over high-cost, low-carbon alternatives can significantly affect the final carbon footprint of the products.

CELM Principle 1: Consumers bear the cost of carbon emissions, and the back end of the industry chain is liable for the total carbon emissions generated at the front end. This mechanism is critical within the CELM.

Q8: Is the definition of "consumer" in the CELM and implementation plan limited to individual and household consumers?

A: The definition of "consumer" in the context of the CELM is broader, which encompasses not only individuals and households but also includes enterprises, public institutions, schools, hospitals, and government departments, all of which are considered consumers in a wider sense. These social organizations, much like individual households, purchase vehicles and real estate and serve as the ultimate consumers.

Within the industrial chain, producers are also consumers for their upstream manufacturers. They should equally bear the “consumer liability for carbon emissions” outlined in the CELM. The end consumer is liable for all carbon liability embodied in the product, and the back end of the industry chain is liable for the total carbon emissions generated at the front end.

Q9: The carbon emission liability mechanism shifts the burden of carbon emissions to the user side. How should carbon source enterprises be encouraged to reduce emissions?

A: In an efficient market, it matters little whether the liability for carbon emissions is placed at the front end or the back end, as all stakeholders within the industrial chain will allocate costs and liability according to market mechanisms. However, in a market system characterized by higher transaction costs, the consumer liability mechanism is more efficient in driving the reduction of emissions across the entire industry chain. When end-users bear the liability, they have the right to choose under the market mechanism, which can effectively drive all organizations within the industry chain to implement carbon emission reductions. Additionally, part of the carbon emission costs can be transmitted back to producers and carbon source enterprises. Achieving global carbon neutrality requires international coordination to address the sharing and transfer of liability for carbon emissions in international trade. Consumer liability mechanism is generally more efficient and equitable compared to producer liability mechanism. Thus, in markets with high transaction costs, the ultimate liability for carbon emissions undertaken by the consumers will not wholly exempt carbon source enterprises from their corporate liability, which is determined by the economic market trading principle. Specifically, under the consumer liability mechanism, all carbon emissions in the industry chain that exceed the industry average will be promptly assumed.

Q10: Can the government charge carbon fees at the carbon source?

A: Charging at the source is not advisable. The macroeconomic impact of a government-imposed charge at the source is significantly negative.

Firstly, it increases the burden on coal energy enterprises and coal-fired power plants, thereby disrupting the smooth functioning of macroeconomic operations. These pivotal enterprises are vital for supplying the macroeconomy with its lifeblood (electricity) and necessitate robust health to sustain their operations. Consequently, placing the entire societal burden of carbon emissions solely on their shoulders would have a detrimental effect on the macroeconomy.

One of the key advantages of the CELM lies in its equitable distribution of the social costs associated with decarbonation across all nodes of the social industry chain, minimizing disruption to the macroeconomy by ensuring that the burden is shared proportionately. As a result, high-carbon enterprises bear a more significant share, fostering economic resilience and yielding positive macroeconomic outcomes.

Secondly, charging at the source would lead to a substantial immobilization of working capital within each link of the industrial chain. Given the already low marginal effect of M2 (broad money supply) in China's macroeconomy, such a practice would exacerbate the immobilization of funds, ultimately hindering the overall macroeconomic performance.

Thirdly, due to market failures, some price signals cannot reach the terminal users, leading to inefficiencies in the pricing mechanism. Electricity prices and some markets in China are still influenced by a planned economy. In this context, levying charges at the end-user level proves more effective than front end charges, as it addresses a wider range of market failures. Furthermore, the imposition of carbon tariffs introduces additional market distortions in international trade.

Fourthly, incorporating carbon fees into the trading process inevitably elevates transaction costs at every stage, ultimately diminishing overall macroeconomic efficiency. Conversely, managing the front-end process solely through carbon tickets, without the involvement of capital costs, significantly minimizes transaction costs within the industrial chain, thereby enhancing efficiency.

Thus, the decarbonation mechanism based on the CELM, using carbon tickets to transfer the social costs of carbon emissions, holds significant efficiency advantages.

Q11: Ideally, in a scenario where an organization's carbon emissions are average, and there is a balance between the input and output of carbon tickets, the carbon burden ultimately shifts towards individuals and organizations that receive input tickets but are unable to generate corresponding output tickets. Does this suggest that households and individuals primarily shoulder the carbon liability, while enterprises can often transfer it?

A: At the heart of CELM theory lies the principle of "consumer liability". Production stems from consumption demands and is not arbitrary. Thus, consumers inevitably bear a substantial portion of the costs associated with carbon emissions. While the prevalent notion in decarbonation governance emphasizes "producer liability" or the "emitter pays", which does not exempt consumers from their share of the burden. Economic principles dictate that in an efficient market, costs incurred by front-end producers are ultimately passed on to consumers. Conversely, consumer liability ultimately reverberates back to the production side, reducing producer profits, which in turn incentivizes producers to minimize carbon emissions. Therefore, in an efficient market, the distinction between producer liability and consumer liability becomes blurred.

Under the CELM "1+1" framework, an enterprise with balanced input and output of carbon tickets signifies that its carbon emission intensity has effectively aligned with the industry average, eliminating the need for it to bear direct costs. However, economic principles dictate that it will still incur corresponding costs, impacting its profitability. The liability is not solely transferred to consumers but is shared among consumers and businesses across the entire industrial chain. The distribution between producers and consumers is governed by the elasticity of consumer demand and supply.

For production organizations whose carbon emission intensity exceeds the industrial average, the CELM will compel such enterprises to directly bear the carbon costs of the excess emissions. This efficient mechanism will significantly accelerate the decarbonation process of the whole society.

Q12: How can the CEL be balanced among domestic regions (between energy resource provinces and industrial production provinces, consumption provinces, between eastern and western regions, between renewable energy production provinces and renewable energy consumption provinces, between the eastern and western regions concerning electricity transmission as well as data and algorithms)?

A: The "1+1" Decarbonation System rooted in the CELM offers significant advantages in addressing the challenge of balancing regional interests in carbon emissions.

A pivotal principle within the CELM emphasizes consumer liability, ensuring that the back end of the industrial chain takes full liability for the carbon emissions generated by the front end. The NCMS facilitates the transfer of the CEL, clarifying the obligations of each organization within the industrial chain. This internalizes the external social costs of carbon emissions, directly passing them on to consumers through carbon tickets. By doing so, energy resource provinces are relieved of burdens in the initial journey towards carbon neutrality, thereby alleviating the pressure of emission reduction efforts. Additionally, carbon fees collected through the carbon market are invested in energy resource provinces, encouraging their economic transformation through transfer payments. This approach is favorable for energy resource provinces and also aligns with fairness principles, recognizing that energy resource provinces bear the burden of supplying energy and resources, which naturally often leads to carbon emissions and pollution that require treatment and thus it is reasonable for consumption provinces to bear liability and grant subsidies.

The CELM-based Decarbonation System will generate a substantial revenue stream for the country, empowering policymakers to more effectively balance the regional interests between energy resource provinces and consumption provinces, between the east and the west, between renewable energy production and consumption, as well as west–east power transmission, east data and west calculations. From theory to practice, this system offers enhanced scientific rigor and practicality.

Q13: Should legal persons and corporate entities, as owners/users of real estate infrastructure and fixed assets, share the same carbon liability as individual and household consumers of end products?

A: Absolutely. The cornerstone of the CELM is the "consumer liability" principle, where every consumer, regardless of their position in the supply chain, is accountable for their carbon emissions. Under the CELM, all organizations in society must offset their emissions quarterly, either by passing on the liability to downstream entities through carbon tickets or by settling the emissions themselves. This issue naturally finds resolution within the market mechanism.

Q14: In addition to vehicles and real estate, should enterprises and institutions also bear indirect carbon costs such as those related to production equipment and office supplies? Should the carbon footprint of raw materials and intermediates purchased directly from suppliers, along with the carbon costs associated with energy consumed in the production process, be included in the carbon output tickets? This could potentially increase the carbon reduction level of the production sector itself. Instead, for instance, the carbon footprint of aircraft and ships purchased by the aviation and shipping sectors should not be allocated to the passengers and products being transported, only the direct cost of fuels should be accounted for.

A: It is not so complex. Under the CELM, these issues can be resolved through market mechanisms, and the government does not need to be overly concerned. The CELM is grounded in market mechanisms, meaning that as long as there is CEL in a product, there is a responsible entity, and the government does not have to worry about carbon leakage. The allocation of burdens can be resolved through market principles and trading dynamics, without the need for regulatory intervention.

Regarding how liability is shared within the industrial chain, this can be determined by the principle of free trade, without the need for artificial and detailed prescriptions. For such a public good that involves many stakeholders, fewer policy regulations are better. The greatest failure of current carbon reduction policies is their complexity, which hinders implementation.

Q15: With regard to financial leasing of aircraft, rental housing, high-speed rail lines, and high-speed trains, and the expressways, should they only be charged for operating fees? For example, in rental housing, where water and electricity bills are paid by the tenant, is the carbon fee exempt?

A: Whether the carbon costs of aircraft should be shared with passengers is determined by market mechanisms, and we do not need to debate this. The market will self-adjust and establish industry practices that do not require government regulation.

In principle, any costs incurred by service providers are borne by consumers, irrespective of whether they are listed or how they are regulated. This is determined by market mechanisms, not by policies. The benefit of the CELM is that the government does not need to issue numerous implementation details, allowing the market to decide as much as possible.

Q16: Concerning the housing real estate, infrastructure and process factories with relatively long construction period, the principle of "consumer pays" should apply. "Consumer" should also include "owner". For real estate and vehicles, the costs should be borne by whoever owns them, while tenants should only bear direct carbon costs, such as those for electricity and gas.

A: Similar to the previous questions, the principle of free trade in the market applies here. There is no need for detailed policy prescriptions.

Q17: Regarding housing real estate, who is responsible for neutralizing the carbon tickets, the developer, the owner, or someone else? For retail commercial properties, since there may be a time lag between development completion and retail, should the developer be responsible for neutralization? Similar rules should be applied in building individual homes. Only by doing this, can developers adopt low-carbon materials and products during the design and construction phases.

A: The government does not need to intervene; it is determined by the principle of free trade. Retailers collect and offset their carbon emissions. The CELM requires organizations to settle their carbon emission stock quarterly. When the deadline arrives, organizations will naturally know how to handle it.

This principle applies similarly to individual housings. It is not that developers are responsible for carbon neutrality by incorporating low-carbon materials and products during construction, but that once the costs of carbon emissions are internalized into the product price, market mechanisms and consumer choices will drive developers to strive for carbon reduction. There is no need to worry about this.

Q18: During the construction process of plants, a significant carbon footprint accumulates, which should be neutralized by the project owner rather than internalized into the product. For example, fixed assets like boilers, turbines, and generators in thermal power plants generate a high carbon footprint, which should be neutralized by the plant owner and not factored into the price of electricity.

A: It is similar to the previous questions. If electricity prices are determined by the market, the government does not need to intervene. The amount of carbon tickets exchanged between parties, i.e., the transfer of the CEL, does not need to be set by the government but results from the negotiation and interaction between market participants.

Q19: Can the CELM Solution motivates project developers and owners to minimize the carbon footprint of their projects through low-carbon design, supply chain procurement, and construction measures?

A: Absolutely. There is no need for concern because it is driven by market forces. The CELM internalizes the costs of carbon emissions. The invisible hand of the market will drive the entire industry chain, including developers, to strive for carbon emission reduction.

Q20: Withholding and payment are primary methods for collecting personal income tax and sales tax. Can a similar approach be applied to carbon fees?

A: Yes, the carbon charge scheme for retail terminals is similar to sales tax. Countries have extensive experience that can be directly adopted.

In China, it is more akin to the collection of drainage fees, for which major Chinese cities have demonstrated operational success.

Q21: Will government departments, non-profit organizations, educational institutions, and other entities that cannot issue carbon output tickets ultimately need to purchase negative carbon to balance input tickets? How should financial expenditures be considered?

A: For entities unable to issue carbon output tickets, the input tickets represent the CEL that must be borne by the entities. They will need to regularly purchase negative carbon products from the carbon market to offset their emissions. This means that entities without revenue are not exempt from the CEL from their energy consumption, making carbon fees a fixed cost of energy consumption.

Thus, carbon emission costs should be treated like utility (electricity, water) bills. In the future, whenever an organization consumes energy and generates carbon emissions, it incurs an additional cost, the carbon fee. To achieve global carbon neutrality, it is inevitable that the social costs of carbon emissions must be internalized. The increase in carbon fees for government agencies and educational institutions will be reflected in their annual budgets.

Q22: How can the burden among investment, trade, and consumption be balanced to reduce or eliminate personal and household carbon costs as end consumers?

A: Under the CELM, the burden of carbon emissions among investment, trade, and consumption does not need to be balanced explicitly, which is an advantage of the CELM. challenges arising under the current carbon reduction framework can be automatically adjusted by the market under the CELM, eliminating the need for regulatory oversight. According to the principles of CELM liability and practical circumstances, each party can bear its respective burden which will not produce huge challenges.

Indeed, as long as the upstream entities bear the costs of carbon emissions, under efficient market conditions, the cost of products will be passed on to consumers. Achieving carbon reduction inevitably requires consumers to bear some, or even the majority, of the costs of carbon emissions, which is both necessary and unavoidable.

To address the climate crisis and achieve global carbon neutrality, it is not feasible to entirely eliminate the costs of carbon emissions for consumers. There is no need to worry about this challenge, as the design of a carbon emission cost-bearing mechanism can become an essential tool for governments to foster a better society.

The details of carbon expenditure policies for consumers and individual households must be meticulously studied. The CELM highlights the following four principles:

1. Consumer liability principle: Consumers must bear a certain cost of carbon emissions, which serves multiple purposes:

   - Firstly, the increased price of carbon-intensive products will help regulate and reduce consumption.
   - Secondly, having consumers shoulder the costs of carbon emissions creates a beneficial market mechanism that discourages high-carbon products, leading to their elimination from the market.

2. Progressivity of policy implementation: This means that the wealthy will incur higher costs relative to their income compared to lower-income individuals. Special studies should be conducted. The following strategies could be implemented, such as establishing household carbon accounts with a tiered pricing

structure; the price in the first tier would be very low, increasing progressively with each subsequent tier.

3. Reasonable expenditure proportion: The proportion of total carbon fee expenditure to total household consumption expenditure should not be excessively high, requiring a gradual adjustment process over time.
4. Optimization and adjustment of personal income redistribution: After households incur increased carbon costs, the personal income tax threshold should be raised to mitigate the financial impact.

Therefore, achieving carbon reduction is not about whether consumers should bear the burden but how they should bear it. An illustrative example is the drainage fee, which has risen from a few cents per ton to nearly the same as water prices and is charged separately. Due to improvements in the water environment, people are more willing to bear this cost. Similarly, when it comes to improving air quality and the climate, people can understand and accept such measures.

15.3 Input, Output and Circulation of Carbon Tickets

Q23: What is the basis for an organization to issue carbon tickets? Is it determined by the organization itself, through third-party approval, or regulated by the government? What is the mechanism for forming the carbon ticket?

A: The issuance of carbon tickets by an organization is determined through negotiations between the organization and its counterpart. It does not require verification by a third party or regulation by governmental bodies; instead, the market mechanism plays a key role.

The amount of carbon emissions assigned to a product will be one of the core terms negotiated by the two parties involved in the transaction. As long as both parties agree to the transaction, the government will approve it, and there is no need for third-party verification or governmental supervision. Consequently, CELM-based solutions entail low regulatory costs for the government and maintain high data quality for carbon emissions. This is because the market mechanism ensures an effective mutual constraint between the two parties of the transaction, thereby maintaining a fair market under normal circumstances.

Under the CELM, the government does not need to rigorously supervise the process, similar to the practice of value-added tax (VAT). Regardless of the method how the trading parties at each node of the industrial chain determine the circulation of carbon emissions, the overall system will ensure there is no carbon leakage, and someone will always bear the CEL. Thus, the total carbon emissions within the system remain stable.

The regulation that the government should enforce is to prevent fraudulent activities through fake transactions. The system will intelligently analyze the data, detect anomalies promptly, and continuously upgrade the verification process.

The formation mechanism of a carbon output ticket is straightforward. The carbon output of an organization is based on the total carbon liability of its input, which is then allocated to each product according to the actual energy consumption of each product, and finally the organization issues output tickets according to the sales volume of each order. Therefore, the accounting of the output tickets is a simple task that can be accomplished using basic arithmetic operations such as addition, subtraction, multiplication, and division. This contrasts with the current carbon trading systems, which have become complex practices with substantial costs and multiple rounds of verification, and still instances of fraud constantly occur. Both governments and businesses are often overwhelmed by these complexities.

Q24: The circulation of carbon tickets depends on their issuance, specifically the output tickets. How should an organization's carbon tickets be managed, especially if the organization offers hundreds of products and services, or a single order includes dozens of products?

A: Managing an organization's carbon tickets is quite straightforward. Through basic arithmetic, one organization can determine the total input from upstream suppliers, which can then be allocated to each product and transaction contract via reasonable principles. For example, allocations can be made based on the energy consumption of each product line within the organization and the carbon footprint of associated suppliers, keeping the accounting process simple and inexpensive.

Even with dozens or hundreds of products, the allocation can be relatively precise based on empirical statistics of materials and energy consumption for each product. Additionally, while the distribution of carbon emissions does not need to be absolutely accurate, the carbon content of products will naturally form a social standard value, which organizations can reference.

Currently, calculating carbon emissions across industries has become a specialized field requiring trained professionals to assist companies with their calculations. Such carbon management costs are burdensome for society. Within the CELM, the accounting of carbon tickets becomes an internal matter without the need for additional transaction costs.

Q25: Does the carbon emission level on the carbon tickets of an item represent the baseline carbon footprint for a particular product?

A: Industry experts recognize that to effectively manage carbon emission reduction across society, a comprehensive, accurate, and dynamic database of carbon emission factors for all goods and services is necessary. However, building such a database with current methods and capabilities is impractical.

The CTMS under the CELM can resolve this issue. At minimal cost, it establishes a complete, accurate, and dynamic carbon footprint database covering all societal items. This facilitates the creation of a comprehensive carbon emission factor database, providing a foundation for the formulation and implementation of macro-policies and the evaluation and analysis of projects.

With a robust database for carbon footprints, it is easy to form a carbon emission factor database for all societal items. Whether to take averages or apply other definitions, standards, and rules can be determined by carbon reduction authorities and industry associations, with variations depending on the industry.

Q26: How should terminal retailers deal with carbon tickets?

A: Terminal retailers sell goods to consumers and charge carbon fees. Upon receiving the carbon fees, retailers purchase negative carbon products from the carbon market to offset their carbon ticket stocks. Retailers procure goods from upstream suppliers, accumulating numerous carbon tickets that must be offset periodically (e.g., quarterly).

Generally, terminal retailers procure "Owing Negative CO_2" from the carbon market, which are provided by the government for carbon offsetting of social organizations.

Q27: Owners of infrastructure, fixed assets, and rental properties are not users (consumers). Typically, the cost of these assets is passed on to users through depreciation, and some assets can be depreciated over more than a decade. In this context, how should carbon tickets be issued? If they are not issued and paid for by the asset owner, wouldn't this conflict with the principle of consumer payment? Could we adopt a simpler method by including the input carbon fees in the original value of fixed assets and reflecting it in the user price through depreciation?

A: The carbon fee should be considered a one-time cost akin to material fees embodied into the asset. To avoid complexity, payment over many years is not suggested. Since the externalities of carbon emissions occur at the end of the project, the carbon costs cannot be paid in installments. Therefore, carbon ticket offsets must be completed in one go. The CELM stipulates a quarterly settlement cycle, and any excess stock needs to be offset.

If a fixed asset holder leases the asset, the government does not need to intervene with whether to issue a carbon ticket to the lessee. This is governed by the principle of free transaction, relieving the government of concerns about carbon leakage. Over time, the market will develop its own rules, without the need for government supervision or intervention.

The CELM has a significant advantage in that the government does not need to expend considerable efforts making detailed rules, as many issues can be resolved more easily by the market mechanism.

Q28: Should the purchase and delivery price of fixed assets include the input carbon fee? Can the lease, transfer, or operational income of such assets owned by a legal or natural person also include the offset carbon fee?

A: Based on the principle of free trade, both parties can agree on the terms of the transaction. Carbon tickets can be included in lease, transfer, or operational income, and the purchase and delivery price must include carbon fees. Even if the seller does not set up a separate item, the total cost must include carbon fees. The CELM emphasizes the principles of low-cost policy implementation and free transaction.

The government can abstain from mandating carbon fees in the trading process, as the market mechanism will naturally establish market practices.

This is akin to the principles of VAT. Regardless of which party in the transaction pays, the government will not lose any tax revenue. The carbon ticket system works similarly, allowing both parties in the transaction greater freedom, without the need for oversight by regulatory departments.

Q29: How should service enterprises deal with carbon output tickets?

A: The way service enterprises deal with the input and output of carbon tickets is similar to that of other social organizations. Only the total amount of carbon input tickets needs to be allocated to each service contract based on the contract amount, actual consumption, and other criteria, aiming for accuracy where possible.

For some service enterprises where the input of carbon tickets is negligible, carbon neutrality is considered to be achieved, preventing the passing down of carbon emission liabilities. This approach can enhance their brand reputation and secure their status as being green and carbon–neutral enterprises.

The CELM brings significant flexibility to the handling of carbon emissions by enterprises and organizations, with minimal government intervention and strong upstream and downstream constraints through free trading, ensuring no major issues arise. This is a significant advantage of the carbon reduction mechanism based on the CELM.

Q30: Given the relatively large emissions during the construction process in the long-chain real estate industry, how should we deal with the hidden carbon and carbon trading in the process of holding, leasing, purchasing and dismantling? For example, the number of carbon tickets for a building or project may be very large.

A: Regardless of the length of the industry chain, the carbon footprint data recorded by the CTMS based on the CELM remains accurate and reliable, largely unaffected by the length of the industry chain. Similar to the VAT system, regardless of the number of transaction nodes, the VAT base remains correct.

The circulation of carbon tickets during the holding, leasing, purchasing and dismantling phases of real estate is handled similarly to other industries, following the CELM rules and the principle of free market trading. The industry can manage these processes independently, without presenting any special issues.

The cumulative number of carbon tickets for a building should be substantial, reflecting the actual situation accurately. The CTMS excels in simplifying the calculation of CEL for large and complex engineering projects, making the process both easy and precise.

This advantage of the CELM enables governments to reduce the costs of carbon emission reduction and regulation to nearly zero, an achievement that current carbon reduction mechanism struggles to match.

Q31: Should carbon tickets be listed separately on receipts for large purchases, such as those involving direct electricity, fuel, and gas usage? Would smaller transactions, like buying pancakes (which actually generates carbon footprints), be exempt?

A: The CELM operates flexibly, ensuring no issues arise. Retailers will decide the inclusion of carbon tickets with ease, and the government does not need to impose specific requirements. If a commodity is sold and a receipt is printed, the receipt will include the carbon content and the corresponding carbon fee, which is not overly complicated.

Under the CELM, carbon fees can be collected without causing carbon leakage. To date, the CELM approach is the simplest among the carbon reduction management mechanisms proposed by the academic community. This simplicity is a significant advantage of the CELM solution.

15.4 Carbon Source Management

Q32: Carbon sources such as agricultural fertilizers, animal husbandry, steel, nonferrous metals, cement, and building materials are also significant contributors. How should we consider carbon source data management in these industries?

A: Carbon source management should prioritize large emitters and gradually take small emitters in control. Besides coal mines, oil fields, and natural gas, carbon sources such as fertilizers, livestock, steel, and cement also need to be managed progressively.

The management method is similar to the previously outlined methods for major carbon sources, in other words, carbon source organization and data are managed according to the characteristics of different industries. This is not difficult to implement and can be managed accurately.

For instance, when fertilizers are applied to fields, they release CO_2. Therefore, fertilizer plants should be treated as carbon sources. Fertilizer plants would report their output, which the government would verify, and the government would determine the carbon emissions per unit output for different types of fertilizers. This means the government would possess accurate carbon source data. The government would then issue carbon tickets to the fertilizer plants, which would issue output tickets to their customers when selling their products. In this manner, carbon emissions can be accurately transferred along the agricultural industry chain. Other industries mentioned here can be managed similarly without significant difficulties.

Carbon source organization and data management can be carried out step-by-step, with the government gradually managing all carbon sources. This is a progressive process. Carbon source data management based on the CELM should improve incrementally by focusing on larger emitters first while gradually taking smaller ones into control, which operates differently and fundamentally with the current decarbonation mechanism based on carbon trading rights.

Q33: When the government determines the quantity of carbon sources and issues carbon tickets to enter the system, how should it distinguish oil and coal being used as chemical raw materials or primary energy?

A: This is indeed an issue that requires a specific operational plan. Coal and oil serve not only as energy sources but also as raw materials for the production of many chemical materials. For coal and oil used as raw materials rather than for energy combustion, no CO_2 is emitted into the atmosphere during their lifecycle. Therefore, the carbon content of these products should not be included in the carbon source count.

The proposed plan is that when fossil energy manufacturers sell part of their products to sectors that do not combust them, they would issue output tickets in the same manner to transfer the carbon emissions. Within the CTMS, non-combustion departments would submit applications for the cancellation of input tickets, and after the approval from the government, the corresponding input tickets would be canceled. This process is not complicated.

15.5 Energy and Power Sectors

Q34: How does the CELM factor in incentives for new energy sources, such as hydrogen energy?

A: The CELM addresses this by internalizing the societal costs of carbon emissions. While the carbon price cannot be abruptly implemented due to macroeconomic considerations, the framework ensures that each ton of carbon emitted is accounted for in product pricing. This naturally highlights the cost advantage of low-carbon, new energy sources like hydrogen, which incur no carbon emission costs. If their initial cost advantages are insufficient to drive the energy transition, theoretically, escalating the price per unit ton until it fosters market conditions conducive to the transition is the optimal approach.

However, this ideal scenario may not always be feasible or appropriate. In cases where carbon pricing fails to generate a sustained price advantage for new energy, alternative measures, like targeted tax relief and fiscal incentives, can bolster competitiveness. Notably, direct financial subsidies should be minimized to prevent issues like fraud and rent-seeking. Successful policies include low-interest loans, value-added tax exemptions, income tax incentives, and innovative measures like free license plates for new energy vehicles in Shanghai, effectively subsidizing owners by an estimated 100,000 yuan.

Q35: Given that wind power plants and photovoltaic power plants have achieved full cost competitiveness through price subsidies, which have led to significant government funding gaps, how should we reassess subsidies? Can carbon tickets for fossil fuels address subsidies for new energy?

A: The current carbon emission reduction framework, encompassing carbon allowances and China Certified Emission Reduction (CCER), is fraught with overlap, obsolescence, and gaps. Harmonizing existing policies under the CELM is imperative.

Key challenges include:

1. Lack of a unified top-level theory and guidance: This leads to departmental silos, each striving to craft policies favorable to their interests.
2. Clashing sectoral interests: The policies related to carbon emission rights and carbon emission costs significantly reshape sectoral interests arising from low-carbon transitions.

As coal-fired power enterprises fully absorb carbon costs, in other words, carbon emission costs of all products in the whole society have been internalized, with the increase of carbon price, subsidies for wind power should be phased out to ensure fair competition.

If expedited wind power development is deemed necessary, fiscal (tax deductions) and financial (low-interest loans) policies should be prioritized over direct subsidies to mitigate fraud and inefficiencies. In fact, direct subsidies strain government resources, are costly to administer, and often yield low efficiency.

In conclusion, current new energy subsidies and CCER mechanism are outdated and require reformulation aligned with the evolving CELM.

Q36: What strategies should the CELM employ to incentivize carbon emission reduction in coal-fired power sector and mitigate power groups in reliance on these traditional sources?

A: The CELM and its solution are well-equipped with effective incentives aimed at fostering carbon reduction in coal-fired power sector, addressing the issue comprehensively without significantly disrupting the macroeconomy. In contrast to the current allowance policy in the coal-fired power industry, which is inefficient, costly, and economically burdensome, the CELM offers a more refined approach.

Specifically, the CELM "1+1" Decarbonation System ingeniously circumvents direct cash outflows for coal-fired power enterprises by allowing them to issue carbon tickets to the grid companies. But this does not mean that coal-fired power enterprises do not have to bear their CEL and carbon costs, rather, this mechanism subtly incorporates the costs of carbon emissions into the product pricing, thereby internalizing external costs. Under the premise of separation of power generation and power transmission as well as access to the grid by total costs, naturally, grid companies tend to select electricity offers with lower total costs (including carbon fees), therefore, a dual benefit emerges:

1. Encouraging carbon reduction: Coal-fired power enterprises are incentivized to reduce emissions to enhance their competitiveness in the market, as the carbon cost becomes an integral part of their offering.
2. Mitigating economic impact: Currently, coal-fired power remains the primary source of electricity supply and carries the significant responsibility for peak load regulation and supply security. Objective technical conditions and macroeconomic necessities dictate that coal-fired power production must be well-coordinated. At present, the decarbonation efforts in the coal-fired power sector and other key industries are rash actions that significantly influence the macroeconomy. The CELM has devised an optimal plan, incorporating carbon emission

costs into coal-fired power products while promoting carbon emission reduction without imposing an immediate heavy financial burden on the coal-fired power industry, thereby ensuring its sustainable operation.

The reliance of power groups on coal-fired power is largely due to technical factors at this stage.

Within the CELM, coal-fired power products carry an increasingly higher cost associated with carbon emissions. The market mechanism ensures that power purchasing companies will naturally reduce their procurement of coal-generated electricity, alleviating governmental concerns. Presently, the capacity for renewable energy substitution is constrained, and the grid's power supply capability is limited by technical factors. While the cost of renewable energy has declined, its generation remains characterized by randomness, volatility, and intermittency, coupled with technical limitations regarding power supply duration and energy storage. Consequently, power companies primarily depend on coal-fired power plants for their supply. Additionally, traditional coal-fired power technologies are more advanced, possess stronger technical capabilities, offer lower generation costs, and excel particularly in peak and frequency regulation, thus stabilizing the grid. As such, coal-fired power continues to serve as a "pillar" and "stabilizer", ensuring the secure and stable provision of electricity.

Certain issues truly require resolution through technical advancements. Prior to solving the technical challenges associated with renewable energy, it would be imprudent to overly suppress the coal-fired power industry, thereby affecting the macroeconomy.

Q37: The mechanism for determining the price of water may appear relatively straightforward; however, the power pricing takes into account a range of factors including nuclear, hydro, coal, oil, gas, offshore and onshore wind, solar thermal photovoltaic, biomass energy, waste incineration, and other sources. These factors affect their on-grid prices and meanwhile, on the consumption-side, the differing prices are offered for agricultural, industrial, and commercial sales. Given that carbon tickets could potentially be tied to electricity and oil and gas charges, how should the sales price of electricity be made to reflect the inclusion of carbon across diverse power sources?

A: The primary strength of the CELM lies in its simplicity, avoiding the complexities often found in carbon accounting systems. The calculations required are basic arithmetic operations (addition, subtraction, multiplication, and division), making it feasible for anyone with a basic understanding of mathematics to grasp the carbon pricing implications throughout the entire social industrial chain.

Contrary to the MRV system currently employed in carbon reduction mechanisms, which has evolved into a specialized field demanding substantial consultancy teams and significant implementation costs, the CELM offers a stark contrast.

As an important part of the industrial chain, the power supply sector is no different from the other commodities in dealing with carbon pricing. The power supply enterprises procure a variety of power sources, each accompanied by a corresponding carbon ticket. These tickets are aggregated to form the total input of carbon tickets. Based on internal requirements or strategic considerations, the power supply enterprises may devise principles for allocating the total carbon liability, perhaps proportionally according to the carbon emission factor of the grid. This price could either be uniform or differentiated based on the usage time. It all depends on the power supply enterprises.

Once the CELM is implemented, each entity must specify the carbon content of its products. With numerous products, companies must establish guidelines to allocate the large numbers of carbon tickets accurately. The allocation should factor into the following principles:

1. Ensure the total input of carbon tickets is allocated among products. Any unallocated portion becomes a carbon stock, which must be offset through the purchase of negative carbon products from the market on a quarterly basis.
2. Conform to practical situation: Given that organizations produce multiple products with diverse carbon input sources, they should manage these effectively by allocating carbon tickets based on the actual carbon consumption of each product. This is a feasible task within an organization.
3. Market competition and downstream acceptance: If a company's carbon intensity exceeds the industry average, it will need to procure negative carbon products to offset the surplus emissions. This increases operational costs, reduces profits, and penalizes high carbon emitters.

Under the CELM, the market mechanism plays a pivotal role, from the outset to the conclusion, rather than relying on government-set carbon emission factors or incurring significant expenses to engage professional consultants for calculations.

Q38: It appears that under the CELM, the NCTM is primarily geared towards funding carbon sequestration and CCUS projects. Is there a necessity to support additional projects like CCER initiatives, similar to wind and solar energy projects?

A: The CCER has fulfilled its historical mission, and the government should cease using it as an incentive.

Under the CELM, all items bear the societal costs of carbon emissions, and low-carbon projects should compete in the market based on the cost advantages derived from their reduced carbon footprint. They should no longer rely on incentives from certified emission reduction programs, as this creates an overlapping mechanism that fails to ensure market fairness.

The carbon removal certification system based on the CELM overlaps with CCER, covering aspects similar to forest carbon removals and the absolute emission reduction achieved by CCUS. However, it does not include relative emission reduction. Thus, only relevant considerations are included, ensuring a rational approach. There is no longer a need to impose an offset ratio limit, such as the current 5% for CCER. Instead, the focus should be on creating ample space for negative carbon products.

Furthermore, the CCER is complex, non-standardized, problematic, and costly to operate, making it challenging to internationalize. It should be phased out promptly.

Future resources should be directed toward building a robust "Real Negative CO_2" certification system.

15.6 Carbon Pricing

Q39: Is carbon pricing under the CELM a tax or a fee? Is it necessary to pass legislation through the National People's Congress?

A: Carbon pricing within the CELM is structured as a fee rather than a tax, similar to the drainage charge included in water bills. Drawing parallels from the drainage charge system, the imposition of carbon charges requires legislation by the National People's Congress. However, adjustments to the fee rates do not necessitate new legislation, and annual changes can be established through public hearings organized by the National Development and Reform Commission.

The CELM theory proposes an Integrated Carbon Pricing Strategy (IPCS) where the carbon price is determined by the country after considering the carbon neutrality timeline and macroeconomic affordability. The government acts as the first issuer of output tickets and primary provider of negative carbon products (Owing Negative CO_2) in the carbon market, akin to the operator of a sewage treatment system. By selling negative carbon and levying carbon fees, the government wields strong pricing power in the negative carbon market.

Q40: What is the relationship between carbon price and carbon peaking and carbon neutrality?

A: Currently, the cost of "Real Negative CO_2" is relatively high, and the market primarily offsets carbon liability through "Owing Negative CO_2". As we progress toward carbon neutrality, the price of "Owing Negative CO_2" will gradually rise. Simultaneously, with the large-scale development of the carbon removal industry and technological advancements, the cost of "Real Negative CO_2" will decrease. When the price of "Owing Negative CO_2" equals that of "Real Negative CO_2", the market will be able to achieve complete offsetting via "Real Negative CO_2", signifying the attainment of carbon neutrality.

It should be noted that this does not mean carbon peak is reached when the amount of carbon tickets issued by the government has risen to the point where it can't go any higher, nor does it mean carbon neutrality is achieved when the amount of carbon tickets issued by the government has fallen to the point where it can't go any lower.

15.7 International Trade and Carbon Tariffs

Q41: What role does the CELM play in addressing the upcoming carbon border regulation mechanism similar to that of the European Union?

A: The CELM provides a comprehensive solution to carbon tariffs as stipulated by CBAM, and China should implement it as soon as possible.

The CELM introduces a consumer liability mechanism, clarifying the relationship between the CEL of producing and consuming countries. There is a market failure concerning carbon emissions arising from international trade. The mechanism of "producer liability" that Western countries in Europe and the United States have insisted upon has serious flaws. The CELM theory rectifies this by attributing a portion of carbon emissions to the consumer countries. As a result, approximately 10% of China's carbon emissions would be attributed to consumer countries in Europe and the United States.

The CELM addresses two key issues related to carbon tariffs in international trade:

1. Providing reliable data on carbon footprint: The CELM-based CTMS delivers reliable data on the carbon footprint of all goods within society, solving the problem of verifying carbon emission data for internationally traded goods. Low-cost, precise, and dependable data will help reduce disputes over data accuracy.
2. Facilitating domestic carbon offsets for exporters: The NCTM established under the CELM assists Chinese exporters in offsetting their carbon domestically, thereby avoiding foreign carbon charges. Export companies can purchase negative carbon domestically to offset their emissions at the agreed-upon price of "International Negative CO_2", thus being exempt from paying carbon tariffs abroad.

Q42: How does the CELM theory balance the interests of the stakeholders involved in carbon tariffs? Stakeholders include energy (oil, natural gas, iron ore etc.) resource exporting countries (such as Brazil, Australia, Canada, Russia, Middle Eastern countries, etc.), major consumer countries (such as EU countries, the United States, etc.), and manufacturing exporting countries (such as China, India, Southeast Asian countries, etc.).

A: The general principle of the CELM when dealing with both international and domestic carbon reduction stakeholders is that consumers assume liability, and the downstream part of the industrial chain takes overall liability for emissions from the upstream. Following this principle, it is not difficult to rationalize the global CEL system both between countries and within regions of countries. Under the CELM, the only issue countries need to address is the phased negotiation of carbon pricing, which is practical and easy to implement.

The current carbon emission rules dominated by Europe and the United States emphasizes "producer liability" for emissions, which poses difficult challenges. For nearly three decades, the United Nations Climate Conferences have expended resources, time, and generated carbon emissions in the wrong direction by focusing on the allocation of carbon emission rights, leading to significant failures.

The CELM views the global community holistically, avoiding the allocation of carbon emission rights among countries, regions, and organizations. It fully utilizes the market mechanism to regulate both upstream and downstream activities, driving the international community towards global decarbonation.

For fossil energy exporting countries, under the CELM, the costs of carbon emissions are internalized, increasing the actual cost of using fossil energy, which will discourage its use. Specifically, the government issues carbon tickets to oil importers, treating them as carbon source entities. If the exporting country has completed offsets with International NegativeCO_2, the carbon ticket is exempted.

For product manufacturing countries, under the CELM, when goods are exported to other countries, the costs of carbon emissions should, in principle, be borne by the importing country. However, this will increase the total costs of their products and weaken their competitiveness. Therefore, manufacturing countries must strive to reduce the carbon content of their products.

For consumer countries, they should pay for the carbon emissions embodied in products, but they have the right to choose products, encouraging those with lower carbon emissions and reasonable costs to gain more traction. This drives carbon reduction from the demand side in the global market.

15.8 Differences Between the CELM and Existing Carbon Reduction Systems

Q43: Why is it inefficient to build a carbon reduction system around the concept of carbon emission rights?

A: The carbon emission allowance system has numerous limitations and cannot achieve efficient carbon emission reduction on a global scale or within societies.

1. High requirements for government capacity and investment: Allocating carbon emission rights to hundreds of millions of organizations and individuals across society is impractical, and governments lack the capability to undertake such a task. The method of allocation is a profoundly academic challenge, and despite numerous research papers, there is virtually no feasible solution. Regardless of the method chosen by the government, issues of fairness and efficiency arise, leading to extremely high operational costs. Additionally, the distribution of administrative power can easily lead to rent-seeking and corruption in governmental departments, resulting in serious consequences.
2. Non-standardized concept and difficulty in standardizing and capitalizing the concept: The concept of "carbon emission rights" is flexible and scalable, and the connotations vary significantly across countries, regions, and over time. Consequently, it cannot become a standardized carbon asset nor serve as an asset with

a significant role in carbon emission reduction. The trading of global carbon emission rights in the past two decades illustrate this point.

3. Challenges in internationalization and international cooperation: Achieving global carbon neutrality requires coordinated efforts on a global scale. As a critical tool for achieving this goal, carbon emission rights must be highly standardized across regions and over time to be effective. To date, the international carbon reduction mechanisms have struggled to unify and foster international cooperation, having minimal impact on actual carbon emission reduction. The primary reason lies in the fact that the current mainstream carbon policy instrument, carbon emission rights, cannot fulfill this role. If a policy instrument with significant responsibilities cannot facilitate international coordination, it is targeting the wrong objective.
4. Difficulty in expanding the carbon market based on carbon emission rights: Due to the aforementioned challenges with carbon emission rights, the carbon trading market that carries high hopes remains difficult to expand globally. The fundamental problem is that the object of trading in the carbon market is chosen wrongly. The CELM suggests that changing the object of trading to "negative carbon" could yield vastly different outcomes.

Q44: Why should the CCER system be discontinued?

A: The CCER system was effective during the initial phase of carbon reduction efforts but is inefficient given the current carbon neutrality goals. China should transition to a comprehensive carbon removal certification system based on "negative carbon".

CCER represents a relative quantity and cannot be uniformly standardized, making it difficult to internationalize. The determination of reduction is not objective enough, and the methodologies are still evolving, numbering in the hundreds. Such a complex system results in uncontrollable quality and extremely high operational costs, rendering it without promotional value. Indeed, the international community limits offsets to 5% of the total amount. Furthermore, with the internalization of carbon emission costs, the incentive provided by certified emission reduction theoretically should not exist. Therefore, the CCER system has unpromising future, is excessively costly, and should be discontinued as soon as possible. The Chinese Government should not expend significant efforts to build a new professional CCER market, as doing so would be entirely without value.

Q45: Carbon neutrality should align with international standards, and currently, countries are vying for the right to set methodologies and control various databases. Will it be easy for the CELM to compete with existing systems?

A: It will certainly be a significant challenge. However, the current mechanisms are inefficient, and the CELM can substantially improve efficiency, making it worthwhile to pursue.

Currently, not only Europe and the United States but all countries are competing for influence on climate issues. In comparison, China's academic and practical fields have contributed relatively few innovative ideas and have had limited impact on international climate discourse. Given that China is a major carbon emitter, the cost of not exerting effort to shape academic theory and policymaking is high. In terms of foundational theories and solutions, the CELM has laid the groundwork for China to take a leading role in the global response to climate change and has created favorable conditions for enhancing China's voice. If China takes the lead in implementing the CELM and achieves tangible results, it will significantly bolster China's standing on global climate issues. This is the direction that the Chinese government must strive toward.

Q46: How do you view the current carbon trading markets in several cities and the national unified carbon market? How can we unify various trading products such as emission rights, CCERs, carbon removals, carbon credits, and carbon taxes?

A: Due to a lack of research on the fundamental economic theories needed to address climate change, there are shortcomings in the self-innovation of theoretical concepts and top-level design. The top-level designs by relevant departments are still largely imitating European and American models, and the overall progress has not been satisfactory.

We need to harness the creativity of the Chinese people and, through thorough discussions, identify the optimal path to carbon neutrality for China. Based on this, the top-level mechanism and supporting systems should be re-designed to accelerate the process of achieving carbon neutrality while reducing societal costs and resource waste.

The current system is experimental, involving substantial investment costs but with unclear benefits.

The provincial carbon trading markets lack theoretical guidance and professional support, each operating in isolation during their pilot phases. This fragmentation disperses market resources and yields counterproductive results. Such inefficiencies should be addressed and halted promptly.

Efficient carbon market is a national NCTM.

There is a need to promptly upgrade the existing market for carbon emission rights to a negative carbon market. The market for carbon emission rights has largely fulfilled its historical mission and can no longer support the targets of carbon neutrality in China and worldwide.

Similarly, CCER represents a transitional necessity, whereas negative carbon aligns with the development of carbon neutrality. China's certification system should transition fully to negative carbon certification. Presently, many incentive mechanisms are redundant, complex, and riddled with loopholes. And the government struggles to administer and the financial investment is enormous. All together, these mechanisms require a comprehensive reform.

Q47: What is the relationship between the CELM-based carbon market and the existing market for carbon emission rights and CCER trading? Is it disruptive or complementary?

A: The carbon market within the CELM is a negative carbon trading market, while the existing market (CEA) operates on carbon emission rights and includes some voluntary emission reduction (CCER) trading. The top-level designs of these two systems differ significantly.

The CELM-based NCTM represents a reform and enhancement of the current market for carbon emission rights, overcoming many of its limitations with a simpler, standardized model that can scale up effectively and drive effective carbon emission reduction.

Thus, implementing the CELM carbon market necessitates abandoning the CEA trading model and the CCER framework. In other words, the CELM negative carbon trading market is an alternative to the current carbon market, not a supplement.

Q48: In which direction should carbon market reforms proceed since carbon markets proliferate everywhere?

A: Current carbon emission rights, CCER, and other carbon markets must transform and upgrade into a "negative carbon trading market", thereby achieving sustainable development and international harmonization. The primary function of the carbon market is to help the government internalize the costs of carbon emissions and assist enterprises in achieving carbon offsets. Consequently, a negative carbon trading market supports carbon neutrality, becoming a standardized sustainable asset capable of international integration.

The proliferation of carbon markets is misguided. China needs only one carbon market, a national negative carbon trading market, which should be unified across the country. Provincial carbon markets should be phased out, and there is no need to establish separate CCER trading platforms; otherwise, this would lead to significant new inefficiencies.

Q49: Various carbon emission reduction mechanisms proposed by different experts are being implemented, and local governments are also conducting pilot projects. How should enterprises respond?

A: Indeed, at present, multiple plans are being proposed by various experts, and local governments are experimenting with different strategies with the assistance of these experts. This piecemeal approach to carbon neutrality presents significant shortcoming, that is, it lacks professionalism, and constructing fragmented systems is costly and unsustainable. Most of the schemes put forth by experts remain conceptual and lack practical application.

A major challenge in the current journey towards carbon neutrality in China is the proliferation of duplicative and inefficient programs and systems, which consume vast resources. Even many of these initiatives generate considerable negative impacts yet yield minimal positive outcomes, seriously undermining macroeconomic performance.

Addressing climate change and achieving carbon emission reduction is an unprecedented challenge in dealing with public goods, far more complex than many experts suggest. The essence of carbon emissions is that carbon emissions represent a large-scale complex public good with temporal and spatial externalities. Carbon neutrality is a national and global systemic task requiring rigorous economic and scientific theoretical support, global thinking, top-level design, and international coordination alongside national planning. Therefore, approaches that lack a systemic perspective and focus only on isolated aspects are unlikely to solve practical problems, and most explorations tend to yield minimal results.

Given the severity of climate change, the need to find the most efficient and equitable path to carbon neutrality and accelerate its implementation becomes increasingly urgent. The current CELM and its Solution offer a globally competitive approach to carbon neutrality. It is recommended that the government expedite research and validation of this approach. If validated, it could serve as the cornerstone for comprehensive top-level design, help restructure the existing system, and accelerate implementation.

Currently, enterprises are relatively passive participants in this process, and there are two key principles they need to bear in mind: firstly, if their products involve carbon emissions, they must bear the associated costs; secondly, low-carbon products will be foundational for securing their brand reputation. Once they are clear about these two principles, it would be easier for them to adjust their business philosophy and strategy.

Q50: Presently, green electricity and green certificate are traded in some provinces and cities, and some are still engaged in offline trading. Can carbon tickets integrated these practices within grid price?

A: These mechanisms are fraught with numerous overlapping, unscientific basis, and inefficiency. Under the CELM, these mechanisms need to be systematically evaluated, adjusted, and integrated accordingly.

Q51: The carbon burden borne by consumers is primarily the carbon cost embodied in the energy used during the production process. Besides the carbon footprint, there is also the concept of the "water footprint". Could it be integrated into the carbon ticket system?

A: The value of CELM extends beyond providing a breakthrough in the top-level theory and solution for carbon emission reduction; it also offers significant theoretical and practical references for the policy design of other public goods.

Specifically, the CELM brings the following three critical contributions to the realm of public goods:

1. Liability mechanism design: The CELM concept and framework overcome the limitations of insufficient market information and market failures, securing both fairness and efficiency.
2. Quantified liability sharing: By utilizing a digital information technology system, the CELM approach enables low-cost, self-operated acquisition of comprehensive carbon footprint data. This ensures that each entity's liability is precisely and equitably determined.
3. Market mechanism for positive and negative externalities (negative carbon trading market): The negative carbon trading market serves to offset the externalities inherent in carbon emissions. This helps liberate the government from

administrative burdens, reduces administrative costs, and combats rent-seeking behaviors.

These effective methodologies can be adopted in the design of policy instruments for other large and complex public goods, such as mechanisms for reducing the emissions of another major greenhouse gas, methane, following a similar principle.

15.9 Implementation of CELM Solution

Q52: As a concrete manifestation of top-level design, the CTMS requires full support from the country to break down barriers between different ministries. This is particularly challenging given the current environmental governance process, despite years of effective air control, information sharing remains constrained within individual systems. Can the CTMS overcome this constraint?

A: The establishment of the CELM, including the CTMS based on the CELM, represents a historic project akin to China's "Golden Tax Project", serving as national infrastructure and a top-down national carbon emission management system. Achieving this necessitates breaking through all existing boundaries.

Undoubtedly, realizing the "Golden Carbon Project" poses significant challenges, and its success hinges on national resolve. From a technical and operational standpoint, the Golden Carbon Project is less complex than the Golden Tax Project. The CTMS acts as a transaction recording system for carbon footprint data without direct financial transactions, thereby simplifying the process. Thus, provided there is national will, implementation is feasible.

Considering the impact and human toll of the climate storms experienced in 2022, these challenges, though significant, boil down to a matter of perception. Moreover, the existing system is inadequate in addressing the issues, and we are standing at a point where transformation is imperative.

Q53: How long will it take to establish the CTMS in China? What resources are required?

A: The principles governing the input and output of the CTMS are analogous to those of China's current VAT system. Given our experience with the construction and operation of the Golden Tax Project, the implementation of the CTMS is relatively straightforward, making the establishment of a national CTMS neither overly complex nor excessively costly.

The system should be capable of entering trial operations within a year, significantly faster than the current governmental carbon reduction management systems.

Once established, the CTMS can rapidly integrate all organizations and individuals into carbon reduction efforts. The time and resources invested will yield substantial returns.

The CTMS is essentially "a management system + a software system", which requires the following inputs:

1. Legislative efforts to establish a supporting decarbonation management framework.
2. Establishment of a corresponding operational system, designating competent departments and setting up operational organizations at all levels.
3. Development and operation of a national-level carbon ticket management system, the CTMS.

Q54: Will the CELM Solution be piloted in several large industrial sectors, similar to the CEA?

A: It is appropriate to pilot the CELM Solution in a single city or region. A reasonable pilot scope for the CELM Solution could encompass a country or an entire industrial chain, such as the power industry.

However, piloting at a single point within the industrial chain, as has been done with carbon emission trading, is not advisable. The evidence shows that such localized pilots, like those conducted in China's CEA market initially focusing on the coal-fired power industry, have been unsuccessful.

A nationwide CTMS can be piloted directly with minimal risk and without undue concern. It is suggested to construct a national carbon ticket management system, the CTMS initially. During the pilot phase, focus is solely placed on data collection, implementing a data-driven reward and penalty mechanism. The carbon price during the pilot phase is set at 0 yuan/ton or 1 yuan/ton. Such an approach minimizes the impact on the macroeconomy while still achieving a pilot effect.

Provided that the CTMS generates dynamic, complete, and accurate big data on the carbon footprint of the entire society without altering economic benchmarks, a beneficial carbon reduction outcome can be achieved. For instance, ranking the carbon emission intensity per unit output value and per unit output of 100,000 construction enterprises and even revoking business licenses for those with excessively high carbon emission intensity could produce highly effective carbon reduction impacts.

Q55: There is a vast array of products, with new ones emerging daily. Verified carbon footprints for completed products via Environmental Product Declaration (EPD) account for only a small fraction. How can we rapidly promote the verification of product carbon footprints?

A: Internationally, there is growing support for and adoption of EPD, which provide third-party verified, scientific, comparable, and internationally recognized comprehensive disclosures of a product's environmental impact throughout its lifecycle.

However, in the era of big data, this traditional solution has become outdated, costly, and unable to keep pace with rapid changes. The solution based on the CELM involves establishing a national CTMS, allowing for the creation of complete, accurate, and dynamic carbon footprint big data at low cost and high efficiency, thus addressing this challenge.

Q56: Long-chain manufacturing industries, such as automobiles, shipbuilding, aircraft, mobile phones, and computers, have very extended supply chains. How can they avoid the overlapping statistical efforts concerning Scope 1, Scope 2 and Scope 3?

A: This is precisely where the advantage of the CELM "1+1" approach comes into play. The CTMS grounded in CELM, prevents carbon leakage and avoids overlapping statistical efforts.

The CTMS records the circulation of carbon emissions (carbon footprint) based on actual transactions. Provided that the source data of carbon emissions is verified, the integrity and reliability of the data across society and the entire industrial chain can be assured. Similar to the value-added tax system, the mutual checks between upstream and downstream entities ensure the accuracy of the data.

The circulation of carbon input and output tickets within the CTMS accompanies real transactions, thus eliminating the possibility of inconsistent and redundant statistics.

Q57: Many people are concerned about the potential for social resistance if the costs of carbon are passed on to consumers. What measures should be taken?

A: To achieve carbon neutrality and emission reductions, it is inevitable that consumers will bear some of the costs. This is a necessary step and can be accepted by consumers. Drawing parallels from the acceptance of drainage charges, it's clear that the notion that governments alone should fund carbon neutrality and climate change mitigation is unrealistic; ultimately, these costs are covered by taxpayers.

All organizations and individuals must shoulder the costs of carbon emissions, which is a standard component of product pricing, akin to logistics and freight costs. Consumers can not only bear the cost of materials, but not bear the freight cost. Similarly, they should understand that the price of goods inherently includes related carbon costs. For example, when purchasing pork, consumers implicitly pay for its refrigeration costs, which are factored into the final price. There needs to be an educational campaign to mobilize public support. The global climate crisis in 2022 highlighted the urgency of environmental protection, emphasizing the need for collective actions.

In 2022, the government conducted large-scale social surveys, and the results of the data analysis were more optimistic than expected. As people's understanding of climate change deepened, along with a greater appreciation of the concept and importance of carbon neutrality, they expressed willingness to accept a reasonable increase in the costs of commodities.

Moreover, the household carbon account mechanism underpinned by the CELM serves as an innovative tool to enhance social equity, benefiting low-income groups and promoting shared prosperity. With the implementation of the CELM, the risk of social resistance is minimal.

Q58: Would it be more troublesome to implement terminal charge since there are numerous items? Historically, China has favored adding charges to the production phase, such as consumption taxes. Both source and terminal charging have their pros and cons. Is it difficult to change this habit?

A: Charging carbon fees at the terminal is not only simpler but also more effective in driving carbon reduction. Consumer choices can significantly influence carbon reduction efforts. Furthermore, adding carbon fees at the consumer side addresses some of the inefficiencies of the market. Hence, the CELM opts for terminal charging rather than source charging.

In practice, introducing terminal charges is not substantially more complex than current systems. We can consider a carbon fee as an additional component on goods. Currently, the price for every commodity includes a tax, which consumers typically accept without finding it overly complicated.

Present: price paid by consumers = commodity price + tax.

Future: price paid by consumers = commodity price + tax + carbon fee.

Adding a carbon fee merely adds another line to the receipt, without significantly increasing complexity. The advantage of terminal charging is its immediate and visible impact. Consumers generally compare the total price when choosing products. In the future, environmentally conscious consumers might also consider the carbon content, which could exert significant pressure on companies to reduce their carbon footprint. This aligns with the rationale behind terminal consumption taxes in countries like Japan and the U.S., where the local tax can be easily adjusted.

The carbon cost is borne by the consumer at the terminal, similar to how sewage treatment fees are handled currently. Other associated costs are typically included in the price of goods, and the government takes this into account when calculating the VAT payable by suppliers. In the United States, this type of charge is referred to as a sales tax, which is collected at the terminal by some states, though some states do not impose this tax.

Q59: Is the "1+1" system based on the CELM exceptionally intricate? In the short term, involving the entire society, sectors, and national households in carbon emission reduction might appear to be more complex by several orders of magnitude than the existing fiscal and tax systems and securities trading systems. How should we simplify the system?

A: To achieve the dual carbon targets, we must accelerate the reduction of carbon emissions across society. We need to move away from the current approach of focusing only on large emitters, and instead mobilize the entire population to participate in carbon reduction efforts immediately. The government has spent over a decade concentrating solely on the carbon emission reduction of the coal-fired power industry, which only accounts for approximately 5% of the total societal carbon emissions. This approach has proven to be extremely inefficient and detrimental to the macroeconomy, leading to issues such as power rationing and allocation of energy usage rights. This demonstrates a lack of foresight within the entire carbon–neutral industry.

In the era of big data and artificial intelligence, incorporating the whole society, every sector, and every household into carbon emission reduction is not as complex as one might think. The key lies in having the capability for fundamental theoretical innovation, top-level mechanism design, and technological implementation. This would enable the total implementation cost of the societal carbon emission reduction system to be lower than the current cost incurred by targeting a single industry. The "1+1" system based on the CELM can achieve this effect.

By utilizing the national CTMS and a unified national NCTM, we can offer the top-level management system for carbon emission reduction across society. This will significantly mobilize the engagement of all organizations and households. The full utilization of digital information systems, along with the power of digitization and market mechanisms, can greatly reduce the intensity and difficulty of government oversight, enable the autonomous operation of the system, and simplify the overall system considerably.

Q60: The Golden Carbon System seems similar to the Golden Tax System. However, the difference is that the Golden Tax System pertains to the relationship between enterprises and the government, whereas the Golden Carbon System involves the relationships among enterprises, the industrial chain, and the government. For enterprises where energy costs represent a significant portion of overall expenses, there is a concern about leaking sensitive information such as production costs and output, since it is easy for competitors to infer this information from the carbon footprint data.

A: Information security is a legitimate concern, but there is no need for excessive worry. The CTMS, or the Golden Carbon Project, is a national data management system and a critical piece of national carbon–neutral infrastructure controlled by the government. Its security is rigorously maintained, ensuring a high level of data protection. For an enterprise, the data relationship within the CTMS is akin to that within the Golden Tax Project, which also reflects the relationships between enterprises, the industrial chain, and the government. In this respect, the two systems are similar. Since businesses already operate within the Golden Tax Project, adding the Golden Carbon Project will not introduce additional risks.

The development and operation of the CTMS platform are overseen by the state, and the data security of CTMS is paramount and fully assured.

Q61: It appears that the CELM is so efficient that it might render many carbon consultants unnecessary. What should we do with the tens of thousands of professionals who have been working in carbon research for the past two decades?

A: The current policy framework is inefficient. Its impact on carbon reduction is limited, while the management system is extensive, incurring high societal costs. The transaction volume of national carbon emission market only reached over 10 billion yuan despite of two full years of operations. Some experts predict that the carbon reduction consulting industry will soon reach a scale of 10 billion yuan, which is unreasonable given the current context.

Many existing policy mechanisms seem designed not to genuinely reduce carbon emissions but rather to create new markets and business opportunities. Countless methodologies, rules, and algorithms have been developed, making the system overly complex and necessitating the involvement of expert advisors, thereby artificially creating a market for carbon consulting and finance. These practices violate social values and squander societal wealth, rendering them unsustainable.

The CELM and its Solution, however, are straightforward. An organization should take liability for its carbon emissions, and a clerk can do this using simple arithmetic operations (addition, subtraction, multiplication, and division), without needing experts or investing excessive time.

Those working in the carbon consultancy sector need not despair. They should shift their focus towards assisting society in accelerating carbon emission reduction, rather than focusing solely on tasks, such as carbon stocks and emission calculations, which can be automated through big data systems.

Here are three key directions for the carbon consulting industry:

1. Assisting organizations with decarbonation management systems: All societal organizations need to establish decarbonation management systems and will benefit from the expertise of professional consultants.
2. Verification of carbon source organizations and carbon source data: As the government begins to track carbon sources from coal mines, oil fields, and natural gas sectors, the need for consultants to verify support detailed data will grow.
3. Supporting government in managing carbon removal organizations and verifying carbon removal capacity: The workload here is expected to be substantial, as the government aims to develop carbon removal management initiatives. Given the international dimension, the scale of this effort will be significant and will require a large number of consultants.

Q62: Will the implementation of the CELM pose challenges to the government's supervisory capabilities? After all, the supervision of volatile organic compounds (VOCs) has been a long-standing issue for local governments, with scientific management always seeming to be a work in progress.

A: The CELM Solution presents a significant advantage in addressing these challenges, reducing the regulatory capacity and investment required by the government by at least two orders of magnitude.

Carbon reduction represents one of the most complex and large-scale public goods initiatives, testing the limits of national governance. It involves all industries, organizations, and individuals, demanding substantial governmental oversight and resource allocation. Despite nearly two decades of efforts, both domestically and internationally, carbon emission reduction management has only achieved robust control in select sectors, even with the support of numerous industry consultants. Many problems still exist, and this has become a considerable burden for both enterprises and the nation.

The CELM, guided by advanced climate change economics, leverages digital technology to establish a comprehensive digital carbon footprint for society. It utilizes market mechanism to assign CEL to all organizations and coordinate macroeconomic and carbon–neutral processes with integrated carbon pricing. This minimizes the regulatory requirements and resource input needed by the government.

1. By utilizing the CTMS, it becomes straightforward to build a complete, accurate, and dynamic carbon footprint database for the entire society. This reduces the complexity of current carbon emission accounting, simplifies the accounting process, significantly decreases the workload, and mitigates the various issues encountered during carbon emission accounting. Presently, managing carbon emissions within just one industry, the coal-fired power industry, requires substantial resources from consulting firms and still faces issues with data quality. A CTMS based on the CELM can streamline these processes while maintaining high data accuracy.
2. It reduces the difficulty in allocating the allowances for emissions and eliminates the need for huge investment. The current carbon reduction mechanism relies on allocating carbon emission rights, a process fraught with difficulties, heavy administrative burdens, and high regulatory costs, which the government struggles to manage effectively. The CELM directly removes the need for the allocation of carbon emission rights, relying instead on market mechanisms for regulation. This approach is efficient, equitable, and requires minimal input.
3. It avoids the challenges of dynamic carbon pricing. Setting the carbon price too low impedes the carbon neutrality process, while setting it too high places undue strain on the macroeconomy. Determining carbon pricing is a highly technical and systematic undertaking. The current mechanism lacks scientific rigor and faces operational difficulties. By integrated carbon pricing strategies, the CELM uses the CTMS to determine the carbon liability of all societal organizations. The government can then utilize negative carbon measures to balance the carbon neutrality process and macroeconomic performance, adjusting carbon prices efficiently, precisely, and dynamically via the negative carbon market. This reduces the complexity of pricing and enhances the effectiveness of carbon emission reduction efforts.

Q63: Companies collect carbon fees on behalf of consumers, similar to the principle of Extended Producer Responsibility (EPR). However, despite many years of implementing EPR in the refrigerator industry, the collected funds do not seem to have played a significant role. Will the CELM face a similar situation?

A: Extended Producer Responsibility (EPR) is an environmental policy that mandates producers to take responsibility for the entire lifecycle of the goods they produce, from design to disposal (including waste collection and disposal). Under EPR regulations, responsible entities are required to minimize the environmental impact of their products throughout their lifecycle. The primary objective is to incentivize manufacturers to design more reusable and recyclable products.

While both the CELM and EPR involve costs, their operational strategies differ significantly. Since the CELM enables the precise internalization of external costs, it aligns with economic principles and should, therefore, lead to reduced carbon consumption and effective resource allocation.

The limited effectiveness of the EPR policy in the refrigerator industry highlights a lack of a robust scientific mechanism.

Q64: How does the government generate revenue from the carbon fees?

A: The government derives its carbon fee revenue from the carbon market. It provides "negative carbon" products to the carbon market, allowing organizations to offset their carbon emissions. Essentially, the government sells negative carbon products in the negative carbon market to generate income.

The quantity of negative carbon supplied by the government to the carbon market annually is approximately equivalent to the total annual carbon sources in the country minus the amount of "Real Negative CO_2" provided by carbon removal organizations. If the current carbon price is 50 yuan per ton and China's carbon emissions are around 12 billion tons per year, the government would receive about 600 billion yuan in carbon revenue. When investors purchase negative carbon assets, the government raises revenue, which is initially invested in carbon reduction efforts and later used for buy-back purposes.

15.10 Integration of the CELM with Global Carbon Neutrality Solution

Q65: What is the core idea of the CELM?

A: The core idea of the CELM is centered around three key aspects:

- Firstly, consumer liability: Historically, all carbon reduction mechanisms implemented globally have been based on producer liability, a framework largely established by Western developed countries. This approach has been found to be inefficient and unfair. The CELM introduces a fairer and more efficient consumer liability system, which can better distribute CEL throughout the industrial chain and facilitate the handling of carbon tariffs in both domestic and international contexts.
- Secondly, negative carbon basis: Traditionally, carbon reduction systems worldwide have been built on the concept of carbon emission rights. These systems tend to be complex, unfair, and costly to implement. In contrast, the CELM is entirely based on negative carbon, offering superior fairness, efficiency, and lower implementation costs compared to previous carbon reduction solutions.
- Thirdly, market mechanism: Current carbon markets based on carbon emission rights essentially function as a large planned system with a small market component, resulting in low marketization levels, significant administrative intervention in the macroeconomy, adverse impacts on economic growth, and extremely low efficiency. The NCTM based on the CELM features high marketization levels. Through controlling "Owing Negative CO_2" resources, the government exerts influences on carbon prices but does not interfere with the determination of CEL or the allocation of emission rights across the industrial chain. This results in

a fully market-driven mechanism with minimal government involvement, lower operating costs, and higher efficiency in resource allocation.

The CELM incorporates three significant innovations:

1. Utilizing the ticket input and output mechanism and carbon ticket management system, the CELM efficiently and cost-effectively determines the CEL of the entire society. With innovative frameworks and digital systems, it addresses the current issues of heavy workload, poor accuracy, and high costs associated with monitoring, reporting, and verifying (MRV) carbon emissions. While existing systems have been limited to covering just one industry (coal-fired power) over more than a decade, the CELM can rapidly encompass the entire society, all organizations, and households in carbon emission reduction efforts, thereby accelerating the progress to carbon neutrality.
2. CEL offset mechanism: Once the CEL of each organization is established, the enterprises with carbon emission stocks are required to offset their surplus carbon emissions by purchasing negative carbon products on a quarterly basis. Those with negative carbon stocks can sell their negative carbon for profits. This provides efficient and timely bidirectional incentives for carbon emission reduction across the industrial chain.
3. Negative carbon trading market: Unlike the current carbon market, which is inadequate for achieving carbon neutrality, the negative carbon trading market based on the CELM directly facilitates two-way incentives for "carbon emissions" and "carbon sequestration" activities. It is highly marketized, and the government gains substantial financial revenues to support the goal of carbon neutrality effectively.

Q66: Who benefits most from the CELM-based Carbon Neutrality Solution? And who might be disadvantaged?

A: The CELM-based Carbon Neutrality Solution represents the most efficient and equitable pathway towards global carbon neutrality that the government can currently adopt, benefiting the broader situation and society as a whole.

Certainly, the impacts of the CELM-based Carbon Neutrality Solution vary across different industries. The most positively impacted sectors (those most favorably affected) are currently those focused on carbon reduction, export industries, as well as energy provinces and carbon removal regions. Under the CELM, there are no disadvantaged industries, as the sharing of carbon emission reduction liability is optimized for fairness. However, high-carbon organizations will face higher costs because their products contain more carbon content, leading to higher carbon charges in the total product cost. Consumers with high carbon consumption will also incur higher carbon expenses, thus elevating the overall carbon emission costs for society. Additionally, regions that are net importers of energy will incur higher costs for carbon emissions.

The sectors, regions, and organizations that will experience the greatest positive impact include:

1. Coal-fired power, steel, and cement industries

These industries are currently under significant pressure to reduce carbon emissions, bearing a substantial portion of the costs. For instance, the power market has not fully adopted market-oriented pricing, leading to failed cost transmission and thereby increasing the losses for coal-fired power enterprises in carbon reduction efforts.

Under the CELM, the coal-fired power industry is not a primary target for government regulation of carbon emissions. As long as the input and output of carbon tickets are balanced, there is no direct burden of carbon emission costs. Moreover, there is no need for complex carbon data management; determining the CEL of enterprises through carbon ticket input and output is much simpler than the original Monitoring, Reporting, and Verification (MRV) process.

Consequently, the coal-fired power sector will be entirely liberated by the CELM. Similarly, the so-called eight major carbon-emitting industries will face comparable situations.

2. Export enterprises

Chinese export enterprises confront the issue of the carbon border adjustment mechanism, akin to CBAM of the European Union. The "1+1" system based on the CELM can effectively address two crucial problems: providing reliable carbon footprint data and bearing an acceptable carbon emission cost domestically.

3. Energy-producing provinces

Under the CELM, the CEL is transferred through the entire industrial chain via the CTMS system to energy-consuming regions, along with the associated costs. The state collects fees for carbon emissions, and invests them in energy-producing provinces and carbon removal regions, creating a more effective means of transfer payments.

4. Carbon removal enterprises

Organizations involved in carbon sequestration, including forest carbon removals and CCUS technologies, will have ample opportunities for development. The more carbon they absorb, the better. The demand for carbon sequestration will rapidly expand to market sizes measured in gigatons of CO_2e. The cap on the percentage of offsets (currently 5%) used by carbon organizations will no longer apply.

There are three categories of industries, organizations, and regions that will see an increase in their liability:

1. High carbon emission enterprises

If high carbon emission enterprises are unable to issue all the input tickets, they will immediately have to bear the costs of carbon emissions (with quarterly settlements). The CELM compels every enterprise, organization, and household to focus on carbon reduction.

2. High carbon consumers

High carbon consumers will bear a greater portion of the carbon fees. Once household carbon accounts are established, the carbon fee will rise according to per capita carbon consumption. This mechanism helps promote a resource-saving society, regulates distribution, and contributes to building a better society.

3. Net energy importing regions

Provinces with high consumption and manufacturing activity, i.e., those with high energy consumption, will bear a greater share of the social costs of carbon emissions. The current liability mechanism follows the principle of "emitter liability", whereas the CELM adheres to the principle of "consumer liability". Therefore, net energy importing regions will bear the corresponding carbon emission costs according to their actual energy consumption.

Afterword: Simplicity Leads to the Greatest Truth

Following two years of dedicated efforts, bolstered by the collective support of numerous contributors, our research team has surmounted countless obstacles, culminating in the successful completion of this book. While the cost has been significant, our sense of achievement is profound.

Several years ago, the software development team at Lubansoft collaborated with Professor Xiao Jianzhuang's team from Green Construction Research Center of Tongji University to pioneer a software solution tailored for calculating the carbon footprint for engineering projects. The software Building Information Modeling (BIM) enabled precise quantification of materials and equipment used across the entire design scheme. However, a critical challenge emerged: both domestically and internationally, the absence of a comprehensive, accurate, and dynamic database for carbon emission factors hampered the seamless evaluation of carbon footprints across diverse engineering designs. Accordingly, this lack of a reliable database for carbon emission factors has become a pervalent issue, complicating the assessment of carbon footprints in engineering projects worldwide. We had to resort to makeshift approaches, such as using fragmented data, replicating information from various sources domestically and internationally, to bridge the gap. Consequently, the database for carbon emission factors stands as a formidable challenge in the government's carbon emission management efforts.

To address this gap and develop a digitized and intelligent framework for calculating carbon footprints in the engineering sector, our R&D team delved into foundational theories of climate change economics and global carbon reduction mechanisms. We discovered systemic flaws in the top-level design of the international community's approach to combating climate change and reducing carbon emissions. Despite decades of concerted efforts by millions of researchers and policymakers, there has been no fundamental breakthrough in either the theoretical underpinnings or practical solutions for carbon neutrality, still revolving around the principles of "producer liability" and "carbon emission allowances" established by Western nations. They failed to provide the international community with fair and efficient basic theories on climate change and feasible carbon neutral solutions.

B. Yang, *The Carbon Emission Liability Mechanism*,
https://doi.org/10.1007/978-981-96-3612-9

Furthermore, the prevailing global carbon reduction policies pose a significant risk to economic growth and do little to advance climate equity and justice. Tackling climate change, arguably the largest academic endeavor in human history, has seen massive investment in research funds and carbon emissions, yet may stand as the least effective research initiative in academic history, with the worst input-output ratio of research funds and the worst input-output ratio of carbon emissions. The annual COP conferences, attended by tens of thousands, serve as a stark reminder of the lack of progress due to the absence of a fair and efficient theoretical framework, resulting in ineffective negotiations. On the other side, the hand of the weather is pounding on our fragile glass windows.

Confronted with these realities and the increase of the number of victims in climate disasters, I, even as a newcomer to the field of climate change economics, feel a profound sense of urgency. For China, achieving the ambitious "3060" dual carbon targets remains challenging, with time being of the essence.

Driven by a passion for institutional economics and over two decades of experience in the digital domain, we begin to take a fresh look at the global climate change and the domestic dilemma of carbon neutrality, we are strongly aware that there exist serious problems with the current carbon policy system and that there ought to be better solutions. Upon recognizing the deficiencies, we embark on a mission to seek a superior solution. With the backing of Tongji University, we promptly establish a research team and commit substantial resources to conduct specialized studies. In 2022, I transitioned from an entrepreneur to a dedicated researcher in climate change economics.

As our research progresses, we arrive at several pivotal insights regarding the international community's predicament in addressing climate change:

Firstly, due to the limited perspectives and ideas of different interest groups, it is inevitable that they encounter obstacles when addressing the governance of climate change, a large-scale and complex public good with spatial and temporal externalities. In the field of climate change economics, current research predominantly relies on the Pigouvian Tax principle, Coase Theorem, and traditional methodologies like those proposed by Nordhaus, employing mathematical models to analyze social costs. The academic community has yet to introduce significant innovations or upgrades to the top-level governance theory of climate change, lacking a higher-dimensional perspective, advanced systemic thinking, digital thinking, Internet-centric approaches, and integrative innovative thinking to comprehend the challenges we face, thus failing to identify a suitable path forward.

Traditional economists tend to adhere to conventional thinking patterns, seeking to resolve societal issues through economic theories and mathematical models. However, they often fall short in leveraging Internet and digital thinking and lack the capability to integrate knowledge tools from other disciplines to solve problems. For many dilemmas related to large-scale and complex public goods, in the era of big data and digitization, obtaining comprehensive data on a public good is not particularly challenging, and the cost can be minimal. Solving these issues often doesn't necessitate complex theories or data models; rather, it requires designing a relatively simple liability mechanism and methods for offsetting liability, thereby resolving the problem.

Secondly, to overcome the challenging triangle of "global coordination, efficiency and equity, and national sovereign interests" demands that every social leader, scientist, economist, and head of economic entities embrace a spirit of global vision and a vision of a shared future for mankind. There exists a viable pathway towards rapid carbon neutrality and a definitive resolution to the climate crisis. The international community will never achieve a balanced solution if it continues to adopt unilateral strategies in the pursuit of its own interests.

The history of over three decades of negotiations over carbon emission rights underscores this point. Carbon emission rights are intrinsically tied to equality of human rights and the right to development, making the balancing of interests exceedingly difficult. Fortunately, over the past three decades, advancements in green energy technologies and the evolving developmental aspirations of nations have alleviated some of the tensions surrounding climate issues. Consequently, the international community has adopted a bottom-up voluntary commitment mechanism for emission reductions, known as *The Paris Agreement*. There is a growing recognition that developed countries must assume responsibility for developing nations, and that the affluent must advocate for the less fortunate, a principle that ultimately benefits everyone. In the context of climate change, the vision of "building a community with a shared future for mankind", as proposed by China, has demonstrated remarkable resilience and vitality.

It is imperative to note that on matters of climate change, scholars and policymakers should adopt a broader perspective and abandon the creation of unnecessary academic imperatives and commercial markets.

Thirdly, simplicity leads to the greatest truth; only straightforward theories and solutions can resolve problems arising from large-scale complex public goods. Complicated frameworks are inherently incapable of solving such issues. The current carbon reduction systems worldwide are a testament to this flaw. The reason is straightforward: because the carbon reduction policy framework necessitates the coordination of approximately 200 countries and the endorsement of countless stakeholder organizations, unless the system is sufficiently simple, consensus cannot be achieved, regardless of the number of participants or the duration of discussions. After more than three decades, with each session involving 30,000–50,000 participants, the outcomes remain far from ideal. Currently, the international community is exploring the policy pathways of carbon taxes and carbon markets, but the complexity of these systems and the multitude of policy variables result in long-term failure to reach consensus, unable to form concerted action.

Drawing on the aforementioned points, our research team breaks through the existing theoretical constraints both domestically and internationally, leveraging the strengths of interdisciplinary integrated research. Our approach aims to find a multi-disciplinary integrated solution to global climate change, encompassing philosophical, legal, sociological, political-economic, informatic, and digital perspectives.

Fortunately, the efforts of our team soon yield significant breakthroughs. Building upon prior theories and integrating innovative approaches, we discover promising avenues for addressing global climate issues. Our research indicates that the international community can achieve global carbon neutrality at minimal cost, or even derive positive benefits. Furthermore, by integrating a carbon currency system based on the CELM framework, there's potential to entirely eliminate atmospheric CO_2 accumulations after industrial era.

Thus, the new Carbon Emission Liability Mechanism (CELM) and its Global Carbon Neutrality Solution are conceived.

The introduction of CELM theory offers the international community fresh perspectives. Grounded in the three foundational principles of "consumer liability, immediate accountability for exceeding the industry's average carbon intensity, and offsets via negative carbon products", it becomes feasible to address most of the current challenges posed by global climate change. This approach not only accelerates the journey towards carbon neutrality, promotes economic growth, and enhances social welfare, but it also does so at a manageable cost, ensuring fairness and efficiency, while facilitating international cooperation. The CELM represents a comprehensive innovation in the systemic design of both global climate governance and national carbon neutrality strategies, holding the promise of becoming a unified solution for global climate governance.

Confronting the global challenge of survival, the CELM is capable of resolving issues arising from large-scale, complex public goods featured with spatial and temporal externalities, providing implementable solutions across approximately 200 countries worldwide. The fundamental principles of the CELM are remarkably straightforward, reinforcing the notion that simplicity leads to the greatest truth. For over three decades, progress on global climate change has been limited due to differing stances among stakeholders and a failure to fully leverage human ingenuity. Today, we must focus on the essentials to achieve theoretical and practical breakthroughs. The resolution to our climate crisis necessitates employing the simplest principles to identify the greatest common ground that enables the international community to attain its objectives.

The CELM does it.

The CELM equips us to confront both international and domestic challenges with greater composure as we strive toward carbon neutrality. It aids in achieving the temperature control goals outlined by the IPCC and enables China to transition more swiftly from a passive to an active stance on climate issues, thereby making a greater contribution to solving the global climate crisis.

After more than three decades of development, the extensive international and domestic carbon reduction systems now require substantial reform, and in some cases, a complete overhaul, involving imaginable resistance and complexity. We have thoroughly assessed the difficulties and challenges associated with implementing these solutions. As a scholar, I have fulfilled my duty by publishing my research findings. However, we will not stop here; we will continue to allocate resources to communicate and promote our theories and plans to the international community. We are acutely aware that we cannot rush the process, as numerous experts, friends, and leaders have cautioned us about the immense difficulty of altering such established systems. We are convinced that there are always individuals whose work is driven by ideals, where success or failure is secondary.

The urgency of climate shocks grows stronger with each passing day. The CELM is nascent and requires refinement in many areas. We look forward to collaborating with more colleagues to contribute wisdom and strength toward China's "3060" dual carbon targets and the comprehensive resolution of global climate change.

Broadening horizons, breaking through limitations, embracing shared global destiny;

Simple, problem-focused, fair and efficient;

Consumer liability, negative carbon offsetting, market-driven mechanism;

We believe this is the solution to global climate change.

Bibliography

1. IPCC AR6 SYR. Climate Change 2023[R]. Switzerland: IPCC, 2023.
2. IPCC AR6 WG III. Climate Change 2022: Mitigation of Climate Change[R]. Switzerland: IPCC, 2022.
3. IPCC. Special Report: Global Warming of 1.5℃[R]. Switzerland: IPCC, 2018.
4. WMO. State of the Global Climate 2022[R]. Switzerland: WMO, 2023.
5. China Meteorological Administration. China Climate Bulletin (2022) [R]. Beijing: 2023.
6. China Meteorological Administration. State of the Global Climate (2022) [R]. Beijing: 2023.
7. IEA. CO_2 Emissions in 2022 [R]. Paris, France: 2023.
8. IEA. Global Energy Review: CO_2 Emissions in 2021[R]. Paris. France: 2022.
9. IEA. Energy Technology Perspective 2023 [R]. Paris, France: 2023.
10. IRENA. World Energy Transitions Outlook: 1.5°C Pathway [R]. Abu Dhabi: 2021.
11. World Bank. State and Trends of Carbon Pricing 2023 [R]. Washington, USA: 2023.
12. Carbon Pricing Leadership Coalition. Report of the High-Level Commission on Carbon Prices [R]. New York: 2017.
13. United Nations Environment Programme. Emissions Gap Report 2022: The Closing Window—Climate Crisis Calls for Rapid Transformation of Societies [R]. Nairobi. https://www.unep.org/emissions-gap-report-2022, 2022.
14. UN. Climate change: No "credible pathway" to 1.5C limit, UNEP warns [EB/OL]. New York: UN, [2022–10–27]. https://news.un.org/en/story/2022/10/1129912.
15. Du Sisi. Xie Zhenhua: China-U.S.-Europe Cooperation on Energy Transition Enjoys Broad Prospects [EB/OL]. Caixin.com. (2022–06–16). https://www.caixin.com/2022-06-16/101899683.html.
16. CICC Global Institute. Carbon Neutral Economics[M]. Beijing: CITIC Press Group, 2021.
17. Xinhua News Agency. China's major measures to address global climate change [EB/OL]. (2015–11–30). https://www.gov.cn/xinwen/2015-11/30/content_5018396.htm.
18. Kripa Jayaram, Chris Kay, Dan Murtaugh. China reduced as much pollution in 7 years as US did in 30 years [EB/OL]. Bloomberg, https://www.bloomberg.com/news/articles/2022-06-14/china-s-clean-air-campaign-is-bringing-down-global-pollution.
19. Liu Zhenya. UHV Mission in the New Era [J]. Outlook Weekly, 2021(11): 40–45.
20. Gong Ming. Adhere to Green and Low-Carbon Development, Build a Clean and Beautiful World (Shared Future) [N]. People's Daily, 2021–10–30(3).
21. Drew Johnson, Tennessee Center for Policy Research. Al Gore's Personal Energy Use Is His Own "Inconvenient Truth"—And Replies [EB/OL]. https://www.chattanoogan.com/2007/2/26/102512/Al-Gores-Personal-Energy-Use-Is-His.aspx,2007-2-26.
22. One on One. Ding Zhongli: What Is a Fair Approach to Emissions Reduction [EB/OL]. CCTV network, (2010–02–31). http://tv.cctv.com/2010/03/31/VIDEdgu5EUoJiNv6LWsou3Yz100331.shtml.

B. Yang, *The Carbon Emission Liability Mechanism*,
https://doi.org/10.1007/978-981-96-3612-9

23. Sharanya Hrishikesh, Meryl Sebastian. Delhi suffers at 49C as heatwave sweeps India [EB/OL]. BBC, (2022–05–16). https://www.bbc.co.uk/news/world-asia-india-61242341.
24. Aniruddha Ghosal. South Asia's intense heat wave a "sign of things to come" [EB/OL]. AP, (2022–05–24). https://apnews.com/article/climate-science-politics-pakistan-a015aa2a05a1a433afde43414e3d16b4.
25. Jiang Wei. William Nordhaus and Climate Change Economics[J]. Climate Change Research, 2020, 16(3): 390–394.
26. Huang Jing, Fu Yan, Liang Yu. Review *The Stern Review* and the Challenge of Climate Change[J]. China Sustainability Tribune, 2021(12): 19–24.
27. Hu Angang, Guan Qingyou. Four Feasibilities for China to Fight Global Climate Changes[J]. Journal of Tsinghua University (Philosophy and Social Sciences), 2008, 23(6): 120–132.
28. Bill Gates. How to Avoid a Climate Disaster[M]. Beijing: CITIC Press Group, 2021.
29. Lu Shuling, Bai Yanfeng. International Practices of Carbon Taxation and Its Enlightenment to Achievement of Carbon Peak in 2030[J]. International Taxation in China, 2021(12): 21–28.
30. Wei Tao, S. Glomsrod. Impacts of Carbon Taxation on China's Economy and Greenhouse Gas Emissions[J]. World Economics and Politics, 2002(8): 47–49.
31. Su Ming, Fu Zhihua, Xu Wen, et al. China's Path to Carbon Tax[J]. Environmental Economy, 2009(9): 10–22.
32. Su Ming, Fu Zhihua, Xu Wen, et al. Research on the Levy of Carbon Tax in China [J]. Review of Economic Research, 2009(72): 2–16.
33. Su Ming, Fu Zhihua, Xu Wen, et al. Problems about Levying Carbon Tax in China[J]. China Finance: 2009(24): 40–41.
34. Carbon Research Team. Feasibility Analysis of Carbon Tax in China[J]. China State Finance, 2009(19): 52–53.
35. Carbon Research Team. Framework Design of China's Carbon Tax[J]. China State Finance, 2009(20): 38–40.
36. Carbon Research Team. Design and Conception of China's Carbon Tax Policy Under the New Situation[J]. Sub National Fiscal Research, 2010(1): 9–13.
37. Fang Jiaxi. Carbon Tax! It Will Be Introduced in 2012[N/OL]. Economic Information Daily, (2010–05–28), http://www.jjckb.cn/gnyw/2010-05//11/content_220733.htm.
38. Li Guiqin. In the Global Context of Low-Carbon Economy, Carbon Tax Is Gradually Coming[N/OL]. China Business Journal. (2010–05–31). http://www.cb.com.cn/index/show/jj/cv/cv114153474/p/license/10001.html.
39. Guo Xia. Don't Take the Poor as an Excuse When You Oppose a Carbon Tax[EB/OL]. www.cn.cn, (2012–0614). http://views.ce.cn/view/ent/201206/14/t20120614_23406099.shtml?from=groupmessage&isappinstalled=0.
40. Zhang Xiaona. The "Green Tax" Controversy Comes[N/OL]. The Democracy and Law Times, (2018–01–20). http://e.mzyfz.com/paper/1002/paper_21545_5655.html.
41. Wu Xiaohui, Zhao Yang. Leveraging the Effective Pricing Function of the Carbon Market[R]. Beijing: CICC Global Institute, 2022.
42. Anyong Carbon Neutrality Research Team. A Path Guide to Carbon Neutrality[M]. Beijing: China Machine Press, 2021.
43. Gou Hongyang. Low-Carbon Plot[M]. Taiyuan: Shanxi Economy Press, 2010.
44. The State Council. Action Plan for Carbon Peak by 2030[EB/OL]. [2021–10–24]. http://www.gov.cn/zhengce/content/2021-10/26/content_5644984.htm.
45. The State Council Information Office. China's Policies and Actions to Address Climate Change[EB/OL].[2021–10–24]. http://www.scio.gov.cn/zfbps/32832/Document/1715491/1715491.htm.
46. Institute of Climate Change and Sustainable Development, Tsinghua University. China's Long-term Low Carbon Development Strategies and Pathways Comprehensive Report[M]. Beijing: China Environmental Publishing Group, 2021.
47. Yang Yanqing, Cheng Guang. Economic Analysis of Carbon Neutrality: A Compilation of Zhou Xiaochuan's Dissertations[M]. Beijing: China Financial Publishing House, 2021.

48. Yang Shuying, Cai Bofeng, Cao Shuyan. Carbon Tax: International Experience[M]. Beijing: Chemical Industry Press, 2011.
49. Bernard Salanié. The Economics of Taxation[M]. Beijing: China Renmin University Press, 2017.
50. Dai Yande, Kang Yanbing, Xiong Xiaoping, et al. Carbon Trading System Research[M]. Beijing: China Development Press, 2014.
51. Chen Hongyan. Study on Carbon Tax in the Context of Multilateral Trade System[M]. Beijing: Social Sciences Academic Press (China), 2015.
52. Zhao Aiwen. Economic Effects of Carbon Taxes Under the Constraints of Carbon Emission Reduction[M]. Beijing: China Financial & Economics Publishing House, 2021.
53. Bjorn Lomborg. Welfare in the 21st century: Increasing development, reducing inequality, the impact of climate change, and the cost of climate policies[J]. Technological Forecasting and Social Change, 2020, 156: 119981.
54. Nordhaus, W D. To tax or not to tax: Alternative approaches to slowing global warming[J]. Review of Environmental Economics and Policy, 2007.
55. Liu Shangwei. The "Nursery School Experiment" in Climate Governance[J]. Caixin Weekly, 2022(4): 18.
56. Global Energy Interconnection Development and Cooperation Organization. Tackling Climate Crisis[M]. Beijing: China Electric Power Press, 2022.
57. Chang Jie. The Research on Pricing for Carbon Emission Trading Market[D]. Beijing: Central University of Finance and Economics, 2015.
58. Wang Dongfeng, Zhang Li. A Review of the Economics of Climate Change[J]. Economist, 2011(11): 83–89.
59. Zhang Haibin. History of Global Climate Governance and Path Towards Sustainable Development[J]. Contemporary World, 2020(6): 15–20.
60. Tian Chengchuan, Zeng Hongying, et al. Case Study of Carbon Inclusive Development and Practice in China[R]. Beijing: Center for Environmental Education and Communications of Ministry of Ecology and Environment, Beijing Green Inclusive Network Technology Co., LTD, 2023.
61. Luo Nan. Research on Household Carbon Accounting - Trading System[J]. Contemporary Economics, 2016(23): 123–125.
62. Wei Y M, Liu L C, Fan Y, et al. The impact of lifestyle on energy use and CO_2 emission: An empirical analysis of China's residents[J], Energy Policy, 2007, 35(1): 247–257.
63. Treasury H M. Stern review: economics of climate change[R]. 2006. https://mp.weixin.qq.com/s/_a5gHoSE3cV5NwrSquLrxw.
64. Lucas Chancel. Global carbon inequality over 1990–2019[J]. Nature Sustainability, 2022, 5: 931–938.
65. OXFAM. Carbon emissions of richest 1% set to be 30 times the 1.5°C limit in 2030[EB/OL].[2021–11–05]. https://www.oxfam.org.uk/mc/zyd5iv/.
66. Shan Chong. Study on Reform of Urban Drainage Fee System and Conversion of Operation Model[J]. Urban Roads Bridges & Flood Control, 2017(11): 104–107.
67. Zhou Jianliang, Zhu Dajian. Thinking About the Adjustment of Wastewater Charge in Shanghai[J]. China Water & Wastewater, 2004(10): 87–90.
68. Ding Meirong. Analysis of Carbon Emission Status in Cement Industry and Its Path to Emission Reduction[J]. China Cement, 2021(7):46–49.
69. Wang Jingjie, Hu Yan, Li Dai. Analysis of the Impact of Carbon Trading Market on Power Generation Enterprises in China[EB/OL]. [2021–8–31]. https://www.gzf2010.com.cn/uploadfiles/file/20210904/20210904010456_6708.pdf.
70. Household Carbon Account Research Group of the First Affiliated High School of Tongji University. Establish Household Carbon Accounts and Mobilize the Whole People to Reduce Carbon[R]. Shanghai: 2022 Shanghai Youth Dual Carbon Proposal Competition, 2022.
71. McKinsey. A blueprint for scaling voluntary carbon markets to meet the climate challenge. [EB/OL]. [2021–01–29]. https://www.mckinsey.com/capabilities/sustainability/our-insights/a-blueprint-for-scaling-voluntary-carbon-markets-to-meet-the-climate-challenge/.

72. Robinson Meyer. Not Even Free Money Can Fix a Carbon Tax? [EB/OL]. The Atlantic, [2022–01–26]. https://www.theatlantic.com/science/archive/2022/01/carbon-tax-rebate-policy/621363/.
73. Xie Fuzhan, Liu Yaming, et al. Annual Report on Actions to Address Climate Change (2020)[M]. Beijing: Social Sciences Academic Press (China), 2020.
74. National Academies of Sciences of the G7 states. Decarbonization: the case for urgent international action[R]. Germany: 2022.
75. Pierre Friedlingstein etc. Global Carbon Budget 2022[R]. Australia: Global Carbon Project, 2022.
76. Hainan Green Finance Institute. Paths of Cement Enterprises to Reduce Pollution and Emissions in New Development Stage[EB/OL]. (2023). https://mp.weixin.qq.com/s?biz=MzI3NzQ1OTA3Ng==&mid=2247515589&idx=2&sn=6f6d66e80a40118914138203e5774ee7.
77. Zhan Chen, Huang Qifan. The Construction of Shanghai Financial Center under the Background of Dual Carbon[EB/OL]. [2021–12–25]. https://qzs.stcn.com/zixun/202112/t20211225_4010358.html.
78. China Construction Industry Association. Statistics Analysis of China's Construction Industry Development in 2022[J]. Journal of Engineering Management, 2023, 37(1): 1–6.
79. China Association of Building Energy Efficiency, Chongqing University. 2022 China Building Energy Consumption and Carbon Emissions Research Report[R]. Beijing: 2022.
80. Christian Wigand, Katarzyna Ko Lanko, Jördis Ferroli. Screening of websites for "greenwashing": half of green claims lack evidence[EB/OL]. [2021–01–02]. https://ec.europa.eu/commission/presscorner/detail/en/ip_21_269.
81. Viktor Tachev. Financial Greenwashing: What is it and How Does It Happen? [EB/OL]. Energy Tracker Asia, [2022–06–01]. https://energytracker.asia/financial-greenwashing-what-is-it-and-how-does-it-happen/.
82. Wang Hailin, Huang Haidan, Zhao Xiaofan, et al. Key Problems in Global Climate Governance and China's Countermeasures[J]. China Population,Resources and Environment, 2020, 30(11): 26–33.
83. Tencent. Tencent Carbon Neutrality Target and Roadmap[R]. Shenzhen: 2022.
84. Xinhua News Agency. China's Renewable Energy Generation Will Increase by about 8.4% Year-on-year in 2020[EB/OL]. (2021–01–30). https://www.gov.cn/xinwen/2021-01/30/content_5583790.html.
85. State Grid Corporation of China. 2022 Social Responsibility Report[R]. Beijing: 2021.
86. Xia Caiyan. Big Data Panorama of China's Electricity Sales Enterprises in 2022[R]. Beijing: Prospective Industry Research Institute, 2022.
87. China Electricity Council. Analysis and Forecast Report of National Electricity Supply and Demand Situation in 2021–2022[R]. Beijing: 2022.
88. Huang Wenzhong, Zhang Yetong. The Economy of the Power Generation Side and the User Side May Benefit the Upstream Manufacturers[R]. Great Wall Glory Securities, 2023–04–25.
89. Brandon Graver, Kevin Zhang, Dan Rutherford. CO_2 Emissions From Commercial Aviation, 2018[R/OL]. Washington: ICCT (2019), https://theicct.org/publication/co2-emissions-from-commercial-aviation-2018/.
90. Liu Heng, Huang Zhixiong. On the Reasons and Enlightenment of EU Aviation Carbon Tax "Shutdown"[J]. Research on Rule of Law, 2023(10): 63–70.
91. Fan Ruohong, Zhao Xuan. Difficulties in Incremental Distribution Reform[J/OL]. Caixin Weekly, (2023–06–12). https://weekly.caixin.com/2023-06-10/102064173.html.
92. Feng Difan. How much will carbon pricing be to drive emissions reductions? The IMF President says $75 a tonne is neededl COP27[EB/OL]. Yicai, (2022–11–08). https://www.yicai.com/news/101586986.html.
93. Xinhua News Agency. President Xi Jinping Chairs the 36th Collective Study Session and Made an Important Speech [EB/OL]. (2022–01–25). https://www.gov.cn/xinwen/2022-01/25/content_5670359.htm.
94. Planning and Development Department, China Electricity Council. Research on the Development Path of Carbon Peaking and Carbon neutrality in Power Industry[R/OL]. (2021–12–27). Beijing: China Electricity Council, https://www.cec.org.cn/detail/index.html?3-305486.

95. Wang Kuaijie, Hu An, Li Dai. Analysis of the Impact of carbon trading market on power generation enterprises in China[R]. Guangzhou: Guangzhou Futures Research Center, 2021–08–31.
96. National Energy Administration. Coal-fired power will continue to play an important role in ensuring power security for a long time[EB/OL]. (2022–04–29). http://www.nea.gov.cn/2022-04/29/c_1310579709.htm.
97. Marginal finance laboratory. Former central bank adviser: "Carbon neutrality" will cause the default rate of coal-fired power companies to jump from 3% to 22%[EB/OL]. (2021–04–21). https://www.163.com/dy/article/G83PD92J0539BX8Z.html.
98. Sun Mingchun. Carbon neutrality focuses on the demand for carbon credits, why not make a carbon currency?[EB/OL]. Yicai, (2021–03–17). https://www.yicai.com/news/100989532.html.
99. Liu Dongxiann, Zhang Dingyuan, Li Jinghua. China's contribution and impact analysis in the Sixth Assessment Report of the IPCC[G]//Policies and Practices to Implement the Dual Carbon Goals: Annual Report on Actions to Address Climate Change (2022). Beijing: Social Sciences Academic Press (China), 2022.

The manufacturer's authorised representative in the EU is Springer Nature Customer Service Centre GmbH, Europaplatz 3, 69115 Heidelberg, Germany. If you have any concerns regarding our products, please contact ProductSafety@springernature.com

Printed and bound by CPI Group (UK) Ltd, Croydon, CR0 4YY
01/10/2026
02225930-0018